The Winds of Change:
Macmillan to Heath, 1957–1975

A History of the Conservative Party

A History of the Conservative Party

This series, originally to have been published in four volumes, is now complete in six. It was established by an editorial board consisting of John Barnes, Lord Blake, the late Lord Boyle of Handsworth and Chris Cook.

The Winds of Change: Macmillan to Heath, 1957–1975

John Ramsden

Longman
London and New York

Longman Group Limited,
Longman House, Burnt Mill,
Harlow, Essex CM20 2JE, England
and Associated Companies throughout the world.

Published in the United States of America
by Longman Publishing, New York

© Longman Group Limited 1996

First published 1996

ISBN 0 582 27570 9 CSD

British Library Cataloguing-in-Publication Data

A catalogue record for this book is
available from the British Library

Library of Congress Cataloging-in-Publication Data

Ramsden, John, 1947–
    The winds of change: Macmillan to Heath, 1957–1975 / John Ramsden.
      p. cm. — (A history of the Conservative Party)
    Includes bibliographical references and index.
    ISBN 0–582–27570–9
    1. Conservative Party (Great Britain)—History.
    2. Great Britain—Politics and government—1945–
    I. Title. II. Series.
JN1129.C7R24 1996   95–14489
324.24104′09′045—dc20   CIP

Set by 5EE in 10/12½ pt Bembo
Produced by Longman Singapore Publishers (Pte) Ltd.
Printed in Singapore

Contents

Part II Heath and the Heathmen

Acknowledgements

To a great extent, my thanks are due to the same people whose assistance was acknowledged in *The Age of Churchill and Eden*. Without the leave granted by Queen Mary and Westfield College, the research grant awarded by the then Social Science Research Council and the hospitality of Corpus Christi College, Oxford, this volume too would have been seriously handicapped. The work of Chris Stevens in collecting most of the material from local Party minute books and other dispersed records has made an even more central contribution to this volume than to the previous one, and to all these people I am deeply grateful.   A work of this sort that tries to look intensively at a complex organisation over a longish period needs to rely on the published secondary sources as well as the institution's own archives, and my references acknowledge these. The footnotes also indicate my especial debt to Philip Norton's books on voting and dissent within parliament, Michael Pinto-Duschinsky's thesis on local Conservative associations, and the Institute of Contemporary British History's splendid series of witness seminars. I have relied most of all on the six volumes of the Nuffield College Election series that fall within these years; David Butler has authored or co-authored all of the Nuffield volumes since 1951 (as well as helping to supervise my own initial research into the Conservative Party) and I had in 1970 the opportunity that he has extended to many Nuffield students of working on the study of that election. Like many others, I owe to David a huge debt for personal kindnesses as well as for that series of books which have become an incomparable resource for the historian of post-war Britain.

   When dealing with such recent subjects, the contemporary historian can derive much material too from personal interviews, not least in the avoidance of gratuitous error that can otherwise be re-cycled from the press into works of serious history. I am grateful to the following for giving up their time to discuss some of the matters covered in the book, recently or in time past: Rt Hon. Lord Barber, the late Rt Hon. Lord Boyle of Handsworth, Rt Hon. Lord Carr of Hadley, Rt Hon. Lord Deedes, Lord Fraser of Kilmorack CBE, Rt Hon. Sir Edward Heath MP, Rt Hon. Lord Howe of Aberavon, Rt Hon. Lord Jenkin of Roding, the late Rt Hon. Lord Joseph, Rt Hon. Enoch Powell MBE. If I single out from all of these Michael Fraser, it is because his kindness to me over the writing of what is now five books on the Party has gone far beyond the call of duty either to history or to the Conservative Party.

Friends and colleagues have looked at this text in whole and in part. While what remains is my responsibility alone, I have gained much from the comments and advice of Stuart Ball, John Campbell, Peter Hennessy, Chris Stevens and John Turner.

For permission to see and quote from the Conservative Party's papers, including a number that are not normally open to scholars, I gladly acknowledge the approval given by Dr Alastair Cooke of the Conservative Political Centre; for permission to see the minute books of the 1922 Committee for the period after 1964, I am especially grateful to Sir Marcus Fox MP. For permission to quote from private collections of papers, I am grateful to the following: the Librarian, Leeds University Library (for extracts from the papers of Lord Boyle of Handsworth); the Master and Fellows of Trinity College, Cambridge (for extracts from the papers of Lord Butler of Saffron Walden); Sir Nicholas Hedworth Williamson (for an extract from the papers of Lord Hailes); Lady Miranda Cormack (for an extract from the papers of the 1st Earl of Kilmuir); the Earl of Woolton (for extracts from the papers of 1st Earl of Woolton).

John Ramsden
January 1995.

Abbreviations used in the text and footnotes

ACC	Association of Conservative Clubs
ACML	Anti-Common Market League
ACP	Advisory Committee on Policy
AGM	Annual General Meeting
BBC	British Broadcasting Corporation
CA	Conservative Association
CAER	Conservative Action for Electoral Reform
CAJ	*Conservative Agents' Journal*
CBF	(Conservative) Central Board of Finance
CBI	Confederation of British Industry
CCO	Conservative Central Office
CND	Campaign for Nuclear Disarmament
CPA	Conservative Party Archive
CPC	Conservative Political Centre
CPRS	Central Policy Review Staff
CPS	Centre for Policy Studies
CRD	Conservative Research Department
DN	*Daily Notes* (issued during election campaigns)
DTI	Department of Trade and Industry
EC	Executive Committee
EEC	European Economic Community
EFTA	European Free Trade Area
F and GP	Finance and General Purposes (Committee)
GDP	Gross Domestic Product
GLC	Greater London Council
GNP	Gross National Product
ICBH	Institute of Contemporary British History
IEA	Institute for Economic Affairs
ITA	Independent Television Authority
ITN	Independent Television News
ITV	Independent Television
LCC	Leader's Consultative Committee (shadow cabinet)
LSE	London School of Economics and Political Science
NCP	*Notes on Current Politics*
NEDC	National Economic Development Council

NF	National Front
NFU	National Farmers' Union
NHS	National Health Service
NIC	National Incomes Commission
NOP	National Opinion Polls
NSA	National Society of (Conservative) Agents
NUCC	National Union Central Council
NUEC	National Union Executive Committee
NUFGP	National Union Finance and General Purposes (Committee)
NUM	National Union of Mineworkers
ORC	Opinion Research Centre
PAR	Programme Analysis and Review
PEST	Pressure for Economic and Social Toryism
PLDF	People's League for the Defence of Freedom
PM	Prime Minister
PPS	Parliamentary Private Secretary
RPM	Resale Price Maintenance
SACC	Standing Advisory Committee on Candidates
SNP	Scottish National Party
TUC	Trades Union Congress
UA	Unionist Association
UCS	Upper Clyde Shipbuilders
UN	United Nations
VAT	Value Added Tax
YC	Young Conservative

Introduction

By 1955, when the Eden Government was re-elected with an increased majority, the Conservative Party faced the future with confidence. It had survived the catastrophe of 1945, when many even in its own ranks had feared for its future electability, and it had survived fifteen years of Churchillian indifference to its corporate prosperity. It had also developed a myth about the recovery of the Party itself that would last for years ahead, a myth that offered assurance about the Party's own inherent adaptability in a changing world. Oliver Poole, who was Party Chairman in 1957, thought that the recovery after 1945 'was the biggest change for a hundred years, between those who were anxious to put the clock back as far as possible to the pre-war world and those who preferred the post-war. Intellectually, we captured the party.' Harold Macmillan, whose credentials as a Conservative who was open-minded about the future went back to the start of his career, was fond of describing the same process in a different way, emphasising economic progress and consumerist benefits, most notably in the valedictory message that was read to the Blackpool Conference at the time of his 1963 resignation:

> Since 1945, I have lived to see the party of our dreams come into being . . . I have seen our policies develop into that pragmatic and sensible compromise between the extremes of collectivism and individualism for which the party has always stood in its great periods. I have seen it bring to the people of our own country a degree of comfort and well-being . . . such as I and my comrades could not have dreamed of when we slogged through the mud of Flanders nearly fifty years ago. Thus, the silent, the Conservative revolution, has come about.

(Much of Heath's later Conservative stance derived from this period in which he served under Macmillan, and perhaps his 'quiet revolution' offered in 1970 drew on this too?) For Iain Macleod, the Party's recovery of confidence after 1945 derived from its ability to recognise its own mistakes, because it was at heart pragmatic rather than ideologically dogmatic. As Party Chairman, he told the Conference in 1962 that 'it would have been impossible for the Conservative Party, after its defeat in 1945, to reform and reorganise itself if it had contemptuously said that the electors had chosen wrongly. Instead, we started from the assumption that it was we, the Conservative Party, who were at fault and not the people of this country.'[1]

Such confident statements were all very well when the Party had been in office for more than a decade, but in 1955 a sharp recession and the onset of foreign difficulties sapped at such confidence very quickly after Eden won the Election, as the previous volume in this series has described. In the longer-term history of the Conservative Party, the Suez crisis that prompted the downfall of Anthony Eden and allowed Harold Macmillan to seize the leadership in January 1957 was a relatively minor event. Even before President Nasser nationalised the Suez Canal Company, Eden was a beleaguered Leader whose ministerial colleagues were already anticipating his early downfall. As a Prime Minister unfamiliar with the small-change domestic issues of prices, jobs, rents and interest rates, and consequently unable to persuade the public or the Party that he was an effective leader in the difficult economic circumstances he inherited, Eden could not compensate (as so many Tory predecessors had done in the past) by demonstrating his diplomatic skills on the world stage. Henceforward, as Sir Alec Douglas-Home's partial reversion to Eden's political position was to show, Tory Governments would stand or fall on the domestic economy and its ability to deliver the goods to an electorate encouraged to expect effortless affluence.

Within six months of succeeding Eden, in the 'Never had it so good' speech at Bedford that has been signally misunderstood as no more than an electioneering appeal to materialism, Macmillan was actually trying to warn his Party that sacrifices could be needed to maintain prosperity, and he kept on offering similar warnings on other occasions too: he told a group of backbenchers on 25 June that 'the country simply did not understand that we were living beyond our income, and would have to pay for it sooner or later'. Within another half-year, the Macmillan Government would be rocked to its foundations (as successive disputes over foreign and colonial policy had so clearly failed to rock it) by the long-postponed debate about the irreducible level of public spending for peacetime. Since 1951, Tory Ministers had managed to combine the running down of a war economy with the country's favourable international trading position and growth in the domestic economy to facilitate increases in social spending *and* tax reductions. That easy road terminated in the economic downturn of 1955–56 and would never be open again, though the defence review of 1957 demonstrated a determination to milk the Churchill–Attlee war/Cold War military establishment for the last drops of expenditure reductions. In December 1957, Tory Ministers remained committed to their basic 1951 formula of paying for both spending increases and tax cuts from the proceeds of economic growth, but in that month they also decided by default that if economic growth could not be achieved at a

---

[1] Anthony Sampson, *The Anatomy of Britain* [all books cited were published in London unless otherwise indicated] (1962), 77; John Ramsden, 'From Churchill to Heath', in Lord Butler (ed.), *The Conservatives* (1977), 425, 450.

fast enough rate to square that political economy circle, then their priority would lie with maintaining social expenditure rather than in cutting both expenditure and tax; although the sum of money finally at issue when the Treasury Ministers resigned in January 1958 was a mere £50 million, and although the Chancellor overplayed his hand and antagonised his colleagues, the principle involved was arguably a strategic one of importance. In 1958–59, public expenditure as a proportion of Gross National Product (GNP), which had been falling since the Tories returned to power, began an increase that would continue until they left office in 1964. Facing a strategic choice on an equally narrow issue in 1951, Attlee's Government had decided to stick with its Chancellor and to part company instead with the defenders of social spending; but in 1957, rather than agreeing to raid family allowances or to postpone the end of conscription, Macmillan's Ministers cheerfully let their Chancellor go. This can be seen – according to taste – as evidence of a consensus of conviction between the parties on the minimum social programme inherited from the post-war settlement, or it can be seen as evidence of the Conservatives' deep-seated fear of the electoral consequences of such harsh policies as cutting family allowances. The effect is the same on either view.[2]

By 1960, Thorneycroft was wryly pointing out that public expenditure had actually risen by fifteen times as much as the sum he had resigned over, and that his Party had therefore taken a much bigger decision than appeared in 1958. That fact was masked by three factors. First, the arrival of a long-awaited economic upswing during 1958, developing into a full-scale boom in 1959–60, encouraged the belief that it had been wise to avoid harsh choices which subsquent evidence had shown to be unnecessary: growth would pay for both public and private affluence, the prospectus on which the Macmillan Government fought and won the 1959 Election, winning the largest Tory majority for a quarter of a century precisely by ridiculing Labour's tax plans as being unnecessary as well as dangerous. Second, Macmillan's virtuoso political skills in the years in which he was dubbed 'Supermac' had also done much to steady Tory morale and to divert attention away from strategic choices; his inspired choice of Poole and Hailsham to run the Party machine in improbable partnership had contributed signally to the same process of recovery. Third, in the Party's electioneering there had been a sea-change of method and approach; the 'You're looking at a Conservative' posters of 1957–58 were the storm petrel that heralded the modern world of media and public relations campaigning. The Woolton period of Party recovery up to 1955 had largely been characterised by the restoration (in far more effective form) of traditional methods and approaches, but in 1957 the revolution actually began. In the continuous between-election campaigning that Macmillan, Hailsham and

---

[2] Nigel Nicolson (ed.), *Harold Nicolson's Diaries and Letters, 1945–1962* (1968), 335.

Poole started in that Summer, in the carefully-researched and professional advertising campaign that dominated the hoardings and the press, and even in the rapid change of broadcasting and press-management strategies adopted by the Conservatives under pressure during September–October 1959, the Tories approached the formation of electoral opinion as no Party had ever done before – but as all serious parties would have to do in the future. Having once embarked on this route, the Party would henceforth be faced by the continuous need to stay one day's march ahead of its political opponents in the steady move downmarket; at the centre this would present few problems except the financial one, for the new campaigning methods were to prove ruinously expensive, but in the backwoods there would be an increasingly desperate struggle to modernise Party machinery that had been created for another world, a struggle that would never entirely succeed. None of this modernising impetus in electioneering had much to do with the presentation of hard choices to the electorate, except insofar as it related to the alleged programme of the Labour Party. The Party's determination not to have a debate, or even indeed a policy, on immigration in these years is a case in point. All of this is discussed in Chapter 1.

Behind the scenes though, if carefully kept off the boil until the 1959 General Election had been won, the Macmillan Government was edging towards the making of real strategic choices in what Macleod had called earlier in the year 'matters involving the long-term re-education of the Party'. The resignation of Lord Salisbury and the repudiation of the Tory whip by the right-wing Suez rebels in 1957 were early attempts by the discontented to demonstrate the way in which the wind was blowing. In both cases, the mismanagement of the issue by the rebels, the adroit footwork of the Prime Minister and the resolute determination of most Conservatives not to allow the boat to be rocked in the year after Suez combined to prevent a wider debate from taking place. By the time that the Party returned from the 1959 campaign, implementation of the 1957 Defence White Paper was making it impossible for Britain ever again to embark on a military operation on the scale of Suez. Though that shift had not been acknowledged either in the White Paper or in the subsequent debate, Britain had settled for the subordinate status in the Western alliance that Suez had shown to be the best now on offer. Yet, as Macmillan was photographed in Moscow and then chatted patronisingly with his wartime chum 'Ike' on primetime TV on the eve of the 1959 Election campaign, it was easy for the British people to miss the point. Nigel Nicolson had reported to his father the shift of approach in Macmillan's first Prime Ministerial address to the 1922 Committee, but also the subtlety with which it was concealed:

> It was superb. His whole speech turned upon the distinction between pride and vanity in the conduct of international relations, and there was not much doubt what he had in mind. . . . He said that the greatest moments in our history have not been when we have conquered but when we have led. You see the subtle

change? I was delighted. I said to the Chief Whip [Heath] as we were going out, 'What a pity it is that now we have the most intelligent Prime Minister of the century, he has to conceal his intelligence from the public for fear that they will suspect it, and that only we, on such occasions as this, can be given the full quality of his mind.' 'Yes', said the Chief Whip, 'Yes.'

However, Macmillan's inability to play an effective independent role at the 1960 Summit, and the regular public debates over weapons systems purchased from the United States in the early 1960s, made the claim to lead as a substitute for conquest increasingly difficult to sustain.[3]

It was equally difficult from 1960 to misunderstand the drift of Conservative colonial policy, against which Salisbury had so ineffectively warned in 1957, but about which there had been little active debate before the 1959 Election. Macmillan's choice of Iain Macleod as Colonial Secretary after his return to power placed in the hot seat the archetypal modern and liberal-minded Tory in place of the more traditional (and more right-wing) Alan Lennox-Boyd, who would shortly join the new Monday Club to indicate his displeasure at what had happened after he departed. Tory colonial policy, which had in fact been shifting ever since Macmillan took over from Eden, was accelerated by Macleod. More importantly Macleod saw it as his task to win support for his policies by the open advocacy of the case for decolonisation where Lennox-Boyd had proceeded more by stealth. Colonial policy was in 1961 as contentious as it had been relatively harmonious in 1957. The Macmillan–Macleod conviction was that Britain's remaining Third World colonies could not now be retained once they demanded independence, since Britain no longer had either the will or the defence resources to resist such demands; they saw the proper and most *conservative* course as being to steer colonies towards self-government before such demands led to bloodshed and visible British humiliation. But if this was actually only a change of pace since Lennox-Boyd, it seemed to be more to a Party which, since successful military campaigns in Malaya and Kenya in the past decade, had been taught to believe that Britain would at least choose the method and the pace of its own retreat from Empire. The elder statesman Lord Halifax, who had known plenty about British weakness even twenty years earlier at the time of Munich, thought in May 1958 that 'the difficulty of the Government is that they are tied by their local Conservatives, who do not yet realise that we are no longer a Great Power, and that the days are past when we could assert our authority with a Maxim gun'. Macmillan's 'winds of change' speech to the South African Parliament in 1960 was in part an attempt to remove that sort of illusion; it was a big political success for the Prime Minister, but the subsequent formation of the Monday Club (in direct opposition to his policy and taking its name from the day on which the speech had been delivered) heralded a running battle

---

[3] Robert Shepherd, *Iain Macleod* (1994), 155–61; Nicolson, *Harold Nicolson Diaries*, 331.

over African policy in the Party that would last for a generation. Alongside the conventionally right-wing elements that formed the Monday Club, and overlapping with them to a great extent, were the many Tories of all types, highly placed throughout the Party (especially in southern England) for whom the future of South Africa and Southern Rhodesia presented other problems, since so many of them had relatives who had chosen to settle there or had economic interests that they wished to preserve. As other policy areas were soon to show, the modernising impetus in the colonies ran counter to the *conservative* wish to defend property rights and special interests. Against the uncompromising official view, first of Macleod and then of Maudling when he succeeded him at the Colonial Office, that Britain's future role was not to be a colonial power and that that future should be embraced with enthusiasm rather than with dread, the right – and instinctively very many more in the Party too – felt only an uncomfortable reminder of Britain's decline and a betrayal of the 'kith and kin' who had been encouraged to migrate to Africa by previous Tory colonial secretaries. In place of Churchill's confidence-building doctrine of three circles of British internationalism (Empire, American Alliance and Europe) which intersected only in London, there was now within five years of his retirement the recognition of a Special Relationship that existed only on American sufferance and an Empire whose days were numbered. Macmillan's reassuring rhetoric continued to obscure some of these truths, but the struggle to defend actual policies without admitting to their primary motivation became more and more desperate. As Anthony Sampson pointed out at the time, the discussion of this shift of policy direction was enmeshed in the perception of the changing personnel of Conservative governments in the generation after Maxwell-Fyfe. The bitterest attack on Macleod's colonial policy, as 'too clever by half', came in March 1961 when he was assaulted in the House of Lords by Salisbury; in the subsequent furore, Macleod was backed by Lords Kilmuir and Hailsham (the latter in what Salisbury himself called 'a speech of extreme violence') and Salisbury's supporters included the Duke of Montrose and the Earl of Arran. One peer who observed it thought that 'it wasn't really about Africa. It was pure class warfare – the upper class peers against the middle class peers.' Sampson's own view was that 'it was not only a conflict between classes, and between old and new Conservatives: it was a conflict between a generation strong enough to stand up to its enemies, and one preoccupied with solidarity and survival.'[4]

Such worries might have been assuaged more successfully if the Government had managed to put momentum behind an alternative focus for Britain in the world, had in effect (in Dean Acheson's words) 'found a role' after having 'lost an Empire'. Entry to the European Common Market had been intended by Macmillan to fulfil precisely the inspirational focus of identity which the Empire could no longer supply (and which few Conservatives

---

[4] Nicolson, *Harold Nicolson Diaries*, 349; Sampson, *Anatomy*, 81–2.

felt for 'Commonwealth'). A sense of Britain's relative economic weakness contributed to the same strategy: whereas British policy-makers had allowed the early moves towards European integration to proceed in her absence under the twin illusions that the European Economic Community (EEC) without Britain could do her no economic harm, and that an alternative could be constructed in the European Free Trade Area (EFTA) that would bring equal benefits, by the time of the 1961–62 recession few Tory Ministers doubted that Britain must some day join the Common Market for her own economic security. A second economic downswing during the thirteen years of Tory government was crucial here, for it concentrated attention on the accumulating evidence that, while the British economy had performed impressively in the 1950s when compared to the 1930s (Macmillan's own constant point of comparison until 1960), then it had not done at all well when compared to the current rates of growth achieved by her industrial competitors. There was an almost inescapable conclusion that Keynesianism in one country was not going to prove to be the economic philosopher's stone and deliver affluence for all; with the increasing pace of decolonisation and the steady drift of the dominions away from traditional ties, Britain must anyway expect greater competition in the future in what had been her best markets. Once again economics and politics came together; without steady economic growth, the awkward choice that had faced Macmillan's Cabinet in December 1957 would recur with increasing frequency; how to sustain levels of social spending on which general Conservative popularity was thought to depend, without over-taxing the economic interests of the middle-class voter on whom the Party relied for money and work as well as support at elections, or borrowing to an extent that would induce inflation to the disadvantage of the Tory rentiers. The tensions involved in this strategic change of direction are looked at in Chapter 3.

However, the diagnosis of Britain's declining economic performance did not only rest on her international partnerships. Increasingly, the British economy was being said to be held back by its roots in an old-fashioned political and social culture, archetypally presented to a mass readership by Penguin Books' *What's Wrong with Britain?* series (which concluded that just about everything needed putting right). Macmillan himself was no natural conservative – Clement Attlee thought him to be the most radical man he had encountered in British politics – and was quite ready to embrace this prospective gospel of change. The shift to a neo-corporatist doctrine of indicative planning in 1961–62 by the Macmillan Government was to the premier an opportunity to bring to political centre stage ideas which he had advocated since he co-authored *Industry and the State* in 1927, and which now seemed to be paying off in the faster growing economies of France, West Germany and Japan. The 'New Approach' of Summer 1962 was an attempt by Macmillan to devise a domestic policy that would run alongside entry to the EEC in propelling Britain into modernity; the ministerial reshuffle of July 1962 was intended to provide the political counterpart to this economic strategy by highlighting new, younger faces at the cutting edge of Government policy. It was only the belated and reluctant recognition that there was no place for Selwyn Lloyd in this brave new world of Tory modernising, and the catastrophic mishandling of his dismissal by Macmillan, that diverted attention from the policy initiative on to political and personal battles. Nevertheless, by late 1962, the Government had changed course towards a European future, and had begun to put in place the domestic mechanisms of reform to underpin it. As John Campbell has pointed out, it is a significant pointer for the Party's future that Edward Heath was close to Macmillan while this shift of gear was being achieved, for the pursuit of economic growth achieved by domestic reform and of European integration was to remain Heath's political agenda throughout his front-bench career – and indeed afterwards too.[5]

There were though three serious difficulties with such a shift of direction, quite apart from the Party's sentimental attachment to a colonial past and the economic self-interest of some of its members in the colonial world. First, while Macmillan was indeed a man with a radical mind second to none, and with a ruthless determination to press through his 'new approach', he was also a man who had only recently traded most successfully on his own visible embodiment of Britain's past. The 'Edwardian style' of dress, walk, language and political persona that he had consciously adopted in the 1950s had been deeply reassuring to a Party that was quite happy *not* to confront the true lessons of Suez, preferring to accept Macmillan's confident assurances that Britain was still a great country, that she could remain a world power by cultural superiority, example and diplomatic skills even if no longer able to dominate by economic and military power. The significance of the cartoon character 'Supermac' lay in this collision of the romantic past and the tough-minded future in the real Macmillan. But the 'New Approach' (as even the name he gave to it suggested) had to eschew the past and welcome the future with open arms, to advocate change with enthusiasm and without regret. To a large extent Macmillan was incapable of doing this convincingly, and the problem only increased as he himself aged, at just the moment when sweeping changes in the popular culture of the Western world were bringing forward the spirit of youth. Even without the terminal damage inflicted on his Government by Vassall, Profumo and the failure to get into the EEC, Macmillan would in 1963 have had increasing difficulty in maintaining his ascendancy in a Cabinet that was a generation younger than he was, and against an Opposition Leader who was even younger than that (and who constantly harped on the fact), in a world where political leaders were measured against John F. Kennedy rather than 'Ike'.

---

[5] John Campbell, *Edward Heath* (1993), 134.

Macmillan was further disabled by increasing complaints (mainly from the press, but with echoing voices in the Party too), that for all his modernising rhetoric, he was actually a snob who filled his Government with extremely un-'modern'-looking ranks of relatives and Old Etonians, and thereby denied real influence to the Party's rising meritocrats. In this context, his determination that he should be succeeded by Lord Home when he eventually had to step down in October 1963, and deep suspicions that he had rigged the contest so that the 'establishment' candidate would win, were a fatal legacy from Macmillan both to his Party and to Home himself. For *The Economist,*

> the major national misgiving must be that [Home's] accession could retard the progress of modern Conservatism as a radical innovating force . . . . The new Prime Minister also claims to be by nature a Tory radical. He has in the past defined this himself – in a revealing phrase – by saying that he sees change as a fact of life, not merely to be recognised but welcomed. But he has not so obviously seen change as something he should strive to initiate and bring about. And herein lies the great divide, one which liberal Conservatives like Mr. Macleod are right to emphasise and which at least some of those who have sponsored Lord Home's candidature still seem loth to recognise.

When the symbolic Tory meritocrat Iain Macleod, a co-author of One Nation's 1954 publication *Change is Our Ally*, first refused to serve under Home and then penned the most informed press attack on what Macmillan had done in October 1963, such claims could not be ignored. Home himself, though he actually lacked 'side' to as great an extent as any Tory Leader between Baldwin and Major has ever done, seemed to epitomise through his background and social position the backward-looking side of Macmillan that he himself had been striving to subordinate.[6]

Home's narrow failure to win the 1964 Election, which was anyway a huge task after the ructions of 1963, and his poor performance in the rougher world of opposition in 1965, prompted his early downfall. In Edward Heath, the Party elected in July 1965 a Leader whose meritocratic origins were reflected in his 'blessed are the pacemakers' rhetoric, and for whom the modernisation of Britain and entry to the EEC were twin poles of the policy of a true believer. He won the leadership contest over Reginald Maudling whose language and policy preferences were remarkably close to his own; both men had emerged at the top at the end of the Macmillan period, and both of them saw Britain's future along the lines that the Macmillan Cabinet had embraced in 1962. For many of the younger generation of Conservatives, Heath's advent therefore seemed a golden opportunity to unite the future they believed in with a political style that did not distract with its over-the-shoulder nostalgia; and he was a man whose leisure pursuits would not locate him photographically among the country's landowners. A letter received at Central Office in December 1963 from a 44-year-old industrial manager put

6 *The Economist*, 26 Oct. 1963.

just this viewpoint, and very persuasively. In choosing Home, the Party had, he felt, showed that the

> 'establishment' . . . would rather lose the election than lose their power in the Party. We are looking for a 1963 leader. Do you remember Kennedy? We liked him. We are sick of seeing old-looking men dressed in flat caps and bedraggled tweeds strolling with a 12–bore. For God's sake, what is your campaign manager doing? These photographs of Macmillan's ghost with Home's face date about 1912. The nearest approach to our man is Heath. In every task he performs, win or lose, he has the facts, figures and knowledge. We don't give a damn if he is a bachelor. He is our age, and he is capable, he looks a director (of the Country), and most of all he is quite different from these tired old men, their 19th century appearance and their 18th century platitudes. Capable as we think Mr. Heath is, we don't believe he or his kind will ever be allowed to take the reins from the tired, old men, or the Etonians.

The loss of votes by the Conservative Party in 1964 from exactly the type of young manager for whom this correspondent claimed to speak (and for which there was abundant evidence at the time) undoubtedly helped to get Heath's leadership campaign rolling. Heath's election as Party Leader therefore seemed a belated denial of these claims that the 'establishment' would ever give up its power to such a man. It was easy in all of this not to notice that Heath's rise through the ranks had been very much as an insider, in the successive positions of Chief Whip, trusted confidant to Macmillan as Prime Minister and main domestic prop to the Home Government. He had permeated the establishment rather than overturning it, as say Macleod or Powell might have done, and as Heath's own successor in the leadership would quite deliberately attempt.[7]

The second problem with the Macmillan 'new approach' as carried forward to Heath's leadership election was the specific policy area of industrial relations. Throughout the 1950s, and especially at the end of the decade, the Party leaders had stifled or ignored the increasing demands of the rank and file for legislative action to curb the freedom of the trade unions. Successive Tory Ministers of Labour after Walter Monckton, with only the partial exception of Macleod and Heath, had seen it as their job to encourage and strengthen trade union leaders against their own shop stewards, and to do nothing that would make their position weaker. As the union leaderships entered on a more left-wing phase of activity, and as unofficial strikes and demarcation disputes made the unions a favourite Tory scapegoat for Britain's poor economic performance, the Government's position became steadily more difficult to maintain. But the 'New Approach' required the cooperation of union leaders in corporate harmony with the Government and the leaders of industry in the pursuit of economic growth, harmony that would not be encouraged by legislation that the unions themselves

---

[7] John Ramsden, *The Making of Conservative Party Policy: The Conservative Research Department since 1929* (1980), 225–6.

opposed. The creation of the National Economic Development Council and the National Incomes Commission by the Macmillan Government therefore provided both a further, pressing argument for keeping the Trades Union Congress (TUC) in cooperative mood and – to Tory critics of this policy – fresh evidence that the unions would not give up anything in return for being involved in a national governing partnership; such schemes were therefore only delaying the moment when the Government would have to take responsibility for modernising industrial relations practices by law. The failure of the Home Government to face up to this issue during its short life – when it was quite ready to deal with the equally contentious matter of Resale Price Maintenance (RPM) which hit the Tory shopkeeper vote hard – was seen by some of its Tory critics as evidence of its poor political strategy. After power was lost in October 1964 the dam burst within weeks, and by Summer 1965 the Conservative Party was irrevocably committed to trade union legislation that would if necessary be imposed. But that dramatic shift was once again easily misunderstood, for neither Heath, who largely engineered the policy change before he became Leader, nor the successive Party spokesmen on industrial relations, had actually abandoned the 'partnership' approach to the maintenance of low inflation and high growth rates that they themselves had followed in office. That approach was no longer unchallenged within the Party high command, for by 1965 Enoch Powell had laid out the full prospectus for a 'deflationist' economic strategy – and this fact too led to a blurring of Heath's intentions and to new possibilities of misunderstanding – but neither Heath nor his closest advisers ever abandoned in their own minds the instinctive corporatism that they had practised since 1962. Much of this is explored in Chapter 5.

The third problem with the modernising thrust of policy from the early 1960s was that many Conservatives at every level of the Party did not actually like it very much. Quite apart from those whose personal interests might be threatened by a meritocratic Toryism, there were many who disliked the rhetoric of modernising change simply because they were natural conservatives who did not therefore see it as their Party's business to preach the opposite viewpoint. As each area came up for review – economic policy, education, industrial relations, transport, local government – it was possible to educate the Party to the need for the reforms proposed, but it was far less easy to make Conservatives into enthusiasts for change as such. Indeed, in 1964 Oliver Poole told David Butler that this was the main fault-line in the contemporary Conservative Party, separating

> those who positively like modern British society, with its motor cars, modern buildings and egalitarianism, and those who do not. The traditionalists recognise that change is necessary and seldom try to impede it, but they do not welcome it, and their lack of enthusiasm is always a force to be reckoned with. Much of the Party's history from 1960 onwards becomes intelligible only in the light of this division.

In 1970, congratulating Edward Heath on his victory, Robert Blake felt the need also to remind him of Lord Coleraine's recent book, *For Conservatives Only*; this had shown 'the folly of the Conservative Party posing as the party of "change" in order to attract to its side a largely fictitious, minority progressivist floating vote.' William Deedes was arguing something very similar in 1973 when he diagnosed the same worries as being at the heart of the Heath Government's problems with 'faithful Conservatives outside Westminster'. The Party had 'permanently adopted, so to speak, the banner of the One Nation Group pamphlet . . . "Change is Our Ally",' but 'change is an anxious, disturbing process and perpetual change becomes alarming to many.' He conceded that 'it is plain enough that the old world *has* come to an end', but argued that 'far from regretting it', Conservative leaders 'seem to be making a good thing of it'. This, he felt, gave Powell's more pessimistic and more traditional messages a strong appeal. In 1963–65, Macmillan could instinctively appeal to Tory progressives as well as to the traditionalists, Home only to the traditionalists, Heath only to the progressives. The young technocrats to whom Heath appealed could though not easily be attracted without the loss of votes elsewhere; Iain Macleod reminded the Party Conference in 1966,

> Let us remember that we are not all pace-setters, we are not all competitors, and let us remember that change when it comes as it must is often a very cruel thing to an individual or a township or a country. So competition needs compassion.

These issues are explored in Chapters 3 and 4, though many of them recur in later chapters too.[8]

In 1969, James Margach thought that

> Heath was lucky. The Tories were in the mood to swing from the high breeding of the great aristocratic families with rolling acres and grouse moors to the lower middle-class artisan breeding with a mere third-acre at the back of the semi-detached. Heath fitted the bill as to the manner born by breeding. Basically, the party wanted a Tory Wilson, a grammar-school boy who, like Labour's leader, had been to Oxford too for finishing. Heath was the identikit model for the abrasive pace-setters who were supposed to be on the voters' rolls in their millions.

With Heath as Leader, the Party therefore embarked on a policy review that positively relished the new rather than the traditional. But it had to do so in Opposition, and in a hurry that discouraged the careful move from general principles to policy detail that had been adopted between 1946 and 1949. As a Leader elected in Opposition, Heath had continuing difficulties in gaining full authority in the Party, very much as Thatcher was to do between 1975 and

---

[8]   D.E. Butler and Anthony King, *The British General Election of 1964* (1965), 79; Robert Blake, 'Mr. Heath's Triumph', *Spectator*, 27 June 1970; William Deedes, 'Conflicts within the Conservative Party', in *Political Quarterly*, vol. 44 (1973), 435; Robert Shepherd, *Iain Macleod*, 438.

1979. Even supportive colleagues found the 'government in exile' approach that Heath adopted to be restrictive, and the Party rank and file were for much of the time discontented with Heath's public relations performance – a field in which he had few natural skills and even less personal interest. The failure of the Wilson Government to maintain its popularity and the consequent avalanche of Conservative gains in opinion polls, local and by-elections masked this problem and allowed Heath to continue without any actual challenger to his leadership before 1970, but it was always an uncomfortable ride. The increasing estrangement of Heath and Powell culminated in the 1968 sacking of Powell from the shadow cabinet when he stirred up a furore, for *and* against his views, on the race issue. This explosion of feeling on a sensitive subject on which (at least in certain regions) the rank and file felt very differently from most of their leaders, distracted attention away from even deeper cracks that were opening up on economic policy, and which with Powell's departure could now be papered over. Rab Butler had noted that the members of Macmillan's 1963 Cabinet encompassed two distinct philosophies, already identifying Keith Joseph as a spokesman for the anti-interventionist wing, and a keen reader of Conservative frontbenchers' speeches could by 1968 perceive this from the outside too; in that year Arthur Seldon of the free-market Institute of Economic Affairs felt that Conservatives spoke with two different voices, only one of which differed significantly from that of the Labour Government. After 1968, and especially after the return to office in 1970, the unorthodox, unKeynesian strain of policy was again marginalised, when Joseph in particular stopped arguing the Powellite case, but the Party's official rhetoric between the Selsdon Conference of January 1970 and the Election in June suggested that economic Powellism had made at least some impact on the official Party and its Leader. This is analysed in Chapter 5, and provides an essential background to an understanding of the Heath Government's record in office and its subsequent repudiation by a section of the Party's leadership in 1974.[9]

The 1970 General Election seemed to mark the termination of all these difficulties. In the latter opposition years, Heath had finally been persuaded to act on good professional advice on presentation, and as a result one of the least media-minded premiers of modern times was propelled into office with the most elaborate media campaign to date. Heath though seemed more aware of having won a personal victory, against the expectations of everyone but himself, than of the means by which it had been achieved, and in office he more than reverted to type. Taking their cue from the Prime Minister, and seriously damaged by the death of the master communicator Macleod within weeks of entering office, Heath's Ministers were rarely able to present a persuasive account of their policies and the reasoning behind them to an increasingly hostile public and Party. Although the 1970 Government

[9] James Margach, *The Anatomy of Power* (1969), 8.

was unusually assiduous in the carrying out of its pledges, and remarkably single-minded in the pursuit of such consistent policy objectives as entry to Europe, stability in Ulster and economic growth, it was also unusually pragmatic about the means used to achieve these ends. As a result, it had by 1972 acquired the catastrophic reputation of being an administration that was all too ready to reverse its policies at a moment's notice. For some Conservatives the 1972 U-turns on incomes policy and/or on industry were the crucial point, for others it was acceptance of the Ugandan Asians, all issues on which methods of policy in 1972 conflicted with the rhetoric of 1970, and arguably contradicted explicit promises too. More often, Tory mutiny derived from the accumulation of grievances and the sense (reinforced by the Government's public relations failures) that the Party leadership did not itself quite know what it was doing or why. These problems came to a climax in the first General Election of 1974, which the Party so desperately wanted to win in order to tame the unions and purge the humiliations of the past few years, but which instead led to the loss of office when – as in 1923 – an Election need not even have been held. This is discussed in Chapter 6.

Alongside the conventional story of the Party's policy and campaigning relationship with its voters and with the country at large there was a domestic side too. Chapter 2 describes the way in which the Party itself operated and was managed in Macmillan's heyday, and may be set alongside similar chapters contained in earlier volumes of this series. By 1960, the Party had passed on from the heroic phase of post-war recovery from the nadir of 1945, and was strong and confident in its own self-image. It still had a very large membership, healthy finances that allowed it to be the least conservative party in electioneering practices, and a traditional view of its own centrality to the British political and social system; honours received by Party activists for 'public' as well as 'political' services were a twice-yearly reminder of that fact. The Party's leaders and managers were though uneasily aware that it was already proving increasingly difficult to maintain the momentum of Party activity in the constituencies without a radical shake-up – which the local parties did not want and which the central agencies were unable to insist on. Progress was certainly made, as for example with the spread of model rules to guide local parties, so that some of the more haphazard ways of running local associations and selecting their candidates became steadily more unusual, but such developments were slow and piecemeal, and came only by consent. Edward du Cann's chairmanship (1965–67), marked the first drive towards a comprehensive modernisation of the machinery since the 1940s. At the centre, these changes achieved a great deal, if not always immediately, but out in the sticks the forces of inertia were more resistant. By the early 1970s therefore, Conservative organisation in Scotland and in most English cities was in a dangerously run-down condition, membership had declined to less than half of its peak level of 1952, and the Party was seriously short of money. There was an increasing dislocation between the outgoing electioneering approach of the central Party offices, geared to the latest professional advice from the marketing and media industries, and the traditionally-introverted socialising and fundraising activities of the local associations (which were anyway of decreasing effectiveness as their memberships fell). And to date all attempts to bridge the gap had been politely rebuffed by the constituencies or simply not implemented in practice. Faced with this dilemma, and while continuing to pay lip-service to the importance of constituency activity, the Party's central organisations would have to place more and more reliance on their own electioneering in future campaigns: whereas in 1951 (*after* the Woolton recovery and when the Party was flush with funds) Central Office had still spent only a fifth of the Party's total election budget, the rest being spent by candidates in the constituencies, in 1970 central spending was over half of the Party's total and by 1979 it would be about two-thirds. The speed with which this process took place should not be exaggerated, but the evidence of the long-term trend was clear enough by February 1975. These domestic affairs are examined in Chapters 2, 5 and 7.

Once Heath lost the authority of the Prime Minister, he was a beleaguered leader. His attempt to do a deal with the Liberals to retain office (and the simultaneous rebuff to Unionists who had been Conservative allies for a century) would surely have provoked a severe Party crisis if it had come off, but in the event only deepened the sense of failure when it fell through. The attempt poisoned Heath's last year as Leader, for it was impossible to argue against an all-party government in Summer 1974 after Heath himself had tried to create one in March. It was equally impossible wholeheartedly to advocate such a coalition without probable Conservative rebellions and certain loss of Party morale. The shaky and obscure forms of words adopted for the October 1974 campaign were testament to that fact and were also the source of severe recriminations directed at Heath himself when the Party lost again. From October 1974 the ground slipped away from the Leader at a speed that astonished observers both inside and outside the Party. In part that simply reflected his record of losing so many elections, something for which the Conservative Party has rarely been forgiving, but in part it also followed from the refusal of Heath and his closest advisers to accept that much academic and press opinion had moved sharply in the direction of the alternative economic strategy that Conservative leaders had successfully marginalised ever since 1945. For market economics the hour had come, with Keith Joseph becoming the bearer of the message. Even after losing three elections of his four as Leader, Heath offered his Party no change of direction to indicate that he had learned from what the electorate considered to be his mistakes, while his chief critics offered both an apology for past errors and a recipe for a different future. The refusal of Heath to stand down in favour of a Leader of whom he could approve, his apparent reluctance even to face re-election, and the rapid, skilfully managed rise of Thatcher as 'the only man amongst them', the only frontbencher whose candidature would allow the

Party to get rid of a Leader that Tory MPs no longer wanted, completed the process of Heath's fall. All of this is related in Chapter 7.

It is clear that when MPs voted for Margaret Thatcher in February 1975 they had – as in July 1965 – only the haziest real idea what the new Leader would do when installed in office a few years later. In each case the new Leader had been chosen for oppositional and presentational skills as much as for real policy alternatives, in each case as a reaction against what had gone before and as a reaction too against the Labour premier who had to be faced across the despatch box. Nevertheless, the election of Thatcher can reasonably be seen as a turning away from the policy package that Macmillan had evolved as Prime Minister and Heath had striven to pursue; henceforward, neither Europe as a focus of British identity nor the modernising lessons that could be learned from the economic performance of other countries would figure prominently in Conservative rhetoric; the need for change and reform would become even more insistent, but the inspirational models for those changes would be sought in the past and within Britain rather than in the future and abroad. This volume therefore charts the progress of the Conservative Party from the Edwardian style of 1958 to the espousal of Victorian values after 1975, via the aggressive adoption of the perceived demands of the twenty-first century in the years in between.

Part I

The Macmillan Ascendancy

I had myself to take a staunch decision to back the Common Market. This meant overcoming my anxieties on domestic agriculture and Saffron Walden. Once done I found that I could be of great service to the PM who needs and likes a companion . . . I said I felt as at the time of the India Bill, that here at this [Commonwealth] Conference was a choice between the future and the past. I told the PM of my talks with Baldwin, and how he, despite Churchill's opposition, had said 'India is so big a subject that I would be glad to go down for it.' Harold was pleased with the description that here was a matter for the future.

(Note by R.A. Butler, 23 October 1962)

I spent some time in the House assessing the position and could not but register that there was very strong tide flowing in favour of a new generation. This is partly a reaction against Macmillan's age and partly a desire to match Wilson in this country and Kennedy in America. . . . The turn on Macmillan is, of course, typical of the ingratitude of politics. They were lauding him only a few minutes ago at the 1922 Committee Private Members' lunch and they have owed most them their present positions to his ability in the past.

(Note by R.A. Butler, 19 June 1963)

There is an inherent dilemma in the construction of a Conservative election policy for 1963–64. On the one hand, the record of our past achievements and the pejorative comparison of Socialist achievement and policy have become boring to the point of irrelevance. Twelve years' worth of the electoral roll have never voted on a Socialist record, nor can recall, as adults, anything but the present series of Conservative administrations. What we need, more than ever before, is the momentum and attraction of bold new policies. On the other hand, the longer our continuous period of office extends, the harder it becomes suddenly to propound such policies: the question 'Why have you only just thought of this?' becomes increasingly embarrassing, and the practical administrative problem of disengaging from policies in force becomes more and more intractable.

(Enoch Powell paper, Chairman's Policy Committee, March 1962)

Chapter 1

The rise of 'Supermac', 1957–59

The Macmillan Government

When Harold Macmillan became Conservative Party Leader in January 1957, few expected his Government to survive for long, especially when Lord Salisbury – widely though wrongly seen as January's kingmaker – resigned only a few weeks later. When in May the Prime Minister summoned John Wyndham to Downing Street to join his personal staff, he explained why he had not done so earlier: 'The fact is that I did not really think my administration could last for more than a few weeks; but we seem now to have got over a number of jumps on this Grand National course, and having just managed to pull the old mare through the brook and somehow got to the other side with the Cecil colours fallen, I am plucking up my courage.' Lord Hailsham had told the Macmillan Cabinet when it first assembled that 'we should be extremely lucky, in the confused state of public opinion at the time, if we were not skittled out by July'; the Party Chairman, Oliver Poole, had warned Macmillan that there was 'a considerable sense of confusion and uncertainty in the ranks of the Party', even among those who had been loyal throughout the recent crisis; at Saffron Walden the Conservatives discussed a possible return to recruiting, but decided that 'unless something spectacular in favour of the Government took place, it would be quite impossible to work up any enthusiasm for such a campaign'; in Derbyshire, the High Peak Tories discussed in March 'the growing discontent of supporters with the Government and consequent refusal to re-subscribe at present'.[1]

Relying on the support of Poole and on the Chief Whip Edward Heath, Macmillan's objective for that first few months was simply to hang on; some controversial legislation such as a Shops Bill was ditched, though the difficult Rent Bill could not go without too great a loss of face. Macmillan was unlikely to lose his own nerve: Harry Crookshank, who had served with Macmillan in the Grenadier Guards in the Great War was fond of quoting in

[1] Lord Egremont, *Wyndham and Children First* (1968), 161; Lord Hailsham, *The Door Wherein I Went* (1975), 149; Alistair Horne, *Macmillan, 1957–1986* (1989), 17–18; Saffron Walden Conservative Association (CA) minutes, 19 Feb. 1957; High Peak CA minutes, 1 Mar. 1957.

the 1950s the Brigade's catchphrase for any special act of courage, 'nearly as brave as Mr. Macmillan'. The new Prime Minister spent much time in the Smoking Room, soothing raw nerves, and in his first year he was also an unusually regular visitor to the 1922 Committee. So attentive was he to the Party that he even turned up unexpectedly at a Sussex Young Conservative (YC) dinner at the Commons – and achieved his objective, for one of the guests reported that 'the Prime Minister was in great form. He was brimful of confidence for the future and imparted the same feeling to us all.' The strategy was explained to Poole after a by-election defeat in February, which Poole had attributed to 'the climate of opinion in the country': Macmillan replied that 'what we have got to work upon is the Party at Westminster and the Organisation in the Country. This should in time have its effect among the people as a whole. However, we must face the fact that we have a lot of very unpopular things to do. What I am trying to arrange is that we should get them all done as soon as possible, so that when the more attractive things come along, we have the troublesome things behind us.' Meanwhile, the public face of the Prime Minister was confident; his first television address to the nation ridiculed the idea that Suez had demonstrated British weakness in a world of great powers, but it also offered the first full-length viewing of his soon-to-be-familiar theme of 1950s affluence contrasted with 1930s unemployment.[2]

It was a rocky ride for the first year, punctuated by the Salisbury resignation in March, another Suez rebellion in May, and a December split on economic policy that led to the resignation of the entire Treasury team. Nevertheless, although in 1957 opinion polls and by-elections went badly, Macmillan was quietly pursuing the strategy he had explained to Poole; a year after he became Prime Minister, the difficult legislation of the Parliament was on the statute book, the effect of Suez had been neutralised, the Party's colonial policy had been fixed on a path that produced little dissent for the next two years, and the stage had been set for economic recovery. Alongside these policy successes, which won few votes at the time, Macmillan had begun to emerge as a Tory vote-winner on a scale that can only be compared in Conservative Party history to Baldwin in and after 1924.

Within hours of becoming Leader, Macmillan had reappointed the whole team of Chief Whip, Party Chairman, Vice Chairmen and Party Treasurers, so that they could continue without interruption in the urgent task of steadying the ranks. Heath, who would have liked to move from the Whip's office to a department of his own, was told that 'the Government is like a regiment. You

2 Gerald Nabarro, *Nab 1: Portrait of a Politician* (1969), 32; Philip Goodhart, *The 1922: The Story of the 1922 Committee* (1973), 176; John Campbell, *Edward Heath* (1993), 104; Andrew Roth, *Heath and the Heathmen* (1972), 115; Central Office Chairman's department file CCO 20/8/2, Correspondence with Macmillan, 1957; George Hutchinson, *The Last Edwardian at Number 10* (1980), 42–7.

cannot change the CO and the adjutant at the same time.' But a severe pruning of the company officers was carried out. There had been many arrivals and departures since the return to office in 1951 but no really comprehensive reshuffle, and this Macmillan now undertook. As a result, his team was his own as Eden's never had been. Anthony Head was summarily sacked from the Cabinet, probably because he was unlikely to fall in with Macmillan's desire to reduce spending and reorientate defence policy, and four other Ministers were removed – Gwylim Lloyd George, Patrick Buchan-Hepburn, Walter Monckton and James Stuart; the last two were quite ready to go, and the first three went straight to the Lords, Stuart joining them in 1959; with Selkirk's demotion from the Cabinet and Eden's departure, this removed seven Cabinet Ministers, a purge comparable to 1962. The key placement was Butler, and here the Prime Minister won a triumph of the will that was to characterise all their future dealings. Butler wanted the Foreign Office, a post he might well have insisted on but which would have brought clashes with the premier, as Eden had clashed with Churchill and Macmillan with Eden. Macmillan was in any case determined not to sack Selwyn Lloyd, since over Suez 'one head on a charger [was] quite enough', and insisted that Butler take the Home Office instead. This also placed Butler in a department from which he would continue to be attacked by the Party's right wing for his liberal views. Peter Thorneycroft's move to succeed Macmillan at the Treasury opened the way for the general reshuffle. Only five Cabinet Ministers now remained who had served in the wartime coalition and only four who had sat in Cabinet in 1951; when Salisbury left in March 1957, only six Cabinet Ministers even held the same post as in the previous December. This provided room to bring in new faces: Lord Hailsham, Henry Brooke, Harold Watkinson and Charles Hill joined the Cabinet, while Reginald Maudling, Ernest Marples and Enoch Powell were all promoted outside the Cabinet. The average age of the Cabinet fell to 53. Powell's appointment as number two at the Treasury was prophetically welcomed by the *Daily Express* as 'a faint beam of hope for those who fear the pro-European bias in the Administration'. There was also some fine political tuning in the encouragement of both Edward Boyle and Julian Amery, representing opposite groups of dissenters over Suez. Norman St. John Stevas later recalled attending a dinner called to celebrate Boyle's principled resignation in November, which was 'somewhat marred by the fact that he was back in office by the time the celebration was due to be held'. Boyle characteristically amended Central Office's discreet draft of its standard biographical details for him as a Minister, so as to include a paragraph still explaining why he had resigned in 1956, but turned down invitations to speak outside his constituency while 'the Suez controversy is a pretty live issue'.[3]

[3] Central Office Chairman's department file, CCO 20/8/2; Roth, *Heath* (1972), 118; James Stuart, *Within the Fringe* (1967), 179; Lord Butler, *The Art of the Possible: The Memoirs of Lord Butler* (1971), 196; Gerald Sparrow, *Rab: Study of a Statesman* (1965), 152; Anthony Howard,

A few weeks later, Salisbury's resignation threatened the new team before it got into its stride. The immediate occasion was the Government's decision to release from detention the Cypriot leader Archbishop Makarios, without securing any promise of good conduct; to Salisbury this signalled a lack of determination in Government policy towards the colonies – and in the sense that it prefigured the release of Jomo Kenyatta in Kenya and Hastings Banda in Nyasaland it did indeed prefigure a readiness by the Macmillan Government to talk to violent opponents of British rule in an accelerated process of decolonisation. Macmillan had made clear to colleagues within days of becoming Prime Minister his entirely pragmatic approach to decolonisation; he circulated a Cabinet paper on 28 January calling for a 'profit and loss' account to be drawn up for each colony, 'so that we may be better able to gauge whether, from the financial and economic point of view, we are likely to gain or lose by its departure'; he foresaw that some colonies would become 'ripe for independence over the next few years' and that others which 'are not really ready for it, will demand it so insistently that their claims cannot be denied'. It seems remarkable that Macmillan had succeeded to the premiership only days before writing this, as the candidate of the right wing of the Party, a fact which helps to explain later disillusion with him in that quarter. Salisbury entirely failed to make clear these deeper issues involved in his resignation – having heard his explanation, Woolton thought it 'a somewhat feeble reason' – and since he had threatened to resign at regular intervals in the past he probably did not expect to depart anyway. John Wyndham wrote that 'Lord Salisbury, very upset, tendered his resignation, and in those years in Downing Street there was probably nothing to equal the astonishment when Mr. Macmillan accepted it.' By calling his long overdue bluff Macmillan ensured that Salisbury left over a containable issue. A month later the Prime Minister was noting privately that it had been extremely helpful of Salisbury to go over Cyprus, when he could have done so much more damage by waiting to resign over Suez, but at the time his diary showed both deep animosity and the inherent ambivalence of the historically-minded Macmillan to aristocratic allies: 'all through history the Cecils, when any friend or colleague has been in real trouble, have stabbed him in the back – attributing the crime to qualms of conscience'. Anthony Howard overstates the case somewhat in arguing that Salisbury 'vanished from the British political scene almost as though he had never been', for his interventions in the Lords on colonial subjects and his readiness to articulate white settler opinion made him a man who had to be watched

continued

RAB: The Life of R.A. Butler (1987), 149–50; W. Gore Allen, *The Reluctant Politician: Derick Heathcoat Amory* (1958), 168; Earl of Kilmuir, *Political Adventure* (1964), 288; Andrew Roth, *Enoch Powell: Tory Tribune* (1970), 162–3; Boyle's correspondence with Central Office, January 1957, Boyle MSS 22502, 22504; Norman St. John Stevas, *The Two Cities* (1984), 40.

carefully for the next seven years, but it is certainly true that his leaving of the Government caused only a small splash. Lord Kilmuir recalled that 'one Area Chairman, forewarned by telephone of the impending announcement, enquired, with genuine incomprehension, who Lord Salisbury was'; this too is surely exaggerated, but does convey the Party mood in 1957. Since 1852, when the 2nd Marquess of Salisbury took office under Derby, the Cecils had played a continuous part in Conservative ministerial politics but they were not to do so again for nearly forty years; the long historical shadow of the Hotel Cecil had masked the post-war reality – that political respect for the family's past services had long gone. Now Salisbury's departure provided only a platform on which Macmillan could show his authority; Richard Crossman, looking back at the beginning of May, saw that the March week-end of the Salisbury resignation was 'the moment when [Macmillan] consolidated his leadership and stopped the collapse of the Tory Government'. It was also a moment of significance for another reason, for Salisbury's departure meant that Home became Leader of the Lords and was able to demonstrate his own leadership potential as a result; in notes for a talk on 'The Macmillan Epoch', Kilmuir, who watched this in the Lords, gave as one of the five factors that stabilised Macmillan's administration in 1957–58 'the extraordinary development of Lord Home in the House of Lords'.[4]

In May though, Crossman was being characteristically perceptive, for he was writing before the Suez issue had been neutralised. Macmillan himself, in another of the racing analogies he favoured, told his diary that 'I don't see how we can fail to take a toss at the Canal hazard. The best we can hope for is to pull the horse, rather vigorously, to the other side and then scramble back into the saddle.' The normalisation of international relations, especially with the US Government, had been a priority since November, but the final climb-down, when the Cabinet advised British shipowners to use the Canal and pay dues to Egypt, was the truly difficult moment; this inescapably demonstrated that all the efforts of 1956 had failed, something that Eden and Macmillan had refused to acknowledge and had so far managed to conceal from view. Fourteen Tory MPs abstained in the vote and eight resigned the whip to sit as independents; they were disconcerted to find that they were immediately struck off mailing lists for Party briefings and deprived of their places and the right to speak at the Party Conference; Poole and Heath were careful though not to widen the breach, since 'the Party is not fond of sanctions', as Poole put it, and Party speakers were sent into the rebels' constituencies to defend the Government only when actually asked for by the local Conservative associations; all the rebels who stood for re-election

[4] John Turner, *Macmillan* (1994), 178; Woolton MSS, diary, March 1957; Egremont, *Wyndham*, 161; Harold Macmillan, *Riding the Storm, 1956–1959* (1971), 235; Horne, *Macmillan*, 38; Howard, *RAB*, 254; Kilmuir, *Political Adventure*, 293; Janet Morgan (ed.), *The Backbench Diaries of Richard Crossman* (1981), 588; Kilmuir note, undated, Kilmuir MSS, 6/8.

in 1959 were by then once again official candidates. The continuing dissent of the Suez rebels was in any case only part of a gradual increase in the tendency of backbenchers to rebel; in the 1955 Parliament as a whole, half of all Tory MPs defied the whip on one or more occasions, a figure that rose to three-quarters in the more difficult Parliament of 1959. Despite the activities of the Suez rebels, the mocking of Selwyn Lloyd by Labour helped to rally the Conservatives. Macmillan made a fighting speech and had an ovation from his own side; he saw this as 'an extraordinary and spontaneous act of loyalty . . . How odd the English are! They rather like a gallant failure. Suez has become a sort of Mons retreat.' No Conservative MPs voted for Labour's critical motion, and there was an overall majority of forty-nine for the Government. Macmillan's own feeling later was that 'we had turned the corner. We should now be able, with ordinary luck, to run till the normal end of the Parliament.' *The Economist* agreed: 'the Prime Minister has cleared his own Suez Canal.' There was a successful Party Conference in October, with Macmillan cheering up his supporters with an attack on Labour. Aneurin Bevan had spoken of the British as 'an embittered and frustrated industrial mass', but Macmillan now asked 'where he got that impression from. Has he never seen any of those six million TV aerials which have gone up since 1951? Has he never come across any of the extra two million cars or motor bicycles? Does his view not embrace any of those houses he didn't build and we did?' The Government's answer to Suez would be to bang on about domestic affluence.[5]

Macmillan and the 'Edwardian style'

By this time, Macmillan's approach to government and his political style had begun to operate in his favour too. Colleagues were complimentary about his handling of Cabinet, the private office and the government machine. He can even be seen as re-establishing Cabinet government after six years of eccentric management. Thorneycroft reported him to be 'a superbly sensitive and businesslike chairman'; Watkinson admired the skill of his summing up in Cabinet, expressing the will of the majority while also giving a clear lead; Hill felt that 'if he dominated it (he usually did), it was done by sheer superiority of mind and of judgement. He encouraged genuine discussion provided it kept to the point'; Kilmuir's view was that Macmillan was 'businesslike and firm. . . . He imparted confidence to his colleagues and the Party in Parliament. . . . It was a remarkable example of

---

5 Macmillan, *Riding the Storm*, 231; R.J. Jackson, *Rebels and Whips: Dissension, Discipline and Cohesion in British Political Parties since 1945* (1968), 158–9; Kilmuir, *Political Adventure*, 289; Horne, *Macmillan*, 18, 40; Roth, *Heath*, 172; Central Office Chairman's department files, CCO 20/1/5, Correspondence with the Chief Whip, and CCO 20/8/2; Central Office *Notes on Current Politics* [hereafter *NCP*] 28 Oct. 1957.

how a political revival must start from the top'. Butler, who rapidly settled into a good working relationship as Macmillan's acknowledged deputy, also found much to admire:

> My description of the Prime Minister as being the Restoration Monarch of modern times is, I think, just. He has the characteristic of working extremely hard and conscientiously at his problems and then spending infinite time without apparent fatigue in the Smoking Room, talking to his critics or friends, as the case may be. He has an infinite capacity for elasticity which might tire his friends, if they did not realise that he is ruthless in his determination to carry the disaffected along with him at all costs. This would not lead to great cosiness, were it not for an urbanity which accompanies his manner.[6]

Alongside skilled management of the Cabinet went effective liaison with press and Party. There has been no more successful working relationship in this crucial area than between 1957 and 1959. The private office was ably staffed, the appointment of Wyndham being critical for Party work; the Prime Minister insisted both on an atmosphere of unhurried calm in the office (hence his famous motto from *The Gondoliers*, 'quiet calm deliberation disentangles every knot') and on the efficient dispatch of daily business before the end of the day, setting a good example by a scrupulous punctuality in his own paperwork. Within Parliament, the Prime Minister's Parliamentary Private Secretary (PPS), first Robert Allan and from 1958 Anthony Barber (both of whom had the added advantage of coming to the post from the Whips' office), was pro-active in keeping open avenues of communication with the backbenchers; those defending marginals could be encouraged with occasional visits to Number 10 that produced photographs on the doorstep shaking Macmillan's hand, and many backbenchers received congratulatory notes on speeches they had made in the House – after the PPS had drawn it to the premier's attention. None of this conveys though the sense of purpose and fun that Macmillan inspired among his personal staff and closest Party contacts; Anthony Barber, who saw him almost daily, recalls how far the Prime Minister enjoyed the mutual encouragement that such small-change Party activities involved when it was all on an upbeat in 1958 and 1959. For big speeches, the combined resources of the Conservative Research Department (CRD), Central Office's George Christ, and John Wyndham would be enlivened by the intellectual input of the Prime Minister himself; Wyndham took to tape-recording Macmillan's off-the-cuff remarks at less prestigious occasions to provide copy for the next set-piece oration. How sharp was the political cutting edge of the Downing Street staff and the Prime Minister in these years can be seen in correspondence between Leader and Party Chairman, for at least as much political input flowed down from

---

[6] Alan Thompson, *The Day Before Yesterday* (1971), 162–3; Roth, *Powell*, 168; Harold Watkinson, *Turning Points: A Record of Our Times* (Salisbury, 1986), 74; Lord Hill, *Both Sides of the Hill* (1964), 235; Kilmuir, *Political Adventure*, 308; Howard, *RAB*, 259–60.

Number 10 as in the reverse direction. On occasion, the Chairman was given a blinding glimpse of how far electoral politics was going on without the need of his advice: in April 1959, Lord Hailsham suggested that with an election imminent Macmillan might like to invite into Downing Street a few key newspaper proprietors. Macmillan replied that he already met several of those named more often than monthly and had talked to all of them since the start of the year, added a longish list of the editors with whom he was also in regular touch, and rounded it off with the news that he had lunched twenty-four Scottish editors only the previous Friday; an abashed Hailsham could only respond 'Thankyou for your impressive minute about press owners. I had no idea you had been so busy.' A few months later, Macmillan was already meeting Roy Thomson, just embarking on his career in British newspapers, a contact set up by Canadian Conservatives. The Party did not need to know about such contacts, and the combination of Party and Government worked well.[7]

The Liaison Committee (created in 1952 to link Party and Government in the presentation of policy) functioned more effectively than under Churchill or Eden, because Macmillan took a personal interest in its work and Charles Hill was a good chairman; Hill was, as Chancellor of the Duchy of Lancaster, almost entirely free to work on presenting the Government's case, a task he had been given in the dying days of the Eden administration and would continue with until 1962; Hill also selected Harold Evans to be the Prime Minister's press officer, another conscious effort to improve both coordination and the improvement of the presentational side. Each Liaison Committee meeting discussed coming ministerial speeches and ways in which they might put across positive points even in bad weeks, what Michael Fraser called 'blow softeners'. In June 1957 Fraser, following Macmillan's strategic lead, urged that a batch of unpopular White Papers be all published together and 'the good ones spread out over a period'. Careful coordination of Party and Government publicity was set up to deal with the Rent Bill, with the Defence White Paper, and with the Suez debate. In July 1957, the broad line that Macmillan took for his major speech at Bedford derived from discussion in the Liaison Committee. One organisational feature was entirely new, the creation in 1957 of a Steering Committee that aimed to do for medium-term strategy what the Liaison Committee did for tactics. This at first upset Butler, for it threatened to impinge on the policy-making system that he had managed since 1942, and threatened even the sensitive borderline between the Conservative Research Department and Central Office. In the event, such fears proved to be groundless. Macmillan took the chair of the Steering Committee personally, with Butler as deputy – but still chairman

[7] Hutchinson, *Last Edwardian*, 52–3; Egremont, *Wyndham*, 168, 170, 176–7; interview with Lord Barber; Central Office Chairman's department file, CCO 20/8/4, Correspondence with Macmillan, 1959.

both of the Advisory Committee on Policy (ACP) and of the CRD – while Michael Fraser of the CRD became secretary of the Steering Committee. Together with its manifesto sub-committee under Macleod, another guarantee that Butler and the CRD would not be sidelined, the Steering Committee laid the foundations of the 1959 election policy.[8]

Macmillan's advance in public estimation owed as much to image as to policy content and organisation. Larry Siedentop wrote in 1970 that 'the langour, irony and careless elegance that made up Macmillan's "Edwardian" style hardly need to be emphasised. They were quickly recognised when he became Prime Minister and the act of recognition seemed to make them more pronounced.' John Boyd-Carpenter found that 'as a Prime Minister everything he did had style. Everything was done with an air. Cabinet papers were often headed with a well-chosen literary quotation. . . . Government was a great game, played in a high eighteenth century style.' The word 'style' was almost universally applied, though with a variety of qualifying adjectives. One characteristic was ostentatious calm: Macmillan was characterised by Hailsham as 'unflappable', and the word and its derivatives stuck and were widely applied to him. Many colleagues realised even at the time how far the surface calm belied a nervous tension within; more did so as they got to know him better, and the private words of Macmillan's diaries prove just how far the studied exterior was indeed an act. Selwyn Lloyd recalled that on a diplomatic negotiation, Macmillan 'was desperately anxious. . . . He worked himself up until he was really quite ill; a cold, a temperature and all those things. As soon as there was a successful communiqué and a good press conference he became himself again.' There was an element of self-parody about his detachment; at one of their first meetings, each Minister found a small packet of tranquillisers laid on the Cabinet table in front of his place. On the other hand, the assumption of a detachment that he did not feel led on to the questioning of how much of the rest of Macmillan's manner was also assumed for the occasion, particularly after 1959 when the actor seemed to some to replace the man. But however genuine it was, the Macmillan manner proved, as Siedentop put it, to be both a deep reassurance to the British people in a period of rapid change and a powerful electoral asset.[9]

Macmillan's dated style was put across above all by a modern medium that he himself hated, television. His first broadcast as Prime Minister was strong on content but criticised by television buffs for its lack of professionalism. He responded by recognising that he had to master the new medium, and

---

[8] John Ramsden, *The Making of Conservative Party Policy: The Conservative Research Department since 1929* (1980), 190–201; Hill, *Both Sides of the Hill*, 177, 186; Central Office file, CCO 4/7/62, Liaison Committee, 1956–68; Howard, *RAB*, 260.

[9] Larry Siedentop, 'Mr. Macmillan and the Edwardian Style', in V. Bogdanor and R. Skidelsky (eds.), *The Age of Affluence* (1970), 17–52; Egremont, *Wyndham*, 163; John Boyd-Carpenter, *Way of Life* (1980), 151; Lord Hailsham, *A Sparrow's Flight: Memoirs* (1990), 318; Thompson, *Day Before Yesterday*, 173; Watkinson, *Turning Points*, 73.

soon discovered that, approached in the right way and with good advice, he had a real talent for performance on the air; in December 1957 Hailsham reported to Heath that Macmillan's recently-recorded broadcast was 'a great advance technically' and 'much more relaxed'. He adjusted his schedules, particularly the regular departures and arrivals at airports, to fit in with the demands of television news-gatherers too. The *Observer* felt that these television appearances had 'transformed an Edwardian relic into a modern character'. Like Baldwin on 1930s newsreels, the regularity of Macmillan's relaxed appearances became an asset in itself in familiarising the public with his personality and 'style'. He adapted well to the new practices of television interviewing too, dealing expertly with Reginald Bosanquet over a by-election defeat, with Robin Day when he was asked to sack Selwyn Lloyd, and especially with Ed Murrow in a lengthy American interview in 1958. A few months later, the National Union President, introducing Macmillan's Party Conference speech, was clear about his achievement to date: 'In the course of the last eighteen months, Mr. Macmillan has impressed his personality first on the Party, then on the House of Commons, then on the Nation, and month by month he is impressing his personality on the world. How has he done it? Well, of course we all know he is a pastmaster at television . . .' With his new confidence, Macmillan's appearance had altered too; Alistair Horne notes that 'gone were the little Commissar-like spectacles; the "Colonel Blimp" moustache had been ruthlessly pruned; the disarrayed teeth fixed – which somehow transformed the toothy, half-apologetic smile; the hair had assumed a more sophisticated shapeliness. Here was a new, almost dapper figure, with instant authority. The television "personality" had arrived.'[10]

After the Murrow interview in May 1958, Macmillan's personal poll ratings increased dramatically, from 37 per cent approving of his performance as Prime Minister to 50 per cent. Indeed, over the whole period 1957 to 1959, there was a steady improvement in the Prime Minister's ratings which indicated that he was pulling ahead of the Party itself in popular esteem; by October 1958, 57 per cent of voters, and by August 1959, 67 per cent, approved of Macmillan as Prime Minister. When he spoke to the 1922 Committee in July 1959, he was given 'a prolonged and enthusiastic ovation'. But even though Macmillan's soaring popularity and Labour's sorry performance in Opposition were positive features, there remained enough negative factors to leave the Conservatives in a weak position, well into 1958. Labour gained North Lewisham in February 1957, the first Tory seat lost at a by-election for twelve years, and there were heavy swings to Labour in other contests, as well as a worrying upsurge in Liberal voting; what was especially

---

[10] Michael Cockerell, *Live from Number Ten: The Inside Story of Prime Ministers and Television* (1988), 55–7, 60, 62–3; Central Office Chairman's department file CCO 20/8/2; Roth, *Heath*, 125; Central Office General Director's file, CCO 120/1/4, Broadcasting, 1958–59; John Ramsden, 'Churchill to Heath', in Lord Butler (ed.), *The Conservatives* (1977), 449; Horne, *Macmillan*, 145.

galling in North Lewisham was the fact that a candidate from the right polled more votes than the Labour majority. The League of Empire Loyalists, known by Central Office to be linked to Mosley and other fascist politicians, caused regular embarrassment, including a demonstration against Macmillan's 1958 Conference speech (which with considerable irony generated an unsuccessful legal action by these neo-fascists against the Tory agents who as stewards forcibly removed them from the hall; although the legal action was defeated, there was strong press criticism of the stewards' behaviour, especially from Bernard Levin in the *Spectator*). The sophistication of the League's political reasoning may be deduced from their denunciation of the 'Lenin–Macmillan line' on economic planning in 1956, but extensive efforts were made to prevent further embarrassment, including the collection of photographs of League leaders so that Tory stewards and police could deny them access to any later Party meetings; in December 1957, the London Area, when planning a rally, instructed agents that 'special care must be taken in the distribution of tickets'. In May 1957 there were heavy defeats in the local elections as the middle class continued to stay at home. In the same month as Lewisham, a big Liberal vote at a by-election in Edinburgh provoked the following report from the Chief Organisation Officer: 'I do not believe that this is in any sense a Liberal revival, although it might have the effect of encouraging one. It is largely a revolt of the middle classes against the Government. It is also a revolt against the South Edinburgh Unionist Association' for being so 'complacent'. Another bad result at Ipswich in November was attributed to middle-class disaffection, though Gallup helpfully reported that many voters who switched to the Liberals were already saying that they would vote Conservative in a General Election: Poole refered to 'the "Poujadeism" which is at present infecting ordinary Tory voters' (a reference to the current populist upsurge in France). In June, North Dorset was held largely because Liberals and Labour both attracted Tory votes but neither could claim to be the main challenger; *Time and Tide* noted that 'in this essentially Suez territory' the Conservatives should anyway do well, but spitefully pointed out that neither Nigel Nicolson nor Lord Hinchingbrooke, both local MPs, were helping the Tory candidate – but for opposite Suez reasons.[11]

Economic policy

The Government's chief difficulty derived as in early 1956 from the economy, but this was reinforced by the unpopularity of legislation, deliberately pressed

[11] Cockerell, *Live from Number Ten*, 63; D.E. Butler and Richard Rose, *The British General Election of 1959* (1960), 31–2; Minutes of the 1922 Committee [hereafter 1922], 24 July 1958; London Conservative Union, F and GP, 11 Dec. 1957; Chris Cook and John Ramsden (eds.), *By-Elections in British Politics* (1973), 195; Central Office Chairman's department file, CCO 20/8/2; Central Office files CCO 3/5/88–93, League of Empire Loyalists, CCO 4/7/250, local elections, CCO 4/7/62, Liaison Committee; Central Office General Director's files on by-elections CCO 120/2/60 and 63–7.

through by Macmillan in the first year of his premiership. At the Ministry of Labour, Iain Macleod continued to pursue a cautious policy that upset both Tory voters and industrialists: a climb-down over engineers' pay did particular damage after the Government had encouraged employer resistance at the start of the dispute; *The Economist* called this 'another blow to everybody's standard of life', while Macleod pragmatically told his officials that 'I never fight battles I can't win'. Butler at the Home Office showed great skill in steering a Homicide Bill into law (greatly reducing the types of murders for which hanging remained a possible punishment) and went on to launch in March 1957 a wide-ranging scheme of penal reform; Macmillan, who regularly taunted Butler with his liberalism, accepted these plans with typical cynicism: 'I am all for it. No doubt it will cost money, but I do not suppose the money will be spent very quickly. I take it, it will mostly be building new prisons, but they will take some time, especially if the Ministry of Works have anything to do with the plans.' The Party was less relaxed: Butler reported in August 1958 that 'I am to answer 28 bloodthirsty resolutions at the Conservative Party Conference at Blackpool. With the greatest difficulty we have chosen one out of the 28 that is at least moderate. On this I can make a reasonably calming speech.' The baiting of Butler at Party Conferences became a fixed feast of the political year between 1957 and 1962. His White Paper, published early in 1959, was a landmark of penal policy in its insistence on research into criminology as the basis for future policy, but this made little appeal to Party activists. His resistance to the reintroduction of corporal punishment and his gradual conversion to the abolitionist case against hanging did little to improve either his Party standing or his future prospects.[12]

The Rent Act, which sought to reintroduce market forces into housing, was a very different matter. This policy had impeccable Conservative principles behind it but was difficult to sell to tenants whose rents might be raised and anyway offended some in the organisation who disapproved of its principles; the chairman of Liverpool Walton wrote to Hailsham that it was 'the wickedest piece of social legislation ever inflicted upon the people of Great Britain'. As it went through in this difficult year, the Party's nerve only just held. It was intended to extend the rent decontrol that had been tentatively started by Macmillan in 1954, a conscious effort to draw private landlords back into the housing market by giving an incentive to invest in new building for rent. The economist Peter Oppenheimer later believed that 'towards the mid fifties it became reasonable and indeed urgent to deal with private rents, which were still frozen at the 1939 level'. The Act was relatively modest, decontrolling altogether only new tenancies, and giving Ministers further powers to decontrol by order that were scarcely ever used; the Act's main provisions were also delayed into 1958, to allow tenants time to adjust to

---

[12] Nigel Fisher, *Iain Macleod* (1973), 120; Robert Shepherd, *Iain Macleod* (1994), 122; Howard, *RAB*, 253, 255, 264; Butler, *Art of the Possible*, 198, 200, 202.

higher rents, and most of the early implementations applied only to better-off tenants; even where rents were increased it was to well below their real value in 1939; and the fact that 2 million more tenancies were revalued upwards between 1957 and 1964 as a result of properties falling vacant indicates that many tenants could afford to pay more. Such rational arguments cut very little ice at the time. There was a great row in 1957, especially in the London area where controlled rents were furthest out of line with market prices, and considerable Party opposition built up. The Government imposed only a two-line whip on one difficult amendment and found eleven Conservative MPs abstaining against the Bill's provisions. As Chief Whip, Heath had to warn Central Office in December 1957 that there were fourteen MPs who should not be used for Party speaking engagements, as they were likely to do more harm than good. There were cold feet at the National Union too; at the Executive Committee in February 1957, William van Straubenzee found it 'very depressing that we should be having this discussion. I remember Mr. Poole being cheered when he said "More Conservatism, more quickly", but now we get a considerable number of people throwing up their hands in horror. . . . There is an ice-bound block in housing, which somebody has got to break.' By the Autumn the Bill was through, and Central Office was turning to the difficult task of publicising its actual impact on rents, in the hope of discrediting Labour's scary predictions. In December it was noted that, now that tenants could see what was actually happening, hostility to the Act was fading: a Labour protest march in London had had to be cancelled for lack of support. None the less the Act was blamed for the loss of Glasgow Kelvingrove at a by-election in March 1958, and it remained a factor in the London area; when London did not swing to the Conservatives as much as the Midlands in 1959, this was attributed to housing issues, and the abuse of the Act's vacancy provisions by unscrupulous landlords like Peter Rachman caused the Party difficulties in the early 1960s.[13]

None the less, prices and jobs had more significance than any other policy to the Party's chance of being re-elected. Initially, Thorneycroft seemed to be a Chancellor in the Macmillan mould. Although he held office for only a year, Samuel Brittan detected a Thorneycroft I, pursuing in Spring 1957 plans that Macmillan had begun, and a Thorneycroft II, increasingly in collision with Macmillan in the Autumn. The Budget reduced taxation but planned an increased surplus, and so continued the broadly deflationary policy of the previous year. Macmillan's Bedford speech in July was chiefly noticed for its rousing defence of 'never had it so good' prosperity (the phrase itself coming from Alf Robens on the Opposition front bench); but most of the speech was

---

[13] Central Office constituency file CCO 1/12/113; Peter Oppenheimer, 'Muddling Through: The Economy', in Bogdanor and Skidelsky, *The Age of Affluence*, 155; Jackson, *Rebels and Whips*, 144; Central Office file CCO 20/1/5; National Union papers, NUA 4/3/1, Executive Committee papers; Central Office file, CCO 4/7/62.

devoted to pointing out the perils that inflation posed to the continuation of that prosperity, a view with which Thorneycroft concurred. (In view of the later fame of Macmillan's Bedford speech, it is interesting to note that the Central Office report of the meeting at which it was delivered concluded that 'the audience of two thousand were slow to respond and there was no great enthusiasm' – but they would of course have absorbed the full speech and its downbeat message, not just its most famous line.) Also in July, Thorneycroft appointed a three-man Council on Prices and Incomes, the first institutional development of Conservative incomes policy; Macmillan, no opponent of interventionist methods, could go along with this despite the implication that it denoted a policy that would target inflation as the major evil to be resisted, and at that stage the Prime Minister was also urging colleagues to go along with the Chancellor's tough views on public spending. The TUC on the other hand were suspicious and boycotted the Council altogether when its intentions became clear. In August Poole was warning Macmillan that the good effect of his Bedford speech was being undermined by 'reaction against the "appeasement" policy of the Ministry of Labour' and by the negative tone of speeches by the Chancellor. The evidence of Summer resolutions from constituencies suggests though that Thorneycroft had considerable backing among Party activists, for the Conference agenda contained seventy resolutions on prices, most of which called for public expenditure cuts. A parting of the ways came with an Autumn sterling crisis that prompted Thorneycroft to reimpose high bank rate levels and credit restrictions; after the humiliation of Suez, he saw the defence of sterling as a crusade to save Britain's great power status. Macmillan now sensed that the economic rationale of his Treasury Ministers – Nigel Birch and Enoch Powell as well as Thorneycroft – was unduly dogmatic, and that in pursuing a rigidly deflationary policy to stem inflation, they would imperil employment, prosperity and the Government's political recovery. Thorneycroft had though set out the issues for his Cabinet colleagues in stark terms from the outset, warning them in January 1957 that:

> For many years we have had the sorry spectacle of a Government which spends too much, drifts into inflation, then seeks to cure the situation by fiscal and budgetary measures. These attempts in turn lead to flagging production, taxes are reduced, and demand is stimulated; but we shrink from the measures necessary to cut expenditure decisively and inflation starts again. There is only one way out of this unhappy circle, and that is to cut expenditure and not to increase taxation . . . but to reduce it.

The issue came rapidly to the boil in late Autumn because Macmillan's plan to start 1958 with a long Commonwealth tour meant that public expenditure for 1958–59 had to be finalised both earlier than usual and more quickly. Thorneycroft demanded a cash freeze in public spending, in effect a stiff cutback in a time of inflation. Through December the Cabinet crisis deepened, though with no hint of it reaching press or public. The Treasury Ministers achieved big cuts in expenditure, but the agreed package fell short of their demands by about £50 million – around one per cent of the total budget and well within margins of error in any forecast out-turn figures (though since other proffered reductions also fell through when this last cut was not achieved, the sum really at issue was some £200 million); one argument that encouraged the rest of the Cabinet to resist was Lord Mills' view that further economies would lead to compensating public expenditures on dole payments and elsewhere in the system. It was eventually less an argument over figures than a battle of wills. The Treasury Ministers believed that the triumph of the spending departments over the Treasury would have seriously inflationary effects through increased public borrowing, while the rest of the Cabinet felt that no great issue was at stake and that Thorneycroft was being unduly inflexible; Iain Macleod compared Thorneycroft's demands for cuts to 'Hitler tactics', and the Chief Whip became convinced that the Chancellor was actually trying to bring down the Prime Minister. If Thorneycroft had won the argument, other Ministers would certainly have resigned and at least one had his letter already written. With no compromise, events took their course; the three Treasury Ministers resigned together on 6 January 1958.[14]

In retrospect, these 1958 Treasury resignations came to acquire a symbolic significance as the moment when Macmillanite Conservatism chose the primrose path of inflation rather than the narrow gate that led to sound money. That interpretation owed something to Powell's legacy to Keith Joseph and Margaret Thatcher after 1975 (when Powell was no longer a Conservative) and to Thatcher's appointment of Thorneycroft as her Party Chairman when she herself was in the full flood of monetarism. In 1966 Powell himself put the case at its strongest:

> The year 1958 was the great turning point which marked the beginning of the true Macmillan era. . . . The year 1958 was even statistically a turning point. . . . At that point the State's share of the national income, which had been declining since 1951, began to rise again and has been rising ever since. . . . Harold Macmillan . . . defeated his Chancellor of the Exchequer, Peter Thorneycroft, and settled for inflation.

Reviewing Macmillan's memoirs in 1980, Powell added that in 1958 'Macmillan already aimed at winning in 1959 on public expenditure', and that he had sacked Selwyn Lloyd in 1962 with the same intention in mind for 1963–64. Powell's insistent post-1963 analysis of the great issue at stake in 1958 contrasts with his loyal reticence between 1958 and 1963, when he was either

---

14 Samuel Brittan, *Steering the Economy* (1969), 128–35; Central Office file, CCO 3/5/88; T.F. Lindsay and Michael Harrington, *The Conservative Party, 1918–1970* (1974), 202; Hutchinson, *Last Edwardian*, 59–61; Central Office Chairman's department file, CCO 20/8/2; National Union papers, NUA 2/2/23, Central Council reports; Oppenheimer, 'The Economy', 135–6, 140; Thompson, *Day Before Yesterday*, 165–7; Turner, *Macmillan*, 228; Roth, *Powell*, 176–80, 186–9; Boyd-Carpenter, *Way of Life*, 139; Macmillan, *Riding the Storm*, 369; Horne, *Macmillan*, 71–2.

in, or wanted to be in, Macmillan's Government. Birch, who correctly saw little chance of his own return to office, became Macmillan's most persistent critic on the backbenches at once, but widened his attack to encompass all of Macmillan's policies and style, so that the public expenditure argument was lost in a welter of invective. Thorneycroft, who certainly did see a ministerial future for himself, steered a middle course; he lost few later opportunities to vindicate his 1958 resignation and was far from discontented when the wheel turned to give his views greater validity after 1975, but his resignation letter of 1958 was moderate in tone and was anyway not published, his resignation speech was careful not to increase the damage, and he led all three ex-Ministers to vote with the Government in the censure debate occasioned by their own resignations. At the time then, whatever it seemed to be subsequently, the resignation *issue* was not presented publicly as one of great consequence. The departing Ministers had in any case not enjoyed much support from civil servants or economists at the Treasury, and the Radcliffe Committee which reported in 1959 gave an official imprimatur to the case against their economic reasoning. The new Chancellor, Heathcoat Amory, did not publicly repudiate Thorneycroft's policy objectives, but, as Samuel Brittan put it in 1969, he 'quickly dropped the fanaticism and the monetary metaphysics'. The year 1969 was still just before the new popularity of Chicago school economics gave a retrospective respectability to the 1958 Thorneycroft line, but the tide then turned with remarkable rapidity: as Powell remarked only ten years after Brittan had written of Thorneycroft's 'fanaticism', 'economists have been awarded Nobel Prizes for demonstrating what Thorneycroft was ridiculed for asserting'. The policy at issue in 1958 made little impact precisely because it was so far ahead of – or so far behind – academic *and* political fashion.[15]

In any case the resignations were politically ineffective: they did not change the direction of policy and did not enlist Party support for their cause; this was partly because the resigners chose not to spell out what was at issue in a divisive way, partly because of the Prime Minister's handling of the affair. The rearrangement of senior posts was carried out by Macmillan in the few hours before his Commonwealth departure, and Butler then sorted out the junior posts. The Cabinet turned out in force to be photographed at Heathrow Airport waving Macmillan off, to show collective solidarity. Macmillan had privately visited Churchill to ensure his support in the crisis, but had assumed in his private office a degree of calmness that was exaggerated even for him, and he now announced at the airport, in a carefully contrived exit line, that he would not be deflected by 'these little local difficulties'. Hailsham later described this remark as having 'more panache than accuracy', but the trick worked, and political comment on what had been an unprecedented political

[15] Roth, *Powell*, 190; Enoch Powell, *Reflections: Selected Writing and Speeches of Enoch Powell*, (1992), 140; Jackson, *Rebels and Whips*, 145; Horne, *Macmillan*, 237; Oppenheimer, 'The Economy', 136; Brittan, *Steering the Economy*, 136; Hutchinson, *Last Edwardian*, 69–70.

event was short-lived and muted. From the United States, Randolph Churchill telegraphed Macleod with the news of a 'total lack of interest in Washington about recent resignations. My secretary does not know who Thorneycroft is or was or will be'.[16]

The Party remained firm as well as the press, fortified by some quick action by the Party Chairman. Telegrams were sent out to every Area and constituency chairman, explaining the Government's side of the case and suggesting that nothing of importance was at stake, before the resigners themselves had had a chance to say anything. In South Aberdeen, which received Hailsham's letter with the endorsement of James Stuart as Scottish Party Chairman, the association chairman read the letter to his association: 'this message asked that all Party Members give their fullest support to the Prime Minister and the Government in what was inevitably a most worrying and exacting time, pointing out that Party Members' duty to the Country and the Party demanded no less', a view with which the meeting strongly concurred. On hearing the telegram, Rugby helpfully cancelled a meeting that Powell had been booked to address in the constituency later in January, on the somewhat unconvincing ground that as he was no longer a Minister he would not be a big enough name to attract an audience. There was a heated exchange of views with Dulwich, which had written to the Party Chairman to argue that 'a bold programme of planned retrenchment would greatly increase public support and enthusiasm for the Government'. Going well beyond his normal brief, Hailsham belligerently demanded to know whether they would like such a 'bold programme' to include the abolition of family allowances, lowering the school leaving age, abolishing welfare foods, or abandoning the promise to end conscription; the Dulwich chairman replied in hurt tones that 'frankly we were much concerned with the tenor of your reply'. Hailsham also crossed swords with the chairman of Thorneycroft's own constituency at Monmouth, which had passed a resolution congratulating its Member on the stand he had taken; the Party Chairman loftily told Monmouth that they could not know what the dispute was really about because they had not sat in on the Cabinet's debates; Hailsham was however forced to gloss a remark made in a letter to *The Times* linking Thorneycroft's views to 'Micawber's delightful but disastrous nonsense', and admit that he did not actually reject Mr Micawber's belief in sound finance. Bradford Conservatives were more typical in both regretting Thorneycroft's departure, and resolving to support the Government, on Hailsham's assurance that there would be no change of the Cabinet's 'monetary and financial plans'. Writing back home from India, Macmillan expressed his thanks for all the measures taken to steady the Party 'at rather a critical period. From what I can judge the situation is improving

[16] Howard, *RAB*, 158; Thompson, *Day Before Yesterday*, 167; Fisher, *Macleod*, 122.

and other subjects and personalities from Bulganin to Fuchs are superseding the notoriety of Thorneycroft.'[17]

'Supermac' turns the tide

Macmillan's return to Britain though coincided with a new low point for his Government. At Rochdale on 12 February 1958, a Conservative marginal seat was taken by Labour with the Conservative pushed into third place by the Liberals; the Conservative vote fell from 26,518 to 9,827, in a contest which attracted attention as Britain's first televised election campaign; in advance of the contest, the Attorney-General had still been trying to warn television off such coverage, with dark hints that the Director of Public Prosecutions might feel obliged to test the matter in the courts; after ITN (Independent Television News) had called his bluff he conceded that 'the chances of a successful prosecution would appear to be remote'; Central Office was still anxious that if television extended its forays into constituency electioneering at a general election, then the parties rather than the broadcasters should choose which candidates should be interviewed. A month after Rochdale, the Party lost Glasgow Kelvingrove to Labour following the death of Walter Elliot, and before the end of March Torrington fell to a Liberal – three seats lost in six weeks, all of different types and at different ends of the country. The Rochdale defeat had been foreseen; Hailsham minuted in December 1957 that 'we shall lose this, but let us put a first class candidate in the field. Some of our gallant supporters who are bellyaching for safe seats ought to be encouraged to do a Duff Cooper here.' A month later, before Macmillan left for his overseas tour, Hailsham warned him to expect a Liberal win, which 'will be hard to bear, and for some part of my pessimism we shall have to blame our former colleagues'.[18]

Macmillan nevertheless thought the Rochdale result a 'tremendous shock', and Hailsham (who had been Party Chairman for only six months) reported sadly that the scale of defeat had been foreseen by the *Daily Mail* but not by Central Office. He offered his resignation: 'I had hoped until Peter [Thorneycroft]'s resignation that I was beginning to draw the threads to-gether. . . . However, this result disposes of any such flattering belief. . . . There is something to be said for the rolling of heads when a knock like this comes, and I shall not complain if you select mine for the purpose.' In reply, Macmillan asked him 'not to construe the result too personally'. In

[17] Macmillan, *Riding the Storm*, 367; Hailsham, *The Door*, 163; South Aberdeen CA minutes, 13 Jan. 1958; Rugby CA minutes, 22 Jan. 1958; Central Office constituency files CCO 1/12/6 and 1/12/544; Bradford CA minutes, 21 Jan. 1958; Central Office Chairman's department file, CCO 20/8/3, Correspondence with Macmillan, 1957–58.

[18] Cockerell, *Live from Number Ten*, 59; Cook and Ramsden, *By-Elections*, 195–6; Central Office, General Director's files on by-elections CCO 120/1/4 and 120/2/69.

some panic, the Steering Committee debated even the question of offering the Liberals an electoral pact, for which the chief supporters were Home and Heath, the most articulate opponents Macleod and Hailsham. The Torrington defeat confirmed fears that were already present in the South West, where Liberalism had never entirely died away. North Cornwall grimly noted that the situation was 'composed in the main of Westcountry Liberal fervour, a psychological attitude', while Cirencester and Tewkesbury reported that 'there was a very hard core of Liberal diehards in the constituency, particularly in the Chapel areas, and that in this part of the world Liberalism was regarded as a religion more than a philosophy'. North Cornwall, North Devon and Torrington began to hold meetings to coordinate their anti-Liberal efforts, but resisted Central Office direction; anti-Liberal posters were turned down as 'circus tactics', and when Poole offered anti-Liberal literature in any design favoured locally this was turned down too; he was sternly told that local Tories preferred the positive approach, 'that the right answer was to put better policies in the shop window than other parties'. But that would take time.[19]

There were poor county council results in April, which wiped out the gains of 1955, but distinctly better borough results in May. By June, Poole was reporting that another series of by-elections had gone rather well, indicating 'that support for the Government is steadying'. Weston super Mare in particular had 'enormously exceeded our expectations' and was 'the first really pleasant electoral surprise we have had for some time'. Nevertheless, in August Hailsham was cautiously urging Macmillan not to appoint the Attorney-General to the vacant post of Lord Chief Justice (as was customary) since a by-election in his marginal seat was the last thing the Party needed; the appointment was not made, but Macmillan was then so unimpressed with Lord Parker in the post that he regretted his decision: in November 1959 he asked Kilmuir, 'Can you do anything about the Lord Chief Justice? How I wish I had appointed the Attorney-General in his place.' Torrington was actually the summit of this Liberal revival and, since it was a former National Liberal seat, an untypical contest anyway. In the last eighteen months of the Parliament, no further seats were lost and adverse swings steadily reduced. It was at this late stage, on 6 November 1958, that Vicky's cartoon of Macmillan as a flying 'Supermac' appeared, only then that there was a full understanding of his electoral appeal. The only electoral worry came at Norfolk South West in March when the intervention of Andrew Fountaine, an ex-Conservative candidate disowned by the Party in 1950 and now on the far right, threatened to reopen old scores from Suez;

---

[19] Horne, *Macmillan*, 88; National Union papers, NUA 2/2/24, Central Council reports; Central Office Chairman's department file, CCO 20/8/3, Correspondence with Macmillan, 1958; Shepherd, *Macleod*, 146–7; North Cornwall CA minutes, 15 Apr. 1958, 20 Jan. and 17 Feb. 1959; Cirencester and Tewkesbury CA, minutes 6 Mar. 1958.

but swings to Labour in 1959 by-elections were never large enough to indicate a change of Government. Local government results moved the same way; York Conservatives, preparing to defend a knife-edge marginal constituency, thought their municipal results in May 1959 to be 'very satisfactory and encouraging'; the problem now would just be 'to keep the tide of opinion in our favour'.[20]

The turn of the tide could be seen too in opinion polls: in July 1958 Richard Crossman noted that the Conservatives had drawn level 'as anyone who has a feeling for such trends must have expected'; by October he was noting that his own leader Hugh Gaitskell was 'in a panic about the Gallup Polls'. The Conservative recovery thus came both suddenly and late in the Parliament. What turned the tide in Spring 1958? Looking back, Edward Boyle believed that the change of mood took place at this time because of the Macmillan interview by Ed Murrow and the defeat of a London bus strike. Tory activists had certainly been calling for a tougher line on the trade unions, and Poole had foreseen in 1957 that the arrival of Frank Cousins as a left-wing militant leader for the Transport Workers could be turned to advantage if handled right. Macleod now at last had an opportunity quite different from the cautious policy adopted since 1951, and he handled the tactics of a prolonged strike skilfully. In the London bus strike of 1958, as in the miners' strike of 1984, neither side made much effort to avoid a showdown; in 1958 as in 1984 the battleground favoured the Government. The dispute became more significant when Labour tabled the first motion of censure on a Minister of Labour since before the War (in itself a remarkable comment on seven years of Tory Government); Macleod delivered a blistering attack on Gaitskell and scored one of his greatest parliamentary triumphs; the Opposition spokesman Alf Robens privately congratulated Macleod on 'the best speech you've ever made in your life'. Other trade unions and the TUC rejected Cousins' efforts to widen the dispute by involving railways and oil tankers, while the Government signalled its determination by cancelling army leave. After seven weeks, the strike was abandoned on 21 June. Macmillan noted that 'although we had treated the TUC delegates with courtesy and understanding in private, in public we had taken firm action.' His friend John Vaizey (who felt that Macleod had been allowed to confront the union only because Cabinet Ministers never actually used buses – they had recently been much more conciliatory over the railways), argued that the dispute gave Macleod 'a wholly undeserved reputation for toughness'. The official policy remained one of partnership in industry, and Party resolutions demanding the continuation of confrontation were shrugged off; Macleod told the Advisory Committee on Policy that the law had no part to play in reducing strikes,

---

20 Central Office General Director's by-election file, CCO 120/2/83; Macmillan to Kilmuir, 1 Nov. 1959, Kilmuir MSS 6/8; Hutchinson, *Last Edwardian*, 64; York CA minutes, 21 May 1959.

and that trade union reform could come only by consent. At the Steering Committee in November, Macmillan responded to those who asked for Government action by using the traditional argument:

> But aren't you more worried about the weakness of the trades unions? Poor old trade union man who comes along at £750 a year and gets laughed out of court by the bummarees. But really the role of the Minister of Labour is to strengthen the trades unions to keep control of those chaps.

The minutes record that 'discussion was again adjourned inconclusively'. But if policy was unchanged, the demonstration of Government resolve in a high-profile dispute in the capital may still have done something to restore the morale of Party workers, to convince Tory voters that the action they wanted was at least on the agenda, and to reduce the wage-push influence on inflation.[21]

There were other policy successes that could be pointed to clearly enough in the second half of the Parliament. At the Ministry of Transport, the relaxation of public expenditure controls allowed Harold Watkinson to push ahead with a road-building programme, easily the biggest civil engineering scheme that the country had ever attempted. The first phase of the M1 motorway was built at the rate of three miles of road and three bridges every fortnight. The M1 opened only shortly after the 1959 General Election, but Britain's first motorway, the Preston by-pass, was opened by Macmillan in person in December 1958. The programme was needed simply to provide road space for the ever-increasing number of cars, another way in which new roads drew attention to prosperity.[22]

A similar record of successful building could be seen in Education, where David Eccles had laid foundations for the policy that Hailsham and Geoffrey Lloyd now carried through, to provide places for the largest ever number of pupils. In January 1959, Macmillan wanted more attention given to 'the education drive' and asked Fraser to consider planting paragraphs about it in all the ministerial speeches drafted at the CRD. The policy was traditional in focus, with careful provision being made for denominational schools. Lloyd was the last Conservative Minister of Education to hold office without meeting serious trouble over the future of the grammar schools; a few comprehensive schools were introduced, but only as experiments or in rural areas that could be described as special cases, and Macmillan was careful to reassure the National Union in 1959 that 'we are certainly determined

---

[21] Morgan, *Crossman*, 687, 720; Thompson, *Day Before Yesterday*, 168; Central Office Chairman's department file, CCO 20/8/2; Fisher, *Macleod*, 126–30; Shepherd, *Macleod*, 138–9; Lord Butler, *The Art of Memory* (1982), 102; Macmillan, *Riding*, 346; Horne, *Macmillan*, 90; John Vaizey, 'Iain Macleod', in his *In Breach of Promise* (1984). 46; Advisory Committee on Policy minutes [hereafter ACP] 30 Apr. 1958; Ramsden, *Making of Conservative Party Policy*, 196.

[22] Watkinson, *Turning Points*, 81, 83, 87.

to uphold the grammar schools, which we regard as the best guarantee for maintaining high standards in secondary education and as the main source of the scientists and technologists we need.' Nevertheless, Lloyd wanted to 'steer' the Party away from 'adopting an educational policy which would appear as doctrinaire in one way as the Labour policies in another': during the thirteen years of Conservative Government, the number of comprehensive schools rose from 5 to 195; by 1964, nearly two-thirds of all local education authorities had either introduced comprehensive schools or were in the process of doing so. Conservative rhetoric allowed the Party to become distanced from progressive educational opinion while the policy of Ministers in office simultaneously inflamed Party activists; by 1961, the first educational pressure group of the right was being formed, by Harry Greenway and Rhodes Boyson, to resist educational egalitarianism and the erosion of the remaining grammar schools.[23]

The Government's foreign and defence policies were also sources of short-term political strength. Duncan Sandys had been given a brief to make substantial cuts in the defence budget and in personnel. The Sandys Defence White Paper of 1957 announced a more integrated and professional defence force, and the ending of conscription. Though conscription was not actually phased out until 1960–62, the popularity of the policy was considerable. The ferment on the left occasioned by fears of the Hydrogen bomb made few inroads into the Conservative vote and may well have scared potential defectors back into the fold when confronted by the Campaign for Nuclear Disarmament (CND) and the Labour left's alternative defence policies. Central Council in March 1958 resolved to 'deplore the present attempt to create an atmosphere of emotionalism concerning the nuclear deterrent. It resembles similar activities in the years before 1939 which undoubtedly encouraged the enemies of freedom to embark upon a war of aggression.' There were no speakers against the motion, which was then carried without dissent; despite their over-use in 1956, arguments drawn from the lessons of 1936–39 could still produce the desired response, just as the most effective way to damn a cooperative policy towards trade unions was to call it 'appeasement'. Sandys was a good choice for this portfolio, a tough Minister of Defence who forced through his reforms in the teeth of service opposition. The attempt to form a counterweight to the EEC in the European Free Trade Area, and the subsequent doomed attempt to link these two organisations together created both an impression of activity and the hope of an achievement that would neutralise the setback of 1956–57. Macmillan's

23 Central Office Chairman's department file, CCO 20/1/5, Correspondence with the Chief Whip; CPA, National Union papers, NUA 3/2, Leader's replies to resolutions, 1959; David Dean, 'Preservation or Renovation? The Dilemmas of Conservative Education Policy, 1955–1960', in *Twentieth Century British History*, vol. 3, no. 1 (1992), 21, 24, 30–1; Christopher Knight, *The Making of Tory Education Policy in Post-War Britain, 1950–1986* (1990), 14, 16.

visible role in summit diplomacy, notably his Moscow visit of February 1959, gave him the profile of a world statesman, and his attention to the media ensured that the maximum was made of this; his arrival in Moscow in an outsize white fur hat would have irritated the Russian leaders had they realised that he had acquired it in the Russo-Finnish War (from their viewpoint, on the wrong side), but in Britain it was a public relations triumph of the first order and, according to Robin Day, 'the picture of the year'. When the Labour leader Gaitskell visited Moscow in August it was scarcely even reported, in part at least because Macmillan had enticed President Eisenhower to London in the same week and was staging a foreign policy jamboree of his own.[24]

Inaction on immigration

One overseas policy that could not be claimed as a success was Commonwealth immigration. It is remarkable how persistent was the belief that this was fundamentally a Commonwealth issue rather than about the future of British society. Another persistent belief was that if the issue could be avoided or delayed then so much the better. There is much to be said for Peter Rawlinson's confession about large-scale immigration at this time: 'That all in public life over this period were so ignorant of its significance while it was occurring is an indictment that none of us who served in Government or Parliament during these years should ever be allowed to forget.' In fact, the undercurrent of dissent was clear enough and the Party tried its best to attract Ministers' attention to it. In 1954, Michael Fraser had warned the Liaison Committee about letters of protest being received, and the parliamentary Labour and Commonwealth committees had both discussed it; in November 1955, the West Midlands Area Council resolved that 'in view of the over-crowding of large centres of population and the possible effect on public health, this meeting is of the opinion that the Government should take some steps to control immigration into the United Kingdom.' The Churchill Cabinet had already considered the question since the Prime Minister himself favoured introducing controls, but this was obstructed by the Colonial Office.[25]

Eden's brief for the 1955 campaign provided him (in the foreign policy section) with stalling replies to possible questions, but in fact no such questions were raised in the national campaign anyway. Nevertheless, the Liaison Committee's post-mortem on the campaign decided that the issue had been forced to the attention of so many Tory candidates by voters that

[24] Anthony Sampson, *Macmillan: A Study in Ambiguity* (1968), 133; National Union papers, Central Council minutes, 1958; Siedentop, 'Mr. Macmillan', 38, 52; Reginald Maudling, *Memoirs* (1978), 67, 78; Cockerell, *Live from Number Ten*, 64; Horne, *Macmillan*, 48–50, 122.

[25] Ramsden, *Making of Conservative Policy*, 177–8; Peter Rawlinson, *A Price Too High: An Autobiography* (1989), 84; West Midlands Area Council minutes, 19 Nov. 1955.

they should now report this to the Colonial Secretary. They did not perhaps all know that the Home Secretary was even then preparing a Bill, but this was then rejected by the Cabinet in July 1956; the majority felt that 'control will eventually be inescapable, but the balance of advantage lies against imposing it now'. Salisbury more tough-mindedly argued that 'the longer we delay, the worse the position is bound to become'. In May 1957 Poole was reporting to the various Ministers involved that the Party's North West Area had also now passed a motion calling for immigration control: 'I hope you will give some thought as to whether reciprocal restrictions should not be imposed, as I believe there is a growing demand in the country for this to be done. If the Government has decided not to do this, I should be grateful if someone in your Department could let me have a brief on the matter, as at present I find it very difficult to answer the many complaints and questions which I am getting.' Butler responded with the complacent reflection that 'this is a subject that comes up from time to time' and referred Poole to a recent speech in the House of Lords in which his junior minister had set out the reasons against taking action. Lennox-Boyd, Colonial Secretary, welcomed Poole's acceptance of the fact that (white) Canadians would have to be treated exactly like Nigerians, but offered no support for legislation anyway. Alec Home, Commonwealth Relations Secretary, feared that any unilateral action by Britain would lead to the retaliatory removal of the right of British citizens to enter Pakistan and India (a worry that rather belies his claim to 'quite understand the anxieties in certain areas', for their own right to go to Karachi was hardly what worried immigration campaigners in Birmingham); Home concluded that 'it would be a red-hot question within the Commonwealth and we must if at all possible avoid it'. A Central Office committee under Barbara Brooke reported in June that investigations in the cities indicated that there were very real housing, social and health issues in areas where immigrants had concentrated; concentration in itself invalidated the Government view that total numbers were too small to matter: 'what we ignore at our peril is the very real resentment often felt by the local white English citizens'. But it concluded lamely that there was little the Party could do except keep warning the Government.[26]

Eventually there was a more public debate, prompted by riots in Notting Hill, Dudley and Nottingham in 1958, leading on to Sir Oswald Mosley re-entering politics as candidate for North Kensington. Mosley was easily seen off by the major parties and again race did not figure prominently in the 1959 campaign, but the numbers of immigrants did now constitute a part of the electoral battleground. In November 1958, the MP for Bradford North asked his city party for advice about a meeting for Asian voters; it would not be good to make distinctions between different types of voters,

---

[26]   Richard Lamb, *The Failure of the Eden Government* (1987), 16–24; Central Office files, CCO 4/7/166 and 4/8/138, Immigration.

and might open the Party to the charge of making special arrangements for 'these people' that many Bradford electors did not want there in the first place, but the alternative was to leave the new electors outside the normal party machines and under the influence of militant leaders. Despite reservations, the Bradford Tories agreed to provide chairmen and speakers for such meetings, so as to open up channels of communication, a positive step towards political integration that preceded both the largest influx of numbers and the most intense period of debate. Successful contacts were however opened up only where sitting Tory councillors had a vested interest in the time and effort required, one for example learning Urdu for the purpose; when their enthusiasm flagged, or when in 1962–63 they lost their seats, the Party's contacts tended to disappear too. Meanwhile one of the Conservative anti-immigration campaigners, Sir Cyril Osborne MP, did manage to raise the issue at the 1958 Party Conference; Rab Butler's reply indicated that there could be no legislation in the coming session, but the Conference nevertheless passed a motion calling for entry controls. Enoch Powell was at this time one of many wrestling in their minds with the implications for British citizenship and the future of the Commonwealth if changes in the immigration rules were to be made unilaterally by Britain, and he took no part in these debates. The Cabinet's response to the 1958 riots was to welcome the stiff sentences handed out to rioters and to begin a new round of consultations with Commonwealth governments to see if restrictions could be introduced by agreement. This postponed any controversial legislation until after the 1959 General Election, but when an angry association chairman had to be pacified, Central Office decided not to use Butler's letter from the Home Office saying that it was still all 'under review' on the ground that it would do more harm than good; the Party and the Government now had a quite different sense of the urgency of the matter.[27]

The Party's convolutions on immigration reached a droll climax in the framing of the 1959 manifesto. First, the Lord Chancellor demanded a ruling on the future of immigration controls, since ministerial answers to questions were beginning to diverge and in an election campaign this would be dangerous. The Steering Committee's first draft (by the liberal-minded Rab Butler and Peter Goldman) proclaimed that 'we are proud that discrimination on grounds of race and colour has never been a part of our life and law, and we intend to uphold that principle'. This was not popular with some colleagues, and almost everyone thought that such a pledge would unduly raise the profile of the issue in the campaign. After numerous re-drafts, during which the phrase 'irrespective of creed or colour' was successively removed and reinserted, the paragraph was eventually transferred to the manifesto page

---

[27] Bradford CA, F and EC minutes, 14 Nov. 1958; Central Office constituency file CCO 1/14/220; Roth, *Powell*, 206, 208–10; Butler, *Art of the Possible*, 205; Butler and Rose, *General Election of 1959*, 173–4.

on law and order with only this phrase now surviving at all. The reference eventually ran as follows: 'It will continue to be our policy to protect the citizen, irrespective of creed or colour, against lawlessness'; this pledge did not actually relate to immigration at all. However, being forced to listen to their supporters on the doorstep in October 1959 did then begin to change the minds of rather more Ministers and backbenchers, and, as the numbers of migrants increased sharply after 1959, so did the calls for controls. The 1950s refusal to acknowledge that the Government must either plan for the consequences of large-scale immigration or legislate to prevent it is a sorry story indeed; either policy stance could have been justified, but there could be little excuse for doing nothing at all while antagonisms accumulated. In view of the Party's vocal response to the situation there could be no claim either that Ministers had not been fairly and squarely warned.[28]

Ironically – in view of the high levels of unemployment in some immigrant areas in later years – an argument often used against immigration control was an economic one; with unemployment so low and the country experiencing a boom in 1958–60, there was a heavy demand for colonial labour to fill vacancies in the public sector; there was for example a conflict between the need to use free market forces to keep down wage rates (as Powell was to argue for when confronted with the nurses after 1960) and the social consequences of coloured immigration; at the 1970 Selsdon conference, Geoffrey Rippon argued mischievously that there had been nothing wrong with the 1961 incomes policy except that the Government had mismanaged it in the public sector and 'listened to Enoch's argument about not paying the nurses more because of the black girls'. But the economic recovery that this dilemma indicated was the final policy success that pointed forwards to Macmillan's triumphant re-election in 1959. Heathcoat Amory, a mild-mannered and generally popular man who seemed more like a civil servant than a politician, gave Macmillan none of the troubles he had had with Thorneycroft; the new Chancellor had himself converted from Liberalism to Conservatism under the influence of Macmillan's *The Middle Way* (1938), and had sat with Butler and Macmillan devising *The Industrial Charter* in 1947. He would not fail to understand the importance of promoting economic growth, and was regularly reminded of it by Macmillan in any case: after six months in office Macmillan felt that he was 'worth 20 Thorneycrofts!'[29]

The 1958 Budget marked only a cautious move from Thorneycroft's deflationary policies, but did not of course incorporate the further deflationary medicine for the economy that Thorneycroft would have wished to see; there were substantial reductions of stamp duties on property transactions, which provided encouragement to homeowners who had been so critical of late. Poole thought that the Budget 'gives us a firm base from which to start to

---

[28] Ramsden, *Making of Conservative Policy*, 204.
[29] Leader's Consultative Committee papers, 1970; Horne, *Macmillan*, 139–41.

regain the confidence of our supporters who have been wavering'. The steady reduction of credit controls had a stimulating effect and the 1959 Budget was unashamedly expansionist, encouraged by the personal intervention of Macmillan: income tax fell by ninepence in the pound, purchase tax and excise duties were reduced, and once-for-all bonuses were offered in the repayment of post-war credits (a form of compulsory wartime savings frozen since 1945, and the subject of many Party resolutions since). When even the 1960 Budget, after the Election, did not indicate any sharp reversal of policy, Macmillan and his new Chancellor were fairly roundly attacked by Thorneycroft himself in the House. The coincidence of a generous Budget in 1959 and an election year led to inevitable charges that the electorate were being bribed; but Samuel Brittan argued in 1969 that 'the real error of the 1959 budget is not so much that it gave away too much but that it came too late'. In his view the mistakes of policy in these years arose mainly from the failure to respond quickly enough to the changes in economic indicators, a technical failure of judgement by political economists learning to use new tools of management rather than a political error influenced by electioneering. Some indication of the intentional targeting of economic benefits is given in Macmillan's celebrated minute to Michael Fraser in October 1957: 'Dear Michael: I am always hearing about the Middle Classes. What is it they really want? Can you put it down on a sheet of notepaper, and I will see whether we can give it to them?' He might of course have asked Angus Maude, who had co-authored a book on the subject and who would have appreciated a question posed in that tone of voice. In 1949, Roy Lewis and Maude had foreseen precisely the problem that was now arising:

> The whole meaning of middle class incentive will be missed unless we face the fact that, rightly or wrongly, justifiably or reprehensibly, the middle-class breadwinner is seeking more than an *absolute standard* of achievement. . . . He seeks a *relative advantage* over certain other groups. This is as true of the lower-middle-class man, seeking to raise his family above the working class, as of the upper-middle-class professional man striving to move away from the more obviously suburban suburbs and to send his son to a public school. How grievously these cherished ambitions conflict both with the egalitarian philosophy and with recent political tendencies!

As their status had already been eroded since 1939, it is not surprising that the middle classes were angry that inflation had now eroded their financial lead over wage-earners as well. Fraser accordingly replied to Macmillan that the middle classes wanted something that they could not be offered – as comfortable a standard of living as they had enjoyed before the War and the restoration of pre-war differentials between them and wage-earners. Nevertheless, a further detailed CRD paper on the problems of those on fixed incomes did lead to targeted concessions in the Budget. Macmillan did his bit too, reminding the Chancellor that 'measures which are merely intended to annoy what is left of the possessing classes are not attractive to our supporters and are best left to a Socialist Chancellor'.[30]

There remained one persistent regional problem that nagged at Macmillan's mind, unemployment in Lancashire where so many marginal seats were situated. In 1955 the same problem had motivated Woolton's concerns about the economic paragraphs of the manifesto: without consulting either the Chancellor or the President of the Board of Trade he 'did a deal' with Eden about cotton quotas for the benefit of his home county. In June 1958, seven Conservative MPs from Lancashire abstained in a vote to draw attention to the continuing problems of cotton; rather than disciplining the rebels, the Party tried to help them in their constituencies. In March 1959 the Party Chairman went to Lancashire to meet representatives of thirty-four constituencies and see if the Party's electioneering operations could help them, and reported to Macmillan on what he had heard. The Prime Minister was not satisfied with these efforts. In September he minuted that there must be a special leaflet, since 'the references in the manifesto are *not* enough'. He added sagely that although only 10 per cent of Lancastrians were now employed in cotton, it 'still has great psychological significance in the county'.[31]

Hailsham rings the bell

The Party therefore had an excellent record to defend by 1959, but due attention must also be paid to organisational activity that took place in the Conservative machine to ensure that the record was understood. The key component here was the partnership of Poole and Hailsham. In Summer 1957, Macmillan concluded that the Party needed a more flag-waving Chairman than Poole if it was to win back the initiative. He persuaded Hailsham to accept this role, and then managed to get Poole to stay on as Hailsham's deputy. Poole now managed the machine and the money, while Hailsham made high-profile appearances at Party meetings and laid into the Opposition. Despite very different personalities they made a good team; in 1959 Hailsham observed privately that 'we are an oddly assorted couple of hounds, mais nous allons bien ensemble'. One of Hailsham's advantages was one that Woolton had also enjoyed; as a Cabinet peer he had access to the Government's deliberations without being tied to daily attendance and votes to keep it in office, and he had no seat of his own to defend in a general election. He had the considerable advantage too of being the first Party Chairman ever to run

---

[30] Horne, *Macmillan*, 62–3; Gore Allen, *Heathcoat Amory*, 187–8; Turner, *Macmillan*, 230; Brittan, *Steering the Economy*, 139–40; Michael Pinto-Duschinsky, 'Bread and Circuses? The Conservatives in Office, 1951–1964', in V. Bogdanor and R. Skidelsky (eds), *The Age of Affluence* (1970), 69; Roy Lewis and Angus Maude, *The English Middle Classes* (1953 edn), 220; Turner, *Macmillan*, 239.
[31] Woolton MSS, diary, 5 Apr. 1955; Jackson, *Rebels and Whips*, 146.

the machine from a well-equipped and purpose-built headquarters; Central Office moved from Victoria Street to 32 Smith Square in early July 1958.[32]

Hailsham devoted his advocate's skills to the presentation of the Party's case, and decided that he should do all the things that Macmillan could not do for the Party: 'Where he would understate, I would be strident, where he would be serious, I would be humorous, and vice versa. Where he would play the Duke's son-in-law, and even the Duke, I would be elegant and ostentatious to the point of vulgarity. On the other hand, where he was devious, I would be plain-spoken.' The Prime Minister had to appear as the head of Government seeking to unite the nation, but the Party's spokesman needed to 'dramatize differences, point contrasts and challenge opposition'. Despite his memoirs' disclaimers, Hailsham obviously rather revelled in the publicity he now attracted at Conference time, bathing in the sea with photographers in attendance, ringing bells to the delight of delegates, and being photographed eating gigantic sticks of seaside rock; he was certainly a natural for this showman's role. A good representative sample of his style would be his 1957 Conservative Political Centre (CPC) lecture, placing current events in a historical context in none too reverential a style.

> We have been abused by many opponents, and our backs are broad. We were abused by the Roundheads, and we remained to see a popular Restoration. We were abused by the Whigs, and we lived to see them swallowed up in the Liberal Party. We were abused by the Liberals, and we have survived to see them degenerate into a little, heterogeneous mutual admiration society, which singularly fails in its main purpose, since they appear neither to admire one another nor to agree. . . . We are now abused by the Labour Party, and without being in the least impatient we realise that one day we or our successors will stand, crepe-hatted and mournful, beside their open grave which, like all their predecessors, the Socialists will have dug for themselves.[33]

It was the Chairman's traditional task to present a commemorative bell to the Conference chairman and to sum up the Conference proper at the Saturday morning session. This could easily be an anti-climax, for there was little left to say by then and delegates were impatient to get out for lunch before the Leader's afternoon rally. Hailsham's decision to ring the bell in 1957 was a deliberate shot at a dramatic climax, even if the actual method was spontaneous. The *Sunday Pictorial* account of what happened was typical of the Conservative press:

> Bouncing and beaming, Hailsham stood on the platform, swinging the chairman's bell wildly while 4,000 delegates rose and cheered. This mixture of emotion,

---

[32] Macmillan, *Riding the Storm*, 415–16; Kilmuir, *Political Adventure*, 310; Hailsham, *The Door*, 150; Central Office Chairman's department file, CCO 20/17/1, General Election, 1959; Lord Windlesham, *Communication and Political Power* (1966), 36, 44–5; Central Office file CCO 4/8/99, Finance.

[33] Macmillan, *Riding the Storm*, 420; Hailsham, *The Door*, 151–2, 162; Hailsham, *Sparrow's Flight*, 322; NCP 28 Oct. 1957.

Churchillian rhetoric and knockabout humour was exactly what they were longing for. . . . At the end of the speech [he] gripped the large handbell and swinging it above his head said, 'Let us ring it for victory'. The Tories loved it. As the delegates rose to their feet Hailsham shouted 'Let us say to the Labour Party, "Seek not to enquire for whom the bell tolls" – it tolls for them.' Then more cheers. This was what they wanted. 'Now let us go forth to the country with uplifted hearts', he added. Yes, this has been Hailsham's Conference.

Summarising the Conference for Butler (who was in hospital and so missed all the fun), Pat Hornsby-Smith MP reported that Hailsham had rung the bell 'for two whole minutes', and so worked the representatives up 'into a frenzy' that he forgot that he was supposed to be thanking the Conference chairman and had to be reminded to give her the bell; but she also quoted a constituency representative who had said to her as they left that 'the audience gave [Hailsham] the mantle of Churchill. His star rose like a rocket'. A few months later, Tynemouth Tories named their headquarters 'Hailsham House', an honour generally granted only to Churchill and Woolton since 1945, and other associations followed their example in 1958.[34]

The effect on the Prime Minister was less positive, for it was Hailsham and his bell that provided the lead story in the Sunday papers, and not Macmillan's more traditional speech the same afternoon. Macmillan's congratulatory note to Hailsham was not in his most effusive tone – 'you must be gratified by the reception you have had' – and the Prime Minister later referred to Hailsham's personal assistant, without much cordiality, as 'the bell boy'. In 1958, John Wyndham made discreet attempts to ensure that Brighton's upstaging of the Leader was not repeated at Blackpool, but for once his diplomacy did not work, for, arguing that Blackpool deserved at least equal treatment to Brighton, Hailsham again rang the bell. There were occasions when Macmillan had to soothe those that Hailsham's speeches had offended, as for example when his undiscriminating attack on Liberals upset Dorset Liberals who now tended to vote Conservative, and Hailsham did not campaign in the Torrington by-election for the same reason. After the 1959 election, Hailsham was summarily removed from the Chairmanship and took some offence at his treatment, attributing it to a purely personal misunderstanding with Macmillan. Hailsham had an immodest (and exaggerated) view of how much he had contributed to the 1959 victory, claiming most of the credit for himself, and, when the campaign was over, he intended to remind Macmillan of how useful it had been 'that some of the rougher work could be farmed out to someone who was not the leader'; because of his sacking the letter was not sent. But despite such tensions, the period between 1957 and 1959 marked the appearance of the modern Chairmanship in its cheer-leading role; Woolton had done something similar, and with an equally damaging effect on

---

[34] Windlesham, *Communication*, 38; Hornsby-Smith to Butler, 12 Oct. 1957, Butler MSS, G31; Central Office constituency file, CCO 1/12/70.

his relations with the Leader, but he had also run the machine. Increasingly after 1957, the actual management of the Party was left in other hands while Chairmen metaphorically rang the bell.[35]

Hailsham's main job was thus to rally the Party's morale and in this he was a great success. Butler wrote to Patrick Buchan-Hepburn, now Lord Hailes, in October 1959, that 'we have certainly had a wonderful victory, and all credit must go to the Hailsham/Poole partnership which did so much to strengthen the morale and organisation of the Party'. Before accepting the Chairmanship, Hailsham had already been lined up to deliver the annual CPC lecture at Brighton. He used this televised occasion to deliver a strong philosophical defence of current policy and a ringing attack on the Labour alternative. This fitted exactly with Macmillan's objective of turning round opinion in the country by persuading the Party first and then using the active membership to sell the message to the voters. Shrewsbury Conservatives were told by their chairman in December 1957 that Hailsham's appointment was 'a matter of great importance to the Party' and they resolved to get copies of his CPC lecture for all the branches in the constituency. During his two years as Chairman, Hailsham visited every Area to address meetings of constituency leaders, spoke at dozens of constituency meetings and dinners, and introduced what became the permanent practice of sending out periodic Chairman's letters to constituency and Area officers on current political topics; when the first such letter arrived in North Cornwall in November 1957, it was sent on to all branches in the constituency, with the association chairman telling her members that 'where we have had doubts . . . we must have faith.' Hailsham addressed in all thirty-nine mass meetings before the 1959 campaign, and spoke at every by-election but Torrington; he also agreed to Heath's suggestion that he should see groups of MPs, 'made up into suitable batches', though he privately minuted, 'what a bore!' All of this was effective: the intelligence summary provided for the Liaison Committee in October 1957 reported a strong rallying after the Brighton Conference, 'and in particular Lord Hailsham's inspiring speech'. The Shrewsbury Conservatives' annual report wrote of Hailsham's appointment as both inspired and inspiring, and West Derbyshire resolved that if Macmillan could not attend their annual rally then Hailsham would be their next choice ahead of Butler, and well ahead of anyone else.[36]

There was a definite effort too to put across the Party's case with a programme of meetings addressed by other Ministers; in April 1957, Central

35 Central Office Chairman's department files, CCO 20/17/1, 20/8/2 and 3; Dennis Walters, *Not Always with the Pack* (1989), 91, 96–7.
36 Butler to Hailes, 20/10/59, Hailes MSS, 4/12; Hailsham, *The Door*, 159, 163; Hailsham, *Sparrow's Flight*, 319; Walters, *Not Always*, 84–6, 89–92; North Cornwall CA minutes, 16 Nov. 1957; Central Office Chairman's department file, CCO 20/1/5; Windlesham, *Communication*, 40; Central Office file, CCO 4/7/375, Public Opinion; Central Office, Chairman's department file, CCO 20/8/2; West Derbyshire CA minutes, 10 Nov. 1958; Shrewsbury CA minutes, 9 Dec. 1957.

Office had found it difficult to persuade Ministers to accept these engagements; at that time the Ministers most generous in accepting speaking
invitations were said to be Macmillan himself, Hill, Brooke, and Kilmuir,
the worst were Sandys and Lennox-Boyd, who rarely accepted invitations
and then usually cancelled at the last minute anyway. By Summer 1958, the
general recovery of morale and discreet prodding by the Whips had ensured
a greater willingness to put heads over the parapet. Hailsham was also able
to use his position to stamp some of his own liberal ideas on the Party; he
was one of the few Conservatives to sympathise with Ian Harvey after his
disgrace in 1958, and he intervened actively on behalf of Peter Goldman
when it appeared that anti-semitism might be holding back his selection as
a Conservative candidate.[37]

Alongside the recovery of morale came the return to recruiting. A campaign
called 'Roll Call for Victory' was launched at the 1958 Party Conference and
ran until the end of the year. As in 1948 and 1952 this was a coordinated
national effort in which nearly all constituencies took part. The coincidence
of similar stories in all corners of the Conservative press in September 1958
suggests that a briefing had taken place. The *Daily Telegraph* welcomed the
chance to verify statistically the claims 'of a falling off of membership and
interest'. In January 1959, these same papers collectively speculated on the
results of the recruiting which were due to be released shortly; the *Yorkshire
Post* said that 'the last time the Conservatives counted heads was in 1952 when
they numbered nearly three millions. It is thought that the new figure will be
well ahead of that.' In fact no figure was ever released. The reason was clear
enough: although the campaign itself was a success and enrolled a quarter
of a million new members, the actual counting of heads was a tremendous
embarrassment. It emerged that *before* the campaign membership had fallen
by nearly 30 per cent in six years. Even after the 1958 recruitment the total
membership of the Party in England and Wales was down to 2.2 million
(a reduction of two-thirds of a million compared to the equivalent count at
the end of 1952). The regional pattern was also disturbing, for it showed
that the biggest falls had taken place in industrial areas and that the Party's
rural and suburban strongholds had remained relatively the strongest: the four
Southern English Areas outside London (out of a total of twelve Areas in
England and Wales) had already had 43 per cent of the Party's members in
1950 but now had almost half of the total. Put another way, the Party had
lost 6 per cent of its members in the South West but nearly 40 per cent in
London. In Yorkshire as a whole, there was a loss of about a quarter of the
membership, while in rural Barkston Ash the fall was 10 per cent of ordinary
members but a third of YCs. Hampstead was apparently typical of the pattern
in the strongest areas; membership was 7,105 plus 696 YCs in 1954, but fell

[37] Central Office Chairman's department file, CCO 20/1/5; Walters, *Not Always*, 101–4.

by almost a thousand in 1955–56, and further falls then took place despite energetic annual campaigns; after taking part in the 1958 national campaign, the senior membership was 5,850, and there were still 661 YCs; the next period of Party unpopularity reduced the senior total to 4,197 by 1964. After 1957–58, not only were national figures never announced at the end of recruiting campaigns, but nor were the press ever led to believe that they might be. For many years after 1958, Central Office did not compile official national figures: it was safer to stress constituency autonomy and say 'don't know'. Since, as Michael Pinto-Duschinsky found a decade later, only a tenth of the constituency associations even gave the number of their members in annual reports, it would not now be easy to collect such information without a special effort.[38]

Quota payments indicated the same geographical pattern, though since full lists were not yet published, this had to be deduced from the bouquets handed out to the good payers; in 1956, 110 associations overpaid their quotas, and 16 actually paid more than twice what they had been asked for; this latter group contained, in addition to Sutton Coldfield and Knutsford (both very untypical of the Area in which they lay), only West Dorset and thirteen associations in the South East; that pattern continued each year in the later 1950s, financial health being a good index of organisational strength (since the quotas were already calculated to allow for the different numbers of Conservative voters in each constituency). Against this generally disappointing scenario, it should be stressed that the 1958 recruiting campaign did in places produce impressive results; in affluent South Coventry, 3,225 new members were recruited to take the total up to nearly 5,000, by a long way the highest total in the history of the constituency, but here, as also in Walsall, the association had apparently suspended its minimum subscription (which was only half a crown [12.5 pence]), in the effort to bump up overall numbers, so the level of commitment from newly-recuited members may not have been very great. In the very different constituency of Bury St Edmunds, there were not only a large number of new members but also over two hundred additions to the branch committees; at King's Lynn too the campaign had been 'quite a success. Nothing spectacular, but good solid progress' in which two branches had been restarted from scratch and several reorganised – a reminder that numbers were not the only measurement of progress. It is perhaps significant that it was in East Anglia and the West Midlands that the Party was to do best in the 1959 General Election and through the 1960s. Equally in a stronghold like Guildford the 1959–60 membership of 12,981 was the highest ever, and

---

38 Central Office file, CCO 500/11/7, Recruiting 1958; Central Office constituency files, CCO 1/10/194 and 1/11/189; Hampstead CA minutes, 22 Oct. 1955, 7 Sept. 1956, 19 Jan. 1959, 9 Nov. 1964; Michael Pinto-Duschinsky, 'The Role of Constituency Associations in the Conservative Party', D. Phil. thesis, Oxford University, 1972, 17.

included nearly half of all Tory voters in the constituency; here too there was an excellent result in 1959.[39]

Much attention was paid to one particular recruit. When Field-Marshal Montgomery retired from the army in 1958 and embarked on an extensive round of television, public speaking and writing, he approached Macmillan privately to offer his support. Poole, who had served on Monty's wartime staff, went down to visit him at Alton. It was agreed that the Party would send briefing notes on defence matters but remain at arm's length in public, so that Monty's declaration of support could make maximum impact. Poole treated Monty with care, so as not to risk embarrassment at anything this political loose cannon might say: he recalled that it had been said of Sir William Beveridge that 'he mistook Tuggle Hall for Mount Zion' and added that 'there is always the possibility, though much more remote than in 1945, that the Field Marshal will mistake Alton for Colombey les Deux Eglises'. Monty was jollied along and made his declaration of support to a less-than-amazed press in the run-up to the 1959 Election.[40]

The same diplomatic skills were needed when the Earl of Avon (formerly Anthony Eden) enquired what role the Party would want him to play in the coming campaign; this rang warning bells, for Randolph Churchill had recently reopened old Suez memories in a series of *Daily Express* articles that were severely critical of Avon. Poole again went off to the country and reported with obvious relief that Avon's health would not allow him to do very much; they had agreed that, if health permitted, Avon would make a single speech in his old constituency or issue a press statement; Poole added that this was just as well for he could not possibly recommend using Avon in any more visible role. In the event the press statement that Avon issued in 1959 had to go through several drafts before a text was agreed, and even then he could not bring himself to endorse Macmillan by name. These meetings did though enable Poole to get Avon to hand over to Edward Heath the presidency of the Federation of Conservative Students, which had suffered rather from having only an inactive president, and to satisfy himself that the Suez volume of Avon's memoirs could not be published or serialised in the press before November 1959 – well after the last date for an election that year.[41]

Increased activity brought change as well as expansion. Some old structures withered; the Primrose League was reported in 1959 to do little except hold a couple of dinners a year, though it also retained a social presence in some

[39] National Union papers, NUA 2/2/22–25, Central Council reports; Coventry South CA, report on 1958; Walsall South CA minutes, 14 July 1958; Bury St Edmunds CA minutes, 1 June 1959; King's Lynn CA minutes, 27 Jan. 1959; Guildford CA minutes, 25 Mar. 1960.

[40] Central Office Chairman's department file, CCO 20/8/3, Correspondence with Macmillan.

[41] Central Office Chairman's department file, CCO 20/8/4, Correspondence with Macmillan, 1959; David Dutton, 'Living with Collusion: Anthony Eden and the Later History of the Suez Affair', in *Contemporary Record*, vol. 5 (1991), 204; Robert Rhodes James, *Anthony Eden* (1986), 608.

localities; it had a paper membership of twenty thousand, including ninety Members of Parliament, but was said to continue in existence only through Churchill's patronage as Grand Master, and because the CRD produced its magazine. The Central Office view was that no effort should be expended to keep it going. On the other hand there was a welcome for the Bow Group as a new contributor to the Party. This was rather belated for the Group had been founded in 1950, by former Tory students who wished to continue to meet after coming down from university, and who found a first meeting place at the Bow and Bromley Conservative Club in the East End; founder members included Peter Emery and Dennis Walters, both later MPs. Its purpose was 'constructive thought and research' which would 'provide for the Conservative Party what the Fabian Society provided originally for the Labour Party'; it began with fifty invited members and an age limit of 35 (which immediately put it into friendly competition with the YCs). By 1952, Central Office was already helping the Group to find speakers, and advising the Vice Chairman John Hare that Bow Group members were 'all . . . of the type who may become prospective parliamentary candidates'. However, by 1956 its membership was still only two hundred. In 1957 it began a more active phase with the launch of the magazine *Crossbow* and the advent of a new generation of ambitious chairmen; leading members at this time were Geoffrey Howe, Patrick Jenkin, James Lemkin, Michael Wolff, Timothy Raison, Christopher Chataway and Ian Gow, and by 1960 membership had quadrupled.[42]

The Bow Group thus became an important ladder for the would-be Tory MP. One problem was that the Group explicitly did not take a collective line, seeing its role as the encouragement of debate, and this sometimes raised hackles, particularly over colonial policy; in 1957, there was a row over a Bow Group study of the public schools, and one Party member described it to Hailsham (who concurred) as being 'as socialistic as the Labour Party's own propaganda'. A similar outcry followed the work of a study group led by Julian Critchley that advocated in 1961 the ending of Britain's nuclear deterrent. Bow publications stated clearly enough that their contents did not represent either a Party or a Group view, but they tended to be reported (accurately) as the views of rising young Conservatives. The Group prospered, despite financial and editorial crises, mainly through the self-generated activity of its talented young leaders and because Macmillan himself gave his patronage; he came in person to the launch party for *Crossbow* (where he delivered a speech largely written by Howe for the occasion) and said with characteristic self-mockery that 'I was never able in my time to persuade any Prime Minister to participate in the launching ceremony of one of my projects'; he saw Bow Groupers as the heirs of his 1920s 'YMCA', and allies in the drive to modernise the Party; in considering the moral of

42 Central Office files, CCO 3/2/62 and 3/3/48, Bow Group.

the 1959 campaign after it had been won, Macmillan's own private view was that 'the great thing is to keep the Tory Party on *modern* and *progressive* lines'; Geoffrey Howe's dictum that the Bow Group 'were seeking to make the Tory Party fit for *Observer* and *Guardian* readers to live in' indicates the civilising role that it could play along Macmillan's line of argument. For exactly this reason, not everyone welcomed the Group; in the satirical novel *The Short List*, published by David Walder MP in 1964, a Minister tells the hero at all costs to avoid 'the Stepney Group': 'it attracts all the worst elements in all the parties under our banner so that we find ourselves not only defending our own policy but everyone else's as well.' Howe's conception of the Group's 'broad framework' as being 'economic rigour and social awareness' was indicated by his own remarkably prophetic article on the future of social policy, published by the Group in *Principles in Practice* in 1961. This strategy would find its place at the heart of Tory politics only a generation later when these Bow Groupers themselves got to the top. In 1958 Poole wrote that the Party backed the Bow Group 'because it keeps together a group of intelligent young people whose help we need'. Peter Walker, national YC chairman, opened a debate at the National Union General Purposes Committee in 1957 with the ironic reflection that 'it has been said that the intelligent join the Bow Group while the unintelligent join the YCs', but he accepted that the Group had 'played an important part and have created a good image of progressivism in the Tory Party'. It was agreed that the different organisations offered complementary services, though the YCs continued to complain that the Bow Group's talent for publicity put their own much larger organisation in the shade. The Group's image, unlike that of the YCs for the most part, remained that of a group of serious-minded and ambitious men and women with an active social conscience; Anthony Sampson reported hearing of a girl who joined them, 'thinking they were the "Beau Group", and was disappointed to find them dull and not very sexy'. Sampson himself thought the early Bow Groupers to be

> studious and carefully pedestrian – compared to the more equestrian postures of pre-war young Tories. They write long, well-printed pamphlets full of accurate figures and cautious suggestions, and they give sober parties in Kensington and Chelsea.

This last fact at least proved the cynical wisdom of the Central Office official who had in 1950 noted that 'the idea is a good one but . . . will not last if there is too much slumming'. For all its members' social consciences, it did not take the Bow Group long to leave Bow.[43]

---

[43] Central Office Chairman's department file, CCO 20/16/1, Correspondence with Vice Chairmen; CPA, Central Office files, CCO 3/3/48, 3/5/38 and 3/6/38, Bow Group; National Union papers, NUA 5/2/32, secretary's notes of GP committee meetings; Harold Macmillan, *Pointing the Way, 1959–1961* (1972), 16; David Walder, *The Short List* (1964), 10; Geoffrey Howe, *Conflict of Loyalty* (1994), 25, 29; Sampson, *Anatomy*, 88; Central Office file, CCO 3/2/62, Bow Group; interview with Lord Howe.

Advertising and electioneering

The recovery of morale and the relative recovery of membership, together with Poole's special skills, ensured that money continued to come in healthily. This enabled the Party to embark on the other main aspect of its recovery strategy, which was the work of Poole rather than Hailsham. Since 1955 the Chief Publicity Officer had been Guy Schofield, ex-editor of the *Daily Mail*; shortly before his return to Fleet Street in April 1957, Schofield suggested that the Party should consider a massive campaign of press advertising organised and coordinated by a major agency. This made financial sense, for surveys showed that a half-page advertisement in the *People* would cost about £110 for each 100,000 people who read it; even to print that many leaflets would cost twice as much, and they would then have to be delivered and would mainly be discarded unread. Sunday papers were targeted because people were believed to have more time to absorb such messages on Sundays; the Party's concentration on Sunday papers was to lead to rushed tactical decisions made to hit the Sundays' deadlines in both 'the night of the long knives' in 1962 and the Profumo affair in 1963. In May 1957 the Party commissioned Colman, Prentis and Varley to produce an advertising scheme, at an initial cost of £80,000; the first advertisements appeared on Sunday 30 June, a picture of a little girl peering through a five-barred gate, with the slogan 'Will she be fenced in when she grows up?' This was a historic step into a new form of electioneering. In his *Communication and Political Power*, Lord Windlesham wrote in 1966 that 'in the period 1957–9 the Conservative Party developed a pattern of political communication that was to become a standard model in British politics, admired and imitated by political opponents as well as by later Conservative propagandists.' This 1957 experiment burgeoned into an almost continuous two-year poster and press campaign, derided by some as vulgar and dangerous in its use of subliminal images, but feared by opponents like Richard Crossman as completely out-gunning Labour's own efforts – which he thought uncoordinated and amateurish by comparison. Where Labour spent £103,000 on pre-election publicity, the Conservatives spent £468,000. The campaign team used the academic voting studies first appearing in the 1950s to demonstrate ways in which voters formed images of the competing parties. Surveys showed that the Conservatives' chief problem was in winning support from young, married, manual workers, many of whom told interviewers that they considered themselves to be middle class but who had inherited attitudes from their working-class parents. Part of Poole's acclimatisation was to make visits to the archetypally marginal, upwardly mobile constituency of Watford, where he could watch his target voters doing their week-end shopping, but campaign decisions were based more on systematic research, and the Party handed over the management of its advertising to the professionals.

The campaign mainly aimed to distance the Tories from their image as the

Party of the upper class; pictures of housewives, children, manual workers and white-coated technicians all appeared with the caption 'You're looking at a Conservative'. Gallup reported a fall from 27 per cent in 1955 to 17 per cent in 1959 in the proportion of voters associating the Conservative Party with privilege. Not all the campaign ideas worked; the hope of showing voters how lively their rulers were led to strip-cartoons of Butler walking his dogs, Hailsham as a pullovered undergraduate, Selwyn Lloyd playing golf, and the mild-mannered Heathcoat Amory actually bronco-busting in Argentina; Crossman scoffed that Macmillan was being 'sold like a detergent' and these efforts attracted such derision that they did not appear for long. 'You've never had it so good' never appeared as a slogan, but was obliquely used in a forward-looking way in the 1959 series captioned 'You're having it good. Have it better'. There was a final intensive campaign in Summer 1959, when the Conservatives were for six weeks the largest advertiser in the country. Since there is evidence that the overwhelming majority of voters, even in the relatively fluid campaign of 1959, made up their minds before Parliament was dissolved, this long-term projection of favourable Party images was important to Conservative re-election after the trough of 1957–8. Windlesham's sceptical conclusion seems about right; the publicity campaign did not win the 1959 election, but 'people were influenced, events guided, and conditions created which allowed an election to be won.' Butler and Rose in 1960 reached broadly similar conclusions.[44]

The Party could also benefit from publicity campaigns by industries that feared that Conservative unpopularity would again threaten them with nationalisation. In August 1957, Poole reported that the Iron and Steel Federation were realising that they would have to fight if they wanted to keep a Labour Government out of office and would spend 'a very large sum of money to this end'. He also reported that the leaders of industrial assurance companies were coming to the same conclusion: they were 'the most powerful weapon of propaganda in the country. They have 10 million policyholders and an army of 25,000 agents who are constantly in touch with that section of the general public which it is most difficult for us to approach'. This type of politico-industrial activity had not been much seen since 1950–51. In May 1958 Macmillan hosted a dinner, paid for by the Party and organised by Poole, for leaders of the Iron and Steel Federation. Poole's brief reported that the CRD was in regular touch with the Federation for the exchange of political ammunition, that Federation spokesmen had been offered television training at Central Office, that the Federation would shortly embark on an anti-nationalisation publicity campaign, and that it would give the Party 'substantial' extra funds for its own work. The high

---

[44] Windlesham, *Communication*, 35–6, 41, 51–4, 59, 61; Morgan, *Crossman*, 771; Butler and Rose, *General Election of 1959*, 21–5, 28, 33; Sampson, *Macmillan*, 163.

profile of these campaigns makes it easy to overestimate their importance, but because they could only oppose a single Labour policy and (for legal as well as tactical reasons) not endorse the Conservatives, the actual impact was rather limited, especially when it is remembered that in 1959 nationalisation was unimportant to most voters. An extensive attitude survey, done for Central Office in September 1959, not only found that 63.5 per cent of all electors opposed more nationalisation, but also that nationalisation was only the eighth most important issue in the electors' own order of priority, behind prices, unemployment, pensions, housing, taxes, education and rates. The most that the industrial campaigns can have done was to contribute to the generally negative impression of Labour. On the seven more prominent issues the Conservatives had to depend on their own advertising and on their record.[45]

As in 1955, the record was in 1959 the Party's greatest asset. With a few regional exceptions, unemployment was again low and a spending boom, fuelled in part by easily available credit, had roared ahead; between December 1957 and July 1959, total hire purchase credit rose by £294 million. Over the period since the return to power in 1951, the number of white-collar workers (the Conservatives' most loyal support) had risen by a million, and the number of manual workers had fallen by half a million. Mass production and mass consumption over the decade had loosened some of the political affiliations derived from class and narrowed the visible differences in lifestyles. Gallup recorded in Summer 1959 that 38 per cent of all voters did not think it mattered much which party won the coming election, another sign of the decline in the politics of fear that had already been noticed in 1955; significantly too, Conservative voters were far more hostile to the prospect of a Labour government than Labour voters were to a Tory one. At the TUC Conference in September, Richard Crossman found that 'the atmosphere was complacent, detached and completely defeatist about Labour's chances. They all seemed to think a third Tory victory was a bad thing but something inevitable you had to come to terms with'; this was again a world away from 1951. Gallup also found that the Conservatives had a strong lead over Labour when voters were asked which party would be more likely to increase production and prosperity.[46]

Iain Macleod had picked up this theme in a speech in March 1959 at Reading, appealing for support from the socially mobile in such marginal seats:

> they are as surely men of property as if they held broad acres or led great firms. Perhaps they own a house, or, more probably they are buying one through a

---

45 Central Office Chairman's department files, CCO 20/8/2 and 3, Correspondence with Macmillan; Central Office file, CCO 4/8/336, Public Opinion.
46 Butler and Rose, *General Election of 1959*, 12, 14, 19, 69–70; Morgan, *Crossman*, 775; Thompson, *Day Before Yesterday*, 170.

building society. They have a car and a television set – perhaps a refrigerator and a washing machine. . . . At this time of the year you will find them looking at gaily-coloured travel brochures and planning their holidays. But now they do not only think of the English seaside resorts – the pamphlets that they study are of the Costa Brava, the Rhineland, the Italian cities. They are for the most part employees drawing high wages in a prosperous and expanding economy. . . . We can give them the opportunity they long for instead of the equality they despise.

Seven months later, with the election lost by his party, Labour's Patrick Gordon Walker concluded that 'the simple fact is that the Tories identified themselves with the new working class rather better than we did.' The National Union Executive, reviewing the election after it had been won, was quite sure how important the record had been. When a member complained about the quality of the Party's television broadcasts, Evelyn Emmet MP reminded him that 'eight million people who looked at us on television did not have one in 1951. Three million realised that they now had a decent home which they did not have under the Socialists. It was our good national record that won the election.' With a longer perspective, an alternative view of the 1950s emerged, as a time in which Britain's economic growth had lagged decisively behind that of her competitors, a failure of performance partly due to consuming too much and investing too little, but that alternative view was hardly articulated in election year. What was clear as the election approached was that the Party would fight in an upbeat way, and that Macmillan would be central to the appeal to the voters, as the Guildford MP told his supporters on 15 Sepember:

> Whoever represents this country as Prime Minister must feel that he has his Party and Government behind him. Mr. Gaitskell, with his undisciplined left wing which might break away from him at any time, was surely not that man. On the other hand, Mr. Macmillan had brought the Summit Meeting in sight, and he was obviously the man to represent the country. The Labour Party were still preaching the same policies of Nationalisation which were out of date in the Twentieth Century in a country becoming more prosperous. This was the age of the common man, when everyone had the same opportunities whether on the bench or at the Managing Director's desk. Mr. Nugent concluded by saying there was a golden future ahead of us . . .[47]

Macmillan had prepared himself and his Party for the re-election of his Government as thoroughly as any Prime Minister had ever done. He had addressed meetings outside London every year, combining these with receptions for constituency leaders, and he began discreet election tours from Summer 1958. A series of two and three day regional tours was arranged by Poole, with Anthony Barber for the Prime Minister and Anthony Garner for Central Office reconnoitring each tour in advance, checking hotels, meeting

[47] Fisher, *Macleod*, 136; Sampson, *Macmillan*, 166; National Union papers, 4/3/2, Executive Committee minutes; Guildford CA minutes, 15 Sept. 1959.

rooms and schedules in great detail. They were treading a careful line between the Government and the Party side of Macmillan's duties, for these were ostensibly non-political occasions on which the Prime Minister would visit factories, new buildings or sporting events, but they were sited to place him in marginal constituencies and with sitting Tory MPs gathered round him for photo-opportunities; in the evenings there were Party receptions at which he could shake the hands of local leaders, and the size of these was carefully calibrated; the General Director instructed his Area Agents that Macmillan wanted invitations limited to between fifty and eighty people, 'enough to enable him to shake hands with all who are present. When the numbers are extended beyond this sort of figure the privilege of meeting the Prime Minister loses some of its distinction.' His visit to Shrewsbury in 1958 exceeded that total, with forty tickets offered to each of the four Tory associations in the county, but even then great tact had to be exercised in their distribution. Peter Walker, fighting his first contest at Dartford, remembered the fillip which the Prime Minister's visit in 1959 gave to his local supporters, but that encouragement actually worked both ways: Macmillan's diary recorded in April 1959 a visit with 'six or seven speeches' in 'many Lancashire towns, including Oldham, Rochdale, Bury, Stockport, Manchester. . . . It was really a most heartening experience. With the masses of people whom we saw – they waited in large numbers in the streets – there was scarcely a boo.' The fine line being drawn was also indicated by the fact that the Prime Minister agreed to an open-top car for these tours, but not to a loud-hailer, since that would make his visit look too much like campaigning. The 1959 programme completed for Macmillan a full series of visits to rallies in each of the Conservative Areas; the rally in Home Counties North (Essex and Middlesex) at the Alexandra Palace involved every constituency in the Area.[48]

The politically non-political character of his forays away from base is conveyed by the minute Macmillan sent to John Wyndham in July 1959 asking him to list the New Towns,

> and mark those which are hopeless politically or have made the area they are in hopeless, and those where we could have some good hopes. I thought of making a little tour to some of these New Towns. I could easily do so alleging that I took such a great part in building them and would like to know how they are going on. I would not, of course, choose places which we could never win or the places we are bound to win. It would be the doubtfuls. It might be worth doing and would not be too exhausting say at the beginning of August.

One result of this minute was a Prime Ministerial 'non-political' visit to Harlow in August, accompanied by the Conservative MP for the Epping constituency; despite the advent of fifteen thousand additional (mainly work-

---

[48] Central Office Chairman's department files, CCO 20/8/2–4; Shrewsbury CA minutes, 26 Sept. 1958; Peter Walker, *Staying Power: An Autobiography* (1991) 22; Macmillan, *Riding the Storm*, 745.

ing-class) voters to the constituency since 1955, the Tory majority rose at the election in October. Reviewing the results at the National Union Executive, Lady Davidson (who had with her husband represented Hemel Hempstead since 1921) proclaimed that 'the New Town people are not Socialist. We hoped that the people that came to the new towns would become the backbone of the party. We must realise that we have a potential following in these new towns'. Essex (and Hertfordshire) man was beginning to stir.[49]

The 1959 General Election

Macmillan's New Town visits were a bonus, for election preparations had been made on the assumption of a Spring election. Central Office advice which cautiously promised a Conservative majority of only thirteen in a Spring election prompted the decision to go for October instead. The delay was officially attributed to the European situation, but Macmillan disarmingly added that, 'besides, if I may be quite frank, I think my party will do much better later on'. This allowed the Party machine a further period of tuning up, and in the case of television broadcasts time for over-preparation; it also allowed everyone to holiday early to prepare for the fray; Macmillan's note on a policy draft on 20 July was 'Have to be done by the end of the month, or everyone will be in Monaco'. The delay allowed time too for Macmillan's most audacious public relations event, the Eisenhower visit in August. The motorcade from the airport, with the Prime Minister sharing an open car with the President, was spontaneously surrounded by cheering crowds, but then Macmillan persuaded Eisenhower to agree to a live television broadcast of a conversation between them at Number 10. This was an effective way of reminding the electorate that Macmillan was a statesman on cosy terms with world leaders; he was also the first to show how effective a camera in the home could be to a premier.[50]

The Tory unpopularity of 1957–58 and the humiliation of Suez remained in people's minds in considering the likely result. As late as 18 June, the Labour elde. statesman Hugh Dalton speculated on his party's chances and concluded that 'unless we make bloody fools of ourselves, we shall win it easily'. The Conservative lead in the polls over the Summer changed such expectations, yet many Tories were still nervous; Hailsham wrote to Macmillan on 7 September that 'there are disadvantages in starting the race hot favourites. There is always a danger of over-confidence and of a Keep the Tories Tame type of attitude. . . . Have you any advice to offer?' When the

---

[49] Central Office Chairman's department file, CCO 20/8/4; National Union papers, 4/3/2, Executive Committee minutes and notes.

[50] Hailsham, *Sparrow's Flight*, 323; Roth, *Heath*, 130; Lindsay and Harrington, *Conservative Party*, 207; Central Office Chairman's department file, CCO 20/8/3; Ramsden, *Making of Conservative Policy*, 206; Cockerell, *Live from Number Ten*, 66–7.

election campaign was announced next day and with polling a month later, things quickly began to go wrong. Macmillan's objective, as Hailsham later recalled, was to 'play it long, play it down, play it slow', and this strategy was knocked off balance by events. The Party manifesto made a perfectly decent stab at being forward-looking after the Party had been in office for eight years, but struck few sparks with press commentators; as the Prime Minister had earlier observed, 'problem is, how to present what is in fact "Safety First" into a policy which looks as if it is moving forward', and suggested that the Party's line should be 'on the basis of what has been done, move one', which was necessarily unexciting. When the Advisory Committee on Policy (ACP) approved the final draft, Peter Walker welcomed on behalf of the the YCs 'the confident and forward-looking tone of the document and the feeling that one got from it that the Government had done so well it was inconceivable that they would not be returned for another five years'; it was precisely this tone that struck some outside the Party as complacent. The first election broadcasts, some of them filmed as much as six weeks earlier, were generally thought to be stilted and ineffective. And Labour's invention of a daily morning press conference in Westminster to provide issues for debate at the start of the news media's day gave their party a head start for the first two weeks of the campaign.[51]

At one level the carefully thought-out campaign functioned exactly as planned. The Party fought an effective organisational campaign. Butler reported to Fraser at the end of October that 'the Prime Minister had told me that he has never known the briefing and documentation better'. Tory candidates were again younger on average than their opponents, and the Bow Group was now a factor here: ten Bow Groupers were elected, five of them gaining Labour seats in the process, and forty-seven were among the unsuccessful candidates; sixty YCs were also candidates and ten of these won. There were in total 104 new Conservative MPs elected in 1959, representing rather wider social backgrounds than those they replaced. Macmillan fought an active campaign, travelling over 2,500 miles in a month and addressing seventy-four meetings. In the constituencies, though the decline of political meetings and canvassing in a television age was now remarked on, this afflicted the Conservatives less than Labour: about half of all Conservative voters were canvassed by their Party during the campaign (a quarter of Labour voters by their party) and about one in four were knocked up on polling day. In marginal seats the figures would have been very much higher.[52]

51 Central Office Chairman's department file, CCO 20/8/4; Ben Pimlott (ed.), *The Political Diary of Hugh Dalton, 1918–1940, 1945–1960* (1986), 692; Hailsham, *Sparrow's Flight*, 323; Butler and Rose, *General Election of 1959*, 49, 53; ACP, 22 July 1959; Ramsden, *Making of Conservative Policy*, 203.
52 Ramsden, *Making of Conservative Policy*, 208; Butler and Rose, *General Election of 1959*, 125, 130, 140; Horne, *Macmillan*, 151

All the same, the smooth functioning of normal Party mechanisms was not sufficient to offset fears that in the national campaign things were slipping away. This arose from the fact that opinion polls were now being published often enough in the four-week campaign to provide – or seem to provide – a continuous measurement of the electoral temperature. At the outset the Conservatives were comfortably ahead, though few predicted a big Conservative majority. The trend in the polls was then continuously down, and the average lead of about 6 per cent in the first week had been halved by a week before polling. In the last week, the polls detected a little further slippage and then a Conservative recovery; they finally predicted a lead of 2–3 per cent, about half the lead in the actual votes cast on 8 October. When it is borne in mind that in 1959 opinion polls appeared only after a time-lag of about a week between fieldwork and publication, it would appear that the Conservatives lost ground in the first two weeks of the campaign and recovered it in the third and fourth weeks, finishing almost exactly where they had started. This is consistent with the canvass returns telephoned in to Central Office, showing that the position was very promising on the final figures, but after a sticky start. Oliver Poole was keen to point out that the Conservatives were never actually behind in the polls, that all polls were out of date, and that the reported movement of opinion had anyway mainly been from Conservative to doubtful and back to Conservative by voters who had never opted for another party. On this basis, he panicked rather less than others and recognised that the turn of the tide had taken place in mid–campaign and not only at the very end. Those who set the betting odds, and opinion on the stock exchange, reached the same view, with expectations of a Conservative victory building up again about ten days before polling. The daily intelligence reports compiled at Central Office, utilising all sources of press and Party information, recorded the same chronological pattern; on 25 September it was thought that the Labour campaign 'has given us a setback', and on the 28th there were worried reports flowing in from constituencies all over the country, but on 29 September, nine days before the poll, there was confidence that support was increasing and that 'the rot has been stopped'. By 1 October, it was reported that Conservatives now had the campaigning edge in every field but television.[53]

If this was then a campaign of retreat and counter-attack, what was it that shifted opinions? The historiographial consensus has found explanations in television electioneering and in political tactics. Television was a favoured explanation for political trends because in 1959 for the first time half the electorate had access to a set, and because there seemed to be an unusually sharp difference between the parties' performance. In retrospect, nobody

---

[53] Howard, *RAB*, 268; Butler and Rose, *General Election of 1959*, 46, 101; Central Office files, CCO 4/8/252, Sample Canvass, CCO 500/24/135, Canvass 1959, and CCO 4/8/113, Intelligence Reports.

wished to claim credit for the Conservatives' early broadcasts; Hailsham felt, on the day after polling, that these had 'almost cost us the election' and blamed himself for leaving it all to the Chief Whip and the Vice Chairman. Heath, speaking to Michael Cockerell in 1988, seemed to have forgotten his own responsibility for the election broadcasts as Chief Whip, in giving a scathing account of the early 1959 broadcasts, but he too argued that a poor television performance had been losing the Party the election. It is clear that after three of the five broadcasts had been shown things were felt to be going very badly. The fourth broadcast was scrapped, and a new one put together, linked professionally by Christopher Chataway in a way that poured scorn on the slickness of Labour on television (which was in its way a tribute to how good Conservatives thought Labour's broadcasts had been). The final broadcast has acquired a mythic significance as a last-minute virtuoso intervention by Macmillan, who under the expert guidance of Norman Collins is said to have turned the election: Heath claimed 'it changed everything'. This makes a good story, and Macmillan did indeed put in a fine performance and was widely applauded for it, but its significance was much less than has been claimed. In the first place, it had always been intended that a Macmillan solo should round off the campaign, as Eden had done in 1955, and Poole had lined up Collins to produce it several months earlier; it had also been planned to be a broadcast scripted at the last moment, so no plans therefore needed to be changed. Secondly, it attracted an audience only slightly larger than the other broadcasts, and the BBC's own audience surveys found that while this broadcast was significantly more popular with Tory voters than the earlier efforts had been, it made no greater impact than the others on Labour and uncommitted voters. If so, how can it have swung many votes? Finally, the fact that it was delivered only two days before the poll, by which time the Conservative recovery had already been under way for a week, suggests that it cannot have turned the tide.[54]

If broadcasting did affect the outcome in 1959, then it was surely because television and radio reporting of campaign speeches ensured that the ebb and flow of the national debate was more quickly available to the voters than it had been through the press alone in previous elections. Television news bulletins were on every day and attracted larger audiences than any Party broadcast; reviewing the previous few years in December 1959, the Party's Chief Publicity Officer decided that news and current affairs programmes had been far more influential than anything the parties had produced, citing Macmillan's interview with Ed Murrow and a Butler interview on the Hydrogen bomb as the most telling examples; the decision in August to authorise all Area offices to hire a set at the Party's expense, so as to be able to keep up with campaign issues as they arose, had been a recognition of the same

---

[54] Central Office Chairman's department file, CCO 20/17/1; Cockerell, *Live from Number Ten*, 70–4; Egremont, *Wyndham*, 184–5; Butler and Rose, *General Election of 1959*, 88, 93–4.

development. He concluded that technical experts should determine the shape of the Party's broadcasts in future, with only the subject areas determined by Ministers, for 'the great lesson of the Election campaign was that topicality, and up-to-the-minute issues are the lifeblood of good political television'. (Hailsham had reached the same conclusion; colleagues might still 'do the policy input', but they must not 'mess about with the programme formula and layout'.) A Central Office committee chaired by the General Director endorsed these views; it also decided to invest in a new Party television studio in Central Office and to convene a special advisory group of people such as Chataway, Geoffrey Johnson-Smith and Collins, who would be both technically experienced and loyal to the Party's interests. Far more intensive coaching was laid on for the Party's spokesmen than in the more primitive courses run in the 1950s; in January 1960 Edward Boyle was asked to join a panel of junior ministers for eight weekly sessions of television training. For a few years, television was thought especially important because to most voters it was still such a novel experience to see and hear a Minister speaking about an event on the day on which it happened; in September 1964, the North Fylde Conservatives closed a meeting early as 'the members had to leave to see the Prime Minister on the T.V.', hardly something that would have excited anyone ten years later.[55]

In retrospect it was tempting for Conservatives to claim that they had always intended to fight a two-stage tactical campaign, an 'El Alamein' election in which Labour would be encouraged to make the running at the start and then be defeated in a well-timed counter-attack. This was certainly not the case. In the Tory press and in the Party itself, Labour's early momentum caused both alarm and a change of Conservative tactics. Hailsham's memoirs recall Poole ringing him up 'halfway through the campaign. "You know", said he, "we are losing". "I know", said I, and we contrived to warm things up accordingly.' From 27 September the Conservatives put Poole and Hailsham up at daily press conferences to reduce the effect of Labour's similar ploy. And on 28 September, Hailsham urged Party workers 'to wade into the fight. . . . Let there be plenty of hard-hitting above the belt. Just because we fight honourably there is no reason why we should be dull. By all means be pure but for goodness sake do not let us be driven onto the defensive.' There is though a core of truth in later claims to have foreseen and shaped the way in which campaign issues would develop. From early on, and with increasing insistence, Hailsham, Poole and Macleod had all battered away at the cost of Labour's programme and how it was to be financed. If this only paid off at the end, then their earlier work had set up the winning tactic; the Central Office intelligence report of 26 September

[55] Central Office General Director's file, CCO 120/1/4, Broadcasting; Central Office, Chairman's department file, CCO 20/17/1; Kaberry to Boyle, 26 Jan. 1960, Boyle MSS, 22509; North Fylde CA minutes , 24 Sept. 1964.

noted that 'the Socialists have not liked Lord Hailsham's breakdown of the cost of their proposals, and so it might be well to pursue this line'. It was in response to such attacks that Hugh Gaitskell made his fatal promise not to raise income tax, and in response to the added scepticism that this in itself produced, that he went further and proposed actual reductions in purchase tax. Richard Crossman was privately 'appalled at what we felt was a breach in Gaitskell's intellectual integrity', and the Tory leaders saw at once how useful this would be to their campaign. Hailsham, campaigning for Tony Barber in Doncaster, exuberantly announced that, 'The Lord hath delivered them into our hands'. Macmillan, reading reports of Gaitskell's new promises in his car, announced to his speechwriter 'We've got him!', and stopped on Wandsworth Common to make a speech on the subject to the attendant press corps emerging from their cars, before the opportunity passed; he offered a sardonic commentary on all election promises by pledging to the electorate that it would not rain on 9 October. Butler happily suggested that Labour should use the slogan 'a bribe a day keeps the Tories away'. With something to cheer at last, the Conservative press now had a field day; the *Daily Sketch* (which had already being doing rather well for the Party – Butler and Rose commented on its 'fine disregard for fact and for taste') now captured the Party mood perfectly with the headline 'It'll be free fags next!' These events took place with ten days to go before polling day and exactly coincided with the apparent start of the Conservative recovery, though it was another week before the opinion polls reported the fact.[56]

When shown a Research Department paper about average trends in poll leads during recent election campaigns in 1970, Hailsham wrote back to reject its 'underlying determinist thesis' and to cite 1959 as a prime example of a campaign that had been fought and won on tactics, which had shaped rather than been shaped by the opinion polls. He also made in passing some pointed comments on the failure to repeat the trick in 1964.

> I think we not merely could but would have lost the 1959 election, had not Oliver Poole and I got together and (without authority) changed the whole tempo of the campaign as Labour showed signs of drawing level. I always disliked the calm tactics of David Maxwell Fyfe and Harold M. and believe we would have lost if we had stuck to it. I think we could just about have won the 1964 [*sic*] had Alec with Reg Maudling's support not pussy-footed at the beginning. It was then considered cleverer to ask questions about the prices on the menu [of Labour's plans] instead of marking high prices on them and waiting for Labour to scream blue murder (as I did in 1959, despite non-cooperation from the Treasury) and plunge violently (though I did not anticipate Gaitskell's famous blunder on income tax, I did help to precipitate it). Labour's financial inadequacy was the right point in 1959 and 1964.

56 Butler and Rose, *General Election of 1959*, 58–60, 68, 93, 114; Hailsham, *Sparrow's Flight*, 323; Morgan, *Crossman*, 787; Central Office file, CCO 4/8/113; Hailsham, *The Door*, 157; Horne, *Macmillan*, 151; Thompson, *Day Before Yesterday*, 172; Kilmuir, *Political Adventure*, 311.

Passing this on to Heath, Michael Fraser was in 1970 sceptical of all such views: 1964 had been so close that it was possible to argue that almost anything *might* have tilted the balance, but in his view the Party had *never* been losing in 1959 anyway, as Poole, now prayed in aid by Hailsham, had maintained even at the time.[57]

In the outcome, it was indeed hard to believe that the 1959 election had ever seemed to be a close-run thing. The first result showed a strong Conservative performance in the Billericay division of Essex despite the growth of Basildon New Town in the constituency; Basildon thus embarked on its long career as the harbinger of Tory election night victories. Within half an hour the first Tory gain, for Geoffrey Johnson-Smith in Holborn, indicated an increased parliamentary majority. Overall, the Conservatives polled 13.8 million votes to Labour's 12.2 million and increased their share of the popular vote despite an improved Liberal performance; the Party won twenty more seats than in 1955 and pushed up its overall majority to a hundred. These national results masked sharp regional variations; big gains in the Midlands and the south were partly offset by five seats lost in Scotland, the first signs of a long decline. Despite earlier fears of Liberal intervention that had prompted considerable effort to keep the Bolton pact going against local Tory wishes, the increased Liberal vote made little difference to constituency results, and Torrington was easily regained. The variable pattern of swings indicates the extent to which prosperity was the overriding factor, with the Party doing best where unemployment had been lowest and less well where it had fallen least since 1956; Unionists in Dunbartonshire were convinced that it was the level of unemployment in the area that had produced increased Labour majorities in the county. A post-mortem by CPC groups found that, apart from London, where variations in the results were to be explained by housing issues, the variation in swing was due entirely to the national distribution of prosperity. Typical of Party comments was that of the Area Agent from the North West: 'The Conservative theme that "Life is better under the Conservatives" was a winner. Conversely, the Labour theme that only the few had benefited from Conservative prosperity and that in general conditions for the mass of the people were poor was not believed because it was not true.' His colleague in Home Counties South East thought that 'the sense of mission has gone from the bulk of the Labour Party, while at the same time many who previously voted Labour saw no special reason for keeping Tories out, and had nothing much to vote against'.[58]

---

[57] Hogg to Fraser, 17 Apr. 1970 and Fraser to Heath, 18 Apr. 1970, Leader's Consultative Committee correspondence.

[58] Butler and Rose, *General Election of 1959*, 189, 191, 195, 200; Central Office file, CCO 4/7/86, Pacts; Central Office Chairman's department files, CCO 20/8/2–4; Central Office file, CCO 4/8/107, Central Office Agents' reports on the 1959 Election; Dunbartonshire West UA minutes, 16 Nov. 1959.

Re-election for a third consecutive term set new records in modern party politics, and launched a period of recrimination in the Labour movement that left the Conservative Government almost without opposition for the next year. In 1960, there were by-election swings to the Government even above the high water mark of the 1959 victory, and a marginal seat was gained from Labour at Brighouse and Spenborough. The local election results of 1960 were the best all round that the Conservatives had had since the War. Macmillan's popularity continued to increase, and no peacetime Prime Minister before or since has registered satisfaction ratings as high as his were in mid-1960. It was a remarkable three-year upswing, but one that in itself contained the seeds of problems to come. In March 1960, Macmillan's press secretary and the Cabinet Secretary wondered 'is the P.M. becoming too godlike? The last P.M. was ruined by failure. It would be ironical if this one was ruined by success. . . . Will he really retire in two or three years time? Or will the allurements of power prove too strong?' It might also have been wondered whether the magician's touch would remain as sure as it had since 1957, and whether such problems as Europe, decolonisation, immigration and the trade unions might sooner or later require more difficult strategic decisions than the Party had faced up to since Eden's retirement.[59]

[59] Cook and Ramsden, *By-Elections*, 197; Harold Evans, *Downing Street Diary: The Macmillan Years, 1957–1963* (1981), 111–12.

Chapter 2

Macmillan's Party

The Party managers

This chapter steps back from the chronological to consider the ways in which the Party functioned as a social organism, how it was managed, and how in the period of Macmillan's heyday around 1960 it differed from a generation earlier when – as Butler still uncomfortably recalled in 1962 – Macmillan himself had sat in the Commons chamber in 1940 singing 'Rule Britannia' in response to Neville Chamberlain's fall. His reputation for unorthodoxy may well have prevented Macmillan from getting the Party Chairmanship in 1946 for, as earlier in the century, the half a dozen men and women who were entrusted with the management of the actual machine were invariably people of loyal background and opinion.[1]

As in decades past, the key post was that of Chairman of the Conservative Party Organisation, though in deference both to the cumbersome length of that title and to the way in which it had evolved from an organisational to a mainly political role since 1911, and especially during Woolton's long tenure of the office (1945–55) the holder was now universally called 'Party Chairman'. Appointment to the office was at the sole discretion of the Leader, though consultations with top National Union figures and senior Cabinet colleagues were usual; in 1962–63 and in 1966–67 there were semi-public discussions of possible changes of incumbent which indicated how far the Leader's freedom of action was circumscribed. The experiment of a Chairman outside Parliament had not worked in 1955–57, though Poole himself had played a crucial role in the Party's recovery and was made a peer in 1958. Macmillan's Chairmen – Hailsham, Butler and Macleod – were all Cabinet Ministers regarded as good Party men, if with very different personal styles.

It was not generally appreciated how far the Chief Whip also played a role in Party management that went wider than his responsibilities in the Commons and the Government. He was the central figure in the preparation of Party broadcasts, a role that seems to have derived from his ex-officio participation in the meetings between the parties and the broadcasting authorities. He also had a wide remit in appointments; after consultations that had involved all the

---

[1] Butler note, 24 Jan. 62, Butler MSS, G38.

senior Central Office people, it was the Chief Whip, 'at the Prime Minister's suggestion', who approached Paul Bryan about becoming Vice Chairman of the Party. Less surprisingly, the Chief Whip remained closely involved too in any matters of selection or de-selection that involved sitting MPs, as for example in the drawn-out process which removed Nigel Nicolson from Bournemouth in 1957–58; part of Edward Heath's role in that case was to warn off other MPs from seeking the nomination in Bournemouth before there was a vacancy and so weakening Nicolson's position even further. The Chief Whip liaised with the Party Chairman on political honours, and Heath in 1959 suggested that MPs be brought directly into that process so far as it affected their local activists, currently managed by the Area Agents, and reporting to him only through Central Office. Essentially though, relations between the whips and Smith Square consisted of the pooling of useful information on any Party question that arose; they collaborated in 1959 to deal with the financial embarrassment of a West End Tory Club before it had got out of hand; in 1957, Heath and Poole were sharing intelligence from MPs and Area Agents about the likely effect on the Government's popularity of factory closures by the Royal Ordnance. Heath's successor Martin Redmayne liaised with Iain Macleod at Central Office in 1962 to reduce the impact of Gerald Nabarro's maverick activities by dangling before him (but never actually delivering) the prospect of some preferment either in the Government or the Party. Nabarro, a self-confessed 'bounder' with an outsize moustache, regular press columns and ubiquitous broadcast interviews, was easily the best-known Conservative back-bencher of the period. According to Reginald Bevins, who Nabarro himself thought to be a fair judge of colleagues, Nabarro was,

> an ebullient and belligerent debater, a good constituency Member, extremely industrious, sincere and possessed of an unerring flair for publicity surpassing Ernest Marples, which is saying something. He was also immodest, vain, ostentatious, arrogant and in no sense a conformist.

The colour that such an outsize personality brought to the backbenches allowed him an unusual amount of room for manoeuvre – almost as licensed jester – but was a further management problem for the whips. In 1964, Redmayne and Lord Blakenham were cooperating to defend Julian Critchley from attack from his constituency party, for Critchley was just beginning a career almost as irreverent as Nabarro's.[2]

The senior Vice Chairmanship, the post held successively after 1951 by John Hare (who as Lord Blakenham returned to Central Office as Party Chairman, 1963–64), Sir Donald Kaberry, and Paul Bryan, was generally

---

[2] Central Office Chairman's department files, CCO 20/4/2, Correspondence with Vice Chairmen, CCO 20/1/5 and 6, Correspondence with Chief Whip; Gerald Nabarro, *Nab 1: Portrait of a Politician* (1969), 12–13.

given to an energetic backbench MP. The chief responsibility was for the Candidates' Department, but Kaberry and Bryan also kept an eye on the YC organisation, radio and television, and liaison with backbench committees. Alongside him was a second Vice Chairman, invariably a woman and almost as invariably the wife of a senior Party figure, Lady Maxwell Fyfe and Dame Barbara Brooke for example; she took responsibility for the women's organisation, for the speakers' department, for staff welfare within Central Office, and for liaison with the Lord Chancellor's office (for the nomination of magistrates) and with Buckingham Palace (for invitations to garden parties). In practice though, as correspondence files show, the Vice Chairmen generally worked with the Party Chairman and the General Director as part of a single political management team, and any of them could deputise on any matter of Party business in the Chairman's absence.[3]

From 1957, when Poole became Hailsham's second in command, a new post was effectively created, as a backroom deputy to the Chairman (though not always with that title). It was held by Sir Toby Low MP under Butler and Macleod between 1959 and 1963, and then again by Poole, first alongside Macleod and then under Blakenham. The position was financial and managerial; Low explained to Macleod in 1961 that under Butler he had dealt with 'all concern for finance' and he advised Macleod to follow Butler's example and, as a senior Minister, 'keep away from all details of Party finance. I give this advice not because there is anything illegal or underhand about it, but because we do try to keep the collection of finance from bringing pressure on Government policy'. In addition to this practice, which Macleod willingly accepted, Low was responsible for Central Office establishment matters, for Party publications, for keeping in touch with the constituencies, and for day-to-day propaganda. The value of having such a factotum was brought out when Macleod, consulted by John Wyndham over a complaint about Party fundraising in Lancashire, when Macleod was actually Chancellor of the Duchy, was able to reply that he was 'insulated' from all such business: 'I therefore know nothing, am told nothing, and make no enquiries in these matters'. None of this prevented the Chairman's name being used when it was useful to do so; letters of thanks to generous subscribers were sent out by Poole in May 1963 as coming from 'Iain Macleod and I'. The Treasurers were less happy than the Chairman about the insulation of Ministers from fundraising, as one of them told Selwyn Lloyd in 1963 during his investigation into the Party organisation: the Central Board of Finance included some very important people, and

> looking around the room I am impressed not only by the political but also by the industrial and financial influence represented. Because policy has such a very direct bearing on the raising of finance, there are expressed at the Central Board

---

3 Central Office Chairman's department file, CCO 20/4/2.

of Finance comments on Government policy of which notice must be taken. There should perhaps be better communications between Ministers and the officers of the CBF. This is of course a delicate matter because it is clearly important, especially from the point of view of the Civil Service, that Ministers should not be seen to be under pressure from those representing Party finance. Nevertheless, mistakes might be avoided and Party morale strengthened if Ministers were more fully aware of and paid more attention to the opinions of the Central Board.

This did not form part of Lloyd's report, even though the Treasurers told him how difficult their lives had been made by the recent separation of functions. 'Before 1958 the chairman knew about finance. Lord Woolton knew about it and Lord Poole had been Treasurer before, but Lord Hailsham did not attempt to master the subject. . . . Subsequent chairmen have also not tried to understand Party finance.'[4]

Poole was effective in the role of fundraiser and financial manager, but stayed scrupulously on the proper side in the ethical dilemmas that such activities threw up: ethics and Party self-interest were in his view closely related. In December 1963, he warned Blakenham that he was entirely opposed to the proposal to give a peerage to Roy Thomson, proprietor of *The Times* (which had recently been so hostile to the Party), even though Macmillan before his departure had already half-promised this.

> I can think of nothing that would look like a more blatant attempt to suborn a newspaper proprietor than to give Thomson a peerage at this time. For many years, both as Treasurer and in other capacities I have resisted honours being given in this way, and I can hardly conceive of anything that would do the Party more harm.

In 1963, when Poole was organising a lunch for a group of property-developers to meet Macmillan, news leaked to the press, and the Party Treasurers feared that photographers might recognise among arriving guests one whose firm 'has got the reputation of being very bad landlords' – this at the height of stories of 'Rachmanism'. To avoid embarrassment, the lunch was cancelled and the opportunity to raise subscriptions thereby lost; there is some considerable irony in the fact that the same businessman contributed to the Labour Party, and was in due course knighted on the recommendation of Harold Wilson, before allegations of fraud led to his suicide. Macmillan too, while generous in the distribution of honours, was extremely careful about the ethical side. In July 1963, he reported to Poole on a visit to him from 'a Canadian tycoon'.

> He was wheeled in because he had lost the use of his legs. He told me that he had some time ago given £10,000 to the Conservative Party funds. He said that

---

[4] Central Office Chairman's department files, CCO 20/16/1, Correspondence with Deputy Chairman, CCO 20/8/6, Correspondence with Macmillan, CCO 20/22/2, Correspondence with Treasurers; Central Office General Director's file, CCO 120/4/9, Selwyn Lloyd Inquiry.

he had it in mind to give a much larger sum, probably £50,000. He said he wanted to be a GBE. I said that of course he knew all this was quite impossible nowadays. There could be no link between subscription and an honour. He waved this aside in a rather presumptuous way and after a few minutes talk I had him wheeled out. What I am anxious is that he should not get the impression that anything of this kind could be arranged. If, therefore, he sends a donation of any kind to the funds, it must not be accepted.

About a year later, less blatant approaches from a far more deserving candidate did indeed lead to the tearing up of a cheque; the problem was caused by an over-zealous Area official who had told one of his constituency chairmen that something might be done for him in return for £10,000. After the cheque had been destroyed, and the situation sympathetically explained to the applicant, one of the Treasurers explained the policy to the man who had 'fouled it all up':

> It seems to me not only to be extremely dangerous but in practice unworkable to connect money and honours. If a man who is in the running for an honour gives us money, either he can't get the honour or we have to return the money. If anybody makes any approaches to me with a view to getting an honour for anyone, my first reaction is always to say, 'For goodness sake, tell him not to give us any money.' I don't suppose anyone would see anything wrong in someone who had received an honour subsequently making a gift to the Party, provided there was no prior commitment.

This last proviso was much like the policy adopted by Davidson in the 1920s, though now more scrupulously observed in practice: as long as political honours existed, then Party supporters would often get them, and the same people would very probably give the Party money too, but no bargaining must take place and no deals be made. With some embarrassment, the applicant who had inadvertently caused all this trouble now sent another cheque and made it clear that he did not expect anything in return. About ten years later he was knighted, but by that time his unstinting voluntary service to the Party and his other public services would have earned the distinction anyway.[5]

If the Party Chairman was now the Party's visible cheerleader rather than the real manager, the work of the Party Treasurers remained shrouded in secrecy. The chief executive arm of fundraising was the Central Board of Finance, set up in 1946 on the authority of a resolution passed by the National Union Executive in 1944, and then re-formed in 1949. The CBF had the responsibility of raising sufficient money to pay for Central Office, the work of the National Union, Area Offices, Research, the speakers' service, political education (including Swinton Conservative College), Party

---

[5] Central Office Chairman's department file, CCO 20/16/3, Correspondence with Deputy Chairman; Ben Pimlott, *Harold Wilson* (1992), 724–5; Central Office Chairman's department files, CCO 20/8/7, Correspondence with Macmillan, CCO 20/22/2.

publishing (including discounts offered to poorer constituencies and marginals), training of agents, and grants to impoverished constituency parties – in effect the entire range of Party activities except those directly under the ambit of the constituency associations which were *not* impoverished. Its basic method of approach was personal contact, and the justification for its existence was, as a 1952 note put it, that 'many people who are in a position to make a large donation will give, say, £100 to the centre but not more than a tenth of that amount to a local association'. The size of its liabilities, and the businesslike way in which it could be seen to discharge them, was thus in itself an aid to fundraising. In the 1950s it functioned mainly through its Area representatives, working closely with Area treasurers, and instructed to liaise at least monthly with the Area Agent, but jealously excluded from 'closed constituencies' in cities like Sheffield or Leeds which retained industrial money for local needs. In 1955, the CBF had nineteen local representatives, fifteen of them retired officers, including a Vice-Admiral and three Major-Generals, and it functioned very much on an armed services 'need to know' basis; for the 1955 Election appeal, it had seven additional voluntary staff, all working in the same room in Central Office, to which none but CBF staff were ever to be admitted. In 1967, its fifteen representatives still included ten retired senior officers, and advertisements for vacancies were made at well above the agents' salary scale for positions of discretion and responsibility. In other ways though, the CBF functioned as a normal part of the organisation; the CRD produced briefs for it on Labour's nationalisation policy which could be used when talking to potential business donors (the 'horrors of socialism' being a good argument to use in such circumstances), and Swinton College provided a base for conferences of its representatives. The CBF itself was chaired by the Party Treasurers, and its membership included in 1962 the chairman of the 1922 Committee and such National Union veterans as Lady Davidson, whose husband had been such a successful fundraiser in the 1920s.[6]

The CBF was certainly an effective body. In its first ten years it raised about £2 million, over and above special appeals for general elections, and reckoned that about 90 per cent of this was retained to set against Party expenditure, after netting off the cost of the CBF's own activities, establishment and staff bonuses; in election years it did even better – £215,000 in 1954 rose to £333,000 in 1955, three-quarters of which came in during the single Spring quarter in which the campaign took place. In the late 1950s, CBF representatives' total annual target was about £265,000 a year, which would represent a net £200,000 after deduction of their costs and of the credits allocated against constituency quotas; this covered roughly a third of routine central Party expenditure. Since constituency quotas raised a little over £100,000 at this time, this still left about

---

6 Central Office files, CCO 4/5/16, 4/6/20 and 21; CCO 4/7/22; CCO 4/9/10, and CCO 4/10/72, all Central Board of Finance.

half of the overall total to be raised by the Party managers personally. Some came in the form of bequests which, since the Party was not a corporate body that could be named in a will, were channelled through a trust set up by Woolton in 1949, and which remained 'The Conservative and Unionist Trust, 1949', with Woolton until his death one of the trustees; substantial sums continued to come through British United Industrialists which had been providing such a route for corporate donations since the War years. However, a great deal still had to be raised simply by going out and asking for it. In 1964, the Election appeal was carefully graduated, with seniority equating to cash, as a note by Poole in January 1964 set down. The Party Chairman Blakenham would approach the twenty largest donors personally (six wealthy peers, five public companies, and eleven commoners, half of whom were senior National Union figures, past or present, anyway). As Deputy Chairman, Poole would speak to a middle group, fourteen donors who had given about £25,000 each last time; that gifts of this size constituted the *middle* group in itself indicates just how much was raised from the twenty largest donors – probably approaching £1 million. The Treasurers would contact, mainly by letter, the four hundred donors 'who give less substantial sums'. In addition to these approaches to individuals, sympathetic insiders would go the rounds among the merchant banks, the stock exchange, Lloyd's and the brewers, arrangements that were 'already in hand'. An indication of how this last operation was managed comes from another letter that Poole wrote in the same week to a senior City figure, a Bank of England director who was also chairman of a merchant bank: 'at the time of General Elections, the Merchant Banks have always been very good in supporting the Conservative Party, thanks to your making the approach to them.' He stressed the need for money to come in early so that it could be used for pre-election publicity campaigning, and asked for a meeting so that he would have 'the opportunity of telling you how much money we need, and roughly what we spend it on, as I never think it is reasonable to ask for substantial contributions unless they know what it is for.' He was able to suggest one or two other City sympathisers who might assist with this delicate operation, and concluded with a cheeky postscript that says much about Poole's relationship with such City supporters, and indeed about the Party's relations with them too: 'I must confess that we are rather relying on your doing this, and indeed much of the money has already been spent!!' There was much care taken in these approaches. There was for example a rule that foreign companies were not to be approached, and when an oversight led to a request to Fiat to contribute, apologies were made all round. There were no such inhibitions with traditional supporters among British companies: in October 1963, Poole wrote to a supporter who was chairman of a brewing company, to say that though there would be no election appeal until early in 1964, he had already committed the £10,000 that the company had 'always provided in the past' for a special project that needed to start early, and he was therefore calling in the subscription early too; he received it almost by return of post.[7]

Contrasting with the considerable amount of money actually raised from industry, to which little publicity was given, there was a bright spotlight shone on the relatively small constituency quota contributions, for these seemed the part most defensible in a democratic age, and were also the most reliable – the income least susceptible to unplanned reductions during a recession. Quota payments raised by constituencies from Party members were, wrote one of the Treasurers in 1955, 'politically the best money we receive'. The successful constituencies were congratulated at Party Conferences; from 1956, a 'blue diploma' was presented to any constituency paying in full for three successive years, and a 'golden diploma' for success in seven or more years; in 1963, a specially-inscribed chairman's gavel was presented to associations that had paid in full ever since the scheme started in 1949.[8]

In the 1950s, when quota payments were still a recent invention, there continued to be awkward requests for information. In 1953 for example, a new Area Treasurer asked for a breakdown of figures indicating 'what it costs to run the Party' so that he could use the information for arm-twisting purposes in his Area. This request, as Lady Maxwell Fyfe pointed out, 'does raise certain difficulties' and she asked the CBF to provide 'one of your gifted replies' which would satisfy the enquirer without giving anything away. The constituency treasurers and agents in the South East were in 1957 given a complete breakdown of the way in which central funds were spent, but were warned that in no circumstances should the information be circulated in writing; the Area Treasurer, Sir Ambrose Keevil, took to visiting constituencies to brief them on the problem in the hope of eliciting larger quota payments, but the information given was always verbal and unattributable. Later in the decade, Poole provided for the Watford constituency magazine a guarded piece that could then be offered to any other Tory enquirers. In general terms though, the Treasurers argued that there was an essential discontinuity that made any one year's figures unrepresentative. An agent who had enquired in 1958 about press reports of staff cuts at Central Office was told that 'the structure of Party Finance has to be viewed over a period from General Election to General Election. The expenditure is reduced after a General Election and starts increasing again a couple of years or so before the next Election may be expected.' More information did have to be given when efforts were made in 1965 to raise the overall level of quota payments from constituencies; the 'Maxwell Fyfe gap' between what the Party needed centrally and what it could raise centrally was now put at about half

---

[7] Central Office files, CCO 4/6/20 and 21; Michael Pinto-Duschinsky, *British Political Finance, 1830–1980* (1981), 138; Central Office file, CCO 4/8/291, Party Funds; Central Office Chairman's department file, CCO 20/22/2.

[8] Central Office file, CCO 4/9/446, Party Treasurers.

a million pounds a year, but quotas were raised only to £300,000; the largest actual payment to date in a non-election year had been £130,000 in 1960, but in the later 1960s associations regularly met twice that figure. To encourage such efforts, the constituencies were told that nearly all Central expenditure was in effect supporting the constituencies, about a quarter going on direct grants to marginals and poor associations, another quarter on Area offices which reinforced local campaigning, and two-fifths on providing services like publicity and research, so that only a tenth of all expenditure went on Central Office's establishment costs. The accounts – in this period produced for internal use only – bear out the broad truth of these proportions, and also of the Treasurers' argument about discontinuity, even outside election periods; expenditure in 1963 was £1.074 million, up by nearly 50 per cent on the previous year, which reflected huge increases in the category of 'special campaigns' (mainly advertising, posters and missioners), while the amount given out to constituencies through Areas fell sharply in the same period. All such national campaigning was indeed related to the intention of supporting constituencies in their efforts to win parliamentary seats, but the decisions on priorities were firmly under central control.[9]

If secrecy remained the official policy, it was no longer taken for granted. As Party Chairman, Rab Butler had to prepare in 1960 for a Commons debate on the sources of Party funds, after David Butler and Richard Rose's *The British General Election of 1959* (and reviews of the book) had highlighted the Party's heavy spending on advertising before the 1959 campaign, and its alleged influence on the result. When Labour MPs threatened to raise the matter in the House (though never actually succeeded in doing so), Butler found that his only briefing material was a document produced by the Party in 1950, when Labour had last raised the question. The Research Department therefore produced in June 1960 a brief, setting out the arguments both for and against the publication of the Party's accounts, and concluding that since Labour had actually done nothing about the question when in office, it was probably only stirring up the subject now 'to create prejudice against the Conservative Party'. Butler was more sceptical; he accepted that there was no case for the Party going for full publication, but suggested to his senior Central Office staff that over the next decade,

> some step should be taken to make less mysterious the fact that we receive money from industrialists. It is well known that we do; it is well known that the Labour Party does; it is well known that we cannot publish detailed accounts. We cannot keep up an air of mystery for ever, and the question arises whether we should not find some very cautious path through the jungle, while leaving some of the tropical growth untouched.

[9] *Conservative Agents' Journal* [hereafter *CAJ*], 3 Nov. 1958; Central Office files, CCO 4/5/269 and CCO 4/8/291, Party Funds; South East Area Council, 1 June 1957; Maidstone CA minutes, 18 Jan. 1955; Central Office Chairman's department file, CCO 20/22/3, Accounts.

He does not seem to have convinced his colleagues, though Low conceded that there might well be a case for getting British United Industrialists to make a statement about their activities; his stipulation that even this should not come until anticipated by-elections were out of the way was an indication that the time would probably never be judged to be right in practice; the Treasurers' uncompromising view was that 'there is no middle position between declaring nothing and declaring everything', and they thought that they could not publish everything because of the individual donor's right to give in private. Butler and his successor Macleod seem not to have pressed the point, and Poole's return to Central Office ended such initiatives anyway; when in 1963 the Treasurers briefed Selwyn Lloyd for his inquiry they took the traditional view that calls for publication interested only the Party's enemies and should be resisted; Lloyd was told that 'our big business income' was now about £520,000 a year, which, since overall Party income (local added to central) was estimated at £2.5 million, was only a fifth of the total and rather less than Labour received from the trade union political levy. But they would not want to say even this in public as it 'could be damaging'. Since Labour was by this time officially considering proposals that would compel public companies to disclose political contributions, plans were put in train to frustrate such legislation: Poole was told by the Treasurers in December 1963 that 'we are now channelling our funds in such a way as to conceal the identity of our supporters. We doubt if any legislation will force us to disclose the names of those who give us money, except through the Central Board of Finance which is of course already well known and whose activities we consider it would be foolish to try to hide'. As indicated above, those CBF activities were a relatively small part of the total. However, when Labour in office did indeed legislate, the Party found that it had to react to a new situation and that there was now an overwhelming case for releasing more information, as is described in Chapter 5.[10]

Central Offices

Conservative Central Office was all too frequently credited at this time with a vast degree of power over the Party throughout the country (much as the Leader was wrongly credited with autocratic power at the centre), a view that was first, and most persuasively, challenged by Michael Pinto-Duschinsky in 1970. There was, as he pointed out, a huge degree of latent resistance to Central Office's control of the Party in the country, and its practical influence ran only so far as it could be seen to be providing services to the constituencies which they actually needed and could not provide for themselves; elsewhere

---

[10] Central Office Chairman's department file, CCO 20/22/1, Publication of Accounts; Central Office General Director's file, CCO 120/4/9, Selwyn Lloyd Inquiry; Central Office Chairman's department file, CCO 20/22/2.

it certainly had influence but rarely control as such. For example, one of Central Office's most valuable direct services to constituencies was its force of missioners, in 1957 a team of eighty paid canvassers who were drafted into marginal seats, and sometimes into by-election constituencies prior to the actual campaign; over the year, these missioners recruited thirty thousand new members and registered about twenty thousand postal votes.[11]

Part of the reason for the relative weakness of Central Office as a repository of 'power' in the Party was its own internal complexity, and the fact that almost every section of the office had a separate interface with clients in the wider Party, and its own objectives to promote. Figure 2.1 sets out the internal structure of the Office and its various connections in the Party. That plan, derived from one provided for Selwyn Lloyd's review of the Party organisation, already treated the Publicity Department as if it did not come under Urton's control, though in theory it still did; the chart line leading to Personnel, Finance and Registry was the only one that did not lead out of the office to a connection with the professional or voluntary side of the Party in the country. The broad range and relative weight of these different activities may be conveniently summarised through the financial turnover, taking the extant accounts for 1963 as an example. Small sums were spent by the Party on Swinton College, on the Whips' office, and on miscellaneous activities, but even taken together these amounted to under 5 per cent of central expenditure. The CRD accounted for a further 10 per cent, but the whole of the rest was committed to Central Office (£361,392), its Area Offices (£143,765) and to special campaigns, mainly also controlled from Central Office (£419,904). Within Smith Square itself, the overwhelming majority of expenditure went on the staff costs of the Organisation, Publicity and Registry departments; but of the special campaigns, large budgets were controlled by the CRD (opinion research), by Publicity (posters and press advertisements), and by Organisation (literature discounts, by-election campaigns and missioners, all of which involved the Area offices too). It was too large and sometimes too unwieldy a machine to devote to any one internal Party cause.[12]

The key professional appointment was the General Director, successively Stephen Pierssené, William Urton, and Richard Webster (for whom the post was renamed 'Director of Organisation'). All of these were former agents who had risen to be Area Agents and had served in Yorkshire, London and Lancashire respectively, the populous places with plenty of marginals in which senior organisers could show their managerial skills. Each had necessarily developed the ability to relate comfortably to senior career politicians and to the whole range of activities that were coordinated through the Area offices. Nevertheless, as the Party's public relations activities became more

---

[11] Pinto-Duschinsky, *Political Finance*; Central Office file, CCO 4/7/280, Missioners.
[12] Central Office General Director's file, CCO 120/4/10, Selwyn Lloyd Inquiry; Central Office Chairman's department file, CCO 20/22/3.

Figure 2.1 Organisation of Central Office, 1962

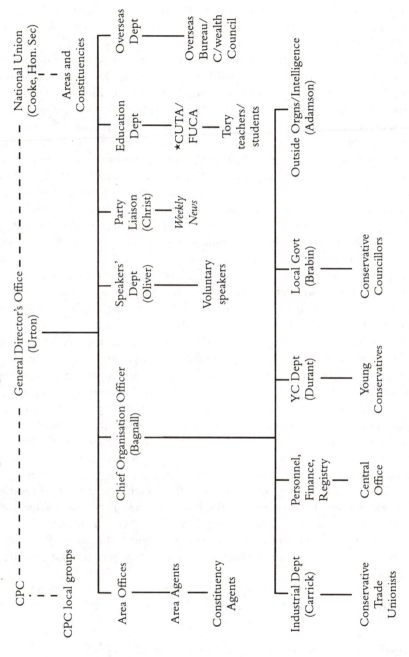

*CUTA was the Conservative and Unionist Teachers' Association; FUCA was the Federation of University Conservative Associations.

sophisticated and as it became more and more necessary to rely on the advice of professionals in electronic public relations, it inevitably became more difficult for people whose original training had been in traditional agents' tasks to exercise the overall control that Robert Topping had achieved in the 1930s. As early as 1960, Urton was in need of considerable specialist briefing in dealings with the BBC.[13]

The Conservative Research Department may perhaps be regarded as reaching its pinnacle in the time of Macmillan's premiership. Despite reductions in its budget after the Party returned to office in 1951, it continued to employ about two dozen graduate research officers (who easily outnumbered their opposite numbers in the other parties), and could persuade the Party to commit to it the substantial additional funds needed to begin systematic opinion polling, to investigate the psephological roots of Conservative voting and the attitudes of Party supporters to Conservative policy. In Michael Fraser it had its longest-serving Director and the man who most shaped its permanent ethos and habits of mind once the necessary scramble of opposition policy-making ended in 1951; by 1959 he was in his second decade of Party work and being consulted on a wide range of issues; by then he should be considered as one of the interdependent team of Party Managers rather than just the director of one unit, a shift that would result in his moving to Central Office as Deputy Chairman in 1964. He also had fairly easy access to Ministers (quite a few of them former CRD colleagues by this time) so that his Department was kept abreast of ministerial thinking and able to prepare itself for policy developments before they occurred. The CRD retained its independence, working in a separate office and with its own more flexible working conditions than applied in Smith Square, but without the jealousies of its separate role that had caused some difficulties in the 1940s and would do so again after 1975. Working relations with the CPC and the Central Office Publicity Department were now harmonious, and the CRD produced many publications such as the fortnightly briefing *Notes on Current Politics* and the equivalent *Daily Notes* produced for candidates during election campaigns. Under a Prime Minister who personally engaged in the policy process and ran an organised, coherent Party policy operation alongside that of his Government, the CRD felt that it was both valued and effective. The network of committees which Macmillan established and which the CRD serviced, most of all the Steering Committee set up in 1957, ran as smoothly as such policy operations have ever done when the Party has been in office.[14]

Alongside the CRD, but with a different role, was the Conservative Political Centre. This 1946 initiative had by the late 1950s already begun

---

13   Central Office, General Director's file, CCO 120/1/5, Broadcasting.
14   John Ramsden, *The Making of Conservative Party Policy: The Conservative Research Department since 1929* (1980), 190–224.

to attract much criticism. The evidence given to the Colyton inquiry into the Party organisation in 1957 suggested that constituency discussion groups had become isolated both from the rest of the work of the local association and from the bulk of the Party's members: 'so far as political education was concerned, there seemed to be an enormous amount of it taking place in a closed circuit, and not reaching the general body of members'. This perhaps missed the point that the CPC's 'two-way movement of ideas' programme had always had two different purposes, to inform and educate the membership and to inform the Party leaders what the members thought. It would always be a relatively small group of local activists who wanted to sit round and discuss policy ideas, and the more commitment that was involved the more self-selected such a group would become. Nevertheless, new efforts did produce an increase in CPC activity, as Table 2.1 indicates. This expansion was not only into the weaker constituencies; Lewes in Sussex,

Table 2.1   CPC activity (England & Wales)

	1954	*1957*	*1962*
Constituencies taking part (of 547)	369	400	481
Active discussion groups	214	525	1,443
Discussion reports sent in	37	1,241	2,530
CPC titles published	9	14	23
Literature service subscribers	910	1,555	1,821

a strong association with healthy finances and a large membership, formed its first CPC committee only in 1969. When in 1963 the CPC groups discussed the future of industrial relations, there were 279 reports submitted by local groups, representing discussions in which about 3,000 people had taken place, a fairly typical degree of involvement for that time. Since expansion took place at a time when Party membership almost halved, the increased activity clearly represented a greater permeation of the constituency associations. But the overall figures were still small; if MPs, Tory peers and adopted candidates, and at least some of the associations themselves are subtracted from the total of literature subscribers, then even the 1962 figure does not suggest that there can have been many more than a thousand (say, two per constituency) among ordinary active members who bought all the CPC's publications; the regional breakdown suggested that these limited numbers were heavily concentrated in London and the South East. Even in such places, there were regular complaints that constituency associations were insufficiently political in their outlook, and had become locked into a round of social and fund-raising activities to the exclusion of all else; in Dulwich in 1961, a member pointedly remarked that the association had not even discussed its

MP's 'courageous decision to vote against the Government on the Common Market', and the debate that this remark started led to a resolution 'that some extension of Political Activity within this Association is considered essential'. The growth in the practice of submitting motions to the Party Conference suggests that extended activity did indeed take place, and that this in turn led some members to envisage a more definite role for Conference in policy-making.[15]

For the more committed, by 1961 Swinton Conservative College had attracted about 27,000 students to its courses, about 2,000 a year since it had opened its doors, and though this was still on an upward trend, reaching 2,465 in that year, this was still only an average of four per constituency each year. The Western Area hoped in 1960 that Swinton would be able to run extra-mural courses in the West Country from time to time, to offset the distance from Plymouth to Ripon; it was reported that only 4 per cent of Swinton's students had come from the West or from Wessex, while three-quarters were from the North and Midlands. In Wales and the West, more emphasis was necessarily placed on constituencies' own efforts in political education, as in Monmouth's all-day constituency CPC school for Party workers in 1962. Ashford was that year typical of better-off associations in founding a special 'Swinton scholarship' to pay for one of its poorer members each year to attend a course in the North, and the Eastern Area was in 1957 already sending thirty-nine 'students' a year to Swinton on Area funds. Even in constituencies not far from Swinton it was not always easy to create a demand; in the Northern Area in 1965, of 114 scholarships offered only 32 were taken up, 30 of them by women. But this approach, even if universally adopted and if all scholarships had been filled, would not have materially altered the numerical situation or the geographical balance. These limited figures need though to be set alongside the original intention that the CPC and Swinton should together be a Conservative Fabian Society, for the Fabians themselves, even at their point of greatest influence, had not generated a greater or more widely-spread record of activity than this.[16]

Area organisations

The aspect of Conservative organisation in this – or any other – period that it is easiest to underestimate is the Area level, least visible to the national or the

---

[15] Stuart Ball, 'Local Conservatism and the Evolution of Party Organisation', in A. Seldon and S. Ball (eds), *Conservative Century: The Conservative Party since 1900* (Oxford, 1994), 278; Central Office General Director's by-election files, CCO 120/10 and 15; Lewes CA minutes, 2 Oct. 1969; National Union papers, NUA 2/2/26, Central Council reports; Dulwich CA minutes, 18 Sept. 1961.

[16] Central Office file, CCO 4/9/111, CPC summaries; Western Area Council, 28 May 1960; Monmouth CA minutes, 25 Sept. 1962; Ashford CA minutes, 1 June 1962; Eastern Area Executive, 29 Jan. 1958; Northern Area Council, 21 Sept. 1965.

local press, and often only dimly understood even by constituency activists. Reviewing the 1945 defeat, Butler had suggested to his colleagues that the Party would best grow back to prosperity if local enthusiasms were given their head in the voluntary organisation, and if effective people were found to lead the Areas. Whatever his original intentions, Woolton soon came to share this view, and the team of new Area Agents put in post by Pierssené in 1946–47 became key figures as a result. In 1948 it was specifically decided that all assistance to constituencies should be routed through Area offices, so that the prestige and influence of the Area Agents would be thereby enhanced. A general review undertaken for Central Office in 1967 concluded that money had been a useful lever in exerting influence, for even strong constituencies would get into difficulties from time to time; experience had shown that Area Agents 'can go a long way to becoming the "managing director" of the Area by the judicious use of pressure and the funds which the Area has at its disposal'. The work of William Urton in London provided a good example of this, prior to his taking over as General Director in 1958. In his case he was also able to control teams of women organisers who could be sent to constituencies at his discretion, and who were paid for (on his initiative) by such bodies as the political committee of the Ladies' Carlton Club. Area influence was needed because of the 'continuous cat and mouse game' played between Areas and constituencies over the upkeep and modernisation of the organisation; Urton wrote in 1956, of Brentford and Chiswick, that 'I am personally quite friendly with the Brentford & Chiswick officials, but the Association as a whole is anti-Area. They are always coming to us for help and loans, and if you asked any one of them why they disliked Area, they would not know'. Of a South London constituency he wrote in 1958 that 'there is no one in this constituency who is prepared to come to grips with the weaknesses of the organisation, so many of which are the results of the agent's laziness. Any help given to the association, eg by the provision of an organiser and/or missioner will need to be used to the best advantage'. In the North West, Bolton was headed off from appointing an uncertificated agent in 1958 not by pressure, nor even by the news that only 11 other associations out of 542 constituencies in England and Wales had done so, but by the Area's offer of money to subsidise the new man's salary. Scarce resources needed to be constantly recycled to maintain Areas' leverage; in 1960, the Western Area was simultaneously phasing out financial support for the agent's salary in Devonport and introducing the same aid for Exeter. Over time, this Area role tended to reduce as the Areas themselves became less successful fundraisers, and mainly limited to passing on money from the centre; the subscription income in Yorkshire was fairly typical, barely keeping pace with inflation until the early 1960s, and then falling even in absolute terms in the 1970s, as the following figures for typical non-election years indicate: 1948 – £4,473, 1953 – £6,701, 1957 – £4,827, 1962 – £9,950, 1968 – £5,050, 1972 – £5,908. The

Area's entire income would have paid for about eight agents in 1948, but only three by the 1970s.[17]

With a regular turnover of the officers running the constituencies, and in some cases a frequent turnover of agents too, the Area officers, voluntary as well as professional, could provide important elements of continuity as well as leadership by example. Area offices could also offer unique professional advice to constituencies if they would take it, and the correspondence with Central Office was full of the badgering of associations to keep up professional standards; when Uxbridge appointed Eric Ward (himself a future Area Agent) as its agent in 1957, it agreed a salary with the appointee, but agreed too that the payment of increments would be made on the advice of the Area Agent who would be most able to monitor his professional performance. The still-continuing vitality of the regional press provided a reinforcement of these regional autonomies, many of them with no hesitation about their partisanship; the *Yorkshire Post* and its evening stablemate were not afraid to declare themselves in the Party's 1952 Conference handbook, as 'pillars of Conservatism in the North'. Likewise, the *Burton Mail* was a staunch supporter, and the company that ran it subscribed £100 a year to association funds in the town; when there was a dispute over the appointment of county aldermen in 1965, Sir Clifford Gothard (Association President as well as the power behind the newspaper) 'promised the cooperation of the Burton Mail if the facts could be supplied to them'. Such support was rarely declared by the newspapers in print, but many were (as were many weekly papers in Wessex in 1959) willing to accept syndicated articles drafted in the Area Office; this was highlighted when the independent *Oxford Mail* indignantly repudiated such a connection, but the Area Office confirmed that this was simply a misdirection – the articles should have gone to the *Oxford Times* which was still happy to print them. A similar private connection in the North West enabled the Party to place columns in the *Workington Star*.[18]

One value of Areas was to filter out embarrassing or contentious resolutions before they reached the national level; in 1956, the London Area received a motion from Peckham deploring the visit to Britain of Russian leaders as likely to do 'nothing but promote the advancement of Communism and treason in this country'; the Area Council returned the motion as inexpedient, though 'concurring very strongly' with the anti-Communist views expressed. In the same year the Eastern Area declined to support Cambridge's demand for a

[17]   Butler note, July 1945, Butler MSS, G17/216; Stuart Ball, 'The National and Regional Party Structure', in Seldon and Ball, *Conservative Century*, 211; Central Office file, CCO 4/10/4, Area organisation; Central Office Area correspondence file, CCO 2/4/1; Central Office constituency files, CCO 1/11/368, CCO 1/12/6 and CCO 1/12/99; Western Area Council, 5 Feb. and 24 Nov. 1960; Yorkshire Area, annual reports.

[18]   Uxbridge CA minutes, 24 Jan. 1957; National Union papers, NUA 2/2/18, Central Council reports; Burton upon Trent CA minutes, 6 Oct. 1965; Central Office Area correspondence file, CCO 2/2/14; Workington CA minutes, 2 Nov. 1963.

root-and-branch review of the system whereby constituency quotas were worked out, deciding that all systems were imperfect but that the existing one was as fair as any. In 1963, the South East Area Council decided that it would not even discuss the principles involved in extending the boundaries of Greater London into Kent and Surrey, which had many of its member associations up in arms, but would provide instead a forum for the practical discussion of consequential reorganisation and leave representations on the principles to more local efforts; since the London Area did the same thing, instead of coming directly into conflict, the Areas channelled local association activity into practicalities and away from the main point at issue. Such actions commanded respect only because the Area bodies themselves were broadly constituted, incorporating membership not only from constituencies, women's, CPC and YC groups, and from the local branch of the National Society of [Conservative] Agents (NSA), but also generally coopting Tory leaders from local government. There were regular efforts to ensure that the officers and committees of Areas did not become remote from the constituencies; in the South East, one vice chairman each year came from each of the counties in the Area, while when the Eastern Area was expanded in 1964 to reflect the addition of Essex, the election of representatives to the new Executive was carefully adjusted to reflect the number of constituencies in each county.[19]

The limitations of Area influence emerged most clearly over payment of quotas. From 1949 these were collected through Areas and totalled as Area figures; but there was only a limited amount that the Area could do if a constituency did not regard payments to the centre as a priority; an Area official noted sarcastically after attending the Twickenham Annual General Meeting (AGM) in 1962 that 'it is pitiful to hear of the misery which has been caused to them by their failing this year to pay their full Quota, alas their investments and deposit assets barely exceed £3000!' Much the same suspicions could occur within associations, dependent on their branches for fund-raising and often setting quotas for their own branches to meet the divisional budget – paying for the agent, office, and so on, as well as the quota for national funds; few associations, particularly in decentralised county constituencies, were confident enough to try the tactic adopted in 1957 by Ripon, which introduced a rule requiring all branches not paying their quota in full to produce their balance sheets for the inspection of the association officers. In 1962, the Upminster branch was horrified when their treasurer reported 'that the Divisional Treasurer seemed of the opinion that Upminster had hidden funds. This Committee took strong exception to this and instructed the treasurer to submit a copy of the balance sheet to the Divisional Treasurer.' Just as associations were sometimes reluctant to

---

[19] London Area EC, 10 Jan. 1956; Eastern Area F and GP, 24 June 1956, and Council, 2 Nov. 1963; South East Area Council, 19 Jan. 1963.

offer Central Office information about their activities and their funds, so that Area Agents took to using their right under the rules to attend association AGMs to pick up a copy of the balance sheet, so branches were suspicious of associations; in Norfolk, branches resisted the adoption of membership subscription books with carbonised duplicate pages, on the ground that they did not wish their own constituency office to have lists of branch members and their addresses. At Horncastle, even attending the AGM did not produce a copy of the association's accounts which were only 'on display' there and not distributed to those present; asked to send a balance sheet to the Area office in 1967, the agent explained that he never gave such information to anyone outside the constituency; he asked pointedly whether the National Union had ever made such a stipulation, and if so what was the date of the resolution. The Area Agent could get nothing out of Newbury either, where in 1962 he reported that only verbal reports were given, and the association was 'rather cagey' about its financial affairs, 'although the agent has promised to let me have a copy [of the accounts], which I rather doubt will arrive'. Against such examples should be set such places as Guildford which hardly needed any persuasion to accept ever-increasing quota targets, which kept up both its membership and its fundraising potential to an enviable extent, and was sufficiently proud of its achievements to tell Area all about them; the Election appeal in 1955 raised £4,154 for a campaign that cost a mere £720, and only £1,447 went on deposit locally; the rest was sent off to Area without prompting to help marginals, and something very similar happened in 1959. Basingstoke was another constituency association that routinely and confidently told Area all about what it was doing. The range of constituency relationships with Areas was as large as the number of constituencies, but the basic pattern tended to be that better and more open relationships existed where the constituency association had the least to hide.[20]

The National Union

The highest profile National Union event of the year was the annual Party Conference in October, not an event that has ever generated critical praise. In 1960, the former Tory MP Christopher Hollis wrote that 'a Conservative Conference is intended to be, and is, the dullest thing that ever happened. . . . Delegates come not to hear their rulers but to see them. One is often tempted to wonder whether it would be the best plan to cut out the speeches altogether.' His point is borne out by Poole's insistence in 1957 that Macmillan spend at least one night in the Conference hotel prior to delivering

---

[20] Central Office constituency file, CCO 1/14/86; Ripon CA minutes, 2 Feb. 1957; Upminster branch minutes, 28 Feb. 1962; King's Lynn CA minutes, 17 Dec. 1964; Central Office constituency files, CCO 1/14/296 and CCO 1/14/449; Guildford CA minutes, 24 Jan. 1955 and 23 Oct. 1959.

his rally speech to the faithful, as 'the representatives and local people like to feel you are in the town even if they don't see you'. Geoffrey Howe was in 1958 even more dismissive:

> Discretion is the besetting sin of the Tory party. Nowhere is this more disastrous than in the selection of motions and speakers to be called at the party's annual Conference. . . . If it is to remain no more than a genteel safety valve for a party machine that has gone off the rails, the constituency representatives might as well stay at home as go to Blackpool.

For the Bow Group, Howe and Lord Windlesham wrote a pamphlet urging such radical ideas as shorter, punchier motions for debate, a Leader's rally that was part of the ordinary week's programme, and even that the Leader should attend ordinary sessions. The key to an understanding of Hollis's comment though lies in the acknowledgement that what he described was also what was 'intended to be'; the 1949 Maxwell Fyfe report had concluded that the annual Conference should be 'a demonstration of solidarity and enthusiasm'. Representatives came from the constituencies knowing what to expect, and as John Biffen pointed out in 1965, the activists did very much want to go to Conference; Denbigh in 1962 was typical in holding a ballot for Llandudno Conference places because demand so easily outnumbered vacancies, even when the constituency had (as a nearby constituency) over a hundred places in the overflow hall for the Prime Minister's rally. Despite Macmillan's generous distribution of honours to Party workers, a week in Brighton or Blackpool metaphorically rubbing shoulders with the Party leaders was the only reward that the majority even of constituency officers ever got for their thousands of hours of voluntary work. Nevertheless, the level of political activity associated with Party Conferences did increase; Poole had also urged in 1957 that Ministers should listen to the debates and make proper winding-up speeches, and not just deliver statements on Government policy that could have been, and probably had been, written in London a week earlier. The number of resolutions submitted by constituencies rose steadily, especially during the 1960s, to the point that it became a real drain on the Party's financial resources to print them all in the handbook.

Table 2.2   Average numbers of constituency resolutions for Conference

1947–50	149	1961–65	555
1951–55	227	1966–70	1,077
1956–60	417	1971–75	1,149

Newark, which had taken little interest in Conference motions in the 1950s, was stirred up by a new candidate in the 1960s, submitting eight resolutions in 1963, five of them proposed by the candidate himself. This rise in activity introduced new difficulties in its wake; in 1971, the Eastern Area had eighty-nine resolutions for Conference, and had to remit them to a sub-committee before forwarding them to Central Office, for at least half were either ambiguous or ungrammatical. Conference might not *make* policy as a constitutional right, but it could not be ignored; Conference resolutions contributed to the decision to go for the 1957 Rent Act and for the subsequent abolition of Schedule A taxation, and, as John Biffen pointed out, by such means as submitted resolutions, and by speeches made (if not by actual votes), representatives at Conference could influence more widely the Party's future direction. Efforts were made to ensure that those chosen to speak would be seen to be broadly representative, and the rest of the week's events also reflected the range of Party interests brought together at Conference. In 1963 there were 126 speakers in total, 24 of them women and about the same number of YCs, 24 adopted candidates and only 16 MPs; 1,500 copies of the verbatim transcript were ordered in that year, over £1,000 was raised for Party funds at the Conference rally, and rather more at a Conference ball in aid of the agents' benevolent fund.[21]

In 1960, William Urton explained in a radio interview that the Conference had two purposes, to express views which the leaders dare not 'totally disregard' (though he was careful to say that it did not 'dictate' policy, for 'the Leader of the Party, especially if he is Prime Minister, knows much more about policy than the Annual Conference does') and to 'whip up the enthusiasm of the voluntary Party workers, who go back to their constituencies full of zeal for the cause'. There is no reason to believe that those who attended Conferences wanted anything very different from this; a survey of the views of representatives at Blackpool in 1966 produced over two thousand replies; on the issue of policy-making, about a quarter wanted longer debates, but as many wanted shorter ones and half wanted no change; asked what issue they would have liked to spend more time on, answers covered nearly every item on the agenda, with no obvious bunching on any one issue; finally, asked what the real value of the Conference was, 38 per cent said that it kept the leaders informed of the Party's views, 25 per cent that it boosted morale and 17 per cent that it got the Party good publicity; about the same number therefore saw Conference as a demonstrative body

---

21 Richard Kelly, *Conservative Party Conferences: The Hidden System* (1989), x, 2, 15; Rupert Morris, *Tories: From Village Hall to Westminster* (1991), 122; Central Office Chairman's department file, CCO 20/8/2, Correspondence with Macmillan; National Union papers, NUA 2/2, Central Council reports; Michael Pinto-Duschinsky, 'The Role of Constituency Associations in the Conservative Party', D.Phil. thesis, Oxford University, 1972, 266; Newark CA minutes, 15 July 1963; Eastern Area Council, 6 Nov. 1971; Richard Kelly, 'The Party Conferences', in Seldon and Ball, *Conservative Century*, 247; John Biffen, 'The Conservative Party today', in M. Wolff (ed.), *The Conservative Opportunity* (1965), 186–7; Denbigh CA minutes, 19 Feb. 1963; National Union Executive Committee minutes [hereafter NUEC], 3 Nov. and 1 Dec. 66, 2 Nov. 1967; interview with Lord Howe.

as saw it as a deliberative one, and hardly any questionnaires indicated deep dissatisfaction. Occasionally, the unpopularity of a Tory Government could produce a different attitude, as when Hexham Tories in 1961 deplored Macmillan's 'cavalier' disregard of Conference motions on law and order, but this was still unusual, and when the Yorkshire Area included the 'insufficient notice taken of Conference resolutions' among the causes of the 1964 Election defeat, they were complaining as much about the actual policy as about the mechanism by which it was made. From the later 1960s though, as is shown in Chapter 5, demands began to be made for greater powers for Conference, leading to the 1967 rule change whereby ballots could be demanded from the floor for the first time, and then to the work of the Chelmer Committee. In 1967, 107 representatives spoke at Conference, but 503 had sent in slips asking to be called, suggesting that there was indeed a greater wish to participate than had yet been accommodated. The constituency activists gathered at Conference could have one other informal influence, and by their reactions to speeches affect the pecking order at the top. Both Hailsham and Macleod enjoyed enhanced roles as frontbenchers through their ability to electrify Conferences with their oratory (which contributed to the case for making each of them Party Chairman), and Butler's inability to do so correspondingly damaged his chances. Hailsham's failed candidature for the leadership in 1963 demonstrated, though, the limitations of such a powerbase once Conference was over.[22]

In any case, as Richard Kelly has suggested for a later period, the press's single-minded concentration on 'the' Party Conference tended to miss altogether the more limited but significant roles of the other annual conferences, for councillors, trade unionists, YCs and women, which had been a regular feature of the National Union year since the 1940s; in 1963 for example, the YC Conference had twelve hundred present, roughly the same number of YCs who attended the October 'Party Conference', and was addressed by six members of the Cabinet. The same point might well be made for the National Union's Central Council, which because it met for a shorter time and with a smaller attendance than the Autumn Conference was also easy to underestimate. However, since it always met in London in this period, it generated a mainly south-eastern audience, to a far larger extent than the annual week in a coastal resort.[23]

If Conferences were the most visible National Union activity, then the Executive Committee was the most influential. In the 1950s, the Executive contained 156 members, with an average attendance of about 80, and over 30 of its members were also MPs, but this was a consequence of so many

---

[22] Central Office General Director's file, CCO 120/1/5, Broadcasting; National Union Finance and General Purposes Committee [hereafter NUFGP], 6 Nov. 1963; Hexham CA minutes, 18 July 1961; Yorkshire Area Council, 2 Nov. 1964.

[23] Kelly, *Conservative Conferences*, 179; NUEC, 4 July 1963.

National Union figures having gained seats in 1950 and 1951, and that degree of overlap with the parliamentary party did not last for long; in 1963, efforts had to be made to increase the number of MPs on the Executive, and to get them actually to attend meetings, to improve communications. The size of the Executive allowed it to remain broadly representative of the Party, but militated against debate on detailed management issues. From 1951, most such matters were devolved to the smaller Finance and General Purposes Committee, which effectively became the body that administered the National Union itself, arbitrating on the rules and running the Conference, while the Executive remained the interface between the National Union and the rest of the Party; that trend was reinforced when the Selwyn Lloyd report of 1963 recommended that the chairman of the Executive should be the channel through which voluntary members of the Party liaised on policy with the Advisory Committee on Policy, and he was now empowered to pass on resolutions from Areas and constituencies to the appropriate Minister, without awaiting a meeting of his committee. The terms of reference, which had become lax over time, were tightened up so that the Executive would be more political and the Finance and General Purposes Committee exclusively administrative. Executive members were among the most generously honoured for their services, though this undoubtedly reflected the calibre of its membership and the wider work that they did for the Party rather than being just a sort of non-pecuniary attendance allowance. In June 1960, four members of the Executive were knighted in the same honours list. In June 1963 seven members were honoured – one Privy Councillor, one baronet, and (in the Order of the British Empire) one CBE, three OBEs and an MBE – so that when nine more were honoured in January 1964, and thirteen in June 1964, about a sixth of the entire membership had been honoured in just over a year. Writing in 1963, Peter Richards suggested that the annual number of awards given by Macmillan 'for political services' or 'for political and public services' was 'remarkably constant at about 130. One has an impression of loyal Conservative supporters queueing up for a place in the ration made available to their party organizers. It is not a pretty thought.' He also pointed out the devaluation of the currency, for whereas Attlee had given no political knighthoods, and the three CBEs of 1948 had all gone to Labour MPs with years of public service behind them, the equivalent Tory MP of 1962 would expect to become a knight or a baronet; on average, fifteen years as a quiet backbencher would produce a knighthood. Niceties were still observed though, and such averages concealed the careful use of patronage to encourage loyalty. Some embarrassment was caused when an Area Chairman wrote to Poole in 1959 with a lengthy recitation of his services to the Party, urging that no notice be taken of his enemies' slanders; from Number 10, John Wyndham wrote that 'the kindest thing is to suppose that [he] was drunk when he prepared his letter', and Poole minuted that 'I would say either (a) it means he wants to be a peer, or (b) something disagreeable is going to happen which we do not yet know of.' It was finally agreed, on Chief Whip Heath's suggestion, that Macmillan should send a letter of fulsome thanks – but take no other action. Honours often flowed to National Union leaders, but it was not the done thing to ask for one.[24]

Central Office was careful never to trespass on the National Union's acknowledged area of activities, and this sometimes necessitated convoluted decision-making, for example in a recruiting campaign which would have to be set up and coordinated by Central Office through its Area offices, but which, since it would involve voluntary workers finding more voluntary workers was technically a matter for the National Union. Butler was briefed in 1961 that the National Union's officers had already been sounded out, that they had agreed to pass a resolution asking for a recruiting campaign in 1962, and that when he received that resolution Butler would as Party Chairman set up a special organising committee (on which the National Union would then be represented); the committee would work out all the details and report back to both Central Office and to the Executive, but in the mean time Central Office (which unlike the National Union had the money to pay for it all) would get literature designed. Thus were all the procedures observed, and constituencies could be told that this was a National Union campaign, originating from a National Union resolution; a similar brief for the National Union's officers ensured that they too knew exactly what was happening and in what order; everybody spoke their lines on cue and the campaign was duly authorised.[25]

The least visible activity in which the National Union took part (and which as a hybrid body was not technically part of the National Union) was the Advisory Committee on Policy (ACP). This had a chairman and vice chairman appointed by the Party Leader (the chairman being Rab Butler from its re-formation in 1949 right through to 1965); seven of its members were from the National Union Executive, seven from the parliamentary party (five MPs elected by the 1922 Committee and two Tory peers), with up to four coopted members. This was therefore in principle a link of great significance between the leadership, MPs and the voluntary party. In practice its importance fluctuated with the character and calibre of its membership, but Butler rarely had difficulties in keeping it tame; despite the enormous policy problems faced by the Eden government, the ACP met only six times in 1955 and 1956, and not at all in the second half of 1956. Along with other sections of the Party, the ACP failed to press the Government into action on immigration in the late 1950s or on trade union reform in and after 1962. There was certainly an advantage in having such a broadly-representative (but

---

[24] NUEC, 16 Mar. 1950, 11 Jan. 1951, 6 Apr. 1961, 13 June and 5 Sept. 1963, 9 Jan. and 2 July 1964; Peter G. Richards, *Patronage in British Government* (1963), 215–18; Central Office Chairman's department file, CCO 20/8/3.
[25] National Union papers, NUA 5/2/2, Secretary's notes of F and GP Committee.

entirely discreet) sounding board for the review of manifesto drafts and other policy documents, but the ACP in this period never had much more than that limited role. After 1970, when policy disagreement in the Party became more acute, the ACP was to be a forum at which far more critical debates took place, but debates that remained unreported outside its doors.[26]

The constituency associations

Investigating the London constituency of Baron's Court, Holt and Turner found a paradoxical contrast between the apparently participatory democracy of the Conservative association (described in its rule-book) and the practical oligarchy that actually existed; there were about three thousand paid-up members, but 'only a fraction of these people are even reasonably active', and in the period 1954 to 1966 only two people had held the association's chairmanship. Across London in Greenwich, a decade earlier, a similar phenomenon was noted; the Conservative membership there included more women than the population as a whole; it was also rather older, better educated and better off than the average for the constituency; the profile of Party officers generally diverged from the norm more sharply than members as a whole, but was younger and less female than the membership, in part no doubt a reflection of the YC's local leadership affecting the overall sample of officers (see Table 2.3). Jean Blondel's researches later in the 1950s and Michael Pinto-Duschinsky's in the late 1960s amply confirmed these general patterns, for the country as a whole, as Tables 2.4 and 2.5 indicate. They also confirmed that the constituency parties saw their main function as being social and financial (the two being closely linked, since social events raised so much money), while political action and political discussions were very much secondary to this objective. The Party was best described as an inverted

Table 2.3. Conservative members and officers in Greenwich, 1950

Social characteristic	Total electorate	Party members	Party officers
% female	54	57	25
% over 50	36	48	43
% with high income	21	67	90
% educated after age 14	27	64	59
% Church of England	74	78	88

[26] Central Office Chairman's department file, CCO 20/8/2; Advisory Committee on Policy minutes [hereafter ACP], 1/1.

Table 2.4 Occupations of constituency chairmen, by social class, 1969 (%)

	A	B	C1	C2	DE
Safe Conservative constituencies	81	13	3	3	—
Marginal Conservative constituencies	62	27	6	4	—
Marginal Labour constituencies	69	19	5	7	—
Safe Labour constituencies	56	21	12	9	2

Table 2.5 The social pyramid: % of various groups in social classes A, B and C

	AB	ABC
Total electorate (1964)	16	31
Conservative identifiers (1964)	24	47
Conservative members (1964)	40	70
Party workers (1964)	42	76
Constituency chairmen (1969)	85	94
Conservative MPs (1970)	97	99

pyramid, with Tory voters more socially and occupationally upmarket than the electorate as a whole, and with privileged backgrounds (and maleness) becoming steadily more prominent as the evidence was cited in turn for constituency activists, constituency officers and candidates.[27]

After their spectacular rise in the 1940s, the YCs were always going to be a difficult body to keep on course, and already in 1952 the National Union Executive was debating the problem of YC 'wastage' – the half of all active YCs who did not go on to join a main branch when they became too old to be YCs; it agreed to encourage constituencies to improve liaison between YC and main branches, but the problem remained endemic, as did the allegation (which was at least half true) that the appeal of the YC branches to their members was social rather than political; reporting on the re-starting of a London branch in 1959, the chairman was keen to point out to older members

[27] R.T. Holt and J.E. Turner, *Political Parties in Action: The Battle of Barons' Court* (1968), 31; M. Benney, A.P. Gray and R.H. Pear, *How People Vote: A Study of Electoral Behaviour in Greenwich* (1956), 47, 51; Jean Blondel, *Voters, Parties and Leaders: The Social Fabric of British Politics* (Harmondsworth, 1963), 131–58; D.E. Butler and Michael Pinto-Duschinsky, 'The Conservative Elite, 1918–1978. Does Unrepresentativeness Matter?' in Z. Layton-Henry (ed.), *Conservative Party Politics* (1980), 194–7; Pinto-Duschinsky, 'Constituency Associations', 74–5.

that 'rock and roll were out', but a year later the branch's meetings had been banned from local church premises for being too noisy. Tony Hancock told his radio listeners that he had decided not to join the Young Conservatives since he couldn't play table tennis and was not looking for a wife – funny because it only exaggerated the received view (though the secondary joke was that 'the lad' was well over the maximum YC age too); Julian Critchley remembers the YCs as 'the marriage bureau of the middle classes; 200,000 nubile girls in search of 10,000 politically ambitious young men.' In 1960, Butler as Party Chairman launched an initiative to increase political activity in the YCs, but the inexorable fall-off both in numbers and in activity continued. When Iain Macleod investigated the YC movement for the Party in 1965, he found that the trend towards younger marriages, after which former YCs tended to become absorbed in building homes and bringing up families to the exclusion of active politics, had reduced the average age of members to twenty-one (which meant that at any one time half of them had never voted). He recommended reforming the branch structure so that each branch would specialise in either social or political activity, so encouraging different memberships, and the age limit was raised from 31 to 35 in the hope of arresting the decline in the number of YCs with political experience. These and other changes did provide some new impetus, and the YCs benefited from the general upsurge of youth movements in the late 1960s, but this was only a temporary halt in the long decline. Meanwhile there were also new pressures, and 'the major problem' diagnosed by Geoffrey Johnson-Smith as Party Vice Chairman in 1968 was 'for the YCs to establish a meaningful relationship with the rebellious youth syndrome', something that spilled over into the wider Party, and is discussed in Chapter 5.[28]

To a large extent, the informal nature of local structures had survived the Woolton and Maxwell Fyfe reforms; the National Union offered model rules, and Area Agents encouraged democratic practices, but neither had the opportunity or the authority to enforce their views; as late as 1973, Lord Carrington as Party Chairman was telling a correspondent that 'I have neither the will nor the power to make constituencies do what they resolutely do not want to do'. Mark Benney and his colleagues were surprised in 1950 at the 'rudimentary' nature of the Conservative association's rule-book in Greenwich, which 'quite explicitly' left 'internal regulatory detail to an Executive Council which is largely of the co-opted type'. In 1959, the association in Lichfield actually set up such a restricted Executive, with a total membership of twelve, seven association officers and the other five coopted, but there was also a Management Committee that was much more broadly representative. During the 1950s, many more associations adopted

[28] NUEC, 27 Mar. 1952, 7 Apr. 1960; South West Islington CA minutes, 27 May 1959 and 13 Feb. 1962; *This is Hancock*, Pye record, GGL 0206; Julian Critchley, *A Bag of Boiled Sweets: An Autobiography* (1994), 32; NUEC, 4 Nov. 1965; Eastern Area Council, 24 Apr. 1968.

rule-books based on National Union recommendations, as St Marylebone for example did in 1958, and Bristol North West in 1965 after much Area and Central Office nudging; Aylesbury in 1965 agreed to adopt new rules because their existing ones were said to be now contrary to the rules of the National Union, and it was implied that acceptance of the National Union's rules was a condition of affiliation (which was not strictly true – the National Union had no such power). Adopting model rules did not necessarily change the actual practice; in 1967, West Middlesbrough, noting that Mrs Dawson had been President for the permitted three years, resolved that 'rules were made for guidance' and re-elected her. It was also a matter of finding those who were willing to take office; Pinto-Duschinsky found in 1969 that 56 per cent of constituency associations operated a three–year rule for office-holders, but that the figures were 67 per cent in Conservative-held and only 41 per cent in Labour-held constituencies.[29]

Model rules included among their advantages both a more representative local structure and a means of settling disputes without undue acrimony. When a row erupted in Carlisle in 1964 over the activities of the maverick MP Donald Johnson, the National Union found that it had no basis on which to intervene, for despite Area pressure since 1951 the local association had never adopted model rules which included an arbitration clause (referring disputes to the National Union). With the fine disregard for form that has so often mystified investigators from outside the Party, the National Union Executive chairman, on receiving a petition from discontented members in Carlisle, intervened anyway and sorted out the problem by persuading both sides to accept his (non-binding) ruling. As the adoption of model rules became more widespread, this problem gradually disappeared; when a dispute over the selection of Greater London Council (GLC) candidates took place in 1971, Dulwich referred the matter upwards to Area for arbitration; on the resolution to accept Area's ruling, the losing side abstained but made no further waves, though a later dispute also had to be referred to Area only two years later. The new rules adopted by South Bedfordshire in 1961, after taking National Union advice, indicate the typical character of an association structure at that time. The association Executive was made up of the association officers (chairman, treasurer and secretary/agent), the three women's advisory committee officers and four constituency YC officers, three ordinary representatives from each polling district branch, five from each women's branch and four from each YC branch (both covering larger areas than polling districts), four from each Conservative club, and the chairmen of the local CPC committee, Conservative Teachers' committee and any other

---

[29] Ball, 'Local Conservatism', 262; Benney *et al*, *How People Vote*, 43; Lichfield CA minutes, 28 Jan. 1959; St Marylebone CA minutes, 29 July 1958; Central Office constituency file, CCO 1/14/484; Aylesbury CA, 9 July 1965; West Middlesbrough CA minutes, 13 Jan. 1967; Pinto-Duschinsky, 'Constituency Associations', 78.

affiliated body; the Area Agent was to attend whenever he wished, but only in an advisory capacity. The smaller Finance and General Purposes (F and GP) Committee, set up in the same rules, was to be similarly representative, and was empowered to fix the quotas the branches would have to pay to keep the association's finances going. At its first meeting under the new rules, the Executive elected chairmen for committees to look after membership, publicity, political education and social events, each committee also to be made up of branch representatives. Often though, financial business was kept to a very limited circle of decision-makers; Solihull in 1959 set up a new F and GP Committee that was not at all representational, being in effect a meeting of association officers. In North Cornwall in 1957, welcoming a financial surplus for the first time in many years, the small F and GP Committee resolved not to let word of this reach the rest of the membership lest they should slacken in their fundraising; £250 was put into an election reserve and the accounts presented to the Executive showed the usual deficit. Next door in Truro, even the parliamentary candidate was not allowed to attend F and GP Committee meetings.[30]

One shadowy but important role was that of president, sometimes a purely honorary figure, but often much more. The president might be a former chairman, but was generally a figure of unusual distinction for the constituency and held office for longer than other officers. Rank and station were important: the Countess of Stair succeeded the Earl of Galloway as president of the Galloway Unionists in 1952 and remained in office until her death in 1968; when Lady Apsley retired as president of Cirencester and Tewkesbury in 1965, the names considered for her successor were Lord St Aldwyn (who was chosen), Lord Bathurst, Lady Dunrossil, and Sir Walter Pollen (who had just completed seventeen years as chairman, and now became vice president). A titled president could contribute more than just a name; when affairs were rather heated in the Manchester Conservative Association in 1963, the Area Agent reported of the annual meeting that 'the atmosphere was far from happy, and it was a good thing that Lord Derby was in the chair'. The King's Lynn F and GP Committee met in the home of their president, Lord Althorp, in 1962, and the association chairman joked that it was the best-attended meeting he could remember, but Althorp's duties included leading the election appeal, so visiting him for a finance meeting may not have been purely social. Lord Leigh's duties as president of Warwick and Leamington for nearly thirty years also involved the running of the fighting fund at elections. Many presidents were themselves important benefactors; Sir William Rootes, president of all three constituencies in Coventry in 1954, was reported to put in a great deal of work for them, and to back them 'with a great

---

30 NUEC, 2 July 1964; Dulwich CA minutes, 22 Mar. 1971; South Bedfordshire CA minutes, 9 Feb. and 9 Mar. 1961; Solihull CA minutes, 4 June 1959; North Cornwall CA, 19 Mar. 1957; Truro CA minutes, 13 Mar. 1970.

deal of money'. The Duke of Devonshire's role in West Derbyshire involved both substantial personal generosity and the making available of Chatsworth House for mass rallies and outdoor fundraising events. Other presidents were retired politicians themselves; David Margesson was the president at Rugby, and on his advice the association elected as its chairman in 1956 Sir Hubert Ranch, 'a very distinguished man' who had just moved to the area and was unknown to the rest of the committee; when a parliamentary selection was under way in the constituency in 1958, the president and chairman had 'preliminary interviews' with the applicants and reduced the list to four, apparently without even telling the rest of the association who else had applied. Sir James Lumsden, president of West Dunbartonshire Unionists for decades, had a similar authority; when the chairman, who had himself served as an officer for eleven years, retired on health grounds in 1961, the matter was remitted to the president, whose suggestion of Sir Alastair Young was accepted at once, although Young had played no major role in the association's affairs before becoming its chairman.[31]

Whether in the absence of formal structures or working through them, the association chairman remained the pivotal figure, at least if the chairman was a strong personality who gave an effective lead, and it was a commonplace of Area Agents' reports to attribute organisational success and failure to the lead given from the chair; of a Manchester constituency in 1957 it was reported that the incumbent was 'not an inspiring chairman, and in consequence the Association lacks leadership.' In 1952, the West Midlands Area Council was told that,

> on the whole it was noticeable [in the recent Election] that the efficiency of a constituency election organisation varied in accordance with the interest taken in it by the Association Chairman and Officers. It was highest where they actively concerned themselves in assisting the Candidate and Agent to ensure that arrangements worked smoothly and indeed in those Constituencies where they shouldered a large part of the burden and responsibility. In one or two cases the Association Chairman was not seen between the Adoption Meeting and that on the Eve of the Poll.

Chairmen's influence was not only paramount at election times; when Lord Hailsham needed a seat quickly on coming down from the Lords in 1963, the St Marylebone chairman told his constituency Executive that the sitting MP, Sir Wavell Wakefield, would receive a peerage on the following day, and successfully moved that the Executive conduct the selection forthwith; he then proposed that Hailsham be the only candidate considered, and Hailsham

31 Galloway UA minutes, 17 Nov. 1952 and 4 Apr. 1968; Central Office constituency file, CCO 1/14/178; Cirencester and Tewkesbury CA minutes, 23 July 1965; King's Lynn CA minutes, 22 May 1962 and 18 Sept. 1963; Warwick and Leamington CA minutes, 6 Apr. 1964; West Derbyshire CA minutes, 6 Nov. 1957 and 15 Sept. 1958; Central Office constituency file, CCO 1/10/299; Rugby CA minutes, 20 Apr. 1956 and 23 Sept. 1958; West Dunbartonshire UA minutes, 13 Nov. and 11 Dec. 1961.

was then formally adopted by a Special General Meeting within a week. If the chairman was not so effective then problems could be long-lasting; in the case of a 1957 by-election, the Chief Organisation Officer reported that the association 'chairman (who is no good) telephoned Mr. Poole and said the list of candidates which they had been given was no good and would Mr. Poole immediately send another list. Whilst he was about it he might send a list of agents as well as [the constituency agent] was no good'; this inaugurated an unhappy campaign, but a bad result provided a pretext for forcing the chairman out, after which the association recovered. A chairman's feud with the agent was a real recipe for chaos and ineffectiveness; months of bitter wrangling at High Peak culminated in 1964 with an uninhibited shouting match at an association meeting; the chairman reported that many people were 'disgruntled' with the agent (to which the agent replied 'name them!'), and that there was a litany of complaints from the branches about the agent's rudeness and incompetence. Chairman and agent both had strong supporters in the association, but most members were reluctant to take sides in an election year: one said 'that it was a terrible time to be in such a state. He was rendered speechless by these events', and another 'asked "When does one reach the point of no return?"' This bitter row ended when (as the minutes, duly confirmed as a true record at the next meeting, put it) 'the meeting then disintegrated into respective criticism and argument, mostly personal'. By the next meeting the agent had left, though his supporters kept up the fight, and it took a joint intervention by the MP and Area officers (offering a financial subvention to clear the overdraft and allow a fresh start) to sort things out; it is perhaps not entirely coincidental that the seat was lost shortly afterwards with an unusually adverse swing, and it was only after a period of years and a new chairman was installed that matters finally settled down. A less public but equally bitter row in Aylesbury in 1955 resulted in the departure of both chairman and agent, and again things then recovered. At Basingstoke in 1956, it was the chairman and treasurer who had to go and the agent who survived, developing a better working relationship with the new team of officers then elected.[32]

Long-serving chairmen were a feature that gradually disappeared from the scene in most places; in Twickenham in 1962, the chairman for the past ten years was eased up into the presidency and a three-year rotation rule adopted before his successor was appointed. Ashford adopted a three-year term for all officers except the president in 1960. Saffron Walden adopted a rotation rule when Sir Reuben Hunt, Rab Butler's association chairman for a quarter of a century, retired in 1964. Brighton Kemptown in 1961 had their first

---

[32] Central Office constituency file, CCO 1/12/116; West Midlands Area Council, 17 May 1952; St Marylebone CA minutes, 30 Oct. 1963; High Peak CA minutes, 29 Apr. and 13 May 1964; Central Office General Director's by-election file, CCO 120/2/65; Central Office constituency file, CCO 1/11/453; Basingstoke CA minutes, July–August 1956.

ever election for the chairmanship, after the incumbent had tried to increase the association's control over ward branches in the selection of municipal candidates; in 1970 the same association overthrew another chairman after he had sacked the agent without authority, but in circumstances in which the association became almost impossible to lead. Occasionally these pressures on chairmen boiled over; the South West Islington chairman, thanked for many years of service on his retirement in 1952, replied somewhat tactlessly that 'the best thanks he could be given was for all members of the Association to pull their respective weights and resuscitate the Association. Old grievances should be forgotten, or, if there were any criticism, it should be aired in Committee and not in public.' In 1964, David Walder thought that the typical constituency chairman was 'late forties or fifties, business man, solicitor, perhaps a service background; dark suits in the towns, not too smart tweeds in the country'. Association chairmen were, in the 1950s and 1960s, overwhelmingly middle-class in background, with only a tiny number from manual occupations, but there was an increasing tendency for women to hold these crucial posts during the 1960s. The constituency Executive Council provided the main representative forum for discussing policy resolutions and making strategic decisions; it was for example usually the largest body in the association to be offered any choice of candidates in a selection process. In practice though, the Executive was an unwieldy body for practical discussion, and in many associations practical authority seeped away during the 1950s to a smaller Finance and General Purposes Committee, often including in urban areas the chairman of each ward branch and so concentrating a lot of authority round one table; the Ilford Conservatives resolved in 1956 to delegate 'the general control of the financial affairs of the Association' to such a Finance Committee. As Table 2.6 indicates, Pinto-Duschinsky found that the numbers involved in these various structures tended to reflect the overall strength of the local membership.[33]

Table 2.6 Number of members on Executive Committees and F and GPs, 1950s

	Executive Committees	*F and GPs*
Safe Conservative constituencies	121	20
Marginal Conservative constituencies	88	24
Marginal Labour constituencies	85	20
Safe Labour constituencies	55	14

[33] Central Office constituency file, CCO 1/14/86; Ashford CA minutes, 11 Nov. 1960; Saffron Walden CA minutes, 2 Dec. 1964 and 24 May 1965; Brighton Kemptown CA minutes, 20 May 1961 and 15 Sept. 1970; South West Islington CA minutes, 7 Feb. 1952; David Walder, *The Short List* (1964), 71; Ball, 'Local Conservatism', 270–1; Ilford CA minutes, 10 Apr. 1956; Pinto-Duschinsky, 'Constituency Associations', 69–72.

Below the Area level, there was a wide variety of avenues of cooperation between constituency associations. In 1961, Cornwall, Durham, Kent, Sussex and Surrey still had county federations, survivals from the nineteenth-century pattern that functioned below and alongside the Areas but did not employ staff of their own; they provided a useful forum for the coordination of county council campaigning. Eleven English cities had a 'city party' that was recognised by the National Union (for example, by granting until 1972 additional representation on Area and national committees). In these city parties, control was often ruthlessly centralised, and since they were large and wealthy bodies, Area influence could be held at bay too. The Area Agent reported of Birmingham in 1954 that

> to understand the Birmingham set-up it must be realised that Sir Theodore [Pritchett, who combined the roles of chairman of Birmingham Unionist Association and Tory leader on the City Council], with the Treasurer, Sir Walford Turner, and the Vice Chairman, Alderman J.C. Burman, control absolutely the Birmingham Conservative and Unionist Associations in all matters of any importance. Local Government affairs in the City is their first priority and take precedence over Parliamentary matters. I am on friendly terms with Sir Theodore, but I recognise that very little real co-operation in Area matters can be got from him because he is interested only in Birmingham.

The CBF was not allowed to raise industrial money in Birmingham, and the constituency associations were tightly controlled, with all their agents and other staff paid for by the aptly-named 'Empire House' machine (which had more staff than were based at the Area Office with responsibility for four times as many constituencies). The West Midlands Area eventually gave up the contest and withdrew from Birmingham altogether, setting up offices in Leamington Spa, as unsatisfactory a regional capital as Vichy or Bonn. Birmingham was an extreme but not a unique case; after complaints from the North West, also in 1954, the General Director minuted despondently that 'this is not the first time that we have had requests from the Area office to do everything possible to encourage Liverpool and Manchester to recognise their existence and make use of their services'. Relations then deteriorated further, and in 1957 Liverpool threatened to secede from the Area altogether, withdrawing the threat only when it became clear that this would also exclude them from the Party Conference and the services of Central Office; relations then gradually improved, particularly as the financial strength of the Liverpool Tories became less secure.[34]

Money was at the heart of city party authority; in Newcastle upon Tyne in June 1954, the treasurers of the four constituencies met and constituted

---

[34] NUFGP, 14 Jan. 1961; Central Office Area correspondence file, CCO 2/2/1; Central Office constituency file, CCO 1/8/343; West Midlands Area report, 18 Jan. 1954; Central Office constituency files, CCO 1/11/242–5, CCO 1/10/111 and 1/12/107.

themselves a committee to raise industrial subscriptions; by mid-1955 they had raised £6,557, part of which went into a special deposit account, but £3,000 was passed to the constituency associations; by the following November, the central finance committee was paying the city's entire Central Office quota of £1,000 a year, as well as funding the local elections for the wards, propping up the four constituency associations' current activities and loaning money for the purchase of property. Local elections were the motor of city party activity, for local businesses paying rates had a real interest in the outcome of municipal elections; it was probably the feeling that this relationship could become confused that led Newcastle to refuse to take Wallsend under its control. By 1958, this small finance committee was widening its horizons, running football competitions and sweepstakes as well as an annual appeal, and inviting Viscount Ridley to become its patron. When industrial money dried up, so often did the health and strength of the city party, for unlike constituency associations, city-wide committees were too remote from the average ward member to enable them to feel any responsibility for the whole city's finances; Leeds in 1961 ruled that quotas from constituencies 'must' be raised by £2,000 overall, but had no redress when this did not happen, and the North West Leeds constituency Executive carefully minuted that annual contributions were 'donations' for which no obligation existed. In Nottingham and Bradford there were less dominant city parties which gradually accommodated themselves to an independent role for constituency associations; Nottingham evolved into a confederation existing only to raise funds from large subscribers, and to run city council campaigns, while in Bradford the city party was wound up in 1971 without apparent regret. In Bristol too, a dominant city party gradually moved to a sharing of power with the constituencies, mainly because of the difficulty of raising enough money centrally for the running of six constituencies, and in 1973 Bristol too wound up its city party and replaced it only with a loose coordinating committee. Ten other cities and towns had a 'central association', generally little more than a consultation arrangement for local elections, but sometimes also a basis for agreeing a joint budget for a shared office and agent. However in some towns with a very strong municipal tradition, where, as in Bolton, local rather than parliamentary politics were what really encouraged people to give up their time to run the Party machine, it proved impossible in the 1950s to keep separate constituency associations going with any real life of their own.[35]

Finally in this series of intermediate structures, the grouping of constituencies in Labour strongholds that had been begun in 1930 (but was suspended

[35] Newcastle upon Tyne CA, Finance Committee minutes, 1954–58; Leeds CA, F and GP, 3 Feb. 1961; NW Leeds CA minutes, 1 Feb. 1957; Nottingham CA minutes, 19 Mar. 1968; Bradford CA minutes, 16 June 1971; Bristol CA minutes, 17 Jan. 1973; Bolton CA minutes, 29 Jan. 1960.

in the optimistic days of Woolton) had by the early 1960s produced eight such groups, six in the coalfields of Wales and northern England and two in inner London, covering a total of thirty-six constituencies which could not sustain an independent organisation. When the run-down of Area funding for such constituencies made such a combination necessary in Central Lancashire in 1957, the Chief Organisation Officer welcomed the idea, as 'I have always been in favour of grouping in these sort of seats as being both effective and economical'. It was difficult to keep such hybrid bodies active, and a real challenge to the chief agent, who had to satisfy members in up to six different constituencies that they were getting an equal share of the agent's attention; the first such efforts in East London were unsuccessful for just that reason, but since the constituencies involved were all short of members, the scheme had to be continued and gradually won acceptance. Most were never self-standing; in 1957, the Mid Yorkshire Federation of Dearne Valley, Hemsworth, Pontefract, and Normanton, facing a combined Labour majority of a hundred thousand votes, needed a subsidy of £1,500 a year from Central Office in order to keep an organisation going even when their contributions to an agent's salary had been pooled. A chief agent assisted by relatively inexperienced assistants and with only a single office to pay for could though provide a skeleton organisation for quite a large area; they also provided between them a large enough pool of committed workers to make social events more viable and to fight elections in their better areas; in the early 1960s, Easington was combining with Houghton-le-Spring for a barbeque, and with Chester-le-Street for a summer fête. This group structure though, as with so many facets of the Party organisation, rested on the assumption that agents would be available for such thankless tasks; by 1969, with fewer agents in the job market, the Northern Area had to appoint a trainee agent to take singlehanded control of the several constituencies in the Durham group.[36]

More informal constituency cooperation also took place, for example for mutual aid at election times, or for fundraising events, but could also give rise to difficult disputes. In 1961 West Newcastle was censured by the Northern Area for trying to involve other constituencies in its 'win a car' raffle scheme, which seemed like poaching on the preserves of other associations, but when the National Union investigated it found that constituencies as far afield as Lancashire were involved in the West Newcastle scheme and that most thought it a great help in raising money. There was an increasing tendency for money to be derived from such activities, such as the Grand National draw that was in 1972 bringing in £556 a year in Brentford and Chiswick; that constituency had also run since 1966 an exclusive 'hundred club' which

---

[36] Central Office constituency files, CCO 1/11/106 and CCO 1/7/479; Pontefract CA minutes, 7 Mar. 1957; Easington CA minutes, 4 May 1960 and 2 Apr. 1963; Northern Area Council, 10 Mar. 1969.

gave its members regular access to the constituency MP when they met for lunches, and also raised a good deal of money: there was a waiting list to join. Pinto-Duschinsky found in the late 1960s that nearly half of all branch 'social' activities also had an element of gambling in them – whist, bridge or bingo evenings. At King's Lynn, a constituency that had never in the 1950s managed to bring in enough subscription money to run its normal activities, annual draws on the Grand National and the Cambridgeshire races brought in £929 in 1960, and a Christmas Market raised £523, which together made up half the association's total income and paid the agent's salary. In 1963, King's Lynn was helping to set up an Eastern Area Conservative Supporters' Association as a vehicle for the running of a football competition with bigger prizes than any one constituency could offer (and hence larger sales and larger profits); in the first year the association sold over four thousand cards to members and supporters and added an extra £600 to its funds. A similar scheme in Coventry South raised £9,000 in its first eight years, roughly equivalent to two years' entire expenditure by the association.[37]

Most money continued to be raised from members, either in direct subscriptions or in branch quotas derived mainly from social events, and here the conflict between keeping up overall numbers and raising money in an inflationary period came into play. Most constituencies in the 1950s still had a minimum subscription of 2/6d (12.5p) and even where these provisions were – after much heartsearching – raised to, say, 10/- (50p), it was not unusual for that rule to be suspended during recruiting campaigns. In 1960, Glasgow Pollok had a healthy list of 5,991 members, but even the *average* subscription was not quite half a crown (12.5p), which suggests that more than half must have been paying less than the supposed minimum rate. A neat device for relating subscriptions to the ability to pay, while retaining the voluntary principle, was the 'book scheme', whereby approaches to subscribers were carefully calibrated so as to put them under pressure to be generous. In 1962, the Chief Organisation Officer explained how it worked in recommending Darlington to adopt the scheme as a solution to financial difficulties:

> I myself have built up in constituencies before the war a subscription list of over £1000 a year with the assistance of these books and with the least possible trouble. It must however be very carefully and conscientiously run, and the people selected for approach must be put into categories of what you think they would be prepared to give. The books you use should be matched to people, i.e. it is silly to send a book containing a number of persons subscribing 10/6 to a person who could easily afford £10. That person would send you only 10/6 if you did that. I recommend therefore that the books should be graded and local knowledge should be used to select the class of book for each particular recipient.

37 NUEC, 9 Feb. and 13 July 1961; Brentford and Isleworth CA minutes, 17 Apr. 1972; Pinto-Duschinsky, 'Constituency Associations', 43; King's Lynn CA minutes, 31 Jan. 1961 and 18 Sept. 1963; Central Office constituency file, CCO 1/14/360.

The idea was that subscribers offered the book would thereby be shown what other people that they would be likely to know were giving, hence the importance of getting the peer groups right.

> You will see, of course, the objection put forward that it is political blackmail and so on. The fact is that if it is properly worked it is a moneyspinner, and I used, when an agent, to be perfectly contented to take the occasional abuse for the sake of the indubitable profit.

As a constituency agent, Area Agent, and Central Office official, he had 'never known it to fail', and it was indeed a source of much useful funding. There were some constituencies where it did not succeed, but that was usually because the association concerned was already so weak that it did not have the personnel with the extensive local knowledge needed to promote the book scheme successfully. In Bradford in 1953, on the other hand, a combination of recruiting methods that produced four thousand new members in the city found about a quarter of these through the book scheme, mainly in the middle-class wards where ability to pay made it most effective.[38]

As this suggests, there were constant efforts to hold on to the high membership totals that had been built up in the Woolton period, but on the whole unsuccessful efforts; in South Battersea, the paid-up membership in 1955 was 3,351, a respectable figure for an urban constituency, and more than a fifth of the Conservative vote; in 1965 it was 2,157, of whom 954 were newly recruited that year, which suggested a figure barely over 1,000 at the end of the Party's thirteen years in office; this then rose further during the period in opposition, but rarely exceeded 2,000. Similarly, in the very different Darlington constituency, the 4,226 members of 1952 had fallen to only 1,233 in 1964; in York, the 3,285 members in 1958, a third of them recruited that year and only a fraction of the total in 1952, had dropped again to 2,731 by 1962, by which time the local YC organisation had almost disappeared. The limitations of this type of head-counting were indicated though when a new agent found in 1967 in York that there were 1,048 people actually doing some work for the Party, but that 655 of these were not on the books as paying members. In Scotland, peak figures tended to be reported rather later, but with a 1960s decline in numbers that was not as in England halted when the Party returned to Opposition in 1964: East Edinburgh had 2,425 members in 1953, rising to 3,325 in 1957, then falling after a period of stability to 2,337 in 1963 and 1,696 in 1970.[39]

One legacy from the inter-war years that remained highly problematical

[38] Glasgow Pollok UA minutes, 28 Oct. 1960; Central Office constituency file, CCO 1/14/109; Bradford CA minutes, 11 May 1953.
[39] Central Office constituency file, CCO 1/11/3; South Battersea CA minutes, 8 Oct. 1965, 6 Mar. 1970; Central Office constituency files, CCO 1/12/47 and CCO 1/14/109; York CA minutes, 15 Jan. 1959, 11 Jan. 1962, and 24 Sept. 1967; East Edinburgh UA minutes, 1 Dec. 1953, 11 Mar. 1957, 18 Mar. 1963, and 21 July 1970.

was the Party's trade union wing. In the 1940s revival, this was re-launched, and was from 1953 intended to be an integral part of every constituency, with a committee of trade unionists in every local association and with its chairman alongside the women's chairman and the YC chairman as ex-officio members of the constituency Executive. This prescription was resented in many areas and not universally observed, though in some industrial areas Tory trade unionists had a real presence: in the West Midlands in the mid-1950s there were 23 constituency committees and 138 local groups; the East Midlands also had 23 constituency committees (in 42 constituencies) and 91 'factory groups', each with about two dozen members; in the Northern Area, there were committees in most constituencies, and 108 factory groups with a total of 1,512 members. Conversely, when reminded by Area in 1961 of the importance of trade union organisation, Bradford Tories, whose chief agent had argued in 1953 that 'the organisation of Conservative trade unionists is of real importance' in resisting communism, now replied uncompromisingly that they had been trying ever since 1919 and had now concluded that it just did not work; henceforth they would encourage trade union members to take part in ward branches just like anyone else. In a world of mass affluence and near-universal homeownership, organisations based on the idea of class separation made less and less sense. The root of the problem was that Tory trade union groups suffered from the same schizophrenia that was indicated by national Party policy: were the trade unions to be subverted or appeased? In 1958, the East Midlands Area fought shy of a motion calling on Tory trade unionists to refuse to take part in unofficial strikes, and the amended version eventually passed urged only 'that all Conservative members of Trade Unions should attend, and use their voice and vote, at Branch Meetings with a view to preventing unofficial strikes'. But in practice, while the trade union organisation continued to have several thousand members, still fifteen thousand in the mid-1960s, local organisations often existed only on paper; only two of the forty-two constituencies in the East Midlands refused to implement proposals to revive local structures, but by 1961 there were still many who had not done so in practice; the Uxbridge annual report on 1957 indicated that the trade union committee had continued to function 'in a quiet unassuming manner'. In Cardiff South East, the trade union group was in 1958 'again functioning', but was reported to be poorly attended. The National Union's Trade Union Advisory Committee was given a prominent role, and was generally a mouthpiece for quietist policies on industrial relations – which did not endear it to other members of the Party. When the Party's approach to trade union policy shifted in 1964–65, a change by then welcomed even among Conservative trade unionists, the role of the separate organisation became even harder to justify, and in 1969 North Fylde put their local committee 'into cold storage' when its chairman resigned after years of trying to keep activity going. In 1975 the remaining staff of the Central Office department that had serviced this part of the Area and local structures were paid off. The Party's continuing ability to attract working-class votes did not then owe much to its own trade union organisations, which were consistently treated as peripheral by most constituency leaders – except in the heavy industrial areas where the Party did not win the seats anyway.[40]

One haven of working-class Conservatism that continued to flourish within the organisation was the club movement. In 1948 there had been 1,500 Conservative clubs, and this figure hardly fell in the next two generations, though there was a slow decline in some inner city areas; the Bow Group owed its name to the fact that the Bow and Bromley Conservative Club, even in the early 1950s, was so hard up that it let out premises cheap to the Group's founders. As late as the 1980s, the Association of Conservative Clubs (ACC), with about 1,350 affiliated clubs, was about as large as the *combined* strength of the British Legion, and all the Liberal and Labour clubs. This represented the continuation through sheer inertia of a movement whose impetus was by then a century old; Philip Tether found in 1988 that over two-thirds of the Conservative clubs he surveyed had been founded before 1900 and only 5 per cent since 1918; a few still indicated their origins, like the Reading Curzon Club which did not even have 'Conservative' in its title, though nearly all by then did so. Family connections with the original patrons and benefactors often continued though; the Heathcoat Amory family were still helping in the 1960s the Tiverton Conservative Club that they had helped to found in 1890, much as the Halstead Conservative Club in Essex still relied on the generosity of the Courtaulds. These distant traditions also determined the geographical distribution of the clubs: half of all the Conservative clubs were in Wales and the North West, while there were very few in southern England; in 1958 Lancashire had 277 Conservative clubs (including more than a dozen each in Bolton, Burnley, Bury, Liverpool, Manchester, Oldham, Rochdale and Wigan), while Sussex as a whole had fifteen. On the other hand, the strict hierarchies that had once existed within the world of the clubs were now passing away; the class separation between the Ashton-under-Lyne Central Conservative Club, restricted to middle-class members, and the other five clubs in the working-class wards, and the similar set-up in Bradford, was no longer observed, and as a result of these changes very few clubs now included 'working men's' in their title. The old pattern whereby the clubs had deep local roots in stable communities – each councillor an ex-officio member of the ward club and aldermen having special chairs

---

[40] Andrew Rowe, 'Conservatives and Trades Unionists', in Layton-Henry (ed.), *Conservative Party Politics*, 217; West Midlands Area Council, 26 May 1956; East Midlands Area Council, 13 Feb. 1954 and 13 Dec. 1958; Northern Area Council, 21 Feb. 1953; Bradford CA minutes, 9 Jan. 1961; Central Office constituency file, CCO 1/9/160; Uxbridge CA, annual report, 1957; South East Cardiff CA minutes, 3 Mar. 1958; J. Phillips and M. Wilson, 'The Conservative Party from Macmillan to Thatcher', in N. Nugent and R. King (eds), *The British Right* (Farnborough, 1977), 33–4; National Union papers, NUA 5/2/1, F and GP, secretary's notes; North Fylde CA minutes, 30 May 1969.

in the appropriate club in Bolton – were becoming a thing of the past too. The Club movement had shared in Woolton's modernisation of the whole Party organisation; in 1948, the Association of Conservative Clubs, already more a service organisation than a political body, became a limited company owned by the Party. Though its articles of association stressed commitment to political activity, its priority now was selling to its members the stocktaking, marketing, accounting and other commercial services that had become increasingly significant since its reorganisation in 1933. The ACC continued to be taken seriously by the Party leadership though, with a frontbencher always its President (Peter Thorneycroft in 1958, Selwyn Lloyd in 1963, both ex-Chancellors with time on their hands) and with a Cabinet Minister drafted in to address each annual meeting; in 1963, eighty-nine clubs and eight local club federations sent representatives to that meeting. Other elements of club life had not changed much in the century of their existence; almost all clubs in the 1980s still functioned around a bar which provided both the core of its social activities and the basis of its finances. Almost all in the 1970s abandoned their 'men only' rules, though some retained male zones by convention, usually such places as snooker rooms, and women at last became a numerically significant part of the membership.[41]

When the Party Conference came to Blackpool in 1954, all eleven Conservative clubs in the town opened their doors to Conference delegates who could produce an ACC affiliation card, and a number of fringe meetings were held in them. It is much less clear how political clubs remained in general; the Central Office report on the 1950 Election concluded that clubs had been 'ineffective', and attributed this to the fact that they had been 'infiltrated by Labour supporters'. In the West Midlands in 1952, the Area Agent thought that 'with their large memberships, there should be a great deal of active interest among our clubmen. During the [1951] General Election some of the clubs did very well, but there were many which gave no help at all.' Such complaints continued after every campaign. Conversely, in Oxford, the clubs were still at the end of the 1950s central to the Party's work; most clubs admitted only existing Party members, they raised much of the association's income, and leading clubmen went on to become chairman of the association. In Southport too, the clubs remained at the heart of things, with the association's general purposes committee in 1960 still containing twelve club representatives, about the same number as those elected by ward branches; but by 1973 the clubs were involved in the association (if at all) only through the ordinary branches. Perhaps Darlington, where the Area Agent reported harmonious but limited relations with the clubs, which were 'not entirely indifferent to politics but they are not exactly bursting with political

41 Philip Tether, 'Clubs: A Neglected Aspect of Conservative Organisation', *Hull Papers in Politics*, no. 42 (1988), 2, 33, 40–1, 44–5, 52–3, 55, 58–9, 70; NUFGP, 4 Jan. 1961; Central Office files, CCO 3/5/4, 3/6/3 and 4, Association of Conservative Clubs.

activity', was a more typical case in a socially-mixed marginal seat. Almost all clubs would at least make a donation to a general election appeal, a significant matter in the industrial areas where there were plenty of clubs and not much else in the way of Tory organisation. The *Conservative Clubs Gazette* usually carried an appeal from the Party Chairman in a special General Election issue, though the *reminder to vote* that formed a prominent part of that appeal indicated the low level of expectation that Central Office now had of Tory clubmen. There was little the Party could do to change things, for the clubs had even more practical autonomy than constituency associations; when the National Union debated the issue in 1958, Geofrey Finsberg reported that 'in Lancashire they are behind the Party but not elsewhere', while in South Wales 'you cannot even go into the bar as the majority of the people are socialists', and he was able to name a Conservative Club that had held its annual meeting on General Election polling day, so oblivious was it to politics. Efforts were then made to step up political activity, for example by appointing club organisers to Areas in 1962, with the specific remit of improving liaison with the local Party organisation. Even when almost entirely non-political, clubs could generally be shamed into offering accommodation to the Party, in deference to past associations; sometimes a constituency agent could find a free or subsidised office on club premises, more often the association could get temporary additional space in the clubs for election campaigns: an Area report on Accrington in 1956 noted that 'there are five clubs in the constituency. The Accrington Club possesses large premises and is very prosperous. It provides accommmodation for the Association offices, rooms for meetings and a donation of £150 towards the association funds.' This was a common practice, if not always in so generous a form; of Manchester Withington it was reported that 'the constituency receives no financial help from any of the clubs, but they supply rooms for meetings, whilst one . . . is virtually the headquarters of the Conservative Group on the City Council'; investigators in Greenwich early in the 1950s, thought one of the Conservatives' main organisational advantages over Labour to be 'the usufruct of three spacious clubs inherited from the past'.[42]

Agents

In Summer 1960, when temporary arrangements made for the previous General Election had expired, there were still a few constituencies without

[42] National Union papers, NUA 2/2/20, Central Council reports; Central Office file, CCO 500/24/2, 1950 Election; Tether, 'Clubs', 67; National Union papers, NUA 4/3/2, Executive Committee papers; Central Office file, CCO 3/6/4; West Midlands Area Council, 17 May 1952; Southport CA, 1960 and 1973–74 annual reports; Central Office constituency files, CCO 1/12/476 and 1/12/47; South East Area Council, 10 Dec. 1962; Central Office constituency files, CCO 1/11/93 and 1/11/123; Benney *et al.*, *How People Vote*, 38–9.

an agent – 46 only in England and Wales out of 546 constituencies, and few of these winnable. The position in Scotland was less healthy, since thirty-seven of the seventy-one constituencies had no professional agent. There were at that time thirty-two trainees at various stages of qualification, and moving into the profession, but there were already worries both about the overall wastage of trained professionals to other careers where remuneration was better, and about the drift of the best agents into the strongest constituencies – the Chief Organisation Officer lamented in 1962 that 'the vast majority of them wish to live and work in "Bournemouth"', while the Party needed more of them in Blackburn. These problems were real ones: a National Society of Agents survey in 1952 found that only 58 per cent of agents in post were on or above the recommended salary scales, 18 per cent were below scale rates but with allowances (such as a free house and car) that made up for shortfalls in salary, leaving 24 per cent who were 'not receiving adequate salaries'. It was difficult for Area Agents to press constituencies to pay their agents more if they had also to press for national quota payments, and if the constituency association in question had too little money to meet its obligations anyway; in 1965 in Wales it was noted that an increase in agents' scale rates had been afforded only by making reductions in quota payments. From the East Midlands the Area Agent reported in 1961, when an agent went off to run a pub, that

> his loss to the profession will not be great and his action has really saved the Association the problem of firing him. He leaves [the association] in a very low condition and really they need someone good there to pull them together, but whether I can talk them into this, plus the need to produce the money to pay such a man properly, I do not know.[43]

The result was that those who could pay could also get the pick of the agents, and this factor kept driving up both the agents' pay scales and what constituencies actually advertised when posts fell vacant. Tynemouth were paying £650 in 1956, £800 rising to £1,000 in 1958, and £1,500 by 1968; as early as 1962, the Area Agent had warned the constituency that an advert offering only the standard scale 'would be unlikely to get replies'. More affluent West Derbyshire, which was already paying its agent £825 in 1956, had to pay the scale rate of £1,250 by 1960, but with an additional 'personal merit' payment to keep an experienced agent from moving on; by 1965 that scale salary was up to £1,750 (now with an even larger merit payment on top). But not all constituencies could afford to join in the auction. When Maidstone sought a new agent at national scale rates in 1955, there were thirty-nine applicants, all but one of them fully qualified and several having wide experience; the

[43] National Society of Agents, Annual report, 1960; Ball, 'Local Conservatism', 280, 283; National Union papers, NUA 4/3/1, Executive Committee papers; Welsh Area Council, 20 Mar. 1965; East Midlands NSA branch minutes, 17 Jan. 1952; Central Office constituency file, CCO 1/14/273.

appointee had worked in London and East Anglian seats for twenty years. Basingstoke in 1966 had fourteen qualified applicants to choose from, and conducted a scrutiny of the short-list much as if they had been choosing a parliamentary candidate. When northern industrial seats were advertising they rarely had such a choice. Middlesbrough, a two-constituency association (one of them a critical marginal) had only two applicants for a vacancy in 1963, but decided on Area advice that it was not worth re-advertising. Offering £850 a year in 1964, West Fife attracted only a single, unqualified applicant. East Flint in 1958 also had one applicant, and appointed a trainee; when his failure to pass the examination led to another vacancy there were only three applicants. For the safe Labour seat of Swindon in 1958 replies to the advertisement were 'very unsatisfactory' and, after a series of temporary expedients, an untrained agent had to be appointed; at the next vacancy in 1965, there were four applicants, only one of whom was thought worth interviewing. In October 1966, nearly all Conservative and marginal constituencies had agents in post, but under half of Labour-held seats had Conservative agents.[44]

Stephen Pierssené, as General Director, had told the National Union in 1957 that 'basically . . . it is really an issue between a centrally-employed corps of Agents and the present free market', since all investigations into halfway schemes had foundered; 'experience has shown that the centrally employed corps of agents is incompatible to [*sic*] the constituencies'. The main reason for this fatalist view, as the Chief Organisation Officer minuted in 1961, was the fear that unless they were kept under pressure, constituencies might let up in the fundraising they had done so successfully since the 1940s, for the payment of their agent from any other source would remove their greatest incentive to find money, while the agent's awareness that his salary was not dependent on his own fundraising efforts would have a similar effect. William Urton did though explain in 1961 that 'we try to get the idea around that it is better not to go to the South coast but to take something difficult first of all', so that a young agent would at least have to learn the skills of the trade in a hard contest; he reported that Central Office money distributed by Area offices could influence employment decisions for agents, thirty-one being currently subsidised in their posts in marginals. Nevertheless, the obvious mismatch between experienced agents and marginal constituencies was a constant theme of discussions of the agents' profession from about 1960 and became steadily more shrill as the agents' overall numbers then declined. In 1960, the official scale of pay for agents started at £700 (almost exactly the then average weekly

[44] Tynemouth CA minutes, 8 June 1956, 19 Apr. 1958, and 20 Nov. 1968; Central Office constituency file, CCO 1/14/132; West Derbyshire CA minutes, 12 Jan. 1956, 1 Dec. 1960 and 1 Nov. 1965; Maidstone CA minutes, 17 Oct. 1955; Basingstoke CA minutes, 10 Oct. 1966; Middlesbrough CA minutes, 30 May 1963; West Fife UA minutes, 25 Feb. 1964; East Flint CA minutes, 6 Feb., 14 Mar. and 25 Oct. 1958; Swindon CA minutes, 15 Oct. 1958, 5 Nov. 1959 and 11 Mar. 1965; Pinto-Duschinsky, 'Constituency Associations', 105.

male income, though the availability of additional payments in kind made most agents better off than this in practice) and rose to £1,200 after eleven years' service, which was a slight fall in the real value of agents' income since the Woolton period. In order to get an experienced agent in 1961, King's Lynn had to pay on its own scale, starting at £1,100 and rising to £1,400, £100–200 of this being paid as 'marginal weighting' by Central Office; even this generous offer attracted only eleven applicants. Repeated efforts to raise agents' pay generally between 1963 and 1970 reflected these concerns, as did the eventual introduction of central employment in 1972, half a century after it had first been seriously considered.[45]

The National Society of Conservative Agents, with about five hundred members when Macmillan was Prime Minister, played an important role in maintaining the coherence of the profession, as did the *Conservative Agents' Journal*, for which Arthur Fawcett was editor from 1955 to 1960, fulfilling the role of national spokesman much as Elton Halliley had done in the previous generation; his book *Conservative Agent*, published in 1967, was the first attempt to explain to the wider Party how his profession had developed. Social events such as an annual golf tournament and cricket match, usually linked to the annual agents' refresher course at Swinton College (often oversubscribed, as it was in 1959) helped to maintain the profession's coherence. The NSA had another role in dealing with occasional disciplinary offences, as in the East Midlands in 1957 when the withdrawal of a member's certificate after financial irregularities was done by an NSA panel (rather than by Central Office which actually employed the man), and this confirmed the tradition of a self-governing profession that had been evolving since the 1920s. The status of agents was also reflected in the Prime Minister's attention to patronage; in 1959, eight members of the National Society received honours, one for a staff member at Central Office, two in Areas and five in the constituencies, which as the NSA Council put it, 'must surely be a record and this must give considerable satisfaction to all our members'. In the following year, the record was exceeded, when the NSA's list of 'friends and colleagues' who had been honoured ran to thirteen.[46]

Parliamentary candidates and their selection

There was much discussion in this period of the extent to which the parliamentary candidates – and hence Tory MPs – represented a wide enough cross-section of the nation. As Party Chairman, Lord Hailsham told the *Sunday Times* in 1959 that

[45] Central Office constituency file, CCO 1/11/411; Central Office Area correspondence file, CCO 2/6/1; NUEC, 5 May 1960; King's Lynn CA minutes, 2 Oct. and 10 Nov.1961.
[46] National Society of Agents, annual reports for 1958–60; East Midlands Area F and GP, 21 Feb. 1957.

we need people who understand industry and commerce, but we do not want the Party to be exclusively formed of them; and they should reach Parliament before they are too rigid and set in their ways, otherwise they find difficulty in adapting themselves to political life . . . I have read some critical comments which suggest that Conservative MPs and candidates are drawn from too narrow a social background. I do not believe that most of this criticism is justified.

Researching for the University of Chicago at exactly this time, Philip Buck confirmed that a better balance had been achieved; he concluded in particular that 'Conservative front-benchers in 1955 to 1959, show a wider diversity of education, a more varied range of occupations, and more governmental and political experience than their predecessors of 1918 through 1955. In these respects they reflect the changes which have been gradually appearing in the general character of political activity'. Donald Johnson, however, quoting Hailsham's remarks in 1967, and after Peter Paterson's *The Selectorate* (1967) had made more unflattering comments both on Conservative selection procedures and their output, reached different conclusions. To Johnson, the reforms of the 1940s had swept aside the business interests that had dominated Baldwin's Party but replaced them with

a more archaic concept – rule by the best people, the hereditary and social aristocracy, and those who by arduous endeavour have assimilated themselves to it. The Etonians in fact. So, while other nations moved into the twentieth century, Britain turned back the political clock to the days before the industrial revolution.

The businessmen of the Baldwin age had at least included in their ranks self-made men of humble origins, but the rising Tories of the 1950s were predominantly children of the professional classes; Iain Macleod's father was a doctor, Selwyn Lloyd's a dentist, Quintin Hailsham's a barrister, Reggie Maudling's an actuary, and Enoch Powell's parents were both school teachers. Angus Maude, the son of an army officer, had written in the *Political Quarterly* in 1953 that while recent reforms had 'certainly ended the period during which the Party was largely the mouthpiece of big business', it had generated an influx of middle- rather than working-class MPs.

It is common form at every Party Conference for someone to move a resolution calling on constituencies' Conservative Associations to adopt working class trades union candidates in areas where they may hope to win seats. There is nothing whatever to stop the local committees doing it, for there are no longer any financial disadvantages involved. Nevertheless they do not in fact do it, even in constituencies where there is a majority of working class people on the committee. The reasons are deep and somewhat mysterious. The selection committees do not appear to be imbued with any 'ruling class *mystique*'; more probably they are afraid that a working class MP, lacking the Labour-TUC ticket, will be an object of resentment among his fellows. It is, I think, also felt that entry into Parliament very soon makes a working class man middle class, so the benefits of such a choice do not long endure.

In support of the last point he drew attention to Labour's evolution from a party of miners into a party of university intellectuals in only two generations.[47]

Traditional routes to the top continued to lie through Oxbridge; Oxford in the 1940s (where Edward Boyle succeeded Margaret Thatcher as President of the Conservative Association), Oxford again in the later 1950s, and most spectacularly of all Cambridge in the early 1960s (where the celebrated 'Cambridge mafia' of Fowler, Clarke, Gummer and Howard coalesced), provided nurseries for whole generations of MPs, cutting their teeth in friendly rivalry in the university unions, in public speaking, and in Tammany Hall battles for control of student Conservative societies; at Kenneth Clarke's wedding, the best man was John Gummer and the guests included Leon Brittan, Norman Lamont and Michael Howard. Oxbridge also fulfilled its centuries-old role of integrating young men and women from outside the traditional elite into the manners and customs of their betters; the Ministers who ruled Britain in the early 1990s were the real heirs of the 1944 Butler Education Act, but it was the fact that the grammar schools which the Act fostered provided a pathway to Oxford and Cambridge that really opened career opportunities to Norman Fowler, Michael Howard and Kenneth Clarke. According to John Gummer, 'University was such a liberation, because we all came from backgrounds which had been pretty restricted up until then. We came from small towns and grammar schools where the attitudes were very traditional.'[48]

Much was made therefore of the two Tory MPs who could unequivocally be described as working class, Ray Mawby and Sir Edward Brown. Mawby was an electrician who had to brave parental as well as workmates' displeasure to become a Conservative, and Brown was a laboratory technician, so both were members of genuine industrial trade unions; the National Union Executive minutes described Brown (Chairman of the National Union in 1960) as 'a prominent trades unionist', which was perhaps overstating the case, but the Party certainly spared no effort to make his union membership well known. The fact that Mawby and Brown represented Totnes and Bath respectively, rather than constituencies in which the Party was more desperately chasing the votes of industrial workers, lends some credence to Maude's view that working-class candidates were not necessarily thought to be right for industrial seats, particularly when in the early 1950s trade unionists were still so suspicious of Tory intentions. When the Stoke-on-Trent North by-election of 1953 was fought for the Party by 'a Tory pitman' (splendidly

47 Donald Johnson, *A Cassandra at Westminster* (1967), 45–6; Philip Buck, *Amateurs and Professionals in British Politics* (1963), 94; Angus Maude, 'The Conservative Party and the Changing Class Structure', in *Political Quarterly*, vol. 24 (1953), 139.
48 Peter Riddell, *Honest Opportunism* (1994), 54, 62, 64, 70; Malcolm Balen, *Kenneth Clarke* (1994), 32, 46.

named Sam Middup), the Area Agent reported that he 'may have aroused hostility. There were frequent cries of "traitor" at the meetings' and no great enthusiasm for him among working-class Conservatives, of whom 'several suggested he was a stunt candidate'. When Middup was considered for the more mixed constituency of Newark though, he had strong backing from branch members in the mining parts in the constituency, but was so strongly opposed by the farmers and townsmen that, even after he had beaten all the other candidates, he could not get a majority vote to secure adoption; such candidatures clearly raised strong opinions on both sides. Neither cries of traitor nor claims of a 'horses for courses' stunt would be encountered in the rural South West, but there were other problems there. When Mawby was adopted for Totnes, with supportive pressure exerted by Woolton, the Tory MP for neighbouring Torquay was outraged, arguing in public as well as in private that 'Devon should be the preserve of "Gentlemen" and that trades unionists should not be selected', so that considerable efforts had to be made to keep him quiet, with only partial success. This embarrassment cannot exactly have encouraged other constituencies to select trade unionists, and Woolton told a correspondent that the Party's policy was perfectly clear, but that 'the difficulty is to get constituencies to follow the wise example set by Totnes'. In 1955, the Party claimed to have thirty-seven 'trade unionists' among its candidates for the coming General Election, but of these, ten were teachers and eight were journalists, while others were from such jacobin unions as the National Union of Bank Employees, the Guild of Insurance Officers, and the British Gas Staff Association; only ten were genuine industrial workers, four of them in the Amalgamated Engineering Union. But whatever their union, scarcely any were in seats where they might ever be elected. At least in part, this was because blue-collar workers did not generally have the presentational skill to convince selection committees that they ought to be selected on merit; when in 1952 Gravesend were considering their next candidate, the chairman 'reminded the members that, although some would very much like to see a Trade Unionist, it was practically impossible to obtain one'. The difficulty that Edward Brown had to find a seat, even with strong Central Office support, suggests that this was not the whole story. The number of trade union candidates fell steadily after the departure of Woolton, and after only eleven were selected for the 1964 Election, the Central Office strategy was largely abandoned anyway; by 1967, after the candidates' list had next been pruned and updated, even this list of several hundred *possible* candidates contained only eleven trade unionists.[49]

[49] Riddell, *Honest Opportunism*, 43; NUEC, 8 Sept. 1960, 9 Feb. 1961; Central Office General Director's by-election file, CCO 120/2/9; Central Office constituency file, CCO 1/12/250; Totnes CA minutes, 10 Apr. to 11 July 1953; Central Office file, CCO 4/6/14, Candidates; Gravesend CA minutes, 5 Mar. 1952; J.R. Greenwood, 'Promoting Working Class Candidates', in *Parliamentary Affairs*, vol. 41 (1988), 456.

Whatever the occupational background, there was clearly embarrassment occasioned by the extent to which Conservative MPs were predominantly male and Christian. The National Union Executive, debating the question in 1962, heard complaints that too little had been done to build on the Maxwell Fyfe reforms of 1948–49, and that far too few women and workers were being selected; on the defensive, the Vice Chairman responsible, Paul Bryan, reminded members how much better things were than before the War, but agreed that more could be done to educate association chairmen, since the steering of selections often lay largely in their hands. When the Executive returned to the question in 1966, it was reported that only 12 of 273 adopted candidates even in Labour-held seats were women, and again the Vice Chairman, now Geoffrey Johnson-Smith, pointed out that this was a problem that only the constituencies could solve. The number of women Conservative candidates fluctuated between twenty and forty in the 1950s and 1960s (of which between seven and fifteen were elected, the largest numbers coming in the better years, since women were less often selected for the safer seats); it was not until 1970 that the number of women Tory MPs first exceeded the figure reached in 1931 (for quite a lot of 'unwinnable' seats had actually been gained in the landslide of that year).[50]

If women barely held their own, Jewish candidates were less common than in the great heyday of Tory business MPs before 1939. In 1953, Henry Brooke, MP for Hampstead and hence for many of London's better-off Jewish electors, raised at the Executive what he called 'a growing feeling among the Jewish community that practising Jews have no chance nowadays of becoming Conservative Members of the House of Commons'; this started a nervous debate, and while there was general agreement that a lead should be given to remedy the situation, nobody could suggest action that would not be counter-productive; the secretary's note of the debate included the following contribution from a former chairman – '*Sir N. Colman*, Situation dangerous – what meant by giving lead? (Conservatives against Jews). Nothing must leak out from Executive that we are against Jews.' In 1954, there was correspondence over the selection for Derby North which was illuminating, even though conducted in code. As Vice Chairman John Hare suggested to the Area Office 'What about Sir Henry D'Avigdor Goldsmid. He is really rather good. His name may be against him but he is an extremely competent chap.' The Area reply was that 'his name would make things too difficult – none of them would be able to pronounce it, which might be a bit awkward!' This outraged Hare ('I nearly had an apoplectic fit') but, after calming down, he wrote back that 'I really think it very peculiar that Derby North should take this attitude about such a distinguished citizen. Surely they do not regard

50 F.W.S. Craig, *British Parliamentary Election Statistics, 1918–1970* (Chichester, 1971), 69; NUEC, 3 May 1962, 6 Jan. 1966.

gallantry in battle and distinction in both commerce and local government as meaning nothing?' The Deputy Area Agent then asked rather pointedly why such a 'distinguished citizen' had not been snapped up already by another constituency, which was largely beside the point since he had only just come on to the list, but she did succeed in getting him interviewed (but not selected) by Derby. He was shortly afterwards adopted for Walsall South and was in due course joined in the House by his equally distinguished brother, as MP for neighbouring Lichfield and Tamworth. In 1955, there was criticism of the inclusion of a question about religion on the candidates' standard application form, which Brooke's wife Dame Barbara had to field as Vice Chairman; the question had been raised by a Catholic, but she 'knew that the Jews feel very strongly about it too. . . . Of course we cannot prevent Selection Committees asking candidates what their religion is. But if it is not on the Central Office form we do not draw attention to any dissentient from the traditional cover of C. of E.' Donald Kaberry was not persuaded; the question about religion must stay on the form, and he argued indeed that since candidates would be asked anyway it was better not to give the impression that information was being concealed. At constituency level, there was sometimes less tact, as when Islington Tories reported in 1957 that they had interviewed only five of the six candidates suggested by Central Office as the sixth had been unwilling to come to a meeting during Passover. In view of all this concern, it is not surprising that Keith Joseph's narrow defeat at Baron's Court in 1955 was a disappointment, nor that the General Director should report in January 1956 that Joseph's selection for North East Leeds 'will give great satisfaction to the Jewish community which is of course strongly represented in his Leeds constituency'; it can have done Joseph's chances of selection no harm to have the Vice Chairman for candidates as the only other Tory MP sitting for a Leeds seat, but in Joseph's subsequent career, and in his rapid promotion to ministerial office on merit, the Party was able to signal a positive attitude – both to the Jewish community and to its own members; looking back from a senior position in 1970, Joseph nevertheless felt that being a Jew in the Party had 'forced him to fire on all six cylinders at once' in order to succeed. Nevertheless, there was still only one practising Jew among Tories in the House in 1959, and not till the 1970s did the figure return to the dozen or so characteristic of Baldwin's time. Given their positive historiographical reputation, it is a surprising reflection on the Maxwell Fyfe reforms, that, in freeing constituency selection committees to follow their own preferences, they may well have made the parliamentary party for a generation *less* representative of the nation than it had been before. The National Union notes on the conduct of selection procedures stopped far short of encouraging positive discrimination: they explained that the Party needed more minority, trade union and women candidates, but added that 'constituency associations have complete freedom in their choice. All that they are asked to do is to eliminate prejudice, if any exists, and to include women and trade unionists among the names under consideration. The final choice must be made on merit alone.'[51]

This approach in itself caused some heartsearching; when Falmouth and Camborne in 1955 asked for more women to be added to their list, the Vice Chairman was 'rather appalled at the scarcity of women candidates who can be described as really good'. Oliver Poole told Macmillan in 1957 that the quest for quality in candidates conflicted with the desire to be representative. 'With regard to candidates one is on the horns of a dilemma. If you get "Old Etonians" etc, there is criticism from the Press and from some of the Party; but if you get "red-brick" or working class candidates they tend to be inadequate in by-election campaigns and often of doubtful use in Parliament.' There were, he thought, only about twenty really good candidates, men of whom it could be said that they were more likely to get into the Government than were existing backbenchers, and despite there being five hundred on the list, it was short of the sort of 'people of real distinction' that were needed for such constituencies as South Kensington. He reported that he had his own very small priority list of people he was actually keen to see fighting winnable seats and would try to get them selected.[52]

One of those who was urged on a number of constituencies was Margaret Thatcher, who after fighting uphill contests in Dartford in 1950 and 1951 (impressing the agent, who reported to Central Office on 'her ability, intelligence and charm'), then had the utmost difficulty in getting selected for a winnable seat; asking Holborn and St Pancras South to consider Thatcher, John Hare tried to promote two special cases at once by claiming that she was a trade unionist as well as a woman, for 'she was at one time a member of the Association of Scientific Workers'. Another woman was selected for Holborn, and Thatcher continued her trawl of constituencies in the south east, invariably described as 'Mrs Denis Thatcher' in the minutes of selection meetings (a tribute to her husband's higher profile than her own in Tory circles at that time, as well as a convention that implied women's secondary role), before eventually getting selected for Finchley for the 1959 Election. Coming only second in Maidstone in 1958 was at least partly the result of her handling of the woman candidate question: the Area Agent reported that,

> she was asked about her ability to cope as a Member, having in mind the fact that she had a husband and a small family, and I do not think her reply did her a lot of good. She spoke of having an excellent nanny and that as a Member she would

51 National Union papers, NUA 4/3/1, Executive Committee papers; Central Office constituency file, CCO 1/10/215; South West Islington CA minutes, 7 May 1957; Central Office General Director's by-election file, CCO 120/2/48; Butler and Pinto-Duschinsky, 'Conservative Elite', 192; Michael Harrington, 'Sir Keith Joseph', in T. Stacey and R. St Oswald (eds), *Here Come the Tories* (1970), 78; Central Office file, CCO 4/5/13, Candidates.
52 Central Office file, CCO 4/6/14, Candidates; Central Office Chairman's department file, CCO 20/8/2, Corrrespondence with Macmillan.

have the mornings free (quite ignoring the fact that Members have committees in the mornings). She also spoke of having the week-ends free, and made no reference to spending time in Maidstone at the week-ends. She did say she would have to give up the Bar!

For male candidates, wives faced similar questioning, and needed to give the right answer; asked about her possible participation in constituency events when her husband was up for Rushcliffe in 1966, Mrs Kenneth Clarke replied, 'that it would always depend on satisfactory arrangements for baby-sitting', a response that generated a 'murmur of approval'.[53]

Women who succeeded in getting selected still faced considerable difficulties from the Tory electorate, as illustrated by Elaine Kellett's career; she was first selected for Nelson and Colne, the association executive self-consciously resolving that 'there is as a matter of principle no disadvantage in adopting . . . a woman candidate', but she did not win the seat in 1955. When she was then selected for South West Norfolk in 1959, Poole told Hailsham that 'there is no doubt that a woman candidate in a rural constituency in a by-election loses probably as much as 2%, merely for that reason'. When the result went largely according to the pattern of other contests in that year, the Central Office post-mortem nevertheless concluded that a woman candidate was a problem, 'particularly in a place like Norfolk, where some village women do not hold with mothers of four going into Parliament. Mrs. Kellett made great play about her children and some women were heard to cry "Why does she not look after them instead of going into parliament?" She's also too much of a fireball for Norfolk.' Kellett again failed to win the seat in the 1959 General Election, and then fought Buckingham unsuccessfully in 1964 and 1966, before winning Lancaster in 1970 and holding it for many years; was it a constituency that did not object to having a fireball as its MP, or did her Lancashire connections, as at Nelson and Colne in 1955, cancel out her gender difficulties? Peggy Fenner in Rochester and Chatham was reportedly popular both with the local association and with the press; on the advice of his Vice Chairman, Edward du Cann in 1966–67 took to mentioning her name whenever he was confronted with complaints about the lack of women candidates. By then there were many such complaints; in 1966, Joan Vickers MP and Lucille Iremonger (the wife of a Tory MP) demanded to see Heath to ask him to intervene to improve the representation of women in the Party. The most senior woman in the Party organisation, Susan Walker, thought that there was little point in wasting Heath's time: she argued that 'there is an attitude of mind in the constituencies which will not easily be shifted. The Walls of Jericho will not come tumbling down as a result of a blast or two from the Leader.' The constituencies' attitude to women was

---

[53] Central Office constituency files, CCO 1/9/17 and 1/14/423; Balen, *Clarke*, 73.

neatly summed up by Accrington's decision in 1963 that they would prefer a man as candidate, unless a woman applicant had 'outstanding qualities'.[54]

What was sought was often still traditional values and local ties; faced with a tricky by-election in Hereford in 1956, the Area Agent reported happily that 'David Gibson-Watt is an excellent choice. He won an MC [Military Cross] and two bars in the last war and farms in a neighbouring county.' Since the cumulative effect of such selections was the parliamentary Conservative party, there was still (as Julian Critchley has put it), 'something of "Chips" Channon about the Tory party. The great pre-war diarist would have felt at home', when Critchley was first elected in 1959 (Channon had in fact died, still an MP, only a year earlier):

> Call the roll in the 1922 Committee and it was all Knight, Frank and Rutley. A Tory MP was well-suited. The party still retained something of its pre-war sleekness; elderly gentlemen in Trumper's haircuts, wearing cream silk shirts and dark suits, Brigade or Old Etonian ties. They were all called Charlie. . . . In those days, everyone appeared to be related to everyone else . . . I was forever being accosted while sitting quietly in the Smoking Room . . . by nice old buffers who claimed to have known my father. They hadn't. I did not feel at home among so many Charlies.

He was not the only young MP to be struck by the outward appearances of their colleagues; David Walter wrote in 1964 of a fictional Tory whip that he 'had everything' so that he was 'plainly a Tory MP': 'Black hair, black moustache, [Brigade of] Guards tie. . . . Beautiful blue suit with large white tramlines reproduced in miniature on the shirt, thin gold watch chain. Large bloodstone signet ring, heavy cuff links. British warm on one arm.' These 'Charlies' were very often local to their county constituencies too, but locals were not always so welcome when once selected: when the candidate resigned in a Midlands seat in 1955, the Area office reported that this had been welcomed, for 'he was generally regarded as the biggest bore in the town and I have been told that numbers of business men gave up lunching at the Conservative Club as they were "fed up" with [his] conversation.' Central and local perspectives were frequently rather different; when Derby North picked a local man for the 1962 by-election, the Area Agent thought him 'ideal for the constituency', but the Vice Chairman's view at Central Office was only that he was 'as good as we'll find in Derby'. Local roots could certainly compensate for other shortcomings; in a 1958 by-election the Area Agent reported that the candidate, formerly the association chairman, was 'a bucolic, modest type of man who has spent his time explaining that he really is not up to the job. I understand that Dr. Hill told him this was unnecessary as the electors would soon find it out for themselves. He really is a very nice man

---

[54] Nelson and Colne CA minutes, 1 Sept. 1953; Central Office General Director's by-election file, CCO 120/2/83; Central Office Chairman's department file, CCO 20/48/1, Candidates; Accrington CA minutes, 25 Oct. 1963.

but clearly finds the whole business distasteful and his political knowledge is nearly nil. . . . He is a very likeable man and will I think make . . . an excellent Member of Parliament but as a candidate he is just not with us.' Fortunately, 1958 was not too bad a year for Conservative candidates, though it is only fair to add that he had the second best by-election result of the entire Parliament, and in his safe seat he never had to fight a real contest again in a lengthy parliamentary career. In May 1962, the National Union Executive held a general debate that illustrated many of the current concerns. Clyde Hewlett, shortly to become the Executive's chairman, said that 'he had some diffidence in raising this subject as it was a political atomic explosion at the present time', as a result of discussions of the Liberals' classless 'Orpington Man' candidates and of the relationship of parliament and business; he felt that 'nowadays too many MPs became Directors rather than too many Directors becoming MPs'; he did not welcome the professionalisation of politics that this indicated, in which 'the candidate today was a professional welfare officer'. Geoffrey Finsberg then reviewed the actual process of selection in the constituencies, in which 'the selection committee asked first for a list from Central Office, and then, from the long list sent, looked at the names, then the school, religion, and where the prospective candidates lived as a criterion for selecting them'; there was a crying need to educate the selectors to do their business better. The debate then as usual descended to the anecdotal; Sir Douglas Glover 'said . . . the whole problem was one of human nature. Some people were chosen because of their health record – and that was why he had been selected: his predecessors having given up for health reasons, the selection committee thought he looked healthy.' The reply to the debate by the Vice Chairman, Paul Bryan, was traditionally two-sided; first, it was a matter for the constituencies, who would not take his advice anyway, and so he contented himself with getting the overall list right, and he did this by asking himself of a candidate, 'what has he done with his life so far?' and 'Can I imagine him as an MP, or fighting an election?' Second, the Party should recognise how much progress had already been made since 1945, 'and he thought the intake in the House of Commons was better than before the War, and he went on to name some of the ministers who were of that ilk – Mr. Macleod, Mr. Powell and so on.' At times, Iain Macleod's representative significance to the Party seemed almost as great as Keith Joseph's.[55]

In 1961, embarking on the selection contest that produced Francis Pym as their MP, Cambridgeshire Conservatives were urged by a branch chairman to go for a candidate 'who was strongly anti-socialist and committed to a policy of supporting the interests of the upper and middle classes', but the Executive preferred the less contentious job description that their MP should

---

[55] Central Office General Diector's by-election files, CCO 120/2/42 and 76; Critchley, *Bag of Boiled Sweets*, 64; Walder, *Short List*, 43; Central Office constituency files, CCO 1/11/211 and 1/14/273; National Union papers, NUA 4/3/2, Executive Comitttee papers.

be 'friendly and confident but not cocksure'. North Cornwall decided in 1957 to seek a man between 35 and 45 who would be 'a good mixer' and able to get on well with Cornishmen. Lichfield and Tamworth in 1963 started looking for 'a young man with political knowledge, experience and wisdom . . . and preferably someone local'. York in 1967 decided that 'if possible the person selected should be between 30–45 years of age, have fought a Parliamentary Election, be a good mixer, be accessible, and have a "good" wife'. North Edinburgh in 1960, having to fight a by-election because the previous incumbent had been appointed to the Scottish bench (as was traditional for law officers), resolved not to select any candidate who could become Solicitor-General, and so halved its short-list by removing all the lawyers; the association then made a nonsense of this decision by selecting the heir to a peerage, whose inheritance of the title forced another difficult by-election in 1973. The thorough search for a new MP for Reigate in 1967–68 illustrates the rather more detailed preconceptions that selection committees worked to; the chairman suggested that they should be seeking a candidate who would serve for a minimum of ten to fifteen years and it was therefore agreed that the person selected should be between 30 and 50 years old. The Executive then decided to rate applicants against the following scoring system:

(1) Political experience (worth 25 points) – constituency and Area work, council service, Party employment
(2) Parliamentary/election experience (20) as MP or candidate – public speaking, journalism, writing, TV and radio
(3a) Education (40) – O levels, A levels, degree, courses, professional
(3b) Other qualifications (10) – travel, interests, responsibilities
(4) Marital status (10).

There was nothing in this meritocratic list about opinions, but several criteria against which 'soundness' and the skills needed in a parliamentary career could be measured. When Newark were selecting again in Summer 1957, the Vice Chairman for candidates was upset to find that they were including in their short-list a local YC who had voted against a crucial motion at a YC National Conference, and therefore 'did not support Sir Anthony over Suez'; the Area Agent was asked to bring this to the attention of the constituency and 'to do anything possible to prevent anything further developing about the gentleman mentioned'; the constituency association were unperturbed though by a principled act of rebellion and proceeded to select the man because 'his speech was aggressive, and this suits the mood of the Newark constituency'; the Standing Advisory Committee on Candidates (SACC) then endorsed the choice, but perhaps did so with equanimity only because Newark was then a safish Labour seat. When Horncastle selected Peter Tapsell in 1967, the Area Agent professed himself astonished, for he had thought Tapsell too moderate to win over a rather right-wing constituency party, and yet he had beaten a large number of promising aspirants – several of whom were themselves to reach the Commons. He had done this by exercising precisely the political skills that MPs would need for the rest of their careers: 'I have never seen a candidate sell himself with such efficiency and emotional appeal', so that his speech had constantly been interrupted by spontaneous applause and he had received a standing ovation. Despite remaining resolutely 'left wing', Tapsell was able to retain the strong backing of his local association.[56]

The processes described above could be short-circuited. Jim Prior embarked on a political career in East Anglia largely through personal contacts and had been selected for Lowestoft before even being interviewed by anyone at Central Office; the relative informality of the process may again have reflected the fact that Lowestoft was a Labour seat not then high on the list of the Party's targets. But when the local chairman almost got himself adopted for a Midlands seat in 1958 before getting SACC approval (and with the Area Agent convinced that he was 'not politically stable'), the need for central vetting was used as a lever to get him out of this winnable constituency: the SACC then graded him as suitable only to fight a tough industrial contest (in other words, to lose). Michael Howard was selected for Liverpool Edge Hill in February 1966 while not yet on the official list, and had come into the reckoning only through personal contacts, but had been chosen too late to go through the SACC process before parliament was dissolved; after the Election, the official list was to be reconstructed and Central Office insisted that Edge Hill must not readopt Howard until the SACC had seen his papers; in 1967 he was readopted, having easily gone through the formal procedures.[57]

Most candidates went through national vetting before appearing before any constituency for selection, however, which placed considerable discretion in the hands of the Party Vice Chairman. Aspirants were seen by him (or sometimes women applicants by the woman Vice Chairman) and, only if they passed this first stage, also by two members from a panel of MPs (chosen by the Vice Chairman); papers, references and reports on these interviews were carefully scrutinised, before the Vice Chairman reported to the SACC which (having not seen the applicants) could not easily question the recommendation, though local experience was also fed up through National Union channels into the SACC. In emergencies, the Vice Chairman would anyway act for the SACC, as when he told Pontefract that they could adopt the unlisted Mervyn Pike after she had so impressed Lady Maxwell Fyfe at interview. The verdict on first applications was often that the applicant should go away and get more experience, for example on a local council or by speaking for the Party at outside engagements. For those like John Hunt, who had already won

---

56 Cambridgeshire CA minutes, 20 Jan. 1961; North Cornwall CA minutes, 27 Mar. 1957; Lichfield and Tamworth CA minutes, 27 Feb. 1963; York CA minutes, 15 June 1967; North Edinburgh UA minutes, 4 and 8 Apr. 1960; Reigate CA minutes, 27 Nov. 1967; Central Office constituency files CCO 1/12/250 and 1/14/236.

57 Jim Prior, *A Balance of Power* (1986), 17; Central Office constituency files, CCO 1/12/296 and CCO 1/14/169.

the YCs' national speaking competition, this could seem a quixotic decision, but for such applicants it generally involved only a short delay.[58]

Once on the official list, approved candidates were given a number on a scale from one to ten which could then be communicated to association chairmen when selections were taking place; Area Agents reported back on how potential candidates had performed and were encouraged to suggest changes in the ratings. After Lincoln had selected in 1962, the Area Agent reported on one applicant that 'your rating is B.5, I would recommend B.6 or B.7' and Bryan minuted 'change'. Sometimes the advice was simply to keep a high flyer on the escalator; although Kenneth Clarke was not short-listed at Lincoln – being only 21 at the time – the Area Agent reported that he had performed impressively and justified his high rating; two years later, with an unexpected vacancy falling in because of the illness of the selected candidate for Mansfield in the same Area, Clarke became a candidate while still 23, and, again in the East Midlands Area, he was selected for the winnable Rushcliffe constituency in December 1966, still only 26. That scoring system was used to calibrate the lists of candidates sent to constituencies, so that relatively low-powered (or simply inexperienced) applicants were sent to mining seats and only the best were offered for plum seats in the suburbs and the shires. Central Harrow's 1962 short-list consisted entirely of people who were fighting safe seats by the time of the next General Election. When Wanstead and Woodford were selecting a successor to Winston Churchill in 1963, all the candidates offered by Central Office had scores of nine or above; few of these impressed though, and the association sought and obtained permission also to poach for interview (and then to adopt) Patrick Jenkin, who was already an adopted candidate elsewhere. When South Worcestershire were selecting in 1965, Gerald Nabarro returned to the House after an absence through illness by defeating eighty-six other applicants; the final short-list included, along with Nabarro himself, Maurice Macmillan, Peter Tapsell, and Jerry Wiggin, all of whom had safe seats by 1970; few have gone so far in describing such procedures as Nabarro, who not only named those he had defeated in his autobiography but actually published a photograph of them all taken on the day he won. Some such safe constituencies certainly had a high opinion of what they deserved; after reviewing a very long Central Office list that included some twenty future Tory MPs (half of them destined to be Ministers and one of them to be Chancellor of the Exchequer), the St Marylebone president reported in 1962 that the selection committee thought the list 'falls so very much short even of the mediocre'.

Not one of the candidates . . . is of sufficient calibre in normal times to merit the majority we have to offer. Have we no budding Walter Moncktons, John Andersons, or Oliver Lytteltons, to whom we can go and say (after meeting

---

58 Riddell, *Honest Opportunism*, 105–6; Central Office file, CCO 4/6/16, Candidates; Central Office constituency file, CCO 1/14/291.

the selection committee of course) 'Would you like a safe seat in Parliament, because we think you're the sort of man the Tory Party would like to have'?

Iain Macleod as Party Chairman could not suggest any 'budding Walter Moncktons', and after picking three candidates (none of whom was to have a parliamentary future), the selection committee had the indignity of having their selections referred back by the association Executive. In despair, they asked the sitting MP to stay on, but were ripe for the suggestion of Hailsham as a candidate of real national weight when he left the Lords in 1963. By contrast, even for a critical by-election in Luton in 1963, there was a rather more miscellaneous list with the lowest names scoring only three points. High Peak, a Conservative marginal in the North, was offered only seventeen names by Central Office in 1961, by no means all people with high scores or bright futures.[59]

The effect of this selective distribution of names was that the Candidates Department at Central Office was able to exercise an invisible steering of selections and to promote the interests of those that the Vice Chairman thought were the Party's best prospects for the future. Since association chairmen were under instructions not to reveal personal scores to the candidates (some of whom would no doubt have been outraged had they known their ratings) much depended on the nods and winks that the chairman, agent and (when present) the Area Agent offered to a selection committee. In 1953, the Rugby selection committee received information which not only listed and analysed the twenty-nine candidates suggested by John Hare, but also received guidance on each one, which the agent minuted as 'London's opinion'; these included some remarkable judgements of character, for a future Party Chairman was listed as 'a crank', and three other future MPs were respectively minuted as 'not impressed', 'not popular' and – most damning of all – 'able, but . . .?' None of those four was even interviewed by Rugby, but the limitations of such steering from the chair were indicated when Harold Soref, who 'London' was said to think 'excitable, difficult, vehement', was not only interviewed but also won the nomination (but not the seat). Rebels were not necessarily as unpopular in the constituencies as in Smith Square; though Billericay decided in 1956 that they had had enough of Richard Body (who therefore 'retired' in 1959), he was back in the House in 1966 for a Lincolnshire seat, voting against the Heath Government's European policy in 1971 and still there to resign the whip in 1993. Chairmen could be given actual gradings, but even the agents were not usually so favoured; when the Newbury agent rang Paul Bryan's assistant for advice in 1962, she noted that 'I did not give your "gradings" but said "average", "quite good", "fairly good" etc.'; on such casual conversations much might hang, and not

[59] Central Office constituency files, CCO 1/14/41, 1/14/94 and 1/14/374; Balen, *Clarke*, 49, 73; Central Office constituency file, CCO 1/14/75; High Peak CA minutes, 27 Jan. 1962.

always simply the promotion of merit. When Newbury selected John Astor, a man with extensive Berkshire connections as well as a famous name, Bryan reflected that he would 'never set the House of Commons on fire', but would be a real asset none the less, for he was 'a John Morrison type'; the parliamentary party needed such men just as much as future Ministers for Morrison was Chairman of the 1922 Committee at the time.[60]

There was in any case much self-selection, for not all candidates were willing to go forward for all types of constituencies; an extreme case was Easington in Durham, where the chairman in 1960 rejected a suggestion that the selection be left to 'a more representative meeting. He reported that there were no nominations for the candidature' anyway. A mining seat, miles from London, and with three or four years still to go in which the constituency would have to be nursed, was not an attractive prospect. Peckham in 1960 was offered seventeen names to consider, nine of whom were long-listed, four interviewed by the selection committee, and two then put forward to the Executive, which chose Toby Jessel, a young man typical of the type of candidate chosen to fight hopeless causes early in their careers. At that time, a strongly Tory constituency in the south-east would have been offered about a hundred names. Such young men gave good value to difficult constituencies with their enthusiasm, but naturally saw them more as stepping-stones to better things than as their object in life, and the constituencies recognised this; after selecting Anthony Royle when he was only 28 and not even yet on the approved list, and getting a good result in the 1955 Election, St Pancras North accepted in June that he must be free to go on to a better seat; he then fought but lost the Torrington by-election in 1958, got into parliament for Richmond in 1959 (still only 32 years old) and was a PPS a year later. For the 1959 Election, St Pancras North was fought by David Mitchell (31, on his way to Basingstoke), chosen over Norman St John Stevas (30, on his way to Chelmsford) and Geoffrey Howe (32, on his way to East Surrey via Bebington). In 1964, the candidate for St Pancras North was Kenneth Warren (38, on his way to Hastings) and in 1974 the constituency was contested twice by John Major (on his way to Huntingdon). St Pancras was of course a convenient seat to nurse for a young political aspirant who wished to keep contact with Westminster, and equivalent seats outside the south-east were less lucky. Offered only a limited list of names in 1956, Kettering chose eight for interview, seven of whom refused to come because they had better hopes elsewhere and the eighth was then not passed by the SACC; after the association had in 1961 adopted a London resident as its candidate and agreed to pay his travelling expenses to nurse the seat, there was an accumulation of criticism by 1963–64 about the lack of time that he was spending in the constituency; the chairman interviewed him and

---

60 Rugby CA minutes, 7 Sept. 1953; Pinto-Duschinsky, 'Constituency Associations', 240–5; Central Office constituency files, CCO 1/14/449 and CCO 1/8/182; Nabarro, *Nab 1*, 86.

extracted a promise that he would stand down, but the association then found that they were unlikely to get a 'top rate person' and had to go back to their adopted candidate and beg him to stand after all – in effect accepting that they could run only a part-time campaign with a candidate of whom a neighbouring MP reported that 'he knows nothing about farming and should never have been selected in the first place'. By 1972, when redistribution and improved Conservative performance in the Midlands had made Kettering a winnable seat, the association had a choice of ninety-six names. Regionalism operated rather differently in Scotland; when West Dunbartonshire, a highly marginal constituency, was seeking a candidate in 1962, they were offered only eight names by the Edinburgh office; since one of these had already been adopted elsewhere, the three others from west Scotland were under 36 and deemed insufficiently experienced, and the remaining four were all Edinburgh lawyers, the association abandoned selection procedures and simply invited someone who had not even applied to contest the seat.[61]

At constituency level, selections remained carefully controlled and involved a relatively small number of people; in 1958 and typically, Harrow West set up a selection committee consisting of twelve people, six of them association officers and the other six representing the branches, but in less healthy associations there could be as few as four involved in selection. When Norman Hunt on BBC radio suggested in 1961 that only about forty of a constituency association's five thousand members would ever have any actual *choice* in selections, the General Director argued that this was irrelevant, since all those doing the selection knew well that the candidate selected had to attract the support of all Tory voters; in the respect they accorded to political skills as such, they were indeed doing so. There were few disposed to follow the example of Brighton Kemptown in 1965 or Reigate in 1968 in offering a short-list to a full general meeting of members (something close to the YCs' demand for full primaries, made at the 1968 Party Conference) rather than narrowing the options to one well before that stage. Guildford in 1965 adopted a common procedure; six weeks were taken by the small selection committee in considering the names of sixty-six applicants, eighteen of whom were interviewed over two days; seven were then seen a second time and put through their paces with prepared speeches on education and the National Health Service (NHS), after which they were again interviewed, with their wives also now present, and the list reduced to three; the Executive, with forty-three present, interviewed these final three and overwhelmingly selected David Howell as prospective candidate; he was then unanimously adopted by a general meeting of the association at which the membership saw no other

---

[61] Easington CA minutes, 29 Feb. 1960; Peckham CA minutes, 30 Mar. to 29 June 1960; Central Office constituency files, CCO 1/11/32, 1/12/32 and 1/14/76; Kettering CA minutes, 20 Apr. 1956, 29 May 1961, 13 July 1964, 14 Feb. 1972; Central Office constituency file, CCO 1/14/300; West Dunbartonshire UA minutes, 23 May 1962.

candidate. But general meetings were clearly still seen as important even if they did not exercise much actual choice – just as Conference was important in a demonstrative rather than a deliberative way; the Bradford West association could attract only about 24 to its routine annual general meetings, but 115 turned up to the general meeting in 1964 to readopt Arthur Tiley as candidate. At whatever level, selection decisions were rarely made on grounds of the candidates' views on policy matters; Austen Ranney's conclusion in 1965 was that 'most Conservatives speak of wanting a man of character – solid, loyal, dependable in a tight spot, not flashy or brilliant', and this is borne out by the local evidence, as is the common view that associations were fierce in defence of their independence. Shoreditch and Finsbury in 1960 agreed by five votes to four not to ask about the religious views of potential candidates, but were then offered an even more radical option in self-restraint. 'Cllr. Jones suggested that when members interviewed candidates fewer questions be put regarding their political views, on the grounds that they must be politically sound as they had been passed by the Standing Advisory Committee on Candidates. This did not meet with general approval.' The SACC was though a valuable safeguard against unsuitable candidates, or selections that might have departed from the proper procedures; when Robert Hudson got a peerage in 1951, he consulted the General Director to see if Central Office had anyone that they wished to 'force' on Southport; Pierssené explained that such things were not done, but agreed that the front-runner of the two locals going for the selection might be unsuitable because of marital problems, noting also that 'he is a Mason and the other is not, and about half the selection committee are Masons'; to be on the safe side, Southport were reminded that any candidate needed SACC approval 'beforehand', and they took the hint and chose a different man altogether.[62]

It was generally believed that, once constituencies were choosing from within the official list, there was little more that Central Office could do to influence the outcome, assumed indeed, as John Biffen put it in 1965, that Central Office knew that any such intervention would be 'the "kiss of death"' to the hopes of selection of a candidate that was so favoured; political scientists who investigated selection processes in the 1960s reached the same conclusion. This ignores though the discreet steering that took place in compiling the lists of candidates from which local committees could choose, and the effects of verbal (and usually unminuted) advice on the strengths and weaknesses of particular applicants. If Central Office had tried to bounce a local association

[62] Central Office General Director's file, CCO 120/1/5, Broadcasting; Kelly, *Conservative Conferences*, 30; Riddell, *Honest Opportunism*, 108; Peter Paterson, *The Selectorate* (1967), 140–6; Patrick Seyd, 'Democracy within the Conservative Party', in *Government and Opposition*, vol. 10 (1975), 219; Guildford CA minutes, 4 June to 14 July 65; Bradford West CA minutes, 24 Sept. 1964; Shoreditch and Finsbury CA minutes, 23 June 1960; Central Office constituency file, CCO 1/9/137.

into selecting a favourite candidate, then that would certainly have been counter-productive, but there remained channels through which influence could be exerted. It was largely by controlling the national list from within which constituencies had to choose that the Party's leaders, and especially the half dozen men who were Vice Chairmen for candidates between 1951 and 1970, changed the entire character of the parliamentary party into a team of full-time career politicians very different even from the post-Maxwell-Fyfe parliamentary party in the 1950s; it was through the SACC that the voluntary Party gave its assent to that process of change and it was in their rising expectations of political skills among those who appeared before them for selection that the constituencies implemented it. But at no time was the issue actually the subject of a serious Party debate.[63]

In 1965, Julian Critchley derided this system of selecting the nation's rulers as 'government by greengrocer', but he also detected a reason for its survival: 'a bargain has long been reached in which the Party leaves the choice of candidate to the constituencies, while they, in turn, refrain from meddling in policy'.[64] The balance of forces so described may indeed be taken as confirming that the implicit concordat between national leadership and local autonomy that existed by the 1920s was still the norm by which the Party operated in 1960, and not only in selecting candidates. In organisation, in finance, in the work of the SACC and in policy formation, most active Conservatives were happy to leave the initiative in the hands of their national leaders and organisers. But in matters that directly affected the running of the local structures – selecting candidates and agents, recruiting members, politics in local government, quota payments and how the constituency associations themselves were run – there remained a fierce insistence on localism which the national organisers could break down only when bearing gifts. Increasingly though, the withering of the Party at the bottom as membership continued to fall made the Party's national leaders in Central Office and the National Union impatient with their inability to determine what happened lower down; the increased need for quota payments from the localities led more activists to question what the money was being spent on; and the apparent failure of successive governments to deliver traditional Tory policies in 1963–64 and 1972–73 rendered more and more of the rank and file increasingly unwilling to trust their leaders on matters of policy. The implied concordat here described would shortly be under attack from both ends.

---

[63] Biffen, 'Conservative Party', 187; Ball, 'Local Conservatism', 266.
[64] Julian Critchley, 'Government by Greengrocer', *The Economist*, 5 Feb. 1965.

Chapter 3

'Modernise with Macmillan', 1960–62

Losing momentum in Government

During 1960, when the Party could coast along, practically without opposition and enjoying remarkable popularity, there was a relaxation of grip in both policy and presentation that made a difficult problem to remedy – perhaps an impossible one – when things began to go seriously wrong in 1961–62. The Conservatives lost the tide before they were even aware that it had turned; in March 1960, Butler at the ACP complacently 'summarised the present political situation, five months after the General Election, with the Labour Party still in considerable disarray and the country thoroughly bored by clause 4, and the Conservatives quietly working away without any great publicity'. But by 1962, it was a commonplace of both press and Party that the country had now become 'bored' with the Macmillan regime; his own view in 1962 was that 'the public really are tired of us – of our faces, our caricatured faces, our appearance'. This decline needs to be considered both from the viewpoint of Macmillan and his Party and from the outside.[1]

In his memoirs, Macmillan diagnosed the problem acutely:

> Ministers, once they are 'dressed in a little brief authority', tend to forget the means by which they have obtained office and may hope in the future to achieve a renewed tenure. In Opposition the leaders and the rank and file of a Party are closely bound together. . . . But when a Government is firmly seated in power its relations, both with the back-benches and with the Party organisation, become at once more remote and more delicate.

Between 1957 and 1959, the adversity that the Party faced produced the same binding together as occurs in opposition. But this was not so after a big majority was achieved in 1959, and Macmillan was himself to an extent going through the motions after 1959. Harold Evans, his press secretary, noted in March 1960 that 'the Prime Minister no longer feels any compulsions in his public relations and has largely lost interest', though with dangerous confidence he added that 'the public relations work is so thoroughly organised that it is simply a matter of pressing buttons'. Television appearances in 1960–61 suggest that the smoothly-oiled machine

---

[1] Advisory Committee on Policy minutes [hereafter ACP], 2 Mar. 1960; Michael Cockerell, *Live from Number 10: The Inside Story of Prime Ministers and Television* (1988), 82.

of 1958–59 was no longer fully in operation, for the writing of scripts became a difficult and contentious business. In place of the premier's courting of the press before the Election, there came an increasing resentment that even proprietors of friendly papers should have any call on his time. Anthony Sampson's explanation of the decline in Macmillan's public image was that the Prime Minister came to overact his role, playing along with the stereotype so far that it became impossible to break the habit: this was dangerous in the new world of television that needed a constant supply of fresh images for easily-jaded palates. Julian Critchley recalls that 'even as left-wing a Tory as Humphry Berkeley took to calling him "the old actor-manager", and there was something of the Donald Wolfits about the Prime Minister.' Perhaps too, there is something in Richard Crossman's 1970 verdict that Macmillan's gambler's luck simply ran out.

> Macmillan had a profoundly cynical view of politics and he thought it was only worthwhile being there if you took epoch-making decisions. 'Right', he'd suddenly say, 'get out of Africa' – you know that's quite a thing to decide; and the 'wind of change'; or 'go to Suez' or, even more surprisingly after three days, 'get out of Suez'. He was a tremendous card in that way. . . . A man of that kind is bound to catch himself sooner or later because one of these gambles won't come off, and an unsuccessful gamble is, of course, more devastating than four successes. . . . In politics you're very lucky if you have more than three or four years when the going's good.

James Margach's explanation of Macmillan's decline, expressed by quoting the view taken by both Peel and Baldwin – that five years at the top was the most anyone could hope for without losing effectiveness – comes near to the same point.[2]

After the great recovery of 1957–59, there was an understandable tendency to take success for granted, and to enjoy the grand gesture: John Boyd-Carpenter recalled an occasion on which he was lunching with Macmillan at the Carlton Club, enjoying his wit, his company and the port: 'at this point his admirable Parliamentary Private Secretary, Knox Cunningham, rushed in to tell him that he had only just enough time to get to the House to answer Prime Minister's Questions. . . . Macmillan paused only for a moment in the story he was telling, waved the folder aside, and said to Knox Cunningham, "Ask Mr. Butler to answer them for me".' Cunningham was in any case a strange choice to be the Prime Minister's eyes and ears in the parliamentary party, and backbenchers like Humphry Berkeley noticed that a Prime Minister who liaised with them through Martin Redmayne and Knox Cunningham, as Chief Whip and PPS respectively, was being less well served than by

[2] Harold Macmillan, *Pointing the Way, 1959–1961* (1972), 4; Harold Evans, *Downing Street Diary: The Macmillan Years, 1957–1963* (1981), 111; Alistair Horne, *Macmillan, 1957–1986* (1989), 262–3; Cockerell, *Live from Number Ten*, 77, 80; Julian Critchley, *A Bag of Boiled Sweets: An Autobiography* (1994), 85; Alan Thompson, *The Day Before Yesterday* (1971), 176; James Margach, *The Anatomy of Power* (1978), 120.

their predecessors Edward Heath and Anthony Barber before 1959. There was also an increasing tendency to interfere in the work of Ministers, where in the early days there had been discreet steering at Cabinet. When from 1960 Macmillan had Home as Foreign Secretary and Lloyd as Chancellor he had compliant colleagues in the two busiest offices and an increased temptation to decide both domestic and foreign policy in detail; writing privately at the time of his retirement in 1963, Macmillan himself referred to 'the present policies' of the Treasury and Foreign Office, 'which I initiated, approved and largely directed'. As Alistair Horne points out, dissension in the Government forced him also to become his own 'Minister for Africa'; when Butler was asked to take over this last responsibility in 1961, the Cabinet Secretary told him that the impasse over Africa was exhausting the Prime Minister and threatening the whole system of Cabinet government; when Butler then accepted 'the Central African tangle', Macmillan wrote to say that 'it is very patriotic of you to do it', for 'you will be like Bonar doing all the work for Lloyd George'. Butler for his part privately assured himself that he was *not* taking it on 'because of frustration after 9 years of *acting* head of Government', but because he believed that the Indian experience at the start of his ministerial career might give him a lever on the African situation. The introduction of twice-weekly Prime Minister's Questions in the Commons following the report of a Commons Select Committee on Procedure in 1959, and Macmillan's own decision to be the first Prime Minister who could be interviewed by journalists on the record, both greatly increased the extent to which the Prime Minister became the frontman for all of his Ministers' policies. The cumulative burden that this placed on a man now past the age when most retire, and after ten years of continuous ministerial strain, meant that he was often exhausted; Woolton, meeting Macmillan in May 1960, noticed that he was 'physically and mentally tired', but was pleased to note that unlike Churchill when he reached the same state Macmillan remained polite. He was enjoying it too. Butler noted in January 1963 an occasion when he and Macmillan 'had a short talk on the awfulness of going into business & that politics despite its dangers was the greatest game in the world. He said as PM "strain is awful, you have to resort to Jane Austen . . ."' The second part of these remarks is the sheerest self-parody, but the first part sheds a sinister light both on Poole's attempt to reassure the Party's industrial subscribers that their money was in good hands since the Prime Minister was himself an experienced businessman, and on the sincerity of Macmillan's own adage – 'exporting is fun'.[3]

3 John Boyd-Carpenter, *Way of Life* (1980), 156; Humphry Berkeley, *Crossing the Floor* (1972), 82; Horne, *Macmillan*, 245, 493; Larry Siedentop, 'Mr. Macmillan and the Edwardian Style', in V. Bogdanor and R. Skidelsky (eds), *The Age of Affluence* (1970), 46; Butler note, 10 Mar. 1962, Macmillan to Butler, 9 Mar. 1962, and Butler note, 11 Mar. 1962, Butler MSS G38; Peter Hennessy, *Whitehall* (1990), 60; Margach, *Anatomy of Power*, 118; Woolton MSS, diary, 5 June 1960; Butler note, 8 Jan. 1963, Butler MSS G40; Central Office file, CCO 4/7/23, Central Board of Finance; Macmillan's 1963 memorandum is in PREM 11/5008.

If Macmillan remained polite, he also became more aloof. He was fond of pointing out that as the grandson of a crofter who was also the son-in-law of a Duke, he 'had it both ways', but as time went by the ducal side acquired predominance, even if there always remained a radical, modernising passion beneath the surface. George Hutchinson saw in him a Whig grandee who had strayed into the Tory Party but never quite belonged, a view that was often and fiercely maintained by Enoch Powell who, unlike most Conservatives, knew precisely what he meant by his own 'Toryism'; to Powell, then and later, Macmillan was 'Superwhig', a cynical manipulator of class politics with no Tory belief in traditional institutions. John Grigg felt that in Macmillan there was a permanent contradiction between intellectual assurance and emotional insecurity which produced a tendency to seek a home in a 'kind of enveloping hierarchical establishment. . . . At the time he was Prime Minister . . . he was increasingly finding it in the world of great houses in the patrician establishment of the country.' In this context it was noticed how freely honours became available to backbenchers: about eight Tory MPs a year became knights or baronets, though overall Macmillan created no more peers – and rather fewer knights – each year than either Churchill or Attlee had done. There was a big expansion in the Order of the British Empire and a steady flow of these lesser honours through the Party machine; about a tenth of *all* MBEs, OBEs and CBEs went to Conservative Party workers, more than a hundred a year.[4]

The real focus of criticism on this front was occasioned by ministerial appointments: the offer of a job to his son was generally recognised as justified on merit, but the placing of his brother-in-law, the Duke of Devonshire, at the Commonwealth Relations Office, had a distinctly quixotic air. Baldwin's loyalty to Harrow School in making the Cabinet of 1923 was eclipsed by Macmillan's loyalty to Eton in his own patronage. Even after the axe was wielded in July 1962, in order to give the Government a modern image, half of the new Cabinet were Etonians. The greatest outcry had been two years earlier: the announcement in July 1960 that Macmillan was sending the Earl of Home to the Foreign Office provoked outrage; the *Daily Mail* told Macmillan 'to stop making a fool of himself', and the *Sunday Express* objected to the appointment of 'this unknown and faceless earl'. Lady Home's loyal (and prophetic) reaction was that 'as far I am concerned he is able enough for any post in the Government, even Prime Minister'. Perhaps it was because Home's appointment did turn out rather well that Macmillan encouraged an even more aristocratic look in his Government over the following two years. It was precisely this fondness for men of breeding that led some to wonder

4 Boyd-Carpenter, *Way of Life*, 151; Anthony Sampson, *Macmillan: A Study in Ambiguity* (Harmondsworth, 1968), 174, 177–8; George Huchinson, *The Last Edwardian at Number 10* (1980), 22; Enoch Powell, *Reflections: Selected Writings and Speeches of Enoch Powell* (1992), 139; Thompson, *Day Before Yesterday*, 176; Central Office file, CCO 4/8/363, Titles.

if the Party of 'one nation' was heading in the right direction, and which provided the most deadly line of attack. Anthony Sampson's 1962 book, *The Anatomy of Britain*, tabulated the extensive Churchill and Cavendish family relationships in the 'establishment'. A Minister remarked to Sampson that 'I don't think Harold appoints aristocrats to show off; he's used to their company. But I don't think it does him any good.' Christopher Hollis wrote polemically (but since he was a former Tory MP he was much quoted for saying so), that 'there has been nothing like it in England since the days of the eighteenth century Duke of Newcastle, and the record today is unparalleled in any country in the world, save only Laos, Saudi Arabia, and perhaps the Yemen'. Such things were being said – and read – about Harold Macmillan throughout the second half of his premiership. There was, Sampson himself wrote, an 'extraordinary periphery of peers with ancient titles who form a kind of guard of honour to Macmillan's ministry – the Marquess of Lansdowne, the Earl of Perth, the Earl of Dundee, Lord Carrington and Lord Waldegrave'. The inclusion of Carrington on that list is significant, for one effect of Macmillan's undifferentiating conviction that the English love a lord was that by appointing so many he made it difficult for the ones who had political talent to be taken as seriously as they should have been. Did he even care about this? Sampson quoted Macmillan's insouciant response in 1959 to charges that he was addicted to snobbery: 'Mr. Attlee had three Old Etonians in his cabinet. I have six. Things are twice as good under the Conservatives'.[5]

Macmillan probably only affected indifference to attacks on him: he noted in his diary when criticised for making Devonshire a Secretary of State that 'a Duke of course is always fair game'. Indifference masked though an exaggerated sense of his own vulnerability. He had a parliamentary party ready to express its individuality in strong words and occasional contrary votes, as much the result of long-term trends as of anything inherently to do with 1959–63; he also had unrelenting critics on the backbenches like Nigel Birch and Lord Lambton, and from 1961 there was in the Monday Club an organisation whose very existence challenged a central policy objective of his Government. But although such critics were never more than a small and temporary threat to his majority, the Prime Minister's diary shows how anxious he was about every parliamentary vote and how easily he could convince himself that ex-Ministers were plotting his downfall. Initially his fears centred on the trio who had resigned from the Treasury in 1958, and their good conduct was sought by dangling a return to office before their eyes. The *Sunday Express* reported in 1959 'a message which comes rustling along the Tory grapevine', as it was presumably intended to: 'it

5 Lord Home, *The Way the Wind Blows* (1976), 142–4; John Dickie, *The Uncommon Commoner* (1964), 125; Kenneth Young, *Sir Alec Douglas-Home* (1970), 121–2; Evans, *Downing Street Diary*, 117; Anthony Sampson, *The Anatomy of Britain* (1962), 34–5, 88, 175, 328.

tells how Mr. Harold Macmillan . . . often speaks kindly of his former Chancellor. Musing, as he fingers his moustache, "One day we shall have to have Peter back".' When in 1960 Thorneycroft and Powell did rejoin, *The Times* detected the 'delicate Macmillan touch' in the appointment of these two guardians of the public purse to big spending departments, though the necessity of matching newcomers to available vacancies may well have been at least as important a motivation. They were airily described by Macmillan at the Party Conference as 'one or two who have recently returned to us – wandering souls but happily not lost'. Each reshuffle brought new and equally imaginary plots from the dispossessed; Butler seemed to be the threat in 1961–62, Selwyn Lloyd in 1962–63, and in each case the supposed plotters were offered the prospect of promotion next time. It could all too easily seem like a determination to hang on at all costs. Butler at least, who had gone through the same thing with Churchill in 1951–55, saw it in exactly that way.[6]

Losing momentum in the organisation

The first half of the 1959 Parliament was also a missed opportunity in the Party organisation. With Hailsham removed from Central Office and Poole returning to the City, Macmillan appointed Butler, who for two years was Party Chairman as well as Home Secretary and Leader of the Commons. Butler was by this time a Party man who could keep the wheels turning without undue effort; he was also temperamentally unlikely to steal the Prime Minister's thunder by upstaging him as Hailsham had done, but by the same token he did not have it in him to provide the vulgar flag-waving that the Party had come to expect. It does not do to overstate the limitations in Butler's political style, but by this time he was like Macmillan to an extent acting out a self-parody of his earlier career in which he was 'safe' rather than 'dynamic'; Anthony Sampson recounted a 'favourite parliamentary story' of Butler's instinctive response to being asked the time: he 'would congratulate the honourable member on his question, discuss different measurements of time, heartily endorse the importance of timekeeping, but fail actually to give the answer'. It is not clear whether the most significant part of this story was that most MPs recognised Butler in the parody, or that Butler was said to enjoy it himself. In any case, the placing of three posts in one pair of hands left little time for visits to constituency or Area functions, at least while parliament was sitting; he confessed to Sir Fitzroy Maclean in May 1961 that Scottish meetings were quite impossible for him. The combination

6 R.J. Jackson, *Rebels and Whips: Dissension, Discipline and Cohesion in British Political Parties* (1968), 162, 164; Horne, *Macmillan*, 332, 455; Central Office file, CCO 3/6/16, Monday Club; Macmillan, *Pointing the Way*, 363; Andrew Roth, *Enoch Powell, Tory Tribune* (1970), 215, 228, 235.

of the Party Chairmanship with the Leadership of the House was a strange one anyway, for one post required the cultivation of good relations with the Opposition while the other required him to denounce them at every opportunity. Nor was it especially helpful for the Party Chairman to receive an annual battering at the Party Conference for his own policies at the Home Office. In 1961 for example, there were sixty-five constituency motions on law and order, most of them critical of Butler's policy; in this sense even such triumphs as the 1961 debate, when a helpful amendment moved by Geoffrey Howe persuaded the Conference to stop short of disowning Butler's views on corporal punishment, were pyrrhic victories. Although the holding of the Party Chairmanship by the second man in the Government seemed to enhance its standing, and (thought Macmillan) would prove that the Party would remain progressive after its 1959 victory, it was probably the one post of Butler's three that most suffered from his over-stretch. Things ticked over well enough, but the opportunity was lost of using victory in 1959 to repair serious faults in the organisation, as for example in the lamentable state of organisation in Scotland.[7]

Hailsham wrote after the 1959 results showed a Labour swing in Scotland that 'the matter now brooks no further delay. Their organisation is horrible.' Something of the indifference that Conservatives were increasingly to show for Scottish sensitivities was indicated by Macmillan when, in the aftermath of losing Scottish seats in 1959, he promoted one of the defeated candidates to the Lords and allowed him to take the name of the constituency that had just refused to elect him. The retirement of Colonel Blair as political secretary to the Scottish Party Chairman in 1960 provided an opportunity of modernisation that was not taken; instead his departure worsened the deteriorating relations between the Chairman's Office (in Edinburgh) and the Scottish Unionist Association (in Glasgow) which now made the adoption of any coherent strategy in Scotland more problematic, and Macmillan had to appoint a series of peacemakers when rows erupted over both personalities and finance; the practice followed since 1951, whereby the Party Chairman in Scotland was also the Secretary of State for Scotland, did not allow a separate identity to be claimed for the Scottish Party at times when the Government was unpopular. Lord Aldington, who as Sir 'Toby' Low acted as Butler's deputy at Central Office, told the National Union General Purposes committee in November 1962 that 'the organisation in Scotland looks ghastly from here and when you get there it is worse. Michael Noble is doing great things – they now have a public relations officer. The G[eneral] D[irector] does everything he can from his angle. Please would everybody help Scotland

---

7 Horne, *Macmillan*, 215; Anthony Howard, *RAB: The Life of R.A. Butler* (1987), 269, 283–4; Sampson, *The Anatomy of Britain*, 84–5; Geoffrey Howe, *Conflict of Loyalty* (1994), 33; Butler to Maclean, 10 May 1961, Butler MSS, H26; National Union papers, NUA 2/2/26, Central Council reports; Gerald Sparrow, *Rab: Study of a Statesman* (1965), 162–3, 169–71; Lord Butler, *The Art of Memory: Friends in Perspective* (1982), 96.

whenever possible.' Quite what Sussex or Staffordshire Tories were meant to do for the Scots which Central Office could not do was not explained.[8]

The same lack of progress was true of the English cities; Butler wrote in March 1961 that 'when I first came [to Central Office] I said I was not satisfied with the control of the cities. I have now had striking evidence from Manchester and Birmingham that we are not really in control of the situation. I do not think we can go on like this.' Two years later, Macleod was writing as Party Chairman that the Area chairman was 'concerned about Birmingham, which is as you know a private empire within the Area. It has always kept itself to itself and this is because of organisation and finance. They collect money by hiring people to do it on commission . . . and this is not very suitable for a voluntary organisation'. The problem was that the flight of the rich from the cities had left the city parties without the resources with which they had been created, as Martin Maclaren MP reported to Selwyn Lloyd in 1963, citing the case of Bristol:

> The difficulty from which we suffer, and which we share with the other cities, is that many of the more successful businessmen go and live in the country and are then keen to play the country gentleman, and pay their money to a county association rather than to a city where their money is made.

A forced reorganisation would be highly contentious though, and would be opposed by those who still ran these private empires; reform of the city parties had to wait till 1967–72.[9]

An important exception to the general loss of momentum in the Party organisation after 1959 was at the Research Department, which retained its cutting edge and its readiness to think in new ways. This emerged most clearly from the Psephology Group that Fraser began to convene in October 1960, the purpose of which was to evaluate the technical reliability of survey evidence and to analyse for the Party the output of the infant science of election studies. Its main findings influenced Conservative strategy over the next few years and might usefully be summarised. First, the group's investigations revealed that the electorate contained a latent Labour majority, 'sufficient if activated to cause heavy Conservative defeat'; the victories of 1955 and 1959 had been won against this inherent tendency of most of the electorate to think of Labour as its natural party of allegiance; this sober finding contrasted sharply with the 'Must Labour Lose?' tendencies in the public and academic debates of these years. Second, it was found that three-quarters of Tory voters were aged between 30 and 64, and that these were also the ones with the most fixed opinions; the youngest and oldest electors were not only the most

---

[8] Central Office Chairman's department files, CCO 20/17/1, 1959 General Election, CCO 20/16/1, Correspondence with Vice Chairmen; P.G. Richards, *Patronage in British Politics* (1963), 228; J.T. Ward, *The First Century: A History of Scottish Tory Organisation* (Edinburgh, 1982), 38; National Union papers, NUA 5/2/1, F and GP papers.

[9] Central Office files, CCO 4/9/118, Recruiting, CCO 500/11/10, Recruiting reports 1962; Central Office General Director's file, CCO 120/4/11, Selwyn Lloyd Inquiry.

volatile but also the ones least likely to vote; such demographic trends as the 1947–49 bulge in births would place the Party increasingly at the mercy of more unstable younger voters by the 1970s. Third, there was a great paradox in the class–party polarity: 'though the divisions between the classes have narrowed, people are voting more by class than before the war.' The key borderline for the Party to watch was that between the working and lower-middle classes, for 'the tendency towards a more middle class society has a long way to go', and 'it is still from the working class two-thirds that we get more than half of our votes, and have to if we are to win an Election'. Finally, the key issue in winning over the votes of the socially-mobile was housing, rather than consumption patterns in general: 'it appears that as far as the property-owning democracy is concerned, "l'appétit vient en mangeant".' The key fact to remember was that 'of all working class adults who do *not* vote Labour, a third live in houses which are either already owned by them or are being bought' (which was true only of a very much lower proportion of the Labour-voting working class), while half of all Labour-voting working-class electors lived in council housing (as did far fewer working-class Tories). This solid finding underpinned the Conservatives' steady escalation of pledges in the housing auction, up to 400,000 completions in 1964 and half a million in 1966; it also gave some advance indication of the damage that would be done to Tory electoral prospects in 1961–62 (and again in 1972–73) when high interest rates damaged the interests of young married house-purchasers, and the further damage done by uncertainty about Party policy on land in 1963–64; and it led on to the policy of selling council houses to their occupiers in the next decade.[10]

In October 1961, Butler had two of his three posts summarily removed, when Macleod succeeded him as Party Chairman. This brought into Central Office an ambitious politician who wanted the job, and an attacking orator who could bring the Conference to its feet. At his own insistence though, Macleod continued the combination with the Leadership of the House. He was also Chancellor of the Duchy of Lancaster; he joked that 'the duties attached to this office take me half an hour in a tough week', but it also paid the salary which left him freer than Butler had been for his Party work. Macmillan feared that when Macleod became Party Chairman 'a lot of colonels will resign', and the *Manchester Guardian* later reported that Macleod, 'the least glossy of the Tories', had outraged local activists by urging older constituency officers to make way for the next generation. Despite a lack of sympathy in some quarters, and his unpopularity with the right over Africa, he was seen, at the time of his appointment as Party Chairman, very much as a coming man; James Margach in the *Sunday Times* argued that 'for a man of his intellectual capacity and genius for political organisation, the impact he could make over the next year must be profound'; *The Economist*

---

10 Central Office file, CCO 4/8/331, Psephology Group.

regarded him as 'the best next Prime Minister we've got' and the *Daily Herald*'s cartoonist drew him as 'Supermac Mk.II'. Macleod certainly saw his appointment as the launching pad for future leadership prospects, and was the first Chairman since Davidson in 1926 who had taken up the post in that expectation; he was to find to his disappointment that for a Chairman Central Office did not give the weight in governmental decision-making that came with a major Government Department. He was an extremely active Chairman, bombarding Macmillan and his Cabinet colleagues with political pointers to strategic ways forward; the traffic in political advice between Smith Square and Number 10 was more of a one-way street than it had been in 1957–59.[11]

Unfortunately though, Macleod's arrival at Central Office coincided with the moment at which the Party's popularity nosedived, and the next two years did little to enhance his reputation; the Lichfield and Tamworth association's annual report, having conceded that 'our Party and Government has lost a considerable amount of public support during [1961]', was even more downbeat a year later: 'during 1962, the Government, our Party and our Association had a number of setbacks and it would be idle to pretend otherwise'. After the Orpington by-election in March 1962 Macleod warned constituencies that they must expect 'that the storm has not yet reached its peak', but, in order to boost morale, he soon had to make hopeful claims, as when he told the National Union Executive in June 1962 that the West Derbyshire by-election was 'the end of the beginning', an optimism that was soon disproved by events. In Spring 1963, there was regular talk of Macleod being replaced, the favourite candidates in press speculation being Hailsham, Heath and Selwyn Lloyd, but Number 10 gossip favoured Lord Amory; instead, Oliver Poole returned to Central Office in May, as Joint Chairman with Macleod, dividing up the work much as he had done with Hailsham in 1957–59, 'roughly the division between G. and A & Q'. (It is characteristic that an oblique reference to the two traditional branches of staffwork in the British army should have been for that generation of Tories a natural mode of analysis.) Aldington stayed on until October as 'special assistant'. Poole told Woolton that he had agreed to return to Central Office because 'we *must* win the next election. I believe it could be done, but it will be very, very difficult.' Since they did not get on personally, the partnership of Macleod and Poole was not a success, and it is notable that it was Poole rather than Macleod who represented the Party professionals' viewpoint in the 1963 leadership contest.[12]

[11] Nigel Fisher, *Iain Macleod* (1973), 200–4, 213, 231–2; Central Office General Director's file, CCO 120/4/8, Selwyn Lloyd Inquiry.
[12] Lichfield and Tamworth CA minutes, 23 May 1962 and 7 June 1963; National Union Executive Committee minutes [hereafter NUEC], 7 June 1962; Evans, *Downing Street Diary*, 256; Central Office file, CCO 4/9/118; Poole to Woolton, April 1963, Woolton MSS, box 22; Central Office file, 500/11/10.

The low state of the Party was indicated by the 1962 recruiting campaign which was markedly less successful than that of 1958 (which was in turn less successful than 1948 or 1952). Many constituencies refused even to take part, feeling that the months after Orpington were not an opportune moment at which to invite people to come on board; the High Peak division of Derbyshire agreed in January 1962 to start recruiting, but the agent reported to the same association meeting that 'people are not looking with favour on the Conservative Government at present. Talk is of "lack of courage", "getting fed up with governing" etc', and it is therefore not surprising to find that it was being reported five months later that the recruiting campaign 'had not gained strength as expected'. The Member told his supporters that 'he realised how difficult it was at the present time to go out and call on people, but this was the only way to get things going', but this advice does not appear to have been heeded. Denbigh was unusual in 1962 in reporting that membership levels had been sustained, 'despite the slight chill in the political atmosphere', but here too recruiting was unsuccessful because of 'the apathy of the electorate'. The Wessex Area reported on the year of recruiting that hardly any constituencies had done more than replace the year's normal wastage. The decreasing effectiveness of the successive recruiting campaigns is brought out starkly by Table 3.1, giving the results for the Areas for which comparable data survives. After 1962, the Party never again attempted the high profile, nationally-coordinated campaign of the type inherited from Woolton's days.[13]

Table 3.1 Numbers of new members recruited in 1952, 1958 and 1962

Area	1952	1958	1962
London	16,183	9,082	11,753
Home Counties North	41,688	33,821	c.16,000
Home Counties South East	70,757	46,656	19,754
West Midlands	34,047	24,502	8,886
Yorkshire	27,626	11,678	9,200
East	22,103	21,450	c.10,000
The six above areas	212,404	147,879	c.76,000

As membership and activity fell away so did income; the Treasurers reported worryingly that 1961 was 'the first year in a between-election period that the quota contribution in one year has been less than that of the previous year'; in Gravesend, for example, both membership and subscriptions rose in

13 High Peak CA minutes, 15 Jan. and 21 June 1962; Central Office files, CCO 4/9/446, Treasurers, CCO 500/11/10; Denbigh CA minutes, 27 Apr. and 6 Nov. 1962.

1960–61, stabilised in the following year and then fell as the Government became really unpopular in 1962–63, and there was a similar pattern in Harrow and in Hampstead. Constituencies were ready to blame the Government for their lost momentum; York attributed the loss of municipal seats in 1962 to national issues, when 'the political climate had been very much against us' and West Derbyshire decided in February 1962 not even to run their usual fundraising ball that year 'in view of present circumstances'. Ruislip decided in May to hold up sending any further quota payments because of heavy local criticism of the Government (centring in this case on the very specific issue of local government reform). Not only did the overall quota totals reduce, but so did the number of constituencies meeting their targets, and it seems likely that Poole's return to Central Office in 1963 was intended to arrest this financial decline. In 1962 there were again many resolutions on the Conference agenda complaining about poor public relations; in March, Central Council not only passed overwhelmingly a resolution 'call[ing] upon the Government urgently to improve its ability quickly to communicate essential facts in convincing fashion and in clear, simple terms', but also noted in its minutes that there had been an unusually large number of those present who had wanted to speak *for* the motion. After receiving this resolution, Macmillan responded that such matters were for the Party rather than the Government, which was rather disingenuous since he was the leader of both, but he added that 'it is, I believe, a fallacy to think that policies which are bound to be unpopular can be made popular by better presentation'. He urged the constituencies to play their own part by buying and distributing more Party literature, which did present the case clearly. When Macleod picked up Macmillan's phrase about the 'fallacy' that unpopular policies could be made popular, and included it in a Chairman's letter to constituencies, Bristol Tories replied sharply that better presentation would still achieve a great deal, and added that it was the lack of a spirited presentation of the Government's pay pause that was at the root of the Party's problems.[14]

Macleod did though launch in Autumn 1962 a far-reaching inquiry into the state of the Party, turning the temporarily unemployed Selwyn Lloyd loose on a one-man consultation exercise as 'a new Maxwell-Fyfe'. (There had in fact already been a second Maxwell Fyfe in the report commissioned in 1957 from Lord Colyton, formerly Henry Hopkinson of the Parliamentary Secretariat, but this had made little impact and even so keen a Party man as Macleod had by 1962 completely forgotten its existence, as had the officers of the National Union.) Lloyd agreed to take it on as a job done personally for the Chairman,

---

[14] Gravesend, Hampstead and Harrow West CA minutes, various dates; York CA minutes, 17 May 1962 and 14 Feb. 1963; West Derbyshire CA minutes, 23 Feb. 1962; Ruislip CA minutes, 29 May 1962; National Union papers, NUA 2/2/28, Central Council reports; National Union Central Council minutes [hereafter NUCC] 15 Mar. 1962; Central Office constituency file, 1/14/484.

not then feeling too keen on doing favours for the Leader, and made it clear that this Party work would not commit him to remain silent in debates on Government policy. On this understanding he set to work on a massive consultation; he met and talked to about three thousand Conservatives, in Areas, constituencies, agent groups, the National Union, Central Office and affiliated bodies. An invitation to submit written evidence produced an avalanche of paper that was carefully analysed and cross-referenced. Not all the findings were at all palatable; he wrote in February 1963, with permissible *Schadenfreude* since they had contrived his own sacking in the previous July, that 'feeling against Macmillan and Macleod as both Chairman and Leader [of the House] continues to accumulate'. Macleod, passing on to ministerial colleagues an early Lloyd recommendation that Tory leaders should pay more attention to the views of the Party, prefaced it with his own exasperated comment that 'there is, perhaps, a certain irony in Selwyn suggesting that Ministers do not do enough to let the Party grumble to them, but let that pass.' The whole exercise was in part what Lloyd himself called 'a lightning conductor', for it showed hundreds of Party workers at a difficult time that one of the Party's major figures had made time to travel the country to listen their views.[15]

The Selwyn Lloyd Report was published on 6 June 1963 but did not make much of a splash, since that was also the day on which John Profumo resigned; Lloyd's planned television appearances were unceremoniously cancelled and the report itself was buried away on the inner pages of the newspapers. It was in any case a far from revolutionary document; Lloyd reported to the *Sunday Telegraph* that 'the most striking and refreshing impression which I have received was one of deep loyalty to the Party'. He had found that there was general agreement that the basic structures were sound, and had contented himself with recommendations of ways to make them work better; the posts of Chairman and Leader of the House should not be combined; more effort should be put into marginal seats; agents' pay and conditions must be improved; ministerial speakers must be routed to the places where the Party needed them, and not just go where the network of friendships on the backbenches produced invitations that could not be refused; there should be more use of the Bow Group as Tory 'Fabians'; there was a need to find more active members among the 25–40 age group and to deal with the loss of YCs to the Party when they reached the maximum YC age (a subject that was to be the subject of a separate consultation and report by Macleod himself in 1965); there should be a minimum subscription, a non-residential Party college in London, and a more rapid turnover of office-holders at all

15 Central Office General Director's files, CCO 120/4/1, 3, 4, 9, 10, 11, Selwyn Lloyd Inquiry; D.R. Thorpe, *Selwyn Lloyd* (1989), 365–6; Central Office Chairman's department file, CCO 20/1/6, Correspondence with the Chief Whip.

levels of the National Union; Ministers must be made more available to listen to the Party and to explain Government policies to them.[16]

Though it attracted little attention outside, the report was discussed and largely implemented by the Party; Poole was saying three months before the report came in that 'I certainly intend to act at once, and look as if we are too, on any recommendations [Lloyd] makes. They won't be very radical and will I believe be sensible.' The National Union Executive agreed most of the recommendations on 5 September 1963 and at a special meeting on 4 December, though it rejected the idea of a minimum subscription (which could have had a serious impact on the number of members only a year after a recruitment campaign had failed so badly). It was also decided not to tackle the thorny questions of the city parties and boundaries between Areas until after the impending Election. Discussions with the National Society of Agents produced a new salary scale that gave increases to agents in post of between 10 and 15 per cent, taking the top of the scale to a level 40 per cent higher than average non-manual earnings in 1963 (even without making any allowance for agents' benefits in kind, which always included a car and often a house or flat as well); a new clause allowed payment above the top point of the scale for long experience and in 'certain key constituencies'; it was at last made compulsory on all agents and all employing associations to join the agents' superannuation scheme; marginals were given special funding to enable them to attract or retain good agents at the new rates. *The Economist* was thus close to the mark when it suggested that 'the Lloyd Report may therefore be something between a compendium of minor but probably useful suggestions, and a timely safety valve, ensuring that in a trying period the National Union will not blow up, but will content itself with letting off steam'.[17]

The 'return of idealism to politics' and the satire wave

Alongside the problems of modernising the organisation, continued affluence in the 1960s created its own difficulties, for it encouraged a spiralling of expectations that would be hard for any government to meet. After Birmingham Tory leaders had written to Macmillan in 1961 to describe their 'annoyance, bewilderment and frustration' at the country's economic slowdown, Geoffrey Lloyd MP met them in order to calm them down, but received 'a much hotter reception than I expected. . . . They were just very angry! Of course Birmingham people are so used to prosperity that it may be they resent especially any Government action which threatens to interrupt it'. The housing auction is a specific case in point: the 1951 pledge to build 300,000 houses a year was met nearly every year from 1953 and the total

[16] Central Office General Director's file, CCO 120/4/25, Selwyn Lloyd Inquiry; Thorpe, *Lloyd*, 367–8.
[17] Poole to Woolton, April 1963, Woolton MSS, box 22; NUEC, 5 Sept. and 4 Dec. 1963; Central Office General Director's file, 120/4/8, Selwyn Lloyd Inquiry.

number of dwellings rose by 2.3 million in the Conservatives' first decade in office. But by 1964 the Tory manifesto was offering 400,000 as a new target – and one almost achieved that year; with Labour in office and building to the 400,000 target, in 1966 the Tory pledge went up to 500,000 a year.[18]

It is clear that after the 1959 victory there were some attempts to scale down expectations and to downplay the heavily materialist emphasis in Party policy. The National Union Executive debated in May 1960 a motion from the Federation of Conservative Students, 'that "You've never had it so good" gives a false impression of Conservative philosophy'. It was socratically agreed that the phrase was 'a useful summary of the conditions resulting from the work of a Conservative Administration but great care was necessary to guard against the encroachment of the slogan into the philosophy of the Party.' In October, the tone of speeches at the Party Conference was distinctly different from earlier years. Edward Boyle wrote in hopefully to ask whether the emphasis on 'work' and 'duty' in the Conference speeches of Butler and Macmillan 'imply a deliberate departure from the philosophy of "never having it so good"'. Butler replied that there was no inconsistency, merely that the Party needed to talk about responsibility as well as economic growth. The recent past could not be repudiated, and so the change of emphasis was never whole-hearted. Perhaps for Macmillan it was never more than skin-deep anyway: in June 1961 he told a journalist, 'We've got it good. Let's keep it good. There is nothing to be ashamed of in that.' When the Chancellor wanted to go for mild deflation of an overheated economy in the 1960 Budget, Macmillan talked him out of the idea; in his diary Macmillan noted that 'I have won this battle quite definitely'. [19]

Outside government, the public mood certainly did shift in a way that made it difficult for the Macmillan spell to work. Lord Kilmuir felt that 'the return of idealism to politics caught both parties off balance, and the Conservatives, as the Government party, suffered worse than our opponents'. Macmillan himself wrote in 1963 that the Government's 'difficulty is really due to a certain boredom with material success and apparent inability to harness this to spiritual purposes'. The 'return of idealism' fairly describes the surge of support for CND in these years, and such changes among the young as the popularity of voluntary service overseas and fundraising for World Refugee Year in 1963, but is an odd way of describing the almost entirely negative shift in cultural attitudes that arose from the satire wave of 1960–63. The first manifestation was the Cambridge University review *Beyond the Fringe*, which opened at the Edinburgh Festival in 1960, but acquired its sharpest political

18 Geoffrey Lloyd to Edward Boyle, 3 Aug. 1961, Boyle MSS, 20709; Fisher, *Macleod*, 219; D.E. Butler and G. Butler, *British Political Facts, 1900–1986* (1986), 333; Michael Pinto-Duschinsky, 'The Role of Constituency Associations in the Conservative Party', D.Phil. thesis, Oxford University, 1972, 75.
19 NUEC, 5 May 1960; Central Office Chairman's department file, CCO 20/1/9, Correspondence with Ministers; Sampson, *Macmillan*, 167; Macmillan, *Pointing the Way*, 222, 225.

sketches for its London run in the following year, including Peter Cook's devastating parody of Macmillan's election broadcast of 1959. Poking fun at politicians was hardly new – a Peter Sellers record had some time earlier included affectionate mimicry of Eden's oratory, and the film *I'm Alright Jack* was one of several that included a parody of an upper-class Tory MP in its cast. What was new in 1961 was the venom with which such attacks were made and the impact that they made: Michael Frayn recalled two Tory audience members 'neighing away like demented horses, until the middle of Peter Cook's lampoon on Macmillan, when the man turned to the girl and said in an appalled whisper, "I say! This is supposed to be the Prime Minister," after which they sat in silence for the rest of the evening.' The review ran for five years and launched a whole new mood in the public's relationship to its rulers, not least because the Queen herself came to see it. Peter Cook was also a founder of the 'Establishment' night club, which soon had 11,000 members, and of the magazine *Private Eye* which began regular operations in February 1962 and achieved a fortnightly circulation of 80,000 in the following year.[20]

The climax came with the BBC's *That Was The Week That Was* (*TW3*), which ran from November 1962 to early 1964, and not only clocked up 12 million viewers, but for many changed the social habits of Saturday evenings too. Although the satirists spread their attacks widely, Macmillan was the most popular single target (until Home succeeded him as Prime Minister), both because these young meritocrats took it as a personal affront that the country should be led in the 1960s by an Edwardian both in age and manner, and because he happened to be Prime Minister at the time in which it became acceptable for youth to cock a public snook at age and authority. When his Postmaster-General, Reginald Bevins, announced that he would get the BBC to restrain *TW3*, Macmillan stopped him with a laconic minute saying, 'Oh no you won't'. He took this liberal view partly because he had a radical's sympathy with *TW3*'s iconoclasm, but partly too because he underestimated its effects; Bevins later thought that this was a mistake, and that *TW3* had rather proved that some publicity is indeed bad for politicians. Apparent indifference only increased the savagery of the attacks. After the Cabinet purge of 1962 Macmillan had to read approving reviews of a new stage show, *SuperMacbeth*, in which Selwyn Lloyd was cast as Banquo, a type of political satire not seen on the London stage since Walpole censored the theatres in the eighteenth century. Boyd-Carpenter and Soames were among the many who complained regularly about the BBC's 'diabolically-biased attitude'. The BBC was a Tory devil figure at this time; in October 1963, Yorkshire Tories were asked to help the Area's publicity officer monitor *Mrs*

---

[20] Earl of Kilmuir, *Political Adventure* (1964), 322; Alan Bennett, Peter Cook, Jonathan Miller and Dudley Moore, *The Complete Beyond the Fringe* (1987), 7, 116–17; Macmillan's 1963 view is in the memorandum of 15 Oct. 1963 in PREM 11/5008.

Dale's Diary and *The Archers* 'with a view to discovering whether or not they had any political bias'. In the regions, the new local news programmes were often even more suspect; York replied to the above enquiry 'that the ITV programme *Scene at Six* was far more dangerous from this point of view'. Spies and other scandals in 1962–63 added the press, including most of the national Tory papers, to the hate-list, as Chapter 4 describes. The last time that the Tories had felt so persecuted by the mass media was in wartime, before the electoral disaster of 1945.[21]

The treatment of Ministers when they addressed meetings in the universities was further evidence of the remoteness from the concerns of the young that was to dog them throughout the Parliament. Butler at Glasgow and Watkinson at the London School of Economics and Political Science (LSE) were just two of the Ministers who found themselves faced with very hostile receptions. The attempts to get back on terms with the popular culture of 'the swinging sixties' became steadily more desperate. In May 1964, Poole hoped to get Maudling to present a golden disc to the Beatles (to recognise their services to exports), and in October the Party's election record, *Songs for Swinging Voters*, included a track with a Mersey beat and a backing group singing 'Yeah, yeah, yeah!' But the most remarkable response was from the constituencies, where there was an unusual desire to find show business and sporting candidates to enable the Party to compete for attention in the new mood. Unfortunately those actually chosen were a misguided response to that public mood and were put in the wrong places. Robin Marlar, the former Sussex cricketer, fought the by-election in industrial Leicester North East in 1962, but he at least already had a longstanding record of work for the YCs. The selection of Ted Dexter to oppose Jim Callaghan in Cardiff was harder to comprehend, for Dexter had no previous political experience and little apparent knowledge either. The most surprising of all was the choice of the comedian Jimmy Edwards to fight North Paddington; he drew large audiences for his meetings, but audiences that went away disappointed when they found an intelligent and earnest campaigner rather than a comic trombonist. The Vice Chairman for candidates suggested consulting the Chief Whip 'about the extent to which Edwards could go on being a comedian if he became an MP', but the Party Chairman minuted simply that 'after all, we have Nabarro!' In fact both Dexter and Edwards performed quite respectably as candidates but had little chance of gaining Labour seats in 1964: the swing in their constituencies was much as in adjoining areas.[22]

21 Cockerell, *Live from Number Ten*, 85–6; Richard Ingrams, *The Life and Times of Private Eye* (Harmondsworth, 1971), 8, 11, 15, 17; Reginald Bevins, *The Greasy Pole* (1965), 20–1; Thorpe, *Lloyd*, 357; Central Office Chairman's department file, CCO 20/1/11, Correspondence with Ministers; York CA minutes, 17 Oct. 1963.

22 Sparrow, *Rab*, 160; Harold Watkinson, *Turning Points: A Record of our Times* (Salisbury, 1986), 155; Central Office Chairman's department file, CCO 20/1/9; Central Office file, CCO 4/9/378, Records; Peter Rawlinson, *A Price Too High: An Autobiography* (1989), 107; Central Office constituency files, CCO 1/14/69, 282 and 425.

Empire or Europe?

Iain Macleod told the National Union Executive in April 1962 that what made the people most unhappy was that 'at a time when we are ceasing to be the greatest Imperial power in the world the Country as a whole was not sure where it was going as a country'. Macleod and Macmillan had no doubt that where it was going was away from Africa and towards Brussels, and they also agreed that this was the idealistic, unifying theme that would restore the Party's momentum. Unfortunately, both ends of the transition had to be disguised and as a result the strategy as a whole never emerged clearly enough to offer that inspiration; thanking Eward Boyle for his support over Europe in July 1961, Macmillan wrote that 'my son Maurice, who has quite good judgement in these affairs, feels that the worst thing of all would be to dither along'. But that was nevertheless what seemed to be the policy for the next eighteen months.[23]

   The withdrawal from Africa was always going to be difficult for the traditional Party of Empire. Macmillan, relieved that his Party had 'just succeeded in "getting by" on this' in the 1959 Election, felt that it was 'the biggest problem looming for us here at home'. The National Union Executive held a special meeting to discuss overseas policy in July 1960: it was noted that the Conservative Commonwealth Council was mainly made up of ex-Colonial administrators, which made it a powerful vehicle for the expression of white settler opinion, and thus made life difficult for the Government; the Executive also rejected a call for the Government to declare its intentions and timetable for decolonisation. At this time though, it was still possible to avoid strong dissent: there were seventy constituency motions on the Commonwealth on the agenda for the 1960 Party Conference, but few of these were critical of moves towards self-government and the one chosen for debate spoke approvingly of 'guiding the colonies towards self-government', which neatly attracted both wings of the argument. At Scarborough Iain Macleod delivered as Colonial Secretary a strong speech in defence of 'the road we must walk, and we can walk no other', which earned him an ovation; he continued to proclaim his policy in unapologetic terms, ending his term of office with a ringing declaration of the 'international brotherhood of man'. In 1961, the hostile motion from Horncastle which denounced 'appeasement in Africa' was still untypical of the overall mood. What was characteristic of 1960–61 though was that an increasingly vocal minority on the right of the Party singled out the Colonial Secretary for abuse over the accelerated pace at which decolonisation was now taking place, especially because independence for Kenya and Southern Rhodesia was now within sight and this would imperil the interests of their substantial white

---

[23] NUEC, 5 Apr. 1962; Macmillan to Boyle, 21 July 1961, Boyle MSS, 23001.

settler communities: Macmillan had told the Cabinet Secretary in 1959 that 'Africans are not the problem in Africa, it is the Europeans'.[24]

Macleod was sent to the Colonial Office precisely to accelerate the pace, and was quite unrepentant about that policy; he told Peter Goldman that he intended to be the 'last Colonial Secretary'; Roger Louis later thought that 'Macleod was to Africa what Mountbatten had been to India'. Macmillan characteristically offset his liberal influence with the parallel appointment of Duncan Sandys to the Commonwealth Relations Office where he would act as a brake to Macleod's accelerator in Africa. For both Macmillan and Macleod decolonisation was a *conservative* policy that had to be pursued in order to avoid something worse: Macleod argued that 'any other policy would have led to terrible bloodshed in Africa. That is the heart of the argument.' Britain must concede independence while still in a position to influence the shape of the successor states, and so keep together a Commonwealth that could be both a vehicle for British influence (and trade) for decades to come and a genuinely optimistic experiment in multi-racial cooperation; this liberal ideal was some justification for the unwillingness to upset the whole apple-cart by imposing unilateral restrictions on immigration to the UK. After Lord Salisbury in the Lords denounced Macleod as 'too clever by half' for advancing such arguments, Macleod only cautiously defended himself on television: 'Salisbury might say "the pace in Africa is dangerously fast. It would be better if we went more slowly." And I might say "the pace in Africa is dangerously fast but it might be more dangerous still if we went more slowly".' This was also the thinking behind Macmillan's 'winds of change' speech in Cape Town in 1960, though the Sharpeville massacre and the reaction of other Commonwealth countries to it imparted a greater urgency than he had foreseen and brought about the train of events that took South Africa out of the Commonwealth; the 1922 Committee, which was to give Macmillan's African policy some difficult moments, agreed in February 1960 to cable to him a resolution 'congratulating him on the success of his African tour and especially the success of his speech to the South Arican Parliament'. But while Macleod gave the policy a strong progressive gloss, Macmillan's speeches were more ambivalent and he became irritated by the strength of Macleod's convictions and his resignation threats when Sandys obstructed or the Cabinet expressed reservations; in February 1961 Macmillan 'thought I was going to lose a Minister and a continent'. Eventually Macmillan replaced Macleod with Maudling, whose equally progressive instincts made him just as difficult a colleague; Macmillan now thought Maudling to be 'plus noir que les nègres'. The deadlock was resolved first by giving Butler the overarching responsibility for Central Africa, and then by giving Sandys responsibility for both of the Government departments involved; from 1962 the Government

[24] Robert Shepherd, *Iain Macleod* (1994), 159, 255; NUEC, 14 July 1960; National Union papers, NUA 2/2/25 and 26, Central Council reports; Siedentop, 'Mr. Macmillan', 35–6.

was still unable to deal with Southern Rhodesia but had set its path firmly in the decolonising direction in the rest of Africa.[25]

The right on the other hand saw only a policy of 'scuttle', the driving of South Africa out of the Commonwealth, and the bloody civil war that had followed Belgium's too-rapid withdrawal from the Congo. The ninety MPs who signed a critical Early Day motion on Central Africa in early 1961 were a sign of how many critics there could be if the going got rough. A cocktail party on 25 September with a white Kenyan speaker was the leadership's first warning that such opinion was now being organised; a Central Office staffer who had attended reported that the new grouping had been founded by former Bow Groupers, 'who held extreme right wing views'. In November 1961 a circular sent to all MPs, accompanied by a pamphlet on African affairs, announced that 'the Monday Club had been formed by a group of younger members of the Conservative Party who believe in the implementation of policies based on Conservative principles'. The Central Office view was that 'their main aim appears to be to discredit the policy of the Government in Africa', and in particular to attack Macleod. In December, Central Office was replying to the many enquiries it was receiving by asserting that it had 'no connection whatever' with the Club. It was noted that the Club's printing was done for it by Edward Martell's 'Free Press' and that Martell's *New Daily* was giving it a great deal of attention. Nevertheless, it was not yet taken very seriously; a brief for the General Director in January 1962 reported that the Club was 'a group of young people of extreme right wing views who operate in Chelsea/South Kensington and . . . hold their meetings at the Onslow Court Hotel by way of roughing it'. The position then changed rapidly, when Lord Salisbury agreed to become the Club's patron, announcing that 'there never was a greater need for true Conservatism than there is today', and by then ten MPs had also joined; as a result of these more established figures taking part, the *Daily Telegraph* began to report its activities. Some of the Club's attempts to form local branches were successful, for example in St Ives (Cornwall), where the local Conservatives (as the agent shamefacedly reported) saw it as 'a genuine attempt to "keep the Conservative Party Conservative".' Whereas the Bow Group was encouraged, the party machine was always careful to avoid any contact with the Monday Club; the YC Department at Central Office was instructed not to keep up contacts, and the Chief Organisation Office wrote in 1962 that the Club was 'obviously not to be encouraged', because of its explicit opposition to Government policy.[26]

---

[25] Shepherd, *Macleod*, 161–2, 256; Horne, *Macmillan*, 188, 201; Hutchinson, *Last Edwardian*, 111; 1922 Committee minutes [hereafter 1922], 4 Feb. 1960; Butler, *Art of Memory*, 105, 107; Howard, *RAB*, 287; Fisher, *Macleod*, 141–2, 155, 165, 170–3; Evans, *Downing Street Diary*, 139; Reginald Maudling, *Memoirs* (1978), 89, 97, 99; John Turner, *Macmillan* (1994), 185.

[26] Central Office file, CCO 3/6/16, Monday Club.

If the Monday Club was uncooperative, the opposite problem arose with another right-wing initiative that had to be kept at arm's length despite its offers of help. Edward Martell, quiescent since the East Ham by-election of 1957, was also unhappy about decolonisation, though in his case domestic policies, and trade union reform in particular, were more important. In 1960, Central Office warned MPs to keep their distance from Martell's People's League for the Defence of Freedom, which was now offering support to Conservative candidates, though it conceded that 'we have not found the League to be any more than a slight nuisance'. In 1962, Martell formally joined the Party; he was soon a ward chairman in Hastings and planning to take Conservatism over if he could. By 1962–63, Martell's *New Daily* was beginning to make an impact that could not be ignored, with a circulation approaching 100,000 copies a day, and his various organisations had been brought together as the Freedom Group; he claimed 160,000 members, and the letterhead included ten peers, twenty knights and dames, and a lot of retired generals; it also included Sir Adrian Boult and T.S. Eliot, and two Tory backbenchers, but no political figure of any real weight. His aim was proclaimed to be 'a sound and traditional Conservatism'.[27]

Sir Alec Douglas-Home was as Prime Minister advised not to correspond with Martell, since he would print extracts of any correspondence in his paper, out of context, and make it seem as if he was a confidant of the premier. Martell met the Party Chairman in February 1964 and promised help to 'keep the socialists out'. The *Yorkshire Post* quoted him as saying he would work humbly for the Party, but adding 'that in the next four or five years . . . we will do everything we can to persuade the Conservative Party to drop its pink socialism'. Two months later he was grandiloquently offering workers to any Conservative candidate that needed them, and promising that he would unseat Harold Wilson in his own constituency; the Party Chairman now told candidates to accept the offer of help but also to keep a watchful eye on what helpers actually did in the Party's name. Martell's bluff was then called by a Tory candidate in Liverpool – little help ever appeared. Over the Summer Martell caused further concern over the legal implications of his campaign against Wilson, and with his 'Plan 50', by which he promised to put up fifty additional candidates at his own expense, and thus earn the right to his own television election broadcast which he would use to tell voters to back the Tories; this fantasy was abandoned only on 2 October when, as he said, the Conservative Party was 'now in a winning position and no extraordinary measures are needed'.[28]

Within a few months of the Conservatives' 1964 defeat, the Party adopted the trade union reform platform that had been Martell's main campaigning

27 Central Office files, CCO 3/6/128 and 136, National Fellowship and PLDF (People's League for the Defence of Freedom).
28 Central Office file, CCO 3/6/101, Freedom Group.

asset over the past decade, and the press was reporting that Martell was appealing for funds to keep his organisation afloat; the *New Daily* was now only a weekly token publication. This time, Martell did not manage to restore his fortunes, and Central Office was beset by those who had invested in one or other of his enterprises and could not get their money back. By October 1966, Martell had again severed all links with the Conservative Party, and was denouncing Heath as much as Wilson; he was now working for a new National Party which would fight all by-elections, but which in fact vanished after losing its deposit at the first attempt. It is hard to estimate the impact and importance of such South-Sea-Bubble politics as Martell's, but it seems likely that the Party gained little from his support and lost little from his hostility. It is a great tribute to his skills as a self-publicist that he was able to persuade Central Office to take him at all seriously for so long. But one effect of his activities was undoubtedly to divert disaffection from channels that could have been much more dangerous to Party unity. When his organisation finally folded, the Monday Club became considerably more numerous and more effective.[29]

Arguments over Africa in 1961–62 had a number of other consequences. One was to undermine the claims of Macleod, Maudling and (once again) Butler to become Party Leader, for in all three cases their policy on Central Africa turned right-wingers into implacable opponents. Butler accepted the responsibility for Central Africa with a heavy heart: 'it seemed simple to think that there were any runs to be made. It occurred to many commentators that there was a reputation to be lost.' There was also some increased criticism of the Prime Minister, for right-wingers were bitter when they saw Macmillan – the supposed strong man of Suez – apparently presiding over the liquidation of Empire. The Foreign Secretary was perhaps the only Party leader who was able to extract political benefit from decolonisation: in 1961 Home made at the United Nations an attack on double standards in international affairs, and in particular on Russian (and by implication American) complaints about Britain's colonies while they retained subject peoples of their own. This went down well with Conservatives.[30]

In one way though the rapid pace of decolonisation did allow the Government to get back in touch with opinion at the grass roots. The lower profile that imperial issues would take in the future helped to change views on nationality: Enoch Powell, though still not involving himself in the debates on immigration, drew some hard-headed conclusions in a 1961 speech: the imperial phase was over, 'so plainly ended that even the generation born at its zenith . . . no longer deceive themselves as to the

[29] Central Office file, CCO 3/7/21, Freedom Group; Central Office Chairman's department file, CCO 20/52/1, Edward Martell.
[30] Lord Butler, *The Art of the Possible: The Memoirs of Lord Butler* (1971), 210; Thompson, *Day Before Yesterday*, 179; Home, *Way the Wind Blows*, 163.

fact'. The years 1959–61 were decisive not only in shifting opinions on Empire but also in demonstrating a growing tide of domestic opinion about immigration. Birmingham MPs elected in 1959 grouped together to press for action after their experience on the doorsteps (though with Edward Boyle and Aubrey Jones declining to take part), and in Brixton, Birmingham and Smethwick local Conservatives began to campaign openly for immigration controls, using local government elections to highlight their views; in Smethwick the Tories took control of the Council against the national trend in 1964. The 1922 Committee had its first serious discussion about immigration only in 1960 and the issue scarcely figured in the 1960 Party Conference, when only seven resolutions had been submitted (as there had been only six in 1958). But opinion was now hardening; demands for action in May 1961, from industrial supporters, were met by Fraser with the response that it would be embarrassing to have to take unilateral action in the year of West Indian independence, but that the Government was 'watching the whole situation with care and concern'; his questioner replied tartly that 'people are getting very tired with the perpetual "watching the whole situation with care" and are only hoping that a firm conclusion will be reached before it is too late'. There were forty Conference resolutions in 1961, and a tough call for action submitted by Hayes and Harlington was selected for debate. There were even more motions in 1962, but by then legislation had been introduced and carried into law in July. Macmillan seems to have woken up rather late to the increasing level of discontent, noting only in May 1961 that 'immigration . . . is becoming a serious problem', though by November he was also saying rather unfairly that 'Rab hasn't done it very well, has he?' His biographer points out that at this time Central Africa occupied ten times as much space in his diary as immigration. Action was eventually inescapable, as the number of entrants increased dramatically in 1961 during a period of high unemployment, and as polls showed an overwhelming public demand for entry controls. When the Commonwealth Immigration Bill eventually appeared, there was confusion about the Government's intentions concerning Ireland; if Irish immigrants were excluded along with West Indians, then controls would be impossible to enforce along the Ulster border, but if they were not excluded the Bill could be portrayed as a form of colour prejudice, as Labour alleged. Thirteen Conservative MPs on the left of the Party voted against the deletion of Ireland from the Bill on these grounds, and four on the right voted against controls as such, since they still valued the common citizenship that they saw as the core of Commonwealth identity. Ministers like Macleod – who had recently said that it would be 'extremely distasteful' to have such legislation, 'which would run counter to the long-established position of Britain' – were far from happy to be defending these provisions, and in November 1961 he suggested taking the unusual step of publishing the CPC groups' collective recommendation of legislation, to show that 'the thinking people in the party' accepted the Government's case. Although the

1962 Act at first reduced intakes sharply, amendments made to meet criticism during the course of enactment allowed increases in later years that ensured that the issue continued to rumble on. Rhodesia and immigration controls remained running sores from the retreat from Empire which were to plague Conservative leaders for another generation. And the constant reiteration of the right's concerns in these areas made it more difficult to proclaim Europe as an alternative focus for Britain's future.[31]

As soon as the 1959 Election was over Macmillan began putting the pieces in place for a shift of British policy towards the developing European Community. The reshuffle of posts occasioned by Heathcoat Amory's retirement from the Exchequer in May 1960 provided the first opportunity. Sandys went to Commonwealth Relations, Soames to Agriculture and Heath to the Foreign Office, so that all the key departments had strongly pro-European Ministers. The more sceptical Butler, having sat for Saffron Walden for thirty years, had become receptive to the views of farmers. Macmillan, whose fertile imagination saw Butler as the Disraeli to his own Peel, feared a split in the Party like 1846 and kept Butler well away from any relevant portfolio. After considerable hesitation Butler joined the pro-Europeans in Summer 1961 and was then sent round the country to talk to branches of the National Farmers' Union (NFU) and convince farmers that they would not be betrayed. The Chief Whip, Redmayne, was another sceptic. Macmillan privately committed himself to an application to join the EEC at the start of 1961, and the Cabinet resolved to apply on 22 July, Macmillan noting with relief that the decision had been unanimous. The National Union Executive received the news of a Conference debate without much enthusiasm, while a sceptical member asked 'that in the selection of motions . . . no overriding weight would be given to the Government's views'. Despite the lateness of the policy announcement, there were forty-two EEC motions on the Conference agenda, several like Peter Walker's Worcester resolution stressing the damage that membership of the EEC could do to Commonwealth trade. The Conference passed a motion from Brighton Conservatives calling for a 'closer association' with the EEC, the selection of which neatly aligned the right wing pro-European Julian Amery with the new official line.[32]

This inaugurated a difficult eighteen months; the Government had not

[31]   Roth, *Powell*, 220, 256; Harold Gurden to Edward Boyle, 9 Aug. 1960 and Boyle to Gurden, 17 Aug. 1960, Boyle MSS, 20704, 20705; Philip Goodhart, *The 1922: The Story of the 1922 Committee* (1973), 179; National Union papers, NUA 2/2/24–26, Central Council reports; Central Office file, CCO 4/8/138, Immigration; Nicholas Deakin (ed.), *Colour and the British Electorate 1964* (1965), 4–5, 9, 23, 80; Evans, *Downing Street Diary*, 175; Howard, *RAB*, 281; Sparrow, *Rab*, 182; Horne, *Macmillan*, 422–3; Philip Norton, *Dissension in the House of Commons, 1945–1974* (1975), 193, 196; Central Office file, CCO 4/9/225, Immigration; Central Office Chairman's department, file, CCO 20/1/9.

[32]   Horne, *Macmillan*, 255, 258–9, 353; Sampson, *Macmillan*, 205–8; Butler, *Art of Memory*, 107; Samuel Brittan, *Steering the Economy* (1969), 147; NUEC, 13 July 1961; National Union paper, NUA 2/2/26, Central Council report; Thompson, *Day Before Yesterday*, 183, 185.

quite decided to apply for membership of the EEC, only to open talks to see what the terms for membership would be if Britain did apply. This meant that throughout those long negotiations it was difficult to proclaim a commitment to European integration, which might have assisted the negotiations themselves and helped the Government in setting up Europe as a new focus for Britain's future. Anti-Common Market MPs had no such disadvantage, and the campaigning of the Tory 'antis' (with some encouragement from Lord Avon) made considerable headway; there were anyway a hundred or so Conservative MPs who would have found it difficult to vote for entry unless satisfactory arrangements had been reached for British farmers. An Anti-Common Market League (ACML) was formed in June 1961, largely the brainchild of Peter Walker, who had been elected to parliament only three months earlier. The danger to the Government was that this body would mobilise opinion on the left of the Party like Walker himself, idealistically hostile to any weakening of the Commonwealth experiment in inter-racial collaboration; if to these were added the old colonial hands and domestic interest groups like the farmers, they could accumulate a grouping right across the Party spectrum. The ACML conducted an active campaign, circulating as much literature on the European issue as the official Party in 1961–62, and mounting a big series of public meetings. It also raised some hackles; when Anthony Fell MP attracted an audience of some 350 people in Tunbridge Wells and told them not to vote for their pro-EEC MP next time, the Party Chairman wondered whether this did 'not go beyond the very wide limits of tolerance that we have been giving in this issue?' In the first debate after the Government's approach to the EEC, only Fell voted with Labour, but more than twenty Tory MPs abstained; as the 'anti' campaign went on, numbers swelled and forty-seven signed an anti-Common Market motion in December 1962, though there were by then no cross-votes in actual debates. The 'antis' had demonstrated their clout and the Government was restrained in its own language as a result.[33]

If the Government's rhetoric was inhibited, the will to carry through the policy did not waver. Indeed, the longer that negotiations went on at Brussels the more prestige it had to invest in ultimate success. Central Council in March 1962 was asked only to pass a neutral resolution calling for the closer association of Britain with all her international partners – Europe, America and the Commonwealth – but by then a hard choice could not be delayed, and a Macmillan speech at Stockton in April indicated that he was coming off the fence. Privately he was telling Home that same month that on the European

33 Peter Walker, Staying Power: An Autobiography (1991), 30; David Dutton, 'Anticipating Maastricht: The Conservative Party and Britain's First Application to Join the European Community', in Contemporary Record, vol.7 (1993), 534, 538; Lord Windlesham, Communication and Political Power (1966), 171, 174–5, 178; NUEC, 5 Apr. 1962; Norton, Dissension, 189; Jackson, Rebels and Whips, 175; Central Office Chairman's department file, CCO 20/1/6.

issue depended 'the fortunes and probably the life of the Government'. Without a clear lead, most constituency associations, understanding little of the complex issues thrown up by this wholly new political debate, seem to have followed whatever line their own MP or candidate took, unless a local interest such as fishing determined their response. Burton upon Trent Conservatives heard in October 1962 that their MP would 'reserve judgement' until the final terms were known, and unanimously resolved to support his eventual decision, thus in effect backing him either way; Derby South backed the Government strongly on its MP's recommendation, and Lewes passed a resolution supporting the EEC when its MP assured the association that this was quite compatible with the safeguarding of Commonwealth interests; despite serious local disaffection that led to the collapse of a branch committee, the Totnes Conservatives also remained loyal to their MP's pro-European views and his wish to back the Government; in York the association backed the local MP's wish for a resolution strongly endorsing entry to the EEC, but only after 'discussion of the effects [of entry] on the chocolate industry'. In a few places though, local opinion or the strongly-held views of an influential member could carry the day against the sitting MP; in West Dorset, Simon Wingfield Digby MP was sceptical about Britain's European future, but his association resolved to back the Government, a key figure in the debate being Jim Spicer, who would later be association chairman and MP for the constituency, before becoming a Member of the European Parliament himself. In May 1962, the National Union's General Purposes Committee noted the general bafflement in the constituencies; they called for a simple leaflet in straightforward language that would explain the options – but while negotiations proceeded this was just what was most difficult to produce. In the same month, the Executive Committee recorded their view that 'people wanted a definite lead from the top'.[34]

The discontent of 'Orpington Man'

With discontent over Africa, and the running in the European debate largely left to the 'antis', it was difficult to sustain the Government's popularity. The cause of unpopularity lay mainly in the country's economic performance. Seriously adverse swings in by-elections began only in March–April 1961 but then continued remorselessly. Because only safe constituencies fell vacant, no seats changed hands in 1961, but in the last months of the year Liberal candidates once again began to do very well and the Conservative vote to fall alarmingly. Opinion polls told the same story, and Liberals gained many

[34] NUCC 3/62; Turner, *Macmillan*, 221; Hutchinson, *Last Edwardian*, 85; Jackson, *Rebels and Whips*, 280; Burton upon Trent CA minutes, 5 Oct. 1962; South Derby CA minutes, 16 Nov. 1962; Lewes CA minutes, 4 Oct. 1962; Totnes CA minutes, 8 Mar. 1962; York CA minutes, 23 July 1962; West Dorset CA minutes, 30 Nov. 1962; National Union papers, NUA 5/2/1, GP minutes; NUEC, 3 May 1962.

seats in the 1961 local elections. But the real crash in Tory electoral fortunes began only in 1962. On 8 March there was a bad result at Lincoln; on the 13th a Liberal came within a hairbreadth of taking the safe seat at Blackpool North. The news from Blackpool was published alongside an Orpington constituency poll that showed the Liberals poised to take the seat; the Liberals cannily bought up thousands of copies of the *Daily Mail* containing this news, and gave them away to returning commuters to encourage switching to their candidate. On the 14th, the Liberals took Orpington with a sensational swing of 27 per cent while on the same day the Tory candidate barely saved his deposit in Middlesbrough East. Macmillan made an unplanned appearance at Central Council to steady nerves, and the 1922 Committee held an anxious post-mortem.[35]

In the following week, the frisson of panic that swept through the Party was associated mainly with Orpington, for an actual seat lost was more worrying than any number of statistical swing figures, and, since the turnout there had been over 80 per cent there was no relief to be had in theories that Tories had simply abstained to express temporary discontent. But it was the cumulative impact of four bad results in less than a week that made Orpington such a chilling climax. The bandwagon rolled on: NOP found in the week-end after Orpington that a national survey of voting intentions yielded the result Liberals 35.9 per cent, Labour 30.5 per cent, Conservatives 27.4 per cent, a finding so improbable that they dared not publish it; a week later they did publish a poll showing the three parties nearly level nationally. As in 1956–58, Conservatives simply could not find the Liberal vote, which at Lincoln was ten times the size recorded in the canvass; this made it impossible to address potential defectors with targeted leaflets or even to find out what type of people they were. As after Rochdale, National Opinion Polls (NOP) were commissioned to carry out a special survey in Orpington, to find what had gone wrong, and to analyse the 'Orpington Man' who had deserted the Party. Most instant press analysis argued that Orpington showed the Conservatives to be out of touch with modern trends, dismissed as a backward-looking class party, but this misunderstood the nature of the constituency, which had actually gone through a period of destabilising social change and had already experienced significant Liberal successes in local elections. The contrast in the candidates actually argued entirely against the popular analysis, for Eric Lubbock, the Liberal who seemed to have an appeal to all classes, hailed from Eton, Balliol and the Guards and was to inherit a peerage, while his Conservative opponent Peter Goldman was the epitome of meritocratic Toryism; Lubbock was local to the constituency, however, while Goldman was an outsider, and this contrast at least may have mattered. Macmillan's consolatory letter to Goldman agreed that, if he had lost by eight votes it

[35] Ken Young, 'Orpington and the Liberal Revival', in Chris Cook and John Ramsden (eds), *By-Elections in British Politics* (1973), 204–6.

might have been the candidate's fault, but when he lost by eight thousand it could only be blamed on the Government. After their deep survey, NOP told Central Office that none of the popular reasons for the result had in fact mattered very much: Macleod reported to Macmillan that 'incomparably the leading factor was the dislike of the pay policy and general dislike of the Government, which I suspect more than anything else is also connected with this.' Letters received by Central Office after Orpington bore out this analysis, for the most common explanation cited by correspondents was economic policy, prices and taxes, though a significant minority also mentioned 'fears of the EEC' and the 'betrayal' of Rhodesia, issues which could not be neutralised while Heath continued his negotiations in Brussels and Butler his attempts to cut the Gordian knot in Central Africa.[36]

Macmillan's soothing verdict on Orpington was that 'we have lost a number of skirmishes, perhaps a battle, but not a campaign. In war it is a characteristic of this country to concentrate on winning the last battle.' Charles Hill, coordinating Government publicity, also refused to panic, seeing simply an inevitable trough in Government popularity that would right itself in time. Nevertheless, the fact that the Orpington by-election had been caused by the appointment of the sitting MP to the judicial bench was taken to heart: few Conservative MPs after Orpington benefited from such preferment. When vacancies did occur in 1962, the contests were awaited with trepidation even in Labour seats, for the performance of the Tory candidate relative to the Liberals was now a factor almost as important as the majority of the winner. In April Macmillan intervened personally at Stockton, touring his old constituency during the campaign and addressing a rally of fifteen hundred supporters; the local press reported the Prime Minister's 'sentimental journey' and his pointed references to the 'remarkable change from poverty to prosperity' in the town, so that 'you wouldn't think you were in the same country'. This may have helped a little, but sights were now set very low; the constituency chairman was able to write of local Conservatives being 'so delighted that we beat the Liberals into third place' – this in a constituency that the Liberals had not even contested since 1950. In the May local elections, Liberals took over a thousand Conservative seats, and the early Summer by-elections were again a trial of strength. In June, Middlesbrough West was lost to Labour but on the same day the former Labour MP Aidan Crawley, with three Cabinet Ministers drafted in to help him, just clung on to rural West Derbyshire for the Tories. His victory was seen as a real triumph and the champagne flowed; Macleod told the National Union that this result would be 'the end of the beginning'. But a week later the Conservative lost his deposit at West Lothian, and the July by-election in North East Leicester was not expected to be at all a happy

---

[36] Young, 'Orpington', 198–221; Goodhart, *The 1922*, 181–4; Central Office Chairman's department file, CCO 20/8/5, Correspondence with Macmillan; Central Office General Director's by-election file, CCO 120/2/89.

event, especially when it became clear that Edward Martell and his *New Daily* were taking a close interest in the contest. The Conservative candidate was warned to have nothing to do with Martell.[37]

In January 1962, the Wessex Area Chairman wrote to Macleod of the growing air of defeatism among Party workers; he attributed this to 'disarray and frustration' over taxation and trade union policy, the 'inadequate presentation of good policies', and (something to be heard more and more as the 1960s went on) the difficulty of distinguishing between the policies of the Government and the Opposition in such areas as the welfare state. Lord Windlesham later pointed out that 'in mid-1962, it had become clear to the Conservative Party Organisation that the Government's economic policy was not so much misunderstood as understood and resented'. Macleod put just this point of view to Macmillan after Orpington: 'I am convinced myself that things are going to get worse before they get better and that the key to it all is the success of our economic policy.' A central problem was that Selwyn Lloyd, Chancellor since 1960, had not inspired the confidence of the public, of economists or even of his ministerial colleagues; in November 1961 Macmillan worried about press attacks, but asked Harold Evans, 'how can I say "Well, if you have a Chancellor who can't explain things, what do you expect?"'. He also surprised Butler, who had regarded Lloyd as a Macmillan protegé, by confessing in March 1962 that Lloyd could not be considered as a possible future Prime Minister, despite his having held two of the great offices of state, for 'when he walked onto a platform nobody felt that here was the ruler of England'. (Was this also a coded message for Rab?) Lloyd's deficiencies had not been so obvious at the Foreign Office, where major decisions involved the Prime Minister, but at the Exchequer they became all too clear, and especially since after 1959 Macmillan devoted an increasing part of his own attention to international affairs. In April 1960, Heathcoat Amory had acceded to Macmillan's request for a 'standstill budget' rather than imposing restraints on the boom then still raging, but at the time of his departure in July, he had warned that tough measures would soon be necessary; with a new Chancellor learning the ropes these were too long delayed. A credit squeeze and a battle against inflation then began, with a heavy-handed pay pause introduced in Summer 1961; at this time, the Prime Minister's press secretary thought that Lloyd had 'had the the most universally critical press that I can remember for any government proposals'. In Lloyd's defence it has to be remembered that he had to face the serious deterioration of the country's balance of payments and could not foresee that this would be a long-term problem in the 1960s as it had not been before. His handling of the economy was hesitant and unconfident, and he was in particular slow to

[37] Sampson, *Macmillan*, 196; Evans, *Downing Street Diary*, 182; Central Office constituency files, CCO 1/14/114, 281 and 282; Aidan Crawley, *Leap Before You Look* (1988), 390; NUEC 7/6/62.

move back to a reflationary policy in 1962 when his earlier restrictions effected a sharper slow-down than he had intended. Worst of all, he was not effective in explaining what he was doing and why. He was ineffective both on television and in the House. Of the latter, Ian Trethowan later recalled that Lloyd 'was undoubtedly a more astute man than he appeared at the despatch box'; at the time, Lloyd had told him after a particularly unsuccessful television interview, 'Well, I suppose that's lost us another million votes.'[38]

The 'New Approach' of 1962

As Chancellor, Lloyd did show considerable open-mindedness about policy methods, and introduced a range of new mechanisms for economic management. The CRD's economic section had been urging on Ministers a more interventionist approach, since 'we have virtually exhausted the Neo-Liberal seam in economic policy' – this being argued at what would now be seen as the very nadir of neo-Liberalism in British politics. Such opinions were increasingly common in the financial press, arguing both from Britain's increasing inability to keep up with growth rates in the developed world and from the example of state planning by the French Gaullists. Interventionism was also becoming popular among business organisations, and a new departure was helped by changes at the Ministry of Labour, where civil service advice was becoming less timid; Heath as Minister of Labour briefly seemed set to reform the unions themselves to deal with restrictive practices. He told the TUC that if they did not put their house in order he would intervene, but also reminded Tory MPs that 'we must first give the TUC the opportunity to deal with its undisciplined minority'; he was shortly afterwards moved to the Foreign Office before this warning period to the TUC had expired. In the Party the mood had changed quite suddenly: in April 1960 the National Union Executive had been unwilling to take a clear position for or against legislation to deal with strikes, but within a few months resolutions were going through calling unequivocally for the regulation of unions by law; likewise, Reigate Tories decided in February 1961 not to pass a resolution on trade union reform when their MP reminded them that industry did not want such a provocative approach, but then passed a tougher resolution only a year later. Intervention to gee up Britain's economic performance could therefore take one of two paths: the Government could either seek union cooperation, or impose a policy on the unions; the second alternative hardly seems to have been debated in

---

[38] Central Office Area correspondence file CCO 2/6/15; ICBH witness seminar, 'Did the Conservatives Lose Direction, 1961 to 1964?', transcript in *Contemporary Record*, vol. 2, no. 5 (1989), 27; Windlesham, *Communication*, 63; Central Office Chairman's department file, CCO 20/8/5; John Ramsden, 'Churchill to Heath', in Lord Butler (ed.), *The Conservatives* (1977), 457; Brittan, *Steering the Economy*, 143, 145–6, 162–3; Evans, *Downing Street Diary*, 153, 175; Butler note, 10 Mar. 1962, Butler MSS, G38; Horne, *Macmillan*, 238; Ian Trethowan, *Split Screen* (1984), 72–3.

1961, and anyway held little attraction for Lloyd or Macmillan, inured to ten years of 'softly, softly' dealings with the TUC.[39]

The key advance was therefore the creation in July 1961 of the National Economic Development Council (NEDC), an optimistic attempt to get the leaders of industry and trade unions to share with government the responsibility for the national economy. This was a form of interventionism that Macmillan had long advocated and which was entirely in the spirit of both his *Industry and the State* writings in the 1920s, and of the *Industrial Charter* of 1947, but it required a great deal of persistence by Lloyd to press it on a sceptical Cabinet; Macmillan told Lloyd that 'I do not think we ought to be afraid of a switch over towards more direction. Our Party has always consisted of a number holding the laissez-faire tradition, but of an equal number in favour of some direction . . . So far as I am concerned I have no fear of it because these were the policies that I recommended before the war.' It was though poor tactics to introduce a bid for union cooperation alongside a determined attempt to hold down incomes, for this almost ensured that the trade unions would offer little commitment to its operations. Attempts to produce a balanced package of 'social justice' measures to cement a new partnership failed miserably; reductions in super-tax were overdue and economically justified, but they certainly gave the impression of favouring the rich, while the tax concessions intended to balance them in the package could, according to Samuel Brittan, 'hardly have attracted less popular attention if they had been deliberately drafted with that in mind'; even in Basingstoke, where an affluent Tory association must have included many super-tax payers, the constituency Executive 'found it difficult to reconcile' the inequalities of the pay pause with super-tax relief. The failure then was a political one. Without statutory powers, the Government's attempt to hold down incomes inevitably focused on its own employees, and here a number of disputes with such popular groups of workers as teachers and nurses did much political damage.[40]

Before the NEDC first met in March 1962, it was already clear that it was unlikely to sustain the hopes that had surrounded its birth, since neither unions nor employers had given any promises to heed its decisions; meanwhile the pay pause announced in July 1961 would expire in April 1962. The extreme unpopularity of the Party in the months after Orpington ensured that the debate about long-term policy would entangle political and economic reasoning; Harold Evans wondered 'what progress can be made when there is no policy and Selwyn Lloyd is so maladroit'. Wrangles over future policy

[39] Brittan, *Steering the Economy*, 146, 150–3, 162–3; Horne, *Macmillan*, 247; John Campbell, *Edward Heath* (1993), 110–11; Andrew Roth, *Heath and the Heathmen* (1972), 134, 139; NUEC, 7 Apr. 1960 and 7 Sept. 1961; Reigate CA minutes, 3 Feb. 1961 and 16 Feb. 1962.
[40] National Union papers, NUA 5/2/1, GP papers; Turner, *Macmillan*, 244; Gerald Dorfman, *Wage Politics in Britain, 1945–1967* (1974), 111, 115 Thompson, *Day Before Yesterday*, 187; Central Office constituency file, CCO 1/14/470.

on incomes produced only a feeble White Paper in February 1962 that set a 'guiding light', a recommended percentage limit that had no backing except the Government's own weakening authority. Party activists were also restive about the Government's poor defence of its policies: London Area Conservatives resolved in February that, while appreciating the necessity for a pay pause, they regretted 'that HM Government did not do more at the beginning to explain the matter more clearly to the electorate'. In these circumstances, the 1962 Budget was to be a key moment, not only because its actual provisions could hasten the economic recovery, but also because the opportunity that a Budget provided could be used to reaffirm political confidence. From Central Office, Macleod was badgering Macmillan to make Lloyd sound more encouraging in the way his policies were put across: on 2 April he urged that the Budget should be expansionist, but also that the words in which it was expressed should clearly show 'that we really want growth'. To Lloyd himself on 3 April, Macleod reported deep dissatisfaction with the pay pause ('and the feeling that this is unfair to the people of this country') described in NOP's Orpington survey; he asked for a few sweeteners (such as a small sum of money for sport) to be included in the Budget, 'which is going to be of critical importance for the Party', and stressed the need for 'complete confidence in the future in what you say'. The Cabinet on the eve of Budget day was stormy; Hailsham called the Budget 'unsaleable' and when other Ministers joined in Lloyd had to promise to add tax concessions he had not wanted. The Budget on 8 April remained cautious; it did not foresee the steep increase in unemployment that followed over the next year, and assumed that a decision in favour of British entry to the EEC by the Autumn would in itself stimulate the economy by producing a boom in private investment; there was to be no relaxation of credit, and the only real innovation, a tax on sweets and ice cream, was easily attacked by the Party's opponents; 'the toffee tax' was as damaging a phrase to hang round Lloyd's neck as 'the pots and pans Budget' had been for Butler in 1955. As to language, Lloyd took more pains to warn of troubles ahead than to encourage or enthuse, and over the next three months he continued to set his face against credit relaxation. Macmillan himself noted that 'Selwyn, though an admirable Minister and a splendid colleague, somehow fails to "put it across".' Spurred on by Macleod, Macmillan concluded that his Chancellor would have to be replaced, though his congratulatory letter to Lloyd after the Budget did not give the intended victim any hint of the fact. On 28 May Reginald Maudling was added to the Cabinet's Economic Policy Committee, a little-noticed hint of what was to come. In the mean time Macleod continued to apply the spur to Lloyd, and Macmillan minuted all Ministers in May with an instruction to 'forget all our own preoccupations with particular issues and concentrate on claiming success for our economic policies'. The need to restore confidence was underlined by critical speeches demanding changes of Government personnel; on 19 May, Gerald Nabarro called on Macmillan to 'shuffle his pack. He must put new men into office and get rid of the dead wood and rotten Ministers. . . . He must give the Tory Party a new dynamic and get rid of the dunderheads.' This outburst generated quite a bit of press support and provoked the journalist John Freeman to urge prophetically, 'It's time for the knife, Mac'.[41]

Macmillan was irritated above all by the fact that Lloyd carried on talking about the need for pay restraint, and so continued the political damage of that unpopular stance, without actually devising any machinery that could make an incomes policy work and so restore the Government's momentum. Indeed he came to believe that the Chancellor was almost paralysed: by July Lloyd was being described as 'by nature more of a staff officer than a commander. But lately, he seems hardly to function.' Macmillan therefore seized the reins personally, summoned meetings of civil servants with himself in the chair, and devised an even more ambitious package than the NEDC had been. Edward Boyle recalled Macmillan's excitement at getting back to the policies of *The Middle Way*, and this certainly comes across in the Cabinet paper that Macmillan presented to outline the new approach. On 28 May, Macmillan took the unusual step of opening a Cabinet meeting by reading a six thousand word analysis of the economic outlook and the way in which the Government should respond to it. Enoch Powell's caustic description of this occasion in 1980 was that

> Macmillan entertained his Cabinet, instead of going through the agenda, with the reading of an essay he claimed to have composed over the week-end. From that paper derived a series of socialist measures, such as 'contracts of employment' and 'redundancy payments' which were seen by him, entirely in the spirit of *The Middle Way*, as the *quid pro quo* to the workers for cooperation in an inflation-free planned economy. I still relish recalling how the heads which were to roll not long afterwards nodded like cuckoo-clocks in sycophantic approval.

Powell was struck by the lack of economic rigour in Macmillan's exposition as well as by the policies proposed. But the Macmillan Cabinet paper was an impressive piece of *political* reasoning, expertly constructed to set those heads nodding. It began by outlining the basic task as the combination of full employment, stable prices, a strong exchange rate and economic growth; since no Government had ever managed to do this, there was no shame in the Conservatives having so far failed, and there had anyway been successes along the way. Incomes control for public employees could not continue if the private sector did not follow suit, for that would be inequitable and politically unpopular, so the problem was how to involve the private sector.

---

[41] Brittan, *Steering the Economy*, 165, 167–8; Evans, *Downing Street Diary*, 179; Thompson, *Day Before Yesterday*, 189; Central Office Chairman's department files, CCO20/1/10, Corrrespondence with Ministers, and CCO 20/8/5; Horne, *Macmillan*, 338; London Conservative Union Council, 21 Feb. 1962; Thorpe, *Lloyd*, 333–5, 358; Gerald Nabarro, *Nab 1: Portrait of a Politician* (1969), 35.

He rejected statutory control as unworkable, and rejected controlling the economy through higher unemployment as politically unacceptable; there would therefore have to be 'a permanent incomes policy' based on cooperation rather than compulsion. He presented this approach as a 'leap forward in the same kind of way and in the same kind of spirit that we should have done had we been now in Opposition instead of in power for eleven years. We must appear full of life and vigour with some new plans to put before the people.' Both the defence of the policy and its implications were spelled out bluntly:

> Everybody knows . . . that the growth in incomes must be parallel to the growth in production. And therefore anyone who is against an incomes policy should be denounced as either being an anarchist, in favour of a sort of 19th century liberalism or free-for-all and the devil take the hindmost; or willing to accept all the risks of continual devaluation, the difficulties of exports, perhaps an almost national collapse . . . or, and this is the class that we have got to address ourselves to, he may be ready to accept an incomes policy in principle, but he may be sceptical about whether it will in fact be enforced fairly in practice. And since labour has the power to wreck any incomes policy the first task seems to me to persuade the Trades Unions and those who speak for labour that it is fair.

The rest of the paper sketched in the inducements that would be needed to persuade 'the working classes as we are apt in this room to call them' to cooperate with a flexible policy of incomes restraint, the measures to which Powell in 1980 took such exception. The middle classes, or 'the Orpingtonians' as the Prime Minister described them, would benefit above all by the restoration of stable prices and lower interest rates (which 'should be pushed as soon as we feel it is sound to do so'), though he would also offer them lower consumer prices through the abolition of retail price fixing. The most difficult problem would be the 'special cases', those groups who as the economy changed would deserve larger than average (or smaller) increases in pay, and the avoidance of leapfrogging and of norms that rapidly became every trade union's target. This all led up to the need for a permanent machinery for the evaluation of individual pay claims, what was eventually inaugurated as the National Incomes Commission. The final inducement to the country to join such a collaborative venture, 'and I hope the Chancellor of the Exchequer will not think me too ambitious', would be the promise of immediate reflation to secure economic growth. He concluded by setting out the harsh choice, either to abandon incomes restraint with the passing of the 1961 emergency, and so lose an opportunity, or to 'develop our policy, saying not only that it is not an emergency but that the modern world requires something of this order, as part of the machinery for running a society like ours'. [42]

---

[42] Brittan, *Steering the Economy*, 165, 170; Horne, *Macmillan*, 342; Hutchinson, *Last Edwardian*, 115; Thompson, *Day Before Yesterday*, 187; Powell, *Reflections*, 140; Macmillan's paper is in PREM 11/3930, drawn to my attention by Peter Hennessy.

This was all in the spirit of *The Industrial Charter*, in many ways reflecting its detailed reasoning too, and the shift away from the more cautious and less interventionist policies pursued in office since 1951 was faced up to as a step towards modernity, a deliberate change of direction. Lurking behind the debate lay Europe (which was not even mentioned in the Macmillan paper), for it was taken to be axiomatic that entry into the Common Market would be an economic opportunity for Britain only if the economy was first streamlined. Macmillan was setting out the governmental framework for that process of industrial modernisation; he was also suggesting an approach that would have put British practices alongside the indicative planning of France and the social market policies of West Germany. That 1962 debate also cast a long shadow forward, for when Edward Heath's Government faced exactly the same problem of re-entry into economic normality after a crisis period of incomes control in 1972, it reverted to a very similar bid for social market cooperation with the unions. By 1972 the European perspective was actual rather than anticipated, but the industrial relations mood was infinitely less promising. Heath may well have imbibed much of the reasoning of 1972 from his earlier participation in Macmillan's Government, despite lurches in very different directions in the mean time. When, during a debate at Swinton in 1973, a Tory critic told Heath that many Conservatives were upset and bewildered by his industrial policy, Heath rejoined that intervention had always been Conservative policy, and cited as an example the Macmillan Government's policy on cotton.[43]

Offered this major strategic choice towards interventionism in the economy, Ministers went along with Macmillan's reasoning; Powell's head may not have been one of those nodding in appreciation, but neither he nor Thorneycroft resigned in protest this time; on the other hand, neither he nor Thorneycroft was now in a department where he would have to take personal responsibility for the policy. During June, the package was refined and worked through in detail. By 18 June, after a Chequers week-end with colleagues, Macleod was 'sure the outline that we settled was the right one', and three days later he sent comments on a speech that Macmillan would soon be making, which 'although it doesn't let the cat out of the bag, does show clearly that there is a cat in the bag'. He urged that thought be given to fending off the press speculation that this would provoke, but also made a suggestion that indicates how far Macmillan's 'new approach' package was already coming apart, in urging the deletion from Macmillan's speech of any reference to ending Resale Price Maintenance (RPM). In response, Macmillan asked Macleod on 4 July to assess 'the effect electorally' of abolishing RPM, and Macleod took this as an invitation to attack the whole idea. He argued that the Board of Trade overstated its likely effect; that a majority of people

[43] Campbell, *Heath*, 100; Central Office file, CCO 500/32/21, Heath Correspondence.

did not favour it; that Conservative MPs 'would bitterly resent legislation to abolish it', a view shared by the Chief Whip (who as a former retailer had special knowledge); and that the most the package should say was that the Government had an open mind on the subject (which he at least clearly did not). No commitment to abolish RPM was given by Macmillan, and at the end of 1962 Central Office was listing the threat to RPM as one of five possible ways of attacking Labour, only for their own Party to take up the policy again in the following year. Difficulties in working out details of the other policies in the package, many of which would also be contentious, produced similarly fudged results. The Chief Whip indeed now opposed the whole thing, arguing that 'this is not Conservatism'. The Prime Minister's final plan was presented to the Cabinet on 20 June, but was not announced until a ministerial crisis had transformed the political landscape. Macmillan noted that Lloyd's reaction to his package was 'rather chilly'. How could such an economic initiative go forward without the Chancellor's enthusiastic advocacy, and how could the package be sold to the electorate unless the Treasury would agree to relax the credit squeeze, which Lloyd was only now beginning even to plan for? On 21 June Macmillan noted in his diary a meeting with Butler that indicated that they shared a common view, 'that the present grave political position is due entirely to the bad handling of the economic problem (or rather its bad presentation) by the Chancellor of the Exchequer and the Treasury. [Butler] felt that drastic action was necessary to save the situation. This means the problem (an immense human and political problem) of replacing the Chancellor of the Exchequer.' Butler, though urged on by Macleod, reported this as Macmillan's view as much as his own. The Party's leaders were nerving themselves to remove Lloyd and encouraging each other to take the view that they had no real alternative.[44]

'Selwyn Lloyd ausgebootet' and the July purge

The urgent need to change the Chancellor now became tangled up with Macmillan's less urgent wish to reconstruct the Cabinet as a whole; the discontented mood that was gathering head in the Party was pointedly brought out in the Peckham Conservatives' CPC discussion on 28 June, when it was agreed that 'the way to meet the Liberal challenge could be summed up in one word, "backbone".' Macmillan had discussed with a number of colleagues, mainly the older ones but including Watkinson who was only 52, the possibility that they might leave the Government in a reshuffle later in the year, and several had agreed to this without demur; Harold Evans had also been urging him to do something about the problem of Government publicity, with which Hill was no longer dealing in a very

---

[44] Central Office Chairman's department file, CCO 20/8/5; Horne, *Macmillan*, 340–1; Evans, *Downing Street Diary*, 199; Butler, *Art of the Possible*, 233.

dynamic manner – and for which he now had insufficient time anyway since he had taken on the Housing Ministry in October 1961. The need for such a reconstruction was seen as deriving from the electorate's 'boredom' with faces who had been seen in office for many years and from the same modernising motivation that underlay Macmillan's economic initiative. George Hutchinson wrote of Cabinet Ministers being 'sacrificed for reasons of stage management, to provide a change of cast, a set of new faces', and this was indeed something for which Macleod was explicitly pressing. On 6 July Butler was asked by Macmillan 'what I would do if I were Prime Minister and forming a new government, since, said Macmillan, "That is what I virtually want to do now".' On the 10th, Butler and Macleod, who were keeping close counsel with each other as events developed, visited the Prime Minister to press for early action. A week earlier, prompted by an assurance from the Area Agent that Robin Marlar at North East Leicester would get at least ten thousand votes, Macleod had confidently claimed that the by-election was a two-horse race between Conservative and Labour. Now, on 11 July, he warned on the 12th that Marlar would almost certainly come a poor third (as he did), and this was the peg on which he now hung formal advice that a Prime Minister could hardly ignore, particularly if he really did suspect a Butler/Macleod plot to oust him from office:

> I feel that I should urge upon you, as Chairman of the Party, that if you are contemplating changes in the Government, that these should be made before we rise for the Recess. I do not relish the idea of the long recess without the guidance of Parliament and with all the propaganda against the Common Market that will certainly come. I think it would help a great deal to steady the nerves of our Party if they could see something of our plans before the House rises.

For Macleod then, the 'new approach' in economic policy and the new team of Ministers were interlinked; it would make little sense to announce a bold new initiative in July and then reshuffle the Cabinet in October. Macmillan's reply, sent through a secretary, indicates that the sub-text had been well understood: 'the Prime Minister was grateful for your letter of July 11, about Leicester North East, and the need for the Government to be seen to be doing something'. By this stage, the need to be seen to be 'doing something' had become almost more significant than what was actually done.[45]

What followed, the 'night of the long knives' or (as Butler dubbed it in deference to Macmillan's crofter blood) the 'massacre of Glencoe', was a sad piece of mismanagement from which Macmillan's reputation never recovered; as the Chief Whip later put it to Butler, 'for once the unflappable actually flapped'. There remains doubt about the exact sequence of events,

---

[45] Peckham CA minutes, 28 June 1962; Watkinson, *Turning Points*, 158–60; Kilmuir, *Political Adventure*, 323; Evans, *Downing Street Diary*, 197; Hutchinson, *Last Edwardian*, 116; Butler, *Art of the Possible*, 233; Fisher, *Macleod*, 220; Central Office constituency file, CCO 1/14/282; Central Office Chairman's department file, 20/8/5; interview with Lord Deedes.

but the main lines are clear. Macmillan determined to sack Lloyd on Thursday 12 June, but probably did not yet intend to do more than make minor conseqential changes. However, the double impact of a leak of his intentions to the *Daily Mail* published on Thursday morning (a leak generally attributed to Butler), and Lloyd's own announcement of the news to his friends after his interview with the Prime Minister on Thursday afternoon, set boundless speculation going. At this point then, to avoid a week-end of unchecked press speculation and the possibility that he might lose control of the situation altogether – might even be forced out of office – Macmillan decided to accelerate the timetable. On Thursday and Friday he terminated six more Cabinet Ministers – Eccles, Hill, Kilmuir, Maclay, Mills and Watkinson. The abruptness of this procedure was breathtaking, as was the scale, and for those directly involved it was most insulting; Kilmuir remarked that he would give his cook more notice than he had received as Lord Chancellor, Eccles thought himself treated like a sacked housemaid, and another of those departing said he was made to feel like an office boy caught with his hand in the till. Lloyd, deeply hurt, refused a peerage and the others were equally determined not to be bought off. They were not much impressed either by the reason given for their dismissal: to Watkinson, the Prime Minister 'painted a picture of a political situation that was beyond my wildest dreams and his forebodings of Ministerial revolt, centred upon Selwyn Lloyd, did not seem to me to make much sense. . . . Selwyn . . . was not the stuff of which rebels are made.' To Hill, Macmillan explained that 'it would be very damaging – even fatal – to the Government to postpone the announcement'. For the casualties, the timing could hardly have been worse, for the sackings were announced on the day after the Leicester by-election; they seemed to have been scapegoated. Nor was it only the seven sacked Cabinet Ministers who were upset; Reginald Bevins later recalled that for days another fifty juniors had the jitters whenever the telephone rang: 'I was uneasily aware that the dangerous political age had fallen from 65 to 50 within 24 hours'.[46]

The outside reaction was one of amazement; the veteran political correspondent James Margach had 'never seen a political party so pole-axed by shock'. A German newspaper headlined its account 'Selwyn Lloyd ausgebootet', but the British press were less amused; headlines, cartoons and political columns all interpreted Macmillan's action as a panic-stricken attempt to retain control of his Government, a bungled piece of butchery. A *Sunday Express* cartoon showed a battered Macmillan on the prow of the good ship 'Never had it so good', saying 'Members of the crew, I have driven the ship

[46] Butler note, 10 Jan. 1963, Butler MSS, G40; Horne, *Macmillan*, 342–4, 346; Keith Alderman, 'Harold Macmillan's Night of the Long Knives', in *Contemporary Record*, vol. 6, no. 2 (1992), 252–4; Thompson, *Day Before Yesterday*, 189–91; Kilmuir, *Political Adventure*, 323; Watkinson, *Turning Points*, 161; Charles Hill, *Both Sides of the Hill* (1964), 201; Bevins, *Greasy Pole*, 135.

on the rocks. For such striking incompetence, you're fired.' Even looking back a year later, the *Daily Telegraph* felt of July 1962 that 'the shooting of so many Admiral Byngs was hardly likely to encourage the rest'. Whereas Gallup had found that 79 per cent had approved of the Prime Minister's performance in office in 1960, and this had already fallen to 47 per cent even before the 1962 purge, it was down to only 36 per cent a week later. Butler privately wrote that Macmillan 'should know by now how to handle Selwyn. He has favoured him and cared for him for six years. He has made Chequers available for him. And now he has made him a martyr.' For Lloyd, Nigel Birch was on hand with memories of 1958, and persuaded him to write a letter of resignation and publish it, a letter that made it absolutely clear that he had been pushed out against his will, and an act that made changes of policy more difficult in the weeks that followed. Lord Avon emerged from retirement to tell the world that Lloyd had been badly treated, and to advise Lloyd to get a resolution of confidence from his constituency, which he easily managed a week later; he somewhat disingenuously told his Wirral supporters that 'the Prime Minister asked for my resignation. I gave it willingly', but an eloquent speech of support from his chairman generated 'a tremendous ovation' for their Member. Lloyd also received an ovation from Tory backbenchers when he next entered the Commons, not a good sign for Macmillan. Birch, who had sardonically congratulated the premier for keeping his head when all about were losing theirs, also penned a philippic to *The Times* with an insultingly brief message: 'Sir, For the second time the Prime Minister has got rid of a Chancellor of the Exchequer who tried to get expenditure under control. Once is more than enough.' For the *Daily Mail*, 'Supermac' was now 'Mac the Knife'. Kilmuir had recently told a political researcher that 'loyalty was the Tories' secret weapon', a phrase much anthologised by later writers on the Conservative Party; after the purge, as his memoirs wryly put it, 'I doubt if [loyalty] has ever had to endure so severe a strain'.[47]

These reactions inevitably meant that the positive side of the reshuffle was not much noticed. Few of the Ministers who had been sacked had been outstanding successes and none had recently been very effective communicators of Government policy. The average age of the seven who left the Cabinet was 60, the age of those who joined was 49; the reshuffle fulfilled Macmillan's secondary purpose of ensuring that, if the Party lost the next election, then there would be enough experienced men of the next generation to take power again in due course; and since only eight of the Cabinet survived with the same job, there was now rather less excuse for boredom. Maudling reached the Exchequer at 45, younger even than Lloyd George had

[47] Alderman, 'Night of the Long Knives', 243, 251; Butler, *Art of the Possible*, 232–3; Thorpe, *Lloyd*, 350–2; Watkinson, *Turning Points*, 164; Sampson, *Macmillan*, 201; Sparrow, *Rab*, 189; Evans, *Downing Street Diary*, 209; Horne, *Macmillan*, 350; Margach, *Anatomy of Power*, 121; Wirral CA minutes, 29 July 1962; Kilmuir, *Political Adventure*, 264.

been in 1908; Powell and Boyd-Carpenter were promoted to the Cabinet; Keith Joseph at 44 and Edward Boyle at 39 were both imaginative Cabinet appointments; Macmillan told the Queen that 'I have been very glad to have had the opportunity to bring in men like Sir Edward Boyle and Sir Keith Joseph, who represent active and energetic youth'. Since they were both baronets, from Eton and Harrow respectively, youth and a modern face for the Government in the swinging sixties were perhaps uneasily yoked together. Boyle was the popular choice of a widely-admired and respected politician, but with an image that reinforced the ambiguity of Macmillan's own. Anthony Sampson in 1962 thought that Boyle had

> a nineteenth century look to him; he is a huge rubicund baronet who wears formal clothes, and talks with unconcealed learning, assuming others to be equally learned. He walks like a bear, with a formidable shuffle, and he has the broad interests and leisureliness of a cultivated squire. But, behind this Victorian appearance, he is one of the most radically-minded men; he . . . has a dislike of Conservative snobbery, and a belief in the purposive role of government, which is rare in his party.

Less ambiguously, the replacement of Charles Hill by William Deedes, as Minister responsible for government information, brought a man with good press contacts into a key post.[48]

When the dust had settled, Butler joked about feeling his neck from time to time to make sure that his head was still on its shoulders, but he had in fact moved to a less prominent role; he had for the past year ensured that colleagues understood that the Home Secretary was the senior Secretary of State, but he now left the Home Office and became just 'First Secretary of State'; he was formally recognised as Deputy Prime Minister, but had no department of his own. Since he continued to be much involved with Africa and was often abroad, the Deputy Prime Ministership meant very little, except when Macmillan chose to leave him in charge, as he had been doing since 1957 anyway. Butler and Macmillan were now the only two who had sat in Cabinet since 1951, and were distinctly older than the rest; the Prime Minister was a generation older than the average age of the Cabinet. For the next year the rationale of the Government's membership was to be that Macmillan and Butler provided the vital leavening of experience while a team of energetic younger men (called 'the beavers' by Macmillan) would provide the modernising thrust. Some sign of the difficulties to come with this relationship in 1963 had been foreseen when Macmillan confessed to Butler in January 1962 that 'as Prime Minister his main problem was in dealing with the temperaments of his comparatively young and inexperienced' colleagues; the generation gap remained a visible problem, but there would be a balanced approach that stressed both continuity and drive, a strategy that

[48] Alderman, 'Night of the Long Knives', 246–8; Howard, *RAB*, 292–3; Horne, *Macmillan*, 347, 349; Morrison Halcrow, *Keith Joseph: A Single Mind* (1989), 28; Sampson, *Macmillan*, 202; Sampson, *Anatomy of Britain*, 89.

fell apart only in the new crises of Summer 1963. William Rees-Mogg in the *Sunday Times* was one of the few who picked up the real point of the reshuffle: 'in the last year, one has often felt, even from his speeches, that the Prime Minister wanted a better administration than his senior Ministers were actually giving him. By choosing the men who most obviously know what the modern world is about he proves and emphasises the quality of his understanding.'[49]

The immediate worry was a censure debate on 26 July. Macmillan's opponents on the backbenches seem to have made a spirited effort to get as many as fifty Conservative MPs to abstain, enough both to ensure safety in numbers from any subsequent persecution, and to force Macmillan himself to resign. There is no doubt that some MPs felt mutinous; when Macmillan spoke to the 1922 Committee on 19 July, there was 'little sign of undue deference', and he was much on the defensive. When it became clear that few would demonstrate dissent when the press was already so hostile, the revolt collapsed. The Conservative majority in the debate was ninety-eight, much as usual. As wounded feelings were soothed with time, the departed ministers accepted the consolation prizes normal to more low-key reshuffles; as Peter Richards put it, the 1962 sackings finally produced 'two new peerages, three Companions of Honour, one Dame, and the Promotion of Lord Kilmuir from a viscount to an earl'. None of the departed became Macmillan's long-term foe, though the early acceptance of directorships in defence industries by both Watkinson and Kilmuir caused him considerable embarrassment.[50]

In the hothouse atmosphere of a July censure debate after a ministerial crisis, the policies announced as Macmillan's 'new approach' attracted little attention, but they (and the European issue that lay behind them) were central to what had been done. When the National Union's General Purposes Committee held a special meeting on 1 August to consider the situation, it accepted that a team of Macmillan as leader with younger Ministers to back him was an effective one, but calls were made for a clearer statement of the Government's strategic intentions and a more positive explanation of their case. John Gummer for the Tory students argued for an idealistic focus of policy: 'young people want to take part in something that is above the level of ordinary politics. The ideal of the Common Market could fill this need.' This perhaps provoked Macleod, who had been pressing a similar argument on his colleagues all year, to an unguarded statement of the way in which he saw the immediate past and the future (as the Secretary's notes indicate):

> It is very difficult to get people to understand that the days of Empire are over; it was a great act of statesmanship to turn the Empire into the Commonwealth.

[49] Butler note, 24 Jan. 1962, Butler MSS, G38; *Sunday Times*, 15 July 1962.
[50] Horne, *Macmillan*, 349–51; Goodhart, *The 1922*, 185–6; Richards, *Patronage in British Government*, 182; Andrew Roth, *The Business Background of Members of Parliament* (1963), i–vii.

This is not fully appreciated. The natural destiny of this country lies in Europe. Very difficult to get this over to the public, as we cannot embarrass Mr. Heath [in Brussels] by pronouncing that we shall become the leader of Europe.

Increasingly in 1962 Europe became the pivot on which all other policies turned, though the Government's official position was never more than that Britain would enter if acceptable terms emerged from Heath's negotiations. The Chief Whip suggested the vulnerability that this situation created and suggested that an alternative position be worked out in case the Brussels talks failed: 'I used to be scolded for suggesting a fall-back position. If we were fighting a battle . . . then we must maintain the objective, and therefore there was no fall back position to discuss.' Other Ministers felt that preparing for any other eventuality would only encourage the anti-marketeers at home and perhaps feed French suspicions of British policy too.[51]

Macleod circulated his ministerial colleagues with a note on public opinion and the European issue on 18 September, concluding that there was a need for an idealistic approach; the support of the young and the key opinion-formers could be won on this tack. He urged that it be proclaimed 'with trumpets' as the nation's next great step forward; the Government should 'say flatly that we were convinced of the advantages of joining the Community and were prepared, if the country would support us, to lead Britain into the Common Market'. In a covering note he warned that there was no more time for hesitation. A few weeks later, he circulated briefing notes obligingly provided by the Board of Trade which set out the economic case for British entry and urged colleagues to use them in speeches; meanwhile Deedes was quietly mobilising the Central Office of Information, not only to inform such critics as the farmers but also any other interest or occupational group that could be identified, always with the positive side of the case on Europe. Also in September the Labour Leader came out against entering Europe, and a tricky meeting of Commonwealth Prime Ministers was successfully negotiated. In October the issue became much clearer, for Labour's decision to oppose entry to the EEC at its own Conference opened up an opportunity that Conservatives found irresistible. Only a few weeks earlier Macmillan had argued in a television broadcast that 'a lot of people look backward, but the real test you must bring to this question is – are we going to look forward?' Harold Evans saw this as 'the night when the PM finally and publicly cast aside caution and reservations on UK entry into Europe'. It was still though a qualified enthusiasm for Europe; in a letter of endorsement for Heath's candidature in the Glasgow University Rectoral election, written on 25 September, Macmillan still stated that 'I absolutely reject the view that Britain is faced with a choice between the Commonwealth and Europe'. At

---

[51] National Union papers, NUA 5/2/2, GP papers; Thompson, *Day Before Yesterday*, 185, 192; interview with Sir Edward Heath.

the Conservatives' Llandudno Conference, a strongly pro-European motion was passed with fewer than twenty dissentients, pro-EEC speeches were made by Butler, Heath and Home, and Macmillan himself finally did come down in favour of entering the EEC in his rally speech. Europe occupied most of the speech, and the demands for greater efficiency, modernisation and change with which the speech were peppered were all set in this context.

> The European Community is not a static but a growing and dynamic body. In many respects its policies and future have still to be worked out. If we wait too long it will be too late. Now is the opportunity and we must seize it. . . . It is our sincere hope – which I know you overwhelmingly share – that these negotiations may be successful.

For once Butler managed to outdo Macmillan at a Party Conference, for the aphorism he used to contrast Conservative and Labour policy on Europe perfectly captured the contrast that Macleod had wanted the Party to establish: 'For them a thousand years of history books. For us the future.' There was even consideration of the calling of a snap election in October, to catch Labour out. The Party had burned its boats, for it was now clear from their own leaders' statements that a failure to get into the EEC would imperil both Britain's future and their own political strategy. While Macleod had regularly commented on the need not to say anything that would damage Heath's negotiating position, it seems not to have occurred to him that Britain might be excluded even if the negotiations succeeded. The stakes were therefore very high: as Michael Fraser told David Butler in 1964,

> Europe was to be our *deus ex machina*: it was to create a new contemporary political argument with insular Socialism; dish the Liberals by stealing their clothes; give us something *new* after 12–13 years; act as a catalyst of modernisation; give us a new place in the international sun. It was Macmillan's ace, and De Gaulle trumped it. The Conservatives never really recovered.

The overall policy stance that Fraser was summarising remained though the core of the Conservative identity and of Conservative electioneering for the next ten years.[52]

---

[52] Central Office Chairman's department file, CCO 20/1/10, Correspondence with Ministers; Fisher, *Macleod*, 223–4; Windlesham, *Communication*, 171; Central Office *Notes on Current Politics*, 29 Oct. 1962; Evans, *Downing Street Diary*, 212, 221; Central Office Chairman's department file, CCO 20/8/5; Campbell, *Heath*, 134; Sampson, *Macmillan*, 213; D.E. Butler and Anthony King, *The British General Election of 1964* (1965), 79; interview with Lord Deedes.

Chapter 4

Macmillan to Heath, 1962–65

The New Approach of 1962 was a package that involved policy, the means of implementing it, and presentation. The new Cabinet team combined the experience of Macmillan and Butler with the middle managers of the Class of 1950, and dynamic younger 'beavers'. The thrust to modernise the British economy was linked to the increasing perception that Britain was ripe for radical reform – and Europe was both the carrot and the stick in the drive to transform Britain. A constructive task in Europe was seen as a way of keeping the Party in touch with the idealistic young and with centre opinion in general. Finally, this package would enable the Conservatives after eleven years in office to portray themselves as the Party of the future, while Labour was locked into the past. This last point acquired a new significance when John F. Kennedy's election to the US Presidency heralded the advent of a younger generation; until then Macmillan was younger than most of his foreign counterparts; in January 1962, Butler noted after a conversation with the Prime Minister that 'he sees around him Adenauer, De Gaulle & others & does not see why he should go before them'. Kennedy was not only young for a world leader, just 43 when elected, but also determined to stress youthfulness, modernity and lack of formality; he was immediately adopted as the international symbol of the emerging global youth culture, and it is no coincidence that the British satirists were stunned into sentimental elegy by his assassination in November 1963. Macmillan actually got on well with Kennedy and was not at first especially damaged by the new mood; the Labour leader Gaitskell was twelve years younger than Macmillan but hardly seemed a modern young man in the Kennedy mould. Even so, Macmillan may have felt that his time was passing, saying to Dennis Walters 'I wish I could talk to some of the younger people'. Gaitskell's death and the election of the 46-year-old Harold Wilson to replace him in January 1963 was a far more dangerous development. Wilson specifically sought comparison as 'the British Kennedy', and if this was far-fetched, his public image did share something with Kennedy's – an easy informality that impressed working journalists and came over well on television, an impatience with traditional ways of doing things, and a frank ambition. For the next two years, Wilson relentlessly exploited against Macmillan and then Home this generation gap of years and manners; at different times Wilson told friends that he most feared Heath, Maudling or Macleod as premier, any of whom would have removed his main campaigning advantage just by being there, though he was also confident that the Conservatives would never bring themselves to do their Party this service. When the Conservatives finally nerved themselves to replace Home with Heath in 1965, for exactly the reason that Wilson had earlier feared, it was after power had already been lost, and after they had therefore also lost the ability to shape the political agenda.[1]

Almost exactly at the time that Wilson first faced Macmillan across the Commons Chamber, the bottom had in any case been knocked out of the 1962 New Approach by De Gaulle's veto and the failure of Britain to get into the Common Market. There had been no planning for this, no fall-back position, and hardly any forethought. For a time the Government was knocked sideways and had little direction to its operations. There were then clear signs, after Easter 1963, that things were back under control; Macmillan and his Party were gearing up for a general election campaign with renewed confidence. It was into this scenario that the Profumo scandal erupted, terminally damaging Macmillan's confidence and seriously wounding the Party's self-esteem. That crisis had in turn been weathered when the Prime Minister's illness, his badly-timed resignation and the public split over the selection of Home as his successor once again negated all attempts to campaign for the future; these events also upset the finely-balanced package of personnel worked out in 1962 and, because the 1963 leadership crisis provoked rumblings for months after the event, it delayed into Spring 1964 any concerted attempt to regain the political initiative. The narrow electoral defeat of October 1964, and the subsequent need to re-form the troops under fire in the expectation of a second election within months, led to the hasty dropping of what remained of the old guard and the Party's uninhibited plunge into the politics of modernisation and youth in July 1965.

Those snakes and ladders of 1963 make it important to recognise aspirations at the start of the year, again in May and finally in September, when in each case there were reasonable hopes that the way was clear for a positive way forward; on each of these occasions that way forward would have been through a version of the New Approach of 1962. The appointment early in 1963 of Hailsham to take special responsibility for the North East as a trouble-shooting Minister to suggest interventionist measures to deal with regional unemployment was exactly in keeping with Macmillan's ideas in May 1962. Polls and by-elections at the end of 1962 seemed to indicate that the worst was over and that the Government could now work its way back to popularity as in 1957–58. By November Gallup polls showed that Labour's

[1] Peter Oppenheimer, 'Muddling Through: The Economy', in V. Bogdanor and R. Skidelsky (eds), *The Age of Affluence* (1970), 149; Butler note, 24 Jan. 1962, Butler MSS, G38; ICBH witness seminar, 'Did the Conservatives Lose Direction?', transcript in *Contemporary Record*, vol. 2, no. 5 (1989), 28; Nigel Fisher, *Iain Macleod* (1973), 206; Janet Morgan (ed.), *The Backbench Diaries of Richard Crossman* (1981), 1005.

lead was back into single figures and that the Liberal share of the vote had almost halved since the Spring. On 22 November, five by-elections in Tory seats were held simultaneously, a 'little General Election' and the first polling since July. The Conservatives lost Glasgow Woodside (a marginal seat won from Labour in 1950) and, in rather special circumstances, Dorset South, but held Chippenham, Norfolk Central and Northamptonshire South. It is a sign of how panicky the Party had become that the retention of three seats that had been held even in 1945 was greeted with much relief. These results also confirmed that the Liberal wave was on the ebb, for only in Chippenham did a Liberal manage second place. Dorset South was a Party disaster of sorts but hardly a precedent: Angus Maude was the official Party candidate, having now returned from Australia, but found himself opposed by a local man standing as an anti-Common Market Conservative, backed by the same Lord Hinchingbrooke who had been Maude's old Suez Group colleague and whose inheritance of a peerage had caused the vacancy; the Independent Tory polled over 5,000 votes while Maude lost by 704; Macleod reported that 'Hinch's influence in the villages was too strong'. Maude's subsequent selection (and election) for Stratford-upon-Avon when Profumo resigned indicates that he was not blamed for the South Dorset defeat. The narrowness of Ian Gilmour's majority in Central Norfolk also owed something to anti-Common Market voting on agricultural issues: turnout was lowest in the Tory farming villages, but there was plenty of discontent there on other issues too. But with Labour now again the enemy rather than the Liberals, politics could return to the normality with which the Party professionals felt more comfortable, and in this context average adverse swings of about 7 per cent were much like early 1958, also three years into a Parliament, from which the Conservatives had recovered to win very comfortably eighteen months later.[2]

Failure to enter the EEC and its consequences

The Common Market issue remained difficult, for while the leadership could get an endorsement in a loyalty call at the 1962 Llandudno Party Conference, by-elections showed that there were still discontents locally, and as long as the 'anti' campaign went on alongside negotiations in Brussels neither the Party nor the country could be rallied with a strong statement of the case for going in. Macleod concluded on 27 November that the country was still 'suspicious and neutral' towards the Government, if no longer actually 'hostile'. It was, he thought, all rather like 1958 except for two things. First, the Party had been in power for longer, 'and less therefore is forgiven us. We have no margin of

---

[2] Lord Hailsham, *A Sparrow's Flight: Memoirs* (1990), 337–8; D.E. Butler and G. Butler, *British Political Facts, 1900–1986* (1986), 258; Central Office Chairman's department file, CCO 20/8/5, Correspondence with Macmillan.

error left.' Second, 'we are awaiting events in Brussels. . . . We are upon a painted ocean until the end of these negotiations. Having achieved our success at Llandudno, we still cannot give out the trumpet call that would, I believe, gather people to us.' His assumption was still that the talks would succeed, and that in the Spring the Party could move back into a concerted propaganda drive centred on entering the EEC, on 'caring', and on 'efficiency' – again the balanced New Approach. At this time, the Party took a great deal of steadying; the North West Area chairman told his Area Council in November 1962 that this was 'no time to panic'.[3]

The Brussels talks had not gone well over the last months of 1962, and while remaining a tough negotiator Heath had had to concede much to keep the application alive. By January 1963 Macleod was no longer sure that the terms on offer would be at all easy to sell to the Party, and he opposed offering more concessions to buy off French resistance. Macleod and Macmillan had at last understood that Britain might not get in even if Heath's negotiations succeeded. Only on 23 January did Macmillan ask for 'a political assessment of the line to be taken, assuming that the Brussels negotiations break down', which was sent to him on the 25th by the Party Chairman after consultations with MPs and with the CRD; Macleod's letter was closely based on a draft by Fraser, though the draft itself was written after they had lunched to discuss its contents. This was the first formal consideration of a fall-back position, and came only a week *after* De Gaulle's 14 January press conference rejecting British entry and at about the time that Adenauer's acceptance of the French veto removed any real doubt about the outcome. Macmillan's broadcast to the nation on 30 January was along the lines of the Party advice received on the 25th, and this completed the story; his broadcast was given a higher profile by its publication in full by Central Office as a glossy leaflet. What then did the Party say? Macleod urged that the 'latent xenophobia and jingoism of the Parliamentary Party and in the constituencies . . . should be firmly discouraged'; Labour's 'told you so' reactions should be rebutted by placing the blame firmly on France, but without rancour, and the Party should 'stress our conception of a democratising, liberal and outward-looking Europe in contrast to the Bonapartist view'. But the crucial advice was about alternatives, given that Europe had been the central Tory aspiration of the past year:

> I am sure that we should not minimise the blow to our hopes, and to the hopes of our friends in Europe, which such a decision represents. Many people may feel some relief at the ending of worrying negotiations and the fear of a plunge into the unknown. But the building of a united and outward-looking Europe is felt by many of the best elements in our society, and by centre opinion generally, as the great task and adventure that faces us. To shrug it off, turn our backs on what

---

[3] Conservative Central Office Chairman's department file, CCO 20/8/5; North West Area Council, 24 Nov. 1962.

we have been trying to do (and indeed on much that has been achieved since the war), would be politically damaging and would involve the hazard of leaving the Liberals as the only 'European' party in Britain.

His advice was to be wary of 'dramatic new moves' and to ensure that any policies now pursued should remain consistent with 'the ultimate objective' of joining the EEC at a later date. The best thing might well be to wait 'for some weeks' before deciding whether 'some broader politial initiative would be advisable'. It was better to do nothing than to risk such a badly-thought-out démarche as a special Commonwealth trade conference (as the press were now urging), whose failure would be 'worse than inaction'. Heath in Brussels on 29 January, Macmillan on television the next day and Government spokesmen in both Commons and Lords on 12 February stuck to this line. Private feelings were even more downbeat: Macmillan wrote in his diary that 'all our policies at home and abroad are in ruins', a clear indication of the centrality of Europe to the new approach. Powell's reflection in 1970 was that 'perhaps this was the moment that he should have declared before history that his act had ended. At any rate from January 1963 onwards one had this continuous sense of slipping, and never being able to regain a hold.' Cummings in the *Daily Express* drew Macmillan as 'MacMoses', ditching tablets with the words 'To Promised Land via Common Market' and substituting tablets with the inscription 'To Promised Land via Macmoses "visions"'; in the corner of the drawing a shifty-looking Macleod is telling Hailsham that 'if you ask me, it's not a new tablet we need but a new Moses'. A *Sunday Telegraph* poll in March found that nearly half of Conservative voters thought that Macmillan should retire. Since the EEC setback was also a severe blow to Macleod's strategy, this was the point at which speculation began about a change of Party Chairman too. There was even talk of bringing in a ministerial chief of staff to assist Macmillan at Number 10, Powell's name being mentioned in the press for the job – but surely not by Macmillan himself.[4]

Macmillan was certainly downcast by the defeat; 'I do not remember going through a worse time since Suez'. He also understood the extent of the damage; after talking to him on 10 January, Butler could already record that 'there is in his mind a certain fin de siècle atmosphere which reflects philosophically that the two-party system was created for a purpose and that at the end of this parliament it may have to give evidence of its operation'. Macmillan told the nation on 30 January that 'a great opportunity has been missed. It is no good trying to disguise or minimise the fact.' A few days later he was noting privately the strategic dilemma: 'the great question remains

---

4 Central Office Chairman's department file, CCO 20/8/6, Correspondence with Macmillan; John Young, *Britain and European Unity, 1945–1992* (1993), 83; John Campbell, *Edward Heath* (1993), 131–3; Alistair Horne, *Macmillan, 1957–1986* (1989), 447; Alan Thompson, *The Day Before Yesterday* (1971), 196; Harold Evans, *Downing Street Diaries: The Macmillan Years* (1981), 256–7, 262, 264.

"what is the alternative?" to the European Community. If we are honest, we must say that there is none – had there been the chance of the Commonwealth Free Trade area we should have grasped it long ago.' Deprived of the strategic spine of their policy, Ministers continued gallantly to proclaim the vitality of the limbs. Heath addressed the YC Conference in London in February with a call to steam on ahead: 'we must be just as ready to face change, to adapt ourselves, now that we are not in the Community, as we were when we were prepared to go into it. Indeed we need to be more ready to face change.' His shopping list of proposals included an end to the sheltering of industries 'which cannot stand on their own feet with efficiency', the ending of the 'luxury of bad industrial relations' (though with no indication of how this would be achieved), an end to 'cosy' restrictive practices, and a drive to lower costs through innovation, better training and more efficient management. As John Campbell points out, this personal manifesto carried him through the rest of his front-bench career, but it was also typical of the way in which Ministers responded to the failure in Brussels in January 1963. Heath failed to persuade Macmillan to switch him to the home front to tackle some of these urgent tasks, partly no doubt because others were already pursuing the same objectives.[5]

There would have been several difficulties with this modernise-to-be-ready-for-Europe-sometime-in-the-future strategy, even if it had not been derailed by Profumo and other extraneous events in 1963. First, as Macleod had argued in November, 'we have no margin of error left', so the Brussels failure could not just be manfully avowed as a gallant failure which taught no lessons. Unlike Suez or the collapse of the 1960 Summit, failure to get into the EEC did not become another Mons retreat or Dunkirk, for which sympathy could be enlisted to the Government for at least trying. With the perversity that characterised British popular opinion about the EEC throughout the 1961–73 period, the public, which opinion polls had shown to have moved steadily against entry while it seemed probable that the negotiations would succeed, now blamed the Government for their failure. The Prime Minister's stock fell and so did that of his Party; Labour's Gallup poll lead doubled to 17 per cent between November 1962 and March 1963. Second, the gospel of modernising change without the European ideal at its heart was a cold doctrine which did not necessarily win votes anyway. Dr Beeching's pruning of the railway network was a case in point; when the Transport Bill was debated in the Commons in November 1961, several Conservative MPs were already expressing their concern about the application of 'purely commercial considerations' to the railways; one voted against and two more abstained; there was more widespread concern when Beeching's wholesale axeing of branch lines threatened MPs' constituency interests in 1963; a disgruntled

---

[5] Horne, *Macmillan*, 448–9; Butler note, 10 Jan. 1963, Butler MSS, G78; Campbell, *Heath*, 134–5.

Area leader wrote of these as plans that would now have to be defended as 'unpopular but necessary'; this was hardly an inspirational tone of voice.[6]

Much the same took place over local government reform. The Government's decision to act on the Herbert Commission's recommendation of a strategic regional authority for Greater London, supported by enlarged second-tier boroughs, was conceived very much as the modernising of an antique system so as to plan more thoroughly and to deliver services more efficiently. It also had the incidental Party advantage that the new Greater London Council, taking great swathes of outer suburbia into 'London', would be easily the most powerful local authority in the country and was more likely to be Conservative controlled than the old London County Council had been. The problem was that Tory suburbs did not take kindly to being removed from their historic affiliations to Essex or Middlesex; few felt any affection for the proposed new boroughs, so faceless that they were not even allocated names until a late stage of the process of legislation. In parliament, there was a running battle against the Bill, with rebellions on eighteen divisions involving fourteen Conservative MPs; Hornsey was so upset at the idea of joining what became Camden that the local Tories threatened to pull out of the National Union in protest; in the interests of efficiency, the Government found itself deliberately overriding the views of the Tory inhabitants of such places. The same principle was forced through in the East Midlands, where the Soke of Peterborough and the Isle of Ely were rationalised into Huntingdonshire and Cambridgeshire respectively, also against local protests. Rutland was luckier, even though its case for survival was the flimsiest when set against the rationalising doctrine of efficient larger units, for its champion was the Party Chairman. The Conservative local chairman reported a 'serious withdrawal of support by our members' when it seemed likely that the county would be dragooned into Leicestershire, and the chairman, agent and MP met Macleod at Central Office in February 1963. After consulting Keith Joseph who was the Minister responsible, Macleod took it up directly with the Prime Minister. He apologised for raising 'such a small problem, in every sense of the word' but explained that he had an 'instinctive feeling that this might turn out very badly indeed'. Macleod's argument was purely pragmatic: with a population under thirty thousand, Rutland as a county was an 'absurd' anachronism for which there was no justification in the modern world, but its very 'insignificance' would make it a dangerous foe to the government – and if Rutland's people did not mind being inefficiently governed why should the Government force the issue? Macmillan had a wary regard for Macleod's instincts in such cases, but replied that it would have to be argued out in

---

[6] R. Jowell and G. Hoinville, *Britain into Europe: Public Opinion and the EEC* (1976), 19–20; Butler and Butler, *British Political Facts*, 258–9; Harold Macmillan, *Pointing the Way* (1972), 369.

Cabinet and committee; along the way, the Government's nerve failed and Rutland lived to fight another day.[7]

Resistance to the argument that larger units would bring efficient, modern management was equally characteristic of Conservative resistance to educational reforms but was a theme that ran completely against the modernising grain of Government policy. Oliver Poole thought in 1964 that 'much of the Party's history from 1960 onwards becomes intelligible only in the light of this division. Whatever the merits of the opposing points of view, the traditionalist–progressive tension could never be ignored by the Conservative leaders. Mr. Macmillan was, of course, a progressive in these terms.' Macmillan demonstrated the difficulty himself in a note to the Minister of Transport in September 1962, pointing out that 'while we must not hesitate from the slogan "Growth means change – innovation and change are all the time necessary", yet we must not let it be thought that so far as men and women are concerned they are to be treated in the Victorian happy-go-lucky way when they thought of humans almost less than they thought of machines'.[8]

The third problem with modernisation as a policy focus was that the very idea of popularising 'change' as a political theme was double-edged for a Government that had been in office for over eleven years and called itself 'Conservative': Martin Redmayne reported to Macleod in February 1963 that a meeting of whips had been very sceptical about centring an election campaign on some slogan such as 'the challenge of change' since it could so easily be confused by Labour with 'time for a change'; they counselled against the use of the word 'change' anywhere in the Party's propaganda. Finally, the stance adopted after January 1963 sat uneasily alongside Macmillan's increasingly battered political image. In the year after July 1962, Macmillan seemed to age by a great deal more than twelve months; the satirists' spoof slogan 'modernise with Macmillan' was a much sharper barb in mid-1963 than it would have been a year earlier.[9]

The Government's continuing unpopularity in early 1963 owed something too to the coincidence of bad weather and spy scandals. As Chancellor from July 1962, Reginald Maudling had been instructed by Macmillan to expand the economy and get unemployment down, but there was a time-lag between Government changes and the reaction in the economy; and Samuel Brittan argued that Macmillan's replacement of Lloyd actually delayed the change of policy. Recovery did not get properly under way until the middle of 1963,

[7] Philip Norton, *Dissension in the House of Commons, 1945–1974* (1975), 191–2, 200–38, 249; National Union papers, NUA 5/2/1, GP Committee papers; Central Office Chairman's department file, CCO 20/8/6.
[8] D.E. Butler and Anthony King, *The British General Election of 1964* (1965), 79; Central Office Chairman's department file, CCO 20/8/6.
[9] Central Office Chairman's department files, CCO 20/1/6, Correspondence with the Chief Whip, and CCO 20/8/6.

and in the mean time the worst winter for sixteen years produced a hike in seasonal unemployment that pushed the overall figure up to three-quarters of a million, easily the worst position since 1947. Three March by-elections produced bad results and even the humiliation of the Conservative candidate coming fourth in East Swansea, but these were all in safe Labour seats. In May the borough elections showed a further fall in the Tory vote compared to the poor performance in 1962, but with Labour rather than the Liberals now the beneficiary; Conservative candidates did worse than at any time since 1945.[10]

Recovery begins

Yet around Easter the mood shifted. The shock of the European failure became less immediate; from Central Office, Lord Aldington, occupying the main backroom role until Poole returned, began discreetly to steer the British wing of the European Movement towards EFTA (European Free Trade Area) rather than the EEC. Maudling's first Budget continued the expansionist thrust of economic policy begun in Autumn 1962 and expounded the policy with a confidence that Lloyd had never managed. Maudling was embarking on a programme of expansion designed to break out of the cycle of boom and slump that had bedevilled the British economy for the past ten years; it was, he later recalled, a glittering prize that was aimed at. 'My policy has been described as a "dash for freedom". I think that is ascribing to me, rather unusually, an excess of energy and enthusiasm. In fact the whole policy was deliberate, calculated and coherent.' By this time though the National Incomes Commission (NIC) was being bogged down by the same lack of trade union cooperation that had already hindered the NEDC; it limped on and gestated into a quite different animal under the 1964 Labour Government, but did little more than give the appearance of inaction under Macmillan and Home. The powerhouse of economic management remained the Treasury and the chief weapons remained budgetary policy and credit controls. The 1963 Budget included new interventionist policies to assist areas with particularly high unemployment, and, together with the earlier measures, these generated in the Government confidence that momentum was being recovered after the January setback.[11]

At the end of March, the Prime Minister minuted colleagues to urge them 'to take greater risks than in the past' when broadcasting; they should be prepared to talk on subjects wider than their own briefs for 'appearances on occasions of general interest have great value in publicising the personality

[10] Samuel Brittan, *Steering the Economy* (1969), 173; Reginald Maudling, *Memoirs* (1978), 103; Central Office *Notes on Current Politics* [hereafter *NCP*] 1 Apr. 1963; Central Office file, CCO 4/10/192, Pacts.
[11] Brittan, *Steering the Economy*, 171, 174–7; Maudling, *Memoirs*, 112–16.

of Ministers'. On 16 April, after a successful trip to Swansea, Macmillan asked Central Office to start laying on 'meet the Party workers' sessions whenever he had official visits outside London, and such arrangements were laid on for a coming visit to Wolverhampton. In early May, Butler was asked to shoulder more of the Prime Minister's routine business, both in chairing Cabinet committees and on the 'formal, representational side', so as to clear Macmillan's diary, 'as the campaigning season has suddenly come upon us'. Macmillan also got Butler's agreement to the secondment to the CRD of two special speechwriters whose main job would be to provide texts and ideas for the Prime Minister, an idea that led to the arrival of Nigel Lawson and Eldon Griffiths later in the year. A week later, Central Office was investigating how Wilson managed press coverage for his speeches and discovering that the Labour leader's practice of holding informal press conferences was more effective than either releasing complete texts or giving the press short hand-outs; Ministers were advised to follow this practice. The Party was even strengthening the Prime Minister's own nerve; when his Bromley supporters asked for the drafting in of junior ministers to address meetings in his constituency because Macmillan's own meetings might well 'develop into rowdy scenes and bring us bad national publicity', Macleod and Poole thought this capitulation to CND to be 'chicken-hearted' and told Macmillan he should not allow himself to be driven off his home territory; a few television pictures of the Prime Minister being shouted down by student hecklers might even do him some good with Tory voters.[12]

In late April there was a strategy week-end at which the thirty senior Ministers met at Chequers without civil servants, and discussed the strategic way forward. Butler's laconic note of the business transacted at the Saturday sessions suggests that few decisions were taken, but it also indicates that a number of divisions normally associated with a rather later phase of Conservative history were already in Ministers' minds, and might well have come forward in the run up to a normal election had one been possible in 1963–64. He thought that,

> The discussions morning and evening . . . were not epoch-making. They came to this – in the morning on economics the time-honoured discussion between those who believe in the power and majesty of the State and those with Sir Keith Joseph on [*sic*] private enterprise. Oliver Poole joined in and with great wisdom asked for a synthesis. I said that a managed economy was here to stay. The afternoon was devoted to social questions which became very muddled between those who wished to adapt Beveridge and get rid of universality and those like me who warned of the difficulties. The last session was concerned with Government organisation and did not get very far. I said that Walter Bagehot was still hard to beat.

---

12 Central Office General Director's file, CCO 120/4/1, Selwyn Lloyd Inquiry; Central Office Chairman's department file, CCO, 20/8/6.

It is striking that it was Joseph rather than either Powell or Thorneycroft who seemed to Butler the most memorable spokesman for the free market position.[13]

At Number 10 in May, Harold Evans was reporting on the work he had been doing since February on the refurbishment of public relations strategy. The themes would be '(a) achievement, (b) forward planning, and (c) the youth, cheerfulness and vigour of the administration under a wise, confident and experienced leader of international repute'. The timing of announcements, White Papers and planted parliamentary questions would be coordinated to enable the Government to shape the flow of the debate; the Prime Minister might experiment with open, televised press conferences in the French and U.S. style (though the British press was known to be hostile to the idea); Macmillan should step up his programme of meetings with proprietors, senior journalists and suitable editors, and should find opportunities to make pronouncements on non-Party issues with a moral content, 'to undermine efforts to portray you as no more than an adroit politician concerned only with material well-being'. This extensive programme was approved at a meeting with Poole, Macleod and the Chief Whip on 14 May, when further dishes were added to the menu: the press would be carefully managed with regard to speculation about the election date; the Party would send targeted mailings to those in marginal constituencies who most influenced the opinions of others; the CRD would produce a brief for Macmillan on the 'philosophical aspects' of a forthcoming housing White Paper to enable him to take the moral high ground; Poole would see Lord Robbins to pump him for details of his forthcoming report on higher education and work out a convenient timetable for its publication; Macmillan would minute Ministers urging them to speak more outside parliament, and William Deedes would provide them with drafts, as he was also doing for the premier; Macmillan would be used more often to wind up debates that Wilson had opened; and Ministers would be added to the backbench mailing list for Party briefings for Commons debates, so as 'to be prepared to include in their speeches the political arguments as well as the administrative and bureaucratic points with which they are so copiously provided'. Macmillan had spoken to Butler of 'moving into a more energetic phase of the political situation'; the decks were now cleared for a high-pressure campaign like that of 1958–59. Fortified by the knowledge that plans were in train, Macmillan handed over to Butler at the end of May and went off on holiday in Scotland to rest up for the intensified campaigning ahead. On 26 May, Harold Evans noted 'the feeling in Westminster that the Tories are pulling up fast'. While Macmillan was away, as Evans would shortly put it, 'out of the clear blue sky came the Profumo thunderbolt'.[14]

13 Butler note, 28 Apr. 1963, Butler MSS, G40.
14 Central Office Chairman's department file, 20/8/7, Correspondence with Macmillan; Horne, *Macmillan*, 477; Evans, *Downing Street Diary*, 268, 271.

The Vassall and Profumo scandals

Some of the explanation both of the Government's mishandling of the Profumo scandal and of the press's over-reaction lies in events months earlier. Several Russian agents had been caught and tried in 1961–62 which, as Macmillan wearily explained to his spycatchers, earned the Government only questions as to why they had not been caught quicker. These difficulties acquired a political edge when in September 1962 a minor Admiralty official called John Vassall was exposed as a homosexual and a Russian spy. A press already hostile to the Government in the aftermath of the July purge turned its attention to Vassall's political contacts in the Admiralty and enjoyed itself in much speculation and innuendo, all of which was incorrect and at least some of which was invented. Battered by recent events, on 8 November Macmillan accepted and possibly even demanded the resignation of the junior minister named in the case, Thomas Galbraith, who was later entirely exonerated, and came near to losing his First Lord too. As the facts of the case emerged, and Ministers realised how they and the wider Party had over-reacted to press hysteria, there was a determination to clear names and find the culprits. Alan Watkins heard Macmillan himself say, 'now we'll get the journalists'. In the Commons he was not much more circumspect: 'the time has come for men of propriety and decency not to tolerate the growth of what I can only call the spirit of Titus Oates and Senator McCarthy.' A judicial tribunal under Lord Radcliffe was encouraged to take a strong line by the attendance of the Attorney-General to press the Government's case and to cross-examine the pressmen who appeared as witnesses; two journalists were sent to jail for contempt for refusing to name their sources (if indeed there were any). For this, the odium fell on the Government. *The Times*, whose high moral tone had always been uncomfortable with Macmillan's encouragement of materialism, and which had recently been austerely critical of 'the apparent ease and rapidity with which retiring Ministers slip into plum jobs in the City or in industry', was now openly calling for a new Prime Minister. The *Mail* and the *Sketch*, whose journalists were in prison, were especially hostile, but the whole of the press united to defend its freedoms from attack. In the *New Statesman* Paul Johnson asked, 'I wonder if Mr. Macmillan understands what he has let himself in for? . . . Between now and polling day political news reporting (and, of course, the slanting of news) will be heavily pro-Labour. At the same time any Tory Minister or MP . . . who gets involved in a scandal during the next year or so must expect – I regret to say – the full treatment'. Other papers deplored Johnson's declaration, but the event justified his prophecy rather more than others' promises of fairness. Macmillan was now a target, for, as Bernard Levin later wrote, the Radcliffe report 'had left most of the press resentful of the way in which its less reputable methods, of building a tower of innuendo upon a foundation of rumour and labelling the result a house of fact, had been exposed. There could now be little doubt that the man at the head of the Government which had put them on such public trial would, if he were ever caught in their trap, be shown no mercy.' Macmillan was correct in maintaining that the imprisonment of journalists was the sole responsibility of the judge, but he himself had framed the tribunal's dangerous line of inquiry and his Attorney had helped to precipitate the actual disaster from within its hearings. Lord Carrington, who as First Lord was also vindicated by the tribunal, was persuaded by Macmillan not to make matters worse by suing the *Daily Express* for libel; a quiet settlement was arranged by which his costs were paid by the *Express* but no damages sought. But it was now too late to calm the press down. When the Commons first heard of the Profumo business in March 1963, for Richard Crossman 'the real interest in the affair [wa]s the hostility between the press and the Government, which makes the press willing to leap at anything'.[15]

In the mean time, the reaction of active Conservatives in the constituencies, before the truth about Vassall was known, was one of shock. The resolution adopted in January 1963 in the Newton Division of Lancashire gave eloquent voice to such feelings, particularly prevalent in the north where suspicion of metropolitan moral standards added to the outrage.

> This executive, reconfirming its support for the Conservative Party and the Prime Minister, is most concerned about the recent incident in which a Minister of the Crown has been involved. The Minister's behaviour was a betrayal of conservative [sic] philosophy of service to the Queen and Country.
> We believe that private and public life cannot be distinguished and that unless the conduct of our leaders is beyond reproach they are security risks and cannot have our support.

When such instinctive feelings were even more sharply antagonised by the next scandal, and in this case a real one, the resulting wave of Party discontent would almost blow Macmillan out of office.[16]

The Vassall case had another consequence too. When Macmillan appreciated that he had accepted Galbraith's resignation unnecessarily and so appeared to condone the attacks on him, he seems to have felt personal shame at his betrayal of the honour of a colleague. This undermined his judgement when faced with a real threat four months later. He was determined to give Profumo every benefit of the doubt and predisposed not to believe what the press alleged against him; the press had cried wolf in 1962, and this time he did not look to see if the wolf was at the door. He also kept himself aloof from the details of the Profumo case until too late, from an austere

15 Thompson, *Day Before Yesterday*, 214; Horne, *Macmillan*, 463–4; Peter Rawlinson, *A Price Too High: An Autobiography* (1989), 89; David Thurlow, *Profumo: The Hate Factor* (1992), 125; Andrew Roth, *The Business Background of Members of Parliament* (1963), ii; Evans, *Downing Street Diaries*, 64, 66–7; Central Office constituency file, CCO 1/14/211; Bernard Levin, *The Pendulum Years: Britain and the Sixties* (1977), 62; Lord Carrington, *Reflect on Things Past: The Memoirs of Lord Carrington* (1988), 173–5; Morgan, *Crossman*, 989.
16 Central Office constituency file, CCO 1/14/211.

distaste for prying into the peccadilloes of a colleague. As a result, when increasing rumours about the War Minister's 1961 affair with the call-girl Christine Keeler, and the possibility that there had been security risks from Keeler's simultaneous relations with a Russian diplomat, the Government spectacularly under-reacted. At first there was no willingness to respond at all, assuming that it would all blow over if ignored, and then, when questions were formally raised in March 1963 under Commons privilege, the reaction was rushed and inadequate. A hastily-gathered late-night group of Ministers decided that scandalous allegations raised on a Thursday evening must not be allowed to reverberate around Sunday's papers without answer, and a personal statement was concocted for Profumo to deliver on Friday morning; because a personal statement (the only kind that cannot be debated) must be at the start of business, this meant being ready by 11 a.m. (on a Friday) rather than 2.30 p.m. (on any other day) which would have allowed more opportunity for daytime consideration of the implications. All but half a dozen words in Profumo's lengthy statement were true (though most of it was to be disbelieved over the months ahead); what was fatal was the claim that there had been no personal impropriety, words that Profumo maintained to be true but which he demurred at using until worn down by the Chief Whip and the law officers. The Ministers involved had no thought of challenging Profumo's word, reinforced by his promise to sue anyone who repeated allegations against him outside the House. As the Solicitor-General Peter Rawlinson has recorded, the Attorney-General felt that in honour he could do no other than believe what he had been told by Profumo; the fact that they hailed from the same school, Oxford college *and* regiment cannot have made any belief in Profumo's dishonour easy. When told about the decision that Profumo would read a full denial to the House, Butler's reaction was 'not on a *Friday morning* surely!' To him, the sensible course would be not to magnify the issue, but to make a holding statement and to gather the facts before going public in detail; this was precisely the caution in Butler that the Party least admired and which at that moment it most needed. He was over-ruled, and when Profumo spoke he was flanked by Macmillan, Macleod and Butler to give the statement the authority conferred by their presence. Most MPs, like the Ministers consulted, could not believe that a lie would have been told in this way and so concluded that the press had again made it all up; even so wary a Minister as Macleod rounded on his own PPS when he tried to warn the Party Chairman of the continuing rumours about Profumo, and bawled him out for listening to press tittle-tattle. The press, mystified, held its fire. If David Thurlow is correct, the real villain of the piece was enraged into redoubling his efforts to bring out the truth.[17]

[17] Thompson, *Day Before Yesterday*, 214; Rawlinson, *Price Too High*, 93–4; Anthony Howard, *RAB: The Life of R.A. Butler* (1987), 298; Thurlow, *Profumo*, 65, 136–41; Andrew Roth, *Enoch Powell, Tory Tribune* (1970), 281–2; Robert Shepherd, *Iain Macleod* (1994), 295.

Over the next two months, the steady sapping away at Profumo's story eventually undermined it altogether, and by early June there was no maintaining his innocence, but Macmillan still misunderstood the depth of the pit opening up in front of him. Telephoned by Butler with the news that Profumo would shortly admit that he had lied to the Commons, he could 'hardly believe this was a major issue' and when he arrived back in London he airily announced that it all looked much less important when viewed from Scotland. For Profumo, the fall was total, from being one of the bright stars of the Party with a good chance of reaching the Cabinet, he became a pariah; he resigned his seat, left office without meeting either the Prime Minister or the Queen, and was struck off the Privy Council. For Macmillan, as the truth eventually dawned, there was a great sense of betrayal; what Andrew Roth had recently dubbed 'the "gentlemen are above reproach" attitude of the Prime Minister' was shattered for ever. Other Ministers reacted in panic, several demanding that the blame should be shared by those who had advised Profumo in March, but Macmillan said that if those five Ministers resigned he would have to go as well. Hailsham was overwhelmed by moral outrage – 'a great party is not to be brought down because of the scandal of a woman of easy virtue and a proved liar' and hinted that moral values were no more secure among the leaders of other parties – while Macleod stood by Profumo and saw it simply as a personal tragedy.[18]

The rational truth was that nothing central to the Conservative programme was involved in the Profumo case and nothing of policy significance was involved in his personal conduct either. As Macmillan sententiously observed, Ministers had 'nothing with which to reproach ourselves, except perhaps too great a loyalty. That is not, in my view, a serious accusation against any man.' Rationality had though little to do with the case from 10 June onwards, as others perceived more quickly than the Prime Minister; the Chief Whip had offered to resign even before Macmillan got back from Scotland, and was dissuaded only by Macmillan's declaration that 'if you resign, I shall resign'. For the next month, Macmillan was actually fighting for his political life, as he had only imagined himself to be a year earlier. The earlier press attacks had been tame by comparison with what now ensued, particularly when in June and July further spy stories, and allegations about the unscrupulous practices of the London landlord Peter Rachman (who had also shared a mistress with Profumo) could be added to the simmering pot. The combination of press speculation and voracious popular rumour fed on itself to produce ever wilder stories. In Manchester on 23 June Poole argued that,

> it is essential that the large number of rumours surrounding the Profumo scandal should be disposed of as quickly as possible. I never remember a time when

---

[18]   Howard, *RAB*, 299; Lord Butler, *The Art of the Possible: The Memoirs of Lord Butler* (1971), 235; Roth, *Business Background*, viii; Rawlinson, *Price Too High*, 97; Thurlow, *Profumo*, 157, 159; Evans, *Downing Street Diaries*, 273.

so many or so varied a number of rumours were circulating in Fleet Street or Whitehall. These rumours are disgusting in detail and probably disreputable in origin. There are certain curious aspects about them, and certainly most of them are untrue. But rumour and doubt and suspicion are horrible things – where and when possible they should be cleared up.

Poole's speech helped to steady the Party, by reinforcing the fear already felt by many Tories that rumours were being deliberately stoked up by political opponents and a malign press, but his claim was surely exaggerated; reporting his speech, the *Sunday Times* more plausibly suggested that the likely cause was the 'simple human failing of taste for scandal, especially that concerning the great or the famous'.[19]

Speculative witch-hunting came close to forcing another Minister out of office, this time from the Cabinet, and when Lord Denning was appointed to inquire into the affair, his terms of reference were so wide as to include any and all 'rumours affecting the honour and integrity of public life'. The Home Secretary told John Boyd-Carpenter that from his reading of the papers it appeared that the two of them were the only Cabinet Ministers 'not at the moment the subject of scandalous rumours'; Boyd-Carpenter was not entirely pleased to be bracketed with the old-maidish Henry Brooke. As David Thurlow puts it, 'the general tone was the typically British one of saying how disgusting and awful it was, with a lingering longing that if they had not actually been there, they would have liked to have known it was going on so that they could have had the choice'. On 17 June the Opposition had for tactical reasons concentrated on the security aspects of the case, though Harold Wilson had still managed to claim that the revelations had 'shocked the moral conscience of the nation'. The press were more honestly interested in the sex and violence, but from this they still drew damaging political conclusions. *The Times* had a much-quoted leader on 11 June, entitled 'It *is* a moral issue.' It argued that 'eleven years of Conservative rule have brought the nation psychologically and spiritually to a low ebb. . . . The Prime Minister and his colleagues can cling together and still be there a year hence. They will have to do more than that to justify themselves.' The *Sunday Citizen* asked 'What can you expect when a nation is debauched in this way? You can expect what we have now got – a Profumo'; the *Daily Mirror* declared that the affluent society had become 'the Effluent Society'. This line of attack could be repulsed only with great difficulty since it was so unspecific. Later in the year, a Penguin Special by Wayland Young made the same generalised connection between the fall of Profumo and a wider Party malaise – and sold a lot of copies for its tale of 'lays, leaks and lies'; the cover blurb claimed that 'the very title, *The Profumo Affair: Aspects of Conservatism*, makes clear that, behind the obvious fascination of so heady a mixture of sex and politics,

---

[19] Horne, *Macmillan*, 479–80, 486; Thurlow, *Profumo*, 31.

there are important issues of moral, social and political consequence'. Young's conclusion was that although it was all about one man, 'we were heading for it; it could hardly not have happened, whether like that or in some similar form. It was the natural fruit of a period of government when convenience was set above justice, loyalty above truth, and appearance above reality.' Young was a Labour supporter who would shortly take office under Harold Wilson, though his book did not identify his politics. But the 'Insight' team of the Tory *Sunday Times*, which had done much the best investigative reporting in Summer 1963, also produced a book later in the year, *Scandal '63*, which reached the similar conclusion that 'before the crisis broke the surface, much was wrong underneath'; its narrative of the nation's moral decline began with Macmillan's 1957 speech at Bedford. A *Private Eye* cartoon by Trog made the same link more succinctly, with the words 'You've never had it so good' being amended by Macmillan himself to read 'You've never had it so often'.[20]

The degree of moral outrage against the Party genuinely felt by individuals may be seen in three letters sent to Edward Boyle between 13 and 15 June, addressed to him as a Conservative who had a personal reputation for integrity, and by people outside the Party who were urging him to give the country a moral lead by resigning. Professor John Vaizey suggested that

> none of us can know the complexities of the situation and your position in it. But surely it is clear that this scandalous business is just the tip of the iceberg – certainly anyone who has lived where we did [Welbeck Street, London W1] can't help but be aware of a number of your colleagues' morals – and that any attempt to 'hush it up' is not only profoundly dishonourable but will *fail* [triple underlining in original]. Your position as the Minister responsible for children is quite clear.

Some of the outrage was directed at Boyle himself for apparently condoning Hailsham's claim that there was also adultery on Labour's front bench, support that he later withdrew. Brian Walden, a Birmingham candidate but not yet a Labour MP, told Boyle that 'we all have those we admire . . . outside our own ranks, and I have always believed you to represent the more humane and enlightened side of contemporary Toryism. I was therefore shocked and horrified by your reported statement that you endorsed the statements of Lord Hailsham made on BBC television'. Finally, another friend told Boyle that 'the moral issue is far clearer than it was at the time of Suez' (when Boyle *had* resigned), for

> whatever Lord Hailsham might say, the fact is that Macmillan tolerated in his government someone whose morals were well known to leave a lot to be desired,

20 John Boyd-Carpenter, *Way of Life* (1980), 153; Thurlow, *Profumo*, 160–1; Evans, *Downing Street Diaries*, 68; Wayland Young, *The Profumo Affair, Aspects of Conservatism* (Harmondsworth, 1963), 7, 112; Clive Irving, Ron Hall and Jeremy Wallington, *Scandal '63* (1963), 1, 3, 219; Howard, *RAB*, 301; Richard Ingrams, *The Life and Times of Private Eye* (Harmondsworth, 1971), 79.

and who associated in very dubious circles. Much more important, there were several of them. Either Macmillan has got to clear up the whole lot or he must give way to someone who will do the job. The Conservative Party has many failings but it has always at least been respectable. Macmillan's fault is that he has turned a blind eye too long.

Significantly, since he was indeed considering resigning, Boyle sidelined the last two sentences of that letter.[21]

Macmillan's leadership challenged

Long-term damage from the Profumo case trailed on for a year, but the immediate crisis was short and sharp. In the Commons debate on 17 June, Macmillan made an effective speech which demonstrated that he and his colleagues had not colluded with Profumo's lie, had known little of his activities, and had been told little by either the security services or the police; he in effect appealed to MPs for sympathy with Ministers who had been as much taken in by Profumo as the House itself had been. The truth of this statement was later demonstrated by Lord Denning's judicial inquiry, and has not been challenged since, (though the press inevitably focused on the single paragraph of Denning's report that criticised the Government, with such headlines as 'Mac blamed'). Macmillan's speech certainly rallied Party sympathy: a meeting of Area chairmen reported to Macmillan on 27 June the unanimous view that 'there is a strong and widespread sympathy and support for yourself in the difficulties which were felt to have come upon you unfairly'. This view was confirmed by soundings drawn together at Central Office on 20 June by the Chief Organisation Officer:

> There is some good evidence that opinion is hardening behind the Prime Minister. Brigadier Mellsop [Dorset] rang me this morning and told me that in his part of the country support for the Prime Minister is marked among all classes, Miss Walker says that in Flint the women passed a resolution of confidence in the Prime Minister. Mr. Slinn [Western Area] says that in his opinion the same thing is happening, and that the Bristol Finance Committee passed a resolution of support for the Prime Minister. . . . Mr. Webster [North West] also says there is a big swing of support. This does not preclude the wish for a change, but it does exclude the wish for an immediate change.[22]

Local feelings were in fact more variable than that report would suggest; in York and in Islington Conservatives did resolve to support Macmillan, and Lewes resolved to deplore attacks on him, but the reasoning behind these moves may well have had more to do with Party self-defence in a crisis

21 Letters to Sir Edward Boyle from John Vaizey, 13 June, from Edward Palmer, 14 June, and Brian Walden, 15 June, Boyle MSS, 5481, 5482, 5485.
22 Larry Siedentop, 'Mr. Macmillan and the Edwardian Style', in V. Bogdanor and R. Skidelsky (eds), *The Age of Affluence* (1970), 49–50; Central Office Chairman's department file, CCO 20/8/7.

than with real support for the Leader; in York, for example, 'the Chairman said . . . he did not see why because one man had defaulted we should not have faith in the Conservative Party, and indeed it would be a tragedy in this country if the socialists were returned'. Other associations took a critical view, even after the hardening of support for Macmillan detected at Central Office. On 18 June, for example, the Liverpool Conservative Association, representing eight constituencies, decided that 'there should be a change in the Leadership, and as soon as possible'. At Denbigh, there was a discussion of the whole affair with the MP present on 11 June, when,

> there was general agreement . . . that this case had done great harm – much greater than 'ground-nuts' or abandoned missile projects. People were angry and dismayed. Action was necessary quickly to restore the good name of the Government and it was vitally necessary that Mr. Macmillan should clear himself. If he could not do so he should resign. . . . Among other comments made were allegations that the Government image was one of an elderly administration, out of touch with the people, too 'old school tie', and badly in need of new Blood.

A month later, when the association had heard Macmillan's explanation, it endorsed its MP's abstention in the confidence debate, and resolved by twenty-eight votes to eight that there should be a change of leader before the next election. West Dorset also backed its rebel MP, when he told his supporters that the Profumo affair was 'nothing to do with morals, all to do with security'. There were many associations that reached a conclusion as double-edged as Truro did on 1 July; half the speakers in the debate wanted Macmillan to go, some of them using extremely hostile language, and the other half wanted him to stay on, but 'all were agreed that it would be a mistake for the Prime Minister to resign immediately and precipitate an immediate general election. All agreed that the Prime Minister's honour and integrity were not at stake and it would be wrong and unfair for him to go as a result of the sordid Profumo affair'. The implication of such discussions at the local level was that Macmillan should not go *because of* the Profumo affair, but should still go once it could be claimed that Profumo had not been the cause.[23]

Not only was Macmillan's tactic failing to produce more than a temporary respite; it also had a double edge in itself. In order to restore his Government's claim to have acted honestly, Macmillan had to damage its reputation for competence. For many, now that they knew the facts, the focus shifted from moral issues to the question of competence: how could Ministers have so entirely failed to prevent their own embarrassment? Butler noted on 19 June of Macmillan's explanation in the Commons that 'while the PM's honour

---

[23] York CA minutes, 17 June 1963; South West Islington CA minutes, 18 June 1963; Lewes CA minutes, 20 June 1963; Liverpool CA minutes, 18 June 1963; Denbigh CA minutes, 11 June and 11 July 1963; West Dorset CA minutes, 13 Sept. 1963; Truro CA minutes, 1 July 1963; ; Howard, *RAB*, 307; Central Office constituency file, 1/14/459.

shone clearly throughout, his lack of knowledge of what had happened made a disagreeable impression upon back-benchers. . . . I think he has also given the impression, partly owing to age and decency of living, that he is out of touch with some of the underground so ably canvassed and represented in the daily press.' Macmillan was not the only one whose reputation for good judgement was dented: as the Solicitor-General involved in drafting Profumo's March statement, Peter Rawlinson recalled that 'the deceived were well mocked'. And backbenchers also still felt let down; to Jim Prior, a new Member in the 1959 Parliament, 'it was as if those in whom we had placed our faith and hope had suddenly become rotten'.[24]

On 17 June, before the crucial Commons debate, Poole and Redmayne attended a crisis meeting of the 1922 Committee, of which its secretary Philip Goodhart recorded just that 'there was widespread criticism of the Government's handling of the issue'; as a result of that meeting and of the whips' other soundings, the Chief Whip predicted that the usual majority of ninety-seven could fall as low as forty, in which case he would feel compelled to resign; the final majority of fifty-seven was not quite so bad. The whips received an unusual degree of public attention in this, with the actual document summoning Tory MPs to vote in the debate on the Government's own motion of confidence being published in the press. Replying on television to claims that Ministers were coercing their backbenchers into ensuring their own survival, Hailsham claimed that a three-line whip was only a summons to attend and not an instruction to vote. This was technically correct, but far from the customary meaning in 1963, and it gave Conservative dissidents both additional irritation and in some cases an alibi for their abstention. Whipping had though whittled down the rebel group, pressurising some like Henry Kerby into conformity by the threat of an early general election; it was reported that twenty-seven had deliberately abstained, but another dozen seem to have been absent unpaired. The dissidents included all of Macmillan's regular critics, notably Nigel Birch, who made the most effective attack on him in the debate by quoting Browning's bitter assault on Wordsworth, 'The Lost Leader', but they were joined by others from right across the Party spectrum; it was also clear to those who abstained that many more would have joined them but for the whips' promise that Macmillan would step down in the Autumn anyway. Macmillan noted that the abstainers included 'a lot of worthy people who had been swept away by the wave of emotion and indignation'. Donald Johnson, the Carlisle MP with a record of maverick behaviour going back to his time as a Liberal, was photographed by the *Daily Express* playing golf on the day of the debate, so ignoring the whip even on Hailsham's eccentric view of its meaning; despite trouble with his local Party, he was unrepentant, declaring a little later that 'the Conservative Party is

---

[24] Butler note, 19 June 1963, Butler MSS, G46; Rawlinson, *Price Too High*, 99; Jim Prior, *A Balance of Power* (1986), 29.

clearly undergoing a great sickness. . . . I have encountered nobody but Rip Van Winkle still living in the days of Harold Macmillan.' The dissidents did not though include Enoch Powell, who had earlier considered resignation, as had Brooke, Joseph and Boyle. In the event Powell's vote for Macmillan reinforced the view that Macmillan had acted with integrity. What one Tory MP called 'Enoch's outsize conscience' was on the Prime Minister's side, once he was satisfied that the Prime Minister bore no responsibility for the misleading of the House. There were no resignations.[25]

Talk of a moral collapse went on through the Summer, was revived by Lord Denning's report in September, kept alive by other books for the rest of the year, and rounded off by a racy account of the scandal in Randolph Churchill's *The Fight for the Tory Leadership* early in 1964. This in itself prevented the political crisis from dying away after the Commons vote on 17 June. The U.S. ambassador's contacts told him that Profumo had holed Macmillan below the waterline. He reported on 18 June that,

> Macmillan's admission that he did not know what was going on at critical times was in circumstances pitiable and extremely damaging. He did not try to shirk responsibility, but on his own account did not give impression that he knew how to exercise it . . . nearly everyone in Parliament appeared to be better informed than the Prime Minister. . . . On present indications . . . his replacement cannot be long delayed for . . . Prime Minister has become . . . an electoral liability.

This was clearly a widespread view; when Macmillan went to the Smoking Room after the big debate, only Julian Amery and Maurice Macmillan (both relatives) went over to speak to him, and his PPS warned of 'disloyalty to him at a very high level'. Harold Evans thought that Poole and the Chief Whip, whose primary loyalty had to be to the Party rather than the Prime Minister, had told Macmillan he would have to retire within the next few months. Questioned by Gallup, only 23 per cent of the public thought he should stay on as Prime Minister. On 18 June a wave of hysteria swept through the parliamentary party when the officers of the 1922 Committee pressed the case for an immediate succession by Maudling; the theory behind this was that the Party should skip straight to the next generation and play safe by going for a safely married man; a few weeks later, Macmillan himself referred to Maudling as having the attraction of being 'a respectable Wilson'. After interviewing fifty 'representative' Tory MPs, the *Daily Telegraph* on 20 June reported their votes on the succession as: Maudling twenty-one, Hailsham eight, Heath six, Butler four, Powell three, Home and Macleod one each, undecided five. Supporters of Maudling included two-thirds of the

25 Philip Goodhart, *The 1922: The Story of the 1922 Committee* (1973), 186–7; Rawlinson, *Price Too High*, 98–9; Thurlow, *Profumo*, 163–9; Humphry Berkeley, *Crossing the Floor* (1972), 85; Horne, *Macmillan*, 483; R.J. Jackson, *Rebels and Whips; Dissension, Discipline and Cohesion in British Parliamentary Parties since 1945* (1968), 169–71, 273–4; Evans, *Downing Street Diaries*, 274; Roth, *Powell*, 186–91.

1922's Executive, and a *Daily Express* poll of MPs also put Maudling well ahead of all the others. At this stage, Macmillan was telling his intimates that he would not resign over a sex scandal – he could not allow himself to be 'brought down by two tarts' – but he was also hinting that after a decent interval he would go quietly. If this was a tactic to buy time, it succeeded; returning from Africa a month after the confidence debate, Butler noticed how far things had calmed down; while he was away, Macmillan had taken the opportunity of his Wolverhampton visit to announce that 'all being well, if I keep my health and strength, I hope to lead the Party into the election. Of course I must have the support of the Party and I think I have it.' He noted privately that this had caught his backbench critics off guard, before their 'Macmillan must go' campaign had made much headway; it was a challenge to them to do their worst, but shrewdly timed for just before the Summer recess. By then too, the signing of a nuclear Test-Ban Treaty in Moscow had given him a much-needed policy success, and his press secretary had thought the end of July to be 'Macmillan's week'. Nevertheless, when Macmillan met the 1922 for the usual end-of-session meeting on 25 July his reception seems to have been cool, and in a meeting attended by some 250 MPs rather than the more typical attendance of about 60: *The Times* reported that only one MP had risen to cheer Macmillan and concluded that 'it seems possible that Conservative leaders have received greater ovations at an end-of-term occasion like this. . . . Mr. Macmillan had not enjoyed a Roman triumph.' His PPS Paul Channon reported to Butler that the Test Ban success had saved Macmillan from a much worse ordeal, and that the only actual call for his resignation, from Lord Lambton, had been 'greeted with cat-calls'; even so, 'almost unanimously, I found that Members thought the Prime Minister would nevertheless go before the election'. There were no doubt many Party loyalists who reasoned as unsentimentally as the correspondent who told Poole on 7 September: 'I have reluctantly come to the conclusion that if things get to the stage where we are almost certain to lose the election, then we *must* have a change as being the only hope. I am one of his greatest fans, but it's a tough life.'[26]

Over the next few weeks, potential successors were discreetly jockeying for position; Butler told a television interviewer that 'I am pretty well aware that people want us to give a fresh impression of vigour and decision before the next election'; Maudling drew attention to his own qualifications in telling the crowd at a Summer fete that 'We have not been successful in obtaining the allegiance of the younger generation of voters, because we have not yet found a way of talking to them in language they understand or in terms of the

---

[26] Horne, *Macmillan*, 483–4; Evans, *Downing Street Diaries*, 274, 284, 294; Butler, *Art of the Possible*, 236–7; Maudling, *Memoirs*, 124; Michael Cockerell, *Live from Number Ten: The Inside Story of Prime Ministers and Television* (1988), 92; Goodhart, *The 1922*, 187–91; Roth, *Powell*, 291; Channon to Butler, 27 July 1963, Butler MSS G41; Central Office Chairman's department file, CCO 20/22/2, Treasurers.

ideals they cherish'. Meanwhile the chairman of Colman, Prentis and Varley admitted to the press that 'we can't plug the leader just now. We don't even know who he is going to be.' A Central Office official told David Butler in 1964 that in 1963 the Party had lived 'from week to week, with no time at all for thinking of the future'. When possible leaders were discussed, the key figure, or so it appeared from the outside, was Rab Butler, who as the second man last time, deputy Prime Minister for six years, and still younger than Macmillan had been in 1957, was clearly the man to beat. He had much the same disadvantage as Macmillan himself, however – age and length of service; Macmillan had warned Butler in March that criticism of the Prime Minister actually included criticism of Butler, since they were seen as inseparable, and that 'the combination of the Kennedy image plus Harold Wilson at 46 was a potent force in favour of a younger man'. The Chief Whip had also spoken to Butler about the possibility of his becoming a caretaker Prime Minister, but indicated that MPs were more likely to go straight to the next generation; the chairman of the 1922 told him more brutally that the parliamentary party would not want a Butler Government – 'the chaps won't have you'. It was already apparent then that Butler suffered from the same double handicap in 1963 as he had done in 1957: not only were the right implacably opposed to his views, but also there was little enthusiasm for him as a potential leader among centre and left MPs who agreed with his policy views – in October the One Nation Group was to decide not to support him. With this discouraging advice, Butler had by the end of July already thought himself into a frame of mind in which he would settle for staying in second place: 'it is no good thinking there is no life left if one is not elected Pope. One can always be a respected Cardinal'. Nevertheless, he did not quite abandon hope, and was gratified to note from a conversation with Macmillan on 11 September that they both wanted to preserve the Queen's freedom to choose, and that they both 'agreed that almost no PM had chosen his own successor, and that the issue might have to be thrashed out, if he decided to go, without his having the final word.' This was to be far from the case. Macleod seems to have decided that his own best chances of the Leadership lay with Macmillan sticking it out a little longer, while Heath, after talking to the chairman of the 1922 Committee, had reinforced the emerging 'draft Home' camp with the experience and contacts of the former Chief Whip.[27]

Macmillan's own view of Butler, communicated to Hailsham at this time, was 'on no account. Rab simply does not have it in him to be Prime Minister.' The fact that Macmillan had discussed the issue at all with Hailsham was

[27] Anthony Sampson, *Macmillan: A Study in Ambiguity* (Harmondsworth, 1968), 241; Lord Windlesham, *Communication and Political Power* (1966), 77; Butler and King, *General Election of 1964*, 80; Butler, *Art of the Possible*, 237, 239; Butler note, 7/3/63, Butler MSS, G40; Goodhart, *The 1922*, 191; Howard, *RAB*, 302–4; Shepherd, *Macleod*, 305; interview with Lord Carr.

significant. Since Summer 1962 he had toyed in turn with Macleod, Maudling and Heath as possible successors, and in conversations with Butler had regularly mentioned Home, but had never fixed on any name for long. In 1963, he picked out Hailsham, seeing in him (as he wrote in October), 'what I was like in my stronger period, am to a greater extent than people appreciate behind the scenes, and would like my successor to be'. Hailsham thus became the Government's trouble-shooter in a series of highly publicised roles, in the North East, in sport, and in finalising the Test Ban Treaty in Moscow, the Government's most signal success in the Summer months; this both raised his profile and widened his ministerial experience; then in July, quite fortuitously, the House of Lords rejected the Government's advice and voted to include in the Bill which allowed peers to disclaim their titles at succession an additional provision that would allow existing peers to avail themselves of the same right if they did so at once. Suddenly, one of the two main arguments against Hailsham as a potential premier vanished, though the other argument – his questionable judgement – remained and was fatally to damage his chances. Since Macmillan had encouraged Hailsham about the leadership in June, while the Government was still strongly resisting that change to the Bill, he was actually running Hailsham to be a Prime Minister in the Lords at that stage; he told Hailsham that his original choice had been Home, but that he was now backing Hailsham. Poole was Macmillan's original emissary to Hailsham, and Aldington was also involved in the preparations for a Hailsham succession. Dennis Walters MP, Hailsham's personal assistant when at Central Office, urged him to agree and offered to help run his campaign. A Hailsham team was in place with the best possible Party contacts. When the peerage rules changed, Poole arranged with the sitting MP for the St Marylebone constituency to be vacated if Hailsham needed it in a hurry.[28]

All this was contingent on a vacancy that did not yet exist. Butler noted on 1 September a call from Poole, 'asking for a joint talk between myself, Alec Home, Chief Whip and him with PM tomorrow afternoon, "so that we can all say the same thing". Exactly what that same thing is I do not know since I get the impression that while all think the PM should go, all except Oliver would be prepared to see him stay, owing to the doubts about the succession.' From the constituencies, unhappy rumblings went on; there were critical resolutions from Esher, Tonbridge and South Buckinghamshire, and several MPs made speeches around the country calling for a new leader; when South Bedfordshire actually wrote to Macmillan telling him to go, he replied with some asperity that 'I receive a constant flow of advice, the chief general feature of which is the diversity of the advice expressed'. From all

28   Dennis Walters, *Not Always with the Pack* (1989), 110–14; Hailsham, *Sparrow's Flight*, 348–50; Howard, *RAB*, 303; Horne, *Macmillan*, 531; Butler, *Art of the Possible*, 240; Shepherd, *Macleod*, 304; Central Office constituency file, CCO 1/14/75; Macmillan's view of Hailsham is in PREM 11/5008.

sides though, he was being urged to decide one way or the other. Macleod, who remained convinced that Macmillan should lead the Party beyond the next election, got permission on 24 September to make a speech ruling out an election in 1963; by then Labour's poll lead had fallen to less than 7 per cent, but Central Office calculated that a Tory lead of 5 per cent was the minimum needed before calling an election safely. Macleod's speech changed the nature of the question rather than the urgency of an answer, particularly with the Party Conference due in mid-October, when Macmillan would need to indicate his intentions. Poole was urging Macmillan that if there were to be a change then it must be before the end of 1963, so as to allow a new man time to prepare for a 1964 election, and this insistent advice troubled Macmillan greatly, for he could neither make up his mind whether he really meant to go on nor delay much longer. Through September, he several times 'finally' made up his mind, but it seems that at the start of October he had decided to tell the Conference that he would carry on, 'for two or three years' – what he privately called 'operation limpet'. It is not clear that this final decision was any more final than the others, and several colleagues, notably Poole, Redmayne and Home, were becoming very impatient for a decision to be made and published – of whatever sort. Perhaps, as he later felt, this uncharacteristic indecision derived from his undiagnosed illness, but, like Churchill in 1955, at the last moment Macmillan wanted to stay on and retire as a hero after an international triumph. Macleod though, seeing the polls turning the Party's way and hopeful that the scandal would at last die away after the Denning report, wrote optimistically to Boyle: 'looking ahead to Conference time, it occurs to me that there is very little of major importance to occupy us this year. The Common Market has disappeared. Africa is no longer a bone of contention and one way and another we look like having a dull Conference. This may not be a bad thing.' It is barely credible that Macleod was here anticipating the bear-garden that was to take place at Blackpool.[29]

The leadership crisis of October 1963

The situation was transformed at the beginning of Conference week by the sudden onset of Macmillan's illness. On the morning of Tuesday 8 October, Macmillan both announced to the Cabinet his plan to confirm in Blackpool that he would lead the Party through the next election, and was then struck down by a prostate condition; he entered hospital on Tuesday evening for

---

[29] Butler note, 1/9/63, Butler MSS, G40; Butler and King, *General Election of 1964*, 80; Central Office file, CCO 4/9/238, Leaders; Fisher, *Macleod*, 232; Horne, *Macmillan*, 531–3, 535–40; Thompson, *Day Before Yesterday*, 218; Butler, *Art of the Possible*, 241; Harold Macmillan, *At the End of the Day* (1973), 492–3; Central Office Chairman's department files, CCO 20/8/6, and CPA 20/1/11, Correspondence with Ministers; Evans, *Downing Street Diaries*, 293, 297.

a Thursday operation, and wrote to the Queen on Wednesday, stating his intention to resign but not actually doing so: 'the conduct of the Government I have handed over to Butler but I shall take this back as soon as I am able to do so'. Also on Wednesday he sent to Blackpool with Home (who happened to be President of the National Union for 1963, and so was a convenient liaison with the voluntary party) a letter reporting his resignation and urging that the Party's 'customary processes' for choosing a new leader be set in train at once. The supreme irony was that within a few days of his operation, Macmillan had made a rapid recovery and by Tuesday 15 October was fully in control of events if still weak; he might well have carried on as Prime Minister if different doctors had advised, and if the illness had not struck in the very week in which he had to put on a public show of his health and vitality in Blackpool.[30]

The news that filtered through to Blackpool, confirmed when Home read Macmillan's message to the assembled representatives late in the Thursday session of Conference, set off an explosion of speculation and lobbying, and turned the normally stage-managed event into something like an American convention. Ian Trethowan recalled that, for reporters,

> for a few happy days we enjoyed something akin to the delights of American politics, with all the plotting and manoeuvring out in the open, at least within earshot of the alert reporter, and sometimes even within range of the camera. The politicians loathed it all, but I would argue that, in this populist age, it was no bad test of the contenders to see how far they were able to keep their nerve, and maintain their authority, under the pressure of those teeming days.

Butler was probably the one who loathed it most. He suspected Home of having extracted the Macmillan letter from the Prime Minister by using undue pressure on a sick man, and later noted that 'I cannot imagine an atmosphere less suited to such a declaration. . . . After that there was no peace'; his own, characteristic reaction to the febrile atmosphere was to hide for as much of the time as possible in his hotel room, and 'in order to avoid creating the wrong impression' he strove to create no impression at all. William Rees-Mogg wrote that at Blackpool the Tories 'ceased to be gentlemen without becoming democrats'. It would have been perfectly possible, and by far preferable, for Macmillan to admit his illness but say nothing about resignation until the operation and the Conference week were over. Anthony Howard has argued that opening the issue at Blackpool was done deliberately to 'put wind in Hailsham's sails', and Harold Evans' diary suggests that this was the crucial influence on timing. But only illness and the fear that he might not survive his operation led Macmillan to such a misjudgement, for he had not the slightest intention of allowing the Conference to determine the succession. Oliver Poole later felt that 'allowing' Macmillan to make

---

[30] Horne, *Macmillan*, 540–6.

the announcement was 'probably the biggest blunder I've ever made in politics', Michael Fraser that the mistake 'did the Party severe long term damage', and Humphry Berkeley that it was entirely Macmillan's fault 'that the Conservative Party had a nervous breakdown in public'. In hospital in London, Macmillan could now only watch in amazement as television showed what was happening in Blackpool; each ministerial speaker was in effect making his pitch for the leadership, and the failure of Maudling to raise the Conference temperature was eagerly contrasted by the press with the success of Macleod, Hailsham and Home; Butler had the double indignity of having both to fight for the right to address the final rally in Macmillan's place and then of failing to sparkle when he did so. Once Conference was over, Butler gratefully returned to London to prepare for more normal succession arrangements to take place the following week. A *Daily Express* poll taken at the week-end found Butler ahead with 39.5 per cent, followed by Hailsham 21.5, Maudling 11, Home 9.5, which seemed to bode well for Butler when the Party needed a vote-winner for an imminent election. All the same, the Conference had transformed the field, though in fact by destroying the chances of the most popular candidate and ensuring that a new runner emerged in his place. On the Thursday evening, odds quoted at Blackpool had Hailsham as odds-on favourite, Butler at 2–1, Maudling at 5–1 and Home a rank outsider at 33–1. A week later Home was to form a Government.[31]

Hailsham's campaign seemed to have everything going for it; he was the Prime Minister's candidate, a fact confirmed to him personally at the start of the week, and then noised abroad at Blackpool by Maurice Macmillan and Julian Amery; he was anyway the darling of the Conference; he had a team ready to run his campaign. The membership of that team – Dennis Walters, Peter Walker, Tony Royle and Ian Gilmour – disproved the theory that Hailsham was the candidate of the right. Hailsham was still the Tory progressive he had been in his Tory Reform Group days, and his critics had, as so often, mistaken partisanship for extremism. Yet within twenty-four hours it had all gone irrevocably wrong, so suddenly indeed that at 2 a.m. on Saturday, between editions, the *Telegraph* headline 'Support for Hailsham grows' was reversed to read 'Support for Hailsham wanes'. In part this stemmed from the over-zealousness of his campaigners, particularly of Randolph Churchill, who arrived in Blackpool with a stock of 'Q' (for Quintin) lapel badges that were pinned not only on supporters but also on bystanders, on other contenders for the leadership, and even on the Lord Chancellor's ample posterior. Randolph also sent several telegrams

[31] Horne, *Macmillan*, 546–52; Ian Trethowan, *Split Screen* (1984), 107; Butler note, 20 Oct. 1963, Butler MSS G40; Morrison Halcrow, *Keith Joseph: A Single Mind* (1989), 32; Butler, *Art of the Possible*, 241–2, 246; Thompson, *Day Before Yesterday*, 217–29; Berkeley, *Crossing the Floor*, 85; Howard, *RAB*, 312–13; Evans, *Downing Street Diaries*, 298; Anthony Howard and Richard West, *The Making of the Prime Minister* (1965), 72; Maudling, *Memoirs*, 126–8; Gerald Sparrow, *Rab: Study of a Statesman* (1965), 193.

to Butler purporting to come from constituency associations, urging him to back Hailsham. For his prearranged address to the CPC on Thursday evening, Hailsham stuck to the printed text, but in answer to a question he announced that he was going to disclaim his peerage, which provoked a reaction that Ronald Butt thought to be 'more like a Nuremberg Rally'; Butler, meeting the Hailsham entourage outside the CPC meeting, noted that Hailsham had been 'surrounded by hysterical and weeping women on the lines of a Hitler campaign'. Significantly, the Party dignitaries on Hailsham's platform were noticed to be either embarrassed or displeased by the reaction that his announcement had provoked; Martin Redmayne and William Deedes, seated on the platform, decided that it would be less embarrassing to join in with the ovation for Hailsham than to remain seated, but reports suggest that they too did not manage to simulate much enthusiasm. The effect of this was heightened by a similar reception for Hailsham later in the evening at a YC Ball and by television pictures of Hailsham with his wife and young baby; these last were entirely innocent but were easily misinterpreted as a piece of low campaigning to build up the image of a family man. His team did not perhaps realise how far all this antagonised those who already suspected Hailsham's judgement; the suspicious would have been even more hostile if they had known that the Hailsham campaigners were being urged by Maurice Macmillan to bounce Conference itself into passing a 'Hailsham for Prime Minister' resolution.[32]

Some critics felt some distaste for Hailsham's style of politics: as Boyd-Carpenter later wrote, 'the Conservative Party still then retained the concept that gentlemen don't throw their hats, or their coronets, into the ring. It preferred the convention, however artificial, that leaders come forward in response to the pressure of others.' Others were anyway frightened by the thought of a Hailsham Government. Over the week-end, Richard Crossman met Marcus Worsley, a Yorkshire MP who was PPS to William Deedes: 'Worsley is convinced that Hailsham with his hands on the nuclear button would be a menace to world peace and he is determined to try and prevent this.' Keith Joseph was said to feel much the same. Overall, those who were pressing Home to make himself available were convinced that Hailsham had made 'an imperial bog' of his chances (in his own phrase). Back in London, Macmillan was appalled to hear of such antics and decided, as Nigel Birch put it, to 'swap peers in mid-stream'; he does not appear to have told Hailsham of his change of mind, nor informed even 'his own clan' (as Ian Gilmour later put it), for Maurice Macmillan continued to press Hailsham's claims long after his father had switched to Home. Macmillan saw in Hailsham something of his own youthful iconoclasm – 'what Stanley, and John Loder, and Boothby and

[32] Shepherd, *Macleod*, 309; Walters, *Not Always*, 121–30; Howard and West, *Making of the Prime Minister*, 75, 80; Hailsham, *Sparrow's Flight*, 352–5; Boyd-Carpenter, *Way of Life*, 177; Butler note, 20 Oct. 1963, Butler MSS G40; interview with Lord Deedes.

Noel Skelton tried to represent from 1924 onwards', but he had now decided that there was a fatal 'excess of boyishness'.[33]

The popular impression of the front-runners and the Party reaction to them was neatly captured at a mass meeting addressed by Sir Gerald Nabarro in Bolton while the Conference was taking place in nearby Blackpool; Nabarro thought Maudling to be 'manly, matey and money-wise' (and the mention of his name produced no audience reaction at all), Butler to be 'donnish, dignified and dull' (audience groans), and Hailsham to be 'ebullient, erudite and erratic' (which brought the audience to their feet, cheering). The problem was that the front-runners each had embattled groups of opponents as well as staunch supporters; of the four MPs who ran Hailsham's campaign, two were for Butler as second choice but two were against him at any price. As Nigel Birch put it, 'the trouble . . . was that those who liked Rab didn't like Hailsham and those who liked Hailsham didn't like Rab'. Birch was one of many who drew the conclusion that the Party would unite only behind a third candidate, a *tertium quid* like Bonar Law had been in 1911. Initially he pinned his faith on Maudling but decided after Maudling's Conference speech had flopped that he would not do either. Like the Lord Chancellor, the Chief Whip, John Hare, Duncan Sandys, the 1992 Committee chairman and Edward Heath, he now saw the best unity candidate as Home; the active adherence of Selwyn Lloyd to the 'draft Home' camp was particularly significant, for his recent travels around the constituencies in search of material for his organisation report had made him a respected authority on what the Party activists felt. Alec Home had been urged to stand by Macmillan himself many times, but at the Tuesday Cabinet he had apparently ruled himself out altogether, which was one reason why such keen observers as Macleod later failed to pick up his late run on the rails; under increasing pressure to come to the aid of his Party, Home wavered and then agreed to consult his doctor, a fact that was disconcertingly communicated to Butler just before he addressed the Conference rally in Blackpool. The word had already got about the bars and corridors, and the applause given to Home for his foreign policy speech earlier in the week was now dwarfed by the reception he had when as President he chaired Saturday's rally; the chairman's ovation overshadowed that of Butler as the speaker. Encouraged by his doctor, Home agreed to be drafted if that is what the Party as a whole wanted; it was, taking Boyd-Carpenter's view quoted above, exactly the attitude that was most likely to appeal, a uniting choice of a reluctant candidate, for if Home had fewer supporters than other candidates he also had fewer opponents. Home's amateur status is amusingly confirmed by the Lord Chancellor's report on Cabinet Ministers' views on the succession, which counted both Butler and

---

[33] Morgan, *Crossman*, 1031; John Dickie, *The Uncommon Commoner* (1964), 172; Butler, *Art of the Possible*, 218; Horne, *Macmillan*, 553–4; Gilmour review in *London Review of Books*, 27 July 1989.

Hailsham as having voted for themselves, but did not include Home as voting for anyone. It would be foolish to present Home as a political virgin unaware of his opportunity, for unambitious men do not devote forty years to politics, however strong their sense of duty. But Home had few personal enemies and hardly anyone who suspected him of underhand motives; Butler later mused that he might have made a better fight of it if he had not been up against 'such a terrific gent'; after the recent claims about the lack of integrity in public life, this was Home's strongest suit. As Lord Carrington so delicately summed up Home, 'No more honourable man has ever climbed to the top.'[34]

West Dorset was one of the few constituency associations to discuss the leadership issue and minute local views before the outcome was known; after a discussion at the association F and G P Committee on Monday 14 October, 'Mr. Pope said that he was not in favour of Mr. Butler as he felt he would not be able to inspire the Party workers. Major Spicer said that on the other hand between 1945 and 1951 Mr. Butler was indeed the architect of our recovery'. On the main issue, thirteen votes were cast for Home, four for Butler, three for Maudling and one each for Hailsham and Heath. But Home was still not actually a candidate; on the train back from Blackpool on the previous Saturday evening, the Lord Chancellor, who was himself urging Home to stand and who was to do as much as any man to make him Leader, bet Mollie Butler five pounds to five shillings that Home would not stand. With Conference over, the deadlock remained. Macmillan recorded in his diary after briefings on Monday the 14th: 'the party in the Country wants Hogg [Hailsham]; the Parliamentary Party wants Maudling or Butler; the Cabinet wants Butler.' It is notable that in this summary of reports to him *no* group was mentioned as collectively wanting Home, and that the statement of the Cabinet's views flatly contradicted what Macmillan was to tell the Queen three days later. This was because the real contest only now began, in London, with Macmillan determined to stage-manage the show. This was neither secret nor underhand. After seeing Butler, Macmillan painfully constructed a minute outlining his proposals for consulting the Party, which was read to Cabinet on Tuesday morning. Even at the end of a long agenda, it is scarcely credible that, as Anthony Howard suggests, Ministers did not give their attention to this particular item. Butler reported back that 'they all agreed that this was the right procedure'; Macleod, who was to be the severest critic of the consultations, received as Party Chairman personal copies of Macmillan's minute and of Butler's report. The premier's minute could hardly have been clearer. Not only did it set out the channels by which Party views would

[34] Gerald Nabarro, *Nab 1: Portrait of a Politician* (1969), 40; Walters, *Not Always*, 122; Thompson, *Day Before Yesterday*, 218; Campbell, *Heath*, 143; Shepherd, *Macleod*, 318; D.R. Thorpe, *Selwyn Lloyd* (1989), 375–6; Lord Home, *The Way the Wind Blows* (1976), 183; Dickie, *Uncommon Commoner*, 172–5; Howard, *RAB*, 322; Carrington, *Reflect on Things Past*, 183; the Lord Chancellor's report is in PREM 11/5008, drawn to my attention by Peter Hennessy.

be collected – through the Lord Chancellor for the Cabinet, the two Chief Whips for MPs and for peers, and Poole and Lord Chelmer (chairman of the Executive) for the National Union – but also it laid down what would happen next: Macmillan 'would like to be informed when they have been completed and I will at that time decide according to the state of my health what steps should then be taken. I may see the people concerned myself or I may make other arrangements for their advice to be coordinated. I will let you know.' It is certainly possible to argue that this was not the 'customary processes', since nothing like it had ever been done before; when the change of leaders was over, the National Union Executive noted with pleasure that it had been formally consulted for the first time, so this was certainly not seen by them as a traditional exercise. What could not be maintained though was that Cabinet contenders had not been told what to expect; if they did not object on Tuesday when Macmillan told them that he would control the next stage if fit enough to do so, then they could hardly complain later; the procedures did not add up to what Macleod later called 'the tightness of the magic circle'. The only real ground for complaint was in the last five ambiguous words of Macmillan's message; he did 'let [Butler] know' what procedure he was following – and Butler still neither resisted nor insisted on taking it back to Cabinet colleagues – but Macmillan did not reveal the content as opposed to the form of the consultations' outcome. Butler's acquiescence is not surprising in the light of an *aide-mémoire* that he had composed for himself in the previous July; he wrote that in the event of a leadership contest there should *not* be a ballot, and that he preferred the collection of opinions by the whips, the results of which should be 'conveyed to the present leader'; he added significantly that 'if there is clearly a big majority for one candidate then I think the rest of us should pull in and help'.[35]

In view of the later charges of fixing the succession that were thrown at Macmillan's head, it is worth pausing to consider what his own feelings were at this stage when the formal soundings began on Tuesday 15 October. This emerges from the mind-clearing *aide-mémoire* that he dictated on that morning, effectively the first draft of the one that he was to read to the Queen on the Thursday. It began with a review of the precedents and went on to review the candidates. Those in favour of an orderly handover of power and the continuity of policy were expected to favour Butler, while the same people would think Hailsham to be 'impulsive, even arrogant, in his handling of business', mainly from his habit of talking too much on subjects about which he knew little. Hailsham's strength was seen to lie in

---

35 West Dorset CA minutes, 14 Oct. 1963; Butler note, 20 Oct. 1963, Butler MSS, G40; Horne, *Macmillan*, 555; Howard, *RAB*, 316; Central Office Chairman's department file, CCO 20/8/7; National Union Executive Committee minutes [hereafter NUEC], 25 Oct.1963; George Hutchinson, *The Last Edwardian at Number 10* (1980), 131; Butler note, 12 July 1963, Butler MSS, G40.

his electioneering appeal as a Leader to take on Wilson, and in the fact that any alternative might be thought likely 'to float upon events' rather than taking charge of them. Lord Home, thought Macmillan, 'is clearly a man who represents the old governing class at its best. . . . He is not ambitious in the sense of wanting to scheme for power although not foolish enough to resist honour when it comes to him. Had he been of another generation he would have been of the Grenadiers and the 1914 heroes.' This last was a remarkable private tribute from Macmillan to one of the 'men of Munich', though doubtless entirely justified. Macmillan added a candid assessment of Home's disadvantages, however, notably the extent to which he was 'free . . . from many of the difficulties that beset modern people today', and he thought that the pro-Home mood that had emerged at the end of the previous week at Blackpool would prove to be 'just a mood'. No conclusion was reached by the premier at this stage, but he was clearly hoping for a result from the sounding that would favour Home, even if not yet confident that he would receive one.[36]

Over Tuesday and Wednesday the various soundings were taken; many of the Cabinet visited Macmillan in hospital as well as being interviewed by Lord Dilhorne; 90 per cent of MPs were said to have been interviewed personally by a whip, the rest by telephone or if abroad by telegram, and some were seen more than once. The consultations were complete by Thursday and taken back to Macmillan in hospital. The peers reported strong support for Home; constituency opinion divided between Butler and Hailsham (though most soundings had been taken at Blackpool before Home was a candidate); MPs, like constituencies, were reported to include strong opponents of Butler and Hailsham as well as supporters, but Home was said to be the most favoured candidate, in Macmillan's words 'not by much, but significant'; Martin Redmayne's report showed that although only 87 MPs had actually plumped for Home as first choice, compared to 221 for other candidates (86 for Butler, 65 for Hailsham, 48 for Maudling, 12 for Macleod and 10 for Heath), Home had the highest number of second preferences and the smallest number of 'definite aversions', and was anyway backed by more senior and experienced MPs and by a wider spectrum of opinion than Butler or Hailsham. Finally, the Cabinet was said to have expressed ten voices for Home (or twelve, a clear majority, if Macmillan and Home himself were included) and with no more than three first preferences for anyone else; there were also calculations showing preferences on different scenarios, but giving a majority for Butler only if both Home *and* Hailsham were eliminated. Only on that Thursday did other contenders for the leadership begin to suspect what was happening, but their late attempts to halt the process by calling for a round-table meeting of candidates or a full Cabinet discussion were ignored

---

[36] Macmillan's memorandum is in PREM 11/5008, drawn to my attention by Peter Hennessy.

by Macmillan as merely the manoeuvrings of 'all the *unsuccessful* candidates', which both assumed that the Queen would inevitably take his advice, and that that advice would accurately represent the Party view anyway. A late-night meeting of discontented Ministers at Powell's house established that at least eight of the Cabinet strongly opposed Home's appointment, but this failed to halt the Home bandwagon. Macmillan then presented the results of his consultations to the Queen in a formal resignation interview on Friday 18 October, together with a summary of his own which made a strong case for Home; he made it quite clear that Home was being put forward as the least divisive candidate, the one who 'would be best able to secure united support'. Home himself, who had consented to be drafted only if the Party clearly wanted him, was now embarrassed by evidence that he was to some at least a highly unpopular choice; he himself suggested delay – an idea that Macmillan impatiently brushed aside: 'Go ahead. Get on with it'. In accepting Macmillan's advice, the Queen would have had to ignore the information telephoned in to the Palace by Dennis Walters for the Hailsham camp, and by others too, that Ministers were dissatisfied with the Party consultations. When summoned to the Palace, Home did not kiss hands as Prime Minister; he was asked only to try to form an administration and then report back, an idea that came from the Queen rather than from her prospective premier, despite many subsequent claims to the contrary. He returned to Number 10 to face his colleagues.[37]

How accurate then were the soundings on which Macmillan based his advice? As with all measurements of opinion, an answer to that question depended on exactly what questions had been asked, when, and in what order. Constituency preferences were *not* for Home, because he was not in the running when many opinions were expressed, and this was taken as a reason to discount them as now out of date. Several MPs recalled that it was the whips who introduced Home's name into their own consultation and some were called in a second time after Home's candidacy was definite to see if this had changed their preferences. Consulted at Blackpool, Jim Prior opted for Maudling as first choice and Butler second; the Chief Whip then twice asked him about Home, 'if he does renounce', to which Prior replied, 'I suppose he would be possible'; reflecting on this conversation later, Prior had 'little doubt that even at this early stage I was put down as an Alec supporter'. William Whitelaw, Humphry Berkeley and Reginald Bennett were all asked for their views in a similar manner; Whitelaw, who was shortly to be Chief Whip himself, thought that the questioning was 'totally irregular'. Gerald Nabarro opted for Hailsham, Butler and Macleod in that order, but

37 Dickie, *Uncommon Commoner*, 182; Horne, *Macmillan*, 555–66; Enoch Powell, *Reflections: Selected Writings and Speeches of Enoch Powell* (1992), 135; Kenneth Young, *Sir Alec Douglas-Home* (1970), 167; Walters, *Not Always*, 135; private information; Lord Chancellor's and Chief Whip's reports are in PREM 11/5008.

agreed to 'accept Alec Home if none of the three I named could secure a clear majority' when pressed by the Chief Whip. Since the whips were counting votes against as well as votes for each candidate, it is not difficult to see how such discussions appeared to be the 'making' of a majority for Home as the least unpopular candidate. When interviewed on the radio in December 1963, Redmayne emphatically denied that it had been 'a black-ball system', but agreed that 'since the object of the exercise was to find out under what Prime Minister the party could most unitedly and enthusiastically move on in the pre-election period, one had obviously to think with which man there would be the least number of dissentients'. He also conceded that it was not simply a matter of counting votes, but of weighing the voters too, for 'in every organisation there must be people on whose opinion one would more strongly rely on than on others'; this would mean that the senior backbenchers now backing Home would have a disproportionate effect on the outcome. So far as the Cabinet were concerned, Dilhorne certainly failed to understand the depth of actual opposition to Home as Prime Minister because there was so little hostility to Home the man, and he too may have misreported some who had acquiesced when his name was mentioned as first preferences for Home. The inclusion of Macleod's name in the list of Home supporters when it is clear that, even *before* the outcome was publicly known, he was already expressing implacable resistance to Home being appointed at all, seriously undermines the credibility of Dilhorne's document; Alistair Horne's suggestion that Macleod was being too clever for his own good in playing some devious game is hardly convincing. And Horne cannot in any case explain away how Boyle also came to be on Dilhorne's list as a Home supporter when he too was a known opponent and was a man who quite clearly said what he thought; on 17 October, the day on which he saw the Lord Chancellor, Boyle added a postscript to an MP's copy of the standard letter that he was sending to friends who wrote about the leadership, in which he said that 'I am personally for Butler and hope for both the Party's and the country's sake that he gets it'. How could even a misunderstanding have recorded Boyle's views on that very day as a vote for Home? More generally, as with MPs so with the Cabinet, the result of complex conversations may well have been, as Macleod later argued, 'that the expressions of genuine regard for [Home] somehow became translated into first preferences'. At the time, Hailsham was livid; recollecting the same events in tranquillity, he came to the conclusion that 'there would certainly not have been anything improper' if the Party managers had 'decided that Alec Home was the ideally safe compromise candidate to hold the Party together instead of the supposedly weak Rab and the supposedly flamboyant Hailsham'. This may very well be how the whips and the Lord Chancellor perceived their duty to the Party, though as late as 1989, reviewing Alistair Horne's biography of Macmillan, Ian Gilmour still believed that Dilhorne had deliberately falsified the Cabinet's views – a view that the evidence of Boyle's views would certainly support. However, even in his hostile 1964 *Spectator* article, Macleod was more charitable than this, taking the view that men acting conscientiously and in accordance with their idea of duty had simply produced the wrong result by asking questions in a particular way. In a still gentlemanly Party, few can have answered the consultation questions in a way as derogatory to the popular Alec Home as did the Postmaster-General: Reginald Bevins had hardly been able to believe that the whip's question about Home being a candidate was other than a joke; he told ITN that his agent had told him that the Conservatives would scarcely hold a seat in Liverpool if a fourteenth earl was chosen; Bevins himself was to be one of the Tory casualties in Liverpool in 1964, one of many in the parliamentary infantry who suffered for a decision that they had never wanted to be made.[38]

When offered places in Home's Cabinet, Butler, Hailsham, Maudling, Macleod, Powell and Boyle all either refused or reserved their position; since this group included the Deputy Prime Minister, the Chancellor of the Exchequer, the Leaders of both Lords and Commons, and the Party Chairman, they had considerable collective weight as well as numbers. Edward Boyle's pencil note on the Friday evening records the then state of play: 'RAB & RM won't say. QH, IM, EP – No'. He also noted that Maudling and Hailsham were now behind Butler, that Powell was also keeping in touch, and that he himself had 'appealed to RAB this afternoon not to let us down'. But Boyle's note also concluded simply, 'overtaken by events'. The fact was that from Friday afternoon, Home was the *locum tenens*, and anyone who placed a high priority either on his own career or on the unity of the Party had to come to terms with the fact. Butler was now the only alternative, for Maudling and Hailsham had both agreed to back him against Home even before Macmillan formally resigned; Butler also had the support of Poole, Aldington and Fraser, all of whom had been drawn more into the contest the longer it went on, and who had doubts about their ability to project Home as an election-winning Leader. Writers on the fringe of active politics but who knew the contestants as friends were also stirring the pot: Alan Watkins telegraphed Boyle to 'stand fast', William Rees-Mogg on Friday night offered the view that 'I think it's quite open', and Kenneth Harris wrote from the *Observer* that 'we are terribly upset here. The whole thing is quite extraordinary. We were RAB to a man as you probably know'. Meanwhile, Home's supporters were also moving to stiffen his nerve. On the same

---

38   Thompson, *Day Before Yesterday*, 218; William Whitelaw, *The Whitelaw Memoirs* (1989), 46; Fisher, *Macleod*, 239; Reginald Bevins, *The Greasy Pole* (1965), 143; Prior, *Balance of Power*, 32–3; Shepherd, *Macleod*, 323–4; Nabarro, *Nab 1*, 45; Bogdanor, 'The Selection of the Party Leader', in A. Seldon and S. Ball (eds), *Conservative Century: The Conservative Party since 1900* (Oxford, 1994), 76, 78; Alan Beattie (ed.), *English Party Politics, vol. II, 1906–1970* (1970), 542; Dickie, *Uncommon Commoner*, 182; Boyle MSS, 5581; Walters, *Not Always*, 143; Butler, *Art of the Possible*, 247; Gilmour review, *London Review of Books*, 27 July 1989; Hutchinson, *Last Edwardian*, 128, 140; Hailsham, *Sparrow's Flight*, 355; Howard and West, *Making of the Prime Minister*, 86.

day, the following message was given to him: 'Mr. Hare telephoned to say that he and Mr. Heath have heard that you "may be meeting difficulties". They say you must realise that you have friends – of whom they number themselves.'[39]

Butler was exactly the wrong man to be placed in this situation. Like Home he wanted to have the Leadership without fighting for it, but unlike Home he had no Macmillan to stage-manage the succession in his favour; without a lead from him the resisters crumbled away. Powell later spoke dramatically of having given Butler the loaded pistol, only to find that he could not bear the thought of blood on the carpet; Hailsham noted caustically that 'Ferdinand the bull had preferred to sniff the grass rather than take what would have been his if he had wished it'. Dennis Walters found it frustrating that Butler could not even bring himself to telephone supporters to urge them to stand firm, and Poole exploded to him, 'I tell you . . . if you had seen [Butler] yesterday morning, dithering about in a gutless sort of way, you would not want him to be Prime Minister of this country. I was quite appalled; quite disgusted.' Geoffrey Lloyd, who had also tried unavailingly to strengthen Butler's nerve, finally told him to his face that 'if you are not prepared to put everything to the touch, you don't deserve to be Prime Minister'.[40]

To be fair to Butler, there was a positive side to the case; unlike the situation in January 1957, he had it entirely within his grasp to become Prime Minister in October 1963, for if he had stood out, several others would have done so too, and Home would then have had to report to the Palace his failure to unite the Party; but once Home had been given first try to form a Cabinet, his failure could have been brought about only through a constitutional crisis involving the monarchy, and with a Party split; it is inconceivable that a Butler team formed after Home's public humiliation would have been able to unite the Party to win the coming election. For Butler, Party unity had been a creed he had lived by throughout his political life – he later told Elizabeth Longford that Peel's splitting of his Party was for him 'the supremely unforgettable political lesson of history. . . . I could never do the same thing in the twentieth century, under any circumstances whatever.' Introducing him to speak at Blackpool a week earlier, Home himself had pointedly remarked that 'everyone knows that no-one has given more loyal or more unselfish service to the Party than Mr. Butler'. Having failed to deter Home by sulking, Butler himself now urged Boyle to join Home's Government to save his career, and during Saturday Maudling, Hailsham and then Butler himself followed suit. After hesitation, Poole agreed to Macmillan's personal plea to stay on as deputy to the new Party Chairman. Only Powell and Macleod eventually refused

[39] Note by Boyle, telegram from Watkins, and notes from Harris and Rees-Mogg, all 18 Oct. 1963, Boyle MSS, 24077, 5582–4; the note for Home is in PREMS/426.

[40] Walters, *Not Always*, 136–8, 143; Butler, *Art of the Possible*, 240, 250; Thompson, *Day Before Yesterday*, 219; Hailsham, *Sparrow's Flight*, 356.

office. Powell's motives had something to do with the affront to the Lords implied by removing a hereditary peer to the Commons to be Prime Minister, and to his extreme distaste for the way in which Macmillan had managed the succession over the previous week, but also rested on his insistence on personal consistency: when asked a second time by Home, he replied 'Well, I don't expect, Alec, you expect me to give you a different answer on Saturday, from one I gave you on Friday. I'd have to go home and turn all the mirrors round.' For Macleod, the reasons had more to do with the maintenance of a progressive image and policy for the Party. Perhaps too, as Nigel Fisher suggested, Macleod was affronted that it had all been arranged behind his back even though he was Party Chairman at the time.[41]

Although Home gave free rein in his Government to Maudling at the Exchequer, and foregrounded Heath to demonstrate that the Class of 1950 was close to the heart of Conservatism in the 1960s, the loss of Macleod and Powell, the archetypal new men of talent, was a severe blow; two years earlier James Margach had written of Macleod as 'the leader of the new forces that make up modern Toryism' and of his 'persuasive appeal to the uncommitted and middle-class voters'. One immediate problem was the chairmanship of the Party, which was refused by Selwyn Lloyd and John Boyd-Carpenter before being accepted by John Hare, now made Lord Blakenham; even among Home's admirers, there was no rush to be his election manager. As a result of having to beg colleagues to serve under him, Home had also lost any room for manoeuvre in appointments; he needed Heath and Lloyd so badly that each practically wrote his own job description. Butler at last went to the Foreign Office, and Anthony Barber and Joseph Godber were promoted to the Cabinet to replace Powell and Macleod, but there were otherwise only minimal changes.[42]

The problem with carrying forward Macmillan's 1962 team beyond the 1963 leadership crisis was that Macmillan himself had been its keystone; for all his snobbishness and elegant Whiggery, Macmillan had a first-class brain that could engage with issues and provide intellectual stimulus to 'beavers' like Boyle and Joseph; when he retired, the *Financial Times* thought that 'though a man of traditional values, Mr. Macmillan was totally modern and pragmatic in his approach', while Julian Critchley thought that in the Macmillan regime, 'the Prime Minister's kinsmen were in office as were the brighter of the middle class – an alliance of the Devonshires and the Research Department'. Anthony Sampson had described in 1962 the bizarre contest for the Oxford University Chancellorship in 1960, in which the premier in office had campaigned as the anti-establishment candidate and won (by hard work and a professional drive to get the vote out); when it was over, the

41 Howard, *RAB*, 320–1; Bogdanor, 'Selection', 95; Dickie, *Uncommon Commoner*, 176; Central Office Chairman's department file, CCO 20/8/7; T.F. Lindsay and Michael Harrington, *The Conservative Party, 1918–1970* (1974), 224; Powell, *Reflections*, 11; Fisher, *Macleod*, 243.
42 Fisher, *Macleod*, 200; Boyd-Carpenter, *Way of Life*, 180–1; Thorpe, *Lloyd*, 381–2.

weeklies continued to debate whether Macmillan had or had not been the establishment candidate; they would never have had that doubt about Home, for as October 1963 had shown it was only as an establishment candidate that he was prepared to stand anyway. With Home taking over then, the aristocratic surface of Macmillanism triumphed over the radical iconoclast with personal memories of Stockton's unemployed. Macmillan might enjoy being photographed on the grouse moors but Home actually owned them. He could not, and did not want to, affect the vulgar populism that Macmillan had cultivated, and which would be crucial in expounding economic policy in an election year.[43]

As Kenneth Young explained, Home

> was at his best when he was most himself, chatting with people on whistle-stop tours, at fetes, in factories or fields. . . . Yet this is very curious. He could scarcely be thought by the public as 'one of us', and was not. He had never nipped in for a quick one or a cup of tea at Lyons. He had nursed babies, his own and those of his children, but he had never pushed them in a pram in the park. Sir Alec filling the boiler or standing in a queue in the pouring rain waiting for a bus was inconceivable. He did not borrow books from the public library; the books flooded in, mint new, from authors and publishers. He did not try to make ends meet. They met.

Hence the satirists were outraged by Home's appointment; Richard Ingrams later remembered 'an outbreak of hysterical rage in the *Private Eye* office which has never been paralleled. It seemed like Macmillan's final gesture of contempt for democracy to elect this half-witted Earl who looked and behaved like something out of P.G. Wodehouse.' *Private Eye* thus carried an obituary notice stating that 'the death occurred on October 18th 1963 of the Conservative Party. The Conservative Party had been suffering from severe Macmillan for the last seven years and although this had finally cleared up, its condition was so debilitated as a result that a sudden attack of Lord Home caused its immediate demise.' Gerald Scarfe's accompanying cartoon portrayed Home as a death's head, setting a fashion for others of his trade, while on television Bernard Levin dismissed Home as a 'cretin'. These critics would keep up their attacks right to the end; on the two days before polling in 1964, Levin explained to the Tory readers of the *Daily Mail* why he would vote Labour. Julian Critchley later believed that he had won Rochester and Chatham (by 1,023 votes), 'surprised but uncomplaining', on Macmillan's coat-tails in 1959, but lost it again (by 1,013 votes this time) because of Sir Alec in 1964. On the day of Home's triumph, Butler had foreseen the whole thing, in telling Home gently that a peer as Prime Minister 'spoilt the image of modernisation'.[44]

43 Donald Johnson, *A Cassandra at Westminster* (1967), 59; Julian Critchley, 'Strains and Stresses in the Conservative Party', in *Political Quarterly*, vol. 44 (1973), 239; James Margach, *The Anatomy of Power* (1978), 116; Anthony Sampson, *The Anatomy of Britain* (1962), 216.
44 Young, *Douglas-Home*, 187; Ingrams, *Private Eye*, 15, 91; Butler and King, *General Election of 1964*, 189; Butler note, 18 Oct. 1963, Butler MSS, G40.

It is necessary to labour the extent to which Home did and did not resemble Macmillan mainly because the single year he had in office meant that it was mainly a hand prepared for Macmillan that he had to play. This is brought out by an *aide-mémoire* that the Party Chairman Blakenham circulated to ministerial colleagues on 8 November to inform their speeches in the 'current campaign' and for months ahead. The themes to be stressed were:

1   New Prime Minister; first-class team; vigorous plans.
2   We are embarked on an unprecedented programme of national recon-
    struction and modernisation. The details make an impressive list and are
    well worth reciting.
3   The increasing tempo of advance is based on the harvesting of plans put in
    hand long ago. There has been no change of direction, simply a dramatic
    acceleration (see pamphlet, *Acceleration*). Growing impact of long-term
    policies (Beeching, for example, appointed early 1961, Stedeford in 1960,
    Buchanan began work in October 1960, Robbins and Newsam began
    early 1961, Robens to Coal Board same year. NEDC foreshadowed
    July 1961. Rochdale began March 1961. Local Government reorganisation
    started in 1958.)
4   The dramatic acceleration of public and social service spending makes
    nonsense of Socialist allegations of private affluence in the midst of public
    squalor.

This was certainly a forceful case, but it was not really Sir Alec's case because he was not at heart an interventionist or a big spender anyway, and he certainly had more regrets for the old world that was being modernised out of existence than Macmillan had ever had. Obedient to instructions, and no doubt thoroughly approving of them anyway, Edward Boyle sent to Number 10 a few weeks later a brief for the Prime Minister's speechwriters on 'the Tory philosophy of education' which placed the greatest emphasis on increases in spending. There was no room now for a change of direction.[45]

The succession crisis just would not die away. After refusing to serve, Macleod and Powell kept silence about their reasons – one commentator said they had been 'reticent to a fault'; they were though provoked by the publication of Randolph Churchill's *The Fight for the Tory Leadership* in January 1964. What irritated them most was that Churchill had been assisted by Macmillan, and they felt that this removed their obligation to silence: Macleod, now editor of the *Spectator,* dubbed the book 'Mr. Macmillan's trailer for the screenplay of his memoirs', and reviewed it himself: he dissected October 1963 in detail, alleged manipulation by a 'magic circle' of old Etonians; consequently, 'the Tory Party for the first time since Bonar Law

---

[45] Blakenham *aide-mémoire* for Ministers, 8 Nov. 1963, and Boyle to Eldon Griffiths,
      26 Feb. 1964, Boyle MSS, 22528, 22684a.

is being led from the right of centre'; despite his avowals that all had acted honourably, Macleod stirred the pot without restraint in the language he used; even to the sympathetic Nigel Fisher, Macleod, 'having first cooked his goose . . . now stuffed it with sour grapes'. The review was censured by his own constituency party and for some time hardly any Tory MP would associate with him. Powell, more cautiously, just confirmed that Macleod had got his facts right, but this was important; Hugh Massingham in the *Observer* remarked that Powell was 'the sea-green incorruptible of the Tory Party. In the unaccountable absence of the Archangel Gabriel, Mr. Macleod could not have found a more powerful or convincing sponsor.' Powell was in any case regularly in the headlines by then for speeches in which he developed what was soon called a 'Powellite' economic doctrine, each public appearance a reminder of his exile from the Cabinet. Replies to Macleod's review kept the issue alive, with Randolph Churchill describing him in the *Evening Standard* as 'the insensitive, ungracious, clod-hopping Macleod' who 'will not soon be forgotten or forgiven'; Churchill also mischievously claimed that Macleod had checked facts with Maudling, thus reintroducing the dispute back into the Cabinet, though he cannot have known that Butler had also assisted by reading Macleod's review in proof.[46]

The damage and the discontent that it epitomised remained a feature of the Party for months. At Central Council in March 1964, an anodyne resolution pledging support for the Government and its policies was easily passed – but not unanimously; in April, *The Times* printed anonymous articles by 'a Conservative' (generally assumed to be Powell, and neither confirmed nor denied by him on numerous occasions since) that were highly critical of Government policy and leadership; the National Union Executive in May and again in July discussed 'the behaviour of Members of Parliament' and the need for Party loyalty, an awkward issue for an election year. John Grigg felt that, given the closeness of defeat in 1964, Home might well have won but for Macleod's allegation that he was a right-winger who had been selected unfairly, and Home himself in his memoirs felt that the Party could have won if Macleod and Powell had 'pulled their weight'. In January 1964, Gallup reported that 48 per cent of electors thought the Conservatives more divided than Labour and only 22 per cent saw Labour as more divided, a perception that reversed a regular Conservative advantage. As late as Spring 1965, the debate about October 1963 went on, with the publication of Reginald Bevins' *The Greasy Pole*. He claimed that 'a party . . . led predominantly by a group of Old Etonians . . . makes a bad joke of democracy' and recalled a Chequers week-end where 'only Ernest Marples and I were without landed estates, Ernest because he had no use for one and I because it was beyond me'. By

---

[46] Randolph Churchill, *The Fight for the Tory Leadership* (1964), vi–xvi; Howard and West, *Making of the Prime Minister*, 113–14; Hutchinson, *Last Edwardian*, 125, 141; Fisher, *Macleod*, 253; Powell, *Reflections*, 135; Roth, *Powell*, 304–5, 311.

then Bevins was well out of touch: he predicted that if the Party ran true to form Christopher Soames would be its next leader, but within weeks of the publication of his book the Party had actually chosen Heath, in a contest where *all* the contenders were outside any 'magic circle' of Tory tradition and where none had attended a top public school.[47]

There is an important qualification to this general point, which is that the debate about what had happened in October 1963 was largely confined to the press and the lobbies; in the constituencies, and more generally in the National Union there was a rallying to Home as soon as he became Prime Minister, a reluctance to believe that anything improper had taken place, and a strong call for unity and loyalty. The Western Area Council agreed that press reports that said that all association chairmen had been consulted had been incorrect, but when the Area Chairman said that it had been easier at Blackpool to consult whoever happened to be the constituency representatives, and that with the Area Agent 'they came to the conclusion that the general feeling was that Lord Home was the most popular choice', there was no further protest. The Guildford association readily agreed with its MP that 'it must be assumed that [Home] had a majority in the Cabinet, and members in the Commons, House of Lords and the Constituencies for Mr. Macmillan to have given the Queen the advice that he did'. The same meeting feelingly endorsed his reminder that 'the Labour Party's fortunes [in this Parliament] had risen and fallen with party dissension, and now the same had happened to us'. The very different constituency of Shoreditch and Finsbury on 21 October welcomed 'Hume' as Leader (though the secretary could not yet spell his name correctly), as did Aylesbury four days later; when the prospective candidate for Accrington publicly criticised Home's selection, the constituency association dispensed with his services forthwith and passed a loyal resolution of support for the new Prime Minister. A few extravagant claims were made, as when their president told the Wessex Area that the Party had proved itself a model of democracy from which the Labour Party could take lessons. There was little disposition then to challenge the closing of ranks that all this indicated, and constituency activists became increasingly frustrated by the refusal of MPs and of the press to let the leadership issue fade from memory.[48]

A final area of fall-out from October 1963 affected the *system* for choosing Leaders. Macmillan's claim that he had followed precedent to preserve the royal prerogative hardly stood up to scrutiny. In 1957, the canvassing of Party views had been partial and informal, with Eden by his own choice taking no

---

[47] Central Council minutes [hereafter NUCC], 6 Mar. 1964; Central Office Chairman's department file, CCO 20/1/6; Butler and King, *General Election of 1964*, 22, 83; NUEC, 14 May and 2 July 1964; Horne, *Macmillan*, 570; Home, *Way the Wind Blows*, 186; Levin, *Pendulum Years*, 217, 246.

[48] Western Area Council, 22 Nov. 1963; Guildford CA minutes, 19 Oct. 1963; Shoreditch and Finsbury CA minutes, 21 Oct. 1963; Aylesbury CA minutes, 25 Oct. 1963; Accrington CA minutes, 25 Oct. 1963; Wessex Area Council, 26 Oct. 1963.

part, and with more than one Conservative advising the Palace; something similar had occurred in 1923. Macmillan ensured in 1963 that all Party advice flowed through his own hands, but collected that advice while still Prime Minister; technically, he resigned office before advising on his successor, but only seconds before. To choose anyone but Home, the Queen would have had to disregard this coordinated advice, and either personally choose a different successor from the one recommended by Macmillan or seek a different adviser, either of which procedures would have been practically difficult. Macmillan was well aware that he was forcing a card on the Queen that she would not otherwise have chosen, for he had told Selwyn Lloyd two days earlier that 'it was all very bad luck on Rab, because had he been run over by a car he assumed that the Queen would automatically have sent for Rab'. Powell, who had a more real belief in the prerogative than Macmillan ever had, was an unrelenting critic on these grounds; his 1973 review of Macmillan's memoirs was headed 'How Macmillan Deceived the Queen'; from the opposite pole of British politics (at that time), Paul Johnson asked in January 1964, 'Was the Palace to Blame?' and concluded that it was. Few would go that far, but it is quite clear that Macmillan in 1963 unintentionally ensured that the monarch would never again have more than one option when there was a Tory parliamentary majority. If only one name was to be communicated to the Palace, and through a single channel, then there was an overwhelming case for that name to be chosen openly, so that fairness could be verified and so that losers would not be able to cry foul. Under a more open system, a new Leader could still 'emerge' as a unifier, as 1990 was to show, but only with a countable majority of MPs taking their share of responsibility for the decision. Even before October 1963, Party discussions of Macmillan's probable retirement had involved speculation about the system of election. After October, these discussions redoubled, for example in the Western Area Council, and at Hexham; Butler's Saffron Walden association wrote to the Party Chairman in December to suggest a new approach, after a meeting at which one member was quoted as saying that 'the present system would not work in the 20th century'. City of Oxford Tories debated long and hard a motion demanding 'a revision of the present far from satisfactory method of electing a Leader of the Party' and eventually agreed that what was needed was 'a democratic election more in keeping with modern practice and which reflects favourably on a Party with a progressive outlook'. Macleod argued in the *Spectator* in January 1964 that 'the procedure which has been adopted opens up big issues for decisions in the future. . . . I do not think it is a precedent that will be followed.' Crucially, Home took the same view; he was wounded by claims that he had entered Number 10 'by the back door', and 'didn't think that any election after my election by the same methods would ever carry any public confidence again'. He promised Humphry Berkeley that he would tackle the question, and waited only for the General Election to be out of the way before initiating action, as did others: in December 1964, the National

Union forwarded to him Bassetlaw Conservative Association's resolution that, while 'in no way criticising [Home's] appointment, it nevertheless regrets the *method* used in selection and the appalling picture presented to the electorate at the time the appointment was made. It suggests that a more open method that can be more readily understood by the rank and file of the Party should be formulated for use on future occasions when the leadership is in question.' After October 1963 that question was bound to be asked, and only one answer could now be given. [49]

Sir Alec as Prime Minister

The Government of Sir Alec Douglas-Home (as he became by renouncing his peerage to return to the Commons) was a twelve-month election campaign against the odds. He assured the Party meeting that elected him Leader on 11 November that 'there is nothing that I like so much as a real, tough political fight – that is what I have to offer you in the months ahead'. At this meeting, Butler had for the third time to propose a colleague for the leadership, but some MPs refused even to turn up; his PPS reported that MPs were now expressing very strong admiration for Rab's recent conduct, and considerable dissatisfaction for that of Hailsham, Powell and Macleod. Sir Alec had no time to play himself in, starting his premiership with a by-election to return him to the Commons. That contest went well enough in a rural Scottish constituency and provided good publicity through forty-eight speeches delivered in a month; it also produced a good result, with a bigger majority than the last three-cornered contest in the seat in 1950. Campaigning in the cities, in English and Welsh marginals, and on television, was to prove altogether different. Sir Alec's political style did not lend itself to modern electioneering, while the circumstances of his accession ensured that his style would always be under observation. He certainly had a great appeal to the converted; Maudling later recalled that 'he inspired an extraordinary affection among the rank and file of the Tory Party who regarded him as the sort of man they would like to be themselves: a good athlete, not brilliant but intelligent; a man of charm, integrity and balance.' Selwyn Lloyd had already picked on these traits when promoting Home as a candidate, pointing out that he would be the only Prime Minister to have played first-class cricket; friendly newspapers were to make regular references to Sir Alec's sixty-six runs in ninety minutes, for Eton against Harrow on a saturated Lords wicket, as evidence of character: having quoted *Wisden* saying in 1922 that Home had

---

[49] Fisher, *Macleod*, 241; Thorpe, *Lloyd*, 378; Powell, *Reflections*, 134, 136, 153; Howard, *RAB*, 319; Walters, *Not Always*, 115; Goodhart, *The 1922*, 201; Western Area Council, 22 Nov. 1963; Oxford CA minutes, 14 Jan. 1964; Hexham CA minutes, 20 Jan. 1964; Saffron Walden CA minutes, 10 Dec. 1963; Young, *Douglas-Home*, 224; Shepherd, *Macleod*, 385; NUEC, 3 Dec. 1964.

had 'the courage of his convictions and could hook and pull the turning ball effectively', the December 1963 *Conservative Clubs Gazette* added that, 'now, over 40 years later and in a different field, Sir Alec is still very much the same sort of person. When things are difficult he gets down to it.' But it was exactly the type of elector who did not think that Eton against Harrow was really first-class cricket who was so hard for Sir Alec to reach. It was also Lloyd who suggested that ridicule for a fourteenth earl as Prime Minister should be met by pointing out that his rival was equally 'the fourteenth Mr. Wilson', which Sir Alec duly did in an early television interview and so held off that taunt for some months; in January 1964 though, Macleod's *Spectator* claim that 'we have confessed that the Tory Party could not find a Prime Minister in the House of Commons' re-started the attack. It was only two days later that Wilson ridiculed the 'grouse-moor conception of Conservative leadership' and the 'Edwardian establishment mentality' in a speech at Birmingham: Labour would 'replace the closed, exclusive society by an open society . . . in which brains will take precedence over blue blood, and craftsmanship will be more important than caste'. As this suggests, Sir Alec was as often mocked for incompetence as for class, with repeated references to his 1962 *Observer* interview in which he had explained that he analysed economic problems by counting matchsticks; as he himself later wrote, 'Harold Wilson was not likely to miss a trick like that'. The CRD found it hard to brief the Prime Minister or produce drafts for speeches, since unlike Macmillan he neither engaged in intellectual exchange with speechwriters nor read their drafts very convincingly. The 'political testament' he provided for them to describe his philosophy was little help: his preferred definition of Conservatism was 'doing the right thing at the right time'. His one year in office was punishing, and tiredness undoubtedly produced slips that critics pounced on: he spoke patronisingly of pensions as 'donations', he refered to computers as 'imputers', he accidentally conferred a knighthood on Geoffrey Rippon during a speech, and when congratulating one colleague he clapped another on the back. When he spoke at Birmingham in October 1964, the demonstration outside included a huge dinosaur wearing half-moon glasses like Sir Alec's, with the slogan 'too much armour, too little brain, now extinct'. For a year Sir Alec had to contest the presupposition that he was out of date and not very bright. If 'modernise with Macmillan' had been a good joke, 'modernise with Home' was not at all funny.[50]

There were particular problems with the House of Commons and with television. After only eighteen months in the Commons in the previous eighteen years, there would have been difficulties in returning straight to the

---

[50] Dickie, *Uncommon Commoner*, 196. 201, 213; Howard and West, *Making of the Prime Minister*, 102; Maudling, *Memoirs*, 130; Thorpe, *Lloyd*, 381, 388; Central Office file, CCO 3/6/4, *Conservative Clubs' Gazette*; Hutchinson, *Last Edwardian*, 141; Home, *Way the Wind Blows*, 184, 187; Young, *Douglas-Home*, 185, 210.

front bench, but a House that resented a Prime Minister coming from 'the other place' was especially sensitive; Wilson, who had given even Macmillan a difficult time, was an opponent well placed to take advantage. Gradually, Sir Alec found his feet and with the vocal backing of Tory MPs was able to hold his own at Question Time, but he made only four major speeches in the Commons as premier, and was never master of the House nor adept at using its proceedings to generate a favourable press. The broadcasting problem was even worse; he later confessed that he had 'never thought I was going to be Prime Minister, so I had never practised television. I hated it, it was a burden all the time.' Here too he gradually acquired some of the arts, and did well in a full-dress interview with Robin Day in February 1964. The Party's electioneering professionals gradually worked out that their best way forward was to highlight differences between Wilson and Home rather than to claim improbable similarities that they might have got away with for Macmillan or Butler. *That Was The Week That Was* had described the Home–Wilson contest as 'Dull Alec' against 'Smart Alec' and this is in effect what Central Office eventually saw as the best tactic, to set Sir Alec's modesty and integrity against his flashier rival's trickiness. A further aspect of the strategy emerges from the note written by William Deedes for the Party Chairman in February. For him,

> the main question . . . is whether fundamentally we wish the Prime Minister to be compared or contrasted with Harold Wilson. We shall not get the best of both worlds. The more I study Harold Wilson's form, the more I favour contrast. Wilson's total authority over the Labour Party is beginning to strike a rather chilling note. 'No bird sings'. . . . It suits their book to have a gladiatorial contest. . . . It does not suit our book. The Prime Minister's character is in an entirely different mould. He is not a party boss by nature or appearance. He is a relaxed figure holding the reins lightly but skilfully over a team of horses whom he encourages to make a pace of their own. He is in reality much more comparable to Attlee than Wilson. He is not a presidential candidate but a traditional parliamentary leader.

Sir Alec should thus be marketed much as Baldwin had been, but unfortunately the demands of the media now made this impossible. This discussion indicates how far Wilson's media dominance was now one of the given facts of the situation to which Tories must respond. In the central area of projecting the Leader, Conservatives remained on the defensive; over time Sir Alec attracted much affection, but his personal poll rating remained well behind Wilson's; the Leader was riding on the Party's coat-tails rather than the other way round.[51]

---

[51] Home, *Way the Wind Blows*, 187; Dickie, *Uncommon Commoner*, 205–6; Howard and West, *Making of the Prime Minister*, 104; Cockerell, *Live from Number Ten*, 96, 98, 101; Boyd-Carpenter, *Way of Life*, 184; Central Office Chairman's department file, CCO 20/1/12, Correspondence with Ministers; Butler and King, *General Election of 1964*, 15, 94–5.

As Deedes indicated, Sir Alec ran the Cabinet on a loose rein, and much would therefore depend on his colleagues. The paralysis of Summer 1963 and the change of Leader meant that the Queen's Speech for 1963 had to be thrown together at the last moment and with little time for thinking through the best programme for an election year; with various inquiries set in hand earlier in the Parliament now reporting (Robbins on Higher Education, Buchanan on Traffic and so on), the theme remained 'the modernisation of Britain, covering many of the economic and social aspects of our national life', but with the emphasis on extensions to the public provision in such areas as education, housing and the health services. In his Perthshire by-election, Sir Alec made it clear that he had no inhibitions about fighting on a policy of public expenditure increases; even at that time, the *Sunday Telegraph* asked if it was wise for the Prime Minister to 'underplay everything that distinguishes Conservatism from contemporary socialism'. After the 1964 defeat, *The Times* made the same point in declaring that Labour's losing policy in 1959 had been more or less what the Conservatives had lost on in 1964. At the Exchequer, Maudling pursued his expansionist policy through the 1964 Budget and, though he then began to fear the economic consequences if some reining back of imports was not put in place, he continued with reflation until the 1964 Election. By the end of 1963, the economy had picked up sufficiently for more than half of the population to expect that in 1964 they would become better off (while only 7 per cent thought they would be worse off). This evidence of optimism was an electoral benefit, reinforced again by Party advertising that pictured the happy, smiling faces of ordinary families, but once again the boom was the delayed effect of earlier measures rather than of an electioneering Budget in 1964. This was still, if not a 'dash for growth', then at least a conscious attempt to break out of the stop-go cycle by refusing to imperil growth for the sake of the currency, an experiment interrupted by the change of government in 1964, but tried again as a 'dash for expansion' by Heath in 1972 (and again interrupted half way through by losing office). The overall argument about 'thirteen wasted years' could be tellingly countered by statistics of consumption: the number of cars on the road had increased fourfold since 1951, the number of televisions thirteenfold; almost twice as many pupils stayed on at school beyond the statutory age and there had been a 60 per cent increase in university places even before the Robbins programme of university expansion got under way.[52]

Nevertheless, there remained a difficulty at the heart of the economic strategy. Since trade unions in the NEDC and NIC were making little contribution to overall economic policy, the Douglas-Home Government

---

[52] Butler and King, *General Election of 1964*, 24, 37–8, 80, 88, 299; Howard and West, *Making of the Prime Minister*, 97; Maudling, *Memoirs*, 114, 116–17; Brittan, *Steering the Economy*, 177–81; Michael Pinto-Duschinsky, 'Bread and Circuses? The Conservatives in Office, 1951–1964', in V. Bogdanor and R. Skidelsky (eds), *The Age of Affluence* (1970) 56.

missed a political opportunity, perhaps hardly noticed that it had one. Within the Party, demands for action against unofficial and 'unnecessary' strikes had continued to grow: in 1962, the parliamentary Trade Union Committee demanded legislation before the next election. Aidan Crawley had concentrated on trade unions when he returned to the Commons; at the 1962 Conference his speech on this theme was going well in the hall but not with the platform; when his five minutes ended, the chairman instantly switched on the red light, but an outcry from the floor ensured that he was given extra time. A month later a survey of CPC groups indicated that industrial relations was the issue they most wanted chosen for early discussion. Opinion was also building up at the ACP, which had set up a committee to propose action in 1962, only to be stalled by the then Minister of Labour, John Hare; in February 1963, the ACP again pressed for action:

> Mr. Macleod said he felt frankly schizophrenic on this subject. He would like something definite to be done about unofficial strikes, provided it was effective and sensible, and he knew it would be welcome in our Party, and also with opinion which had moved to the Liberals. But it must be remembered that a Conservative Government could not be elected without the support of something like 4½ million trades unionists and their wives. . . . Mr. Butler said there was no doubt this subject was of great interest at present, particularly in the cold weather. He would inform the Minister of Labour of the view of the Advisory Committee that the position could not be left as it was.

In March 1963 the CPC groups reported strong backing for legislation to compel secret ballots before strikes, and more generally there was 'a very strong demand for legislation to reduce strikes'; further discussions by 279 constituency groups in November produced overwhelming support for strike ballots and even a majority for the Monday Club's proposal that trade unions should be made generally liable for damages caused by their members. Also in November, the National Union's Trade Union Advisory Committee, usually the least hawkish body, demanded legislation to amend the law to reintroduce 'contracting in' for the political levy. The earlier reason for avoiding this issue, the hope of drawing the unions into sharing economic responsibility, had evaporated in 1963, and only fear of the loss of working-class votes now held the Party back.[53]

A bold decision to take – or at least publish proposals for – legislative action on trade unions would have been extremely popular in the Party, a unifying move; the opinion polls suggest that it would have been more widely popular too. Many Conservatives did not just want legislation to

---

[53] John Ramsden, *The Making of Conservative Party Policy: The Conservative Research Department since 1929* (1980), 214–15; Aidan Crawley, *Leap Before You Look* (1988), 392, 394; Central Office file, CCO 4/9/111, CPC summaries; Central Office General Director's file, CCO 120/4/11, Selwyn Lloyd Inquiry; Advisory Committee on Policy minutes, 6 Feb. 1963; NUEC, 9 Jan. 1964.

control the trade unions but were by now becoming increasingly impatient. In January 1963 a Midlands agent asked the Monday Club's chairman,'what is the reason for the cowardice of our Government in regard to the Trades Unions?' It was, he said, a nonsense to say that you could do nothing against unofficial strikes without the unions' consent, for the same argument might just as well be applied to burglars; 'is there nothing we can do to galvanise the rank and file of the Tory Party to revolt against Macmillanism and Macleodism? . . . The rank and file of the Tory Party are ready to be led, but it must be by true Conservatives.' Such frustrations were understandable when, as in January 1964, Joseph refused to accept a suggestion from the National Union that action be taken against the political levy, on the ground that nothing should be done to upset the unions and undermine progress towards good industrial relations. In retrospect, Home felt that, 'I don't think it was a thing we could have tackled in those short nine months'; this is certainly a persuasive viewpoint in the sense that a trade union Bill would have been complex and would have taken months to produce (since none had so far been planned), whereas the Board of Trade, especially with Heath driving it onward, was quick to produce a Bill on RPM and had been thinking about one for several years. The result was that in 1964 the Party had no pay policy worthy of the name, which removed a central plank of 1962's 'New Approach'. Conservatives could and did blame the unions for irresponsible pay claims, but offered no remedy to deal with the disease that they diagnosed. The Government did refuse to legislate to reverse a legal decision given against the unions in the case of *Rookes* v. *Barnard*, which irritated the unions, but this was so technical as to make little impact on the public or the economy. In July 1964, the One Nation Group demanded a statement on trade union law and practices before the election, but none was forthcoming; the 1964 manifesto promised only that an inquiry into the issue would be held if the Party was re-elected, a half-hearted stance for a Party after thirteen years in office. In opposition after October, a tough trade union policy was devised within a few months, but this was a year too late. After the 1964 defeat, the London Area chairman argued that the Conservatives had lost the Election rather than Labour winning it, and that the main reason was that the Party 'did not deal with trades union reform'. The speed with which moves were then made to repair the gap shows how many agreed with him. In 1965 his Area, now including over a hundred constituencies, demanded in a Conference resolution 'an assurance that the next Conservative Government will govern by true Conservative principles, not seeking electoral popularity by the adoption of quasi-Socialist measures'.[54]

The issue was settled by default by the allocation of portfolios in October

[54] Young, *Douglas-Home*, 208–9; Central Office Chairman's department file, CCO 20/1/6; National Union papers, NUA 4/3/2, Executive Committee papers, and NUA 2/2/29, Central Council reports.

1963. Whereas Heath could have been pitched into the trade unions with interesting results, Godber was a relatively timid Minister where a tiger would have been needed to tackle the unions head on. Heath had moved well forward in the Government's line-up when in October 1963, as John Campbell puts it, 'all of those who would in normal circumstances have been his rivals' were removed or seriously weakened politically, and he was determined to use his opportunity at the Board of Trade both to enhance his own claims and to restore the Government's reputation for dynamism. He hit on a modernising part of the 1962 package not yet pursued, the abolition of Resale Price Maintenance. However, the effect of attacking retailers' restrictive practices rather than trade union ones would be to divide rather than unite Conservatives. To an extent, his hand was forced by a Labour private member's Bill that would have forced the Government to show its hand, but, once he took it up as a Government measure, Heath's commitment never wavered. This was far from true of the Cabinet or the parliamentary party; Ministers were not very pleased that Heath had told the Sunday papers about his plans before they had Cabinet approval: Butler, Hogg (as Hailsham again was after disclaiming his peerage), Lloyd, the Party Chairman and the Chief Whip all worked to get Heath's Bill postponed until after the Election; since Heath would not back down and the Prime Minister 'with many misgivings' backed him, they secured amendments but no delay. With MPs, Heath was even tougher and would not accept amendments: at the 1922 Committee, 'there was almost unanimous criticism of the Government's proposals on the ground of timing. Members appeared equally divided on the merits.' When the Bill was published in February 1964, Conservative MPs took the rare step of tabling a motion calling for its outright rejection; on second reading twenty-one Tory MPs voted against it, and thirty-five either abstained or were absent unpaired – so that a fifth of all backbenchers rebelled. Heath had apparently threatened to resign if the Prime Minister did not give his support and he now steamed straight ahead with his Bill; George Hutchinson, then the Party's Chief Publicity Officer, later recalled that 'I have never . . . heard a Cabinet Minister so much abused by his colleagues, so badly spoken of and so widely condemned in the party, as Heath was then.' Backbench rebellions continued throughout the Bill's passage, and one amendment was defeated by a single vote, when the usual majority was about ninety. John Boyd-Carpenter at Kingston was just one MP who found that the small shopkeepers who were usually staunch supporters and Party members were in 1964 extremely critical; opposing the Bill in the House, Sir Frank Markham claimed that 'the great heart of our party is dead against the Secretary of State', as is certainly confirmed by resolutions sent to the National Union; Dennis Walters was on the receiving end of it all as the newly-adopted candidate for Westbury, and recalled in 1989 that RPM 'caused more anger, more letters than practically any single issue that's taken place in my time in Parliament'. In nearby Bath there was also strong feeling against Heath's Bill; a debate was postponed in March 1964 because the MP could not be present, but, despite his loyal support of the Government, the next meeting resolved to dissociate itself from the abolition of RPM; when Heath responded to this resolution with a defence of his policy, 'discussion of Mr. Heath's letter [in July] showed that many members of the Executive did not accept Mr. Heath's arguments'. York, a marginal with many shopkeepers, contented itself with pointing out that January 1964 'was hardly the opportune moment to introduce this highly controversial measure'. East Newcastle thought that the RPM Bill 'had done irreparable damage to our chances' in another highly marginal constituency that would be lost later in the year. Reigate merely 'deprecate[d] most strongly the introduction of controversial legislation' so near to a general election, and drew attention to 'the demoralising effect on Party workers in the constituencies'. Receiving the Reigate resolution, the National Union Executive met with Heath and expressed its concern, but he gave no ground. Among CPC groups, by April there was 72 per cent support for the principle of the Bill, but still heavy criticism of the timing. The Government got its Bill, Heath's doggedness in the face of resistance reinforced his reputation as a fighter, and the measure did help to hold down prices, but Party warfare in the lobbies throughout the first half of 1964 was a desperately dangerous scenario for a Party struggling for re-election.[55]

The 1964 recovery

Morale remained low; Shoreditch and Finsbury Conservatives decided in December 1963 'that a good fight be put up this time [in the coming borough elections] so that if we were defeated at least we would go down with flying colours'. After Tory candidates had been soundly thrashed in the new Borough of Islington in May 1964, they planned for the coming General Election in even lower spirits, deciding to hold only one meeting, purely for the benefit of the local press, as any more would be 'a waste of everybody's time'. The Party did recover nationally during 1964, however, and almost pulled off a victory for which the odds had seemed impossibly long. On 7 November 1963, the Party lost Hill's Luton seat (Hill having retired from politics to become chairman of the Independent Television Authority (ITA), an appointment made against strong Central Office advice); a swing to Labour of almost 10 per cent in a key marginal hinted at electoral catastrophe to come, but Sir Alec's Perthshire victory on the same day allowed him to proclaim that

55 Campbell, *Heath*, 139, 148–9, 151–6; Home, *Way the Wind Blows*, 189; Andrew Roth, *Heath and the Heathmen* (1972), 176–7; Goodhart, *The 1922*, 197–8; Norton, *Dissension*, 250–2; Lindsay and Harrington, *Conservative Party*, 227; Boyd-Carpenter, *Way of Life*, 185–6; Bath CA minutes, 12 Mar., 15 Apr. and 9 July 1964; York CA minutes, 20 Jan. 1964; Central Office constituency file, CCO 1/14/129; Reigate CA minutes, 21 Feb. 1964; NUEC, 6 Feb. and 2 Apr. 1964; Central Office file, CCO 4/9/111; ICBH witness seminar, 'Did the Conservatives lose direction, 1961–1964?', in *Contemporary Record*, vol. 2, no. 5 (1989), 31.

'Luton was the last page of the old chapter and Kinross and West Perthshire is the first page of the new'. The last five results of 1963 were all in safe seats where swings were lower and no seats changed hands.[56]

During 1964 the fall-out from the disputed leadership was finally settling and an organisational build-up for the election could be intensified. Lawson and Griffiths arrived as speechwriters just as the Leaders changed, so their services were at Sir Alec's disposal, the team augmented by John MacGregor when Griffiths entered parliament at a by-election. They were kept busy: Sir Alec made 174 Party speeches in the eleven months before he called the 1964 election – in addition to his appearances as head of the Government. The Liaison Committee came back into an intensive phase of operation, chaired by the Party Chairman; the key advisers on Party matters were Blakenham (much influenced by Poole), Redmayne and Lloyd. An innovation was the 'Daily Committee' under the Chief Whip's chairmanship, always attended by either Poole or Blakenham and with a fluctuating ministerial cast depending on the flow of events; its function was short-term tactics in parliament and the country. The Steering Committee continued its medium-term approach and was the forum from which the 1964 manifesto emerged, with Heath playing an important role in pushing for modernisation to remain the defining stance. The machinery was all there, but it did not work as effectively as in 1959. Housing and Land policy indicates the point; as Minister, Joseph was one of the most active in exchanging ideas with Central Office about his policies, on which Labour was mounting a determined attack; despite this, and mainly because of the Government's inability to decide either way on taxing increased land values, a policy area which had since 1950 been a big Conservative bonus was in 1964 producing poll after poll in which Labour was seen to be preferred; housing was, wrote Joseph in December 1963, 'proving a trump in socialist propaganda'. In April 1964, Fraser thought Housing to be still 'one of our three main minuses in terms of policy subjects'. Only at the start of 1964 did Poole's serious fundraising for an election begin, but there was no shortage of funds for special projects before that date. Redmayne feared that industrialists might not be willing to contribute in case Labour embarrassed them after the election with a retrospective requirement to publish details of all political donations, but that fear proved groundless and much money came in. A full national advertising campaign on the 1957–59 model had started in May 1963 but then been cut back in the Summer, with a move to negative anti-Labour posters while the Conservatives' own house was being put in order. From January 1964 the campaign shifted back into a higher gear, taking the promotion of Sir Alec and 'straight talk' as its theme; from May it intensified with a coordinated campaign of posters and press

---

[56] Shoreditch and Finsbury CA minutes, 16 Dec. 1963 and 20 July 1964; Dickie, *Uncommon Commoner*, 199; Chris Cook and John Ramsden (eds), *By-Elections in British Politics* (1973), 382.

advertisements that highlighted the rising standard of living. Overall, the eighteen-month campaign before the 1964 election cost the Party just under £1 million, about double the amount spent for equivalent purposes in 1957–59. Since Labour was now competing in this area for the first time, some increase in Conservative spending was needed if the Party was to retain the edge it had had in 1959. There was some innovation in the way that money was spent on television; an August 1964 broadcast was derided by the quality press and by several Ministers as being worse than a soap opera in its appeal to the low-brow, but was undeniably effective: Poole unrepentantly proclaimed that 'if you don't parade the circus down the street no one will by a ticket for the night'.[57]

There was also a gearing up in more traditional ways. Sir Alec was being sent round the country on tours like those Macmillan had undertaken in 1958, visiting factories and other scenes of economic activity, and combining official visits with evening receptions for Party workers; the trips were not entirely successful, and one of them, a visit to South Wales, was embarrassingly mismanaged. He was also using every opportunity to show off his strongest policy suit, with trips abroad to meet international leaders. A friendly journalist was feeding information into the Party's intelligence summaries from a contact within Wilson's office. Special effort was put into preparing for the first Greater London Council elections due in April 1964, and extra money was made available, for the London constituencies would have to fight three elections in six months. Assistance in cash and in kind was more generally available to marginals, and a special opinion research exercise was mounted from February 1963, after an experiment in Rugby. The objective of this was to use paid canvassers to produce or update a full marked register, and to create a 'climate of interest' in the Party by their operations; there were also fringe benefits from such a complete canvass in the finding of new members, activists, and postal votes, but £154,000 was a large sum to spend on activities without verifiable results. This general gearing up of the machine in the constituencies, which had suffered badly from the difficulties of 1962–63, certainly helped in such areas as postal votes; Blakenham later claimed that these Party efforts had saved about eleven seats in 1964, a view approximating to that of David Butler, and had thus prevented Labour from winning a secure majority. Experiments with new publicity methods led to the production of a Party gramophone record for 1964, devoted to lighthearted 'knocking copy' against Labour and the Liberals. Once again the threat of a Labour Government provoked industrialists into action: in April 1964, Charles Curran MP wanted 'to see the steel industry and the road hauliers doing to the Socialists over nationalisation exactly what the chemists have

[57] Windlesham, *Communication*, 69–78; Campbell, *Heath*, 160; Central Office Chairman's department files, CCO 20/1/6, 20/22/2, 20/1/11 and 12; Butler and King, *General Election of 1964*, 89; Howard and West, *Making of the Prime Minister*, 136.

been doing to us over RPM – postcards, telegrams, petitions and so on'. There was not such a big campaign, but there was again £1 million worth of anti-Labour industrial spending on posters and press advertisements.[58]

The greatest problem with the coming election was choosing the date. Since the Party's recovery was slow and discontinuous, opinion polls never produced the steady Tory lead that would have merited a decision to dissolve parliament. There was no Conservative lead at all reported before Summer 1964, and by then an election had to be held within a few weeks anyway. Central Office advice was therefore consistently to wait for a later date, and so allow the recovery to build into an election-winning position. After discounting holiday periods and important dates in the parliamentary calendar, the only possibilities were March, June or October. In early 1964, the Party was still trailing by about 7 per cent, and the March option was quickly discarded as 'suicidal'; it would also allow the Opposition to claim, as Nigel Lawson pointed out, that a tough Budget was ready for April and that the Government wanted to get the Election over first. But there was no easy agreement after that; constituency chairmen in the Wessex Area, consulted in March, came down sixteen for May and fifteen for October. Poole was arguing as early as January that the key date of the year was 9 April when the new GLC would be elected; if those polls of a fifth of the entire UK electorate went well, there could be an election in June, otherwise Autumn was the only option. June was more difficult to rule out than March, not least because this was the Government's last chance to exercise any choice at all; several ministers, including the Chancellor, urged an election before the Autumn and a contest took place for Sir Alec's ear. Maudling had been unsure about the economic position if the election was delayed and felt that uncertainty about the Government's future was in itself undermining its authority. On 2 April Blakenham forwarded Poole's strong advice: polls and canvass returns suggested that the Party would do badly in London, and it would therefore be better to say there would be no Summer election *before* the GLC results, lest it should look too obviously like cowardice when announced afterwards. For a week the decision hung in the balance through a series of ministerial meetings (one of which prompted the terse note brought into the Cabinet room, 'The BBC are outside the front door. Ministers should leave by other exits'), but Sir Alec was not the sort of Leader to over-rule Poole's advice that 'I do not consider there is the slightest chance of the Party retaining a workable majority if an election is held in June'. This argument also determined the judgement of Blakenham, Hailsham, Sandys, Thorneycroft, Lloyd and Heath; a note of

---

58 Howard and West, *Making of the Prime Minister*, 115–18; Central Office files, CCO 4/9/208, Intelligence summaries, CCO 4/9/219, GLC elections, CCO 4/9/317, Marginals, CCO 500/42/1, Opinion Research, CCO 4/9/378, Records; Central Office Chairman's department file, 20/1/6; National Union papers, NUA 4/3/2, Executive Committee papers; Butler and King, *General Election of 1964*, 227, 376.

a meeting on 7 April recorded that 'the main argument of these Octoberists was briefly that there was no chance of winning in June therefore one should not have the Election then. It was as simple as that. When all was said and done as to what might happen in October nobody knew. But whereas there could be a chance of winning in October there was no chance of winning in June.' Eventually, while GLC votes were actually being cast on 9 April, Sir Alec announced that the General Election would be in the Autumn. The heavy Tory defeat announced that night confirmed the wisdom of the decision; Conservatives took only a third of the seats and did unexpectedly badly in outer London areas containing many parliamentary marginals: the *Daily Telegraph* reported a 'suburb warning for the Tories' and agreed that it was a wise choice to delay national voting until the Autumn – 'it has become evident that he had no real choice'. The borough results in May confirmed that Labour was still about 8 per cent ahead – York Tories noted that their results were 'a long way' from the May 1959 performance that had preceded holding the seat – and had another effect too; where outer London Tories had unsuccessfully opposed inclusion into the new GLC area, they were now incensed that their own Party had put them in boroughs under socialist control: affluent Ruislip had never previously experienced such a thing, and demanded the sackings of those responsible.[59]

It was not at all helpful that these disagreements were reported in the press, nor that similar arguments broke surface about the timing of by-elections. Central Office wanted to postpone the filling of four Conservative vacancies until after the General Election, lest the loss of seats should depress morale and again create an impression of a Government on the rocks, but on this Sir Alec was firm and the contests were held on 14 May. The Scottish marginal Rutherglen was lost, but an anticipated defeat at Devizes was avoided and the other two were safe enough anyway. *The Times* reported that the stock exchange had rallied because Devizes had given such a 'fillip to equities', and the quoted odds on the Conservatives retaining power shortened. Harold Macmillan had offered to campaign for the Party at Devizes but this was more easily evaded than Eden's offer in 1959, since Macmillan already understood that, as he put it, 'old actors should retire from the scene, and maybe my appearance, at this moment, would seem rather out of tune with the new conditions in the Party'. Now he was elated, writing to Blakenham that 'we have, at last, got the initiative. *We must keep it!*' Nevertheless, taking the four contests together with the two Labour seats that polled in June, average swings still indicated that Labour would recover office. Only in July and August did polls indicate that the Conservatives had caught

---

59 Howard and West, *Making of the Prime Minister,* 119; Central Office Area correspondence file, CCO 2/6/15; Central Office Chairman's department file, CCO 20/16/3, Correspondence with Vice Chairmen; Maudling, *Memoirs,* 131; Central Office file, CCO 4/9/219; York CA minutes, 25 May 1964; NUEC, 2 July 1964; Nigel Lawson's minute and the notes of ministerial meetings are in PREM 11/4755, drawn to my attention by Peter Hennessy.

up, and never was the Party clearly ahead. Disagreements between Party and Ministers went on to the very end; on 3 September Poole argued against announcing the election earlier than on the planned date of 15 September. Since the Party had at last got the initiative, it was vital to dictate the shape of the campaign, and for this events already organised for late September, including twelve rallies to be addressed by Cabinet Ministers with local candidates in attendance (after the election announcement but before the actual dissolution of parliament would make them election expenses), would be crucial. This final battle he won; the election was announced on 15 September with polling on 15 October.[60]

The 1964 General Election

After such a bruising three years, expectations were mixed; there was elation to be back in with a chance after any hope of a win had seemed wildly optimistic only weeks earlier, but there was also an awareness of how frail the recovery might be; the CRD warned on 1 October that the Party had largely won back those who had defected over Profumo in 1963, especially women voters, but was still having trouble winning back those lost over economic issues in 1962, mainly the young marrieds. Earlier in the year, Fraser had reminded Poole that the Party generally fell back during actual campaigns, so that an appreciable lead at the outset would be the minimum safety margin; since in mid-September the two most recent polls had produced a 2.5 per cent Labour lead and a 1.6 per cent Tory lead there was clearly no such margin. When the campaign began, Poole's private prediction for Blakenham named thirty-four seats as 'certain' losses, fifteen more as 'likely' and seventeen that were 'possible' or 'dangerous'; the first two categories alone would put Labour into office with an overall majority, but he was confident that there was now no chance of a big Labour win. In the event, his lists were very close to the mark: the Party lost thirty-two of his thirty-four 'certains', and nine of the fifteen 'likelies', along with nine others that went down largely because of variable regional swings. As to tactics, Poole had been arguing since the end of 1963 that the Party needed to abandon the quiet campaigning with a last minute counter-attack that had been characteristic of recent elections; 'our secured position is not strong enough to sit behind as we did in 1959'. The first election broadcast should be scripted at the last moment and should aim to set the campaign alight with a professional product to grip the audience; the Prime Minister should take centre stage throughout and should personally take press conferences; Ministers must be ready to alter speeches at the last minute to respond to Labour's electioneering – just

---

Young, *Douglas-Home*, 208; Butler and King, *General Election of 1964*, 27; Central Office Chairman's department files, CCO 20/16/3 and 20/8/6; Cook and Ramsden, *By-Elections*, 382–3; Central Office by-election file, CCO 500/18/78.

pressing on with the Tory campaign would not do; the manifesto should be given a launch on television to splash the news that the Conservatives still had plans for future policy. Hardly any of this materialised, and it would indeed have been hard to hang such a campaign around a Leader who was so ineffective a television performer, on whom technical advice was largely wasted. When Sir Alec was interviewed on television about the manifesto, the Party's Vice Chairman, Paul Bryan, pointed out that 'he seemed to emerge from the fog' and Blakenham agreed that 'Alec was not well lit'. Technique remained shaky, and perhaps because of this the idea that the Party should come out of its corner fighting was dropped in place of the traditional quiet campaign before a counter-punching finale.[61]

Television continued to be Sir Alec's bane. A dispute between colleagues produced the compromise whereby Maudling chaired press conferences and Heath was anchorman for television broadcasts (for he was thought to be good on television after successful reports to the nation on the EEC negotiations, and had as Chief Whip had many dealings with the BBC); this was surely the wrong way round, for Maudling's warmth of personality was better suited to direct communication with the viewers while Heath performed better in question and answer with professionals. Apart from a final TV broadcast that was a major ordeal for both the Leader and his advisers, and was only a moderate success if compared to Eden in 1955 or Macmillan in 1959, Sir Alec was kept away from television studios as much as possible, in particular refusing a personal debate with Wilson. Unfortunately though, the cameras followed him round the country.[62]

The Douglas-Home campaign seemed to have been set up so that he could meet as many electors as possible in small groups; there was an abundance of whistle-stop tours and few big speeches; this ensured that not many people actually saw him, and made poor use of his time, since for less than two hours of a whistle-stop day was he actually in front of any voters. At the end, inexplicably, he eased off; he made no big speech, appeared at only one press conference and spent only two days in whistle-stop campaigning over the crucial last week. Labour had already worked out that he was not good with hecklers and now exploited the fact; his meetings were packed with rowdy hecklers who on occasion made it impossible for him to be heard, and the television impression of a Prime Minister unable to make himself heard was devastating. Blakenham later thought that the Prime Minister's humiliation at Birmingham on 8 October was the point at which the election was lost, for he made no later public speech that could have retrieved the situation.

61 Central Office Chairman's department files, CCO 20/17/9, Prime Minister and 1964 General Election, CCO 20/16/3 and 20/4/2, Correspondence with Vice Chairmen; Butler and King, *General Election of 1964*, 96, 208.
62 Campbell, *Heath*, 60–1; Butler and King, *General Election of 1964* , 96, 172; Cockerell, *Live from Number Ten*, 102–7, 109–11; Young, *Douglas-Home*, 213.

The Conservatives' hope of portraying Labour as a Wilsonian one-man band, whereas 'we bat right down to number eleven', was vitiated by the media's insistence on reporting the election mainly as a presidential contest (exactly as Labour would fail when it tried the 'team' approach in order to hide Michael Foot in 1983). In news bulletins and press reports, the Prime Minister continued to be quoted almost as much as Wilson, and no other Conservative Minister achieved remotely comparable exposure. When colleagues did grab the headlines, it was not always with views that the Party wanted to put to the electorate; Hogg (highlighted by the Party in its last-week counter-attack) made injudicious remarks that brought the name Profumo back into the campaign and said that anyone who voted Liberal was 'bonkers', while Butler gave a frank interview of 'matured indiscretions' which informed *Daily Express* readers that Sir Alec did not get on well with Heath and that the Tories would probably lose the election. Too much should not be made of these negative features of the Conservative campaign – Butler and King concluded that 'its weaknesses were minor slips rather than major missed opportunities' – but for all that the Party did not seize and hold the initiative in October 1964 in a campaign that might well only have been won that way.[63]

As before, but perhaps because legislation had now been enacted, immigration played little part in the national campaign; Sir Alec was the only major politician to address the issue directly, in a speech at Bradford that was little reported and provoked few replies; in the constituencies though, increasing antagonisms had forced the issue on to local agendas. The Act of 1962 won votes in some areas with high concentrations of immigrants, largely because Labour had violently opposed it at the time but were now accepting that it would not be repealed.[64]

If any issue other than the leadership turned the knife-edge campaign, it was the Conservatives' increasing difficulty in defending their economic record against Labour attacks; bad trade figures published during the campaign undermined the Government's claims that economic recovery was well-founded; after the stop-go experience since 1955 it was relatively easy for Labour to argue that a Conservative election victory would be followed by deflation and recession. Against this, Conservatives slowly made headway with their costing of Labour's programme and the claims that a Labour Government would impose increases in direct taxes. The economic recovery won back Tory votes but doubts about the permanence of the recovery limited

63 Cockerell, *Live from Number Ten*, 107; Home, *Way the Wind Blows*, 214–15; Young, *Douglas-Home*, 211; Butler and King, *General Election of 1964*, 120–2, 147, 150–1, 155, 170, 175; Central Office Chairman's department file, CCO 20/17/9; Howard and West, *Making of the Prime Minister*, 188–9, 193, 194–6, 219; Howard, *RAB*, 334.
64 Central Office Chairman's department file, CCO 20/16/3; Central Office files, CCO 4/9/187 and 4/9/225, Immigration; Butler and King, *General Election of 1964*, 360–8; Nicholas Deakin, *Colour and the British Electorate, 1964* (1965).

the extent of that benefit, and there was some justification for Hailsham's later claim that the Party did not quite succeed in putting Labour on the defensive about its own plans as it had done in 1959.[65]

The results confirmed the general impression of a close contest. Early Labour gains indicating a sizeable Labour majority were contradicted by Friday's rural results, and at one time it seemed just possible that the Conservatives would remain the largest party; Ministers in London were summoned to Number 10, but had hardly arrived before Labour gained the crucial seats to give a bare Labour majority of four. The Conservative vote had fallen sharply, by 1.75 million (the largest fall for any party at a single election since the Tories' own 1945 disaster), while Labour's vote remained stable, and the Liberal vote doubled to 3 million. The obvious explanation from these crude figures, that Tory voters had gone to the Liberals in droves, was misleading: there certainly were Conservative defections to Liberal, and these may have turned the result in as many as a dozen constituencies (which was enough to explain the change of government), but the real explanation of overall votes, confirmed by poll analysis, was that Liberals gained votes from Labour as well as Conservative, but that Labour replaced its losses from the young, from 1959 non-voters and from ex-Conservatives. The Conservatives regained many of their 1962–63 defectors but won few new votes to make up for their losses since 1959. The regional pattern accentuated the trend of 1959, with low swings to Labour in East Anglia and the Midlands, where regional prosperity now combined with race to push voters to the right; all four Conservative gains could be attributed to one or both of these influences; on the other hand, Norman Pannell MP, the most persistent Tory opponent of immigration, received no electoral benefit and lost his own Liverpool seat. Conversely, where unemployment had been highest, in Scotland and the north, swings to Labour were well above the national average and constituencies not thought to be marginal tumbled like ninepins. Overall, Tories lost sixty-one seats, including several ministers; from the Cabinet only Barber and Rippon were defeated, though Brooke, Soames and Thorneycroft held on only narrowly in seats that were to be lost in 1966. The theory that ministers suffered high swings which were a repudiation of the Government rather than the Party did not generally fit the evidence, but some individual Ministers did do especially badly; worst of all was the result in Hampstead, where the highly untypical electorate, alerted perhaps by the constant attacks on Henry Brooke's illiberal policies at the Home Office, demonstrated their views by reducing his majority from over 12,000 to under 2,000. Brooke, dubbed 'the most hated man in Parliament' by his Labour critics, and subject to critical votes by Conservative as well as Labour MPs, had certainly fallen foul of the spirit of the hour when he deported the

---

[65] Maudling, *Memoirs*, 119; Howard and West, *Making of the Prime Minister*, 215; Butler and King, *General Election of 1964*, 117.

Nigerian politician Chief Enaharo; he now retired from front-bench politics before losing his seat in 1966. A historically significant milestone was reached on Merseyside and Clydeside, where traditional religious cleavages broke down with remarkable suddenness; without militant Protestantism Glasgow and Liverpool soon became almost no-go areas for Conservatives, who hung on to only four of the two cities' twenty-four seats where previously they had held half of them; at Bebington, Geoffrey Howe saw a large majority shrink to marginal proportions as 'people – even Irish people, on Merseyside at least – were more inclined to vote with their class than with their Church'. The slight accidental bias in the electoral system that had favoured Conservatives since the 1948 redistribution of constituency boundaries now disappeared as a result of population movement; had it remained in 1964, it would have kept Sir Alec in office, if only precariously. Perhaps the Party had after all just run out of luck. Sir Alec's own verdict, often repeated, was that 'thirteen years were too much of a drag', and the Party's reaction to defeat certainly indicated that the record had not been seen as an advantage during the recent campaign.[66]

Back in opposition, 1964–65

It would have taken only nine hundred people to vote differently (if perfectly distributed in the right constituencies) for the Conservatives to retain office. With so close a result, it was hard to know how to respond, and relief was one natural reaction; Sir Alec wrote to Dame Barbara Brooke, the Party Vice Chairman, that 'looking back on the events of 1963, it does appear to me a near miracle that we have achieved the present result'. It was also clear that with a small majority, Wilson would call another election as soon as he sensed an opportunity. For these two reasons there were few Conservative recriminations in October–November 1964. Lord Blakenham's view of the future, delivered to the National Union Executive on 5 November and succinctly recorded in the secretary's notes, was 'regroup under fire; short time; long term thinking'. The Party had the difficult task of conducting an Opposition that had to be always ready for an election, while simultaneously using the opportunity to re-examine fundamental options. It would be what Michael Fraser called 're-deployment in the face of the enemy', always a difficult manoeuvre.[67]

Nevertheless, if the tricky parliamentary situation kept dissent under cover for a time, the constituency associations' own post-mortems on the Party's

---

[66] Maudling, *Memoirs*, 131; Campbell, *Heath*, 164; Thorpe, *Lloyd*, 389; Butler and King, *General Election of 1964*, 289–300; Deakin, *Colour*, 161; Levin, *Pendulum Years*, 173; Geoffrey Howe, *Conflict of Loyalty* (1994), 35; Young, *Douglas-Home*, 219.

[67] Central Office Chairman's department file, CCO 20/4/2; Young, *Douglas-Home*, 218; National Union papers, NUA 4/3/2, Executive Committee papers; John Ramsden, 'Churchill to Heath', in Lord Butler (ed.), *The Conservatives* (1977), 468.

defeat did indicate a broad dissatisfaction that would soon come to the surface. Lichfield and Tamworth were typical of many in their findings:

> The committee felt that Sir Alec Douglas-Home had not reflected the modern age as well as Mr. Harold Wilson, that the nuclear deterrent had not been a vote-winning issue, that the policy was not bad but it had not been put over at all well, and that we had lost the vote of young intellectuals and executives. As an instance of this, Mrs. Mills said that she knew members of the Bow Group who had voted socialist.

The deputy Area Agent present at the meeting confirmed that the loss of 'the young and the newly weds' had been general; in the Western Area too, it was felt that the 'artisan' Tory vote had been retained, but that there had been losses in the white-collar section; Guildford found that it was just such people who had defected to the Liberals; the Eastern Area, which had had some rather good results in Norfolk as well as defeats elsewhere, resolved to congratulate Sir Alec on his leadership during the campaign, but it also decided that the lost voters who must now be won back were 'young marrieds' and 'white collar technicians', who were hardly Sir Alec's forte. Along the same lines, Reigate noted that 'Hume' was not good enough on television, while the crucial 'young professionals' had been impressed by Wilson's broadcasts; in January 1965, the association called for an urgent policy review 'so that Party workers and the country in general may recognise the clear image of a modern Party democratically led'. Such verdicts were not good news for Sir Alec's long-term prospects.[68]

Election defeat necessitated a reconstruction of the collective leadership; Barber returned to Parliament and the shadow cabinet in February 1965, and early by-elections also returned Peter Kirk and Geoffrey Johnson-Smith, junior ministers defeated at the General Election. Two of these three vacancies arose from peerages accepted by Butler and Erroll; the departure of Butler to be a Cambridge Master and the retirement in 1966 of Henry Brooke removed the last links with the 1940s policy revival. After temporary arrangements in November, a new pattern had emerged by February: Maudling became deputy leader and shadow Foreign Secretary, while Heath succeeded Butler as chairman of the CRD and ACP to spearhead the policy review, also becoming shadow Chancellor. This seemed a neat balancing act between two heavyweight ex-Ministers, and there was a sense in which the first nine months of opposition were an undeclared war of succession, with the stronger hand dealt to Heath since Labour's Finance Bill provided him with a chance to shine while Maudling had little visible to do. Powell and Macleod rejoined the front bench to shadow Transport and Steel (due to be renationalised, but delayed by Labour's small majority, and so incidentally sidelining Macleod

---

[68] Lichfield and Tamworth CA minutes, 11 Nov. 1964; Western Area Council, 20 Nov. 1964; Guildford CA minutes, 18 Oct. 1964; Eastern Area Council, 31 Oct. 1964; Reigate CA minutes, 7 Dec. 1964 and 18 Jan. 1965.

like Maudling); James Margach in the *Sunday Times* observed that it was a stronger team than Sir Alec had been able to muster as Prime Minister. The inclusion of former rebels left little room for promotions; the only entirely new recruit to full front-bench status was Edward du Cann who succeeded Blakenham as Party Chairman, the deliberate replacement of a safely reassuring figure with a thrustingly ambitious one, more suitable for a period of opposition. The replacement of Martin Redmayne by William Whitelaw as Chief Whip was a move in the reassuring direction after several years with disaffected backbenchers. The election of Sir William Anstruther-Gray to chair the 1922 Committee, when John Morrison went to the Lords, was also of a highly traditional type.[69]

Sir Alec was not a success as Opposition leader; like Baldwin he was not a man to cheer up his supporters with knockabout attacks on policies he had pursued while in office, and he was now facing a Wilson who had added confidence. Kenneth Young wrote of Sir Alec in opposition that 'the sheep looked up to the shepherd and were not fed. . . . It is . . . likely that he simply did not hear the plaintive ba-ba-ba from the patient sheep so far from Whitehall.' Sir Alec himself told James Margach that he 'was never very impressed by the Tweedledum and Tweedledee form of politics in the Commons. It didn't make sense to me to go bashing ahead against a Government's policies, which perhaps had much to commend them, simply to keep backbenchers happy [but] my people wanted a helluva row all the time.' Backbenchers were indeed spoiling for a fight, and memories of 1950–51 were at work in the decision not to ease Labour's problems with a small majority; members of the 1922 Committee were asked by the Chief Whip 'not to ask the Government Whip's Office to find them a pair as this was playing directly into the hands of the Government whips'. This general mood explains why MPs so strongly approved of Heath's aggressive Commons performances and despaired of Sir Alec's more gentlemanly touch.[70]

MPs were also thinking hard about the future, for the system of electing the leader was at last under open discussion. Sir Alec told the 1922 Committee as early as 5 November that there would be a review of the system, which prompted speculation that he was preparing the ground for his own departure; in fact he was doing no more than ensuring that no future Leader would have to start with his disadvantage, 'the accusation that the last result had been jobbed'. Discussions rapidly came to an agreement in principle that there should be open elections with MPs as the electorate (which was in effect moving alongside Labour's then system); Humphry Berkeley MP was associated with this, for Sir Alec had promised him that the issue would be

[69] Young, *Douglas-Home*, 220–1, 223; Central Office file, CCO 4/9/421, shadow cabinet; Thorpe, *Lloyd*, 389; Campbell, *Heath*, 167–8; Fisher, *Macleod*, 259; Whitelaw, *Memoirs*, 50; Goodhart, *The 1922*, 200.
[70] Home, *Way the Wind Blows*, 217–18; Young, *Douglas-Home*, 222, 226; Margach, *Anatomy of Power*, 136; 1922 Committee Minutes, 3 Dec. 1964.

aired after the 1964 Election, and he now published a memorandum that was quite close in its provisions to what was decided, but the principles were rather obvious, and similar proposals came from other sources too. National Union leaders were not happy to lose rights they had acquired only in 1963, and in shadow cabinet Boyd-Carpenter opposed the whole plan as an attack on the prerogative, but the process rolled through all the same. On 25 February 1965, Sir Alec formally announced the new system; since the Party had no constitution, the decision was the Leader's and his alone. The document declared that, 'there shall be a ballot of the party in the House of Commons'; to show fair play the chairman of the 1922 would be returning officer; a candidate could be elected on the first ballot only by getting *both* an overall majority and at least 15 per cent more of the vote than any other candidate, so ensuring that there could be no winner without broad backing; for a second ballot if needed, nominations would start over again (allowing entirely new candidates – a Home could emerge to unite the Party under this system just as in 1963), and only an overall majority would be needed to win; if a third ballot was needed, the top three on the second ballot would go forward and there would be preferential voting to ensure that a majority voted for the winner. There were indications that the National Union and Conservative peers would make their views known informally, but the idea that not all MPs counted equally was now altogether swept away; henceforth the outgoing Leader and the greenest backbencher would have the same weight in selecting a successor.[71]

With an electoral system in place, it was suggested that Sir Alec should offer himself for re-election, which he refused to do. He was perhaps disdainful of the calibre of the critics, and felt that they were only an 'infinitesimal' number of MPs. In January, the newly-formed Pressure for Economic and Social Toryism (PEST), a group of progressive university Conservatives, justified its acronym with an outspoken attack on the Party's 'intellectual sterility' and its 'one-class image'; PEST denounced the 1963 selection of Sir Alec, 'and the forces that lay behind it', and its first publication called for 'an end to feeble opposition'. PEST was refused access to Party money and office space (as were all such groups, which also had to pay rent for a stall at Conferences), but du Cann reported in April that Central Office had 'agreed to give them limited encouragement', presumably because they represented precisely the type of young graduate with which the Party was trying to re-establish its links – PEST's first generation of active members included Michael Spicer, Keith Hampson and Simon Jenkins; Edward Boyle accepted the position of patron when Butler retired and both he and Heath agreed to attend a PEST conference. PEST continued though to be polemical

---

[71] Goodhart, *The 1922*, 200–1; Thorpe, *Lloyd*, 392; Fisher, *Macleod*, 261; Lindsay and Harrington, *Conservative Party*, 237; Berkeley, *Crossing the Floor*, 29; Boyd-Carpenter, *Way of Life*, 189.

in its activities; Lord Salisbury was denounced over Rhodesia, as was the 'subversive rubbish' of Enoch Powell's speeches on economic policy; it called for a 'moral' policy on immigration rather than a quest for votes, the end of selection at eleven and the compulsory requisitioning of two-fifths of all places at public schools for pupils chosen on merit; on 15 July it again called for Sir Alec to step down.[72]

The first PEST complaints and other such grumblings were roundly condemned by Maudling, in a defence of his Leader that only drew more attention to the attacks. In January, Monmouth Conservatives peremptorily demanded 'that the Conservative Party shall make it crystal clear, through the medium of the national press, to the country, who is to lead the Party at the next Election'. In February the Chichester Conservatives resolved to express their disappointment with the conduct of the Opposition to date, welcomed du Cann's appointment and called for the promotion of others 'of similar age, background and experience'. At Finchley the local association, presumably at least with the knowledge of its MP, resolved that 'in view of the fact that the Party manifesto at the last General Election was rejected by the majority of the electorate voting', there should be an early presentation of new and more vigorous policies. In March, Bristol Conservatives felt that it would be good for the Party if Sir Alec 'submitted himself to the modern method of choosing the Leader of the Party, as this would counteract the continual jibing'. It was a mistake by Sir Alec not to ask for a new mandate in February or March, for there was still no uncontainable opposition to him in the Party and a *Daily Telegraph* poll of Tory MPs on 7 February found three-quarters of them wanting him to carry on; if he did resign, 35 per cent wanted Maudling, 28 per cent Butler and only 10 per cent Heath. Sir Alec's opportunity would not recur.[73]

For a time though things went well; on 21 January the Party took the Labour seat of Leyton when the Foreign Secretary, defeated at the General Election, tried to return to the Commons in a by-election much resented by his new electorate as an unnecessary call on their votes; when the neighbouring MP John Harvey detected and publicised a chance of winning, help poured in from seventy-five constituencies, and a narrow win was achieved. Labour's majority was down to three.[74]

Heath becomes Leader

The hard fact was though that the Labour Government, even with its majority reduced by Leyton, now dictated the agenda of politics, and Wilson continued

---

72 Central Office files, CCO 3/6/138 and 3/7/43, PEST.
73 Young, *Douglas-Home*, 224–5; Butler and King, *General Election of 1964*, 299; NUEC 4/2/65; Lindsay and Harrington, *Conservative Party*, 237; Roth, *Heath*, 179; Central Office constituency file, CCO 1/14/484; Monmouth CA minutes, 25 Jan. 1965.
74 Central Office by-election file, CCO 500/18/83.

to outpoint Sir Alec in the Commons. There was no repetition of Leyton to cheer the troops; in March came the loss to David Steel of a Conservative seat on the Scottish borders, Sir Alec's home territory; in May there were Conservative gains in the local elections, but these were only the recovery of some of the losses in the disastrous year 1962. These borough results had a further significance: Labour would not now risk an election before Autumn at the earliest, and that would allow a new Conservative Leader time to take charge; the Party's policy review (which is considered in the next chapter) would also come to fruition by July, so that the transitional phase of Party recovery would effectively be over by the Summer recess. In parliament and in the constituencies, there continued to be critics of the leadership, always a minority and perhaps only a small one, but enough to keep the issue always alive when their activities were reported. In April, Walter Clegg MP asked his association Executive at North Fylde to propose a resolution stating confidence in Sir Alec at the forthcoming annual general meeting, telling the members that the leadership put 'great store' on rank and file opinion, but if so the tactic backfired; various members criticised Sir Alec's leadership image, and it was resolved instead that the Leader should submit himself for re-election under the new rules. Sir Alec, a proud man who had no intention of outstaying his welcome, called for reports from du Cann on the extent of disaffection and received advice that it did not represent more than a minority view. In fact as the soundings taken among constituency chairmen in the Wessex Area show, this was unduly reassuring: some like Wokingham were happy with Douglas-Home, but far more were (like Henley, Winchester and the Isle of Wight) highly critical, and many of those who said they backed Sir Alec were also asking for 'less right wing socialism' in the Party (Eton and Slough), stronger opposition to Labour (Banbury), and tougher attacks on Labour (Buckingham); High Wycombe had 'thought the Opposition was dead' and was pleased to hear that there would be a real attack on Wilson soon; Devizes, which urged MPs to 'repel the attack' on the Leader, also thought that 'people are tumbling over backwards to give the Socialists a chance because we are not presenting a clear and definite alternative'. The Party wanted both to be loyal but also to be more aggressively led; the National Union Executive on 1 April received resolutions from Oldham and from South Worcestershire calling for loyalty to the Leader in the face of media speculation on the 'non-existent question' of the leadership, and a resolution from South Bucks. demanding more forceful presentation of the Party's case.[75]

The success that Heath enjoyed in the policy review and on the Finance Bill added a new factor: the *Birmingham Post* suggested in January that Heath had been given the policy job 'because he may be the man who will ultimately have

[75] Young, *Douglas-Home*, 227–31, 233; Campbell, *Heath*, 170, 173–4, 176–7; Central Office constituency file, CCO 1/14/484; North Fylde CA minutes, 30 Apr. 1965; Central Office Area correspondence file, CCO 2/7/10; NUEC, 1 Apr. 1965.

to present it as leader'. The military precision exhibited by the Opposition finance team, mainly made up of younger grammar school Tories of Heath's type, and the defeats they inflicted on the Government, were increasingly contrasted with the restrained leadership of the Party. Those supporters who wanted to make Heath Leader sensed that this was his opportunity, and began, if without his connivance, to press for a change. Newspaper talk that Heath had a hundred MPs behind him was easily discounted, and on 26 June Sir Alec tried to end speculation by announcing that there would be no leadership election in 1965, but this was soon undercut by Wilson's announcement that there would be no general election, so freeing the Conservatives to settle their leadership without the risk of being caught on the hop. On 5 July, the issue was debated by the 1922's Executive, in what was then misreported as a failed 'putsch' by the 1922 itself. In early July, Sir Alec twice announced his determination to stay on, but opinion polls continued to show poor personal ratings and newspapers to report Party discontent. Perhaps the final straw was a *Sunday Times* piece by William Rees-Mogg, 'The right time for a change'; perhaps it was the poll that showed that the public even thought Wilson more sincere than Sir Alec; perhaps it was a determination not to be pushed out by the critical resolution that the YCs were preparing for the Party Conference; perhaps it was *The Economist*'s wounding suggestion that Sir Alec was hanging on only to protect class interests, instead of handing over the Party to those who did not carry 'the faintest whiff of the gentry'; most likely it was the cumulative impact of nearly two years of personal attacks on a man not used to fighting for his place. Despite strong urgings to stand firm from Lloyd, Whitelaw and du Cann, Sir Alec announced his resignation to an astonished 1922 Committee on 22 July. Generous to the end, he made clear that the decision was his alone, that he had resigned to prevent further disunity and that none of his colleagues had acted dishonourably; it was notable though that whereas the draft for his speech referred gratefully to the Opposition work of Heath, Maudling and du Cann, only du Cann was actually mentioned on the day.[76]

The Party was choosing a new Leader in opposition for the first time since 1911 (not entirely a happy precedent) and the problems that the new Leader had before he became Prime Minister in 1970 were much influenced by the fact that in this very governmental party he had no means of actually *doing* anything for four years. Heath and Maudling were the obvious contenders for the succession. Macleod calculated that 1963–64 had damaged him too much to run, and Thorneycroft was persuaded not to stand by Lloyd and Hogg (who correctly divined that the Party now demanded a younger man than their generation). Of the two serious runners, Maudling was favourite:

---

[76] Lindsay and Harrington, *Conservative Party*, 238; Roth, *Heath*, 185; Whitelaw, *Memoirs*, 53–4; Boyd-Carpenter, *Way of Life*, 190; Goodhart, *The 1922*, 205–6; Home, *Way the Wind Blows*, 219–21; Central Office Chairman's department file, CCO 20/8/8, Correspondence with Douglas-Home.

he had had wider ministerial experience, and his supporters could not be accused of pushing Sir Alec out: a *Daily Express* poll suggested that the public prefered Maudling to Heath by 44 per cent to 28 per cent, with a similar lead among Tory voters; as Party Vice Chairman, Jim Prior found that adopted candidates were mainly for Heath, but that their main concern was to get rid of Douglas-Home. Press comment contrasted Heath's thrustfulness with Maudling's more relaxed style, and both Butler and Macleod (both of whom might have been thought as natural Maudling men from previous experience) came to see Heath's 'rather tougher' qualities as what the Party needed; Maudling was also damaged by the extent to which he had taken up directorships as soon as leaving office, giving the impression that his commitment to politics was less than total. As John Campbell points out, that contrast was visible in the campaigns too, for whereas Heath's was a forceful canvass of the electorate coordinated by Peter Walker, using MPs to contact only those personally known to them, Maudling's was over-confident and half-hearted. The Heath team came close to a correct prediction of the result, while Maudling was left with a pocketful of pledges from those who had promised their votes but not delivered them; comparing notes afterwards, the campaign teams found forty-five MPs in this most difficult of all electorates who had promised their votes to Maudling as well as to Heath. Whitelaw insisted that the whips take no part in the process, so that no allegations like those made in 1963 could follow the result. Perhaps the crucial influence, as Harry Boyne pointed out in the *Daily Telegraph*, was circumstance; for Prime Minister most MPs would probably have preferred Maudling, but since it was a Leader of Opposition that was needed they opted for Heath's more abrasive manner (though as with Hailsham in 1963 political commentators again confused abrasiveness with extremism); even the RPM battle, from which some Tories still had the abrasions inflicted by Heath, could now be cited ruefully as evidence of his forcefulness. And despite the 1964 campaign, it was often said that Heath was 'good on television'. The candidature of Enoch Powell, managed by Nicholas Ridley, indicated that there actually was a policy choice to make too, but it made limited impact at the time, and those who supported him were by no means all economic Powellites anyway; the lack of a strongly-supported third candidate almost guaranteed that Heath or Maudling would win a majority at the first try, which would deter others from throwing hats into the ring later. Powell's small vote may even have weakened his bargaining position, for as Robert Shepherd has put it, after July 1965 'Heath always knew that, in the last resort, he could call Powell's bluff' in the parliamentary party.[77]

[77] Campbell, *Heath*, 156, 177–82; Prior, *Balance of Power*, 37; Peter Walker, *Staying Power: An Autobiography* (1991), 43, 46; Maudling, *Memoirs*, 136; Shepherd, *Macleod*, 402, 404; Thorpe, *Lloyd*, 395; Fisher, *Macleod*, 263; Andrew Alexander, 'Reginald Maudling', in T. Stacey and R. St Oswald (eds) *Here Come the Tories* (1970), 28; Roth, *Powell*, 328–30; Whitelaw, *Memoirs*, 55.

Most of the shadow cabinet backed Heath, as did Douglas-Home and Macleod, who urged his own backers to vote for Heath and whose support probably therefore swung the election to Heath. Soundings of Tory peers and the National Union, and much of the Tory press, supported Heath, again on the basis that it made little sense to get rid of Sir Alec unless the new man was a political bully who could be rude to Wilson; evidence from individual constituencies like High Peak, Reigate and Aylesbury all suggested that either Heath or Maudling would command general acceptance. Constituency associations were active in canvassing the opinions of members and reporting on them to their own MPs, as for example Cambridgeshire to Francis Pym, and this direct route must have been more influential than the more generalised National Union soundings (which included Labour-held as well as Tory-held seats); on the other hand, since local activists were not decisively for either candidate, their views are unlikely to have tilted many votes anyway. Some nervous posing for the cameras by the candidates over the crucial week-end was followed by a single decisive ballot on Tuesday 27 July, in which Heath got 150 votes, Maudling 133 and Powell 15. Heath therefore had a majority of votes cast, if not quite a majority of the electorate of 303 MPs, but the fact that he did not have a 15 per cent lead became irrelevant when the other candidates immediately withdrew.[78]

The decision made in July 1965 was the conscious, and public, reversal of that made in October 1963, the deliberate replacement of an old Etonian patrician with a young moderniser from a grammar school, the replacement of manners with force and purpose. The Class of 1950 and the One Nation Group seemed finally to have come into their inheritance with the choice of a Conservative Leader as unexpected a couple of years before the event as were the successions of 1911 and 1923. An open election also finally purged the divisions of October 1963; the Wessex Area constituency chairmen, meeting in September, happily recorded their view that Heath had accepted office with becoming modesty, that Maudling had been 'statesmanlike', and Sir Alec 'unselfish'; their only concern was that the National Union's role, established in 1963, seemed already to have slipped to the sidelines again by 1965. The *Sunday Mirror* thought Heath 'a new kind of Tory Leader – a classless professional politician who has fought his way to the top with guts, ability and political skill'. Macleod in the *Spectator* enthused that 'the party battle lines will never be the same again'. *The Economist*'s Alastair Burnet (who knew Heath better than most who wrote such pieces) shrewdly noticed that, if the Party had picked Heath as the man 'most likely to bullock their way back into power', it was far from clear what he would do with power when he achieved it. Nevertheless, the change of Leader was enough to switch over

78   High Peak CA minutes, 19 Aug. 1965; Reigate CA minutes, 21 Sept. 1965; Aylesbury CA minutes, 25 July 1965; Cambridgeshire CA minutes, 13 Sept. 1965; Cockerell, *Live from Number Ten*, 119.

the paper's allegiance, which was important both as a weathercock of informed opinion and as an important influence in itself on economic policy; while *The Economist* had come down for Wilson in 1964, it now became Heath's most reliable supporter in Fleet Street and backed both the man and his policies right up to February 1975. There was though some clear anticipation of the likelihood of storms ahead. In *The Times*, David Wood wrote that Heath had been elected by Tory MPs 'at least in part because he will do rough things roughly that they will sometimes not like to have done'. Richard Crossman, who had thought that Maudling would have made 'a far better, wiser political leader', believed that,

> as a result [of Heath winning] we have curiously similar leaders in the Tory and the Labour Parties. Two wholly political politicians, much more tactically than strategically minded. . . . All the disadvantages of Harold Wilson seem to me to be incorporated in Heath – and most of the advantages as well – his drive, energy, skill in debate, his dedication to politics. These are all considerable assets. . . .Certainly it means the electoral battle will be keen. . . .Our parliamentary democracy will continue to run along the strictest Party lines.[79]

[79] Central Office Area correspondence file, CCO 2/7/10; Campbell, *Heath*, 183–4; Roth, *Heath*, xii, 186; Ruth Dudley Edwards, *The Pursuit of Reason: The Economist, 1843–1993* (1993), 838; Anthony Howard (ed.), *The Crossman Diaries* (1979), 129.

Part II

Heath and the Heathmen

All of us at the centre are determined to link the next Conservative Government with the modernisation of Britain and are busy designing a programme of policies for that purpose.

(Sir Alec Douglas-Home, article for the
Manchester University Conservative Magazine, March 1965)

Life with Ted Heath may well be very uncomfortable. The art of running a party has three rules: to give a clear lead, to make sure that your lead is being followed, and to arouse enough loyalty so that your chaps will back you up even when you make the inevitable boobs. Mr. Heath will certainly match up to the first, and probably to the second: the doubt is whether he has the personal charisma to win devotion. It may sound odd about a man who is always being photographed looking jolly, but the Tory party is littered with people still nursing bruises from some Heath brusquerie. The reason is that he does not suffer fools gladly and by his fairly exacting standards there are quite a few of them still around.

(*The Economist*, 26 July 1965)

Private Enterprise has not failed; it has not been properly tried.

(Sir Keith Joseph, speaking at Reading, 26 April 1967)

Enoch was totally idiotic. I don't think he was worse than that although anyone could have told the damage he would do inadvertently to Ted's authority within the Party. People feel very deeply & I fear that a lot are very impatient with those who argue for calm. I fear that a lot of Conservatives, because it is suggested that Enoch's statements were racial, feel that they are so labelled, at least by implication. This will be very troublesome within the Party.

(Sir Alec Douglas-Home to Sir Edward Boyle, 1 May 1968)

Lord Armstrong: [Edward Heath was] a great man, who achieved a great deal of what he set out to achieve and was at a crucial time unlucky.

Lord Croham: And is now at the moment underrated –

Sir Christopher Chataway – And addressed the two big issues of the day, one entirely successfully – Europe – and the other in the end unsuccessfully – industrial relations.

Lord Armstrong: And that was touch and go, wasn't it?

(ICBH Witness Seminar, 1994)

The state of the Tory Party following upon defeat at the next Election does not bear thinking about. In the 'civil war' that could ensue, the Conservative Party as we know it could be obliged to fight for its survival. . . . It is impossible to forecast the result; the party establishment might survive, and the Conservatives continue as a party of the centre, but were the ideologues to win, we could become the party of the aggrieved motorist.

(Julian Critchley on 'Stresses and Strains in the Conservative Party',
Summer 1973)

Chapter 5

A Government in exile, 1965–70

The Party's years in opposition between October 1964 and June 1970 were not a happy time. The change of Leader in July 1965 promised finally to settle an issue that had been debated continuously for three years, but Edward Heath, the first Conservative Leader since Bonar Law in 1911 to have the difficult task of establishing himself in opposition, had instead five years in which his style and his authority were regularly under scrutiny. Organisation was pepped up, much money was raised and the first entirely modern marketing campaign by any party was mounted in 1970. The review of policy was tackled with determination and more comprehensively than any party had ever applied to the preparation for office, but the review either failed to address or failed to settle central strategic issues about the Party's philosophy and core policy. Finally, while the Labour Government of Harold Wilson was disowned by the media and the public as completely as any Government had ever been, bringing big Conservative gains in local and by-elections between 1966 and 1969, the decade ended with an election that almost everyone expected Wilson to win.

The improbable sequel to all of this was a Tory Government elected on a fragile prospectus, but which, because of the unexpectedness of its election and of the extent to which its Leader had fronted its campaign, felt more than usually justified in claiming a mandate for its policies. To a large extent, the seeds of Tory disarray in office between 1970 and 1974, and of Heath's eventual downfall as Party Leader, had been sown by June 1970. This argues no simple inevitability – all seeds that are sown do not ripen for harvesting – but it does suggest that Heath's Ministers came into office with explosives in their knapsacks which would have required a different approach if they were not to avoid the catastrophe that did eventually overwhelm them.

Heath as Opposition Leader

Much of the problem described above had to do with the balance of strengths and weaknesses in Edward Heath himself, as a personality, as a manager of the Party, and as controller of the debate about future policy options. In view of the circumstances of his election, immediate comparisons tended to be made with Wilson, and this did not favour Heath. When Heath was elected,

Tony Benn felt that Labour would 'be able to project Heath as a ruthless, ambitious machine politician without even the aristocratic backing of Home who could always count upon the deferential vote'. A week later, he was jubilantly noting that Heath's first big speech had been the sort 'that might have been made at a Fabian Summer School. . . . It was so dull, and statistical and so full of quotes that he lost the House and bored us all.' In reply, Wilson was at his best, witty, amusing and relaxed, but also suggesting that Heath was indeed just a hard Party man. Describing this first clash, *The Times* wrote of 'the drubbing Mr. Wilson handed out to his new rival. . . . He pulled the rug from under Mr. Heath and left him gasping on the floor'. Wilson also succeeded in riling Heath, and their final speeches took place amid a continuous uproar which initiated a new phase of Commons life in which the two leaders vied for the honour of being the rudest when addressing or speaking about the other; it was, said Andrew Roth, 'something more like a Sicilian vendetta than the normal parliamentary pillow fights'. It was also a tactic that suited Wilson more than Heath, for as Prime Minister he had plenty of other opportunities to look statesmanlike, while Heath depended on his reported Commons appearances to establish a presence in the public mind; in any case Wilson's quicker footwork usually ensured that he won on points even in these brutal exchanges across the despatch boxes. A year later, Whitelaw 'agreed on the foolishness of Heath in trying to down Wilson in verbal exchange', though these increasingly bitter exchanges had the effect of rallying both parliamentary parties behind their leaders, so there may have been some benefit to Heath on that count.[1]

Wilson even went so far as to upstage Heath's first Conference speech as Party leader in October 1965 by making a contrived flight to Balmoral, which set the media off on the idea that he was calling an election; Jim Prior remembered that 'Ted was furious, but I remember him saying with a wry smile, "Good Lord, no one's done this kind of thing since Harold Macmillan".' Alan Watkins heard Tory MPs at Brighton already asking each other 'in their less guarded moments', whether the change of leader had been 'a terrible mistake'. At the Conference, Heath emulated Hailsham in 1957 and rang the chairman's bell, in his case an attempt to stop the ovation; this was the first of a series of annual ovations, each of which re-established him with the Party for a time; in October 1968, Whitelaw thought that Heath had made at Conference 'the best speech of his career, and perhaps the prime ministership is all that is needed to see him in full command'. The confrontational style was stepped down, and gradually, Heath did learn that different tactics were more effective when dealing with Wilson, though Wilson's over-confidence also contributed to Heath's gradual rise towards parity with him. Wilson's

---

[1] Tony Benn, *Out of the Wilderness: Diaries, 1963–1967* (1988), 301, 303; John Campbell, *Edward Heath* (1993), 192, 198; Andrew Roth, *Heath and the Heathmen* (1972), 187, 192; Cecil King, *The Cecil King Diary, 1965–1970* (1972), 77, 99, 213.

complacent broadcast on the 1967 devaluation opened the way for a telling Heath reply; in the House he discovered that a single repeated question to the Prime Minister was a better way of embarrassing the Prime Minister than either blasts of invective or catalogues of statistics, a tactic that was used to great effect over trade union reform in 1969. Nevertheless, if anger was now usually kept under control, much of Heath's approach both to opposition and to the preparation for government still needs to be seen as a reaction to Wilson, a man despised by Heath as a premier whose unprincipled and opportunistic conduct had lowered the standards of public life.[2]

Heath did not enjoy a cordial relationship with his backbenchers, rarely socialising as Macmillan had done in the Smoking Room, and attempts to improve this often did as much harm as good; there were many stories about dinner parties set up to allow MPs to 'meet the Leader' but which deteriorated into silence or obloquy. It is possible to chart this decline even in the guarded language of the 1922 Committee's minute-takers, who noted a 'standing ovation' for Heath in July 1965 when first elected, an 'enthusiastic reception' in December 1965, but only a 'warm welcome' for his visits to the 1922 in 1967–68. Julian Critchley pointed out that Heath 'conspicuously failed to practise the political arts. His parsimony when it came to handing out the twice-yearly honours to clapped-out MPs was bitterly resented by those who sought consolation of a sort. He was also reluctant to flatter the simple.' Supportive friends were all too often taken for granted; when Charles Morrison, who had been a shadow spokesman, was offered no post in 1970, he did not even get an explanation from the Leader; Heath told Peter Walker that Morrison was 'close to him' and would understand. He didn't. Jim Prior has pointed out that there were already Heath enemies on the backbenches dating from his time as Chief Whip, one of whom, significantly as it turned out, was Airey Neave; Prior added that 'if, like Ted, you don't make friends easily, you have to be successful. If you're successful, everything's all right; but, if you're not, they're after your blood very quickly.' There was also a damaging perception that Heath surrounded himself with congenial and like-minded colleagues; in February 1967 the Party's Chief Publicity Officer noted, in friendly spirit, that

> by and large the Leader and the people surrounding him represent the 'liberal',
> avant-garde wing of the Party. There are not, and probably quite rightly so,
> representatives of clubland or the shires close to the Leader. Therefore, the 'old-
> fashioned' wing of the Party must feel divorced from the leadership and unable
> to assert any influence over it.

---

2 Jim Prior, *A Balance of Power* (1986), 39; Nigel Fisher, *Iain Macleod* (1973), 279; Michael Cockerell, *Live from Number Ten: The Inside Story of Prime Ministers and Television* (1988), 140; Andrew Alexander and Alan Watkins, *The Making of the Prime Minister, 1970* (1970), 107; Robert Rhodes James, *Ambitions and Realities: British Politics, 1964–1970* (1972), 143.

This was thought to be dangerous because such people still had great influence in the voluntary side of the Party and could influence the Party's 'diehard supporters' in a positive direction if they chose to do so. One result of such claims was the appointment by Heath of Anthony Kershaw (MP for Stroud) as an additional PPS to the Leader, thereby opening new links to shire Conservatives, but this did not deal with the basic problem.[3]

The apparent lack of success derived from Heath's problem with the wider Party and with the public. There was, as Robert Rhodes James suggested, a paradox here: 'He was the first leader of the Party who had been elected in a ballot . . . and eventually a man of substantial qualities with an excellent record. Yet, to the Party at large, he still seemed vaguely alien, one of them yet not one of them.' This complex man was hard to understand and impossible to pigeonhole: he was, thought Ferdinand Mount in 1970, determined 'to loosen the hold of the class structure on British life', but at the same time 'he [had] a relish for the trappings of the Establishment'. At first there was a lot of criticism voiced at the grass-roots of the Party, attributed by Whitelaw to the open hostility to Heath of the *Daily Express*, still the biggest circulation Tory paper. Several times the breakthrough to popularity seemed to have been achieved, but each time the bandwagon stubbornly refused to keep rolling. His alleged popularity in the constituencies had been one of his strongest cards in 1965, but was now barely visible; by February 1966, Heath's approval rating was lower than Sir Alec's had been when he had lost the 1964 Election. In September 1967, a *BBC Panorama* film showed Heath 'pasting on a grin', as the commentator described it, in a succession of informal constituency events in which he seemed like a fish out of water; a YC interviewed by the BBC remarked that 'When we got rid of Sir Alec we said, "God knows, we can't have anyone worse than Home." Well, we've got someone worse than Home.' This sparked off another bout of Heath-bashing in the media, and on the following evening ITN asked him whether 'you are at all worried by your total failure to make a breakthrough as Tory leader?' Two months later, Whitelaw was arguing that a successful Conference and Heath's handling of devaluation had meant that Heath's 'self-confidence, as well as his standing in the party, has risen no end', but the polls failed to register this. NOP reported in July 1968 that only two-thirds even of Conservative voters wanted Heath to stay on as Leader of the Party. In April 1969, Norman Collins and Robert Renwick, two powerful industrial supporters of the Party who had been keen to see Heath replace Douglas-Home in 1965, lamented 'the complete lack of success Ted Heath

³ Campbell, *Heath*, 216; Alexander and Watkins, *Making of the Prime Minister*, 91–2; Minutes of the 1922 Committee [hereafter 1922], 29 July and 16 Dec. 1965, 20 July 1967 and later meetings; Julian Critchley, *Heseltine: The Unauthorised Biography* (1987), 45; Peter Walker, *Staying Power: An Autobiography* (1991), 119; Prior, *Balance of Power*, 43; Central Office Chairman's department file, CCO 20/8/10, Correspondence with Heath.

has in getting across'. At last in Summer 1969, there was a measurable rise in his popularity, with his approval rating going up to 40 per cent, but by the Autumn this had dropped again to about 33 per cent.[4]

Much of the problem had to do with manner and style. Robert Rhodes James neatly applied to Heath Rosebery's description of Sir Stafford Northcote, who had in the 1880s failed to inspire his Tory followers when in opposition:

> Where he failed was in manner. His voice, his diction, his delivery, were all inadequate. With real ability, great knowledge, genial kindness, and a sympathetic nature – all qualities indeed which invoke regard and esteem – he had not the spice of the devil which is necessary to rouse an Opposition to zeal and elation.

Between 1945 and 1951 it was just this 'spice of the devil' that had been Churchill's main contribution to the Party. Always sensitive to criticism, Heath seemed to Cecil King in 1967 to be 'obviously deeply hurt by newspaper criticisms and the opinion polls, but battling on nevertheless. Was very critical of the newspapers always pulling down, never building up.' Heath was less happy with the large meetings that the press tended to report than with more infomal gatherings, and apart from friends like Alastair Burnet and Ian Trethowan made little attempt to cultivate journalists, for whose calling he for the most part felt only contempt. Interviewing Heath on the radio, Robert Carvel suggested that Heath must find Fleet Street's first editions 'compelling reading', which produced the following exchange:

> *Heath*: I don't find them compelling reading.
> *Carvel*: It's just a habit?
> *Heath*: No, I'm just uninterested.

The lack of admiration soon became mutual. In July 1968, Andrew Alexander of the *Telegraph* wrote to the Party Chairman to explain how difficult this now was for newspapers that supported the Party and wanted to support Heath too:

> I ought to write to you on the subject of Ted Heath's speeches. We all want him to make an impact. But speaking as a journalist, may I say that something drastic needs to be done about his speeches or he will soon end up being totally ignored. Nowadays in Fleet Street, the news that EH is going to deliver a big speech is received with, at best, a yawn, and – more commonly – with derision. A sense of loyalty spurs some on to give these speeches a certain amount of space. But really! Of all the speeches we have to plod through, EH's are the most dreary. Can nothing be done? I raise the matter purely in the interests of our Party.

---

[4] Rhodes James, *Ambitions and Realities*, 100, 111; Ferdinand Mount, 'Edward Heath', in T. Stacey and R. St Oswald (eds), *Here Come the Tories* (1970), 15; King, *Diary*, 26, 29, 77, 160, 254; T.F. Lindsay and Michael Harrington, *The Conservative Party 1919–1970* (1974), 246; Central Office Chairman's department file, CCO 20/8/12, Correspondence with Heath; Cockerell, *Live from Number Ten*, 137–8; Alexander and Watkins, *Making of the Prime Minister*, 110–11.

George Hutchinson wrote in 1970 that Heath's oratorical manner was still 'addicted, perhaps, by now, incurably, to the factual statement, the plain exposition, marshalling and enumerating his policies like a laundry list'. In the same year, the *New Statesman* saw him as 'a walking, talking Blue Book, chattering out statistics and minatory sub-clauses; lecturing the viewer, and making him feel guilty of neglecting his political homework'. This came out neatly at the 1966 Party Conference, when a speaker read out a curt letter from Heath's office which stated that if anyone did not know what Conservative policy was then it could only be because they had not bothered to find out. Attempts to soften the image that such abrasiveness created with a neat phrase or a photo-opportunity were generally met with a brusque 'I do not say that sort of thing' or 'It is not my style' (in part no doubt because it *was* Wilson's); if the neat phrase did find its way into a Heath speech it was generally delivered in a way that killed its impact. Astonishingly, the Conference speech that was Heath's most important Party performance of the year was always a rushed job, and his advisers could not even get him to give it his full attention until the day on which it had to be delivered. Everyone seemed to recognise the Heath problem and to be ready to offer a solution that would do the trick. Sir Anthony Meyer MP, spearheading the Party's attempts to improve contacts in the universities, reported in 1968 that 'many people told me how infinitely more effective Mr. Heath was sitting behind a table and answering questions than mixing at a cocktail party. It made me wonder whether, in future, Albany parties should not take the form of Mr. Heath sitting his guests round the room with drinks in their hands, giving them a short talk and answering their questions'. In May 1967, the Chief Publicity Officer reported triumphantly that in Stanley Clark he had found a publicity professional who might be able to do the trick:

> There is a short term job to be done of digging for human, true-to-character stories about Heath. Portrait of a serious fisherman [*sic*], and as a serious, successful and beloved Army officer are but two examples. Clark can do this. Clark has proved himself able to get on with Heath – an item of no little importance in the circumstances. And it is reported that Clark can make a little go a long way. He needs to.

Trying to sell the idea to Heath, the same official wrote a week later that 'too many people in Britain have completely the wrong idea about the kind of man you really are', but his package of proposals, including greater reliance on professional guidance and the compilation of a bank of jokes and topical references for Heath to use, did not get very far. Central Office advice about media appearances did not transform Heath's approach, but the imminence of an Election in 1968–69 and the arrival of Geoffrey Tucker as Director of Publicity did mark a change. Tucker, who had worked on the Party's account with Colman, Prentis and Varley before 1959, now pondered on 'the Heath problem' and knew that 'No way was he going to be dolled up or be seen cuddling babies. He was against anything schmalzy. I had to work with the grain.' He was much assisted in this by the unsolicited offer of help from the film director Bryan Forbes, and by early 1970 the *Evening Standard* was able to write of another *Panorama* interview with Heath as 'the most impressive of his whole broadcasting career'. His yachting triumph at about this time even made him a relaxed guest on a television sports programme. Richard Crossman thought, when this sporting success was followed by the Selsdon Conference, that 'suddenly Ted is described as a winner'. The paradox is then that, despite himself, Heath had behind him in 1970 the most sophisticated public relations exercise yet mounted in British politics; Ferdinand Mount, noting in 1970 that Heath's posters were the first ever to be mass-produced in Britain in full colour, reflected that this showed 'the technology of affluence' in the Party.[5]

With the Party, Heath also broke down his presentational difficulties. In part this probably reflected the fact that an elected leader would be far more difficult to remove than one selected under the earlier, informal processes; since he would not have been an easy man to dislodge, the Party had to stop grumbling and come to terms with him at least until the next Election. In part though it also reflected the fact that successive years provided accumulating opportunities for Party people to listen to Heath informally on his regular forays around the country and to develop admiration – if never quite affection – for the man they saw when off the television screen; the chairman of Cirencester and Tewkesbury in 1967 urged members who were critical of Heath to go and see him in the flesh at his coming visit to the Area. Douglas Hurd felt that 'by the time of the 1970 election, active Conservative supporters in the country had a clearer understanding of Mr. Heath than most MPs or journalists in London'. This is borne out by the local evidence; in Sheffield Hallam, for example, which had been highly critical of the leadership, Heath's 1967 visit changed perceptions; it was noted that 'all present were impressed by his personality and the clarity of the speech he gave', and decided not to publish a letter of support for Heath only because 'it was agreed that Mr. Heath was now firmly in the saddle and such a letter was not now as important as it would have been a few months ago'; now converted into keen supporters, the Sheffield Tories kept passing resolutions of support even when he became Prime Minister, for example in February 1972 sending the Leader a telegram of congratulations after another appearance on *Panorama*. Heath's visit to York in 1968 produced another positive shift of opinion

---

[5] Rhodes James, *Ambitions and Realities*, 114, 117–18; King, *Diary*, 145; Central Office Chairman's department files, CCO 20/8/10 and 12; Christie Davies and Russell Lewis (eds), *The Reactionary Joke Book* (1973), 27; Sir Anthony Meyer to Brendon Sewill, 22 Feb. 1968, Boyle MSS, 22727; George Hutchinson, *Edward Heath: A Personal and Political Biography* (1970), 186; Prior, *Balance of Power*, 54; Cockerell, *Live from Numbr Ten*, 146–50, 153; Anthony Howard (ed.), *The Crossman Diaries* (1979), 683; Ferdinand Mount, 'Edward Heath', 14.

about him, as did a meeting he had with Burton's officers in 1967; it was perhaps characteristic of local Toryism that when the York chairman asked if all members of his Executive shared his delight with Heath's recent meeting, he was roundly condemned for even asking such a question and the meeting went on instead to argue about the price of printing the tickets. Heath did certainly make himself available, attending Party gatherings, and delivering about 150 speeches a year outside parliament, ten times as many as he made in the Commons. He also sat in on the whole Party Conference, rather than descending god-like for the final rally. As Party Chairman, Macleod had at least twice suggested that Macmillan should do this as a gesture towards evoking a more modern face for the Party, but to little effect; Macmillan knew his rarity value and would have thought the idea of attending a whole Conference to be a deadly bore. From 1965 onwards Heath simply did it, and the first Conference even took place in front of the platform slogan 'Right Ahead With Heath' to emphasise the fact.[6]

The centrality of Heath to the Opposition did not preclude significant roles for the rest of his team. At first, in July 1965, since he still had to expect an early election, Heath had reappointed most of Douglas-Home's shadow spokesmen, though promoting Macleod to shadow Chancellor, and helping to foster unity by persuading Douglas-Home himself to stay on as a foreign policy spokesman. Heath ran a businesslike and organised operation, infinitely more so than Churchill's after 1945; as well as Douglas-Home, his team included three other potential Prime Ministers of his own generation – Maudling, Macleod and Powell – but none of these was particularly close to him, and his nearest advisers were Carrington, Whitelaw and Barber. Many of the reappointments of 1965 were made simply by a telephone call from the Chief Whip, but Heath himself was careful to explain to such as Selwyn Lloyd that his reappointment was conditional and that he would need a free hand after the Election, whether he won or lost. After losing in 1966, he cleared out six of the older frontbenchers, Boyd-Carpenter, Dilhorne, Lloyd, Marples, Redmayne and Sandys. Lloyd had wished to go, having made no secret of his preference for Maudling over Heath, but others like Boyd-Carpenter were less content to see their careers summarily terminated. These were all men who were closely associated with the difficulties of 1961–64; some of them were to be troublesome on the back benches in the later 1960s, though Enoch Powell, who might also have been removed at this time, stayed on to cause Heath even more trouble from the inside. In their place Heath promoted younger men, exposing himself to the criticism that he was surrounding himself with those who owed their promotion only to him and would therefore be deferential.

6 Rhodes James, *Ambitions and Realities*, 123; Hutchinson, *Heath*, 188; Cirencester and Tewkesbury CA minutes, 4 Feb. 1967; Douglas Hurd, *An End to Promises, Sketch of a Government, 1970–1974* (1978), 12; Sheffield Hallam CA minutes, 13 Nov. 1967, 12 Dec. 1970; York CA minutes, 23 Sept. 1968; Burton upon Trent CA minutes, 1 Dec. 1967; Cockerell, *Live from Number Ten*, 122.

Since they were inherently less experienced than their older predecessors this was unavoidable, but it hardly seems appropriate to describe Peter Walker, Geoffrey Rippon and Margaret Thatcher as naturally subservient colleagues. What those three did have in common with Heath was backgrounds less privileged than had been normal on the Tory front bench, and this produced the further complaint that he was re-moulding the Party in his own image. Heath had been dubbed 'the Grocer' by *Private Eye* as early as 1962 when he was negotiating with the EEC over the price of butter, but when the phrase stuck it also had an element of snobbishness about the origins of Heath and his new Conservative 'Heathmen'; a great irony is that Thatcher, 'straight out of the grocer's shop' literally as well as figuratively, was often seen as the epitome of the Heathite middle-class style. Selwyn Lloyd in 1968 felt that another consequence of these developments was that 'the trouble with our party is that the leaders are all S.E. based'; Heath, Maudling and Macleod all had London constituencies and most of the others who sat for seats in the rest of the country 'are in fact Londoners', citing Joseph and Boyle as examples. This was perceptive, for while there were rising 'Heathmen' who had their roots in such impeccably provincial places as Grantham or Taunton, and while Sir Alec's presence demonstrated that Scotland was still at the heart of Tory politics, by 1968 (when Powell left) there was not a provincial accent among them, for these rising stars had been through the Oxbridge mill, and there was nobody whose foothold in the industrial regions matched that of Woolton and Maxwell Fyfe only ten years earlier, or indeed Teddy Taylor and Rhodes Boyson in the 1980s. Walter Elliot had in 1945 predicted 'the rule of the Home Counties' in the Party and this now seemed to be coming to pass. It was perhaps not entirely coincidental that it was to be only in rural and southern England that Heathite (and subsequently Thatcherite) Toryism consistently dominated at the polls.[7]

A further regular complaint was that Heath ran his team less like an opposition than as 'a government in exile'; a Tory backbencher in 1969 told Cecil King that this was 'why the Tories had been such a feeble opposition'. The sacking of Boyd-Carpenter was a case in point, for he was a good House of Commons man who was always more dangerous when on the attack and therefore a natural for a period of opposition, as he had shown before 1951; several MPs wondered why 'spring-heeled Jack' could not be found a post and political journalists decided that he must have committed the sin of arguing in the shadow cabinet. Initially the 1966 shadow cabinet was reduced to sixteen, with only ten additional spokesmen, a long way from the task-forces and teams of speakers appointed by Douglas-Home; this gradually crept back up to forty-five frontbench spokesmen by 1970. Fifteen of the seventeen in the

---

[7] Hutchinson, *Heath*, 171; Lindsay and Harrington, *Conservative Party*, 254; John Boyd-Carpenter, *Way of Life* (1980), 193, 195–6; Alexander and Watkins, *Making of the Prime Minister* (1970), 82; D.R. Thorpe, *Selwyn Lloyd* (1989), 397, 403, 409; Richard Ingrams, *The Life and Times of Private Eye* (1971), 23; Campbell, *Heath*, 214.

shadow cabinet joined the Heath Cabinet after the 1970 Election, in almost every case slipping straight into the job they had been shadowing. Heath intended to run the shadow cabinet on a tight rein, with none of the thinking aloud or kite-flying that could be both useful and enjoyable when freed from the restraints of office; announcements would be made only when thorough debate had produced agreed Party positions, and spokesmen would not speak on each other's areas of responsibility. This was one cause of deteriorating relations with Powell, who would not accept restriction either on his thought processes or on his right to speak. But Edward Boyle also regretted being 'expected to remain on parade as though one were nothing but the alternative Government'.[8]

The Party's policy professionals were among the least happy with this approach; Brendon Sewill, the CRD director, thought that this way of running a shadow cabinet tended to mean that concentration was on next week's debate rather than on a policy strategy for four years hence. Harold Macmillan attempted to persuade Heath to modify his approach, but was also unsuccessful. Macleod also felt that the single-minded preparation for government was not the Opposition's only task, and might not even be the best strategy; he urged Heath to pursue the more flexible tactics that Churchill had used after 1945, but to no avail; in the *Spectator* in August 1966, he argued that the Party should soft-pedal its detailed work and 'wait awhile. For the moment, what is needed is opposition. Just that.' If Macleod later seemed to have been won round to Heath's way of doing things, as George Hutchinson claimed, it was not that he changed his mind, more likely that he realised the impossibility of changing Heath's; when he arrived at the Treasury in 1970 he announced to his officials that 'whatever I may have said in Opposition, I am not interested in Opposition. I am interested in administration.' This flatly contradicted everything Heath had been saying for five years, and even when contributing to the chorus of praise for Heath's determination to plan, Macleod gave it a twist that rather undermined the point; in October 1969 he claimed that 'no party in Opposition has ever done as much as we under Mr. Heath have done to prepare for Government. Let us be fair. No Government has ever done more to prepare for Opposition than Mr. Wilson's.' Planning for Government went beyond actual policy-making; the steel debates were one example of the way in which parliamentary scrutiny of Labour legislation was used to train up junior spokesmen, whips, and backbenchers on particular subjects; Anthony Barber, who led the team as shadow spokesman, picked personally every Tory member of the parliamentary committee that considered the Bill and chose a team so conspicuous for its blend of youth, experience and talent that nine of its twelve members took office in June 1970. As the 1970 Election

---

8 King, *Diary*, 263; Martin Burch, 'Approaches to Leadership in Opposition: Edward Heath and Margaret Thatcher', in Z. Layton-Henry (ed.), *Conservative Party Politics* (1980), 172; Campbell, *Heath*, 214; Alexander and Watkins, *Making of the Prime Minister*, 98, 100.

approached, the governmental thinking of the Opposition actually increased; in January a Future Legislation Committee was set up under Maudling, much as there would be a Cabinet Committee of that name; a detailed programme and timetable for a year's parliamentary session was devised by March, and a copy was sent over to Downing Street on the day Heath moved in.[9]

The policy review of 1964–70

Nevertheless, it was the central task of making policy that lay behind such legislative plans that occupied most of the Opposition's attention, particularly in the first two or three years after October 1964. The timing of this exercise is the most critical factor in understanding its character. Since Labour had such a tiny majority in the 1964 Parliament, another election must come early, and in the mean time the Conservatives (as in 1950) were careful not to bring Labour down too soon, before they had been given a fair chance, and before they themselves were ready with a manifesto more forward-looking than the one on which they had just lost. The very appointment of Heath to mastermind this review as Butler's successor in the chair of the ACP and the CRD indicates a determination to make major changes quickly, for the new policies that were produced needed a tough-minded advocate if they were to override the objections of ex-Ministers who were often far from happy to see their policies immediately disowned by their own Party. Twenty advisory groups had been set up by the end of the first Christmas recess, with the instruction to report proposals within six months; the groups were generally chaired by shadow spokesmen and comprised about half MPs and half outsiders – other Party people, academics and industrialists; there was criticism in the 1922 Committee when Heath refused to list the groups' membership, but he stood his ground with the explanation that they had been promised anonymity to protect their current employment position.[10]

The electoral rather than the philosophical timetable of this review was central to it from the start; the National Union Executive was told by Heath in December 1964 that he was concentrating on 'particular sections of the electorate whose previous support of the Party had been lost at the General Election', and the secretary's private note indicated who were the target voters: '*Future policy*: Owner occupiers, young marrieds, Liberal support.' Electoral urgency thus forced on Heath a basic approach to policy-making which imported flaws into the whole process. With the expectation of an election within months, time was too short to allow the two-stage process

9 John Ramsden, *The Making of Conservative Party Policy: The Conservative Research Department since 1929* (1980), 255, 273–4, 279–83; Hutchinson, *Heath*, 173–4; Fisher, *Macleod*, 284–5, 305; Robert Shepherd, *Iain Macleod*, (1994), 422–3; Robin Oakley and Peter Rose, *The Political Year, 1970* (1970), 137; Keith Ovenden, *The Politics of Steel* (1978), 106, 112–13.
10 Lindsay and Harrington, *Conservative Party*, 242–3; D.E. Butler and Anthony King, *The British General Election of 1966* (1966), 62.

of policy formation that had been adopted after 1945, principles in 1947 and systematic policy in detail only in 1949. In 1965, the Party had to go straight to the detail and, since Heath was in charge of the exercise, it really *did* go for detail; the assumptions were variously that the Party's broad philosophy was well known and did not need to be re-thought, that broader themes would emerge naturally as detailed work was done, and that an open discussion of big issues would only lead to damaging divisions. When setting up the original policy groups, Heath had written that what was needed was 'new Conservative solutions to the problems that the electorate are worried about'; writing to an ACP member he had claimed that 'though our basic principles are well known and easily distinguished from the Statist emphasis even of moderate Socialism, I do believe that we have to find new practical ways in which to apply our principles to current problems'. Heath was always to hold to this 'problem-solving' approach, because in the first place urgency allowed no real alternative, and then after Autumn 1965 the Party had already published new policies and it really would have been damaging to reopen the big issues; when Enoch Powell attempted to question the assumptions behind trade union policy, Heath told him that it was too late, that it had all been gone into and settled, and that he was 'not just going to, at this stage, have it picked to pieces and fought over'. Heath was probably not dissatisfied with this procedure, since it squared exactly with his preferred way of doing things; John MacGregor, working in Heath's private office, reported him saying, 'Let's avoid committing ourselves on anything until we know all the facts, every single one', a defiantly unphilosophical approach. Powell was to remark in 1989, with a characteristically wicked gleam in his eye, that 'if you showed [Heath] an idea he immediately became angry and would go red in the face'. Powell had an unerring facility for making Heath angry on most subjects, but there is certainly truth in his memory of Heath's reluctance to debate concepts rather than policies. A review procedure that was 'all detail' was likely to hide divisions about basic approaches, but these could well emerge when the policies were carried out in office. In the short term, the concentration on detail made it difficult to demonstrate the broad differences between Conservative and Labour policies; Brendon Sewill lamented in 1968 that work was not yet concentrating on 'where the car was going rather than what we were going to do inside the engine' and invited his predecessor David Clarke to 'write to Ted Heath some time and tell him the public want to know where he wants to go as much as how he means to get there'.[11]

If to Heath British politics seemed to be 'the great divide', it was far less clear from the outside on what the divide hinged: it was in 1968 that Samuel Brittan wrote *Left versus Right, the Bogus Dilemma* and in the same

---

[11] National Union Executive Committee minutes [hereafter NUEC], 3 Dec. 1964, National Union papers, NUA 4/3/2, Executive Committee papers; Ramsden, *Making of Conservative Party Policy*, 234–5, 241, 272; Lindsay and Harrington, *Conservative Party*, 242; Hutchinson, *Heath*, 169, 176–7; Campbell, *Heath*, 195, 212–13, 222, 239.

years that the Liberals produced a poster with the faces of Wilson and Heath over the slogan 'Which Twin is the Tory?' (which was mainly intended to draw attention to Wilson's lack of radicalism, but in the process also indicated the indistinct nature of the Tory alternative). Members of the Conservatives' own Advisory Committee on Policy warned in 1970 that placing all the emphasis on detailed policies for efficiency and growth would reduce the difference between the parties to a 'we can grow faster than you can' auction. Angus Maude went public with similar doubts in January 1966, arguing in the *Spectator* 'that a technocratic approach is not sufficient and that we must have some philosophy', to which he added the barb that 'it is obvious that the Conservative Party has completely lost effective political initiative'. Maude's challenge went wider, for in the *Sunday Telegraph* in November 1965 he had written disparagingly of the transformation of the Conservative tradition of 'gradualness' into a readiness to embrace change for its own sake, a statement that defied everything Heath believed in; after a hesitation, Heath sacked Maude from the front bench for his *Spectator* article and made another enemy for life; the fact that the 1922 Committee then elected Maude to represent it on the ACP suggests that the backbenchers thought that he had a point, but he remained on cool terms with Heath; even in March 1972, when Edward Boyle (who did not share Maude's policy views but recognised in him a thinking Tory like himself) suggested Maude as a possible Principal for Swinton College, Fraser replied that he would bear the name in mind 'though I fancy I may encounter a little trouble with it in some quarters, as Angus is not everybody's favourite person'. In February 1966, the North Cornwall Tories, facing the Liberal challenge head on in a marginal constituency, decided starkly 'that there is very little to choose between Socialist and present Conservative policies, and urge[d] a return to real Conservative principles with a far greater emphasis on individual freedom, and less control from Central Government.' Such views continued to be expressed in other places too, if only by other opponents of Heath; in October 1966, Edward du Cann opened an ACP debate with a speech in support of Maude's views and John Biffen called at the same meeting for Conservative economic policy to be about more than 'efficient management'. Even for those who accepted Heath's stance, the gospel of change and modernisation was still a double-edged weapon; in January 1969 Heath told the shadow cabinet that

> the present mood of the country was much more willing to accept change than it had been a year or so ago. Indeed it was interesting to see that much of the informed criticism of the thirteen Conservative years was that there had not been enough change carried out. . . . Mr. Maudling, while agreeing, said that the real problem was that whereas there was general acceptance of the need for change there was not general agreement about the nature of the change that was needed.

Nevertheless, it was the message of change that was taken up in 1965 and remained at the core of everything done in opposition; Michael Fraser told the Guildford Tories in March 1965 that 'in a period of rapid change only a modern and progressive party could provide the answer'.[12]

Whatever its limitations, the policy review was successful in its intention of producing quick results. By Spring 1965 the number of groups had already risen to thirty-six; legal advice could be supplied through the Inns of Court Conservative Association and, for urgent priorities, research could be commissioned from the Economist Intelligence Unit; comprehensive files of papers and minutes of meetings were kept, providing the basis from which the CRD officers acting as secretaries drafted reports. By March 1965 James Douglas was worried that 'too many people are doing too many things too superficially', and pointed out that there was now a group meeting practically all the time, with sometimes three or four groups meeting simultaneously. However, the six-month deadline that Heath had imposed produced its own discipline, and the expiry of the deadline in July fortuitously coincided with his own elevation to the leadership, so that the groups' recommendations would then have the most powerful of advocates in the final stage of consideration by the shadow cabinet and the ACP; a new Leader, especially the first ever elected Leader and one thought to be in tune with the future, was in a strong position to get what he wanted in August and September 1965. There was horse-trading at this stage, but in essentials the document published for the Party Conference relied on the groups' work in the Spring. The title *Putting Britain Right Ahead* was a late change of mind, with the last word added only when Maudling suggested that the draft title 'Putting Britain Right' would invite the question, 'who had put Britain wrong?' A title could be changed, but the presentational difficulty involved in a radical package of policies produced by a Party that had only just emerged from thirteen years in office would not be so easily brushed aside.[13]

This 'approach document' fed into the 1966 election manifesto, in which no substantial changes of emphasis were made and, after the 1966 defeat indicated a full parliament in opposition, the impetus of policy-making naturally slowed; chairmen were told that they could now think of one or two years as the target for further reports. Heath remained chairman of the ACP, with Boyle as his deputy doing more of the detailed work, until November 1968 when Maudling took over the task, but by that stage even the detailed refinement of the 1965 policy exercise was completed. No new chairman of the CRD was appointed by Heath until 1970, so he effectively kept the reins in his own hands throughout; his approval was

[12] Edward Heath, *The Great Divide* (1966), 3; Bernard Levin, *The Pendulum Years: Britain in the Sixties* (1977), 242; Alexander and Watkins, *Making of the Prime Minister*, 168; Rhodes James, *Ambitions and Realities*, 134; Roth, *Heath*, 196; Advisory Committee on Policy minutes [hereafter ACP], 6 Oct. 1966; Boyle to Fraser, 8 Mar. 1972, and reply, 14 Mar. 1972, Boyle MSS, 22617 and 22618; North Cornwall CA minutes, 25 Feb. 1966; Guildford CA minutes, 12 Mar. 1965.

[13] Ramsden, *Making of Conservative Party Policy*, 233, 240–2, 249.

needed before a policy group was set up and he vetted each one's terms of reference. Boyle did though introduce an important alteration of procedures when he convened regular meetings of group chairmen, gatherings which could iron out inconsistencies and overlaps in the reports. The last phase of policy-making also involved some deviations from the original pattern by shadow spokesmen like Walker and Rippon who began to keep the exercise in their policy areas more under personal control. It is doubtful whether this mattered very much, for the process after August 1965 was the refinement of decisions already made. Changes of detail were made, but not many on issues of importance, and new issues like local government reform acquired significance or topicality as a result of external factors, but the bones of the mandate claimed by the Heath Government in 1970 could be found in the work published in October 1965.[14]

Putting Britain Right Ahead, thrown together in six months in the expectation of an early return to office, is therefore the key document of 1964–70, even though none of its proposals could be implemented for five years. A central theme had indeed emerged from the work of the policy groups. Sewill suggested to Heath on 25 March 1965 that the two themes that were emerging were 'Europe – exciting, interesting and novel, but unfortunately with not much sign of being immediately practical' and 'efficiency and competition – this is obviously right and essential but (like modernisation) seems too technical and cold to be inspiring.' His suggestion was to fuse the two so that the aim would be 'to increase our national efficiency so that we can enter Europe from strength and not from weakness'. If the policies as such were new, that central theme was largely the one that first Macleod and then Heath himself had sought to press on the Conservative Party since 1962, a continuity that was perhaps unavoidable in a period during which Heath had insisted that everybody already knew what the Party stood for. A month later, with policy groups coming nearer to the end of their remit, Sewill was ready to be more specific: he advised Heath that the Party could now see its way to making 'a fairly fundamental shift' from past practice, and listed several areas where 'we could also today break our links with the past and build a new framework of policies'. His list consisted first, of a new approach to regional policy and devolution from Westminster, second, more selectivity in social services (where 'we must give up claiming to have made the biggest ever increases in universal benefits'), third, Europe as the central aim of both foreign and domestic policy, and fourth, reform of the trade unions. For the last, the need was

> to take direct action to limit the power of trade unions to push up wages and costs on an industry-wide basis. If we believe in dealing with monopoly power we should clearly also deal with this. It is this power to strike and put up prices

[14] Lindsay and Harrington, *Conservative Party*, 250; Ramsden, *Making of Conservative Party Policy*, 237, 249–50, 254–5, 263.

against the consumer that most people mean when they talk about the need to check the power of the unions. There seems a danger that we may talk big about taking a strong line on the unions but only deal with some of the minor tangential problems (such as the closed shop, trades union law etc) and miss the main abuse of union power.

In a rare indication of his own views, Heath minuted on this note, 'an excellent paper. We must discuss this week. I agree with almost all of it – I had no idea that anyone held the same views as myself.' What is really interesting in this is that several issues that no post-war Conservative Government had dared even to mention to the unions were already by April 1965 regarded as 'minor tangential problems' that were less significant than reducing the unions' economic power. At the 1970 Selsdon Conference, Heath was equally explicit, as the verbatim transcript indicated:

> *Heath*: . . . Never talked about this in public, perhaps we ought to. Point of industrial relations changes is to redress the balance between employer and employee. Up to 1939, balance on side of employer; after 1945 was on side of unions and still on side of unions. . . . Only way is redressing balance between employers and employees.

This need to strengthen the hands of employers was especially needed in the context of incomes policy. Heath went on, though without convincing *all* his colleagues,

> Come more and more to the conclusion we should say we are going to look after Government sector, our responsibility. But is responsibility of private sector to deal with their own wage negotiations. . . . Throw it back at them. If you don't like wages going up don't put them up.
> *Thatcher*: They will.[15]

The presentation of *Putting Britain Right Ahead* to an extent disguised what was being done. Whereas the *Industrial Charter* had been called 'a statement of Conservative policy' (which is what the Party had demanded in 1946–47) but was actually a statement of principles, the 1965 document, conversely, claimed to be 'an approach document' and a 'statement of aims', but was actually a statement of policy. It also adopted the tone of a Party deliberately breaking with the past and made no attempt to disguise this shift from earlier policies, which is just what Angus Maude found so offensive. As Rhodes James puts it, 'Heath had come to believe that the nation, no less than the Conservative Party, needed jolting out of an out-of-date cast of mind and lethargic acquiescence in the status quo.' The document listed a large number of policy proposals but highlighted five priorities: tax reform to reward initiative and merit; the fostering of more competition in industry, reforms of management and new systems of agricultural support; a definition of the trade unions' responsibilities and the elimination of restrictive labour practices;

---

15 Ramsden, *Making of Conservative Party Policy*, 247–8; LCC papers, 1970.

selectivity in social services to give better support to the needy; entry to the EEC. The first three of these were all justified by the fifth, the need to make Britain fit to take the European plunge without drowning. What was just as significant as anything proposed was the omission of any reference to incomes policy, or indeed of any other way in which the Conservatives would manage the economy; in September 1964, on the very brink of the Election, Maudling had circulated a draft statement calling for a comprehensive incomes policy, and pledging to call a national conference after polling day to work out details; this was stalled by sceptical colleagues who did not allow even a guarded reference to the idea to get into the manifesto, and any chance that it would be taken up by the Party after the 1964 defeat was scuppered by Wilson's adoption of the similar policy which became the 1965 National Plan.[16]

In the Party, the impetus of the headlong rush to a new policy under a new Leader carried almost all before it, and the October 1965 Conference produced few policy criticisms. The press were welcoming but uncertain, finding it hard to place the document in the traditional context of British politics. Macleod in the *Spectator* gave up the attempt altogether: 'it is possible to argue that the document (trades unions – immigration) represents a shift to the right. Equally possible to argue (Europe – social services) that it is a shift to the left. These terms have little meaning inside the Tory Party. Basically, the document is an expression of the thinking of the Party's new leader.' Several commentators noticed the similarity of Heath's technocratic language and Wilson's 'white heat' rhetoric, and *The Economist* suggested that Heath had stolen Wilson's 'efficiency consultant's coat'. Heath had invited that comparison in his personal foreword to the document: 'As I go around the country, I find that people are asking for an entirely fresh approach to the country's problems. They are looking for constructive policies – *how* we do things rather than what needs to be done'. In the *Sunday Times* William Rees-Mogg welcomed the document for just this reason, and saw it as an important bid by the Party to get back in touch with important social forces that it had lost: 'The last years of the Macmillan and Douglas-Home administrations did not seem to many of the young managers and technicians to be relevant to their problems. In the first year of Opposition, the Conservative Party has been trying, partly instinctively and partly consciously, to realign itself with these social forces.' Heath had demanded such a response to the document by the way he himself described the new policies at Brighton:

> Nothing great can really be achieved except through the efforts of individual men and women. It is their efforts for their families, for themselves and for their country which give them the sense of purpose which produces achievements. Everything else is a means to an end. Let us encourage the pacemakers by all

16 Butler and King, *General Election of 1966*, 63–4; Central Office *Notes on Current Politics* [hereafter *NCP*], 1 Jan. 1965; Rhodes James, *Ambitions and Realities*, 112–13; Hutchinson, *Heath*, 15–51; September 1964 correspondence, Butler MSS, H 52.

means because they are the people who are blessed with particular skills, with greater imagination, with foresight, with inventiveness and with administrative ability, who can give the lead and who can keep us to the fore in world affairs. Let us never forget that by doing this they are not only helping themselves but are helping . . . the rest of the community, and enabling us also to have our opportunities, to improve our way of life and our standard of living. Therefore, that is the philosophy which we have tried to express in this document.[17]

This general approach, irreverently nicknamed 'blessed are the pacemakers' in the CRD, was seriously undercut by inner Party opposition to the types of policy changes that it would seem to imply. A meritocratic commitment to the preservation of grammar schools from which so many of Heath's high achievers had emerged (himself included) was difficult to maintain when even Tory local authorities were producing schemes to set up comprehensive schools, and when the Party's (Etonian) education spokesman was increasingly unwilling to defend educational selection at all. Edward Boyle was under constant fire from the Party rank and file, but he was quite right in his claim that the real gulf was between constituency activists and their own councillors, with the Party's spokesman merely holding the ring or, as in a particularly nasty dispute in West Bromwich, refusing to get involved at all and urging the Party Chairman to do likewise. Sending him a crop of critical resolutions on comprehensivisation, the National Union Executive chairman joked in 1966 that 'this subject has an almost equal rating with the top one in our correspondence with the constituencies. "Rhodesia" has it by a short head!' In 1969, the limitations on the Party's preference for self-made earners over inheritors of wealth was again brought out by the outrage that greeted Simon Jenkins' Bow Group pamphlet arguing for the forcible integration of the public schools into the state sector, to raise academic standards for all. The best that could be hoped for in secondary education policy at this time was to limit the damage.[18]

A proposed graduated capital tax, in effect a tax on wealth, had been discussed within the policy review earlier in the year; this had many attractions to a Party bent on rewarding enterprise and on shifting the balance of tax benefits 'from owners to earners' in the drive to stimulate the high achievers. However, this was entirely unacceptable to those owners in the Party who still saw the Conservative Party's duty as conserving inherited wealth rather than attacking it. After confidential discussion revealed the breadth of Party opposition, the proposal never saw the light of day, and by 1968 the shadow cabinet had decided that Conservatives would vote against a wealth tax if Labour now proposed one. With such built-in resistances to the systematic pursuit of what Heath declared to be his central motivation, the spine might well prove to be too fragile to hold the limbs of policy together. And many

---

[17] Ramsden, *Making of Conservative Party Policy*, 470–4.
[18] Fraser to Boyle, Oct. 1966, Barber to Boyle, 21 Jan. 1969, and reply, 18 Jan. 1968, Hewlett to Boyle, 26 Jan. 1966, Boyle MSS, 22559, 22580–1, 22842, 22882, 22739.

would anyway not have recognised the rewarding of success as deserving the description of a Party 'philosophy', certainly not one about which it could be said that 'everything else is a means to an end'. Colin Welch in the *Daily Telegraph* was one of the few who at this stage spotted the possible flaws in policies devised to meet Heath's how-we-do-things rather than what-needs-to-be-done approach:

> 'What men and women want, quite rightly, is not theories but results in terms of more dependable service and better performance.' Thus, Mr. Heath in the new statement of Conservative aims. . . . This sounds blunt, businesslike, British stuff. Yet even in this fog-enveloped island there must be grey pedants who suspect that theories and results are closely connected, that wrong theories will produce wrong results and right, right?[19]

The 1966 General Election

Within a few months, this programme was put to the country in a bid to return the Conservatives to power, but in unpromising circumstances. The Party's successes in opinion polls, local government elections in May 1965, and the victory at Leyton in January were not sustained through the Autumn. By November, Gallup showed Labour well ahead, and also found both a strong preference for Wilson over Heath for Prime Minister and a majority expecting Labour to be re-elected. Labour's majority, down to three seats after Leyton, ensured that the Government did not introduce unpopular measures on which the Conservatives might manage to defeat it, and looked to a by-election in Hull North to confirm the public's view. This was a weathervane constituency that had produced a majority of under twelve hundred votes in four of the last five contests. The decline in the Party's poll standing and fears that Wilson would use a Hull victory as a springboard for a snap election produced some faltering of morale; a local supporter wrote to Central Office to ask 'Have you given up?' The Party Chairman replied that, 'in point of fact we are going into the Hull North by-election with all possible effort and speed', and stopped only just short of promising a victory. Twelve MPs were drafted in as a campaign team, nine frontbenchers went to Hull to speak, busloads of canvassers came in from as far afield as London and Liverpool, and a full canvass indicated a close result and the possibility of winning the seat back. When on 27 January 1966 Labour not only held the seat but also quadrupled its majority, the Chief Organisation Officer had to confess that it was 'a great surprise and a tremendous disappointment'. His verdict was that defeat had been due to the 'middle electors' who 'do not trust us', and to 'the legendary Tory thirteen years' muddle and the £800 million deficit [on the 1964 balance of payments]. This is now an accepted truth like the

---

[19] John Ramsden, 'Churchill to Heath', in Lord Butler (ed.), *The Conservatives* (1977), 474; Ramsden, *Making of Conservative Party Policy*, 245–6.

"troops at Tonypandy".' A private note done for the Party based on NOP's recall survey confirmed this analysis: the Labour Government were thought to deserve a longer chance in office, pre-1964 fears of Labour extremism had evaporated, and the electorate had negative memories of the last Conservative Government, which had been kept alive by Labour's deliberate harping on the issue; when in February 1965 his Housing Minister predicted that there would be a consensus on his new Housing Bill, Wilson told him to 'Draft a White Paper which forces them to vote against you by describing the iniquities of the Tory Rent Act and the need to repeal it.' All this was, to say the least, depressing reading when Wilson called the General Election for 31 March. Butler and King observed that 'as the Conservatives prepared to do battle, they reminded onlookers of the army of King Harry on the eve of Agincourt. Their spirits were low and the odds against them heavy.'[20]

After eighteen months in which a snap election had constantly been feared, the technical preparations were well in hand. Heath described the Party's election strategy to the 1922 Committee on 17 February, eleven days before Wilson announced the election. The first objective would be to fight on positive policies, of which the Party now had a plethora, rather than negatively attacking Labour, and the hope was that this forward-looking approach would also remove the 'thirteen wasted years' claim from voters' minds. Second, the intensive media attention on the campaign would be used to remind voters that with Heath rather than Douglas-Home in command the Party had a vigorous, young Leader; the Party's election slogan, 'Action not Words', was chosen to emphasise exactly that point. In any case, with a campaign that few expected him to win, and coming before he had fully established himself, Heath had to do well personally if he were not to be challenged in the Party after a Conservative defeat. A draft of the manifesto by David Howell, director of the CPC, had been in hand since December 1965, and yet the final preparations were difficult, because of the problems of finding overarching themes to give the document a distinctive feel; it had originally been intended that extensive market research would enable the Party to find out more about the public's order of priorities, but this was not sufficiently advanced by the end of 1965 to make much contribution. Brendon Sewill reported to Fraser that 'when I showed [the manifesto draft] to James Douglas and David Dear, one of them commented that it was very well written but that it could equally well have been put out by the Labour Party, and the other that when he had finished reading it he could not really remember what it said'. There was perhaps some jealousy in this, for CRD officers were not entirely happy that Howell rather than they was doing the drafting, and their response to Howell's second draft was even more hostile, but struck notes that were to be repeated in press reactions to the final document; one officer

---

[20] Fisher, *Macleod*, 278; Central Office constituency file, CCO 1/14/232; Howard, *Crossman Diaries*, 82; Butler and King, *General Election of 1966*, 94.

complained that 'we seem to have substituted the university common room for the grouse moor' and another that 'really, ordinary people do not speak this sort of language and the sooner we realise it the better'; several officers made favourable references to the *Spectator* article rejecting 'technocratic' language for which Angus Maude had just been sacked. A meeting at Heath's Albany flat on 17 February agreed that the manifesto would contain only a personal statement from Heath and an action programme of promises which would be listed and numbered. Time was now so short that this document, jointly put together by Howell and Sewill, was never seen by the shadow cabinet, but approved on 25 February when already in proof, and at a meeting that only five shadow ministers attended. As shadow Chancellor, Macleod was alarmed by the large number of promises his colleagues proposed to make, but was sharply reminded by Heath that this would at least confute all the poll evidence 'that people think we have run out of ideas'. It didn't; looking back in November 1967, Macleod himself recalled that 'at the last election the Conservative Party Manifesto contained 131 distinct specific promises. This was far too much to put across to the electorate, and the net result was that everybody thought we had no policy.' Even the most aggressive presentation could not solve this problem: Heath offered 'an all-out war on crime' on 16 March 1966 and a 'war on waste' on the 21st, but neither attracted much attention in the media covering the election, already satiated with other proposals. The title of the document was also the campaign slogan, *Action not Words*, though even Sir Alec enquired subversively 'if "Ideas" ought not to be brought into it'. Butler and King reported dispassionately that 'the younger Conservatives had found that a number of concepts they used among themselves – competition, free enterprise, the pacemakers, the new competitors – were coolly received by the electorate'. Heath himself, writing the introduction, was unlikely to repair this gap; 'our first aim', he said, 'is . . . to run this country's affairs efficiently and realistically', which, as Rhodes James suggested, 'did not seem to offer much in the form of imaginative leadership. The 1966 manifesto exactly fitted John Campbell's diagnosis of Heath's major defect as a politician, that he could not bridge the gap between concrete details and obvious generalities with the imaginative linking arguments needed to seize the public's attention.[21]

It is hard to believe that any of this made much difference to the result in 1966, a campaign in which Labour was continuously ahead in the polls, when almost everyone knew that Labour would win, probably very comfortably, and when the Conservatives' position as the recently ejected governing party bedevilled all attempts to look forwards with new policies. The Party did try to talk down Labour's claims about the thirteen Conservative years and the

---

[21] Butler and King, *General Election of 1966*, 69, 90, 94; Lindsay and Harrington, *Conservative Party*, 247; Ramsden, *Making of Conservative Party Policy*, 251–2; Rhodes James, *Ambitions and Realities*, 97; Central Office *Daily Notes* [hereafter *DN*], 13 and 23 Mar. 1966.

1964 balance of payments deficit; with the issue so much in voters' minds, Conservatives could not ignore it, but did not really want to debate it either; interviewed on television on 7 March, Heath stoutly described the Tory record of growth, housebuilding, and general affluence as 'years of very great achievement', but insisted that 'it is the future to which we've got to look'. It was impossible to avoid the reiterated question 'why didn't you do all this when you had the chance?' and so the legacy of 1951–64 dragged down the Party's future plans as well as its past record. It was also clear that the electorate responded positively to an argument derived from fairness: Nigel Fisher found when canvassing that he was always being asked the question 'You had thirteen years. Wilson has not had much more than thirteen months. We must give him a chance.' Barbara Castle noted, after her party had won, that 'the campaign was merely an unavoidable hiatus in our work, and I think this is what the country felt: they had made up their minds at the start and they remained unchanged'.[22]

One really new issue that the Conservatives sought to highlight was trade union policy; 60 per cent of Tory candidates mentioned this in their election addresses, compared to only 24 per cent in 1964. Likewise Europe was mentioned as a major issue by half of Tory candidates (but by only a tenth of them in 1964); almost every other issue was downgraded. Here too it was difficult to escape the legacy of the past. Heath was asked why, if trade union reform was now overdue, he had not initiated it when he himself had been Minister of Labour. In the event, the press got bored with industrial relations and gave little prominence to the Party's flagship policy after the first week of campaigning, giving instead prominence to Europe. The difference was that on Europe there was no real debate that might sway votes, whereas on the unions, as Heath claimed on 16 March, 'we are the only people who are putting forward specific, concrete proposals to deal with this situation'. As Macleod had foreseen, the cost of the Conservatives' mountain of promises was also a tactical difficulty; Labour claimed that it would add £850 million to public expenditure, while Macleod himself put the figure at £250 million; he was ready to justify his figure with specific lists of Labour expenditures that he would cancel, but it was as difficult to defend this (especially with promised tax cuts as well) as it had been for Labour in 1959.[23]

In the expectation of defeat, it was important to prepare for next time; Michael Fraser later argued that 'in losing, we said the right things, forced Labour on to a number of hooks which were to prove extremely embarrassing to them in the years ahead, and we went a long way towards establishing our credibility for the next battle'. Even at the time, a senior Conservative told David Butler that 'we thought we probably couldn't win this time, but we

[22] Butler and King, *General Election of 1966*, 71, 182; *DN*, 14 Mar. 1966; Fisher, *Macleod*, 282; Barbara Castle, *The Barbara Castle Diaries, 1964–1976* (1990), 58.
[23] Butler and King, *General Election of 1966*, 103, 109–10, 116, 187; *DN*, 18 Mar. 1966.

were going to make sure we were in a position to win next time'. The two key themes here were the economy and Heath himself. The Conservative cry that the economy was *not* securely heading for prosperity in March 1966 was much repeated, though Cecil King found Heath on 21 March 'depressed that nothing he has to say about the perilous state of the economy is getting across': on 23 March at Glasgow Heath argued that 'the threat we are facing is the greatest that any nation can face short of war itself. Unless we take action to avert it, we are faced with the threat of national bankruptcy.' It was, he claimed, a 'vote now, pay later' election, for 'if the present Government gets back it will be the people of Britain who have to pay for it'. The problem for the Conservatives in March 1966 was the popular view of their own record in office, as Richard Crossman noted in his diary on 1 April:

> Heath desperately tried to warn people. He went on saying that we were going bankrupt; but of course this was completely ineffective with an electorate who felt that on this score – the responsibility for our difficulties – honours were pretty even, if not tipped against the Tories. Looking back, I see that timing was everything.

Nevertheless, in response to Heath's onslaught, Wilson was tempted to make ever more extravagant claims about the rosy prospects for the future, claims that looked very hollow when the Election was followed within months by three years of economic crisis, emergency controls, deflation and devaluation. Even before the worst of the crisis struck in July 1966, Heath was mining this seam: on 15 June, he claimed that 'we are already being proved right. Every warning we gave has been justified. . . . The Government said all was well – and the country believed them. That was what brought about the restoration of the Labour Government's electoral fortunes. But here we are again, back where we started.' On 23 July, after the economic storm had really broken, Heath added, in Bexley: 'Vote Labour and pay later, I said. The country has now got to pay.' This was an immediate advantage in 1966 – Crossman now thought in July that 'on the telly even Heath looks more like a leader these days' – and it was a vital launching pad for 1970, when Labour would again have to claim that the economy had recovered from crisis.[24]

Heath's campaigning was relentless, and the entire Conservative campaign hinged on his efforts. He fronted press conferences, made a big speech nearly every evening, and took a major role in broadcasting, which was coordinated by Macleod; there were plans for liaison between Heath, Maudling and Macleod but these came to little, and the central direction of the campaign was much in the Leader's hands. Seventy per cent of all television reporting of the Conservative campaign was of Heath; Douglas-Home, who travelled all over the country and made sixty speeches in support of his successor, was

---

24 Rhodes James, *Ambitions and Realities*, 98–9; Butler and King, *General Election of 1966*, 183–4; King, *Diary*, 62–3; *DN*, 26 Mar. 1966; Howard, *Crossman Diaries*, 195, 232; Heath, *Great Divide*, 31–3.

hardly reported at all, and instead of huge crowds of hecklers in Birmingham he found himself speaking from the top of a milk crate to about twenty farmers. The campaign did therefore give Heath sufficient exposure to enhance his standing; the friendly Ian Trethowan, in *The Times*, wrote later of the 1966 campaign that,

> in so far as it can be said of any politician who leads his party to a thumping defeat, he had a 'good' election. He visibly matured. His speeches got a bit better (as well they might!), he handled himself passably on television, and he was effective at his regular press conferences. He has never been a particular favourite of journalists (he can be distinctly prickly) but during this campaign they rather warmed to him, and never more so than when he conceded defeat with a good grace.

David Wood had told *Times* readers much the same on polling day: Heath was now 'urbane, witty and in rapport with all comers as we have never seen him before', no longer the 'unrelaxing technocrat'. Crossman thought that Heath had acquired 'something of the admiration that Gaitskell got for his gallant 1959 campaign'. Butler and King were right to warn that these changed perceptions were largely at the elite level, and to point out that there was little evidence that the mass of voters recognised a new Heath. It was though the political journalists who would have to present him over the next four years, so elite perceptions mattered a great deal.[25]

Butler and King also wrote of the number of opinion polls, and 'the growing credence given to such evidence' as lending the campaign an air of inevitability that was fostered by a campaign almost entirely devoid of incident. Labour remained consistently in the lead and Wilson continued to enjoy better ratings than Heath (who was given a favourable response only by about two-thirds even of those intending to vote Conservative); Gallup even found that twice as many voters thought Wilson a 'strong, forceful personality' as Heath, a finding which must have troubled Heath as much as the 'sincerity' poll did Sir Alec in the previous July. Irrespective of who was winning, Gallup had found at every election since 1951 that Labour had enjoyed a small lead when voters were asked which party was best 'for people like yourself'; that lead had never previously exceeded 4 per cent, but in 1966 it shot up to 11 per cent. Most crucially, only three-quarters even of Tory voters thought their Party 'ready to return to power', and a much lower proportion of those who did *not* vote Conservative thought so. Most Tory papers remained loyal to the cause, and *The Times*, which had deserted to Labour in 1964, now stayed on the fence and called for as many Liberals as possible to be elected. The increased market dominance of the pro-Labour *Daily Mirror* led to the CRD regularly including in its *Daily Notes* for Tory candidates items of 'sound sense from the *Daily Mirror*' to use

---

[25] Butler and King, *General Election of 1966*, 105, 130, 185; Fisher, *Macleod*, 281; Kenneth Young, *Sir Alec Douglas-Home* (1970), 238; Hutchinson, *Heath*, 167; Roth, *Heath*, 199; Campbell, *Heath*, 209.

in their speeches. The betting odds on a Conservative victory, which had been three to one at the start, had moved up to twenty to one by polling day, and even for a Labour landslide the odds were by then only two to one. The Tory press, themselves printing the polls that told this melancholy story, could not disguise their disappointment; the *Daily Mail* on 17 March found the Labour lead to be 'unprecedented, unnatural and absurd', and the *Daily Telegraph* on the 19th felt that 'for all the good it has done Mr. Wilson's critics it seems the General Election campaign need not have taken place'.[26]

In this context, the results on 31 March, and especially the more rural results on 1 April, were not as bad as had been feared. There was an unusually uniform swing to Labour of 3.5 per cent, and only eight constituencies in the whole country moved the other way. The Conservatives lost fifty-one seats and did not gain a single one (though there was a crumb of comfort in holding one of their 1964 gains against this tide of woe); of by-election changes since 1964, Leyton was regained by Labour; Tory casualties included Brooke, Thorneycroft, Soames, Redmayne, and Amery among current and former frontbenchers, and Chataway and Howe among the rising younger men. The major parties' share of seats in parliament almost exactly reversed the position in 1959, though so far had regional diversity and population movement affected local results that Labour now held eleven seats that Conservatives had held even in 1945, and the Conservatives hung on in such places as Jim Prior's Lowestoft that Labour had held until 1959. The overall Conservative vote had fallen only by about half a million, but this took it to a lower total, and a lower percentage, than at any time since 1945. Probably for the only time since 1945 more women voted Labour than Conservative, and there were disproportionate losses among the younger voters; among the crucial, and large, skilled working class (the C2s), the Conservatives now had less than a third of the vote. Retirements and the loss of seats not usually considered marginal had, as in 1945, the effect of clearing out a large part of the older generation of Tory MPs. After the election, only three-fifths of Tory MPs had served continuously even since 1959, and there were now only eleven who had sat in parliament before the 1945 Election. For his modernising thrust, Heath now had a much younger parliamentary party.[27]

Party organisation, 1964–70

Back in opposition for a full term from April 1966, the Party concentrated more attention on organisation, on completing the policy review at a less hectic pace, and on continuing the battle with Labour in parliament and in the country. Although there was no wholesale reconsideration of Party structure

---

[26] Butler and King, *General Election of 1966*, 97, 100, 108, 159, 160, 266–7; Ramsden, *Making of Conservative Party Policy*, 234.

[27] Butler and King, *General Election of 1966*, 206, 259–62, 265.

as in 1945–51, for the Lloyd Report as recently as 1963 had concluded that there did not need to be, the opportunity was taken to tighten up procedures and ensure that the organisation was in tune with modern approaches. The key figures in this were the Party Chairman, Edward du Cann, inherited by Heath from his predecessor, and Sir Michael Fraser, who had moved up after thirteen years as Director of the CRD to become Deputy Chairman of the Party in 1964, the first time a career professional had held such a post; he was now, as Robert Blake put it, 'a figure comparable only to Gorst under Disraeli or the famous Captain Middleton under Salisbury . . . the lynch pin of the organisation'. With the abolition of the posts of General Director and Chief Organisation Officer, Central Office now came under four directors of equal status, all reporting directly to Fraser and du Cann. Although the CRD remained in Old Queen Street, Fraser's appointment encouraged better coordination than had sometimes existed in the past, and the integration of the CPC into Central Office had a similar effect. Heath's personal involvement in policy-making brought closer together the Party machine and the shadow cabinet, with Fraser acting as secretary. A reorganisation also finally took place in Scotland, with the two old divisions based on Edinburgh and Glasgow abolished and five areas set up on the English and Welsh model; the previous divided management was replaced by a reformed Scottish Central Office, with its own research and publications departments, and, for the first time since 1912, the word 'Conservative' (rather than 'Unionist') appeared in the Party's title North of the border; despite proposals for better integration with Westminster, the Scottish organisation remained separate under its own Chairman (until 1977) and still seemed to the London organisers to be 'terribly feudal'. Only at this relatively late stage did Scottish Tories attempt a wide-ranging attack on local government, though the non-party tradition of supporting progressive, moderate, citizen and ratepayer groups was still entrenched and the debates in such places as Glasgow were a further cause of bad feeling. The idea of creating Fraser's new post, effectively a Managing Director for the Party, originated from Lord Poole, and the general effect of these and consequential appointments was to bring in a very young team; when appointed in 1964, Fraser was 49, Sewill who succeeded him at the CRD was 35, Howell only 29, and du Cann 40, the youngest Party Chairman since Davidson in 1926.[28]

Du Cann had been an imaginative choice for Chairman when Douglas-Home sent him to Central Office in 1964, for he had the youth and drive that the Leader lacked, and a business background that promised efficient management of the machine. It was by no means so good a choice when Heath took over in 1965; their public images duplicated rather than

---

[28]   Robert Blake, *The Conservative Party from Peel to Thatcher* (1985), 302; Rhodes James, *Ambitions and Realities*, 125–6; J.T. Ward, *The First Century: A History of Scottish Tory Organisation* (1982), 40–1, 43; Butler and King, *General Election of 1966*, 53–4, 59; D.E. Butler and Michael Pinto-Duschinsky, *The British General Election of 1970* (1971), 95, 100.

complemented each other, and they did not get on well personally – had not done so at least since they had both been at the Board of Trade and du Cann had wavered in his support for the abolition of RPM when the going got rough; the Chairman had also supported Maudling rather than Heath for Leader. Du Cann was though a difficult man to shift, for he had a programme of reforms he wanted to see through, and he was popular with the voluntary Party; he possessed all the charms that the Leader lacked and had more political guile too. For some time Heath sought a way to remove du Cann; press rumours at the 1966 Party Conference that du Cann was to be replaced brought protests from the National Union leaders and if there was such a plan it had to be abandoned. Eventually, with the Party riding high in Summer 1967, du Cann was ready to go, but even then he managed to block Heath's preferred successor, Lord Carrington, and Anthony Barber was chosen instead. Du Cann voluntarily left the front bench to return to the City, but was promised office in the next Tory Government. Their exchange of letters gives a glimpse of their working relations: du Cann's press release recounted his career to date (without even mentioning Heath except to say that he had confirmed du Cann as Party Chairman in 1965), and concluded that 'if I am asked again to accept any position in the Party after an interval of time, I shall be pleased to accept. For what counts with me is the cause'. Heath's press release was tersely factual and concentrated on the appointment of a successor, but he did also write a lengthy letter of thanks – which was tactful if not warm; in this he said that 'I look forward to the time when once again you will be in a position to resume additional responsibilities in our political activities', a phrase that du Cann picked up and repeated in his reply. In 1970 though, du Cann was not invited to join the Heath Government and became instead a dangerous critic. When a constituency wrote in to complain about the mismanagement of the handover and the damaging press reports of a rift, the new Chairman struck out of a reply drafted for Heath to sign the words that described such reports as 'wholly false in a suggestion made that there was ever a showdown between Mr. Du Cann and myself' – it was presumably no longer worth denying. Nevertheless, when du Cann left Central Office, the National Union and the National Society of Agents paid tributes that, as Butler and Pinto-Duschinsky put it, 'went far beyond the requirements of good form'. Du Cann's popularity with the National Union was an ominous sign for the Leader.[29]

All this semi-public manoeuvring between 1965 and 1967 obscured du Cann's achievements: he certainly ensured a more businesslike control of Party expenditure, but the unleashing of Ernest Marples on Central Office

[29] Lindsay and Harrington, *Conservative Party*, 253; Rhodes James, *Ambitions and Realities*, 132; Prior, *Balance of Power*, 43; Alexander and Watkins, *Making of the Prime Minister*, 85–6; NUEC, 2 Feb. 1967; Campbell, *Heath*, 215; Central Office Chairman's department file, CCO 20/63/1, Resignation of du Cann; Butler and Pinto-Duschinsky, *General Election of 1970*, 98, 100–1, 105, 285.

in a bid to make expenditure more cost-effective was a less successful idea; when Marples resigned from this task in early 1966 he made it clear that he did not really know what he had been expected to do. Substantial economies were made though in 1965. Du Cann was not afraid to pull punches in attacking Labour, and even came under attack from Conservative MPs for being too outspoken when the Party's *Weekly News* in January 1967 described Wilson as 'the man you cannot trust'; the National Union Executive waded in on du Cann's side and dismissed his critics as 'purely destructive and disloyal'. He was also determined in his attack on the Party itself; the Party now held only 22 parliamentary seats out of 122 in the cities run by autonomous city parties, and a review was at last put in train under Henry Brooke in 1965, but met resistance to any proposals to limit traditional autonomy; Brooke reported 'in some cases fairly entrenched inefficiency, in others a record of persistent sourness and friction'. He proposed to bring the cities into the fundraising sphere of the CBF, and to make their chief agents Deputy Area Agents (so bringing them into the Area and Central Office network). Apart from Bristol and Liverpool, which agreed to the proposals largely because of their own financial needs, resistance continued; Sir Frank Marshall of Leeds spoke darkly of proposals to take them over by the back door, but suggested that the city should pay its quota in future to get Central Office off its back. Another modernising scheme aimed at constituency parties as a whole. 'Project '67' aimed to use survey material to show local parties the social make-up of their electorates and to encourage them to adapt the membership of their own officers and committees to reflect more accurately their supporters; it was difficult though to achieve such changes for, as a Central Office official explained, 'in the constituencies in which the leaders were already representative, the campaign was unnecessary; where they were unrepresentative, they dug their heels in' and resented interference. At York, for example, where there was active and regular discussion of municipal politics but otherwise a concentration on the interrelated priorities of social events and funds, an Area proposal that they should start a CPC was firmly rejected on the grounds that 'there were other and more important jobs to be done'. The association did become more politicised, when Harvey Proctor's active branch of the Monday Club spilled over from the university to the city, but this was not quite what Area had had in mind. More generally, there was an advance of CPC activities in this opposition period; in 1967–68, for example, there was an addition of 800 to the total of Party literature subscribers.[30]

The cost of the 1963–64 campaign and of spending before and during the 1966 Election had raised expenditure well ahead of income, so that despite

[30]   Leeds CA, F and GP minutes, 23 Aug. and 26 Oct. 1967; Young, *Douglas-Home*, 240; *NCP* 1 Nov. 1965; Butler and King, *General Election of 1966*, 57; Central Office Chairman's department files, CCO 20/3/5 and 6, Project '67; York CA minutes, 20 May 1965, 24 Oct. 1966; NUEC, 5 Dec. 1968.

economies there was by 1967 an annual deficit and little in reserve. Du Cann had launched an appeal at the 1965 Party Conference, but on a fairly low key and with a target of only £300,000. More serious planning went into a major effort after the 1966 defeat through a new fundraising unit at Central Office. Lord Carrington agreed to spearhead this 1968 bid to raise £2 million, a large target insisted on by du Cann against Central Office advice, and it was attacked with the aid of consultants and the use of senior Party figures to work the regions; Selwyn Lloyd in the North West was one of those who spent eighteen months lunching with contributors and 'eating for the Party'. Labour's new law requiring companies to declare their political contributions may even have helped, for with an unpopular Labour Government in office, some of the Party's industrial backers were happy to seek the support of their shareholders for larger contributions than they might have previously agreed to in the privacy of the boardroom; the very fact of a shareholders' resolution could be a political bonus, as when the *Daily Telegraph* reported in 1968 the shareholders' endorsement of the view of the chairman of Rugby Portland Cement that a contribution to prevent Labour from staying in office to nationalise the industry was a wise investment. In planning the Party's appeal for the 1970 Election, the Treasurers had to take note of the fact that the stock exchange had already been so exceptionally generous to the Carrington appeal that its members could not be expected to cough up again. It was reported at the 1969 Party Conference that a total of £2.4 million had been raised in the appeal, just under £1 million of which came from constituency associations, the other three-fifths mainly from industry; expressed as a proportion of normal quota targets, the constituencies paid over 237 per cent in the appeal year, with all Areas reaching at least 180 per cent of the normal annual target and with six constituency associations from four different Areas each sending in over £10,000. Industry did even better; in the East Midlands, the appeal target of £72,000 was shared out so that constituencies were asked for £19,000 and industry for £53,000 (ten times the figure for a normal year), and when the CBF in due course raised a further £50,000 from industry in the Area a fifth of this also disappeared into the totals as if it were constituency money under the CBF credit system. The success of this appeal finally put some real money back into the reserves; overall the Party raised centrally about £5.6 million in the four financial years up to the 1970 Election, nearly half as much again as in the period leading to the 1964 contest, even with Poole's considerable talents then at work, and constituency contributions were now making up a larger share of the total.[31]

[31] Butler and Pinto-Duschinsky, *General Election of 1970*, 95, 97, 102–3; Lord Carrington, *Reflect on Things Past: The Memoirs of Lord Carrington* (1988), 257; National Union papers, NUA 2/2/33, Central Council reports; Central Office Chairman's department file, CCO 20/8/11, Correspondence with Heath; East Midlands Area GP minutes, 1 Dec. 1967, and EC minutes, 1 Feb. 1969; Michael Pinto-Duschinsky, *British Political Finance, 1830–1980* (1981), 138–9.

Du Cann also forced through a proposal to publish in the Conference handbook the actual quota payments by each constituency, a recognition that encouraged the good payers and shamed those with a poor record into at least doing something. He warned in 1966 that 'every night when I go to bed I say a particular prayer for those constituencies which most urge Central Office to do more and themselves contribute least when they could do so much', and he now carried out his threat to 'name some of them', in fact listing them all. Nevertheless, despite the overall success of fundraising, since there was still an annual deficit on normal operations, less was available for pre-election publicity spending in 1969–70 than had been spent in 1963–64. This information was now relatively open and available, for central Party accounts were published from 1967–68, a reform on which du Cann had again insisted, over-ruling internal advice. On this du Cann and Heath were at one; once the law required companies to reveal their political contributions, they agreed that there was more to be said for openness than for the traditional secrecy, not least because shareholders might reasonably demand to know what their money was being spent on.[32]

In the constituencies and Areas, despite staffing reductions in the Area offices carried out to reduce costs, the 1966 to 1970 period was in general a time of organisational growth and recovery, owing something to the encouragement and prodding of Central Office and its Area Agents, but owing much too to the simple fact that an unpopular Labour Government in itself produced new recruits and a greater willingness to work for the return of a Tory Government. A few examples must suffice, but are underpinned by the steady increase in the Party's local income, always a good index of numbers and activity. The High Peak association, which had been sliding into serious financial trouble in the Macmillan-Home period, now bounced back, paid off its deficit and started building up reserves. Harrow West had a similar surge of fundraising, and Ashford raised twice as much as was asked for in the Carrington appeal. Membership in Swindon almost tripled between 1967 and 1970. The Western Area undertook a major effort to build up CPC groups, and political activity in general, and managed to start fifty-four additional discussion groups and about thirty supper clubs. In Greater London, an Area where organisational decline had been most marked before 1964, there was a highly successful response to the Carrington appeal, and an increase in CPC activities; by May 1967, there were 113 discussion groups in the Area.[33]

---

32 Central Office file, CCO 4/10/72, Central Board of Finance.
33 High Peak CA minutes, various dates; Ashford CA minutes, 28 Jan. 1968; Harrow West CA minutes, various dates; Swindon CA minutes, 8 July 1970; Western Area Council, 27 July 1965 and 4 Feb. 1966; Greater London Area Council, 19 May 1967 and 1968–69 annual report.

Barber could be sure of a closer relationship with his Leader than du Cann had enjoyed and he focused Party publicity more directly on the promotion of Heath after 1967; James Margach thought that Barber was 'perfectly attuned for the type of leadership provided by Heath', and that he had steered the Party in the Heathite direction of youthfulness, energy and technocracy. He also devoted considerable attention to the particular needs of marginal constituencies. A tough-minded view was taken, with only Labour-held constituencies qualifying as critical seats for help in cash and in kind – Sir Harmar Nicholls with a majority of three votes at Peterborough was treated like any other Tory incumbent; sixty-four of the seventy seats listed as 'critical' were gained in 1970, though the average swing in these seats was actually slightly lower than the national average. Barber mellowed du Cann's reforming zeal and listened to the views of the constituencies; 'Project '67' was allowed to lapse, the enforced reform of the city parties was given up as a lost cause, and the shadow cabinet was regularly reminded that they must give the Party in the country more of their time. In most ways though the change of Chairman in 1967 made little difference to the organisational build-up, not least because Fraser remained in post, and (as Poole had done as deputy in 1957–59) took on under Barber more of the internal management of the Party to free the Chairman for the higher profile activities of constituency tours and speech-making. Investigations in 1965, by Macleod into the YCs and Lord Chelmer into the recruitment and remuneration of agents, provided recommendations that could be worked through the machine for the rest of the decade; the agents' salary scales, already increased in 1963, were raised substantially in 1965 and again in 1969; by the 1970 Election, the scale paid £1,080 on entry and rose to a maximum of £2,400, with additional 'marginal weighting' to take skilled agents into the critical contests; at the 1966 Election the Party had 499 professional agents in post and only 80 hopeless seats had to be looked after by trainees or volunteers. The campaign to revive YC numbers was temporarily successful in arresting the decline, but less so in marking any real change of direction. The approved list of parliamentary candidates was severely pruned in 1965, and then built up with new names of men and women more likely to be acceptable to the constituencies in a forward-looking way; du Cann explained that he wanted to attract 'a younger, more broadly based and more representative list of candidates', and the *Yorkshire Post* explained to its readers that 'once and for all the Party leaders are determined to lay the old school tie and family background look'. By November 1969, there were 569 names on the list, 76 of them former MPs who had lost their seats; about a quarter of all names had been removed since the 1966 General Election, and nearly 100 new ones added (about a third of those who had applied in that time); the South Angus chairman welcomed the parallel Scottish exercise, remarking that in 1966 'some of the candidates put forward at the election were just deplorable'. The allegation that Heath and du Cann were re-making the future parliamentary party in their own image was scarcely tenable, since the choice of actual candidates still lay with the constituency associations, but the determination with which this necessary but unpopular policy was carried through by Barber as well as du Cann did demonstrate strength of purpose in a modernising direction; management selection consultants were now used to advise on vetting methods, the first time that the nation's prospective governors had undergone the scientific evaluation that they expected of civil servants and army officers.[34]

There was a new awareness of the value of opinion polling to keep the Party in tune with the public's thinking, imported into Central Office by Fraser, who had convened his own 'Psephology Group' at the CRD since 1959. With the Party's encouragement, Humphrey Taylor of NOP set up his own organisation, which became the Opinion Research Centre (ORC), and had the Conservative Party as its first major client. The object of the programme of deep polling that ORC did for the Party was to find and analyse the 'target voters' that the Party would have to win over. The target electors were found to contain more women than men and more younger voters than old, to be only weakly interested in politics and more aware of personalities than policies, but rated housing as most important, and probably read the *Daily Mirror*. Over years of reinterviewing the large panel sample, the knowledge of their preferences deepened, and along with political scientists at this time, the Party's investigators began to understand that the electorate was actually far more volatile than the net voting patterns at General Elections appeared to indicate. It was now understood that a carefully contrived publicity campaign that used the results of such sophisticated polling might be able to influence a lot of voters. From about 1968, Geoffrey Tucker and the Party's publicity consultants were seeking to do exactly that. ORC's methods and close relationship with the Party offered a further benefit: they worked faster than most pollsters, and could deliver a survey on a Party broadcast to Central Office by midday after it had taken place. It was this speed of reaction that allowed ORC to reinterview its sample in the closing hours of the 1970 campaign and become the only poll to predict a Conservative win, but it may well only have been ORC's awareness that other evidence was encouraging the Party to think it was winning that provoked them to do the reinterviews in the first place; the flow of information went both ways. From 1966, the Party was spending about £30,000 a year on polling, and it was an important part of the organisational effort; Robert Worcester later felt that

[34] James Margach, 'Anthony Barber', in T. Stacey and R. St Oswald (eds), *Here Come the Tories* (1970), 61; Rhodes James, *Ambitions and Realities*, 124, 131–3; Alexander and Watkins, *Making of the Prime Minister*, 118; Butler and King, *General Electon of 1966*, 55, 59, 193; Butler and Pinto-Duschinsky, *General Election of 1970*, 97, 99, 101, 106–7; Roth, *Heath*, 201; Central Office Chairman's department file, CCO 20/48/1, Candidates; South Angus UA minutes, 9 May 1966.

the difference between the parties at this time was that Labour was operating blind, the Conservatives 'with 20–20 eyesight'.[35]

The opposition period provided another novelty in the organisation, in the first audible calls in years for the democratisation of the Party machinery. The Bow Group published a pamphlet, *Less Equal than Others*, which drew attention to the fact that there were only fifty women among the nine hundred on the approved candidates list, even on du Cann's new list, and called for an end to the practice of interviewing wives of candidates along with their husbands in selection procedures. The Greater London YCs, with some sympathetic backing from their President, Iain Macleod, went considerably further in publishing *Set the Party Free*, a trenchant call for democracy at all levels, including open selections and democratic control of the SACC; it argued provocatively that 'the Conservative Party appears to be organised and controlled by a tiny group of people with the object of maintaining that same group in power', and that the Party was 'patrician, hidebound and undemocratic'. The *Daily Telegraph* reported this as an aspect of the wider youth challenge to authority figures in the world of 1968–69, quoting Lynda Chalker as being 'determined to shake off the pin-stripes, bowlers and anyone-for-tennis image'; her husband Eric Chalker, around whom this libertarian movement in the YCs revolved, was also quoted as favouring the legalisation of cannabis. The Bow Group was propagating similar views, notably on the nature of the Party Conference; its chairman wrote in 1967 that 'each year we resolve that next year all will be different, but by Saturday we have succumbed to the euphoria that emanates from the Leader's Rally'. He wondered why the Party went to so much trouble to avoid disagreement, why the final clause of any motion selected for a Conference debate always 'converts it into an unopposable statement'. *Crossbow* offered strong support to the ideas that lay behind Project '67, quoting an Area agent as saying that

> I am often amazed at how little is spent [by constituency associations] on propaganda and political education. The active members of many associations are so busy in social and money-raising activities, that they are almost in despair, while members outside their ranks, and the public, are often unaware of what is going on, and frequently do not even know the location of the office or the name of the agent.

Such reformers were encouraged by the fact that Heath himself had been elected (if on a limited franchise) and by his determination to make the Party seem modern, but so far they represented only a narrow band of Party opinion. Some democratising changes were carried as a result of this new mood, as for example the introduction of ballots at Party Conferences if

---

[35] Lindsay and Harrington, *Conservative Party*, 244–5; Rhodes James, *Ambitions and Realities*, 126–30; Butler and King, *General Election of 1966*, 67; Robert Worcester, *British Public Opinion* (Oxford, 1991), 40–1.

enough members demanded them, and a technical rule change in 1969 which opened up the election of Area officers to wider competition. The prospect of further embarrassment over rule changes was warded off by the decision to set up under Lord Chelmer (former chairman of the National Union Executive, as Sir Eric Edwards, and now Party Treasurer) a committee charged with the task of making the Party structures both more political and more democratic, a committee that would report only with the General Election safely over.[36]

Powell's economic challenge

Party divisions, both private and public, were more common in the continuing policy debate. All too many of these divisions revolved around Enoch Powell, who had begun to preach his own distinctive economic doctrines after his departure from office in October 1963, and then moved on to develop highly personal views on defence, foreign policy and Europe, and above all on race, each of which moved him further away from Heath. It is much less clear that Powell's views distanced him from the man in the local Tory committee room, though the way in which they were articulated sometimes did so. There is the further danger that Powell's subsequent abandonment of his Party, and his later career as an Ulster Unionist, may tempt us to exaggerate his separateness from the Tory leaders at an earlier stage. It is therefore important to be aware that the initial divergence was on economic issues alone, and that Powell's economic views of 1963–65, for which the word 'Powellite' was coined, were supported by other frontbenchers at the time – and blazed a trail for much that the Party sought to do later; both 'Selsdon Man' and 'Finchley Woman' had their ancestors in 1965 in Wolverhampton. These speeches also made quite an impact on the Party; when St Marylebone Conservatives wanted Powell to address a constituency function in April 1966, they were told that he was too much in demand to be spared by Central Office for any but marginal seats.[37]

At first Powell's thrust tended to be defensive, an insistence that a country and a Conservative Party that lived predominantly by free enterprise should stop apologising for the fact. At Bridgnorth in May 1964, he argued that the 'nation lives by capitalism' and that his Party 'was engaged in a life-and-death struggle with political opponents who are pledged . . . at eliminating the processes of capitalism from our economy and our society. Yet the same nation and the same party will stop their ears and turn the other way if they hear mention of the very word capitalism; and even the various synonyms or euphemisms – "market economy", "free economy", "competitive private

---

[36] Oakley and Rose, *Political Year 1970*, 143; Patrick Seyd, 'Democracy within the Conservative Party', in *Government and Opposition*, vol. 10 (1975), 219; Central Office file, CCO 3/7/4, Bow Group; Charles Moore and Simon Heffer, *A Tory Seer: The Selected Journalism of T.E. Utley* (1989), 52; NUEC 5 Sept. 1969.

[37] St Marylebone CA minutes, 26 Apr. 1966.

enterprise", etc. – all share to a greater or less degree in the same denigration.' The post-war consensus around Labour's 1945 agenda obliged 'even a Tory Government to operate within the framework of an implicitly Socialist public opinion'. Not Powell though: he told journalists that 'when I am kneeling down in church, I think to myself how much we should thank God, the Holy Ghost, for the gift of capitalism'. Powell set out to free the debate from these one-sided assumptions and succeeded almost at once in opening up issues that had scarcely been articulated by a major national figure since 1945. This happened in part because, with his reputation for intellectual integrity already well-established, he could now seize public attention, in part because he was a compelling speaker whose arguments demanded answers even from the many who disagreed with his views, and because the publication of his speeches put them across to a wider audience; by 1970 there were three published volumes of Powell speeches, two biographies, and at least three books about his political influence; this extensive literature was matched by an equal readiness of the press to report and analyse his political interventions; he could be opposed but he could not be ignored. From the negative defence of capitalism, he moved on to a complete rejection of state intervention in the economy, dismissed as having produced no more provable results than had the belief in witchcraft. The 'state', which made these grand strategic interventions, was in fact

> a little group of fallible men in Whitehall, making guesses about the future, influenced by political pressures and partisan prejudices, and working on projections drawn from the past by a staff of economists. Of a 'national plan' thus produced we can assert three things with confidence: it is likely to be wrong, dead wrong, in its major assumptions; its errors will do the maximum damage because they will be imposed on the whole of the economy; and they will be persisted with long after they have been revealed, because governments are the slowest of all creatures to admit themselves mistaken.

Intervention was in fact impossibly inefficient, because it depended on knowing the unknown: 'who is to pick not only the industries, but the regions and the firms, in which earnings are to rise faster, and those in which they are to rise slower? It is unknowable – except by the test of supply and demand itself, the market, which . . . happens of its own accord.' Market forces would in the end anyway defeat all government plans because the market was 'irresistible'. Intervention was inflexible and conservative, for it would always seek to freeze the economic system it inherited, while the battle for prosperity demanded constant adaptation to a changing market; 'there is no past pattern of the distribution of employment in Great Britain which could have been "frozen" without economic loss or even disaster.' If Scotland needed more jobs, it should cut the prices of its products – and the wages paid to the Scots. The message was not only economic but political: 'the free enterprise system is the true counterpart of democracy; it is the only system which gives everyone a say'. The consequence of Powell's views was a dismissal by him of the NEDC and its offshoots (to him these 'little neddies' were Trojan horses within the walls of freedom), as of policies to reduce the price of land and houses, or the fixing by the state of incomes or prices.[38]

There were many Conservatives who felt that here at last was the anti-socialist prophet that they had been waiting for. Sir Keith Joseph wrote to *The Times* in 1967 to deny that his views were 'virtually *laissez-faire*' as the paper had reported, since he in fact favoured more extensive and if necessary more expensive social policies, but argued in the same letter for 'a much more vigorous private enterprise economy – with more rewards for success and more bankruptcies for failure', a view far closer to Powell's economic views than to Heath's. David Wood wrote in *The Times* in May 1964 that if Powell seemed 'more and more like a nineteenth century free trader in every speech he makes', yet he had 'given the trumpet blast for the attack, and charging behind him now are many of the ablest and most spirited of the younger Tories . . . certainly the lesson according to St. Enoch has been read eloquently inside [Heath's] study groups.' A few weeks later the *Sunday Times* felt that 'Enoch Powell, as he has always done, is skirmishing ahead of the main forces'; the main body would catch up in due course. When Powell's first book of speeches arrived later in the year, Macleod in the *Spectator* welcomed the contribution they were making to the Party: he praised Powell's mind as 'the best trained and the most exciting' in the Commons, and said that 'there is an attitude of mind which can be called "Powellism" and it is excellent that we now have the evidence collected in a book.' Macleod also followed one of Powell's lines of argument in calling not just for a 'property-owning democracy' but for a 'capital-owning democracy' too; surprisingly for a Party that included both Walker and du Cann on the front bench, men who had in their business careers practically invented the unit trust for small investors, there was no serious thinking about plans to widen share-ownership; even Macleod felt that it would be 'a pipe dream' until taxes had first been lowered. Not everyone was as complimentary to Powell as Macleod had been. Ian Gilmour argued that Powell was not a Conservative at all but a nineteenth-century Liberal; 'for the Conservative Party, which refused to espouse capitalism when she was at her classical and enticing best, to fall in love with her in 1964 would be sheer necrophilia'. Most crucially, Heath, for all his love of competition and his wish to reward success, would have nothing to do with economic 'Powellism': 'the Tory Party', he argued, 'has never been the Party of *laissez-faire*. It has always been the Party of order which enables people to live fruitfully in freedom.' He also made a series of speeches in 1965 that committed the Party to an interventionist regional policy that ran directly contrary to all that Powell was arguing for:

---

[38] Rhodes James, *Ambitions and Realities*, 175; John Wood (ed.), *A Nation Not Afraid: The Thinking of Enoch Powell* (1965), 3, 27, 88, 101, 110; Andrew Roth, *Enoch Powell, Tory Tribune* (1970), 305–6, 311.

'Conservatives realise that direction of public investment can play a large part in affecting industrial expansion'.[39]

Within the shadow cabinet, the person closest to Powell's economic views was Keith Joseph, already making connections with Margaret Thatcher too, and early in 1970 with Alfred Sherman; Joseph had links with LSE economists who had been influenced by monetarist theory, and immediately after the 1970 Election with Alan Walters; he was warmly reported in the *Daily Telegraph* for his anti-intervention speeches, which Tony Benn thought important enough to demand an answer. In view of the extent to which Joseph sometimes later claimed to have discovered market economics only in 1974, it is essential to emphasise the extent of his commitment before 1970. Writing before the 1970 Election, Michael Harrington of the *Telegraph* thought that since 1964 Joseph had moved entirely alongside Powell's free market opinions, and quoted remarkable evidence in support of that view. Joseph had espoused 'economic liberalism' of a nineteenth-century type, and as a result he 'frequently point[ed] out that private enterprise has not had conditions in which it could operate successfully at any time since the First World War'. Joseph was explicitly repudiating the interventionist policies on which the post-war consensus had rested: 'it is his conviction that these policies have failed to harness the full potential of the British economy. . . . The cause of this failure, in his view, is a misconception, by government, of the right relationship between the state and the economy'. In Joseph's view there should be

> more carrots and a bigger stick; which means lower taxes on incomes to stimulate enterprise and risk-taking, and a more intensely competitive environment to penalise the inefficient. He does not believe that the industries of the public sector should be treated as sacred cows, too precious to be exposed to the crude pressures of the market place.

Britain needed, in Joseph's own words, liberation from 'over-government, excessive demand, sloppy central finances, inadequate incentives, patchy competition, and virtually no sanctions against inefficiency and obstruction'. In assessing the development of Joseph's thought, it may well be concluded that he had moved entirely to a belief in market economics, but as with many others of that persuasion by 1970, like Geoffrey Howe, he did not yet accept the monetarist core of theory which was to be so important to him in 1974–75 and afterwards; in 1970 of course few British economists had made that discovery either.[40]

In view of the relative harmony with which the Heath Government

39 Morrison Halcrow, *Keith Joseph: A Single Mind* (1989), 40; Roth, *Powell*, 325–6, 328; Rhodes James, *Ambitions and Realities*, 122; Walker, *Staying Power*, 60–2; NCP 12 and 26 July and 1 Nov. 1965; Hugo Young, *One of Us: A Biography of Margaret Thatcher* (1989), 58.
40 Halcrow, *Joseph*, 37, 39, 42; Benn, *Out of the Wilderness*, 229; Michael Harrington, 'Sir Keith Joseph', in T. Stacey and R. St Oswald (eds), *Here Come the Tories*, (1970), 75–83; interview with Lord Howe.

operated after 1970, it is important to underline the extent and breadth of these disagreements in opposition, for to a large extent they were the fault-lines that were to occur in and after 1974. So for example on regional policy, the group chairman reported in December 1967, 'a somewhat bigger "split" in our ranks than we had anticipated between those who would give top priority to the region, and those who would give the priority to ensuring that there are no obstacles to growth in the "natural growth areas".' A month later he anticipated 'a fairly strong minority report from those who would not intervene in the economy at all'. The chairman in question was Fred Corfield, who would seek to implement one side of this policy divide as Industry Minister in 1970 and leave the Government when the other half came into the ascendant in 1972. The same openings were to be found on broad economic policy; in July 1966 and again in December, Edward Boyle was using his university contacts to set up seminars for shadow ministers to update them on economists' current thinking on planning and intervention. From within the CRD, Brian Reading, who would be a Heath adviser in office, thought indeed that the Party was giving too much attention to the anti-planners in his profession, and in 1965 Boyle himself had written of the danger that the Party would pay too much heed to the 'Jewkes-Seldon-Jack Wiseman group' who were, he thought trying to build a new anti-planning orthodoxy; John Biffen's *Daily Telegraph* article in March 1966, 'When the Planning has to Stop', followed up in *Crossbow* in April, showed that some Tory MPs took the opposite view. Finally, Joseph convened in early 1967 a two-evening 'seminar on the Paish thesis' (which argued that higher unemployment would be needed to achieve low inflation and higher productivity); this was precisely the approach that Macmillan had rejected out of hand as politically impossible in 1962, but which some shadow ministers now felt that they had to evaluate; in the event, the seminar was not a success, for Heath had another engagement that prevented him from attending, Macleod was in Australia, and Boyle in Sweden; it was significant that, apart from Anthony Barber, only Powell and Joseph found the time to come. These were not only differences recognisable by insiders and conducted in private, but quite visible to keen observers from the different tones in which public speeches were made; Richard Crossman had detected the Conservatives' fault-line on economic policy in 1966. In the Party intellectuals' *Swinton Journal* in 1968, Arthur Seldon drew attention to the similarity to Labour's policy approach of Maudling, Boyle, Boyd-Carpenter and their junior colleagues, but added that

> the outsider has some difficulty in reconciling their views with those of Powell, Joseph, Margaret Thatcher, Maude, Macmillan (the Younger), Howe, Biffen, Braine, Jenkin and others who offer a distinctive philosophy and distinctive principles. Conservatives speak with two voices.

With hindsight, Seldon's second list is a remarkable prefiguring of the post-1975 Party leadership. It was also in 1968 that Geoffrey Howe was recruited by his Institute for Economic Affairs (IEA) contacts into the Mont Pelerin Society, its international equivalent founded by Hayek; the Society's only other members who were also British Tory politicians have been Enoch Powell, John Biffen and Rhodes Boyson.[41]

Since this debate about principles went on throughout the six years in opposition, it is hardly surprising that on industrial and economic policy the Party spoke with an uncertain voice. Heath took the chair of the Economic Policy group himself, because of its sensitivity, but it mainly considered taxation policy; in March 1967, the group contained four shadow ministers – Heath, Boyle, Macleod and Maudling – together with Terence Higgins and Lord Harlech and six bankers, economists and tax experts from outside parliament. In April 1967, du Cann noted that the Party could not produce a pamphlet on economic policy, for progress in 'Ted's group' was 'not encouraging', and it was 'still some way from crystallising a distinctive policy, except in the tax field'. Much work was certainly done on the reconstruction of the tax system, but after the failure to press through with the wealth tax idea, it was difficult to see where additional income would come from to offset proposed reductions and planned expenditures. Each later idea for a new tax ran into the same sort of vested interest, and Sewill lamented to Macleod in 1968 that 'if we try to devise a tax system in which all sections of the community are little worse off or little better off than at present, then it must follow that we come back to virtually the present system'. Macleod was though determined to reduce taxes, by which he really meant the headline rate of income tax, and had given the clearest of pledges on this to the 1965 Party Conference: 'I say categorically to you that Conservatives will bring taxes down again. We did it before and we will do it again.' If Macleod had faltered, Powell was always on hand to press for action. While the Party was in Conference at Blackpool in 1968, Powell upstaged the front bench with a speech in nearby Morecambe in which he presented 'Enoch's budget' and explained how income tax could be reduced to 4/3d (21p) in the pound. His plans bore a striking resemblance to the policies Tory Chancellors pursued in the 1980s when a similar target was finally accepted, for much of Powell's tax reduction was to be paid for by wholesale denationalisation – except for 'leaving the mines and the railways nationalised, just for the moment, to show how unacademic and down to earth we can be'. By the end of the Parliament, the Party had detailed plans for replacing what Macleod called 'the general subsidy, soup kitchen world of socialism' with selective benefits, import levies instead of agricultural subsidies, lower

---

[41] Central Office Chairman's department file, CCO 20/8/10; Corfield to Boyle, 7 Dec. 1967 and 24 Jan. 1968, Boyle to shadow cabinet, 25 July 1966; Fraser to Boyle, 20 Dec. 1966, Reading to Boyle, 23 June 1967, Biffen to Boyle, 11 May 1966, Joseph to Boyle, Jan. 1967, and note of meeting, 7 Feb. 1967, Boyle MSS 23479, 23494, 22701, 22706, 22716, 24108, 24109, 23862, 23865, 23866; Howard, *Crossman Diaries*, 167; Arthur Seldon, *The State is Rolling Back* (1994), 46; Geoffrey Howe, *Conflict of Loyalty* (1994), 31.

public expenditure, and lower direct taxation. Increasingly work was done to prepare for the introduction of Value Added Tax (VAT), which would simultaneously move Britain a step towards readiness to enter Europe and provide a lot of income to allow the abolition of Labour's employment tax and the reduction of income tax. Macleod did not aim to match tax increases and tax reductions exactly, for like all shadow Chancellors, he relied on increased growth and the reduction of waste to bridge any gap. The determination to reduce taxation in itself involved some commitments at least to scale down Labour's economic interventionism; there was an early pledge to wind up the Industrial Reorganisation Corporation to save money.[42]

Macleod and Heath, who appeared on neither side in Arthur Seldon's two lists, were trying to steer a middle way between Maudling and Joseph. But the Party reaction when Labour renationalised the steel industry demonstrates how far that middle point of shadow cabinet thinking was from Powell and Joseph. Nearly five hundred amendments were put down to Labour's Bill, which gave the appearance of a spirited parliamentary opposition, but a quarter of these were either withdrawn or never moved. Barber, leading on the Bill, wanted to amend it to make it more acceptable to the industry, rather than letting it pass and promising repeal; he managed to persuade Labour to accept some of the Conservative arguments, and cooperated with its passage to the extent that no guillotine had to be applied. He promised only that a Tory Government would 'provide the maximum scope for competition and the maximum opportunity for those in the industry to exercise their commercial judgement and technical expertise', but added that 'there should be some measure of supervision'. Heath did not think denationalisation a course worth pursuing, particularly after this Act (unlike that of 1951) so scrambled the industry as to make the reconstitution of the private companies a difficult task; he anyway favoured a more interventionist Iron and Steel Board than had existed even under the Conservatives' 1953 Act. Constituency motions calling for denationalisation were not selected for debate at Party Conferences, and representatives were offered only motions promising 'a return to the principles and practices of competitive enterprise', without any hint of a change of ownership.[43]

Similar uncertainty arose when denationalising other industries was suggested; in December 1965, Powell supported plans for the denationalisation of the airlines, but confessed that his own favourite candidate was the Post Office, starting with the telephone services. In 1967, a policy group on nationalised industries was set up under the chairmanship of Nicholas Ridley. Since Ridley had been Powell's scrutineer in the 1965 leadership contest, his

---

[42] Ramsden, *Making of Conservative Party Policy*, 246; Fisher, *Macleod*, 292, 300; Anthony Lejeune (ed.), *Enoch Powell: Income Tax at 4/3 in the £* (1970), 25–38; NCP 31 May, 1 Nov. and 22 Nov.1965; Rhodes James, *Ambitions and Realities*, 136.
[43] Ovenden, *Politics of Steel*, 110, 114–16, 118, 171.

selection was either a pointer in a denationalising direction or just a way of keeping him occupied. Ridley took a more personal control of his group than most chairmen, drafted the report himself, and pressed for a bold policy. Brendon Sewill tried to head this off, urging that Maudling be advised of the group's thinking and the ACP kept informed; while he was careful to accept in writing to Ridley that 'all Conservatives naturally agree' with the group's 'assumption that denationalisation is right in principle', which was hardly true, he also stressed the economic difficulties that a Tory Cabinet would have to face, and hence the need for caution. Ridley himself described the group's policy to the ACP as 'a middle way between those who wished to do nothing about the nationalised industries and those who wished to denationalise them all' – a long way from where Heath thought the middle way to be – and it was agreed that the best way forward might be to pass a single enabling Act which would allow the 'BP solution' of private owners within the public sector to be introduced by ministerial order; this would also mean that no industries need be discussed by name in an election campaign. Powell then stirred the pot by making a speech calling for denationalisation, quoting back at Heath earlier speeches in which he had accepted the principle, but within weeks Heath had declared that large denationalisations were now impracticable; the report of Ridley's group was promptly leaked to the *Daily Mail*. Sewill's view in 1990 was that 'Ted Heath just put a veto on it. He wasn't prepared to consider it. He saw the whole of his policy exercise as improving the efficiency of the British economy and he thought that denationalisation . . . was purely playing politics; he wasn't prepared to do it, and that was that.' This part of the policy review therefore petered out with the approach of the 1970 Election, and no direct reference to its work was made either in the manifesto or in speeches. Ridley's memoirs claim that his recommendations were in the 1970 manifesto, 'suitably disguised', but if so the disguise was impenetrable. The few definite plans for denationalisation, such as the promise to sell off the Thomas Cook travel agency, were made by individual spokesmen in their own fields (in this case by the very *un*Powellite Peter Walker) rather than as an integrated policy across the board.[44]

Another uncertainty occasioned by Powell pervaded discussions of inflation and pay policy. Maudling was a continuing believer in the policy of pay restraint that he had pursued at the Treasury, but offset by Powell and Joseph who condemned such policies out of hand; shortly before the 1966 Election, Maudling and Powell made speeches in which each, without mentioning names, explicitly rejected the views of the other; Heath and Macleod, who had to hold the ring between these two positions, were handicapped by the

---

[44] Ramsden, *Making of Conservative Party Policy*, 260–2, 273; Roth, *Powell*, 318; Advisory Committee on Policy minutes [hereafter ACP] 17 July 1968; Nicholas Ridley, *My Style of Government* (1991), 3–4; ICBH witness seminar, 'Conservative Policy-making 1964–1970', in *Contemporary Record* vol. 3 no. 4, (1990), 35; Alexander and Watkins, *Making of the Prime Minister*, 103–4.

fact that neither had served at the Treasury and neither was an economist. Under pressure they moved towards Powell's views; *The Economist* reported in September 1965 that foreign visitors who had had private talks with Heath were worried to hear 'that he thinks all incomes policy is tosh, that he is a right-wing advocate of "keeping a curb on the money supply and then everything will be solved", that he is almost an old-fashioned Powellite'. In fact, the position Heath spelled out at Bolton on 15 January 1966 was very carefully worded: Labour's policies were failing and that failure would lead them inevitably into 'the introduction of compulsion on wage levels', which was 'a downward path leading to severe restrictions on individual freedom'. Exhortatory interventionism in pay and prices was to be condemned only if it failed, but compulsion was bad in itself. When in July 1966, the Labour Government introduced statutory powers to defer increases in prices and incomes pending investigations of their merits, in effect allowing time for public opinion to be mobilised, Heath, Maudling and Macleod had no rooted objection to the idea, seeing it as a version of the Conservatives' own policies pursued before 1964, but they met fierce opposition to this in the 1922 Committee. Fortunately for Party unity, Labour then made the new controls so extensive that the Conservatives could unitedly vote against them as a threat to freedom; Heath explained that 'compulsion is wrong and we want to move along a path of voluntary action, of consultation', exactly the ground taken by Robert Carr in opposing Labour's further extension of statutory controls in 1968. Heath himself in March 1968 said that compulsory controls were 'wrong in principle' but added mysteriously in the same speech that 'I am quite prepared for a tough incomes policy'. In 1967 Geoffrey Rippon was telling Cecil King that he had no real idea why the Conservatives were so opposed to Labour's policy, and Labour Ministers certainly thought, as Denis Healey put it in 1969, that the Conservative position was 'politically expedient on only the shortest view'. Lunching with King in March 1969, Maudling took much the same view.[45]

Heath used his chairmanship of the Economic Policy group to prevent much dissension breaking out – Joseph pointedly asked at a meeting in 1968 when the group would actually discuss economic policy – and official statements therefore tended to be stronger on optimism than reasoning. Even the sceptical Macleod was driven to argue in early 1970 that if the Government set an example by not encouraging inflationary pay settlements in the public sector, 'as the largest employer in the country', then 'the private sector will follow', which is exactly what had *not* happened either in 1962–64 or in 1964–66. In November 1969, Macleod was still writing privately to the CRD that 'one of the great problems is what we say about our economic policy'. Decisions

45 Fisher, *Macleod*, 276, 284, 302; Rhodes James, *Ambitions and Realities*, 137; Roth, *Heath*, 189; Heath, *Great Divide*, 3, 12; Lindsay and Harrington, *Conservative Party*, 251; Philip Norton, *Dissension in the House of Commons. 1945–1974* (1975), 292; King, *Diary*, 132, 239, 246.

about what to say were made in 1970 only under the imminent pressure of the General Election, and not very satisfactory ones even then.[46]

One consequence of the deadlock into which the Party fell over economic policy was that more emphasis had to be placed on curbing the trade unions, for that policy now had to provide the main Tory answer to the question 'what is your way of reducing inflation?' This placed on the policy a burden that it was not well-devised to sustain. As is shown by the exchange of minutes between Sewill and Heath in 1965 quoted above, it had been foreseen that this might happen. The Party had been keen to establish from the first that there must be a comprehensive piece of legislation, and that Tories would determine their policy on their own, uncommitted by anything Labour did in office. When Wilson set up the Donovan Royal Commission, Douglas-Home announced that his Party reserved the right to take action before it reported if the national interest required it. The first statement of Party policies came out in *Putting Britain Right Ahead* later that year, and the final package, *Fair Deal at Work*, was published in 1968 *before* the Donovan report. The original group under Lord Amory contained three former Ministers of Labour as well as Ray Mawby MP to speak for Tory trade unionists; it also contained one former and one future law officer, and the number of lawyers in the group increased as its detailed work progressed. The discussions assumed from the start a major change from all past practice, and it was rapidly decided that a new legal framework for all trade union activities must be established, policed by a Registrar and a special court. When Joseph became spokesman on industrial relations after Heath was elected Leader, he was anxious to establish that any pressure must be applied to the unions as organisations and not to their members as individuals, so that there could be no danger of creating martyrs; for the same reason the onus of invoking the law was shifted from the Government to the employer. Following Joseph as spokesman in 1967 was Robert Carr, by no stretch of the imagination a class warrior, and he was anxious to stress the benefits that would accrue to the unions from coming under a more defined legal status: for example, there would be an explicit right to belong to a union for the first time – as well as a right not to belong – and a 1965 plan to attack the political levy was now dropped as being too provocative. In Carr's view it was a balanced package in which the benefits to the unions and their members would offset objections to legal interference in their affairs: 'responsible, accountable but also stronger unions – that is the purpose'. The Party was not deterred by public declarations of hostility to the programme by the TUC; the view was taken, and confirmed in private meetings with union leaders, that they had to be seen to oppose the plans while the Conservatives were in opposition, but that if Heath were elected they would obey the law. Carr almost argued that the new laws would not need to be operated anyway, merely to be there as indications

---

[46] Central Office Chairman's department file, CCO 20/1/18, Correspondence with Macleod.

of what the community thought the unions should do, and a conditioning factor in the making of collective agreements. He certainly never envisaged the confrontational set-pieces that took place in 1971.[47]

In Spring 1969 it seemed that all this effort might have been wasted, when the Labour Cabinet produced its own trade union reform plans, which Heath opposed as not going far enough; Jim Prior later argued that by not backing Wilson (which would have embarrassed him enormously, and probably increased the damage in the Labour Party, but might also have enabled him to get his plans through), the Conservatives had missed an opportunity, and had done so 'to maximise our own short-term political advantage'. The fact that the 1922 Committee twice debated this tactical question of whether to back or oppose Wilson's 1969 proposals, suggests that backbenchers thought this a narrowly-balanced tactical decision at the time. There were others who wondered whether the TUC's defeat of Wilson might rather have damaged the Conservatives' own prospects of success: Whitelaw was saying prophetically in July 1969 that this would 'encourage the hotheads in the trade union movement and make the unions that much harder to deal with when the time comes'. Heath was more sanguine, continuing to argue that the trade unions would respect a mandate – he was indeed still arguing this in February 1974 despite four years of solid evidence to the contrary. Heath was far from alone in his view: Peter Jenkins' *The Battle of Downing Street*, after describing Wilson's humiliation by the unions, concluded in July 1970 that 'there is nothing I can see in the experience of the Labour Government which suggests that a Conservative Government need fail to carry through its programme'. All the opinion polls showed that a majority of electors, and even a majority of trade unionists, favoured the introduction of reforms, a preponderance that actually increased between Summer 1969 and the 1970 Election; if mandates ever mean anything, then the plans that the Tories had developed since 1965 did have a mandate in 1970. The small print conveyed a subtly-different message; CRD analyses of polls on industrial relations in 1968–69 confirmed that the Party was pushing at 'an open door for policy', with an electorate 'anxious for any measure of reform to improve industrial relations'. But the polls also indicated that 'the prevention of strikes', while an objective welcome to the public, came fifth – behind keeping down taxes, lowering prices, controlling immigration and achieving prosperity – in the public's own order of priorities. After 1970 when these desirable objectives came into collision, this was not always remembered.[48]

[47]   Phillip Whitehead, *The Writing on the Wall: Britain in the Seventies* (1985), 70; *NCP* 15 Mar. and 12 July 1965; Robert Taylor, *The Trade Union Question in British Politics: Government and Unions since 1945* (Oxford, 1993), 177–81, 183–4; Ramsden, *Making of Conservative Party Policy*, 243, 267; *NCP* 22 Nov. 1965; interview with Lord Carr.
[48]   Prior, *Balance of Power*, 48; 1922, 17 Apr. and 15 May 1969; Campbell, *Heath*, 230; King, *Diary*, 263; Peter Jenkins, *The Battle of Downing Street* (1970), xiv, 170; CRD briefs on opinion polls, Apr. 1968 and Apr. 1969, Boyle MSS 22756, 22761.

Europe, Rhodesia and immigration

Like trade union policy, most aspects of international affairs did not cause deep or public divisions within the Party. It was perhaps one of the most significant negative developments of these years that there was no real debate on Britain's relationship to Europe, with the result that by 1970 the Conservatives had been committed to a European future for Britain for eight years, and were not now likely to shift that position; even some committed 'antis' like Peter Walker now gave up their resistance, in his case borne down by Heath's patient persuasion and by the obvious trend of Brtitish trade away from the Commonwealth and towards Europe. A surprising wobbler at this late stage was Macleod, who toyed with the idea of a referendum on European entry as a device to unite the Party and the country, was persuaded out of this by Heath but came close to suggesting it again in the middle of the 1970 campaign. The 1969 Party Conference produced a strong anti-EEC demonstration, and only an equivocal speech by Douglas-Home in reply to the debate; there were enough hands raised to insist on a ballot, but this merely demonstrated that pro-Europeans outnumbered opponents by more than three to one. As this indicates, there were still many opponents of the EEC in the Party. In 1967 26 Tory MPs voted against Wilson's application to join, but the more important fact is that 216 Conservatives, including Powell and the entire front bench, voted with the Labour Government to apply, giving the largest majority in favour of entering Europe on any of Britain's three applications – the only time of the three that the Conservatives were in Opposition being the only time that the Opposition supported the Government. The Party also steered through a change in the agricultural support system against the suspicions of its farming supporters, another step towards readiness to enter the EEC. If other policy decisions may have been influenced by short-termism, Heath's commitment of his Party to Europe remained undeviating.[49]

If Europe was relatively straightforward under Heath, the Commonwealth remained difficult. At first no policy group was set up in this field, and Paul Williams of the Monday Club wrote to Heath in horror to say that 'this is typical of the worst of the current attitudes of the Tory Party'. When Heath wrote soothingly to tell Williams that policy groups were set up only where a new line of policy was felt to be needed, Williams replied sarcastically that 'if as you say "the general lines of Commonwealth Policy were firmly established and widely accepted in the Party" it would be very pleasant to know exactly what these general lines are, especially in trade matters'. A policy group was then set up in May 1965, but actually did very little. On international matters in general though, a number of Party announcements went down rather well with people like Williams, for example

---

[49] Norton, *Dissension*, 271; Prior, *Balance of Power*, 49–50, 86; Walker, *Staying Power*, 53; Young, *Douglas-Home*, 254; Oakley and Rose, *Political Year 1970*, 138.

Douglas-Home's promise to return troops to bases east of Suez when Labour withdrew them, and the equally immediate promise to resume arms sales to South Africa. But Conservative thinking on the Commonwealth was in any case overwhelmed in 1965 by the crisis over Rhodesia.[50]

The future position of Southern Rhodesia when the Central African Federation broke up and its other two components became independent under black nationalist governments in 1964 had been just held at bay by the Douglas-Home Government in 1964; formally, Rhodesia resumed its earlier status as a self-governing colony, but under a constitution that continued rule by the minority of white settlers organised behind the Rhodesia Front party. The British Government could not allow full independence under these circumstances, but neither could the Conservative right be brought to accept the subordination of 'our kith and kin' to black rule. After the 1964 change of government this became in theory Labour's problem, but in practice still racked the Conservatives, especially when the Rhodesian Government declared itself independent without the sanction of the British parliament in November 1965. The white settler problem which had bedevilled French politics in Algeria, but which had been carefully avoided in Kenya, now remained an open wound for Conservatives for fifteen years. Wilson's reaction to Rhodesian 'independence' was to stress conditions that must be met before Britain would recognise a Rhodesian Government, democratic tests that had been laid down by Douglas-Home when Prime Minister, though Wilson added a new condition that was almost impossible to meet, that any settlement must be acceptable to the Rhodesian people as a whole. Conservatives could generally go along with this response to an illegal act, even if the Monday Club were unhappy, but offence was given to a wider range of Tory opinion by the involvement of the United Nations in the case (which they regarded as simply an internal British and Commonwealth affair – and Tories still deeply distrusted the UN after its policy in the Congo), and by the policy of sanctions adopted to bring pressure on the Rhodesian regime. It was clear even before the Unilateral Declaration of Independence (UDI) that there would be trouble in the Party. In October 1965, at the Party Conference, an emergency motion was moved by Selwyn Lloyd, recognising the close ties between Britain and Rhodesia in the past and urging settlement of the conflict by agreement rather than by force; an amendment by Lord Salisbury to deplore the use of 'penal sanctions' was helpfully ruled out of order by the Conference chairman, a decision that provoked much vocal resistance in the hall. Even so staunch a supporter of decolonisation as Macleod was unhappy with the Labour Government's policy; he drew a sharp distinction between sanctions that naturally followed an illegal act, such as the freezing of assets, and such 'penal sanctions' as a UN oil embargo which would have to be backed by force. Trapped between a left wing that wanted him to oppose the white

---

[50] Ramsden, *Making of Conservative Party Policy*, 247; Young, *Douglas-Home*, 241, 244.

Rhodesians and a right that wanted him to oppose Wilson, Heath took this middle course and opposed only 'punitive' sanctions, though these were the only ones likely to bring a renewal of negotiations. Whitelaw regarded this as 'not in itself a particularly honourable or logical position, but it was the only means of preserving party unity'. Selwyn Lloyd was sent to Central Africa to try to influence opinion there, being careful to have no official contact with a regime that the Party did not recognise; he came back just before the 1966 Election urging the reopening of talks, a position around which Conservatives could rally; later in the same year Macleod was arguing that it must be possible to settle the matter by a compromise, and when Wilson's attempt to do so in 1967 failed, Conservatives tended to blame the Prime Minister as much as the Rhodesians.[51]

The flashpoint came each year with the parliamentary order to impose, and subsequently to continue, oil sanctions against Rhodesia. In December 1965, the Opposition officially abstained, but thirty-one Tory MPs voted with the Labour Government and fifty against, a damaging three-way split and a rare upset for Whitelaw's careful whipping of the parliamentary party. In the Lords, Salisbury was fighting his last battle, but Carrington persuaded the peers to abstain rather than vote against sanctions, mainly on the tactical ground that the Government would not be able to ignore a defeat in the Lords on this sensitive issue, which would thus provoke a constitutional crisis in which the House's powers would be further reduced. A year later the moderate Maudling was put up in the Commons to argue that the Government had erred in bringing in the UN, and that since this would prevent any settlement by compromise the Opposition would now vote against the Government's policy; one or two Conservative speakers deviated from this stance in debate but none voted against the Party line and only two abstained. For the Party Conference in 1969, there were eighteen motions on Rhodesia, only the one from the Conservative students supporting sanctions. In the following month in the Commons, with further compromise attempts having failed, the Opposition were again officially abstaining, but this time twenty-seven Conservatives voted against. By then, Douglas-Home had practically given up all hope that Britain could influence Rhodesia's future anyway, but he officially reserved the position of a future Tory Government to act in any way it thought appropriate.[52]

Conflict over black and white in Africa ran alongside conflict over the same issue at home. Labour's reaction to the race issue in the 1964 Election, and to its own embarrassment in having now to support entry controls that it had bitterly opposed only two years earlier, was to introduce legislation

51 Lord Home, *The Way the Wind Blows* (1976), 223, 252; *NCP* 1 Nov. 1965; Fisher, *Macleod*, 273–4; William Whitelaw, *The Whitelaw Memoirs* (1989), 58–60; Thorpe, *Lloyd*, 399–402; Roth, *Heath*, 192; King, *Diary*, 95.
52 Norton, *Dissension*, 255–6, 261–2, 362–3; National Union papers, NUA 2/2/33, Central Council reports; Carrington, *Reflect on Things Past*, 205; Young, *Douglas-Home*, 246.

to outlaw racial discrimination and machinery to encourage good relations between the races in Britain. Conservatives were divided in response to this initiative, but followed the lead of Thorneycroft as home affairs spokesman, when he supported conciliation but opposed criminal sanctions. The work of the Tory study group had concentrated entirely on the need for further entry controls, and the Party's 1966 manifesto had little to say about race relations. The Party's refusal to welcome Labour's Race Relations Acts led to Humphry Berkeley MP leaving the Conservative Party altogether, but not until after he had lost his seat in 1966; even at the time of the passage of the mild 1965 Act, Joseph departed from the whip to abstain rather than vote against. It would have been relatively straightforward for the Party to adopt a positive stance for, as Hogg pointed out, the 1965 Act was in many ways a natural progression from the Public Order Act of 1936 which Conservatives in the National Government had pushed through against Mosley's anti-semitism. Under Boyle's chairmanship, the ACP then agreed in July 1967 to back Hogg's support for amendments to make the 1965 Act more effective; he received tough-minded backing from Angus Maude who warned members that there was 'a stark choice between making integration effective or sending the coloured minority back to the countries from which they or their parents came; but a policy which failed to do either would be disastrous'.[53]

Although Powell still took no prominent part in these debates, he had by now embraced a firm attitude to the issue. He detested the 1965 Bill as another piece of Government interference with private freedoms; the *Birmingham Post* reported that when Thorneycroft was speaking against the Bill, 'at his side, righteous, eloquent, fearless, sits Mr. Enoch Powell, nodding approval of every forceful word Mr. Thorneycroft lets drop'. The defeat of Powell's fellow-West Midlander Thorneycroft at the 1966 Election and his replacement as shadow spokesman by the more liberal Quintin Hogg certainly widened the gap between Powell and the leadership on what was to be the issue on which they finally parted company, but it is unlikely that Heath and Powell could ever have remained colleagues for much longer. Despite the fact that neither derived from traditional Tory backgrounds, Powell and Heath had little understanding of each other and hardly any mutual respect. Andrew Roth argued in 1970 that

> both were anti-Establishment, but Powell preferred to fight it from the outside, while Heath preferred to infiltrate it. The contrast of their speech was evidence of this: Powell's speech was straight Birmingham, Heath had put a 'posh' top dressing on his native Kent coast.

On race, Powell increasingly believed that establishment Conservatives like Hogg, and indeed Heath too if he had become an establishment Tory, had

---

[53] Roth, *Powell*, 323; Rhodes James, *Ambitions and Realities*, 157; Halcrow, *Joseph*, 41; Lord Hailsham, *The Door Wherein I Went* (1975), 231; ACP, 5 July 1967.

no instinctive comprehension of what Conservative voters thought in the West Midlands; Hogg and Heath conversely felt that Powell was ignoring the politician's duty to lead as well as to represent opinion. A discussion between the two when Heath became Leader and moved Powell from the Transport portfolio to Defence only ensured that each thought that they had agreed different things; and even then Powell calmly refused Heath's offer to arrange the usual service briefings for defence spokesmen. A few months later, Powell's speech questioning whether Britain should still have troops in the Far East outraged Heath, even though it had been cleared in advance with the foreign policy spokesmen who had raised no objection. The size of the gap between them was demonstrated by a trivial incident in 1967; when Black Rod appeared in the middle of a Commons debate on the EEC to summon MPs to witness a royal assent ceremony, Heath was sure that such 'nonsenses' must be ended; Powell, appalled by such a cavalier reaction to centuries of tradition, only provoked Heath to the more extreme declaration that people were tired of ceremonial mummeries when they interfered with getting things done. Neither could begin to understand why or how the other took such a different view. While sticking to the letter of shadow cabinet rules, and subordinating his policy doubts on Europe (on which Heath would certainly have brooked no hesitations), Powell managed to speak on several issues that were not his responsibility. Almost alone in the Party he questioned whether it was the Government's business to reform the trade unions, or whether the policy should have anything to do with economic management. Heath and other frontbenchers were becoming steadily more concerned by Powell's speeches on race, for example one delivered at Walsall in February 1968. Patrick Cosgrave, in his admiring biography of Powell, conceded that between 1966 and 1968, 'in no ordinary sense of the word . . . could Powell be called a good colleague. His interpretation of his duty, exact and honourable as it was, was at least gnomic, if not even Jesuitical'. It was possibly more even than that, for Powell was quoted in the *Sunday Times*, at the start of April 1968, saying that, 'I deliberately include at least one startling assertion in every speech in order to attract enough attention to give me a power base within the Conservative Party. Provided I keep this going, Ted Heath can never sack me from the shadow cabinet.' It was increasingly unclear by then though how Powell saw himself using this accumulating power base in the Party for, as Bernard Levin later pointed out, he was growing 'more and more deeply into the realisation that he could not in good conscience take office in a Conservative Government pledged, and even intending, to follow the paths of State economic interventionism'. Perhaps the Birmingham speech of April 1968 was an unconscious attempt to break out of this dilemma?[54]

54 Roth, *Powell*, 323, 336, 342, 349; Roth, *Heath*, 188, 203; Alexander and Watkins, *Making of the Prime Minister*, 80–1, 83; Rhodes James, *Ambitions and Realities*, 179; Campbell, *Heath*, 240; Levin, *Pendulum Years*, 169.

The catalyst came with the prospective expulsion from Kenya of large numbers of Asians who under current law would have the right to settle in Britain. Powell and Duncan Sandys had helped to whip up feeling about this at the 1967 Party Conference, and Labour's failure to solve the difficulty in talks with the Kenyan Government produced a crisis in the following February; a Commons motion put down by five privy councillors forced the Government into a rushed change of the law to stop a large migration from Kenya. The Bill was rushed through parliament with the Opposition's backing, but fourteen Conservative MPs led by Iain Macleod voted against it; Macleod also told Sandys through the columns of the *Spectator* that he at least would vote to carry out pledges given in Sandys' own Kenyan constitution. No disciplinary action was taken against the rebels.[55]

So far, so good – or so bad – depending on the viewpoint, but Wilson now had to appease his own left-wing with a new Race Relations Bill that went much further than that of 1965 in invoking the law to enforce changes in attitudes. Officially, the Conservatives did not oppose this Bill, but in practice, because hopes of getting amendments during its passage were frustrated by two left wing Tories at committee stage, the Party once again split three ways, and unity was not aided by a petulant speech by Hogg ('when I was subjected to hostile barracking by some of the right wingers') which ensured votes against as well as for the Bill at third reading, just what Whitelaw had been striving to avoid. This was again not just a backbench fight; Macleod was among the rebels, as were eight future members of the 1979 Thatcher Cabinet, three more of whom abstained; on the very evening of Powell's Birmingham speech, Boyle was dining with prospective rebels on the left of the Party to coordinate tactics, his invited guests including Michael Heseltine, John Hunt, Norman St. John Stevas and Nigel Fisher; Keith Stainton also looked to Boyle for a lead and Max Maddan MP urged him to 'persuade Quintin to stick to the party line – no 2nd class citizens'. After Boyle had led the abstainers in the debate, Sir Charles Taylor MP and Stainton both urged him not to resign from the shadow cabinet, as 'you represent there a viewpoint which would otherwise be extinguished'; Boyle's reply to such advice was that 'I don't intend to resign from the Shadow Cabinet (& hope (with some confidence) not to be asked to do so!)'.[56]

By this final stage of the Race Relations Bill, the Powell issue had finally exploded. The shadow cabinet had had extreme difficulty in deciding how

[55] Enoch Powell, *Reflections: Selected Writings and Speeches of Enoch Powell* (1992), 157; Whitelaw, *Memoirs*, 63; Fisher, *Maudling*, 296.

[56] Alexander and Watkins, *Making of the Prime Minister*, 95–7; Hailsham, *Door Wherein I Went*, 231, 234; Fisher, *Macleod*, 297; Lindsay and Harrington, *Conservative Party*, 257; Norton, *Dissension*, 281, 289, 299; Rhodes James, *Ambitions and Realities*, 164; dinner arrangements, 20 Apr. 1968, Stainton to Boyle, 18 Apr. 1968, and reply, 21 Apr. 968, Taylor to Boyle, 30 Apr. 1968, Madden to Boyle, 24 Apr. 1968, Boyle MSS, 7296, 24130, 24132, 7303, 24131.

to vote on the Bill's second reading, and had agreed a reasoned amendment, using a form of words to which Powell assented, in Hogg's phrase, 'with a face like a sphynx'. On this basis, it was hoped to avoid a split, and Heath had so far committed himself to the tactic that he had written an article for a Sunday newspaper to be published on 21 April, explaining the reasoning behind it. That partly explains his own extreme anger when Powell's speech to the West Midlands CPC at Birmingham on Saturday 20 April rocked the boat so violently. Powell's speech contained two separate explosive elements; first, by quoting extensively from letters received from constituents, Powell used (and appeared therefore to condone) language about race that was neither polite nor parliamentary, but which was widespread among the Party's supporters; second, he made extensive use of an official statistic that seemed to show that the immigrant-descended population would rise to over 3 million in a generation, a figure that was bound to seem scaremongering when contrasted with official estimates. A further cause of offence was the fact that the speech was circulated through the Area press officer rather than through Central Office, a practice by no means unusual for provincial events but easily giving rise to the belief that Powell had deliberately avoided warning his colleagues in advance of their seeing the speech on television; as Alexander and Watkins pointed out, it was stark evidence of the different viewpoints held on immigration in Birmingham and in Westminster that no Area official thought it necessary to tip off his Central Office or National Union superior. Powell has always maintained that 'neither in making the speech, nor in any of the circumstances attendant upon it, did I neglect or break any of the rules or conventions which govern honourable behaviour between colleagues'. John Campbell observed of this claim that, 'as always with Powell, there is a certain formal plausibility in his defence, but also a transparent disingenuousness'. Whatever the intention, the text of the speech was widely distributed to the press (four separate copies reaching the Wolverhampton *Express and Star* to ensure that it was not spiked by an unsympathetic reporter) and a television crew was waiting to film its delivery, while Powell's shadow colleagues had to react to questions before seeing the text. If a feeling of betrayal was one reason for the extreme reaction to Powell's speech, the language he adopted was certainly another. Although he never used the phrase 'rivers of blood' with which the speech has been associated ever since (and later argued that one of only two changes he would have made in the speech with the benefit of hindsight was to deliver that particular passage in Latin), it was the language and the lack of restraint in the speech's content that provoked reactions – both for and against. Heath stopped just short of calling Powell a racialist, but he told the *Daily Express* that 'most people will admit it was inflammatory talk'; the official form of words, incorporated in a draft letter to constituency chairman from Heath himself, and used by Barber when speaking to the National Union, was that Powell's speech had been 'racialist in tone, and likely to exacerbate racial tension'. Powell was thereby acquitted by his colleagues only of the intention to do harm and not of the effect.[57]

Within hours of seeing the speech on television, several shadow colleagues had rung Heath to demand Powell's sacking; Hogg and probably others too would have resigned if Powell had not been removed. There is no reason to think that Heath needed encouragement, and the delay before Powell was sacked was due more to the need to ensure that all shadow ministers had been consulted, and to the delay in contacting Powell in Wolverhampton (where he was not on the telephone), than to any hesitation on Heath's part. When the shadow cabinet met it firmly backed Heath's decision; *The Times* loftily declared that 'in dismissing Mr. Powell, Mr. Heath takes the known risk of having Mr. Powell as an enemy that, fortunately, is less grave than having Mr. Powell as a colleague.' The Party as a whole was less sure, not least because the immediate action taken against Powell could be all too easily contrasted with Heath's easy tolerance of dissent from Boyle, Carr, Joseph and Macleod on the liberal side of the same argument. Sir Gerald Nabarro for example was fond of raising at the 1922 Committee the tolerance given to Boyle's conscience on race issues. Acknowledging from Boyle a copy of a resolution from Durham University Conservatives in May congratulating him on his liberal stance, Anthony Barber added a postscript saying that 'you will not be surprised to know that I have received one or two motions supporting Enoch!'[58]

The immediate aftermath of Powell's sacking was indeed a wave of support for him and his views, demonstrated in opinion polls, in an avalanche of correspondence which the Commons mail room could scarcely handle, in support marches from Smithfield meat porters and dockers – and from many in the rank and file of the Tory Party. Central Office received 105 calls on the subject on the day after Powell was sacked, 'all supporting Powell' (as the file note puts it). Heath had 7,000 letters, mostly protesting against his actions and Central Office also had a large delivery of hostile mail, while Powell's own was overwhelmingly favourable; a letter to constituency chairmen, explaining Heath's side of the case, was (as Barber told Heath's own agent, who had written to complain about the lack of guidance from the centre) 'ready, stuffed and franked' but was then abandoned when soundings among MPs convinced Central Office that it would do more harm than good. Angus Maude spoke up for Powell at his own constituency association, and Margaret Thatcher's association backed Powell and deplored Heath's action. Maudling felt a fortnight after the Birmingham speech that Powell was probably preferred

[57] Lord Hailsham, *A Sparrow's Flight: Memoirs* (1990), 369; Rhodes James, *Ambitions and Realities*, 181–4; Alexander and Watkins, *Making of the Prime Minister*, 92–3; Roth, *Powell*, 350; Powell, *Reflections*, 172; Campbell, *Heath*, 243; Central Office file, CCO 4/10/142, Immigration.

[58] Hailsham, *Door Wherein I Went*, 235; Prior, *Balance of Power*, 52; Whitelaw, *Memoirs*, 64–5; Roth, *Heath*, 205; 1922, 25 Apr. 1968'; Barber to Boyle, 23 May 1968, Boyle MSS 22590.

to Heath as Leader by a third of Tory MPs, perhaps an exaggeration but an indication of the impact Powell had made even on a Tory that heartily disagreed with his views; some Labour MPs began to fear even that the surge of public support could sweep Powell into power. In August Macleod told Cecil King that he was 'alarmed by Enoch Powell and all that, and deplore[d] the rising tide of racialism in this country'. In September, T.E. Utley in the *Sunday Telegraph* argued that through his sacking, 'in parliament [Powell's] position has on balance been weakened. In the country, it has been improved to a positively revolutionary extent.' When the National Union Executive discussed Powell's sacking shortly after the event, it resolved unanimously to endorse Heath's action, but five members then voted against a resolution to issue a press release saying so. By the next meeting the Executive had received eleven constituency resolutions backing Powell against Heath, all from constituencies in southern England; three of these had been unanimous and in the committees of the other eight constituencies 288 votes had been cast for Powell against 56 for Heath; many more constituencies all over the country took similar decisions but did not send them in. A step further up the hierarchy where there was always more loyalty to the leadership, both the East Midlands and Wessex Areas backed Heath with unanimous resolutions, but in the South East the chairman argued that there was nothing wrong with what Powell had said, only with his tone of voice, and added that the speech had served a useful purpose anyway in telling the Government what ordinary people thought on the subject; the Area YCs were said to be 'ferociously' hostile to Powell's sacking, while other members present denounced his speech as unacceptably racialist.[59]

For the Party Conference in October, more considered resolutions from Bridgwater, Crosby, Ilford and Newark formally backed Powell against Heath, and many more called for a Powellite policy without mentioning the man himself. In the months that followed the Birmingham speech, it was clear then that Powell had mobilised a constituency of support that went far beyond that attracted personally by any other post-war politician, but he was at the same time regarded with loathing by most of the liberal establishment and by many leaders even on the right. Lord Boyd, previously Alan Lennox-Boyd and Macmillan's first Colonial Secretary, resigned as patron of the Monday Club when it endorsed Powell's Birmingham speech, 'which I think personally was outrageous and intemperate, and with the tone of which I profoundly disagree'. When Powell came out against British entry to Europe, now allowing free rein to doubts he had stifled while on the front bench,

---

59 Central Office file, CCO 500/32/11, Leader's correspondence on immigration; Central Office Chairman's department file, CCO 20/8/12; Campbell, *Heath*, 244–5; Hutchinson, *Heath*, 193; Roth, *Heath*, 205; King, *Diary*, 192, 204, 208, 264; Rhodes James, *Ambitions and Realities*, 193; Moore and Heffer, *A Tory Seer*, 33; NUEC, 2 May and 27 June 1968; South East Area Council, 10 May 1968.

Labour anti-marketeers refused to share public platforms with him despite his acknowledged drawing power. His later activities continued this paradox, for he rarely debated race issues in parliament, preferring to take the defence of his position on to the public platform. When he spoke on immigration at the 1968 Party Conference, there was a huge roar of approval for the announcement of his name, mingled with boos, but in July 1969, the Chief Whip felt that Powell's backers now amounted to only 'about twenty-eight' MPs, a figure that makes it sound as if the whips had been counting fairly closely. After his sacking, Powell still had admirers on the front bench, mainly those who were dismayed that his sacking for a speech on immigration had deprived them of a spokesman for an economic position that they increasingly favoured. Keith Joseph went out of his way in January 1969 to say how much he admired Powell personally, and Geoffrey Howe, also thinking about economics rather than race, told readers of the *Daily Telegraph*, that 'most Conservatives would agree that if Mr. Powell did not exist then it would be necessary to invent him'. On television in December 1968, Nicholas Ridley compared Powell to de Gaulle as a man who might be called back from the wilderness to save the country. Sir Alec even planned to pay a tribute to Powell in the midst of the 1970 Election campaign until persuaded not to do so by Heath, but he did tell Powell in 1971 that he hoped he would go on making speeches on immigration 'because that is so vitally important and you are so right about it'.[60]

Faced with this pressure, Heath did move his position on immigration closer to Powell's, though without conceding an inch either to Powell the man or to the arguments he had advanced. In September 1968, Heath announced that the Party would remove all remaining special privileges from Commonwealth migrants and treat them in the same way as aliens, and that there would also be tighter restrictions on the entry of dependants. Even this shift did not prevent criticism of the Leader from Powell's supporters in the Party; in October 1969 the Party's immigration policy, by then including proposals for repatriation which Powell had demanded, was backed by the Party Conference only by 1349 votes to 954; since there were about 4,000 representatives entitled to vote, it could be argued that well under half had voted for the Leader's policy (or that only a quarter had voted against it – but the actual margin was uncomfortably close). Some who approved of the policies feared the consequences; the Derby Conservatives, fairly right wing on immigration matters, nevertheless noted in January 1970 that 'it would seem that we had lost a certain amount of confidence with the immigrants', which was only partly due to local circumstances. The fear of a drift to the right was certainly current on the Party's opposite wing. PEST complained

---

[60] National Union papers, NUA 2/2/32, Central Council reports; Central Office Chairman's department file, CCO 20/43/4, Monday Club; Alexander and Watkins, *Making of the Prime Minister*, 101, 104, 193; Roth, *Powell*, 360, 379; Young, *Douglas-Home*, 239; Powell, *Reflections*, 19, 153; Howe, *Conflict of Loyalty*, 38.

in November 1968 when Central Office circulated a Powell speech on race; the Party Chairman agreed that 'some passages in the speech were anathema to me personally', but pointed out that Powell was still a Conservative MP, that he had personally provided Central Office with 200 copies of the text, and that they had merely added it to a general mailing, so that no Party money was involved. More generally, PEST's Cambridge chairman felt in January 1969 that

> progressive Conservatism is going through a phase in which it is out of favour with the Party at large. The influence of so-called 'Powellism' has been growing strongly in the past few months, and we know that many MPs of our persuasion and thinking have been having some difficulty with the Party, particularly in their constituencies, The success of the Monday Club in the constituencies has concerned us greatly.

Heath continued to insist that any repatriation of immigrants would be voluntary and to denounce Powell's language and tone, describing a Powell speech in January 1970 as 'an example of man's inhumanity to man, which is absolutely intolerable in a Christian, civilised society'. He was not the only one who felt angry; in 1969 a private brief by a CRD desk officer on Powell reported that the latest speech contained no very new line of argument and that in general Powell produced 'a sensational effect by the tendentious presentation of selected factual material'. Powell could be denounced both in public or in private, but he still could not be ignored; on the eve of the 1970 General Election, a poll of listeners to the BBC's *World at One* radio programme made Harold Wilson 'Man of the Decade' for the 1960s, but Powell came second – ahead of President Kennedy, Pope John XXIII and Martin Luther King; Heath, well down the field, was not even ahead of the Rhodesian rebel leader Ian Smith. But then, as Roy Jenkins put it, Powell spoke in a language of 'demogogic colloquialism', which is something of which no one ever thought Heath to be guilty.[61]

'Selsdon Man'

The sense that Powell's support on immigration indicated a wider swing to the right owed quite a bit to the work of the Monday Club, which had increased both its profile and its membership in the Opposition years; by 1964 it still had only 140 members, but by 1970 there were 2,000, including 17 MPs, a number that rose to 30 (including 3 Ministers) after the 1970 Election. In 1971, the chairman claimed 10,000 members (probably rather hopefully), and the Club also had by then an office in Westminster and a substantial

---

61 Campbell, *Heath*, 245–6; Rhodes James, *Ambitions and Realities*, 208–11; Derby CA minutes, 13 Jan. 1970; Central Office file, CCO 3/7/43, PEST; Chairman of Cambridge PEST to Boyle, Jan. 1969, CRD brief by John McDonnell, 11 June 1969, Boyle MSS 24410, 22745; Norman Shrapnel, *The Seventies* (1980), 86.

budget; its membership was predominantly young, overwhelmingly male and well educated (three-quarters having degrees). Unlike the Bow Group, whose influence it was to an extent trying to counter, but which concentrated its activities on London-based intellectuals, the Monday Club sought to extend its influence into constituency associations and through them to put pressure on MPs. Also unlike the Bow Group, it expanded without Central Office sympathy; when asked to provide office space for the Club in November 1964, the General Director's reply had been 'Not bloody likely!' There was a reiterated claim by the Club that it was being discriminated against by the official Party, as for example when the Bow Group, but not the Monday Club, was invited to send an observer to the YC national committee, and when few if any Monday Clubbers were included in Heath's policy groups. Complaints actually flowed both ways, for Party loyalists were often deeply upset to receive literature claiming that the Club was the only repository of true Conservatism and that the rest had been led astray by 'pseudo-intellectuals of the new Socialist fringe'. The Club gained some Party support for its regular demands for 'more vigorous' opposition to the Labour Government, and now at least efforts had to be made to keep the Party in touch. Heath agreed to attend the Club's annual dinner in 1967, but luckily missed the same event in 1968 when the toast was to 'the Conservative Party coupled with the name of Enoch Powell', and thereafter Heath gave it a wide berth. In October 1969 the Club launched a 'Powell for Premier' campaign. Nigel Fisher in Surbiton was one of the liberal Tories to be given a difficult time by his association because of the Club's local activities, but Macleod and Hogg both leapt to his defence, the 1922 Committee demonstrated its support by electing him to its Executive for the first time, and the Party Chairman visited the association to demonstrate his support. The battle went on though, with local members determining to put up a 'Powell Conservative' candidate after the official association readopted Fisher; attempts were made to get Powell to declare his backing for Fisher as the official candidate, though when Fisher read Powell's own 1970 election address he decided he would rather not have his backing anyway; the unofficial candidate duly stood against Fisher in 1970 but got only 5 per cent of the vote while Fisher increased his majority.[62]

The chief casualty of right-wing attacks was Edward Boyle, not because of pressure from his Birmingham Handsworth constituency association (which there certainly was), but because the right were able to block his future prospects. A hostile member of the 1922 Executive remarked in 1968 that 'opposition since 1966 seems to have been one long sterile debate about

[62] Patrick Seyd, 'Factionalism within the Conservative Party: The Monday Club', in *Government and Opposition*, vol. 7 (1972), 464; Rhodes James, *Ambitions and Realities*, 188, 199, 201, 205–7, 213; Butler and King, *General Election of 1966*, 205; Butler and Pinto-Duschinsky, *General Election of 1970*, 296; Central Office Chairman's department files, CCO 20/43/1 and 4, Monday Club; Alexander and Watkins, *Making of the Prime Minister*, 97.

Sir Edward Boyle'. Boyle espoused *all* the causes that the right disliked – comprehensive education, Rhodesian sanctions, race relations legislation, an end to capital punishment, and Roy Jenkins' liberalising reforms at the Home Office. He was also not a man to disguise his views under pressure of hostile opinions, and Heath seems hardly to have asked him to do so. In September 1968, for example, with the Powell furore only just past its height, Boyle caused offence to the Party's right wingers by being photographed along with the Labour Minister responsible for race relations, wearing Asian costume at a Sikh community event; this produced a formidable hate mail and a public denunciation by Duncan Sandys. Boyle's opponents would have been beside themselves with rage had they known that he had even helped Harold Wilson with material for a speech on race that he had delivered in Birmingham in May in response to Powell. After several years shadowing education, a job he had already done in office, Boyle seems to have become exasperated; Heath would not sack a man he admired but might well not be able to promote him to a higher post in government, and in 1969 Boyle gave up politics to become a Vice Chancellor. His replacement as education spokesman, Margaret Thatcher, was much more to the taste of the right, but the policy on schooling did not change.[63]

New parliamentary candidates of the rising generation were also likely to be on the right; Cecil Parkinson and Norman Tebbit, both first elected in 1970, 'regarded socialism as a scourge and the failure of the Conservative governments of 1951–64 to reverse the Attlee experiment as deplorable', as Parkinson's memoirs recall their mood at that time. Earlier in the Parliament, Central Office had tried to keep on terms with the Monday Club, through occasional meetings of Club officers with the Party Chairman, and in 1969 Douglas-Home told the Club's annual dinner that 'the best government is the least government', a splendidly Powellite phrase which the Party's elder statesman now quoted to them approvingly. In 1968–9, the publications of the Club on immigration heralded a definite drift in Powell's direction that produced several resignations and a yet more extreme profile. The fact that the 1969 Party Conference required three ballots, all called for by opponents of the platform from the right, indicated the strength of Club support in the constituencies. In the years 1967 to 1969 there was an upsurge in Powellite – or what Mike Wilson classified as 'Libertarian (Right)' – motions coming up from the constituencies to the Annual Conference; three-quarters of all motions on the subject fell into this classification, ten times as many as could be classified as 'Collectivist (Left)'. A manifestation of the same drift of politics was the election of right-wing officers by parliamentary committees,

---

[63] Constituent to Boyle, 25 May 1968, critical letters and cuttings, Sept. 1968, Wilson to Boyle, 6 May 1968, Boyle MSS, 7325, 7430, 7311; Michael Pinto-Duschinsky, 'The Role of Constituency Associations in the Conservative Party', D.Phil. thesis, Oxford University, 1972, 293–6; John Vaizey, 'Edward Boyle', in his *In Breach of Promise* (1984), 125–6.

for example Ronald Bell on Education. Heath appreciated that his language, if not generally his policy preferences, had to be shifted to recognise the new direction; when asked by a friend in 1970, 'Are you moving to the right?', he replied, 'Just a bit – but we have to stay in the centre'. This was a dangerous ambiguity, but when a Conservative agent inadvertently embarrassed the Party by saying that there was little to choose between Conservative and National Front policy, Heath's reaction was positively sphinx-like: his PPS wrote to an enquirer that 'Mr. Heath has no precise knowledge of the policies of the National Front but they are in important ways different from those of the Conservative Party'.[64]

There is a danger of exaggerating this resurgence of right-wing opinions; for as Reginald Maudling pointed out when describing 1966–70 in his memoirs, parties in opposition do tend to revert towards their own particular extreme and it rarely indicates much about what they will actually do in office; the Monday Club's membership of about 2,000 at the end of the 1960s was to prove to be the pinnacle of its strength, not the launching pad for a further period of growth. Between 1964 and 1970, with the Rhodesian issue surfacing annually, with race relations legislation added to the immigration question, with the Powell bomb ticking away and finally exploding in 1968, and with the Monday Club active at the grass-roots, Heath had more trouble than Tory leaders have usually had with opinion on the right, but it was still rather a matter of a vocal minority than a take-over of the party by extremists.[65]

The event that appeared to contradict this verdict – but most misleadingly of all – was the Selsdon conference at the end of January 1970, described by *The Political Year* as 'a brilliant piece of window-dressing'. It had had no such intention though, originating in the CRD as a working policy week-end rather than as any form of public display. There had been policy conferences each Autumn since 1966 at Swinton College, but North Yorkshire was a long way from London if a full turnout of the shadow cabinet was to be achieved and earlier week-ends had anyway been larger gatherings at which backbench MPs and other policy group members had also been given the right to be heard. With the Election due Maudling decided to cancel 1969's policy week-end and not to plan one in 1970; the view was that there was now no need to *discuss* policy but only to get final decisions on priorities. For this reason, James Douglas of the CRD reported that 'Brendon [Sewill] and I have a sinister notion which is to incarcerate the Shadow Cabinet for a week-end where they can really concentrate free from distraction on their policy and strategy for the next Election. Swinton would be the ideal place

---

[64] Cecil Parkinson, *Right at the Centre* (1992), 97; Young, *Douglas-Home*, 265; Central Office file, CCO 3/7/33, Monday Club; M. Wilson, 'Grass Roots Conservatism: Motions to the Party Conference', in N. Nugent and R. King (eds), *The British Right* (1977), 90; Oakley and Rose, *Political Year 1970*, 134, 143; Campbell, *Heath*, 236; Whitehead, *Writing on the Wall*, 40; Central Office Chairman's department file, CCO 20/73/2, National Front.

[65] Reginald Maudling, *Memoirs* (1978), 141; Rupert Morris, *Tories: From Village Hall to Westminster* (1991), 105.

for this, but . . . it will be far from easy to sell the idea.' Officers in the CRD were anxious to get guidance before the drafting of the manifesto went much further, for they were uncomfortably aware that the policies already agreed would add up to a tough package; Geoffrey Block of the CRD wrote in January 1970 that

> this is no doubt our policy, but it is not the sort of manifesto with which we can win a General Election. . . . Few people read manifestoes, but those who do have not been accustomed to being told this sort of economic realism at election times for years. One may almost say therefore that we will have to win the next general election in spite of, rather than with the aid of, our manifesto.

The objective was then not to make policy, but, as Sewill put it, to confront shadow ministers with the policies that they had already agreed piecemeal and ask, 'Are you with it?' If the answers were yes, then the decks could be cleared for the election. Selsdon was meant to be a retreat rather than a photo-opportunity. The Selsdon Park Hotel on the outskirts of South London was chosen simply as a convenient location near to frontbenchers' London homes, and the weekend of 30 January 1970 chosen because planning for an election could not now be much longer delayed.[66]

This working session, a 'Chequers week-end' in Heath's government-minded phrase, then became a public relations event by accident, for when Heath addressed members of the press, gathered outside the hotel at Saturday lunchtime – the last moment at which a story could hit the Sunday papers – law and order had been the only major issue so far settled; even this had been a low-key discussion in the context of an overall manifesto draft, and some of those present could not later recall discussing the issue at all. Following Macleod's advice that law and order was always worth a headline, Heath therefore spoke to the press about law and order, and it was reported widely that this would be the Party's key election theme – which in fact it was not, and had never been intended to be.[67]

Extensive plans had been made to keep the real story of Selsdon running through the following week's newspapers, with a stream of press releases on different issues. This in itself was a success quite out of scale with the thousand pounds that the weekend event had cost; on 2 February, an ORC snap survey found that half of the electorate was already aware of the meeting, 'an enormous achievement'; two fifths of the electorate knew that the Party had discussed tax reductions, slightly more even than those who knew that law and order was a Party objective. However, it was not anything the Conservatives did or the press said that made the Selsdon week-end matter in the longer term, but Harold Wilson's reaction to it. Speaking at Nottingham

66 Oakley and Rose, *Political Year 1970*, 141; Ramsden, *Making of Conservative Party Policy*, 275–6; Prior, *Balance of Power*, 58.
67 Walker, *Staying Power*, 52.

on 6 February, by which time press releases had described the full range of what had been agreed by the shadow cabinet, Wilson launched a blistering attack on what he saw as 'not just a lurch to the Right. It is an atavistic desire to reverse the course of twenty-five years of social revolution. What they are planning is a wanton, calculated and deliberate return to greater inequality. The new Conservative slogan is: Back to the free for all.' Wilson's view was encapsulated in the phrase 'Selsdon Man' that he applied to Heathite Conservatism; this suggested both that the Conservatives had reverted to a sort of pre-civilised state of mankind (as in 'Piltdown man'), and that they now spoke only for the South-Eastern, suburban middle class. Wilson's belief that he could immediately start to fight the coming election as 'a vigorous counter-attack based on rousing people's fears about Tory policy', as Barbara Castle put it in her diary, was to boomerang; as Whitelaw suggested to Cecil King in March, 'Wilson's present plan . . . to run the election campaign on the basis of rip-roaring abuse of the Tories . . . may rally the faithful, but will certainly not bring in the doubters'. And by his reaction to Selsdon, Wilson gave the Conservatives the appearance of a Party with a theme around which all their policies were grouped, exactly what they had had so much difficulty in establishing for themselves since 1965. He also publicised Tory policies that opinion polls were to show to have considerable appeal to the electorate. From Selsdon through to the June Election, the Conservatives were able to keep this impetus going. Butler and Pinto-Duschinsky pointed out later in the year that the policies decided at Selsdon and then carried over to the manifesto 'were not new, most of them having been adopted as early as 1965. But this was the first time that they had started to enter the consciousness of the general public.'[68]

As a new candidate, Norman Tebbit was clear that 'the Selsdon declaration . . . marked the Tory Party's first repudiation of the post-war Butskellite consensus', which was 'music to the ears of radical Conservatives like myself'. If, as John Campbell has suggested, Heath never quite believed in the anti-statist rhetoric that he used in 1970, and was adopting it to keep his Party together, then it is not surprising that younger and more right-wing Tories like Tebbit should have felt so betrayed by subsequent events; Campbell's defence of Heath against the charge that he switched course in 1972 opens Heath instead to the much deadlier criticism that he did not believe in what he said to get elected in 1970. There is surely much truth in Robert Blake's verdict that Heath in 1970 and Thatcher in 1979 had a very great deal in common, and that 'both leaders were ideologists in a sense that none of their four post-war predecessors were. The key to the leadership crisis of 1975 does not lie in Heath's programme before 1970, but in his performance

---

[68] Central Office file, CCO 500/2/24, Central Employment of Agents; Rhodes James, *Ambitions and Realities*, 220; Castle, *Diaries*, 383; Butler and Pinto-Duschinsky, *General Election of 1970*, 129–30; King, *Diary*, 316.

afterwards.' In fact. Heath's 'ideological approach' in 1970 was always firmly rooted in down-to-earth practicality rather than pure theory, and to that extent – without being just pragmatically reactive – he was always likely to modify it in office, and rarely attempted to hide the fact.[69]

On one central issue, there was still only a paper-thin cover over a deep disagreement. Joseph's speeches on industrial policy early in 1970 reopened this division, earning him the reputation of the Conservatives' new wild man of the right; as Morrison Halcrow puts it, 'whatever effect he had on [Labour], he did tend to terrify his own side'. With Labour's adoption of statutory controls, the Tories had already committed themselves unequivocally against the sanctions that Wilson had needed to make Labour's pay policy stick. Not until the early months of 1970 did the Conservative Opposition decide what they would themselves do when back in office. At Selsdon, the consensus was overwhelmingly for the rejection of Wilson's interventionist methods; Peter Walker recorded that when Macleod suggested the dismantling of Labour's state control apparatus, only Maudling, Boyle and Walker himself spoke in dissent. The problem was that agreeing to remove machinery did not constitute an alternative policy. The CRD paper calling for decisions to be made on how the Conservatives would keep down pay and price inflation was placed at the end of the agenda for Selsdon and never adequately discussed. The Party could not agree on what it would do, but it could not avoid a decision about what it would say, and once again Iain Macleod's bridge-player's skill in the finesse united the shadow cabinet. Walker has recorded in his memoirs just how that agreement was made. Macleod,

> said that I and others were quite right in one respect. We might have to have an incomes policy, but to explain in a manifesto that you might have to do it in certain circumstances was grey. Manifestoes had to be black or white. Either we said we were going to have an incomes policy and it would be superb or that we would not have one at all. We should say we were not going to have one and if a few years on we changed our minds we would have to explain there were special circumstances. As far as the manifesto was concerned, it should not be blurred. No 'ifs' or 'buts'. Everybody said he was right and so it got into the manifesto.

This debate seems unlikely to have been at Selsdon, not least because it does not appear in the verbatim transcript of the meeting, but others have confirmed the essential accuracy of Walker's account of the way in which the issue was resolved, and Macleod's role in squaring the circle.[70]

Introducing the Party's 1970 manifesto, Heath certainly followed Macleod's advice and went well out on to a limb, with serious consequences for his later credibility. He told journalists that 'we have always been opposed to

---

69 Norman Tebbit, *Upwardly Mobile* (1989), 120; Campbell, *Heath*, 264–6; Blake, *Conservative Party from Peel to Thatcher*, 301.
70 Halcrow, *Joseph*, 43, Walker; *Upwardly Mobile*, 52; LCC papers, 1970; interviews with Lord Carr, Lord Barber and Sir Edward Heath.

compulsory wage control. We opposed it through the House, when the Bill was going through, and we are opposed to it and we will not introduce it. And we believe moreover that these last few years have shown that as a policy it was wrong and a failure.' There was no preparation of any fall-back positions in that declaration, and it was unfortunate that when in 1972 the Heath Government decided that it had to have a statutory incomes policy, Macleod was no longer available to explain to the public what it was that had changed, and generally to advise on tactics. The strategic problem created at once by Macleod's tactical solution in 1970 was that inflation gradually became the centrepiece of the Party's attack on the Labour Government, and the pledge not to have statutory controls was repeated under a harsher and harsher spotlight as the Election campaign progressed; at the press conference on the manifesto, while arguing that to him the key choice at the election was between styles of government, Heath nevertheless added that 'if you are asking for particular topics which are going to be discussed most of all in the election, there's no doubt that probably prices and inflation is going to be the one'. The final issue of *Notes on Current Politics* before the Election was entirely devoted to 'The price explosion: 1964 £ now worth 15s 7d' [78p]; the one page out of fourteen that referred to Conservative policy was on the Party's record before 1964. The CRD's final report on the Election put on record all the occasions in the past four years on which decisions about an anti-inflation policy had not been taken, and concluded that 'this did not . . . prevent us from developing the cost of living as our main election issue, although our credibility was always a bit shaky'. In 1989, Brendon Sewill, more outspokenly, felt that 'we went into the 1970 election totally unprepared on what was going to be the crucial issue . . . I was very unhappy . . . with the enormous advertising campaign about the shopping basket and how the party was going to bring down the cost of living without any clue how we were actually going to do it. In fact most of our policies were designed to put it up.'[71]

The 1970 General Election

Expectations for the next Election had shifted considerably since 1966, but the deep troubles that beset the Labour Government had for most of the period encouraged the belief that Heath was bound to win. From Autumn 1966, his Party led in the opinion polls continuously until 1970, often by margins of over 20 per cent. In local government elections Conservatives did spectacularly well between 1967 and 1969, taking control of the GLC, nearly all the London boroughs, and by the end of the Parliament most of

---

[71] Ramsden, *Making of Conservative Party Policy*, 277; ICBH witness seminar, *Contemporary Record* vol. 3, no. 3. February 1990; *NCP*, 29 May 1970.

the other local authorities too. Yorkshire Tories celebrated in 1968 the fact that they controlled Sheffield for the first time in forty years and Huddersfield for the first time in a century, and had had 'phenomenal results' in the other cities and boroughs. In parliamentary by-elections, there was another tale of Conservative success, often with big increases in the Tory vote as well as defections from Labour: the average swing in all thirty-seven by-elections of the 1966 Parliament was 12 per cent, a swing to the Opposition exceeded by then only in the wartime period which had foretold the landslide of 1945. Conservatives were naturally much encouraged, with four gains from Labour in 1967, five in 1968 and three more in 1969, the peak coming with a swing to Conservative of over 20 per cent at Dudley in March 1968. Kenneth Baker, who gained Acton in that month with a swing almost as large, knew that the campaigning circumstances were in his favour: 'George Brown, the Deputy Leader of the Labour Party, launched the Labour campaign in Acton but during its course he resigned. Roy Jenkins, the Chancellor of the Exchequer, introduced a budget which raised taxes by the prodigious sum of £900 million. There was a run on the pound and . . . all the banks closed for three days. With that background any Tory candidate would have won Acton.' Similarly, ORC, who were commissioned to do a special report on each by-election constituency ahead of the campaign, pointed out in the case of Swindon in 1969 how encouraging it was that one in three of their sample had spontaneously complained about the Labour Government's record on inflation. With such favourable conditions, it was not hard to generate a strong campaign; Baker was an unusually able by-election candidate, most of the frontbench spoke in Acton, there was a team of seven professional agents running his campaign, and a mass of mutual aid from all over Greater London. It cannot be proved that any of this made much difference; on the same day, the Party also won Meriden with a comparable swing, after a campaign in which the local association had been divided, the candidate unimpressive and neither the agent nor the local chairman on top of their jobs (to judge from reports to Central Office).[72]

However they occurred though, these victories did much to keep up morale; the Upminster chairman for example spoke in February 1967 of the accumulating electoral evidence that the public had turned back to the Conservatives, and in Burton a few weeks later there was satisfaction that 'the Conservative Party is very much back in the electorate's popularity'; Crossman thought that the 1967 GLC result was most important as 'a fillip to the Tories and a strengthener for Heath's leadership'. By-election gains could therefore be used to offset continuing attacks on the Leader; in

[72] David McKie, 'By-Elections of the Wilson Government', in Chris Cook and John Ramsden (eds), *By-Elections in British Politics* (1973), 223–53; Yorkshire Area Council, 10 May 1968; Cook and Ramsden, *By-Elections*, 384–5, 389; Kenneth Baker, *The Turbulent Years: My Life in Politics* (1993), 27; Central Office by-election files, CCO 500/18/111, 500/18/68 and 69.

Denbigh in October 1968, the association chairman used recent results to dissuade his association from passing a resolution against Heath and inviting Powell to address them. The only ominous news on the electoral front came with the first substantial upsurge of nationalism in Scotland and Wales; only Labour seats fell to Nationalists at by-elections, but in local government polls Scottish Unionists were as vulnerable as Labour councillors. After the Scottish National Party (SNP) took Hamilton in November 1967, the Conservatives as well as Labour took fright; an emergency meeting was held at Heath's flat to work out a reaction and campaigning in Scotland was immediately stepped up, with several visits by Heath to Scotland planned for 1968; the Scottish Tories themselves had already set up the Thistle Group, a ginger group intended to make the Party more responsive to Scottish interests. Sir Alec Douglas-Home was put in charge of a constitutional committee to suggest ways in which decisions could be devolved from London to Edinburgh; it was not though easy to mobilise support for any one of the many possible constitutional solutions; after Douglas-Home's committee reported, the Scottish chairman reported that seven adopted candidates and seven sitting Tory MPs in Scotland were strongly opposed to the recommendations, one reason why no action followed in government. The urgency of the constitutional review faltered as this first Nationalist tide ebbed in 1969, but the Douglas-Home committee did suggest an elected Scottish 'convention' with limited legislative powers. In 1970, the Party published a separate Scottish manifesto to demonstrate its new concern with opinion north of the border. In view of the relatively small number of Scottish Tory and Welsh MPs, this issue did not affect overall expectations; in November 1969, Whitelaw spoke of 'the virtual certainty that the Conservatives will win the election'.[73]

The problem with a tide of Conservative popularity deriving largely from the Labour Government's extreme *un*popularity was that it was always difficult to foresee how far changing economic circumstances and the approach of the Election would restore Labour's vote. Private Conservative polls even in 1967–68 did not encourage any belief in an inevitable landslide. Nevertheless, the speed and scale of the turnabout in public opinion in 1969–70 certainly did take Conservatives by surprise. In Autumn 1969, the Conservatives' poll lead fell dramatically, and was by the end of the year down to 2 or 3 per cent; it then recovered somewhat, and November 1969 by-elections anyway indicated a weaker Labour position than opinion polls, but there was never again a secure Tory lead. In Spring 1970, the Labour recovery re-started and, in April for the first time in nearly four years, a poll

---

[73] Upminster branch minutes, 20 Feb. 1967; Burton upon Trent CA minutes, 9 June 1967; Howard, *Crossman Diaries*, 343; Denbigh CA minutes, 16 Oct. 1968; Vernon Bogdanor, 'Devolution', in Layton-Henry (ed.), *Conservative Party Politics*, 80; Ramsden, *Making of Conservative Party Policy*, 265; LCC papers, 1970; Young, *Douglas-Home*, 266–7; King, *Diary*, 292.

reported a Labour lead. In April too, the county election results still gave evidence of a strong Conservative performance, but May's borough elections were less encouraging and 352 seats gained in 1967 were lost – though 1,000 of the Party's 1967 gains were held. The problem during such volatile swings of opinion was to know which baseline to choose; analysed sceptically, the 1970 local results contained evidence of the continuing strength of Conservative voting, for the Party had elected far more councillors than Labour, even in May in the boroughs; in the highly politicised county boroughs, for which continuous records of voting had been kept by Central Office, the Tory share of the vote in May 1970 far exceeded that of 1964 which had preceded a very close General Election. But the suddenness of the reversal of fortunes was so breathtaking as to sweep away all such calculations, and, since opinion polls fuelled expectations as well as reporting them, the trend was self-reinforcing; in January, 57 per cent expected a Tory win, but this had fallen to 21 per cent by mid-May when the Election was called and to only 14 per cent by polling day.[74]

Conservatives were shaken by this reversal; Douglas Hurd, working in Heath's private office, noted of the May results that 'all this casts a gloom'. At the shadow cabinet on 11 May, the Chief Whip reported that he was worried about collapsing morale in the Party, and two days later the Party Chairman conceded that 'the recent trend against the Conservatives in the polls had moved more swiftly than anyone had anticipated'. James Margach told *Sunday Times* readers on 17 May that 'I have never seen a party plunged more suddenly and irrationally into black despair as happened to the Conservatives the other night when the Gallup poll figures showed Labour ahead by an astonishing 7.5 per cent. Suddenly groups of bewildered Tory MPs formed in the lobbies and elsewhere in the precincts, stunned and shaken by the news.' The junior trade spokesman Sir John Eden acknowledged that 'when a lead which we have held for three years appears to have vanished in three weeks for no clear reason at all, it is hardly surprising that we are reeling a bit'. At the Scottish Tory Conference over the same week-end, Sir Alec cheered up one member with the reflection that 'in Scotland swings are less than in England, so at least we won't do so badly up here', but bleakly told another that 'in the Conservative Party we always do our best with our backs to the wall. And all I can say is that it's a damned great wall we're up against now.' Macleod felt that defeat was unavoidable; 'We'll go out and have a bloody good fight – but I am worried about Ted', presumably expecting him to be challenged by Powell for the leadership if he lost the Election. Heath was in fact in defiant mood; he told a meeting of Tory MPs on 13 May that 'we've been in worse corners than this before and we've fought our way out before', a message that did much to cheer up those present and set the tone for Heath's defiance of the

---

74 Fisher, *Macleod*, 300; Butler and Pinto-Duschinsky, *General Election of 1970*, 136, 165; LCC papers, 1970; Central Office file, CCO 4/10/193–4, local elections.

poll evidence throughout the campaign. The Election was called on 18 May, with polling fixed for 18 June.[75]

Since the Parliament was in its final year and speculation about a dissolution had been rife once Labour regained a lead, preparations were well advanced. A planning committee had been sitting since early 1969, and had commissioned a theme tune, a 'set' to be used as a backdrop for Heath's rallies and to be transported around the country ahead of his big meetings, and detailed schedules for speaking tours and television appearances (already completed by December 1969). A publicity drive had been devised in Summer 1969, and launched in September, concentrating on big circulation Sunday papers and on local and regional papers that would most effectively reach the critical seats, using detailed survey evidence to find out which press sources the target voters in each constituency were most likely to read. Large numbers of posters were placed in these marginals, in contrast to more expensive national campaigning of 1957–59 and 1963–64. The theme of this publicity was confined to the inflation and taxation questions which the Party's private polling showed to be at the head of the voters' own agenda. In Macleod's words, 'everything that hard work can do has been done. Everything that sophisticated modern analysis can do has been done. Everything that dedication and determination can do has been done.'[76]

The Party's campaigning stance was as straightforward as its advertising. Joseph, writing in the *Daily Telegraph*, gave as the basic message 'we are the radicals now', and several commentators noticed the contrast between the urgent demands for change that characterised the Tory campaign and Labour's complacent advocacy of the status quo. *The Times* pointed out how difficult it was for Conservatives 'to challenge a Government that appears to answer so well the conservative instincts of the voters'. After a week of campaigning, the *Financial Times* felt that 'in so far as serious issues have been raised it has been the Opposition that has raised them, and to the extent that the discussion has risen above the "ouch you beast!" level it has been the Conservatives who have made the more telling points'. Heath's final broadcast of the campaign, broadcast on 15 June, contained a remarkable passage in which bustling campaign pictures of the Leader were accompanied by a voice-over from Geoffrey Johnson-Smith that both hinted at the Party's fears and offered a final warning to the electorate, before coming to an upbeat final message:

> To a man trained to look ahead the election campaign has often been frustrating. The sun was shining and the opposition was pretending that winter would never come. Heath felt differently. He could see the same signs of economic troubles

[75] Hurd, *End to Promises*, 9; Rhodes James, *Ambitions and Realities*, 234; Fisher, *Macleod*, 303; Alexander and Watkins, *Making of the Prime Minister*, 166.
[76] Alexander and Watkins, *Making of the Prime Minister*, 166–7; Rhodes James, *Ambitions and Realities*, 219, 221; Butler and Pinto-Duschinsky, *General Election of 1970*, 108, 289.

that he predicted so accurately in 1966. But the opinion polls continued to show that people were prepared to close their eyes and hope it would go away. Heath confided to a colleague, 'I don't want to be the one to say I told you so again'. And then, as the days shortened, his message seemed to get through, or perhaps it's the quality of the man that's begun to get through.

The campaign preparations were put into effect smoothly, with Fraser taking a central part in management while Barber was usually campaigning in marginals. Increasingly the focus came to be on the reiteration of the Party's economic themes of imminent crisis, inflationary pressures and the need for lower taxes. This in part reflected the refusal of the media once again to run with other Party policies when they were put forward day by day, but the concentration on the economy was evident from the start in the election addresses of Tory candidates: at no election since 1950 had so many Conservative candidates highlighted unemployment or so few drawn attention to the Empire and Commonwealth; never had so many talked about industrial relations, or so few about nationalisation, and there had certainly been no campaign before in which prices were so constantly discussed; 92 per cent of Tory candidates drew the issue of inflation to their electors' attention.[77]

Non-economic issues received little notice. At the outset it seemed possible that the cancellation of a South African cricket tour would be exploited by Labour to highlight Tory divisions, but the issue did not last long. And although the situation in Northern Ireland had forced the dispatch of British troops in 1969, it was hardly discussed by candidates outside Ulster. Likewise, the agreement of the Conservative, Labour and Liberal front benches on Britain's application to join the EEC, for which talks would be resumed straight after the Election, ensured that no great debate took place on the hustings. Even Rhodesia failed to create any sparks, and was mentioned by only a handful of Conservative or Labour candidates.[78]

Alongside the economy, and in the absence of other non-economic issues catching fire, the 1970 Election was about leadership and style, mainly because Heath was determined that it should be. Heath's personal foreword to the Conservative manifesto denounced Wilson's 'cheap and trivial government' in which 'decisions have been dictated simply by the desire to catch tomorrow's headlines'. In place of this he promised, in words that were to come back to haunt him by 1972, that when he had made decisions in office he would 'have the courage to stick to it'. There would be no more 'backing and filling', but 'a new style of government'. Douglas Hurd saw this as one of

77 Halcrow, *Joseph*, 44; Alexander and Watkins. *Making of the Prime Minister*, 171; Rhodes James, *Ambitions and Realities*, 247; Hurd, *End to Promises*, 22; Butler and Pinto-Duschinsky, *General Election of 1970*, 144, 156–7, 248, 439, 442; Central Office file, CCO 4/10/122, election organisation.

78 Butler and Pinto-Duschinsky, *General Election of 1970*, 141, 148, 438.

the periodic English times of puritan reaction to assert 'a strict view of what public life is about', and Peter Jenkins described the Wilson–Heath contest as one between 'the entertainer and the vicar'. Since there was little effort to give prominence to any Conservative but Heath, this contrast appeared central to the choice before the electorate, and Heath continued to stress the difference of style throughout the campaign. Initially his own campaigning had been structured only around major speeches in big cities, ticket-only affairs so as to avoid the disruption feared after recent unrest in the universities; with the same intention of limiting possible damage, Heath was persuaded much against his will not to take questions at his public meetings – his adviser Michael Wolff pointed out that questions might cause unforeseen problems, and that they dare not abandon the practice if once started; from May 1970 he accepted no more invitations to live phone-ins either. Heath flew to these carefully-managed events with a captive cargo of journalists, but he also chaired press conferences at which serious discussion of issues could be attempted, while Wilson appeared only to walk around chatting to people in the fine weather. Polls suggested that this comparison of their approaches had produced more support for Heath than Wilson when they each appeared on the BBC's *Election Forum*. However, it soon became clear that Wilson's walkabouts, copied from those pioneered by the Queen, were producing very positive television images that contrasted damagingly with Heath's austerely issue-based campaigning, even though this was exactly the contrast Heath had sought. On 5 June it was decided that Heath too should go walkabout in crowded high streets, but as with any unplanned electioneering this was dangerously subject to accident, and Heath was anyway not in his element. At Edinburgh he allowed a microphone to pick up his words 'I think that is enough for them, don't you?', while on the following day at Norwich airport two small girls who had been told to get Heath's autograph visibly did not know what to do with it when he had obliged, and the Heath party then arrived in the town centre on early closing day; Chatham, Exeter and Stretford went much better, but it was always heavy going for Heath's staff to get him to show his human qualities in such artificial situations. He had an additional problem that has not often beset would-be prime ministers, a constituency that was not safe; his Bexley majority had been only 2,333 votes in 1966, and with polls showing Labour well ahead it seemed possible he could lose his own seat, especially when an anti-Common Market candidate stood there and changed his name by deed poll to 'Edward Heath'; with the national battle effectively over, Heath's staff spent polling day outside Bexley polling stations bearing placards telling people to beware of impostors and to vote for 'the real Edward Heath'.[79]

[79] Campbell, *Heath*, 271; Alexander and Watkins, *Making of the Prime Minister*, 169, 174; Rhodes James, *Ambitions and Realities*, 242–3, 263; Butler and Pinto-Duschinsky, *General Election of 1970*, 146, 152, 194, 208; Central Office file, CCO 500/24/288, Leader; Cockerell, *Live from Number 10*, 162, 169; Hurd, *End to Promises*, 18.

Television was naturally very significant in such a personalised campaign. BBC and ITV decided at the outset to put all party political broadcasts out at 10 p.m., and this provided a bonus to the Conservatives who had already decided to model their programmes on ITN's *News at Ten* (much as Labour had mimicked the style of *Tonight* in 1959, and Baldwin had made his Party films look as much like newsreels as possible in 1935). As the 'newscasters', Christopher Chataway and Geoffrey Johnson-Smith were by now both experienced politicians as well as professional broadcasters; their light-hearted banter about Labour's record and its campaign provided the 'knocking copy' while leaving the official spokesmen free to speak more positively; between items there were even spoof advertisements, one of which, showing a pound note being snipped away until only half of it was left beautifully encapsulated the Tory view of inflation and provided, as Martin Harrison put it, 'the most telling visual moment of the campaign'. Another broadcast aimed at housewives was close in mood to Poole's 'soap opera' broadcast in 1964; in response to criticism that the Conservative Party was being sold like soap powder, the Party's media advisers were amused: 'the quality of advice that goes into selling detergents the Tories couldn't afford to pay for and would be very lucky to get.' As in 1959, the final broadcast, revolving entirely round Heath and directed by Brian Forbes, was an important summation of the Party's campaign.[80]

It was not though a campaign between only two personalities, for the media also paid great attention to Enoch Powell; when the campaign started, the Press Association assigned one reporter each to Wilson and Heath, but two to Powell. His distance from the Conservative leadership was well known, and he played expertly on the media's interest to build a sense of anticipation before his final declaration. In the mean time he made speeches on immigration and on Communist subversion, which encouraged Tony Benn to compare 'the flag flying over Wolverhampton' to the one that had flown over Nazi concentration camps; Powell made a dignified reply referring to his own (anti-fascist) war service and Wilson afterwards blamed Benn for having lost Labour several Midlands seats by highlighting an issue that Labour should not have raised. Heath refused to disown Powell as a Conservative candidate, and dare not have done so, but he also refused to utter even a syllable of support for him. There was intense speculation about Powell's motives, and a consensus that he – like most others – expected a Tory defeat and was preparing the ground for what would take place afterwards. His final speech, drawing attention to the view that he had been badly treated by Heath and could expect no office if the Conservatives won, but disinterestedly urging electors to vote Conservative because of the greater evil of socialism, has

---

[80] Cockerell, *Live from Number Ten*, 159, 164, 169; Rhodes James, *Ambitions and Realities*, 248–9; Butler and Pinto-Duschinsky, *General Election of 1970*, 221.

to be seen in that context. During the campaign he again received sackfuls of supportive letters. It seems clear from the analysis of that mail that at least some voters supported Tory candidates in 1970 because of Powell's personal plea that they should do so. That conclusion is a long way short of attributing the Conservatives' victory entirely to Powell's influence, as Powell himself was subsequently to claim; Diana Spearman, after analysing the Powell mailbag and relating it to the other evidence, found it 'impossible to resist the impression that without the impact of Powell's speeches, although the victory would possibly have been won, the size of the majority would have been smaller'. This seems about right, but it does not in fact amount to much, for if Powell's influence is reduced to one of many it becomes impossible to separate out and to give it an individual weight. The Nuffield election study found in any case that Powellite candidates did no better than other Conservatives in 1970; if Powell had an effect it benefited even those Tories who had repudiated his views. His supporters were not about to draw such fine distinctions: Maurice Cowling wrote an essay shortly after the 1970 campaign entitled 'Mr. Powell, Mr. Heath and the Future', urging Heath to bring Powell back.[81]

For some days the media would hardly report anything but Powell's eruption into the campaign, but with difficulty Heath wrenched his campaign back on course. That course did not seem to be prospering, for until almost the end of the campaign and with few deviations, the polls showed Labour's lead to be rising: on the week-end before polling, NOP showed Labour's lead up to 12.4 per cent. The following day's Sunday papers included many stories that speculated on which Tory would succeed Heath after the Party's inevitable defeat, Whitelaw being the most favoured candidate; in *The Times* on Monday, David Wood wrote that for the Conservatives 'it is too late to recover lost ground', and almost every editorial and political column took the same view; the only paper that week to publish a poll giving a Tory lead, the *Evening Standard* on polling day, printed alongside it a political column saying that 'Labour will certainly win'. On that final Sunday of the campaign, Richard Crossman's diary entry reflected both the cause of the Conservatives' discomfiture and the underlying but still barely-visible basis of their hopes:

> As in 1959 the Opposition are fighting a fine weather mood and a sense of complacency, yet I have to record that we can't say the electorate has never had it so good. Macmillan could point to two years of economic expansion and a tremendous rise in living standards, five years of Tory easy-going. We have given them three years of hell and high taxes. They've seen the failure of devaluation and felt the soaring cost of living. Yet Harold Wilson is running the

---

[81] John Wood (ed.), *Powell and the 1970 Election* (1970), 5, 19, 29, 35, 49, 56; Rhodes James, *Ambitions and Realities*, 246; Powell, *Reflections*, 195, 197; Tony Benn, *Against the Tide: Diaries 1973–1976* (1990), 8; Alexander and Watkins, *Making of the Prime Minister*, 179–80, 189; King, *Diary*, 333; Butler and Pinto-Duschinsky, *General Election of 1970*, 408.

election in this Macmillan-like way and he has suddenly found that the mood is on our side.[82]

In fact, the news began to change in the Tory direction at just this point, but with only four days to go. Private Party polls showed that Heath's economic warnings were beginning to make an impact and that, crucially, people were coming to believe not only that the economy was weak but also that the Conservatives would be better than Labour in dealing with the problem. On the Monday before polling, monthly trade figures came out which were worse than expected and appeared to undermine Labour's economic confidence; even when Wilson explained that these figures were distorted by the inclusion of two expensive jumbo jets, opinion did not calm again; a columnist in the *Sun*, then still a pro-Labour paper, accepted on 17 June that 'Mr. Wilson was trying to be reassuring. But what he was saying was that the British economy can be knocked askew simply by buying a couple of aeroplanes. This struck me as immeasurably more disturbing than the gap itself.' Kenneth Baker was one of the West London Tory candidates summoned to a meeting with the Leader on Hounslow Heath when the trade figures came out: 'He was a man transformed. He had just been given the overseas trade figures . . . and he used them to flay the Government's supposed economic recovery. It was this lunchtime which marked the turning point of the election.' The Party therefore finished the campaign in fighting mood and hammering home the economic issue with increasing confidence. It was at this time, only two days before polling, after even any late swing must have been well under way, that a CRD document on prices policy was put into the hands of journalists at a press conference. It was, as Hurd recalled, a draft that had 'hung around for several days waiting for the approval of busy men'. This rather technical document included a phrase that said that if its proposals were adopted the *rise* in prices could be slowed 'at a stroke'. The phrase was not used in a Heath speech, and was anyway not a pledge to reduce prices, as was later claimed against him. Nevertheless, there was a certain poetic justice in the Party being eventually embarrassed by its electioneering on prices policy. At the time more attention was paid to another passage in the document in which it was alleged that the continuation of Labour's policies for another four years could bring about another devaluation; this was noticed only because Wilson denounced it as scaremongering, and so highlighted another issue on which the public by then preferred Conservative to Labour policy.[83]

Despite this fighting final round, few expected the Conservatives to win; Heath exuded confidence, but since even his closest aides never actually knew what he was thinking they could not be sure whether his optimism was

[82] Butler and Pinto-Duschinsky, *General Election of 1970*, 166–7, 177; Howard, *Crossman Diaries*, 725.
[83] Campbell, *Heath*, 278; Rhodes James, *Ambitions and Realities*, 258–60, 271; Baker, *Turbulent Years*, 31; Hurd, *End to Promises*, 23.

genuine or assumed. Macleod also affected to believe that the Conservatives would win, but his optimism was generally attributed to the wish to keep up morale and to the gambler's instinct for the dark horse. Whitelaw and Prior, among others, have confessed in their memoirs to having had no confidence in a Tory win even in the final week. Some shadow ministers made plans at Carrington's country home on the week-end before polling for the quick removal of Heath after defeat. Influenced by the succession of opinion polls, opinion outside the Party was even more certain of the result: the betting odds on Labour reached 20–1 on, but for a time it was impossible to get a bet on Labour anyway. When Heath visited Cambridge during the campaign, George Gale noticed that Rab Butler introduced him as '"Mr. Heath, the Leader of the Conservative Party," and paused, while everyone expected to hear the routine "and next Prime Minister of the country", but [Butler] added instead "for many years to come".' When on election night, as Ian Trethowan later recorded, 'the first result showed a swing of over 4 per cent to the Tories, Heath . . . just smiled slightly and murmured to himself, "Well, well".'[84]

What did the 1970 victory mean?

This wave of self-reinforcing pessimism, rooted in the opinion polls, led Tories to pay little attention to other sources of information which pointed in a diametrically different direction and which suggested that the 1970 Election may not have changed course in the final week anyway; the paradox is in Hurd's report of the mood in mid-campaign, that 'reports from the constituencies were good, everything else was bad. The opinion polls were hypnotic.' Peter Rawlinson, campaigning in marginals, toured the northern Midlands, East Anglia, the West Country and finally Rugby, and found that in all these places as well as in his own Surrey constituency the agents were confident that 'all was going well and they asked why everyone in London was so jumpy'. Jim Prior, for whom a bad national result should have meant the loss of his seat, was confident that Lowestoft was in the bag, and his conversations with the Area chairman reassured him that the same was true right across Norfolk and Suffolk. Robert Rhodes James found the same optimism in South London constituencies, as did John Ramsden in Sheffield and in south coast marginals, and John Barnes in Walsall. Robert Carr, defending a 1966 majority of only 538 in Mitcham, was quite confident that he was 'heading for a major majority, and it didn't tie up with the opinion polls', while the canvass returns in Rushcliffe told Kenneth Clarke's local supporters that they were going to gain the seat. The cause of all this optimism was canvass figures, not by any means a reliable indicator

[84] Fisher, *Macleod*, 304; Whitelaw, *Memoirs*, 70; Prior, *Balance of Power*, 61; John Ranelagh, *Thatcher's People* (1991), 95; Butler and Pinto-Duschinsky, *General Election of 1970*, 165; Wood, *Powell and the 1970 Election*, 57; Ian Trethowan, *Split Screen* (1984), 135.

in individual contests but difficult to ignore when as in 1970 they seem all to have pointed so clearly in one direction; Rhodes James quoted in detail the figures for Banbury which certainly indicated (however reliable they may be in general) that there was no traceable movement of opinion in the final week of campaigning; by the time that he wrote his own memoir, Douglas Hurd had become the MP for much of the Banbury constituency of 1970 and was confident of the reliability of Rhodes James' figures. Oliver Poole, as shrewd an observer of these matters as anyone, was confident that the Party had been winning throughout, and the Vice Chairman, Ted Leather, wrote to *The Economist* to argue the same point, on the basis of his talks with candidates from all over the country; most Tory agents said the same in reporting on the campaign to the Nuffield election study, though by then they knew the result anyway. There is another group of straws in the wind that points to the same conclusion, from polls done on individual constituencies, which correctly foresaw the Conservative gains at Orpington and at Oldbury and Halesowen among other Midlands marginals. The polling organisations that were most 'wrong' about the national result also produced constituency polls that were 'right', though whereas they underestimated Tory strength nationally they tended actually to exaggerate it when looking at individual seats. All this evidence cannot simply be ignored. The Party Chairman, having received from all the constituencies reports on progress and having seen much of it in the marginals for himself, had formed the opinion by polling day that his Party would be a good even bet to win the Election.[85]

How then can we reconcile the Party evidence and local polls, suggesting (as Barbara Castle put it nervously in her diary a week before polling) that 'there [was] a silent majority sitting behind its lace curtains, waiting to come out and vote Tory', with the national opinion polls that pointed to an implausible net change of mind by a million and a half voters in four days. Perhaps one explanation may lie in the fact that Labour's recovery of support was very fragile, which is hardly unlikely after three years of massive unpopularity, and would always have been broken down in the intense scrutiny imposed by an election campaign. This would mean that some 'probable Tory' voters, counted as pledges by Tory canvassers, were still telling neutral observers until late on that they were not certain of their intentions; polls had not (and still have not) found a way of allowing for degrees of partisanship, but canvassers want to know only whether a group of voters are more likely than not to support their candidate. Perhaps too, the violence of the attacks on Powell after his 1968 speech led some Conservative voters who were influenced by

[85] Hurd, *End to Promises*, 21, 26; Peter Rawlinson, *A Price Too High: An Autobiography* (1989), 141; Prior, *Balance of Power*, 59–60; Rhodes James, *Ambitions and Realities*, 261, 271; Central Office constituency files, CCO 1/9/17, 1/14/423; Macolm Balen, *Kenneth Clarke* (1994), 76; ICBH witness seminar, in *Contemporary Record*, vol. 3, no. 4, February 1990, 38; Wood, *Powell and the 1970 Election*, 89; Butler and Pinto-Duschinsky, *General Election of 1970*, 156, 176–7, 335; interview with Lord Barber.

his views on race (or indeed simply shared his views and would have held them whether he had spoken or not) to give more honest answers to Tory canvassers who might reasonably be assumed to share such opinions, than to strangers asking their opinions in a public place; that would match with the universal experience that canvassers could never find voters for extremist parties of the right, and that in 1992 (the other Election in which the polls were so 'wrong') a 'shame factor' may have led to the under-recording of the Conservative vote. In the end, the answer to the paradox is unknowable, but the prevailing assumption of 1970, that there had been a late swing of opinion under the delayed impact of Heath's campaign, both reinforced lessons that Heath drew at the time and then magnified some of the embarrassments of 1972. It is therefore important to record that the Party evidence at least did not support that prevailing view before the polls closed.[86]

Within an hour of the closing of the polls, an exit survey of actual voters at Gravesend predicted a big swing to Conservative that would enable the Party to capture this typical marginal seat (as it did), and within minutes of the first actual results it was clear that Heath was heading for an overall majority with a Tory swing in every region. Overall, the Party had a majority of thirty and Conservatives took seventy-three seats not held in 1966, with gains right across the English regions, and more sparingly in Wales and Scotland, though the Ulster Unionists lost a seat in Northern Ireland. Compared to 1955, when a Conservative majority much like 1970 had been returned, there were fewer Tory MPs for inner London and the provincial cities, more for rural and suburban seats. The polarisation of urban against rural, partly overlapping with a North–South polarisation, took another step forward, but with a much stronger Conservative performance, both urban and rural, in the Midlands. The analysis of votes was unusually difficult, for in 1968 the voting age had been lowered from 21 to 18, and that lowest age group was, both usually and in 1970, predominantly pro-Labour. The net swing to Conservative of 4.8 per cent, the largest between the parties at any post-war general election and the only occasion since 1945 when a safe majority for one party had been replaced at one go by a safe majority for the other, therefore actually understated the Conservative performance since it took no account of the net reinforcement of Labour's vote since 1966.[87]

Some general elections mark long-term changes of voting alignment as well as deciding the party in power for four or five years, and in this sense 1970 was a 'critical' election in the way that Professor V.O. Key defined the concept; the 1970 decline of Labour's voting strength, particularly when some allowance is made for the extra number of 18–21-year-old voters that Labour got compared to 1966, was a psephological milestone that pointed forward not just for four years but for a quarter of a century. That fall of the core Labour

---

[86] Campbell, *Heath*, 279.
[87] Butler and Pinto-Duschinsky, *General Election of 1970*, 259, 338, 342, 397.

vote by something over a million was not to be replaced; Labour would still be able to win elections in 1974, on a lowish vote, when the Conservatives were even more unpopular, but evidence of the new electoral balance that was to allow Tory dominance in the 1980s was there to be seen in the 1970 result. Reginald Maudling was derided when he remarked at the time that Britain was now a Conservative country that sometimes voted Labour, but this was to be a remarkably shrewd prophecy about late-twentieth-century Britain. It is extremely unlikely that such a shift took place as a result of the events of four days in June 1970.[88]

In the short term though, reinforced by the conviction that a late swing of opinion brought about by his own campaign had 'confounded the pundits', Heath received most of the credit for his Party's win; the National Union Executive's annual report in October stated that 'undoubtedly the success of our campaign was a personal one for the Prime Minister'. *The Times* thought that 'achieving so big a victory against the odds puts Mr. Heath in a position of great strength', and the *Spectator*'s editorial on the results was headed 'Mr. Heath's triumph'. The National Union chairman, at the first meeting of the ACP after the Election, argued that 'Mr. Heath's was the greatest single political triumph we should live to see'. Jim Prior recalled with great pleasure the Carlton Club's celebration dinner, full of people who cheered Heath as the Party's election winner, 'often the very same people who a few weeks earlier were saying he was no good and should go'.[89]

Reginald Maudling, given a lift home from the ITN studios by Peter Rawlinson, told him 'Now our troubles begin'. Those troubles would be enhanced by the conclusions that Heath himself drew from his triumph. For Heath, 1970 proved that his judgement was better than that of a worldful of political journalists and pollsters; he was now convinced that he could explain things to the British people in his own way and be confident of a considered and positive verdict. He told the Party Conference in October that the Election had been 'a triumph for the common sense of the British people. It was that which sustained me, and it is for that reason that I was always confident of victory.' In believing that he had his own private line to the electorate, it was all too easy for him to forget that he had been assisted to his triumph by the most sophisticated television campaign ever – and by some rather downmarket campaigning on economic policy. Sir Robert Peel had emerged from the election of 1841 with a similar conviction that his win was a personal mandate in which the Party's conventional electioneering had played little part, and Heath's gradual repudiation by his Party over the next four years was to be not at all unlike Peel's fate in 1846–47. One recruit to the

---

88 V.O. Key Jr., 'A Theory of Critical Elections', in *Journal of Politics*, vol. 17 (1955), 3–18; Shrapnel, *The Seventies*, 98.
89 National Union papers, Central Council reports, NUA 2/2/34; Butler and Pinto-Duschinsky, *General Election of 1970*, 343–4; *Spectator*, 27 June 1970; ACP 25 Nov. 1970; Prior, *Balance of Power*, 65.

Party's voting strength in 1970 was the novelist Kingsley Amis, an ex-Labour supporter who was an early indicator of the reinforcement of Conservatism from the intellectual left that would gather strength as the 1970s went on, converts who would often be more right wing than much of the Party they were joining. Amis's explanation of his switch of allegiance, in the *Spectator*, contained a warning as well as a tribute to the Conservative Leader:

> Mr. Heath now looks and sounds quite like a future Prime Minister; my difficulty is that of being sure that he would lead the country in a recognisably Conservative direction. A wetly me-tooing Tory Government would be worse than another Labour one.[90]

---

[90] Rawlinson, *Price Too High*, 142; Campbell, *Heath*, 285; Cockerell, *Live from Number Ten*, 156; Central Office Chairman's department file, CCO 20/8/15, Correspondence with Heath; *Spectator*, 20 June 1970.

Chapter 6

The Heath Government, 1970–74

Heath as Prime Minister

Edward Heath's emergence as Party Leader had been sudden and until the end unexpected; in October 1963 he was scarcely mentioned during a contest in which half a dozen other names were much discussed; by July 1965 he was one of only two electable candidates and won at the first attempt. Yet by 1970, apart from Powell, who had provoked his own removal from the front bench in 1968, there had been no personal challenge to Heath's authority since 1965. Heath's dominance was based on three factors, his own force of character and determination to get his way, the withdrawal of those who had the experience to qualify as near-equals, and the fact that few new men in Heath's team established a weighty political position of their own.

The first of these factors was clear even in Opposition, but was much extended when Heath took on the premiership with its patronage, its isolating security cocoon, and its tendency (through regular international meetings at head of government level) to make incumbents feel that they are not as other men. He became immersed in the detailed business of running his Government, determined to see through its policies, and less and less able to understand why others could not see the world from this angle. In 1960, Gerald Nabarro, profiling the Chief Whip in his *Sunday Graphic* column, had described Heath as 'Ted to all his hosts of friends, and he has more than practically any other politician I know'. When he became Leader all of this began to change. The Permanent Secretary of the Treasury recalled Heath as 'a lonely man, also because he was a bachelor, and I think this added to the pressures on him and probably affected his performance, because he was not very able to judge people's reaction to him . . .'[1]

The lack of heavyweight colleagues was hardly Heath's fault. Douglas-Home was his own man at the Foreign Office, but since the Government's major foreign policy task was entry into Europe which Heath kept under personal control, there was less room than usual for the Foreign Secretary to bestride the stage; it was in any case unlikely that Sir Alec would throw

---

[1] Gerald Nabarro, *Nab 1: Portrait of a Politician* (1969), 56; Phillip Whitehead, *The Writing on the Wall: Britain in the Seventies* (1985), 51.

his weight around on matters beyond his own portfolio. The decision to make Quintin Hogg Lord Chancellor (resuming the title Lord Hailsham), rather than Home Secretary which he had shadowed in Opposition, marked the end of his active Party career. Unlike predecessors on the Woolsack, in particular Kilmuir, Hailsham confined his activities to the Lords, declined Party engagements in the country, and demurred even at the chairmanship of Cabinet committees; he took the view that the Lord Chancellor 'must develop a slightly more remote political persona than the late QH'. Maudling at the Home Office gave the impression of a career running out of steam and comments on his indolence increased; a new backbencher, Cecil Parkinson, thought that Maudling was at this time 'an enormously capable politician for whom the description "laid back" could originally have been invented'; and of an occasion on which Maudling was physically attacked in the Commons by an Ulster MP, Tony Benn noted in his diary that 'it almost woke Reggie up'. As Heath's deputy, Maudling was still committed to wider policy objectives than his own brief, such as the pursuit of an incomes policy, but unlikely to press them to the point of division. In July 1972, he was a casualty of inquiries arising from his business connections in the Opposition period and resigned from the Cabinet. With Maudling gone, Heath appointed no deputy, choosing rather to designate stand-ins for particular policy areas when he was away; Cecil King thought that 'this will isolate him still further'. Despite the urgings of his supporters, Powell was kept out of office, and Keith Joseph, who had seemed ready to carry Powell's economic flag into Government, was rapidly submerged in the work of the Social Services department and was, in his own later words, 'never . . . a very effective cabinet member'; Alfred Sherman sadly thought of him as 'a good man fallen among civil servants'. Thatcher, who had also demonstrated that she knew her own mind in Opposition, gave the impression of going native when confronted by the civil service in the Education department; the *New Statesman* quoted her permanent secretary, 'perhaps apocryphally', saying that 'although she arrived at the Department with five facts in her head (all wrong), within six months he had succeeded in teaching her eight others (all right)'. As Peter Rawlinson has pointed out, 'of the four leading young contenders for Harold Macmillan's crown a decade earlier – Heath, Powell, Macleod and Maudling – now only Heath survived'. And from within his Government there was no challenge from others either.[2]

Most crucial of all was the loss of Macleod who, after stoically coping with increasing pain through the late 1960s, died on 20 July 1970 only a month after

[2] Peter Rawlinson, *A Price Too High: An Autobiography* (1989), 181; Lord Hailsham, *A Sparrow's Flight: Memoirs* (1990), 377; Lord Hailsham, *The Door Wherein I Went* (1975), 250; Cecil Parkinson, *Right at the Centre* (1992), 111; Cecil King, *The Cecil King Diary, 1970–1974* (1975), 218; Morrison Halcrow, *Keith Joseph: A Single Mind* (1989), 46; Richard Cockett, *Thinking the Unthinkable: Think Tanks and the Economic Counter-Revolution* (1994), 206.

becoming Chancellor of the Exchequer. This was the Heath Government's greatest loss; Norman Shrapnel thought it 'Conservatism's sorest loss of the decade' and equated it to the early death of Anthony Crosland on the Labour side. Macleod had the best tactical brain on the front bench, always insisted that his colleagues consider the presentational and electoral aspects of any policy being debated, and was the Party's finest television performer; Robert Carr felt later that

> politically [Macleod] was our trumpeter. Ted Heath was never a great trumpeter, and any party, any government, needs a great trumpeter. And Iain Macleod had a skill unsurpassed in men of any party in my generation of raising issues in a big way, which commanded attention not only amongst his own party supporters, but amongst the country at large. . . . His loss was a terrible blow, and of course caused a very early dislocation of the government set-up, a re-shuffle within the first two months, just when we were all getting settled into our jobs. That was a great disaster.

A few months later, a Party complaint about political bias in BBC political discussion programmes was met with the disconcerting response (from Lord Hill, who had seen all this before 'from the other side of the Hill') that the usual number of invitations had been issued to Ministers but that most of them had been turned down; Carr, whose moderate credentials were impeccable, had no time to go on television and debate the Industrial Relations Bill because he was tied down by endless debates in the Commons. Lord Jellicoe subsequently agreed to accept an invitation to be interviewed, but with great trepidation, pointing out that 'I am quite happy with steam radio, but I am scared stiff of that beastly screen!' The Party Chairman, while arranging coaching for Jellicoe at Central Office, agreed with his preference for radio, but added regretfully that 'those of us who are in politics can't really escape from television'.[3]

In March 1971, the Yorkshire Area chairman urged that greater attention be given to publicising the Government's work, a view endorsed by the National Union Executive. The Party Chairman then circulated his ministerial colleagues with a note on 'the Government's failure to put over its policies as effectively as it might', and urged them to accept more speaking engagements; analysis of the first two months of the year showed that half of the Cabinet had not made a single speech outside parliament or their own constituency, and only three had made more than one. In April Keith Joseph commented on a poll that showed 'an unsurprising but distressing lack of awareness of what we are up to and what we are achieving on the social services front. I say "unsurprising" because so far no sustained attempt to explain has been made. I have not myself embarked upon explanation until we have enough

---

[3] Central Office Chairman's department file, CCO 20/1/19, Correspondence with Ministers; Arthur Seldon, *The State is Rolling Back* (1994), 270; Norman Shrapnel, *The Seventies* (1980), 29; Whitehead, *Writing on the Wall*, 54–5.

evidence to show of new priorities in action'; he promised to make two or three speeches 'during the middle or late summer to show what we are about'. But politics could not simply be put on ice for twelve months while Ministers played themselves in, and it is arguable that it was in that first year that the Heath Government lost the communications battle and never afterwards got back on top of things. By April 1972 most Ministers had had intensive television training, but the unpopularity of the Government ensured that by then they had a rocky ride whenever they ventured into the studios. The Party Chairman told his colleagues at the end of April 1971 that recent polling 'confirm[ed] a good deal of other evidence we have that the Conservative Party is at present seen as unrepresentative, uncommunicative and remote, with little knowledge of or interest in the problems of ordinary people. . . . This underlying feeling, if it is allowed to persist, can do us significant electoral damage.' This had arisen 'as a result of what is apparently a failure to communicate'. It is clear that Macleod's colleagues were not exactly keen to show off their skills in the brass section. But it was because of the other factors referred to above that Macleod's unexpected loss had so great an impact. When the Heath Government reached its nemesis, it contained no Minister but Heath near the heart of its activities who had played a major role in office before 1964, nobody with the weight and will to stand up to the Prime Minister.[4]

The failure to find weighty new figures to replace the passing generation was therefore equally important. There certainly was a change of character; in 1972 Andrew Roth noted that Heath had brought into major Cabinet posts Ministers from unprivileged backgrounds like his own – Barber, Rippon, Thatcher and Walker for example – which marked an advance on the limited roles of Marples and Bevins a decade earlier, but Roth was far from alone in seeing these 'Heathmen' merely as acolytes of the Prime Minister. Writing in 1974, Butler and Kavanagh felt that no new political leaders had emerged through the Heath Cabinet; a Minister had told them that 'We're not a bad Cabinet but, though we've fewer passengers than any post-war Cabinet, I'm afraid we've fewer stars'. Not everyone would have gone so far, for Whitelaw emerged in these years as a significant political figure and Walker, Prior and Thatcher began to attract attention (in Walker's case at a very young age for he was only 38 when he joined the Cabinet), but the gist of that view represented a common opinion. The *Financial Times* wrote in 1973 that 'there will be no true solutions while we continue to be governed by pygmies', in an article headlined 'A Government of Little Stature'. Lord Carrington felt even in August 1970 that the Government needed more 'fifteen-inch guns', and when Cecil King tried out this phrase on a succession of his luncheon guests

---

[4] Central Office Chairman's department files, CCO 20/7/10 and 11, Tactical Committee, and CCO 20/12/8, Broadcasting; National Union Executive Committee minutes [hereafter NUEC], 6 Mar. 1971.

he found much agreement. Jim Prior's memoirs may stand for a number that make this point:

> Without Iain and Reggie, and with Alec fully occupied as Foreign Secretary, much of the political weight, or 'bottom' as Reggie himself would call it, was lost. There was no way that I, or anyone else – however close we were to Ted – could hope to replace them. They were political equals of Ted and could talk to him in a way that even Willie Whitelaw and Peter Carrington . . . found difficult. Willie and Peter were too close to Ted to give the truly independent and detached view which is invaluable in government.

The reaction to the death of Macleod illustrates that point. Heath placed in the two key economic posts men who – at least at first – transmitted little confidence. When summoned to Downing Street to be made Chancellor, Anthony Barber joked that he hoped it was not to be asked to take over the Treasury. He was in fact very pleased by his promotion, but had for several months to struggle against the inevitable view that he was the second choice for the post; not until the 1971 Budget could he expect to be seen as other than Iain Macleod's substitute; *The Times* reported his 1971 tax proposals in exactly that light, as evidence that he was now his own man. Even before the 1970 Election, James Margach had written that Barber had 'a more professional and practical understanding of fiscal policies than almost anyone in the top flight of politics today. . . . Tony Barber's future role in Conservative Government must lie mainly in the Treasury'. He was certainly no stopgap, and in office he carried through the Party's tax reform package with great determination, but on major economic decisions his views were difficult to separate from those of the Prime Minister. John Nott, who served under Barber, was certain that 'the so-called Barber boom was the responsibility of the Prime Minister, Edward Heath', which overstates the case since they disagreed about so little. In later years, when public expenditure seemed out of control, the Chancellor considered resignation, but was reluctant to take a step which would draw further attention to the problem. He had in any case made it clear to Heath in 1970 that he would shortly leave politics, as he duly did in 1974 when the Government left office.[5]

Despite Carr's recollection, the reshuffle of July 1970 was actually rather minimal, Barber replacing Macleod, Rippon taking over from Barber as European negotiator, and Rippon in turn being substituted by John Davies from outside the Government. There had been widespread speculation that Heath would bring non-parliamentarians into his Government as Wilson had done in 1964, the assumption being that businessmen would enter a Tory

5 Andrew Roth, *Heath and the Heathmen* (1972), x; Jim Prior, *A Balance of Power* (1986), 77; James Margach, *The Anatomy of Power* (1978), 159; Peter Walker, *Staying Power: An Autobiography* (1991), 75; King, *Diary 1970–74*, 28, 35, 54; interview with Lord Barber; James Margach, 'Anthony Barber', in T. Stacey and R. St Oswald (eds), *Here Come the Tories* (1970), 64; Lord Howe at ICBH witness seminar, 1994.

Cabinet to make it more businesslike. In the event nothing like this took place, though there were secondments to the government machine to carry out special projects. John Davies' appointment to the Ministry of Technology in July 1970 – an appointment received with incredulity by some Tory MPs – and his transition to an expanded Department of Trade and Industry in the Autumn, therefore assumed great symbolic significance. Davies had been a real captain of industry as Managing Director of Shell and then Director-General of the Confederation of British Industry (CBI) before he entered the House in June. It was a disastrous appointment, for a man with no Party experience and limited oratorical gifts found the House of Commons a terrible trial, while in administration he tended to get bogged down in detail; a senior colleague told Phillip Whitehead that 'I recommended [Davies], and I was a hundred per cent wrong. He couldn't cope with the House'. By November Davies was already showing the strain, and when in 1972 the Government undertook a major review of industrial policy it was done outside his department, if not quite behind his back; later in that year he was moved sideways into a non-departmental post with lesser visibility. In general Heath left ministers in office to continue with their policies rather than moving them around between posts, and of the eighteen appointed to the Cabinet in June 1970, fourteen were still there in February 1974, half of them in the same post. No Cabinet Minister was sacked and none resigned over a policy disagreement. Heath's one biggish reshuffle in 1972 did not produce many new faces and he did not seem to be looking for any. 'In public and in private', as Butler and Kavanagh concluded, 'it was a Heath government throughout'.[6]

In this situation therefore, a great deal would depend on Heath and the way in which he conducted himself. It is necessary to stress, in view of what followed, his intentions on taking office. In Downing Street on 19 June 1970 he told the press that 'to govern is to serve. . . . Our purpose is not to divide but to unite, and where there are differences to bring reconciliation, to create one nation.' There was no understanding among incoming Ministers in 1970 that they would have continuing warfare with organised labour; Whitelaw explained privately in July 1970 that, if the team looked a bit weak on the law and order side, then it would not matter too much for 'isn't it wiser to start by being conciliatory and toughen up later if it proves necessary?' But this was the exact opposite of what happened. The immediate experience of those who worked with Heath in government was of a very tough premier, one who was quite ready to break with the consensus; the *New Statesman* in December 1970 quoted a senior civil servant saying that in replacing Wilson

6 King, *Diary 1970–74*, 236; Whitehead, *Writing on the Wall*, 55, 84; Philip Norton, *Conservative Dissidents: Dissent within the Parliamentary Conservative Party, 1970–1974* (1978), 38; John Campbell, *Edward Heath* (1993), 298; D.E. Butler and Denis Kavanagh, *The British General Election of February 1974* (1974), 25.

with Heath, 'we have swapped an India-rubber ball for a spanner. The new man at No. 10 is the toughest operator since Neville Chamberlain. He knows what he has gone there to do and nothing will stop him. Nothing.' At the Party Conference in October, Heath had declared that 'we were returned to office to change the course of history of this nation – nothing less.' There was thus from the start a tension between a policy that aimed to unite and a manner that seemed divisive. From the start too, there was a commitment to economic growth that was seen by all the Tory leaders as more important than the means adopted to achieve it. This can be attributed to Heath's own conviction, from personal and family experience, that economic well-being should have an overriding priority, but it was also rooted in the conviction, as Brendon Sewill put it, that without growth there would be no room for the other policies to succeed: 'slow growth would tend to aggravate all the social problems of poor housing and education, deprivation, racial tension, violence and crime'. He might have added that slow growth would also force difficult choices between the pursuit of those objectives and the cutting of taxes.[7]

There was from the start, a deliberate reaction – perhaps over-reaction would be a more accurate description – against Wilson's manner of conducting himself in office. Hence Heath's manifesto pledge to 'create a new way of running our national affairs. This means sweeping away the trivialities and gimmicks which now dominate the political scene.' A year into the Government, T.E. Utley reminded his *Daily Telegraph* readers that Heath was 'trying to govern without guile. This is a revolutionary experiment which distinguishes him as sharply from almost all other Tory Prime Ministers as it does from Mr. Wilson.' There arose from this a dangerous tendency to downplay the Party side of politics and to enhance the governmental; the *Sunday Times* 'Insight' team declared in 1976 that the story of Heath after 1970 was 'the history not of a politician but rather of an anti-politician, who rejected his party long before it rejected him'. Heath experimented in merging civil servant and ministerial committees, so that the group that ran the incomes policy on which the Party would sink or swim was a mixed committee of politicians and civil servants. As press secretary he chose the diplomat Donald Maitland rather than a working journalist; Barbara Hosking who had only recently joined the Downing Street press office from Labour's headquarters was kept on by Heath. The head of the new think-tank, Lord Rothschild, was also a Labour supporter, and his unit was an important influence in setting the Government back towards the incomes policies that so many Conservatives abhorred in the 1972 'U-turn'; the point is not to argue that such advisers did not give of their loyal best, but that they could have no

---

7 Robert Rhodes James, *Ambitions and Strategies: British Politics, 1964–1970* (1972), 266; King, *Diary 1970–74*, 22; Roth, *Heath*, 219; Central Office, *Notes on Current Politics* [hereafter NCP] 26 Oct. 1970; Brendon Sewill, *British Economic Policy, 1970–1974: A View from the Inside* (1975), 30.

instinctive feel for what Conservative supporters would stand for. Nor could they draw on a Party background in giving advice on presentation. Maitland's later account was that 'sometimes . . . a suggestion would be made as to what Mr. Heath should do. And the comment would come "but that would look like image-building". This was something that faces had been set against'. Increasingly, journalists were seen at Number 10 as trivialising obstacles to serious policy explanation; 'it was as though', wrote James Margach, 'he blamed the machinations of the media for the failure of his policies'. There continued to be little time kept free for preparing major speeches and this was vital for, as Hurd put it, 'introduce a rostrum, a microphone or a few thousand people', and, 'instead of speaking to people, Mr. Heath would too often speak at them'.[8]

Many commentators have suggested that Heath would have made a better Permanent Secretary than Prime Minister, and Heath himself used to say that if in the 1946 civil service examinations he had been offered the Treasury, rather than the Ministry of Civil Aviation, he would probably not have become a politician anyway. He was, thought Peter Hennessy, 'a permanent secretary manqué'. But surely, such a view understates the extent to which permanent secretaries need the political skills that Heath lacked? What is certain is that in office he was thought to rely too much on civil service advice and too little on his Party. Increasingly, Sir William Armstrong, head of the Civil Service Department, came to be his right-hand man; both politicians and civil servants noticed that Armstrong was 'openly refered to as "the Deputy Prime Minister"', and journalists pointed out that, when Heath conducted his 'Gaullist' press conferences at Lancaster House, Armstrong shared the platform with him. Douglas Hurd minuted Heath in August 1971 to warn that 'there is a general impression at all levels within the Party that this administration is in fact less politically conscious than its Conservative predecessor'. There were attempts to break down this impression, frequently set in motion by Hurd himself, and by Chris Patten, aide to Lord Carrington as Party Chairman after 1972. In 1972–73, Hurd pressed successfully for the appointment of more Party advisers in government departments, to encourage ministers to take Party views into account and to keep a political edge in their work, rather as Sewill had moved into the Treasury with Macleod in 1970; Hurd later thought that this development came too late to make much difference. Michael Wolff, Heath's speechwriter and policy adviser, felt in 1971 that 'the real problem was to get Ministers continuously to present their work within a political framework', and cited as evidence a recent Party

---

8   Douglas Hurd, An End to Promises: Sketch of a Government (1978), 14, 19, 32; Stephen Fay and Hugo Young, The Fall of Heath (1976), 5, 9, 10; Campbell, Heath, 290; Charles Moore and Simon Heffer, A Tory Seer: The Selected Journalism of T.E. Utley (1989), 103; King, Diary 1970–74, 80; Michael Cockerell, Live from Number Ten: The Inside Story of Prime Ministers and Television (1988), 170, 174–5, 190; Tessa Blackstone and William Plowden, Inside the Think Tank (1988), 26, 86.

broadcast that might as well have been written by a civil servant anyway. In November 1972, Geoffrey Johnson-Smith was attached to the Cabinet Office with a ministerial brief to improve Government presentation, the task that Swinton, Hill and Deedes had successively done between 1951 and 1964; William Armstrong was dismissive both of the task and of his chances of success. But these were all fire-brigade activities when what was needed was flame-proofing – or a premier who was not an arsonist himself. Even the civil servant who kept Heath's diary was moved to point out in January 1974 that he was 'worried about the trend of entertainment here at Number Ten', for 'while the Prime Minister entertains a great number of foreign visitors, the people of Britain are not getting their fair share of the Prime Minister's time'; of the fifty-seven dinners and receptions that Heath had hosted in 1973, only nine had involved any British people from outside Parliament, and only two of these had been in the second half of the year; he concluded that it was hardly surprising that the Prime Minister was getting isolated, for he hardly ever heard anyone else's views on the domestic situation.[9]

A minor suit in this self-consciously non-party approach to office-holding was in political patronage. Heath had to make an early decision whether to continue or reverse Wilson's abolition of 'political' honours and hereditary peerages, for these had been abolished only in the sense that no recommendations had been made to the crown since 1964. An inspired leak to the *Daily Telegraph* in October 1970 let it be known that Heath would resume the custom of recommending honours 'for political and public services', but this story already sounded a warning note in its prediction that Heath would be 'less lavish with his political recommendations than some of his Conservative predecessors', as indeed he was. On peerages, the *Telegraph* reported that Heath had 'allowed Cabinet colleagues to understand' that only life peers would be nominated, for on this he was said to agree with Wilson 'that lifetime honours are preferable largely because an inherited title could be an embarrassment to an heir who had to earn his own living in business or in industry'. It would have been strange if Heath's meritocratic instincts had chimed in with hereditary peerages, but he was, both in this and in the reduction of political honours generally, out of step with much of his own Party – and building up trouble for later. Much the same lack of feel for his Party's instincts had allowed him to agree with the Labour Government in 1968 on plans for the reform of the House of Lords, only for his own backbenchers (led by Powell and other traditionalists) to defeat this attack on the hereditary principle.[10]

9   Whitehead, *Writing on the Wall*, 52; Peter Hennessy, *Cabinet* (Oxford, 1986), 74; Hurd, *End to Promises*, 94: Central Office Chairman's department file, CCO 20/8/16, Correspondence with Heath; John Ramsden, *The Making of Conservative Party Policy: The Conservative Research Department since 1929* (1980), 295.
10 Central Office Chairman's department file, CCO 20/10/3, Honours.

Given the nature of his Government, only Heath could provide its public face, but the Prime Minister's absorption in the business of government was again a great handicap. In 1970, with expert media advice he had been able to project his personality successfully, but, as Douglas Hurd put it, 'under pressure of time and in the atmosphere of government between 1970 and 1974 the private voice faded and the jargon returned'. Speeches were a problem partly because Heath was such a difficult man to write words for, as Hurd's diary entry of 9 March 1971 indicated: 'Dictate a bad speech for Newcastle. It is really impossible to do these things without an inkling of what he wants to say.' Hurd's 1978 memoir is a catalogue of the good advice that his master ignored. In particular, all urgings that Heath should use language that ordinary people could relate to, and throw fewer statistics at them, struck no response whatsoever: 'Mr. Heath believed that people deserved the evidence, and, by God, they were going to get it. Sometimes it made for hard pounding.' Since the entire point of holding televised press conferences, which would irritate journalists (as Harold Evans had acknowledged when suggesting the idea to Macmillan in 1962), had been to speak directly to the people, there was little point in pitching the argument over their heads. But by the time of Heath's press conference on incomes policy in 1972, this tendency had become so marked that even some of the professional journalists present felt out of their depth.[11]

The Conservatives in any case intended to change Government by reducing its scope and changing its character as well as by adopting a different tone; there would be a 'quiet revolution' towards less government and of a better quality; in November 1969, Heath told the Executive of the 1922 Committee that the choice to be made in the coming election was 'between greater government intervention or less'. Unfortunately those planning this policy in opposition and implementing it in office were more interested in the 'better quality' part of this package, while Tory supporters in parliament and in the country were more attracted to the 'less government' part. It was not at first clear that the objectives would diverge: the White Paper of June 1970 argued that 'government has been attempting to do too much', and promised to exercise more restraint in order not to overload the machine. The 1970 Government contained only eighty-three Ministers instead of the hundred in Labour's outgoing team, and it was explained that this would save '£85,000 on salaries alone'. However, that number then crept up almost to the Labour level by the end of 1973. Kenneth Baker was given the ministerial task of cutting civil service numbers but managed only to stop those numbers from rising (a claim that in itself required some creative accounting with the numbers of public sector employees). He found that 'each Department behaved like

[11] Hurd, *End to Promises*, 76–8, 81, 94; Kenneth Baker, *The Turbulent Years: My Life in Politics* (1993), 35.

a great feudal army, jealously guarding its own territory', and when he sought the assistance of ministerial colleagues in cutting staff numbers, 'I soon found that not one was remotely interested'. Backbenchers and Party Conferences were soon producing sharp reminders that the pledge to have 'less government' conflicted with the steady accumulation of new agencies and public employees.[12]

There was a considerable reduction in the number of Cabinet Committees under Heath, but this was known only in the insiders' world. More serious work had been done on structures, and the Government therefore came into office with detailed plans for 'Programme Analysis and Review' (PAR) which, it was hoped, would enable long-term savings to be made in Government expenditure, and for a think-tank which would give the Cabinet independent advice on strategic issues and keep their minds fixed on the big issues. PAR was a casualty of departmental territorialism in Whitehall, a prime example of Peter Hennessy's view that 'the story of Heath's "quiet revolution" is of one revolutionary element after another being taken away and shot or allowed to expire because of neglect'. The Central Policy Review Staff (CPRS), as the think-tank was more decorously christened, did manage to establish its own corner, though again the Cabinet Office gave it a character that had not been planned before 1970. Its director Lord Rothschild was an imaginative choice, but, since he did not set out to recruit a staff that was Tory, the CPRS did not remedy the Government's inherent inability to think *party*-politically and there was no sign that Heath wanted it to. As time went by the CPRS became more devoted to dealing with short-term problems – energy, Rolls-Royce, Concorde – and was less used for the long-term thinking for which it had been created. One good idea that never quite delivered its promise was that there should be twice-yearly Chequers week-ends at which the CPRS would confront Ministers with the long-term consequences of their policies; only three were held in the Government's forty-two months, and they were weakened by the presence of civil servants – in whose company Ministers felt obliged always to fight their departmental corners. The CRD worried that the CPRS would be used to prepare the next election manifesto, a logical development of its role but one that reflected its oddly political/non-party stance; it was agreed that the CRD leaders should also attend the next Chequers week-end to inject their own thinking into the process, but all this was in the event overtaken by the political dramas of late 1973. When manifesto drafts were circulating after the Summer of 1973, they were written by CRD staff and by Nigel Lawson, a friendly journalist brought in by the *Party* for that purpose.[13]

12 *NCP*, 28/9/70; 1922 Committee minutes [hereafter 1922], 16 Nov. 1969; Ramsden, *Making of Conservative Party Policy*, 256–9, 300–01; Hennessy, *Cabinet*, 75, 78; Baker, *Turbulent Years*, 34.
13 Jock Bruce-Gardyne, *Whatever Happened to the Quiet Revolution?* (1974), 17, 60, 73, 100, 107, 123–5; Peter Hennessy, *Whitehall* (1990), 212, 221, 235; Campbell, *Heath*, 319; Hurd, *End to Promises*, 38.

The Industrial Relations Act

Selwyn Lloyd, observing the parliamentary scene as Speaker in 1972, suggested that 'Ted's difficulties sprang from his working out his policy in detail before taking office. By the time he was in Downing Street, things had changed and they were stuck with a fixed programme when what was needed was a different performance.' Nowhere was this clearer than in trade union policy. In July 1970, reviewing the failure of Labour's trade union policy a year earlier, the *Guardian*'s columnist Peter Jenkins concluded that 'the Heath Government has a clear mandate and a fresh one. . . . If the Conservative policies stand any chance of working it will not be through fining or locking up strikers but by gradually, over a period of years, breaking down the outlaw mentality of the unions and encouraging the development of more responsive institutions and responsible attitudes in the changed atmosphere of a legal framework.' That was exactly what Robert Carr believed that he was doing, for his Industrial Relations Bill had been framed in the clear expectation that its provisions would allow no sanctions against individual strikers, and in the anticipation that the extensive new framework of trade union law would create a mood for cooperation, rather than a weapon in confrontation. Lord Hailsham, writing in 1975 and admitting to the benefit of hindsight, revealed that he had privately criticised the policy in its preparation stage for confusing the basic necessity of creating a modern framework of law (which would be neutral between employers and unions) with the economic case for using courts to prevent or postpone strikes (which was distinctly anti-union, or would appear to be so to the unions), but as early as November 1965, David Howell had asked, when drafting the 1966 manifesto, 'are we really proposing to strengthen all unions now, or make them efficient now and then strengthen them?' In 1993 Robert Taylor reached a similar conclusion as to ambiguity of intent: the Conservatives should not have confused the collectivising impulse to organise the unions more sensibly with a liberalising wish to weaken their restrictive practices, and should in any event not have tried to gain both objectives by the same Bill. The real problem for Ministers was that since nobody had tackled these issues at all for a generation, and since they did not expect another major reform for years ahead, they were understandably tempted to do the job comprehensively; in the context of US practice in industrial relations which they had intensively studied in opposition, this meant they needed an Act which would do in about three years what had taken the United States three decades to achieve. Trade union policy had an overtly dual function in the Conservatives' thinking in 1970, for as well as affecting the union members and their rights, the policy was central to the Government's pursuit of economic growth, a prerequisite of entering Europe from a position of strength. Robert Carr argued in 1985 that 'no one will understand the Heath Government unless they understand the degree of our commitment to economic growth. . . . The Industrial Relations Act fitted into this pattern.'[14]

So much for the Conservatives' approach, muddled perhaps by the desire to achieve contradictory objectives, but far from seeking a battle with the unions. What, to pursue Selwyn Lloyd's analysis, had changed since the policy had been devised in 1965 and published in detail in 1968? First, Labour had tried to legislate in the same field and failed, a fiasco that both demonstrated the increasingly militant character of the trade unions and encouraged the militants to do their worst when their opponents rather than their allies made a similar attempt in 1970–71. But a second change related entirely to the transition between mandate and legislation, dictated by the fact that the Election had come unexpectedly in June 1970, which meant that a legislative programme had to be prepared very fast for an Autumn session. Having come into office with a detailed plan ready made, with a timetable for legislation that gave a high priority to an Industrial Relations Bill, and with a Party right wing that was already suspicious that this Government like its predecessors would not in the event take action on this issue, Carr had no opportunity for second thoughts. He published a White Paper in October 1970 that allowed only a month for consultation; Heath had already explained in July that 'we are not prepared to delay proposals', and now promised 'the Bill before Christmas and the Act on the Statute Book this Session'. Ministers assumed, as union leaders had earlier advised them, that the unions would oppose Carr's plans until they became law so that there was little point in prolonging this conflictive phase, might indeed be much to be said for shortening it. But the shortness of time for consultation made it clear that the Government would carry out its plans and take no notice of anything said in the meantime; Carr explained that 'we still want, and we will still welcome, constructive consultation about the details . . . but the main principles are firm, and there is no going back'. This gave offence to moderates in the unions and strengthened the hands of the militants for the next round; 140,000 demonstrators attended a 'Kill the Bill' Rally in London in February 1971. Even by November 1970, the North West Area Conservatives were demanding 'authoritative statements to counteract distorted accounts' of the Party's proposals, as they feared that the initiative was being lost.[15]

That first tactical error was compounded by the way in which the Bill was dealt with in parliament. Just as the Conservatives had achieved a short-term political advantage by opposing Wilson's 1969 proposals, so they now sought

[14] King, *Diary 1970–74*, 211; Peter Jenkins, *The Battle of Downing Street* (1970), 170–1; Hailsham, *Door Wherein I Went*, 292; Howell to Fraser, 30 Nov. 1965, LCC correspondence; Robert Taylor, *The Trade Union Question in British Politics: Government and Unions since 1945* (Oxford, 1993), 186; Sewill, *British Economic Policy*, 33; Whitehead, *Writing on the Wall*, 54; interviews with Lord Carr and Lord Howe.

[15] Taylor, *Trade Union Question*, 187; *NCP* 3 Aug., 26 Oct. and 8 Nov. 1970; NUEC, 4 Dec. 1970; interview with Lord Carr.

to drive home that advantage by taking the Committee Stage of their own Bill on the floor of the House, so forcing each Labour frontbencher either to vote with them or to oppose proposals similar to their own. Labour reacted to this transparent tactic by throwing its entire weight behind the trade union opposition to the Bill. Huge numbers of amendments were tabled and when, inevitably, there was no time to discuss them even in the longest debates on anything but a Finance Bill since the War, the Bill was forced through under a guillotine procedure that Labour denounced as a limitation of free debate; theatrically, the Opposition insisted on voting continuously in fifty-seven successive divisions on undiscussed amendments, a process that took eleven hours. All this heat, which the Government could have limited if not avoided altogether, healed the breach in the labour movement created by Wilson's 1969 proposals, and ensured that before the Act was even on the statute book it was bitterly resented by the unions. Given his pledge not to deviate from his chosen course of action, Heath could not now conciliate on this flagship policy even if he had wanted to; despite urgings not to confront the unions from veteran Tories like Macmillan and Swinton, Heath announced that 'we will persevere and we will come through it', adding hopefully that 'it is the storm before the calm'. In these circumstances, the positive side of the new Act for trade unions was hardly noticed, and the TUC set out to neutralise its punitive clauses. The tactical weapon for achieving this was for the TUC to advise, and subsequently to require, unions not to register under the Act. This denied unions the Act's benefits, but it also had the effect of treating the Act as if it did not exist, for every major union de-registered and thereby acted as if the law had not changed. Carr confessed that 'I certainly had a blind spot about this. I never expected the trade unions would oppose the bill on the question of registration. . . . And from their narrow short term point of view it was a damnably effective tactic'.[16]

The punitive clauses of the Act were therefore left to fulfil the Government's aims on their own, without either the new positive mood which it had been hoped that the Act would introduce, or union cooperation with the legal framework that would at least have indicated their acceptance of parliament's right to legislate. The added problem here was that the early 1970s were a period of continued conflict over pay claims, as the Government sought to bring down inflation and the unions fought to protect their members. From the dock strike that broke out soon after he came into office, Heath was faced with a succession of disputes over pay, battles with miners, dockers, postal workers, railway staff and power workers being only the most prominent. Employers were reluctant to invoke the provisions of the new Act since their workforces would have regarded that as provocative in itself, and the

---

[16] Sewill, *British Economic Policy*, 33; William Whitelaw, *The Whitelaw Memoirs* (1989), 76; Rawlinson, *Price Too High*, 249–50; Roth, *Heath*, 219; Whitehead, *Writing on the Wall*, 72–3.

Government did not even ensure that the public sector made use of it; there was no procession of routine references to the Industrial Relations Court that would have made it a familiar part of the scenery. Although new provisions for cooling-off periods were being respected, giving the new Court room to demonstrate its powers and its independence, the Government blundered badly in deciding on a compulsory ballot before a rail strike in 1972, for this produced only an 80 per cent vote of solidarity behind the union leadership, and the gambit was never repeated. Eventually an employer in the dock industry who did use the Act's provisions on picketing persuaded the court to fine the union heavily for its defiance of the law, only for the High Court to rule that unions could not be held responsible for their members' actions. Exactly what the Conservatives had always sought to avoid now happened, with pickets gaoled for contempt of court. This was, as Carr put it, 'a torpedo below the waterline' for the Act, and while the legal system found a way of releasing the imprisoned pickets before a general strike ensued, creating the impression that the Government had had to find a loophole in its own law, this part of the Act also became a dead letter. In discussions with the unions in 1972, Heath himself agreed that these provisions of the Act would not now be invoked by his Government.[17]

Opinion polls demonstrated that a large majority of voters continued to approve of the basic provisions of the Industrial Relations Act, right to the end of the Government's life. Nevertheless, the Act played no part in the climactic industrial disputes of 1973–74 that brought the Government down. In February 1974, the Conservative manifesto offered to amend the Act in consultation with the unions, a clear recognition that a fresh start was needed; even then some confusion of intentions was evident, for the ideas on which it proposed to consult included both a provision to make conciliation compulsory before any legal action could be taken (which the unions would favour) and the withdrawal of social security benefits from strikers' families (which they would oppose to the bitter end). This last idea was a compromise between some Ministers who did not want it at all, and others like Keith Joseph who had long demanded stronger action. Heath argued that the Government had wanted to tackle this question but felt that it needed a fresh mandate before doing so, suggesting that he had learned little about the value of mandates from his three-year battle with the unions. Brendon Sewill in 1975, while arguing that with suitable amendments the Industrial Relations Act would eventually have been accepted by the unions if Heath had stayed in office, conceded none the less that 'the Conservative Government had no answer to the problem of the new over-mighty subject'. When the Tories went out of office in 1974, the succeeding Labour Government had agreed in advance with the unions that it would

---

[17] Taylor, *Trade Union Question*, 189, 191–3, 200–2; Whitehead, *Writing on the Wall*, 78–9; Reginald Maudling, *Memoirs* (1978), 161; Campbell, *Heath*, 463.

repeal much of the 1971 Act, keeping the trade union benefits it conferred but removing all punitive clauses, so that the Thatcher Government of 1979 had to start from an even less-promising baseline than Heath had inherited in 1970, and with a further trade union defeat of a Labour Government having taken place in 1978–79. It did though have some priceless advantages too, for, having seen what happened betwen 1971 and 1974, Conservative Ministers did not repeat their mistakes. After 1979 there was no big Bill that could lead to a once-for-all showdown with the unions, no reliance on the unions having to register under the law, and no way that individual strikers could become martyrs. Rather there was an incremental policy of 'softly, softly catchee monkee' that led from Prior's cautious start, through Tebbit's tougher legislation, on to Walker's symbolic victory over the miners. Without 1971–74 and 1978–79, it is unlikely that the Thatcher Government's trade union policy would have succeeded as it did.[18]

Implementing promises

The Industrial Relations Act, despite its fate, was a clear example of the carrying out of an explicit manifesto pledge. In view of the Heath Government's historiographical reputation as a 'U-turn' government, highlighted for their own purposes by Heath's Tory opponents after 1975, it is as well to point out how many other pledges were carried through. Powell for example wrote in 1976 of 'the systematic inversion by the Heath Government between 1970 and 1974 of every pledge and principle on which it came to power' (and added for good measure that Thatcher was 'irretrievably shop-soiled' by this inheritance, for 'she too said it all before 1970 and then turned with the best of them "when daddy turned".' This was greatly overstated: in January 1972 for instance, Robert Blake, who was soon to be a critic of Heath, wrote that 'the Conservative Party has done as much as could be reasonably expected of a party in power for only 18 months to implement their pledges and put their principles into practice', though he did already add that 'their greatest shortcoming has not been in the legislative field. It has been in the field of management.' Ian Trethowan, too, reminded us in his memoirs that the later reputation of the Heath Government was undeserved, at least as far as its early days were concerned:

> For the first eighteen months . . . [Heath] appeared to be moving surely and confidently towards his two main goals, of entry into Europe and a sensible curbing of the powers of the unions. Read the records of the times and you will find no sense of doom.

The February 1974 Nuffield election study, while accepting that 'the apparent shifts in the government's economic policy were disconcerting', nevertheless

---

[18] Taylor, *Trade Union Question*, 193; Butler and Kavanagh, *General Election of February 1974*, 51, 75; Sewill, *British Economic Policy*, 31, 53.

also felt the need to remind its readers that 'action was taken on a large proportion of the specific promises in the Conservative manifesto' of 1970, highlighting entry to the EEC, housing finance, social services, and the machinery of government as cases in point. From 1970 on, the CRD kept a scorecard of pledges redeemed, which were listed in the Party Chairman's annual speech to the Party Conference.[19]

Entry into Europe would have to be regarded as a centrepiece in any account of the Heath Government, and it was to a large extent the singleminded pursuit of this objective that led to the redirections of other policies. Geoffrey Rippon proved a successful negotiator, and Heath himself established a rapport with the French President Pompidou that improved on any relationship that a British Prime Minister had had with de Gaulle. Within a year, the negotiations had come to a conclusion and entry terms which the Government could unitedly commend to the Party and the country were on offer. The focus therefore shifted from Brussels to Westminster, where because of the relatively small Government majority the Conservative 'antis' felt that they had a chance of defeating the policy in alliance with a Labour Party which had once again reversed its position. The Prime Minister certainly felt that the 1970 Election had given a clear mandate for entry, but that was scarcely true of most Conservative MPs: nearly two-thirds of Tory candidates in 1970 had made no mention at all of the issue in their own election addresses and about a tenth had stated either their outright opposition to Britain joining the EEC or major reservations, while the Party's national manifesto only promised to open negotiations. Forty-four Tory MPs had in 1970 signed an Early Day Motion opposing British entry; Neil Marten refused junior office because of his anti-entry opinions, and Jasper More and Teddy Taylor joined in 1970 only to resign over Europe in 1971. The number of 'antis' was larger than the Government's overall majority. As Uwe Kitzinger put it, all of this 'did not emphasize the picture of a party hell-bent on entry into the EEC'.[20]

In the country, opinion polls showed in March 1971 as many as 70 per cent opposed to British entry, probably affected by the long wait that had been imposed since 1962; a fluctuating public opinion came down narrowly against entry at the critical time in Autumn, but support for entry among Conservative voters hardened now that this long-sought Party objective was within reach. The Burton upon Trent Conservative Association may stand for many in this process of conversion, for where it had been happy to leave the whole matter to its MP in 1962, it was in 1971 determined to back the Government even though its MP was by then strongly anti-European; the

[19] Enoch Powell, *Reflections: Selected Speeches and Writings of Enoch Powell* (1992), 204; *Crossbow*, Jan. 1972, 10; Ian Trethowan, *Split Screen* (1984), 136; Butler and Kavanagh, *General Election of February 1974*, 10–11; Ramsden, *Making of Conservative Party Policy*, 294.

[20] Whitehead, *Writing on the Wall*, 58–64, 67–9; Uwe Kitzinger, *Diplomacy and Persuasion: How Britain Joined the Common Market* (1973), 107, 149, 152, 154, 156–9, 184, 186–7; R. Jowell and G. Hoinville, *Britain into Europe: Public Opinion and the EEC* (1976), 25, 32.

association vice-chairman reported favourably on a rally he had attended in London at which Heath had spoken on the great issues involved, but also 'said that he would rather surrender a certain amount of sovereignty for the Common Market rather than be defeated in Parliament over the Common Market and get a Socialist Government returned again'; when the chairman issued a general invitation to a packed meeting of the association Executive, not a single member present spoke up for the view taken by their MP. Twickenham was another association that turned up the heat on its MP; Toby Jessel was explaining defensively in July 1971 that he had spoken against the EEC only when it had been an open question, but that he would now back the Prime Minister; if a free vote were to take place, he would consult the association officers, but he had to undertake in any case neither to vote against the Government nor go into any lobby with Harold Wilson; the association then capped this by sending Heath a resolution congratulating him on his firmness and his principles. At Hemel Hempstead in July, James Allason gave his own views as hostile to the EEC, but said that he would decide how to vote only after hearing his supporters' views; of fourteen who spoke in the association's debate, thirteen favoured entry, and at the next meeting in October, despite his repeated reservations on the principle, Allason agreed to vote with the Government. In the 1922 Committee, there was a fierce determination to back the Government now that a policy objective pursued for a decade was within sight of achievement, characterised by Rear Admiral Morgan-Giles MP's much quoted advice to his colleagues, 'pro bono publico, no bloody panico'. Such growing Party support was helped by a Central Council meeting attended by two thousand key activists in July which gave Heath a rousing endorsement, by a vigorous campaign of ministerial speakers to hold the Party's loyalty and by a mass mailing of literature to Party members. Even then, Douglas Hurd felt that the choice of a Euro-sceptic as Conservative candidate for the Macclesfield by-election in September 1971 owed something to the local Party's fear of hostile opinion in the constituency. A parliamentary vote on the main issue of principle was postponed from the Summer because of uncertainty about the intention of backbench dissidents, but the number of rebels was gradually eroded in the Autumn as constituency opinion swung behind the Government. At Conference in October, there were sixty-nine constituency motions supporting entry and only four unreservedly against, and it was reported that of 303 CPC groups who had reported constituency views, 269 had favoured entry and only 12 had been clearly against. Powell made an impassioned speech, the main implications of which became clear only in 1974. 'I do not believe that this nation, which has maintained its independence for a thousand years, will now submit to see it merged or lost; nor did I become a member of our sovereign parliament in order to consent to that sovereignty being abated or transferred. Come what may, I cannot and I will not.' Nevertheless, Conference declared overwhelmingly for the

Government's policy, when representatives voted by 2,474 to 324 for Europe (the ballot actually being called for on this occasion by the Leader).[21]

At this late stage Heath agreed to the key tactical decision, to allow a free vote in the main Commons debate on Europe, a tactic suggested months earlier by YCs (who hoped thereby to demonstrate the extent of their Party's free consent to Europe). The idea had also been pressed on Heath by his Chief Whip Francis Pym, who was quite clear that an unwhipped Tory Party would attract more pro-European dissenters from the Labour ranks than the antis it would lose from its own side, and that this would be the best – possibly the only – way to get a positive vote. His advice was well-judged, for the vote for the principle of European entry went through by 112 votes. Two hundred and eighty-four Conservatives voted for entry, thirty-nine against (including six Ulster Unionists), with two deliberate abstentions (one of them du Cann). The antis included only one former Cabinet Minister, Powell, and only two who were to hold high office under Margaret Thatcher – Teddy Taylor and John Biffen; the Party establishment was now almost solidly behind the European idea. In the detailed legislation that then had to be pressed through parliament in Winter 1971–72, the whips were once again hard at work, with Heath seeing nine backbenchers himself and persuading five of them to change their intentions. There were some narrow squeaks in the voting, but, despite Powell's declaration that the Bill 'shall not pass', having once willed the end, Labour's pro-Europeans were never prepared to let the European Communities Bill fall for want of a timely absentee; with Heath threatening to resign if the Government were defeated, whipping and constituency pressure had anyway reduced the Tory antis to a handful. A senior civil servant told Cecil King in January 1972 that 'Heath is very eloquent in private on the possibilities of European union. It gives us a role instead of our Empire. The tragedy is that Ted cannot, but *cannot*, get his ideas on the subject across.' This was not at all fair, for Heath did manage on some of the big occasions to convey exactly what his European vision amounted to: on television he had told viewers that,

> Many of you have fought in Europe, as I did, or have lost fathers, or brothers, or husbands who fell fighting in Europe. I say to you now, with that experience in my memory, that joining the Community, working together with them for our joint security and prosperity, is the best guarantee we can give ourselves of a lasting peace in Europe.[22]

---

21 Burton upon Trent CA minutes, 5 Oct. 1962 and 9 Sept. 1971; Twickenham CA minutes, 19 July 1971; Hemel Hempstead CA minutes, 16 July and 25 Oct. 1971; Norman St. John Stevas, *The Two Cities* (1984), 41; Hurd, *End to Promises*, 65, 67–8; Richard Kelly, 'The Party Conferences', in A. Seldon and S. Ball (eds), *Conservative Century: The Conservative Party since 1900*, Oxford (1994), 250.

22 Whitelaw, *Memoirs*, 73–5; Philip Norton, *Dissension in the House of Commons, 1945–1974* (1975), 397–8; Parkinson, *Right at the Centre*, 110; Lord Pym at ICBH witness seminar, 1994; Campbell, *Heath*, 438; King, *Diaries, 1970–74*, 165; NCP, 22 Nov. 1971.

There was a more serious tragedy of Europe from Heath's point of view. Despite his declaration that 'our historic decision has been made', because of Wilson's second reversal of direction on Europe, leading to Labour's boycott of the European Parliament and a pledge to renegotiate the terms of entry and then submit them to a referendum, Heath's achievement could not be final. The Conservative Government had to take care not to be too 'European' before the next Election, lest the anti-European card be played against them, though the Conservatives' 'European Forum', set up in 1969, was re-formed on a permanent basis in 1970 as the Conservative Group for Europe, and helped to keep the issue at the forefront of the Party's concerns. Nevertheless, as Sewill put it, 'instead of inspiration there was dispute; instead of new confidence, continued and damaging uncertainty'. In February 1974, less than a quarter of Tory candidates made any mention of their Government's greatest achievement in their election addresses; Europe was not seen as a vote-winner even in the hour of its achievement, and indeed in February 1974 the proportion of the electorate who thought Britain was 'right to join the EEC' was outnumbered two to one by the antis. The problem was economic as well as political: when the Tory Government's popularity sagged in 1972–73 and the possibility of Wilson's return to office increased, how could business people invest in 'a European future' while not yet knowing whether Britain would continue to play a part in it? Heath was at this time denouncing industrialists for failing to invest, at a crucial time for the economy, but it was in truth a rational position for them to take while political uncertainty remained. None the less, the formal entry of Britain into the EEC and the Charlemagne prize that Heath was awarded did a great deal to enhance his prestige both at home and abroad.[23]

Other foreign issues were less satisfactorily resolved, even where the carrying-out of pledges was involved. Sir Alec's precipitate moves to resume arms supplies to South Africa in 1970 offended liberal opinion in the Party as well as outside, and when Central Office heard that the Bow Group was holding a Conference fringe meeting to discuss the issue, an official hoped 'that the news media would have plenty of other material that day'. The decision also caused Heath difficulties with Commonwealth leaders; after a Commonwealth Conference in Singapore, Britain did not renege on its announced policy, but it was clear, as Hurd put it, that that policy 'would be very sparingly used'. Attempts to settle the Rhodesian issue seemed though to promise a diplomatic triumph for Sir Alec as he superintended negotiations that almost brought off a settlement. In October 1970, a resolution calling for the ending of sanctions was decisively defeated at the Conference but in November twenty-three Tory MPs including Powell opposed their renewal for another year, and others gave notice that if a settlement was not made

---

[23] Kitzinger, *Diplomacy and Persuasion*, 160–1; Sewill, *British Economic Policy*, 33; Butler and Kavanagh, *General Election of February 1974*, 63.

soon then they would oppose further renewals; the sanctions debate in 1972 was even more sticky, as was a 1973 debate on new financial sanctions. The settlement negotiated in 1972 was not upheld against the test that it must be acceptable to Rhodesian opinion as a whole; after this the Government urged further talks within Rhodesia on an amended settlement, but continued to renew sanctions annually on the ground that a change of policy would seem to favour one side against the other when what was now needed was for Rhodesians to deal with their own problems internally. The same two dozen critics appeared in each debate but the issue was by 1973 making only a limited impact on the wider Party.[24]

The same could not be said about immigration. The Government passed a new Immigration Act in 1971 to tighten the rules of entry, as had been proposed in 1970. In introducing his Bill, Maudling was uncompromising in his refusal to go beyond the position that Heath had spelt out in 1968: 'I do not believe in large-scale repatriation. It is wrong because it would not work and the attempt to make it work would be enormously damaging to what I see as the real objective of our policy, namely, to improve community relations among people already here.' The Monday Club began a 'Halt immigration now' campaign, and the National Front used the issue to launch a period of organisational growth that ran on for the next five years; more worryingly for Conservatives, there was evidence of penetration of the Club by the National Front (NF), and a Club branch in Middlesex had to be dissolved for backing a NF by-election candidate in Uxbridge. When the Club chairman was to be the Party's candidate in a by-election in Lincoln, he was summoned to Central Office by the Party Chairman and agreed to be 'selective' in accepting Monday Club help in his campaign; he conceded that he was 'worried about infiltration' but 'reluctant to try "hounding" members out of the Monday Club'. There was actually a Government defeat on the order to give detailed effect to the Immigration Act, with seven Conservatives voting with Labour and nearly fifty abstentions, critics coming from both ends of the Party spectrum. There was also trouble in Autumn 1972 when the Ugandan dictator Idi Amin expelled Asians from his country, as Kenya had threatened to do in 1968. The Government agreed to take in many of the refugees that this created, and there were serious rumblings on the Tory right; Area Agents all reported resignations and resolutions of protest, most of all from the West Midlands and Yorkshire, and soon discovered that the protests were being stoked up deliberately by critics of the Government; from the Western Area it was reported that 'many of those writing and telephoning agents are known to be (a) anti Common Market, (b) members of the Monday

---

[24] Hurd, *End to Promises*, 51–2, 54; Central Office Chairman's department file, CCO 20/7/10; *NCP* 26 Oct. 1970 and 5 Apr. 1971; Zig Layton-Henry, 'Immigration', in Z. Layton-Henry (ed.), *Conservative Party Politics* (1980), 65–6; Norton, *Dissension*, 381, 522, 523–5, 585, 597–8.

Club, (c) pro-Enoch Powell'. The wide knowledge of the unpleasant nature of the Amin regime almost certainly limited the political fall-out; even so, the platform at the 1972 Party Conference was backed by less than half of the representatives. Criticised by the Monday Club, Heath replied acidly that 'we hold that it is in the interest of the British people that the reputation of Britain for good faith and humanity should be preserved. I had assumed that this was also one of the purposes of the Monday Club.' But the Ugandan Asians issue was something of a special case – and did not as the right feared become a precedent. The Nuffield election study concluded in some surprise that 'by the end of 1973 as little was being heard about race relations and immigration as at any time for ten years'.[25]

A policy area where Government decisions were unexpected, though actually in conformity with pledges of 1970, was Ulster. This was a difficult issue for the Heath Government as it would have been for any Conservative Cabinet, for, since the entry of British troops into the internal conflict in 1969, it was no longer a matter that could simply be left to the Unionist Government at Stormont. On the other hand any policy that divided Conservatives at Westminster from Unionists in Belfast would cut across ties of sentiment and loyalty and make a material difference to the parliamentary arithmetic, since the Ulster Unionists made up half of Heath's margin over the other parties combined, and even more when English seats began to be lost at by-elections. Initially, the Conservatives continued the policy inherited from Labour. Maudling announced on 30 June 1970 that 'our twofold policy must be, first, to see that grievances are dealt with and, secondly, to maintain impartially public order and freedom under the law'. Even that order of priorities was a disappointment to Unionists, who had hoped that their old allies would give them some breathing space on internal reform, but the Cabinet did not flinch from this. As Hailsham, whose own ancestors derived from Ulster Unionist stock, put it in 1975, it had been 'one thing to acquiesce in the continuance of an unjust situation as the lesser of two evils. This is clearly morally right. It is another thing to attempt to restore it and then fail. I was convinced, rightly or wrongly, that any attempt to restore the status quo would fail.' He was also typical in believing that there was still a chance that sensible, non-sectarian reforms could bring about an early restoration of peace and allow Ulster to become 'a normal democracy'. This meant that the Government must remain strictly neutral between Unionist and Nationalist in Northern Ireland – a difficult path to pursue while Ulster MPs from the two communities sat on opposite sides of the House at Westminster. How difficult this was becoming can be seen from a visit the Party Chairman Peter Thomas paid to Belfast in 1971, one

---

[25] Central Office file, CCO 4/10/298, Uganda; Central Office Chairman's department file, CCO 20/43/6, Monday Club; Campbell, *Heath*, 393; Butler and Kavanagh, *General Election of February 1974*, 24.

of a series of reciprocal visits going back to the 1950s and intended to foster understanding between Unionists and Conservatives. On arrival in Belfast, as the *Belfast Telegraph* reported, 'Mr. Peter Thomas, who arrived on the same plane, was left standing on the tarmac as reporters and cameramen crowded round Mr. Powell'; this was a sign how far normal Conservative politics was already ceasing to matter in Belfast, even if the change was not yet clear at Westminster, where it was in any case masked by the appointment of an Ulster Unionist MP to the Government in 1972, the first such appointment for decades.[26]

Not all Conservatives were happy with the pressure put on Unionists in Belfast; when Conservative students debated in April 1971 a resolution calling for an explicit threat of direct rule if reform slackened in Belfast, it was passed by only ninety-two votes to seventy-one. But it was security rather than internal reform that broke the Unionist alliance. Only in February 1971 was the first British soldier killed but by early 1974 the forces' death toll was already over two hundred, and there had by then been killings on the mainland too. The first reaction to this upsurge in terrorism was the introduction of internment without trial in 1971, a policy on which the Westminster and Belfast Governments agreed. The next stage, when the level of killings actually increased, was more difficult, and in March 1972, in what he described as the most difficult decision of his premiership, Heath announced that the Stormont Government would be suspended and Northern Ireland governed from London. Willie Whitelaw became the first of three successive Tory Chief Whips to become Northern Ireland Secretary, it clearly being felt that a tough listener was the right type of governor for the province. When he was appointed, Whitelaw was said to have agreed with Cecil King's view that 'in the end the answer must be a united Ireland', but this was not what he said publicly; the official position was that future constitutional status was entirely a matter for Ulster people, and a Northern Ireland referendum in 1973 produced a resounding (if predictable) vote for the Union. Whitelaw, and Pym when he succeeded him late in 1973, became the first of a succession of Secretaries of State to attempt to secure cross-community political cooperation in Northern Ireland while officially stating their determination to maintain the partition of Ireland for as long as the Unionist majority wanted it.[27]

The Bill that suspended Stormont, intentionally only for a year but for over twenty years as it was to turn out, had the support of Labour as well as Tory front benches and passed the Commons by 483 votes to 20; the minority included Powell and Maude, a few Monday Club right wingers like John Biggs-Davison (who told the House that he was 'deeply

[26] *NCP*, 6 Dec. 1971; Hailsham, *Door Wherein I Went*, 242; Central Office Chairman's department file, CCO 20/14/14, Chairman's visit to Ulster; NUEC, 22 Apr. 1971.
[27] Butler and Kavanagh, *General Election of February 1974*, 17; Maudling, *Memoirs*, 184; King, *Diary 1970–74*, 187, 198.

shocked and ashamed by the Prime Minister's statement'), all eight Ulster Unionists, and Ian Paisley – the sole Unionist outside the official Party in the 1970 Parliament. In private, far more Tory MPs were critical. In the debate, Powell argued for a complete integration of Northern Ireland into a united kingdom, while Paisley 'had no doubt that many of his own electors would feel that they could never really trust a Conservative Government again'. This presaged the end of a century of Unionist cooperation at Westminster, for after years of keeping themselves to themselves, most Unionist MPs had few close friends on the Tory benches and they now drifted entirely apart, seven of the eight formally announcing on 31 March 1972 that they would no longer give general support to the Government – which only increased their distance from other Tories. When Whitelaw's power-sharing proposals were put to the Commons in March 1973, only ten Conservatives joined the Ulster Unionists to oppose the end of the local dominance they had enjoyed in Ulster since 1920, while 251 voted to end it; henceforth the Unionists were often in the Opposition lobby, being well aware that they could be outflanked by Paisley and his hardline allies if they showed any quarter to the Heath Government. It is therefore essential to make it clear that the decision of 1972 was foreshadowed during the 1970 Election, though, given the low profile of Ulster in that campaign, few would have been aware of the fact – the 1970 Nuffield election study made no mention whatsoever of a Conservative policy on Ulster. Having as Prime Minister visited Belfast in 1964 as part of his speaking tour of all four capitals, Sir Alec Douglas-Home also spoke there in 1970; he was by then not only a Tory elder statesman, but also one whose recent involvement with Scottish devolution policy had made him specially qualified to speak on constitutional issues; it is in any case inconceivable that he would have done what he did without clearing it with Heath in advance. In June 1970 Sir Alec explained in what conditions a Conservative Government would feel obliged to close down Stormont; his prospective scenario for direct rule rested on the proposition that it would happen *only* if Westminster became convinced that the continuation of Stormont was in itself an obstacle to the restoration of order in the province. In 1972 this was exactly the point at issue, for it was generally agreed that police and troops must come under a single authority; the Stormont Cabinet was insisting that it be given command of British troops in Ulster, which would have been wildly provocative to the Nationalist community only a few weeks after 'Bloody Sunday', and it resigned when Heath insisted on the opposite policy of uniting the forces of law and order under Westminster control. Conservative MPs were at first restive about this, but quietened down considerably when the army's successful reoccupation of the 'no-go' areas in August 1972 seemed to prove that security was best handled from Westminster. If British politicians could be forgiven for not knowing what Sir Alec had said in 1970, Ulster Unionist MPs could hardly argue that they had not been warned, for many of them had been on the platform when he had said it. Even before the security crackdown of August 1972, the National Union Executive debate in June had shown that 'there was overwhelming support for the policy being pursued by Mr. Whitelaw'.[28]

Alongside developing Government policy in Ulster, there had to be a Party reappraisal of the Unionist alliance, for the organic link of Conservatism with an Ulster Unionism tied to the Orange tradition was in itself an embarrassment now that a Conservative Government had to be seen to be impartial. It was easier to see the need for such a reappraisal than to carry it out, for old loyalties and friendships could not just be discarded or set aside. Douglas-Home's 1970 foray to Belfast had been intended as a warning shot to the Paisleyites who already threatened to outbid the relative moderation on which the Conservative and Unionist connection hinged. In the following year, Central Office ran a training course for Ulster Unionist agents, 'to help them to tackle the Paisley challenge'; it was reported that the event had been a great social success but had been very divided whenever politics was mentioned – 'to be frank almost every Ulster man is a political party in himself'. The division was most explicit at the younger level; the chairman of the Federation of Conservative Students, Andrew Neill, was one of the first to call for the suspension of Stormont and the resumption of direct rule from Westminster, while Ulster's Young Unionists were well to the right of the Stormont Government and backing William Craig's militant Vanguard movement.[29]

By this stage, organisational separation was also taking place. Once Unionist MPs repudiated the Tory whip at Westminster, the National Union considered early in 1973 rule changes to remove Ulster representatives from its own committees, but as this was referred to the Chelmer Committee looking more generally into the Party structure no changes were put to the vote until after 1974; in February 1974, the local associations that backed Unionist candidates with whom Heath refused to work were still affiliated to the National Union. But Central Office warned constituencies not to accept speakers sent by the Ulster Unionist Council, and was privately suspicious of the fact that these offers had been sent straight to the Areas and not through Central Office. In August 1972 Heath asked Michael Fraser to set work in train on four questions: the effects of introducing proportional representation in Ulster, additions to Ulster's representation at Westminster now that delegated government had been wound down, advice on how to keep up an 'alliance with a sectarian party based on, and largely controlled by, the Orange lodges', and finally, advice on how to retain supportive

28 Norton, *Conservative Dissidents*, 84–6, 88; Whitelaw, *Memoirs*, 87; Norton, *Dissension*, 423–4, 537; Lord Carrington, *Reflect on Things Past: The Memoirs of Lord Carrington* (1988), 248; the Douglas-Home speech, as issued in a Party press release, is included in the briefing notes for the Party Chairman's 1972 visit, Central Office Chairman's department file, CCO 20/14/14; NUEC, 15 June 1972.
29 Central Office file, CCO 500/55/2, Northern Ireland.

MPs in Ulster in the new circumstances. Heath suggested that the last of these questions would necessitate either creating a reformed Unionist Party with no formal connection to Protestant pressure groups or the setting up of Conservative branches in Ulster so that the Party could fight the seats itself. Consulted by Fraser, the Research Department's James Douglas concluded that 'the Ulster Unionist Party as we knew it for twenty years has disintegrated'; he reported that Craig and Paisley had now so syphoned off its traditional working-class supporters that 'it is not beyond the bounds of possibility that [the traditional Unionists] would be unable to return a single Member to Westminster'. He accepted the need to create a new party organisation that would be 'distinctively Irish and broad in its social appeal but also moderate on constitutional and religious issues', but, after sketching in possible ways forward, concluded that all of them seemed 'barely more than science fiction'. Fraser, while characteristically urging in January 1973 the commissioning of 'a really good survey' to underpin any policy decisions, warned Heath that the chances of Conservative candidates winning seats in Ulster were 'negligible', and that the only worthwhile strategy was to go for a reformed Ulster Unionism, which would have modernised methods of candidate selection, a stronger central machine and no links with the Orange Order; finally, he warned that it was essential to tackle all of this soon, and well before a general election. In fact the next year was wasted in discussing these issues, but with nobody in Belfast having the authority to take decisions, and with the Government's insistence on a new Ulster Executive in which Catholics would share power with Protestants complicating the questions enormously. Moderate Unionists who were prepared to support power-sharing were finally disowned by the Ulster Unionist Council only on 4 January 1974, leaving these moderates and their Conservative contacts only three weeks to respond to the new situation before an early election (called for reasons that had nothing to do with Ulster) cut the ground from under their feet. The Conservative Party's position remained much as Douglas had defined it twenty months earlier, but only when candidates were actually selected for the February 1974 Election in Ulster, after parliament had been dissolved, did this become clear.[30]

In purely domestic affairs too there were many policies that were implemented from the 1970 manifesto. Direct taxation was cut and its complexities were greatly reduced, as planned in Opposition; taxation and national insurance taken together fell as a proportion of GNP from 38 to 32 per cent between 1970 and 1973; the top rate of income tax fell from 91 to 75 per cent in the quest to improve incentives for pacemakers, but the standard rate also fell. In 1973, a radical proposal was being planned to bring together income tax and social benefits in a single structure of tax credits, or 'negative income tax'; this would have simplified the benefit system and allowed greater selectivity

---

[30] Central Office files, CCO 500/55/2 and 3, Northern Ireland.

by routing payments through a means test for income tax that everyone had to accept, though many of the complexities of this major reform still awaited clarification. In any case this was another casualty of the Government's loss of office before its time was up. The reform of housing finance, removing subsidy from properties and giving it more selectively to tenants in the form of rent rebates was bitterly attacked from the Labour benches at the time, and subject to a bout of 'Poplarism' from the Labour council at Clay Cross which was a harbinger of local council activism in the 1980s, but the core of the Act remained in existence for many years after 1974. Encouragement to local authorities to begin selling off their housing stock, following successful schemes pursued by Birmingham Tories, was less successful, mainly because the Government's unpopularity soon meant that most local authorities were under Labour control anyway. By 1972 over sixty thousand houses a year were being sold, and by 1974, 7 per cent of the total stock had been sold. A more active policy would have to wait until after 1979, but the shift to legislating for a 'right to buy' owed much to the experience of Labour councils' obstruction of permissive policies in 1970–74.[31]

Peter Walker was equally determined in his wholesale redrawing of the map of local government. In place of a Royal Commission recommendation of single-tier authorities, each uniting a city and its hinterland, Walker set up two tiers on a fairly uniform pattern across the country, adopting the London pattern for the conurbations and a system with stronger county authorities for the rest of the country; Conservative strength in the shires ensured that Walker would be receptive to the case for continuing with county councils, even though there were some fierce battles over boundaries and mergers, with a large number of hostile resolutions passed by Conservative associations and branches: the policy provoked the outright opposition of the Tory-controlled Association of Municipal Authorities. As in 1962–63 when Joseph had attempted a more limited rationalisation, this resistance was mainly from areas threatened with abolition as separate entities and from others placed in counties to which they felt no allegiance, notably on the borders of the Yorkshire ridings, where for example the Ripon Tories wrote to Heath about their 'profound misgivings' over Government policy only shortly before having to fight a critical by-election; the Government tried to distance itself from these multitudinous local grievances by placing much of the detailed work in the hands of a local government boundary commission, and nearly two thousand amendments to the Bill were made during its passage. There had been an extensive programme of explanatory Party meetings but the basic scheme went ahead as planned and this time Rutland did not survive. When Lincolnshire was carved up in order to create the new county of Humberside, the Area Agent reported of local Party opinion, 'They are up in

---

31 Sewill, *British Economic Policy*, 34; Shrapnel, *The Seventies*, 37; Walker, *Staying Power*, 88; *NCP* 7 May 1973; Campbell, *Heath*, 379.

arms'. A comparable restructuring of health authorities was carried through in the same modernising spirit by Joseph. Introducing his Local Government Bill, Walker argued that nobody had attempted such a review of boundaries and functions for a century, 'and no one in their right mind would reform it for another hundred years'. In parliament, opposition to these proposals was minimal, but they were not to have the unchallenged longevity that their architects had hoped for.[32]

The 1972 U-turns

In many fields then, the Heath Government got on with its prepared programme, but it would be foolish to argue that on fundamental economic questions there was not a considerable gap between the perceived 1970 programme and the policies being pursued by 1973. Nor was this only a view put about after 1979 by triumphalist Thatcherites. Ernle Money, who held Ipswich for the Tories after 1970 as a loyal Government supporter, reflected a year after his own 1974 defeat on the irony,

> that a Government which had begun its life by producing legislation to denationalise Thomas Cook's and the state pubs in Carlisle should shortly follow this by nationalising Rolls Royce. In the event of what was to come, the initial policy of winding up the government agencies concerned with consumer protection, the Industrial Reconstruction Corporation and the Prices and Incomes Board was to seem an additional irony.

As we have seen, this view dignifies the Heath team's 1970 position with a degree of coherence in its economic policy that was not in fact the case, though it appeared to be so on its published statements. Even Heath's closest supporters, if never the man himself, gave up trying to pretend that there had been no recantation of the *words* of 1970; Willie Whitelaw's memoirs may stand for many in conceding of 1972's statutory control of incomes, that 'as has frequently been pointed out, this was a complete reversal of the declared policies of the 1970 manifesto'. Even when allowance is made for John Campbell's insistence on the small print and reservations in the 1970 manifesto, this has been the predominant view since 1979.[33]

In order to understand this 'complete reversal', and the reason why the Party at the time assented to it with so little audible protest, we need to differentiate between industrial policy and the counter-inflation policy, which have tended to be subsumed in descriptions of a 1972 'U-turn', and we need to

---

[32] Bruce Wood, *The Process of Local Government Reform, 1966–1974* (1976), 96, 122–3, 149; Norton, *Dissension*, 433; Norman Tebbit, *Upwardly Mobile* (1989), 125; Walker, *Staying Power*, 49–50, 79; Central Office Chairman's department files, CCO 20/19/20 and 21, Local Government reorganisation; Ripon CA minutes, 16 Dec. 1971; Ken Young, 'The Party and English Local Government', in Seldon and Ball, *Conservative Century*, 433.

[33] Ernle Money, *Margaret Thatcher: First Lady of the House* (1975), 108; Halcrow, *Joseph*, 54; Whitelaw, *Memoirs*, 125.

see how far modifications of detailed policy were intended as different routes towards the same end – growth without excessive inflation, with Europe always in mind.

On industry, Brendon Sewill argued in 1975 that 'the "lame-duck" philosophy – that inefficient firms should be allowed to go bust – had a comparatively small place in our thinking in Opposition, was never mentioned at Selsdon Park, and achieved headlines only with Mr. John Davies' speech in October 1970'. This ignored Joseph's speeches before the 1970 Election calling for 'more rewards – and more bankruptcies', but the fact that Heath did not then put Joseph in charge of industrial policy, either in June or when Macleod died, did indicate the distance between his views and Joseph's. Ironically, the man chosen instead of Joseph, John Davies, perhaps because his political inexperience led him to less guarded positions than was wise, uttered the phrases that were most to hang around Heath's neck later. At the Party Conference in October 1970 and in the Commons a month later, Davies was widely quoted as intending to let 'lame ducks' in industry go to the wall, but his actual words at Blackpool were more balanced: 'I believe that simply to abandon great sectors of our productive community at their moment of maximum weakness would be folly indeed. But I will not bolster up or bail out companies where I can see no end to the process of propping them up. . . . I will not accept involvement in an open-ended liability.' Even Davies' declared policy on taking office therefore contained an ambiguity, though his description to the 1922 Committee in February 1971 of 'a strategy of industrial disengagement' seemed clear enough, and his junior ministers Fred Corfield, Sir John Eden and Nicholas Ridley were anyway less even-handed in their words. A year later, T.E. Utley was writing in the *Daily Telegraph* of 'two potentially incompatible elements' in the Government's industrial policy, 'streamlined, efficient administration based on long-term planning by experts assembled in large Ministries, and a deliberate attempt wherever possible to disengage the State. In both these respects, the Government, during its first year, has been outstandingly loyal to its mandate.' Davies' permanent secretary at the Department of Trade and Industry, Sir Anthony Part, later recalled receiving a double instruction of the same stripe from Heath: 'the first was "disengage from industry" and the second was "act like Great Britain Limited".' With contradictory words on offer, much was read into deeds; the winding up of Labour's interventionist machinery within the first months in office seemed self-explanatory.[34]

The first tests of that policy seemed to confirm that a hard line would be taken, when for example the Cabinet refused to bail out the Mersey Docks and Harbour Board in November 1970 even though the Minister

[34] Sewill, *British Economic Policy*, 30; Carrington, *Reflect on Things Past*, 255; Halcrow, *Joseph*, 40, 44; Whitehead, *Writing on the Wall*, 56; NCP 26 Oct. 1970; 1922, 18 Feb. 1971; Moore and Heffer, *A Tory Seer*, 103; ICBH witness seminar, 'The Trade Unions and the Fall of the Heath Government', in *Contemporary Record*, vol .2, no. 1, (1988) 39.

of Transport supported the idea. Labour's plan to nationalise the ports was stopped, and the first steps were taken towards the encouragement of a second major British airline to inject competition into a notoriously monopolistic field. The selling of Thomas Cook's to the private sector went ahead as planned, the Home Office gave up trying to influence drinking habits in Carlisle, and investigations were mounted into the possible selling of hotels by British Railways and brickworks by the National Coal Board; the Gas Council was stopped from drilling in the North Sea to leave the fields to the private sector. Conversely, on the most symbolic industry of all, steel, the Government never had any truck with denationalisation and in June 1971 agreed to the extension of British Steel's authority further into the private sector. Davies was a pragmatic Minister who was interested more in efficiency than ownership, and was easily persuaded to back a programme of expansion by British Steel, though he ran into difficulties with backbenchers when British Steel then engaged in advertising to proclaim its success as a public corporation. Keith Ovenden, writing in 1978 with the experience of Labour in office since 1974 at his disposal, believed that the Conservatives' 'final' capitulation to the idea of a nationalised steel industry had actually encouraged Labour's nationalisers to bid higher: it had 'paved the way for the new surge in public enterprise experimentation and expansion which the Labour Government pressed ahead after returning to office in 1974'. So long as the Conservatives had refused to accept steel nationalisation, their resistance had been a barrier to other nationalisation schemes, but 'when the gates had been opened, and when the Conservatives in office had failed to shut them again, the course was prepared for new developments'. Here again the Thatcher Government would have a worse baseline to start from than Heath in 1970 in the pursuit of traditional Tory policy.[35]

Steel actually attracted remarkably little attention in 1971 – considering the bitterness of debates since 1948 – and may fairly be pigeonholed as another policy in which the Heath Cabinet saw through policies announced in opposition. Other public sector schemes were more actively debated. The first was the remarkable decision to take Rolls-Royce Aero Engines into public ownership early in the Government's life, after a catastrophic miscalculation on a single contract had plunged the company into bankruptcy; the Government first put in a great deal of public money and then nationalised the company to protect its assets, though Corfield was careful to emphasise that 'it is not the Government's intention that Rolls Royce should remain indefinitely in Government ownership'. This could easily be presented as a special case, for as put by Peter Rawlinson who gave legal advice on the policy, the Government 'decided that it could not allow Rolls Royce with its prestigious name and its involvement in defence to disappear'.

---

[35] Whitehead, *Writing on the Wall*, 57; Bruce-Gardyne, *Quiet Revolution?*, 38; Roth, *Heath*, 218; Ovenden, *Politics of Steel*, 178, 180, 183, 191; Walker, *Staying Power*, 110.

Cecil Parkinson recalled that this argument 'persuaded the doubters to support the government', while Norman Tebbit remembered of this debate that Enoch Powell spoke against the Government, 'but not even he would vote against the rescue'. But if the vote in the House was uneventful, the jibes against Heath in the lobbies were many. David Wood in *The Times* pointed out that a Government like Heath's which had so clearly set its face against all compromise was peculiarly susceptible to charges of betrayal: by rescuing Rolls Royce, Wood felt, 'the man of principle will seem to many to be a pragmatist and a fixer of a familiar kind. . . . Mr. Heath has been robbed of something of great value to him'. In this broad reaction, which Heath had encouraged by his own earlier speeches, it was easy to overlook the fact that the car division of Rolls Royce, which was not a special case with defence significance, was speedily returned to the private sector.[36]

The second aberration from the industrial strategy was less easy to defend. Initially the Government refused to rescue Upper Clyde Shipbuilders (UCS) when it faced bankruptcy, and made defiant speeches to that effect; in March 1971 Davies stated that 'no new public funds are to be supplied to UCS', a decision he reaffirmed in June; the *Guardian* had fun with a leaked 1969 Party document authored by Nicholas Ridley in which he had specifically argued for liquidating UCS. However, from Summer 1971, a work-in at the shipyard under the charismatic leadership of a Communist shop-steward attracted considerable media attention and put the Government on the defensive, in circumstances in which its legal position was rather complicated. After receiving police advice that failure to rescue UCS could lead to disorder that would be uncontrollable, the Government changed course and in Spring 1972 found more money to keep the yards open. There was no especial strategic interest involved in UCS, and more widespread doubts were felt.[37]

The shift of policy over UCS in any case coincided with a more comprehensive review of economic and industrial policy that led on to the 'Barber boom' and the 1972 Industry Act. The effect of deflationary policies pursued by Labour before it left office and not moderated in Barber's first year was a steep increase in unemployment. Conventional wisdom since 1945 was that no government would be re-elected unless it had delivered full employment, and in any case Heath and his colleagues were of a generation who remembered enough of the 1930s to know at first hand how far joblessness would produce other social evils in its wake; he told businessmen in June 1973 that 'every government has to go for full employment – no government could exist

36 Whitehead, *Writing on the Wall*, 56–7; NCP 8 Mar. 1971; Rawlinson, *Price Too High*, 179; Parkinson, *Right at the Centre*, 113; Tebbit, *Upwardly Mobile*, 131; Roth, *Heath*, 222; Walker, *Staying Power*, 108.

37 NCP 8 Mar. 1971; Bruce-Gardyne, *Quiet Revolution?*, 35; Cockerell, *Live from Number Ten*, 185; Lord Howe at ICBH witness seminar, 1994; Whitehead, *Writing on the Wall*, 80–1; Parkinson, *Right at the Centre*, 113.

on any other terms'. When charged with inconsistency, another Cabinet Minister asked Andrew Roth rhetorically, 'what did they want us to do [about unemployment], go over the cliff with flags flying?' Moreover, since the Tories had themselves complained about unemployment in the 1970 Election, they could expect no quarter from Labour when it then doubled. The announcement in January 1972 that there were nearly a million unemployed, a significant watershed that was far above any experience since 1947, led to disorder in the House of Commons and the suspension of debate by the Speaker; Jim Prior later recalled this as an event that shook Heath considerably. However, the shift to a more expansionist policy was not simply a knee-jerk reaction to high unemployment; rather it was a determination to speed up economic growth because of imminent entry into the EEC, growth which would have the effect of reducing unemployment anyway. As Butler and Kavanagh put it, for the first year the Government's 'major goal was the fight against inflation. In July 1971, Mr. Heath moved on to a policy of growth at almost any price.' Douglas Hurd thought that the confusion about the Government's economic objective arose from the familiar problem, that the Heath Government was better at explaining policies than the reasons for them or the philosophy behind them. Heath was also handicapped by a wish not to appear to change course too obviously; when it was hinted during the 1971 Party Conference that the anti-interventionist junior industry ministers, Ridley and Eden, were to be thrown overboard, Heath denied it, demanded an investigation into the leak, and put off his reshuffle. Andrew Roth, hardly a sympathetic witness, concluded in 1972 that 'people outside may think it scandalous that a government should jettison in its second year principles thought essential and distinctive in its first year. But the target has always been the same, to enter the EEC with the economy at full stretch.' He might indeed have gone further and said that it had been Heath's settled policy objective since about 1962–63. This conforms closely to Christopher Chataway's view in 1994 that when he was asked to implement the new Industry Act in 1972, 'the driver for it was entry into the Community'.[38]

The effect of this was that the tilt in budgetary policy was put in place before the change in industrial policy had been worked out. In 1971, the conventional Keynesian strategy aimed to reduce taxation to deal with a deflated economy. Then in the 1972 Budget, the Chancellor adopted a higher annual growth target, renewed for a further year in Spring 1973, and shortly afterwards allowed the pound to float, which reduced the impact of currency fluctuation on his expansion strategy. This 'dash for growth' underlay the tax-cutting Budget of 1972 and encouraged ministers to plan for big increases in their own expenditure; increased spending on defence, Joseph's plans for

---

[38] Taylor, *Trade Union Question*, 189; Butler and Kavanagh, *General Election of February 1974*, 11; Whitehead, *Writing on the Wall*, 96; Hurd, *End to Promises*, 89–91; Prior, *Balance of Power*, 74; Roth, *Heath*, xvi, 224–5; Sir Christopher Chataway at ICBH witness seminar, 1994.

social service spending and Thatcher's White Paper predicated on years of rising educational expenditure were the most obvious cases, mainly because these were fields which inevitably released pent up departmental pressures once tight Treasury control was relaxed. The Chief Secretary to the Treasury, Patrick Jenkin, explained in February 1973 that because of the rate of growth in the economy 'there should be no serious difficulty about the management of the overall demand on our resources in the medium term'. Meanwhile, credit relaxations in 1971 had unleashed a surge in the money supply and in the prices of commodities. The banks fell over each other to lend money and recorded huge increases in their profits as a result; in two years the size of bank advances doubled, private borrowing trebled and loans to the financial and property markets quadrupled, while industrial investment continued to stagnate; the occasional dubious business practice that this 'new Klondyke' revealed lay behind Heath's reference to 'the unpleasant and unacceptable face of capitalism'. As land prices soared, housebuilding slumped to a lower level in 1973 than in any year since Macmillan had been at Housing in 1952, house prices rose 70 per cent in two years, and the mortgage rate rocketed to an unprecedented 11 per cent. Heath and Barber now diverged in their approach to economic growth, the Prime Minister taking a slightly more upbeat view than the Chancellor, and hoping to break out of the stop-go cycle once and for all; he told the NEDC in September 1973, 'This time we are determined to sail through the whirlpool'. It would be wrong though to suggest that this Government-induced spending boom ran full-tilt into the buffers in Autumn 1973; credit restrictions began to be imposed by the Government as early as November 1972, and were reinforced several times during 1973, before the largest public expenditure cuts ever were made in December 1973.[39]

The increased spending on education and social services flowed naturally enough through goverment departments, and the banks were enthusiastic channels for the credit boom, but new mechanisms were needed to route government investment to industry, not least since the Government had swept away all such mechanisms in 1970 and the responsible Ministers had no wish to reinvent them. The new approach therefore also required a new team at the Department of Trade and Industry (DTI); Peter Walker has recalled the difficulty of knowing for a considerable time that he would go to the DTI but not knowing whether its present Ministers had yet been told. In the mean time, the new machinery was designed on Heath's personal instructions by a team of civil servants under Sir William Armstrong, outside the Ministry that would have to carry it out; Davies knew about this but was not allowed to tell Ridley and Eden; the Chief Secretary to the Treasury, whose duty it was to wind up the Budget Debate during which Davies announced the new

[39] Sewill, *British Economic Policy*, 13, 37, 41, 45–6; Butler and Kavanagh, *General Election of February 1974*, 23; Whitehead, *Writing on the Wall*, 84–5, 91–2, 94–5; Money, *Thatcher*, 69, 73–4; Halcrow, *Joseph*, 48, 50, 55; NCP 26 Feb. 1973; Geoffrey Howe, *Conflict of Loyalty* (1994), 77–8.

policy, learned of it himself in the House when it was actually announced, just a few hours before he would have to defend its provisions. When eventually offered only the post of Arts Minister in April 1972, Ridley left the Government (if indeed he was not sacked outright – accounts differ), as did Corfield, while Eden was re-directed to the Post Office. Davies lingered at the DTI until Walker finally replaced him in November. The Industry Bill that went through in Spring 1972 as a result of these plans and changes laid the Government open to some telling rejoinders from Labour; Davies' announcement of the new policy achieved an ovation on the Labour side and an embarrassed silence on the benches behind him. Tony Benn pointed out that Heath's Bill allowed four times as much spending at ministerial discretion as the Labour provisions he had abolished in 1970. Again this line of attack, particularly wounding to Heath's vanity, led only to increasingly implausible denials of a change of policy rather than to an effective defence of the reasons for the policy now being pursued. In 1973, Corfield even announced that he would not stand for re-election, because of 'a lack of faith in the Government's economic policy'.[40]

Armed with the new powers, and with enough money to induce industry to accept his advice, Walker set about what he has called 'a frantic phase' in which the DTI 'attempted to rationalize and modernise British industry'. Despite Benn's widely reported comment that the new Act would be 'spadework for socialism', the Government encountered remarkably little resistance from its supporters in the Commons; even in a vote on a proposed new clause that would have extended parliamentary scrutiny of ministerial investment decisions, only four Conservatives defied the whip, though a few more expressed reservations in the debate. There were no rebel votes on other divisions, but there were a lot of miserable Conservatives. A *Crossbow* editorial in May 1973 sadly noted that of Selsdon Man, 'nothing of him remains'. Even while reluctantly accepting the Government's reasoning on the need for an incomes policy, it was bitterly critical of 'the great U-turn' on industry:

> If the weakness of the lame ducks policy was that it had not been sufficiently thought out, the weakness of the present 'leave it to the DTI' attitude is that it is even vaguer. . . . The collapse of the attitude and philosophy summed up in the 'Selsdon Man' phase has left a vacuum in Tory thinking. It is partly because the philosophy is weak that the Government gives the appearance of always reacting to events. This may seem hard, in that the Government's 1970 manifesto has been more completely implemented than any party's. But the lack of a Tory philosophy behind many of the Government's actions has left the party confused, and could leave the party vulnerable in the future.[41]

[40] Walker, *Staying Power*, 92; Hugo Young, *One of Us: A Biography of Margaret Thatcher* (1989), 77; Nicholas Ridley, *My Style of Government* (1991), 4; Whitehead, *Writing on the Wall*, 82–3; Norton, *Conservative Dissidents*, 150; Roth, *Heath*, 234.

[41] Walker, *Staying Power*, 95–6; Bruce-Gardyne, *Quiet Revolution?*, 80; Tony Benn, *Office Without Power: Diaries 1968–1972* (1989), 429; Norton, *Dissension*, 510–11; *Crossbow*, May 1973, 4.

By Autumn 1972, when the Government was beginning to implement the Industry Act, it had attracted even more attention to a change of policy in respect of inflation. At first, the Cabinet kept to its 1970 intentions by pursuing a prices and incomes policy by persuasion only, inducing the CBI to agree to voluntary price restraint and using exhortation to lower wage demands in stages, while awaiting the beneficial impact hoped for from the Industrial Relations Act. This policy was derailed partly by the fact that 1971's battles over industrial relations soured rather than improved relations with the unions, partly because accelerating inflation as the boom took off in 1971–72 made it more difficult to get unions to moderate their demands, but mainly because in some crucial disputes the Government was defeated by powerful unions. The critical moment came with the miners' 1972 pay review. The Government underestimated the readiness for a fight of a union that had not been noticeably militant of late; Carr recalled that 'our judgement turned out to be wrong. There was no doubt about it, our intelligence about the strength of opinion within the miners' union generally was not as good as it should have been.' Hence the Government's reliance on the judgement of the Coal Board, which proved to be poor. The Government dug its heels in, only to find that the miners then voted for a strike and achieved considerable public support for their case; flying pickets took the dispute to coal depots all over the country and the unwillingness of other trade unionists to cross picket lines, in this year of deep union antagonism towards the Government, meant that coal stocks virtually ceased to move; the turning point came when the Saltley coal depot in Birmingham was closed down by the police to prevent disorder, after the Chief Constable had advised that he could keep it open come what may. The Cabinet was now looking into the abyss; Sewill, viewing the scene from the Treasury, recalled in 1975 that Ministers and senior civil servants

> saw only a few days away the possibility of the country being plunged into a state of chaos not so far removed from that which might prevail after a minor nuclear attack. If that sounds melodramatic I need only say that – with the prospect of the breakdown of power supplies, food supplies, sewerage, communications, effective government and law and order – it was the analogy that was being used at the time.

Even giving way proved difficult; an inquiry by Lord Wilberforce awarded the miners most of what they had asked for, but they still refused to settle without getting more. Douglas Hurd wrote in his diary that 'the Government are now wandering vainly over the battlefield looking for somebody to surrender to – and being massacred all the time'. When the miners finally went back to work the Government's incomes policy was shattered; Barber saw the settlement as 'a disaster' and Carr thought 'the court of enquiry blew us to pieces'.[42]

[42] Whitehead, *Writing on the Wall*, 74–7, 89; Taylor, *Trade Union Question*, 197–9; Maudling, *Memoirs*, 160; Sewill, *British Economic Policy*, 50; Hurd, *End to Promises*, 102–3.

Heath's very public defeat by the miners in 1971–72 also hemmed him in for the future; Tory backbenchers made it abundantly clear that the next miners' pay round should be prepared for in advance and that they would not accept a second humiliation from the same quarter. The National Union Executive, discussing the situation with John Davies in March 1972, was clearly in an unhappy mood: 'The recent miners strike, and the situation concerning unemployment were referred to by several members of the committee, and other subjects raised included Government public relations, the apparent change in policy concerning the Upper Clyde shipyards and the general economic outlook'. In the same month, the Party's Trade Union Advisory Committee resolved that it was

> both angered and disillusioned by the refusal, even abdication, of the Government to show itself willing to govern during the recent miners' strike. . . . The handling of the whole issue showed a serious lack of political judgement which is both dangerous and frightening for the future of country and party.

Few heavier brickbats can ever have been thrown at a Tory Government by a national representative body of its supporters. Within Government, even men who were far from hawkish had like Jim Prior 'vowed that never again would we "do a Wilberforce",' and Prior himself took responsibility for creating a Civil Contingencies Unit to make government more ready for any similar showdown in future. Also, though it was not much remarked at the time, the miners' pay dispute in early 1972 was the first time in which Heath began to speculate openly about the possibility of countering the abuse of industrial power by an early appeal for a new mandate. In the short term though, Heath did not even attempt to put a brave face on the setback, and his broadcast to the nation was sombre; he declared that 'nobody has really won, everybody has lost', and he finished with a baleful stare at the camera, without even managing a 'Good night'. The Eastern Area sent a message to assure Heath 'that you have their complete support and loyalty, particularly at this time', which in its closing words was rather like many of the resolutions sent to Macmillan in 1963; such forms of words are roughly analogous to declarations of backing by football club chairmen for managers whose teams are doing badly, something only a little better than silence. Heath had also said though that 'we have to find a more sensible way of settling our differences'. Party briefs produced at the Research Department now quietly dropped any references to Tory opposition to an incomes policy.[43]

Heath's 'more sensible way' of avoiding a wages explosion in 1972 was to invite the leaders of the CBI and the TUC into tripartite talks at Chequers and

---

[43] NUEC, 2 Mar. and 20 Apr. 1972; Prior, *Balance of Power*, 73, 82; Cockerell, *Live from Number Ten*, 187; Ramsden, *Making of Conservative Party Policy*, 298; Central Office file, CCO 500/32/19, Leader's correspondence.

then at Downing Street, and hopefully into accepting a share of responsibility for the management of the economy. Taking part in a question and answer session at Swinton Conservative College in 1973, Heath denied that anything had changed as a result of the miners' strike, but admitted that the failure of the tripartite talks had then made a new policy inescapable; he seems hardly to have noticed the real point of his questioner, that the question posed by the miners' defeat of the Government would sooner or later recur. In May 1972 he was saying that 'we still have to find sensible means by which sensible men can reach sensible agreements before there is any question of industrial action, of courts of law, of cooling off periods or of ballots'. This followed logically enough from the experiments of Tory governments between 1961 and 1964. Heath was doing little more than seeking to achieve what the NEDC had originally been set up for, and he had first invited the TUC and CBI to talks shortly after he went to Number 10 in 1970, but he had persuaded Maudling in Autumn 1971 not to circulate a Cabinet paper calling for an incomes policy as such, suggesting that at that point he too was not yet ready for what he was to pursue in the following year. It seemed like another abrupt change of front to union leaders who had barely emerged from the trenches over the Industrial Relations Act and were now urged to act like partners of the Prime Minister, and most of the outside world also interpreted it as a change of policy when it came: Nora Beloff in the *Observer* thought that 'Mr. Heath's efforts at partnership are not just an expedient to deal with the emergency of inflation, nor a temporary suspension of the "quiet revolution". For him, the Chequers meetings mark a silent but profound conversion.' The talks in 1972 were therefore serious in intention, but just as seriously hampered by the legacy of antagonism between Government and unions from the previous two years. They were only so prolonged because neither side wished to be seen to have caused a breakdown – though a senior civil servant who had taken part told Cecil King that Heath had pressed on because he 'showed all the enthusiasm of the convert' for cooperation. In weeks of lengthy discussions, Heath even managed to give the employers the impression that he was really more favourable to the unions than he was to them. In fact, the unions kept pressing for more and more as the talks continued, including full repeal of the 1971 Act, which Heath could never have conceded, but steadfastly rejected any control of wages. At this critical moment in the Government's fortunes, its relative failure to communicate was a source almost of despair to its strategic advisers. On 24 October, Michael Wolff in Heath's private office reported to the Central Office Tactical Committee the likely breakdown of the tripartite talks, and Douglas Hurd unavailingly pressed for a Minister to go on television to give the Government's side of the case and prepare the public for a breakdown. A fortnight later, the Party's Director of Organisation accepted 'the point that the talks had broken down because the union side had not wanted wages controlled had not got across to the public'. But there were no advance plans to react to this breakdown.[44]

The refusal to accept that policy had changed was a cardinal problem in explaining what the new policies stood for. Heath, for example, clearly came to believe that nothing much *had* changed in 1972, and in particular that nothing that had been done had resulted from trade union pressure. At the last ACP meeting that he attended as Leader, in January 1975, he was clearly riled when a National Union representative remarked that 'the trouble was that governments always gave in eventually in public sector disputes. Mr. Heath replied that this was not true. He recalled at a time when unemployment was over 1 million and coal stocks were down to under a week's supply, the government had refused to give in and the unions had eventually accepted the award.' This was certainly not most people's greatest memory of the Government's role in the 1972 miners' strike.[45]

When all hope of agreement had to be given up, Heath announced in the Commons on 6 November 1972 that the Government would control prices and incomes statutorily; 'the responsibility for action now rests with the Government'. At first there was a ninety day freeze of prices and incomes, then, when the TUC would still not come back into productive talks, stage two was announced, to run from February 1973 until the Autumn, and with all the paraphernalia of a Pay Board and a Price Board, much like that abolished in 1970. The Cabinet were, as Prior put it, 'reluctant converts, as we realised the difficulties it would cause, with all the inevitable anomalies and inflexibilities'. Barber 'felt, as I think all of us felt, very sad. After all, we'd set our hearts and minds against it. . . . Therefore it was a very big decision to make.' Reluctant or not, the Cabinet agreed; there was, as Peter Walker has pointedly recalled, 'no free market voice raised', and responsibility for supervising the policy in action went to Geoffrey Howe, usually one of the most free market voices in the Government.[46]

It was less easy outside: in the Commons, Powell asked Heath politely, 'Has the Right Honourable Gentleman taken leave of his senses?', and on television Heath was asked by Robin Day whether a man of principle who had now done what he had categorically promised not to do ought not to resign; a backbencher, Robin Maxwell-Hyslop, asked the same question at the 1922 Committee. Only Powell voted against the initial legislation, one of the 113 votes he cast against the whip during the 1970 Parliament, though four Tory MPs abstained on the second reading and two on the third; Powell's speech

[44] Central Office file, CCO 500/32/21, Leader's correspondence; Campbell, *Heath*, 469; Taylor, *Trade Union Question*, 203–4; Butler and Kavanagh, *General Election of February 1974*, 23; Hurd, *End to Promises*, 104; Bruce-Gardyne, *Quiet Revolution?*, 138; King, *Diary 1970–74*, 219, 235, 245; Whitehead, *Writing on the Wall*, 87; Maudling, *Memoirs*, 191, 263–5; Central Office Chairman's department file, CCO 20/7/16, Tactical Committee.
[45] Advisory Committee on Policy minutes [hereafter ACP], 15 Jan. 1975.
[46] Prior, *Balance of Power*, 75; Walker, *Staying Power*, 123; Whitehead, *Writing on the Wall*, 89–90.

on 29 January 1973 was recognised as an intellectual *tour de force* but it did not attract a single supporting vote. He continued his opposition to the later stages of the policy, always with voices raised in his support but rarely with votes. Despite all this, for a time the statutory incomes policy worked fairly well, if at quite a risk. Sewill thought that

> the statutory policy was in a way all bluff. On the pay side the law was never invoked. Indeed because the Government had realised that all hell would break loose if any trade unionist was fined or imprisoned, the law was so constructed that in normal circumstances it was not actually illegal to strike. What the policy really meant was that the Government staked its whole reputation, its whole authority, indeed the authority of Parliament, on the hope that the unions would accept 'the law' or anyway believe that the Government could never allow a strike to succeed. For 18 months the gamble worked; but when it failed the stakes were lost.

In that sense, it was not unlike the way that Ministers had thought of the Industrial Relations Act in 1971, a policy that would already have failed if its provisions were tested. The prices and incomes policy though was rather more detailed than such a broad bluffing approach might suggest; Kenneth Baker, who as junior minister was responsible for carrying it out, recalled weekly meetings at the Treasury that would fix 'such matters as the rates of pay for plumbers, new tariffs for taxis, the increase in rents for furnished flats as opposed to unfurnished flats'. He added, in 1993 when such approaches were well out of fashion, that 'anyone involved in trying to run this policy would never attempt it again'. The policy was always to be temporary, and hence the arguments in its favour had to be redeployed as each stage was developed, while no work could be done to prepare a manifesto in its defence because it was never clearly enunciated as future policy. Moreover, the technical, bureaucratic terminology was difficult to make into slogans: James Douglas enquired sardonically in November 1973, 'if we outlive this day and come safe home, will we indeed rouse up and stand atiptoe at the name "Stage Three"?'[47]

Party reactions to the U-turns

At the time, like nearly all Conservatives, whether Ministers or backbenchers, Kenneth Baker appeared to be an unshakeable supporter of the Government's policy. *How* was it possible to secure such widespread support for the adoption in office of so many policies that had been damned in Opposition – even when it is accepted that the pursuit of growth and full employment was a consistent aim throughout? Was there an extensive but submerged Conservative opposition to the 1972 U-turn that surfaced only when power

---

47 Campbell, *Heath*, 479; Taylor, *Trade Union Question*, 206; Hurd, *End to Promises*, 105; Tebbit, *Upwardly Mobile*, 160; Norton, *Dissension*, 520–3, 529, 595; Cockerell, *Live from Number Ten*, 187; Norton, *Conservative Dissidents*, 119; Sewill, *British Economic Policy*, 53; Baker, *Turbulent Years*, 37; Ramsden, *Making of Conservative Party Policy*, 300–2.

was lost in 1974, or was it only the failure of the policies to keep the Party in power that retrospectively invalidated them in Tory eyes? At Cabinet level, there are several pointers to the fact that only those directly involved in the new policies felt obliged – or even sufficiently informed – to take up a strong position either way. Jim Prior felt that most Ministers could not 'produce an informed judgement on the very great difficulties of Rolls Royce', and Keith Joseph, when later disowning the policies he had supported between 1970 and 1974, confessed that 'I cannot exaggerate the good intentions of Ted Heath or of us under him. But I failed to lift up my eyes.' When at the end of 1971 he sent Heath a paper drawn up by Alan Walters, showing how far the Cabinet was abandoning its Selsdon 'economic principles' and what the consequence of its credit policy would be in future inflation, it was returned by the Prime Minister with a note saying that he and Barber understood the risk they were taking but considered it to be justified. Joseph then let the subject drop. He was later convinced that the regular support for Heath's policies given by *The Economist* had helped to steady ministerial doubts; the paper had also loaned Heath one of its editorial staff as a speechwriter in 1973; as Ruth Dudley Edwards put it, 'during Alastair Burnet's editorship, there was never any doubt about which party the paper would support; Burnet was a Heath man through and through'.[48]

Margaret Thatcher was another who expressed private doubts, telling Nicholas Ridley that she agreed with his opposition to the Counter-Inflation Bill, but declining his invitation to resign and help fight it on the backbenches. When *The Times* reported that some Cabinet Ministers 'frankly confess their uneasiness about the socialist implications' of the Industry Bill, Thatcher was again mentioned among the doubters. She also expressed reservations on the inside, for example following a Chequers presentation of future economic trends by the CPRS with the remark that 'if we let inflation go on like that, we'll lose the next election'. But she had been a dissenting voice even before 1970 and as a result was not much listened to by Heath; and she did not press her doubts to the point of resignation. Other discontented Ministers, whipped in as part of the 'payroll vote' to see the Industry Bill through, consoled each other over a picnic supper in John Peyton's room at the House, attended by the Minister of Transport (Peyton himself), the Minister of Posts (Eden) and the Solicitor-General (Howe); Lord Howe's reminiscence in 1994 was that 'those of us who were at the picnic voting for [the Bill] were as resentful as those who were voting against it', but again nobody resigned. It seems that Heath's strong-minded leadership of the Cabinet and his patient exposition of the case he felt obliged to pursue overrode whatever instinctive doubts there were in the minds of Ministers not directly involved – who could generally console themselves that it was not their departmental responsibility anyway; those

---

[48] Halcrow, *Joseph*, 46, 54–5; Central Office Chairman's department file, CCO 20/16/11, Correspondence with Fraser; Ruth Dudley Edwards, *The Pursuit of Reason: The Economist, 1843–1993* (1993), 838.

who were personally involved – Davies, Walker, Carr and Barber – were natural pragmatists with a predilection for interventionism, like Heath himself, and men who were anyway unlikely to face him down. There was though a sign before the end of the Government that Howe, Joseph and Thatcher were reaching a more definite point of discontent, if not yet of coordinated opposition. In Howe's case, the necessity to defend his own Government's incomes policies in Commons debates, with only rather 'jejune' briefing available from the Treasury, forced some deep thinking, and in January 1974 he shared his dissentient thoughts with a *Financial Times* conference. As long as the Party retained office, all of this remained distinctly muted though; Charles Hill had written in 1964 that Macmillan had 'a flair for convincing [Ministers] that they were members of a team which must hold together in fair weather and foul', and Heath quite clearly possessed a similar gift of inspiring the loyalty of his colleagues; at the Heath Cabinet's last meeting, it was Margaret Thatcher who spoke in emotional tones of the wonderful experience of team loyalty that she felt she had shared in since 1970.[49]

It must also be remembered that there were Cabinet Ministers and back-benchers who actually welcomed the new policies since they had been calling for them since 1970; Peter Tapsell and Kenneth Lewis were for example long-term advocates of an incomes policy, as was Reginald Maudling. Others reasoned like Cabinet Ministers as to the direness of the alternative to changing course; Kenneth Clarke told Malcolm Balen that in the Whips' Office, 'we were convinced that intolerable social pressures would build up if unemployment went over one million', and therefore, 'I was strongly in favour of the U-turn'. There was in 1972 no large group of visible rebels against the new policies. The commonly used epithet for them – 'Enoch's Privy Council' – indicates how far they were marginalised by their small numbers and their constant criticism. Cecil King wondered how Powell could be seen by friendly reporters as a possible future Leader of the Party, when only two MPs seemed to agree with his views. One of these, John Biffen, on at least one occasion opened contacts with Labour through Tony Benn, but it was never likely that the Tory right and the Labour left would be able to repeat on economic issues the alliance that had made them so formidable on House of Lords reform in 1968. There were though signs by 1972–73 that discontent was spreading beyond these few professional rebels, and the Industry Bill in particular attracted widespread private criticism for its 'socialist implications'. Hugh Fraser was dining out on stories of the discontent on the backbenches, though he rarely cast a hostile vote himself. After leaving the Government, Nicholas Ridley became a regular critic from the backbenches, and made his point by joining Biffen and Bruce-Gardyne in a demonstration against

[49] John Ranelagh, *Thatcher's People* (1991), 106; Ridley, *My Style of Government*, 6; Howe, *Conflict of Loyalty*, 74, 76, 81; Lord Howe at ICBH witness seminar, 1994; Norton, *Conservative Dissidents*, 93; Campbell, *Heath*, 448; Fay and Young, *Fall of Heath*, 8; Charles Hill, *Both Sides of the Hill* (1964), 238; interviews with Lord Carr and Lord Howe.

the Industry Bill which kept the House going in the longest Friday debate since the War. Amendments were made, and the Minister now responsible for Industry, Chataway, conceded that this 'Lame Ducks (Unlimited) Bill' – as another Minister was calling it – could not have been carried through the House without such concessions; the chairman of the 1922 Committee called it 'a Socialist Bill by ethic and philosophy' and indicated that it was only the level of unemployment that enabled him to give it his temporary support. Ridley was given more authority for his own oppositional stance by his election as chairman of the Party's backbench Finance Committee in November 1972, with Bruce-Gardyne as a vice chairman and Biffen as chairman of the Industry Committee. The Research Department was not willing to brief even official Party Committees against Government policy, and so Ridley got his speech material instead from Alan Walters, who had also now left his Government post, and with this backing he proceeded to press his dissenting views on the Government. In the Committee Stage of the Counter-Inflation Bill, Biffen and Ridley succeeded in getting an amendment passed, with Labour backing, to limit the new statutory powers to one year rather than the minimum of three that the Government had asked for. At Report Stage, the Government suggested a compromise whereby the provisions could run for a *maximum* of three years, which suggests that they were nervous of their supporters' views; five Conservatives voted against even this, and at least eight abstained, while some who voted with the Government expressed reservations. This suggests that there were many more backbenchers who opposed controls in anything more than temporary circumstances than had appeared as rebels by the end of 1973, but who would presumably have become more vocal had the policy continued.[50]

In the 1971–72 and 1972–73 Sessions, there were a very large number of dissident votes cast by Conservative MPs on a whole range of issues, historically high even if the European debates are excluded from the analysis; in 1971–72, there were rebel votes cast in one out of every six divisions, which again suggests that the troops were not happy, and officers of the 1922 Committee were often among the discontented. The election to the 1922's chairmanship in November 1972 of Edward du Cann (a known opponent of Heath and a Privy Councillor – the only one ever to be elected to this essentially backwoods post), was a much clearer shot across Heath's bows from the loyalist majority of backbenchers; *The Times* regarded it as a deliberate warning to Heath, and Michael Fraser noted that the Executive elected at the same time by the 1922 included several of 'those least happy about the party's present economic policy posture'. Briefing the Party Chairman before a meeting with the 1922's Executive in May 1973, Chris Patten told Carrington to expect criticism of 'the Government's alleged

50 Bruce-Gardyne, *Quiet Revolution?*, 89; Malcolm Balen, *Kenneth Clarke* (1994), 85; Butler and Kavanagh, *General Election of February 1974*, 25; Prior, *Balance of Power*, 74; Benn, *Office Without Power*, 6; Ridley, *My Style of Government*, 5–6; Norton, *Dissension*, 533–4.

"U" turns and its publicity failures'. Looking back a year later on the 1973 meetings that Central Office had organised with the 1922 Committee, Patten recalled that 'it turned out MPs mostly wanted to grumble about policy'. As chairman, du Cann did not bother to hide his view that, as he told Cecil King in March 1973, 'the Government are in trouble', and in February he told the Commons that expenditure was going up too fast and was too large a proportion of GDP anyway. Douglas Hurd's verdict in 1978 was that the effectiveness of the Party's whipping by Francis Pym had inadvertently done Heath a disservice by concealing from him the fact that 'under the surface the confidence of the Parliamentary Party was gradually being eroded'. Pym's own view for example of the 1972 Industry Bill was that,

> as far as I was concerned it was a fence twice the height of Beecher's. And I started therefore on the basis of getting the jockey to talk to the horse so that they could discuss how they were going to get over it. Nobody liked it. But it did in the end go through.

Hurd's view seems therefore very plausible, but we should not make the mistake of extrapolating forward from 1973 to assume a further weakening of Heath's position in 1974 if no early election had been held, for no evidence exists to make such a judgement possible. If Cecil Parkinson was one young Member who loyally supported the Government, and indeed had to do so as a whip, Norman Tebbit spent the second half of the 1970 Parliament struggling to decide how long he could support a policy he did not believe in. There were doubtless some who took each of these positions, but, like both of these, Tory MPs who disliked Heath's 'socialist' policies were exactly the ones most reluctant to speak or vote in a way that would make a Labour Government more likely. In November 1973, Tebbit gave up the struggle and resigned as a PPS to free himself to speak out.[51]

In the wider Party the evidence of disaffection was clearer. For the 1973 Party Conference, there were 130 constituency resolutions in the 'economic policy, prices and taxation' section; most supported the Leadership and its policies (as has been true of every Conference in the Party's history), but Wolverhampton South West 'urge[d] the Government to return to the Conservative principles on which they were elected', and several London constituencies were equally critical. In Plymouth Alan Clark had trouble over his selection for Sutton, being perceived as too right wing on economic matters, while David Hunt had trouble for the opposite reason in the Drake division next door, and after he had attacked Powell at the 1972 Party Conference he was dropped as candidate: Chris Patten briefed Lord

---

51 King, *Diary 1970–74*, 211, 222, 242, 247, 268; Central Office Chairman's department file, CCO 20/59/2, Meetings with the 1922 Committee; Campbell, *Heath*, 450, 482; Hurd, *End to Promises*, 105; Lord Pym at ICBH witness seminar, 1994; Norton, *Conservative Dissidents*, 40, 92, 94–7, 115, 123; Parkinson, *Right at the Centre*, 114; Tebbit, *Upwardly Mobile*, 154, 158–9, 161–6.

Carrington that 'the situation in Plymouth has certainly been stormy. . . . The accursed Local Government Bill, the Monday Club and local ambitions have created a real witches' cauldron.' This hints at the catalogue of grievances that could be brought out when complaints once got under way. The Ugandan Asians' issue in September 1972 was universally reported in similar terms; branch officers resigned in Taunton over 'the apparent lack of firm handling by the Government of the nation's affairs', and the Government's weak response to strikes was cited as an additional grievance by branch officers resigning over immigration in Stoke, Salford and Marple; the South Walsall chairman asked 'could anything be more dangerous for the Party than when our loyal supporters say "Ted's weak, he's useless, he's one big joke"?' The Oxford agent, who distanced himself personally from the view, reported in September 1972 that many Tory members, especially in working-class areas, now felt that the Government was 'totally indifferent to the housing, employment, and cost of living problems of the British, but sympathetic to those of anyone from abroad'. At its November 1972 meeting, the National Union Executive was deluged with criticisms; Chertsey and Walton regretted 'the failure of Government policy' and Worthing 'the lack of decisive action', while Sutton Coldfield noted 'the weakness and ineffectiveness of the Government' and Chichester 'the growing lack of confidence in the present Party leadership expressed by many Conservative supporters'. From Greater London, where resignations were reported from a large number of constituencies, it was pointed out that industrial relations policy was as unpopular as immigration, and that the phrase most often used about the Ugandan Asians was 'it's the last straw'. There was in many resolutions a sense of betrayal in the U-turn of the year: Harrow West urged the need 'to be stronger in the implementation of all election pledges' and Croydon Central simply restated its 'support for the true Conservative principles put before the country at the General Election and which the Government started to implement in their first months in office'. The former chairman of Preston North wrote that

> in all my forty-odd years of working for the Conservative Party I have never known the morale of the Conservative workers to be so low. It is apparent that left-wing militancy wins every time and since the Government caved in to the miners things have gone from bad to worse.

These opinions were both more deeply critical and more widespread reactions to the experience of Conservative government than supporters had ever sent in during the 1951–64 period, and it is significant that when the National Union Executive debated the Party's February 1974 defeat, 'the need to pay greater attention to the views submitted from the constituency associations was stressed by several members'. Nevertheless, as might also be said of du Cann in the 1922 Committee, critics in the constituencies rarely did more than criticise Heath – they offered no actual alternative to the policies that he was pursuing. It is notable though that the constituencies represented by du Cann, Thatcher and Powell were all listed in 1972 as having had resignations from among key Party workers; at the least, the increasing reservations of such people about the direction of Government policy would be reinforced whenever they attended constituency events. Conversely, the only MP in danger of deselection was Ronald Bell at Beaconsfield, who came under heavy fire not from the right but from loyal Party members for his rebel votes on the European Communities Bill; but he had already been warned by his association in March 1970, and now survived only narrowly when a crowded meeting of his association voted by 781 to 514 to retain him as candidate. Jim Prior, Vice Chairman of the Party, was saying in October 1972 that 'Tory morale in the country is rock bottom'. The income from constituencies fell, reflecting lower levels of activity, and industrial subscribers were also reported to be critical of the Government's incomes policy in 1973. The fluctuating membership position in the Upminster branch of Hornchurch constituency (a critical marginal seat) gives a good, representative example; in 1959 there had been 1,335 paid-up members, a number that fell to a mere 214 in April 1963, but recovered to 545 before the 1964 Election and to about a thousand by 1966, before beginning another slow decline; in 1971 it was 430 and it was reported that 'people were not collecting subscriptions', falling to 290 in 1972 (when it was resolved 'to restore this to 600, but 1000 is the target'); in January 1974 the figure was 220, but then rose when the Party was in opposition, and was back to 760 in 1977. Few branches or associations minuted the figures of *paid-up* membership so rigorously, and so charted so accurately the switchback rise and fall of members' commitment, which clearly reached a very low ebb indeed in 1973–74. Two swallows that did not make a summer, but did perhaps hint at warmer weather to come, were the Economic Dining Club formed by twelve Tory MPs in 1972 to promote the case for monetarism, and the Selsdon Group, formed in September 1973 to urge that 'the basic principle upon which Conservative Policy should rest is that what the public wants should be provided by the market and paid for by the public as consumers rather than taxpayers.' There can be little doubt that the typical Tory branch committee contained many who yearned for such simple truths as these as Heath's term of office drew to a close.[52]

The breadth of disaffection in the Party is best brought out from the proceedings of the Advisory Committee on Policy, never a body that could be ignored by Party leaders since its creation in the 1940s, but never either a body

[52] National Union papers, NUA 2/2/37, Central Council reports; Butler and Kavanagh, *General Election of February 1974*, 209; Norton, *Conservative Dissidents*, 187; Peter Riddell, *Honest Opportunism* (1994), 107; Central Office file, CCO 4/10/298; Oxford CA, F and GP minutes, 11 Sept. 1972; NUEC, 11 Jan. 1972 and 25 Apr. 1974; King, *Diary 1970–74*, 229; Central Office file, 4/10/72, Central Board of Finance; Upminster branch minutes, various dates; Patrick Seyd, 'Factionalism in the 1980s', in Layton-Henry, *Conservative Party Politics*, 235; Cockett, *Thinking the Unthinkable*, 211–13.

that had seen such manifestations of discontent as were evidenced between 1970 and 1974. The ACP was treated with formal respect by the Government, and a senior Minister attended nearly every meeting to introduce the debate on his policy area, as for example Sir Alec Douglas-Home did when the ACP discussed entry to the EEC in July 1971. In principle, it had a high place in the counsels of the Party through its chairman, though nobody after Rab Butler ended his twenty-year chairmanship in 1965 managed to convince its members of the weight attached to its deliberations as he had done; from 1972 the chairman was Anthony Barber and meetings of the committee were held at 11 Downing Street, but since this meant in practice that the Chancellor often opened the meetings and then handed over the chair to somebody else after half an hour (or had to terminate meetings very quickly) this reduced rather than enhanced members' perception that they were being listened to. In December 1971, Sir John Taylor, who had just become chairman of the National Union Executive, complained that the ACP was not carrying out its functions properly, for it was not monitoring long-term policy, only discussing the short term, a view strongly supported by Angus Maude. A few weeks later Maude and Taylor were again to the fore in criticising the weakness of policy on law and order, unemployment and strikes. In July 1972, after another member complained that the Government was 'drifting', they were again on the war-path; 'Sir John Taylor thought the problem was more than a mid-term malaise, and had to do with the fact that there seemed to be a change of mind on so many fronts, and that some policies seemed to be failing'. After the Ugandan Asians row, on which Maude told the ACP that he had received more hostile mail than on any subject over his twenty years in the Commons, there was another heated debate, with members again seeing the issue as symptomatic of the Government's loss of direction rather than merely wrong in itself.[53]

In May 1973, with the critics on the ACP reinforced by Edward du Cann's election as 1922 chairman, the ACP received a report that it had commissioned on the causes of Party and public 'alienation' from the Government and its policies. Presenting that report, Kenneth Baker conceded that MPs had been treated 'in a rather cavalier fashion' and that the Party had been deeply upset by local government reform which seemed to take local autonomy away from rural areas; he expressed the hope that the worst was now over and that the Government was more aware of the need to persuade supporters of the case for its policies. In October though, the ACP, while accepting that the Party Conference had boosted morale, felt that no really clear message had emerged about the long-term philosophy behind Government policy. Finally, at its December 1973 meeting, prompted by the need to discuss the big issues in a draft election manifesto for a hypothetical 'normal' election, there was a widespread rejection of the Government's approach; on the one hand, several

[53] ACP, 4 Dec. 1971, 26 Jan. and 19 July 1972, 21 Jan. 1973.

members backed the national YC chairman in demanding a more robust resistance to the miners and to strikers in general; on the other hand, Maude rejected any manifesto based on 'an essentially materialist approach'; some wanted the manifesto to defend the Government's record more specifically but others argued that this would be a hopeless task that would be best avoided; 'Mr. Du Cann said the general public disillusion with politicians and government should not be underestimated', a shrewd judgement on the Election campaign that was about to begin, and members in general agreed 'that it would not be wise to rely on a continuing sympathy vote'. After an inconclusive discussion on 28 January of items that might figure in a 'crisis' manifesto, the ACP was not called together again to discuss the draft on which the Party fought in February. This makes a melancholy tale, in which the 'U turn' as such hardly appeared by name (though those writing the minutes could hardly have allowed it to do so, since the Party did not acknowledge that there had been one). Even so, and even when allowance is made for the personal hostility to Heath of both Maude and Du Cann, it is clear that from 1972 onwards discontent was deep-seated in the one body that had been created precisely to act as a sounding board for Party opinion on policy, but of which the Heath Government took very little apparent notice. It was also ominous that so many very senior people in the Party hierarchy were voicing such critical thoughts.[54]

Despite all of this internal (but unreported) criticism in Spring and Summer 1973 there was much optimism abroad. Optimism could hardly have been based on a cursory reading of the usual political indicators. The Heath Government had a brief honeymoon of popularity during 1970 but was clearly behind Labour by the end of the year and never back in the lead until late in 1973; the proportion of voters approving of Heath's record as Prime Minister was close to two-thirds in Autumn 1970, but fell to two-fifths during 1971 and then remained at or below that level, while the proportion approving the Government's record in office was rather lower. In May 1971 Labour took a Tory seat at a by-election at Bromsgrove, and in each year the Conservatives lost local government seats, Central Office attributing these defeats to 'rising prices, unemployment and the Industrial Relations Bill'; after May 1973, the Party controlled only a quarter of the newly-constituted local authorities, though it had almost as many actual seats as Labour. Traditional pointers were though more ambiguous than that bald statement of failure would suggest. Labour's lead in opinion polls was never so large as to encourage Conservatives to write off the likelihood of their Party's recovery, never at levels equivalent to that of 1963 or the lead the Conservatives themselves had enjoyed in 1967–68, and was in any case punctuated by occasional recoveries in the Conservative position that placed them nearly level with Labour, in late 1971, in Summer 1972 and again in Spring 1973. By-elections also told

[54] ACP, 16 May, 17 Oct, and 5 Dec. 1973, 28 Jan. 1974.

an equivocal story. Labour took no Tory seat after May 1971, and lost four seats of its own to a Liberal, a Nationalist and two independents.[55]

The factor that explained this mixed bag of results was another Liberal upsurge during a period in which the Labour Party had moved sharply to the left. After a poor performance in 1970, the Liberal Party edged back up to 10 per cent in Gallup polls in 1972, averaged 15 per cent in Spring 1973 and over 20 per cent in the Autumn, with one poll showing the three parties neck and neck. This was comparable to the Liberal revival of 1962, except that it came later in the 1970 Parliament, and *much* nearer to the following Election. A Liberal candidate took a 'safe' Tory suburban seat at Sutton and Cheam in December 1972, with a swing that made even Orpington look small beer, and Patten warned Carrington that this result would 'strengthen the hands of those (especially MPs) who criticise us for the alleged "U-turns" of the last six to twelve months'; one who did not criticise Government policy, but who nevertheless drew conclusions about the Party's manner and style was Kenneth Baker, who told his constituency association that 'community politics were here to stay, which was the cause of losing Sutton and Cheam'. But on the same day the Conservatives held off a Labour challenge in a traditional marginal at Uxbridge a few miles away (the two results reversing the Central Office prediction). Polls in Sutton indicated considerable middle-class dissatisfaction with the Government over prices and mortgage rates and a paradoxical readiness of voters to punish the Government for becoming too 'liberal' by voting Liberal. This set the pattern, for in 1973 it was the traditionally 'safe' seats that suddenly looked the most vulnerable to attacks on the community politics front; a Central Office committee chaired by Fraser listed in June forty-three seats vulnerable in these new circumstances. Liberals then took two Tory seats, at Ripon and Isle of Ely, on the same day in July 1973, and added Berwick on Tweed in November; neither Ely nor Berwick had even been on Fraser's vulnerable list in June. The defeated candidate at Ripon reported that 'the real trouble was the widespread feeling that the Government deserved to be shaken up', a view that was more than confirmed by ORC's survey finding that only half even of those who had voted Conservative were displeased by their Party's defeat; the view of the Area agent, confirmed at a constituency meeting in Ripon, was that the Tory campaign had been lively and efficient, with five hundred workers coming in from outside, while the Liberals had actually run well below par; this was not a cheerful finding, for it indicated that Yorkshire voters in the dales were deserting even to a near invisible enemy. But once again, on the same day as Berwick, the Tories held the more marginal Edinburgh North where the challenger was Labour, and a Labour seat in Glasgow went to the SNP; the National Union Executive thought these results 'considerably better than some might have expected'. Central Office began once again to provide

---

[55] D.E. Butler and G. Butler, *British Political Facts, 1900–1986* (1986), 260–1, 445.

literature on the inconsistencies in Liberal policy, and took heart from ORC's finding that two-fifths of professed Liberal supporters in Ripon could not name a single Liberal policy; there was less comfort in ORC's Ely poll which found that a third even of remaining Conservative voters would support the Liberals if they seemed capable of forming a government. All in all though, confident that Labour was the only alternative government, Conservative organisers felt that they were doing reasonably well for mid-term – even if only because their rivals were even more unpopular – and on past form could anticipate the ebbing of the Liberal tide with the approach of a general election; many of them felt like James Margach, in the *Sunday Times* after Ripon and Ely, that the Liberals were still no general election threat, for 'it is no good having a run of by-election victories if the party is incapable of fighting successfully more than two seats at a time'. Fraser's committee endorsed a paper that concluded that,

> with the presumed increase in the popularity of the Government leading up to the General Election, and with harder and more selective work on the part of all sections of the Party, the current Liberal threat could well prove to be yet another paper tiger. In effect, may not the present threat be the mid-term expression of disappointment by a highly volatile electorate?

In Spring 1973 the Central Office Director of Organisation argued that it all looked much like 1962–63, and Heath, like Macmillan at that time, began to step up the political side of his work with regional tours. Nevertheless, while Hurd noted 'PM now prepared to give more energy to political matters', he had to add 'but not prepared to change his essential concentration on what he thinks important, e.g. Ireland, Europe, even though political gains are obscure'. With Heath in command it was always going to be difficult to gear up for electioneering. And, most crucially, none of the organisers who assumed the ebbing of the Liberal tide envisaged that a general election would be called while it was still at the flood.[56]

There was still optimism about the economy too in 1973, with Britain now safely in the EEC, unemployment falling, and the pay policy apparently respected by both unions and management; days lost through strikes in the first ten months of 1973 were down by three-quarters on the same period of 1972. Hurd wrote in his diary of a Chequers meeting in March, 'PM v. genial and relaxed. . . . Everyone calm and reasonably reflective over the two-year prospect. Prices should come right slowly after mid-1973, and unemployment come right too fast. Balance of payments will get worse, then better. If no horrors occur, Autumn 1974 might be best (for an election).' In

[56] Chris Cook and John Ramsden, *By-Elections in British Politics* (1973), 265–71, 385; Central Office file, CCO 4/10/4, Area organisation; NUEC, 10 Nov. 1973; Ripon CA minutes, 19 Sept. 1973; Central Office Chairman's department files, CCO 20/2/5, Liberals, and CCO 20/55/53, 58, 65 and 66, By-elections; St Marylebone CA minutes, 16 Apr. 1973; Butler and Kavanagh, *General Election of February 1974*, 28, 144; King, *Diary 1970–74*, 269, 306, 310; Hurd, *End to Promises*, 109, 111–12, 115–16; NCP, 15 Oct. 1973.

the same month, Barber told the ACP that 'the economy seemed to be set on about the right course', and *The Times* was hailing 'the striking success of the present policy' on incomes. In June, Walker was still hopeful, telling a sceptical Cecil King that 'the economy is now on the threshold of a golden age'. King, by this time very hostile to the Government, noted sourly on 4 October that 'I imagine the Tories suppose Ted's reckless inflation will somehow come right on the night'. As late as November, Heath himself, in a mood that journalists had christened 'superboom', was telling the Institute of Directors that the country's economic prospects were 'more exciting and more solidly based' than at any time since 1945.[57]

The Oil Crisis and the Miners' Strike, 1973

In fact the mood had changed sharply by the end of October because of two factors, one external and past, one internal and very much to come. The external factor was the Middle East War which provided the final catalyst for Arab oil producers to make their cartel effective and push up world prices; they also threatened to embargo altogether supplies to countries like Britain that had backed Israel – which placed a great premium on home-produced energy like coal, and gave additional bargaining power to those who dug it out. Occasional warnings from Lord Rothschild that big increases in oil prices were likely had been little heeded, but now turned out to have seriously underestimated the problem anyway. This development placed a quite different emphasis on stage three of the Government's incomes policy which had to be decided in October and on the fact that the miners' current pay deal would run out early in 1974. What followed over the next few months was a re-run of the Government's relationship with the unions to date, but in more concentrated form: first, a ministerial intention to avoid a confrontation, demonstrated by informal talks with union leaders; second, a serious misinterpretation of what the miners would do; third, a miscalculation of the practical consequences of standing firm against a coal strike; finally, a confused stance that was neither confrontational nor conciliatory and which lost the benefits that could have arisen from either approach. However good the Heath Government may have been at policy, it was certainly not very good at politics.[58]

The detailed provisions of stage three of the incomes policy, allowing more variations for different working conditions, had been put in place deliberately to allow the miners to achieve a good pay deal without a strike, and Heath believed that a private talk with the President of the National Union of Mineworkers (NUM) had prepared the way for the miners' acceptance of

[57] *NCP* 29 Oct. 1973; Hurd, *End to Promises*, 108; ACP, 14 Mar. 1973; Campbell, *Heath*, 534; King, *Diary 1970–74*, 293, 310; Fay and Young, *Fall of Heath*, 24.
[58] Butler and Kavanagh, *General Election of February 1974*, 27–8.

a compromise within the Government's policy. In this both men failed to foresee the level of militancy in the NUM and Heath in particular failed to grasp that in order to head off a strike the NUM moderates would not only have to get a better deal than anyone else but would also have to be able to say so too. Other unions were not about to let that happen, and the issue was complicated by the fact that other disputes were running concurrently with that of the miners, notably a rail dispute which also led to strike action in January 1974. Once again the relationship between the Government and the Coal Board was prickly, and the outcome was the NUM's rejection in November 1973 of the pay offer made to them and their imposition of an overtime ban intended to reduce coal stocks in advance of a strike in 1974. The Cabinet reacted by introducing a three-day working week, and such energy-saving measures as petrol rationing, early closure of television broadcasting, cuts in public expenditure and lower road speed limits, in the hope both of conserving energy stocks and of bringing home to the public that their own interests were at stake in the coal dispute. The Government could not offer more without ruining the credibility of its pay policy before stage three had got going. The emphasis in negotiation shifted again to the TUC, which offered to make the miners a special case, but not in circumstances that the Government felt able to accept – or felt would be sustainable in practice.[59]

Already feeling extreme irritation that the NUM had not accepted the Government's tacit offer to make them the main beneficiaries of stage three, Ministers were then outraged when during negotiations at Downing Street the NUM's Communist Vice-President McGahey told them that his real objective was to bring down the Government: the Industry Minister Tom Boardman recalled McGahey as having said to Heath 'I'm not interested in your point of view, I'm only interested in getting you out of that chair'. Accounts of what was actually said – and in what tone – have differed considerably, but there is no doubt that the Conservatives present took the statement as a real challenge, evidence that they were dealing with something more than a pay dispute; this reinforced the feeling that had been abroad since 1972, that the Government simply must not be defeated by the miners a second time. Back in June 1973, McGahey had already told the NUM Conference that 'it is not negotiation in Downing Street, but it is agitation in the streets of this country to remove this Government that is required'; in November, he had written in the *Morning Star* that 'we shall break Phase Three and we shall do all we can to bring the Government down'. Believing that they were faced with a revolutionary threat, and that parliamentary democracy itself was at stake, Ministers had a heavy weight of responsibility on their minds; when his family came home for Christmas 1973, John Davies told them to make

[59] Whitehead, *Writing on the Wall*, 100–1; Prior, *Balance of Power*, 88; Taylor, *Trade Union Question*, 207–9, 211; Sewill, *British Economic Policy*, 52; Baker, *Turbulent Years*, 38.

the most of it, 'because I deeply believed then that it was the last Christmas of its kind that we would enjoy'. He feared that an election would be a violent and perhaps even a bloody affair, with Tory candidates pelted with lumps of coal; *The Times*'s political editor thought that 'perhaps no election this century would be so dangerously disruptive'. When an election was about to be called on 21 January, McGahey added fuel to the fire by saying that he and his Communist friends would mobilise 'working-class lads' in the army to prevent the forces from being used to keep emergency services going – which drew Wilson's wrath down on his head and produced a motion dissociating the Labour Party from McGahey's treasonable words. If it was later fairly clear that the Government greatly exaggerated McGahey's influence in the NUM and therefore the political danger to themselves, then so did others who were much closer to the action; the postal workers' leader denounced miners' leaders who said, 'first, we'll destroy Stage Three and next we'll destroy the Government and then we'll go on to the revolution', and urged other union leaders to recognise that 'the fight is not about wages but about revolution'; and a right-wing NUM executive member argued in January that 'this dispute is Communist-inspired. . . . They want to see this country changed completely and, I am sure, will not be happy until we are all taking our orders from Moscow. No matter what we are offered, they will not be satisfied.' It is hardly surprising that Conservatives (who were far less informed about union matters) took fright from all this. When the Election was called, Heath told the public that 'there are some people involved in the mining dispute who have made it clear that what they want to do is to bring down the elected government. . . . The election gives you the chance to make it clear to these people how you feel.'[60]

Under such a threat, whether real or imagined, 'a siege mentality had taken hold of the Government' (as Prior put it), not helped by the regular input of Party urgings that they should hold firm at all costs. Such urgings were encouraged by the Government's own assurances that there were in 1973, as there had *not* been in 1971–72, fuel reserves with which to hold out; Walker told the National Union Executive as late as 6 December of the 'action taken by the Government well in advance of the present crisis, which had resulted in our oil and coal stocks being larger than ever before'. The press also urged stiff resistance, *The Times* arguing that 'it is an issue of authority and political power'. The responsible ministers were by this time becoming overwhelmed by their burdens and seriously over-tired; endless talks with the NUM and the TUC were going on alongside difficult negotiations over the future of Ulster, close Commons votes over a Channel Tunnel proposal, a series of state visits and a European summit. Ministers' political advisers were told less and less of

---

[60] Whitehead, *Writing on the Wall*, 104–5; ICBH witness seminar, *Contemporary Record*, vol. 2, no. 1 (1988), 42; *NCP* 21 Jan. 1974; Fay and Young, *Fall of Heath*, 6, 24, 27; Central Office Chairman's department file, CCO 20/12/10, Broadcasting.

what was going on, and Hurd took to convening meetings of advisers in his Downing Street office to pool information. There was also a reshuffle in the offing, delayed by the impossibility of bringing Whitelaw back from Ulster until a suitable pause in his business there, and by Walker's reluctance to part with the energy powers of the DTI to a new ministry. When it finally took place it was less than successful: Whitelaw took over Employment in mid-crisis but, while respected by the unions, he found great difficulty in getting his exhausted mind round a new problem and was for some time 'a danger to shipping'; the choice of Carrington as Energy Secretary was an eccentric one: as Party Chairman he was under constant pressure to articulate a hawkish viewpoint that conflicted with what the Energy ministry needed to say pragmatically. By this stage, with no solution forthcoming from talks with the NUM or the TUC, and with the Government's crisis measures in place, a new way of reacting to the situation was emerging. On 6 December, the political advisers collectively minuted Heath to the effect that the Government should now stop trying to claim that all was well and should instead 'emphasise the gravity of the situation'. The same strategy had been under consideration in the CRD since October as it grappled with the question of what a manifesto would have to look like if an election were to be called in a hurry. The Central Office Tactical Committee effectively endorsed the same approach on 18 December, deciding that 'the blame should be put fairly and squarely where it belongs'. Under pressure from colleagues to make a broadcast to the nation, Heath agreed to do so in mid-December, and adopted a crisis tone, but without giving much indication of how the Government saw its way forward. He put in a disastrous performance because he was so tired, but it was noticeable that he put the whole blame for the country's problems on the miners, scarcely even mentioning the rise in oil prices. The crisis was to be defined as a political rather than an economic one, and the miners were to be the political enemy. The previous week, Barber had told the Commons that 'it is the coalminers' overtime ban, not the future of oil, which has put Britain on a three-day week and threatened the security of so many of our people.' In practice Ministers were not as hostile to the miners as this way of presenting the story made them sound; when an NUM representative asked Heath why, when they had given the oil sheikhs what they asked for, they could not do the same for British miners, this very good question produced an embarrassed silence.[61]

It was one thing to define the situation as a crisis, and to impose measures that brought the fact home to the public, but if Powell's advice – to pay the

---

[61] Fay and Young, *Fall of Heath*, 6; Taylor, *Trade Union Question*, 212; Prior, *Balance of Power*, 90; NUEC, 6 Dec. 1973; Hurd, *End to Promises*, 117, 121; Walker, *Staying Power*, 115–16; Whitelaw, *Memoirs*, 123; Carrington, *Reflect on Things Past*, 262–3; Ramsden, *Making of Conservative Party Policy*, 301; Cockerell, *Live from Number Ten*, 194–5; King, *Diary 1970–74*, 322, 327, 331–2; Central Office Chairman's department file, CCO 20/7/20, Tactical Committee; *NCP* 21 Jan. 1974; interview with Lord Jenkin.

miners what it cost to settle the dispute, whatever the effect on the price of coal and the number of jobs in the coal industry – was rejected, and if the miners continued to defy the Government, then public opinion could be brought into play against them in only one way. Ever since October, talk of a possible election had been gaining ground among the Party's leaders, and this idea was being openly discussed in the press by mid-December. The real difficulty was that the Government – especially Heath himself – now had the utmost difficulty in making up its mind whether to take the gamble. After much public hesitation Heath ended up calling a snap election that had been discussed for two months, and which caught his own Party more unprepared than the Opposition; his obvious reluctance to take this course also indicated in advance uncertainties that were to dog the campaign when it started.[62]

To go or not to go?

Once the likelihood of either sitting out the miners' industrial action or shaming them into a more moderate stance had faded, by mid-December, there was until early February 1974 a tug of war between Heath's advisers on the question of calling an election; Heath's PPS even found himself being asked by the Party Chairman who was talking to the Prime Minister and giving him what advice. On one side were arrayed the Chairman and Vice Chairman, Carrington and Prior, well aware that Party opinion would not stomach the only other plausible scenario, a capitulation to the miners without an election. The January 1974 *Crossbow* argued that 'the battle lines are drawn and there can be no retreat. The overwhelming message coming from the constituencies is clear. There must be no surrender now. . . . What is at stake is more than a battle for more pay, but a battle for power.' By the Christmas recess, Carrington and Prior were convinced that an election should be held, but at Chequers Prior found Heath reluctant even to discuss the question. By his silence Heath lost the one opportunity he had to quell election fever before it got out of hand; he may indeed have allowed it to build up deliberately in order to encourage Labour to persuade the miners to be more reasonable. But as one of his staff put it, 'it wasn't a battle between his advisers. It was inside Ted's mind. It was Ted against Ted.' Area Agents, consulted early in January, all favoured a quick dissolution, and Central Office began to work up the press in that direction. Peter Walker was another whose instinct told him that if any election were to be held it should be quickly, but there was no collective Cabinet view. On the other side were Whitelaw and Pym, both extremely conscious of the destructive effect an early election could have on the Ulster power-sharing experiment, and Carr. These three were suspicious of the idea itself; Pym later recalled that 'the country was supporting him. I could feel that. . . . They clearly were. And my instinct was that if they were

62 Butler and Kavanagh, *General Election of February 1974*, 28–9.

asked to vote for it they would wonder why'. But published polls now put the Conservatives ahead by as much as five points and this strengthened the case for an election. Hurd noted on 18 December, 'slowly the band waggon for an early General Election is beginning to roll – but EH, so far as one can gather, still unconvinced'. Heath did not want to be trapped into an election that would become a violent battle with the unions, and nor did he want to risk the loss of office unnecessarily. Also, as Michael Wolff told a journalist, 'Ted's real worry is about the consequences of a Tory landslide. It would sweep away the moderation which post-war Tories went into politics to defend. It would be a triumph for the extremists.'[63]

Early in January, ORC, highly regarded because of their success in 1970, advised privately that the Government was 'in with a chance' of winning an early election, though they also prophetically warned that there would be 'next to no chance of winning after a couple of weeks of three day [a week] working'. Hurd, analysing the ORC report for Heath, drew attention to the fact that 'the result of the election would depend on whether the deep dislike of trade union militancy . . . is stronger than the unpopularity of the Government. I agree with Humphrey Taylor et al that it is stronger at present, but will not remain so.' The Party's media team pressed for getting the election in quick, but when the whips were asked they came down seven in favour of an election and seven against. With this conflict of views, and with the Prime Minister inclining to Pym's viewpoint, the opportunity to call a real snap election for the first available Thursday in February 1974 passed by on 17 January. Labour backbenchers were elated, remembering the crisis Tory landslide of 1931 and the French right's recent triumph on the morrow of the *événements* of 1968. Conservatives were puzzled and downcast by the apparent timidity of their Leader. Afterwards, many Conservatives were to see this as a missed opportunity, for newspapers reported on 7 February that the Party remained well ahead in the polls. This was an unprovable hypothesis, for an election campaign might well have changed voting intentions, as it was to do later in the month. Prior's vivid account of this anti-climax is worth quoting at length.

> Late in the afternoon of Thursday, January 17 . . . I went to see Ted at Number Ten: 'If it's any consolation, I'd like you to know that all the Labour Members were coming up to me in the tea room to tell me that we have let them off the hook. They're throwing their hats in the air – they haven't been in that kind of mood for months.' Ted retorted, 'It's all your bloody fault. If you hadn't allowed Central Office to steam this thing up, we would never have got into this position.' 'If you had told us definitely that you were against an election, it wouldn't have

---

63 Whitehead, *Writing on the Wall*, 108–9; Hurd, *End to Promises*, 122, 125–8, 130; Central Office Chairman's department file, CCO 20/27/18, ORC reports; Butler and Kavanagh, *General Election of February 1974*, 32, 35, 37–8, 218; Francis Pym, *The Politics of Consent* (1984), 4; Carrington, *Reflect on Things Past*, 265; Walker, *Staying Power*, 125; *Crossbow*, Jan. 1974, 4.

been steamed up,' I replied. We had already marched the troops up to the top of the hill, ready for combat, and then had to march them down again; it would be much harder to march them up a second time.

Another Minister noted simply that 'a non-decision was not taken to have no election'. With parliament not dissolved that week, the *Daily Telegraph* warned Heath to get on and make up his mind one way or the other, and the *Sunday Times* reported that 'last week was the Government's worst since it came into power'. Over the following week, the proportion of voters saying to the polls that Heath was doing a good job fell sharply. Chris Patten, writing to a former Central Office employee now in Africa, wrote on 28 January that 'we are all well here but somewhat battered by the Great Crisis. I think we would all like an Election to put us out of our misery one way or another.' In the constituencies, many were simply baffled by what was going on and after getting it wrong in January Central Office was reluctant to advise; on 28 January, the chairman of High Peak told his association that it was 'now obvious that no general election would be held in February'. An additional complication was that election preparations were hampered by the fact that anticipated petrol rationing would wreck traditional schemes of mutual aid, particularly in dispersed areas like Cornwall.[64]

Threatened resignations may have influenced the delay; Westminster gossip on 6 January said that Carrington, Prior and Barber had all threatened to resign if more money was offered to the miners, while Whitelaw might go if no more was found; that was no basis from which to start an election. But Heath had anyway hoped for one last chance either to settle the dispute by reason or to show how reasonable he was in failing, and his most trusted adviser, William Armstrong, though as hawkish as anyone, was telling Heath that he had three or four weeks before he need make up his mind. But the NUM now balloted for a strike and voted overwhelmingly to hold one. Hurd felt that Heath now began, 'though still not vigorously, to interest himself in election planning'. By then, as Kenneth Baker noted, opinion in the 1922 Committee had hardened: from being evenly divided on the merits of an election they were now 70 per cent in favour. The formal presentation of the options made by Michael Fraser on 6 February was a sober one that indicated the ambivalent message of the polls, the opportunities and the risks; he made no recommendation. But as Hurd himself put it, 'events had already taken over the argument'; having now allowed a second phase of election speculation to develop the Government had no real choice; Whitelaw recalls that even opponents of an early election knew that they could not avoid one if a settlement could not be reached with the miners; Hailsham records that

---

[64] Fay and Young, *Fall of Heath*, 6, 26; Robert Worcester, *British Public Opinion* (Oxford, 1991), 44; Prior, *Balance of Power*, 90–2; Whitelaw, *Memoirs*, 130–1; Parkinson, *Right at the Centre*, 122; Campbell, *Heath*, 586; Central Office Chairman's department file, CCO 20/74/3, Correspondence with Patten; High Peak CA minutes, 28 Jan. 1974; Truro CA minutes, 12 Dec. 1973.

the final decision was a unanimous one, but in part because the advice was that the parliamentary party would not accept further delay. At a press gallery lunch on 6 February, Prior argued that as 'the miners have had their ballot, perhaps we ought to have ours.'[65]

The February 1974 General Election

On 7 February, the day on which the country would have been voting had the earlier option been chosen, Heath asked for a dissolution and for the shortest possible campaign; polling was to be three weeks later on 28 February. Remarkably though, the relationship of that decision to the crisis that had brought it about was thrown into some confusion by his decision on the very next day to refer the NUM's pay claim to the Relativities Board, a new arbitration machinery for dealing with special cases; before the campaign had even begun, the Prime Minister had both demonstrated that it would not be a fight to the finish with the miners and called into question the point of having an election at all. When the miners accepted this offer and agreed to give evidence to the Relativities Board, Heath was glad that they were 'talking again. The iron curtain has been lifted. Nothing could be better news for the country.' It was not so clear that it was good news for the Party that had called the election. The decision to allow television to re-start normal programme scheduling into the late evenings was made to allow a full coverage of the election, but had the effect of further diminishing the public's sense that they were living through a great crisis. It also allowed the over-saturation of television coverage with election material that led at least some electors to turn their backs on both traditional parties.[66]

On a radio phone-in in 1972, Carrington had rejected the suggestion of a general election on the Common Market, because 'it's very unlikely that you can ever have a General Election in this country on a particular issue, because other things come into it.' This was what he as Party Chairman had now persuaded the Prime Minister to attempt, and without even sorting out the primary issue first. When they formally raised the question of an election on 6 December, Hurd's team of political advisers had noted that 'it would of course be impossible to confine it to any one issue. The Government's election campaign would only be credible if it included proposals which would bring an end to the industrial action. It is not easy to see what these would be.' Looking back from 1989, Whitelaw recalled that he was 'never clear what answer we would give during an election when asked how we would settle the miners' strike if we won'. These dilemmas remained

---

65 Tony Benn, *Against the Tide: Diaries 1973–1976* (1990), 104; Hurd, *End to Promises*, 132–3; Whitelaw, *Memoirs*, 130; Hailsham, *Door Wherein I Went*, 298; Baker, *Turbulent Years*, 38–9; Prior, *Balance of Power*, 93.
66 Whitehead, *Writing on the Wall*, 110; Butler and Kavanagh, *General Election of February 1974*, 67; Central Office *Daily Notes* [hereafter *DN*], 16 Feb. 1974.

throughout the three-week campaign; they were exactly the sorts of questions that an Iain Macleod would have forced his colleagues to think through before opting for an election. Heath's own answer to the question was given in a television broadcast on 7 February:

> Now I know a lot of people have been asking 'What will an election prove?' The answer is this: an election gives you, the people, the chance to say to the miners and to everyone else who wields similar power in Britain, 'Times are hard. We are all in the same boat and if you sink us we will all drown.' Once you have said that the Government you elect will be in a far stronger position to reach a settlement with the miners that safeguards your interests as well as theirs.

This only raised the further question of what the Government would do if the miners ignored the Election result, as the TUC had ignored the Industrial Relations Act.[67]

Labour had finalised its manifesto on 12 December, reacting to the first whispers of a possible election; drafts of the Tory manifesto were circulating long before that date, but with the difficulty of attracting Ministers' concentration on the matter because of the crisis itself, it was much later that a final version was agreed by the Steering Committee on 8 February. When it finally appeared on 10 February some paragraphs were repeated and a pledge on the introduction of a Public Lending Right was accidentally omitted. The Party's *Campaign Guide* was not ready and had to be circulated to candidates in proof. Television preparations also had to be put together very rapidly; the team from 1970 was hurriedly reassembled, but little library material had been accumulated during three years in office that could now be used to present the Government persuasively. True to type, Heath refused either to allow the cameras into Downing Street to film him at work or to call a 'crisis Cabinet' in mid-campaign that would provide material for the television news; this was 'the sort of thing that Wilson would do'. There was even some panic over money, for the snap election did not allow for the usual pre-election appeal to be launched. One attempt to bring in cash misfired badly; in mid-January, letters were sent to Ministers whose constituencies had not paid their 1973 quota in full; this produced indignant questions as to why only Ministers' seats had been targeted, associations who pointed out that the quota year went on till 31 January and that they always paid part of their quota at the last moment (since their own branches paid only at that late stage), and one or two who were deeply insulted to be targeted when they had in fact already paid up (and had in one case paid in full ever since 1949); the explanation that the target lists had been drawn up by weary Central Office staff working by candle-light because of the energy crisis did not win a sympathetic response, and senior Party officers had better things to do with their time than write apologetic letters anyway. On the other hand, the

---

[67] Central Office Chairman's department files, CCO 20/12/9 and 10, Broadcasting; Hurd, *End to Promises*, 119; Whitelaw, *Memoirs*, 130.

eventual response to the Election appeal was positive, with some industrialists writing in to say that the issues at stake in the miners' dispute had persuaded them to make their first ever political donation. The level of morale in the constituencies was high too, once the starting pistol was fired, for here too there was a consciousness that it was an election at which unusually important issues were being fought out. As Peter Walker has put it, from his experience in Worcester and from speaking around the country, 'Party workers were strongly behind us'. In mid-campaign Gallup found that three-quarters of Tory voters expected to win, and two-thirds of them thought the result mattered a great deal, compared to only half of Labour voters.[68]

Announcing the dissolution on television, Heath had said that 'the issue before you is a simple one. . . . Do you want Parliament and the elected Government to continue to fight strenuously against inflation? Or do you want them to abandon the struggle against rising prices under pressure from one particular powerful group of workers?' At the outset then, the Conservative campaign seemed likely to rely on the 'who governs?' issue that had prompted the Election; most Conservative candidates described it that way in their election addresses. Tony Benn's view was that the Government started off the campaign well with 'clear, strong, simple warnings of higher taxation if Labour is elected'. Peter Rawlinson found in Epsom that this core message did very well in working-class areas of his constituency, but that 'in the grander villas' of Epsom, 'support faded as the campaign progressed'; this was borne out by opinion polls that showed that the Conservative performance relative to Labour actually improved among working-class voters but fell in the middle class, mainly through Tory defections to Liberal. The problem was, as the Party Chairman noted, that the Party had to give a tough impression on the one hand, so as to rally support among those who saw it as a simple battle against trade union militancy, while not seeming confrontationist in a way that would offend middle opinion; in trying to create these two impressions, 'there was always a risk that they cancelled each other out'. This emerged most strongly from the mis-match between the Party's alarmist rhetoric about the crisis, blamed squarely on union militants, and the relatively mild prescription that was offered as a solution. When considering this tactical question back in November, James Douglas had complained that a draft of the manifesto had been composed for 'the scenario of Sophocles', but was trying at the same time to appeal to moderates: 'can Oedipus ever be a moderate?' Only once in the campaign did the Conservatives seem to be coming down clearly on the confrontationist side of the argument, when on 19 February a television broadcast by Barber hit very hard at Labour's programme and at extremists in the labour movement. Coming

---

[68] Benn, *Against the Tide*, 77; Butler and Kavanagh, *General Election of February 1974*, 40, 75; Cockerell, *Live from Number Ten*, 198–200; Central Office Chairman's department file, CCO 20/22/20, Finances 1974; Walker, *Staying Power*, 125; *DN*, 16 Feb. 1974.

at a point when the electorate were already registering dismay at the level of 'mud-slinging', this alienated liberal opinion in the press, and the experiment was not repeated, but it was one of the few Conservative attempts to fight this 'crisis election' as if a crisis was actually taking place – though posters displayed at the local level were sometimes pretty militant too. ORC was reporting a large and constant Conservative lead in answer to the question 'who do you trust to run the country when the country is in trouble?', an asset that would be realisable only if the electorate continued to think in terms of a crisis. In this light, Harold Wilson thought that the only mistake the Conservatives made over the Barber broadcast was to apologise for it, since he thought it good electioneering in the sort of election that the Tories had originallly claimed it to be. After the negative reaction to Barber's broadcast, the pendulum swung more clearly in the moderate direction in the final week, not least because the Conservative leaders were convinced that they had already as good as won and did not therefore want to queer the pitch for future relations with the unions. When it was over, one of Heath's colleagues remarked sadly that 'it is impossible for any party leader to win an election by saying, "Be reasonable". But Ted tried it.'[69]

Had the election that ended the 1970 Parliament been a 'normal' one, the Party would no doubt have concentrated its campaigning on the threat of Labour's programme and its cost, but in February 1974 the Conservative manifesto turned to the Labour alternative only at the end, almost as an afterthought. In the event, their own attempt to concentrate attention on the economic crisis focused the electorate's attention on political issues on which Wilson was by many seen as more moderate than Heath, since he would be able to live more amicably with the trade unions; Wilson cunningly campaigned as the moderate between the extremisms of Heath and McGahey. Only a third of Conservative candidates mentioned Heath in their own election addresses. As the campaign went on, it was in any case impossible to continue to focus on the issue that had brought it about, and debates focused increasingly on prices, jobs and taxes, largely because the media would not report stories on the same theme for three weeks; with electors sceptical about the Tory record on prices, which the polls showed to be their greatest single concern, this shift from the crisis to the record was not helpful. Since Heath stuck characteristically to the single theme, chaired every press conference and largely delivered the same speech wherever he spoke, he made less and less impact as the focus shifted.[70]

In the final week, when the Tory campaign was slackening, just as all the

[69] Butler and Kavanagh, *General Election of February 1974*, 61, 73, 99, 117, 231; Benn, *Against the Tide*, 107; Rawlinson, *Price Too High*, 243; Carrington, *Reflect on Things Past*, 266; Ramsden, *Making of Conservative Party Policy*, 302; Central Office Chairman's department file, CCO 20/27/18; Fay and Young, *Fall of Heath*, 28.

[70] Butler and Kavanagh, *General Election of February 1974*, 51, 62, 81, 115, 119; Campbell, *Heath*, 591, 602–3.

news in 1970 had been bad for Labour, in February 1974 it was all the other way round. The CBI director's off-the-record denunciation of the Industrial Relations Act somehow got into the press, an unexpected piece of flanking fire for the Conservative campaign, on an issue that they did not want to highlight anyway. There were figures released which indicated the worst ever trade deficit, a foreseeable trap in the month which the advocates of an election on 7 February had explicitly sought to avoid. Yet neither of these seem to have done undue damage, and may even have helped Conservatives in reinforcing the sense of economic crisis. Much more damaging was a leak from the Relativities Board which seemed to indicate that the Government's own figures on miners' pay were wrong, and therefore that the whole basis on which the battle with the miners had taken place might be equally faulty. Heath, incommunicado on his way to a meeting in Exeter, learned of this only several hours after Labour had begun to use it as a stick with which to beat him, and although there were good explanations for the discrepancies in the figures, the Party never managed to neutralise the issue. Hurd noted in his diary that 'Edward Heath retires to bed in a cloud of stubborn and unconvincing negatives.'[71]

More important than any of this seemed to be the question of what Enoch Powell would do. He had denounced the idea of a snap election as dishonest on 15 January, and, knowing that he was now so far out of line with all that Heath's Conservatism stood for, he had already decided that by May at the latest he must tell his association that he would not defend his seat; the calling of the Election removed this possibility and he therefore dramatically resigned as Conservative candidate for Wolverhampton South West, saying that he could not stand as a Conservative on a programme he did not believe in, and that Heath's calling of a one-issue election had left him no other honourable course of action; this inconveniently highlighted the fact that Heath was demanding support for the policy of pay controls that he had opposed in 1970. Thereafter, as in 1970, Powell expertly played the media and kept them waiting for his views in instalments; an *Express* cartoon showed him as a huge, menacing bird of prey hovering over Heath as he crawled towards Number 10. Too much should not be made of all this; Powell was mentioned only eight times on television news bulletins during the three-week campaign, and only thirteen times on BBC radio, a degree of exposure less than that enjoyed by Carrington, Whitelaw or Barber, and only about one-fifteenth of Heath's number of mentions. Since he was no longer a candidate, Powell found it difficult to get on to television (which was obliged to maintain balance between parties), and Carrington exerted considerable pressure on the BBC to keep him off *Panorama*; his only full interview was on Thames Television, broadcast live only in the south east of

[71] Cockerell, *Live from Number Ten*, 200–1; Butler and Kavanagh, *General Election of February 1974*, 100, 105, 107; Campbell, *Heath*, 608; Hurd, *End to Promises*, 134.

England. The importance of Powell could though be doubly negative; having refused to endorse Heath's campaign, speculation continued as to whether his antipathy for the EEC would encourage him to urge a vote for Labour as the only Party pledged to reopen the question of British entry, something he had hinted at as early as June 1973. Eventually, he let it be known that he had personally voted by post for the Labour candidate in Wolverhampton, and urged others to do likewise:

> This is the first and last election at which the British people will be given the opportunity to decide whether their country is to remain a democratic nation, governed by the will of its own electorate expressed in its own Parliament, or whether it will become a province in a new European superstate under institutions which know nothing of the political rights and liberties that we have long taken for granted.

This position, and the argument that it represented, was to cast a long shadow forward into Conservative Party politics, and had some immediate effect too. The swing to Labour in Powell's old constituency was a massive 16 per cent, the highest in the country, and other Black Country seats also swung markedly above the national average, so that results there in February 1974 almost exactly replicated the Labour landslide of 1966 rather than the close national result registered elsewhere in 1974. This substantial sub-regional swing-back to Labour perhaps indicated how far the 1970 result there had been out of line, and was, thought Michael Steed in the Nuffield Election Study, 'a remarkable tribute to the influence of Enoch Powell in 1970'. It is though much more difficult to demonstrate that Powell had a decisive effect on the national result in February 1974; when the election was so close, it may be surmised that Powell's advice must have tipped votes in marginal seats, though even that is difficult to prove, but there were five seats gained by Labour in the West Midlands at least some of which can be attributed to the Powell effect.[72]

The indirect effect of Enoch Powell's speeches in February 1974 is even more speculative. By leaving parliament, and committing the one unforgivable act of urging electors to vote against his own Party, Powell deprived himself of Party influence at precisely the moment when Tory economic policy began to shift in a 'Powellite' direction and when Heath was for the first time vulnerable to an attack from the right. Powell's role as a Conservative MP in 1974 and 1975 would have been a pivotal one, and he could not have been ruled out of consideration for the leadership itself. It would certainly have seemed even more improbable in February 1974 that Heath would be succeeded within a year by Margaret Thatcher.

None the less, the overwhelming expectation on 28 February was that the Conservatives would win. At the outset, David Butler had told Tony Benn

---

[72] Butler and Kavanagh, *General Election of February 1974*, 35, 67–8, 103–6, 332, 341; Powell, *Reflections*, 121, 198; Cockerell, *Live from Number Ten*, 202; Benn, *Against the Tide*, 44.

that 'he foresaw a Tory landslide; he was afraid that the Labour Party couldn't survive.' This was only a little exaggerated in its tone; the bookmakers made Heath two to one on to win. Halfway through the campaign, Carrington joked with the Prime Minister's private secretary, 'Bad luck, it looks as though you lot have got us for another four years.' This expectation owed much to the continuous – if falling – Conservative lead in the opinion polls, despite the polls' record in picking the wrong winner in 1970. Butler and Kavanagh wrote of 'a general consensus that Labour had little hope of winning', a consensus that was more accurate than it might seem, for Labour did in fact get neither the largest number of votes nor a majority of seats. The Tories' private polls indicated not only a continuing Conservative lead, but also a clear (if fluctuating) firmness of public support on the key attitudinal questions. Indeed after the Election, ORC wrote to Carrington with a fulsome apology for their failure to warn the Party of the vulnerability of its position; because the polls looked so good, they believed that the Party had been lulled into a quiet final week of campaigning during which the Election had slipped away from it. Carrington generously wrote that it was up to the Party to be more sceptical, but he did not dispute ORC's basic diagnosis; ORC's managing director later told *The Times* that 'we very much regret that we misled a great many people into believing that the Conservatives would win by a comfortable majority'. After they had re-analysed their campaign polling, ORC wrote to Central Office again in April to confirm 'that we accept some of the blame for the failure to win the election'; they accepted responsibility themselves, because they had given the wrong tactical advice, and accepted responsibility on behalf of all the polls, because they believed that it was the false expectation of a Conservative win that had led the Labour vote to harden, while Tory defectors to the Liberals had felt they could safely continue with their protest. In fact, in the final week the upsurge of the Liberal vote in all the polls did induce some Tory concern, but there was uncertainty as to how to deal with it. As the press began to speculate on the outside possibility of a hung Parliament, Robert Carr was drafted into the Party's broadcasting programme at short notice to issue an appeal to Liberal voters as 'fellow moderates' to join in the defence of the incomes policy in which both Liberals and Conservatives believed. But Conservative Party strategists were still thinking in terms of an overall majority of thirty or more and the value of having Liberal support above that level; in this they were perhaps in part lulled into a sense of security by a Party estimate that more than half of Ulster's twelve MPs would still be moderate Unionists who would take the Tory whip, whereas in the event there were to be none at all.[73]

As soon as results began to come in, the indications were of a hung Parliament with Labour just in the lead. It seemed very close throughout the

---

[73] Benn, *Against the Tide*, 106; Campbell, *Heath*, 598; Rawlinson, *Price Too High*, 244; Butler and Kavanagh, *General Election of February 1974*, 91, 108–10; Central Office Chairman's department file, CCO 20/27/18; interview with Lord Carr.

counting, and the gap between the major parties continued to fluctuate to the very end, with two Conservative losses and one Labour gain among the very last seats to declare finally giving Labour a lead of five, but leaving Wilson well short of an overall majority. One Cabinet Minister, the Scottish Secretary Gordon Campbell, was among those defeated. In votes, the Conservatives were about a quarter of a million ahead, but with their lowest share of the vote since the 1920s. If an adjustment is made for Northern Ireland, where there were now very few votes counted as 'Conservative', the Party's vote fell by a little over a million, while Labour's vote fell by only half as much, and the main beneficiaries were the Liberals, whose vote rose by almost 4 million. As in 1964, the pattern of voting shifts was far more complex than such totals suggested; there were actually more voters who switched from Labour to Tory than went the other way, and defections to the Liberals may have more or less cancelled out, but Tory losses to deaths and abstentions, and Labour's gains from new voters and previous abstainers gave Wilson the edge. In terms of seats, a substantial boundary revision made direct comparison difficult, but there were thirty-four fewer Tories elected; the reduction was mainly in Ulster (eight fewer seats), Scotland and Wales (three fewer seats), and northern England (sixteen fewer seats).[74]

Why had this happened, and why had it not been foreseen? After the outcome was known, about a third of Conservative candidates told Butler and Kavanagh that the electorate had been unenthusiastic about the Government's record, and another third felt that too many of the electorate, when asked to make a hard choice between the Government and the unions, had refused to opt for either – and voted Liberal as a result; Lord Carrington felt that 'we were clobbered by the head-under-the-bedclothes vote'. The Yorkshire Conservatives were typical in noting that 'we had maintained the support of the lower paid workers and the pensioners' for whom the 'who governs?' appeal had struck home, but lost votes from 'young married and those about to marry' who had gone to the Liberals because of the Government's record on housing and mortgage rates. Richard Rose pointed out in *The Times* that Liberal interventions had probably most determined the result, since in the two hundred seats that the Liberals fought in 1974 but not in 1970 the average swing to Labour was about 2 per cent, while in seats the Liberals fought both times there was actually a small swing to Conservative; some of those interventions took place in Tory marginals captured by Labour. In fact the small number of net losses can be attributed to the accumulation of different influences, hardly any of which involved a shift from Conservative to Labour on traditional policy grounds; some seats were lost because of the Liberals, some because of Powell, several because of the collapse of moderate Ulster Unionism, and there was an element of sheer bad luck in the fact that these unrelated influences coincided, when it would have taken only three more

[74] Butler and Kavanagh, *General Election of February 1974*, 253, 258–60.

marginals to be retained for Heath to command more seats than Wilson, and only the expected half-share of seats in Ulster to allow a two-party deal that could have kept him in office. With such a close result, there was an inevitable tendency for Conservatives to think that the campaign had been there to be won, by a clearer strategy, better tactics, and a more communicative leader. These were all viewpoints that reflected back on the period in office as well as on the last three weeks. It may well be because he thought that he had already won – and did not actually want too large a Tory majority at his back – that led Heath to let up in his campaigning in the crucial final week. *Crossbow*'s editorial in its post-election issue lamented, 'the worrying lack of political judgement, especially at the top.'

> The whole miners strike disaster stems from the breaking of two fundamental political rules. First, don't take on anyone you can't beat. It is not a noble sentiment but it is real politics. . . . Secondly, we allowed ourselves to be boxed into a situation where there was no escape hatch. Or only one – a general election – and that was booby-trapped. There are no policies which can be a substitute for good political judgement.[75]

The outcome had not been foreseen, and especially not by Heath when he had called the election to settle the Government's dispute with the miners. The confused parliamentary arithmetic on 1 March 1974 provided no obvious way forward, for not only had no one Party won the election, but there were not even two parties (except an improbable Labour–Conservative combination) that could make up a Commons majority by acting together. But Edward Heath had called the election for a specific purpose, and if nobody had won the election, then, as the Liberal Leader pointed out, it was clear enough who had lost it. With all the problems that preceded the election still present, with a record as Leader that now read 'Played three, Won one, Lost two', and with another early election inevitable, Heath would have to fight for his political life and for his conception of what Conservatism meant for the next year.[76]

---

[75] Butler and Kavanagh, *General Election of February 1974*, 263; *NCP* 25 Mar. 1974; Yorkshire Area Council, 27 Apr. 1974; Ramsden, *Making of Conservative Party Policy*, 305; *Crossbow*, June 1974, 4.
[76] Butler and Kavanagh, *General Election of February 1974*, 256–7.

Chapter 7

Reversing the trend?

The aftermath of February

When the Conservatives put to the British people in February 1974 the challenging question 'Who governs?' – with whatever reservations – nobody foresaw that the electors might reply 'Don't know'. Now the Party had to respond to such a verdict, with no Conservative MP remaining in the House who had experienced the last hung Parliament in 1929; in the rush to the February Election there had been no contingency planning for such an eventuality either. This was less reprehensible than it may seem from a later perspective. The collapse of the Liberal vote in 1950, and the failure of any third party to make a numerical impact at Westminster in the generation since, meant that the parliamentary arithmetic had been safely two-party in character. Since 1950, there had never been more than twelve MPs who were neither Conservative nor Labour, and it had therefore been difficult for one of the major parties not to win an overall majority. Now, suddenly, because the disappearance of Conservative-supporting MPs from Ulster coincided with an increased number of Liberals and with a breakthrough for Scottish and Welsh Nationalists, there were thirty-seven MPs from parties other than Conservative or Labour. Britain was entering uncharted waters in which, as the Liberal Leader joyfully put it, 'We are all minorities now'. The Conservative Party was not alone in being unprepared for this eventuality; when Geoffrey Howe asked for background material 'on the implications of minority government' from the Commons library in April, they could offer him only a few papers relating to Canada. Relaxed consideration was not aided by the fact that Downing Street was occupied by a crowd mainly chanting 'Heath OUT!' while the Cabinet debated the issue. Ministers who had seemed so exhausted as to be near the limit of their endurance at the end of 1973, and who had then endured a gruelling Election campaign, now had to grapple with these unforeseen circumstances. For Willie Whitelaw the strain of the past few months was too much, and, ordered to bed by his doctor after a near collapse, he took no part in the events of the post-election week-end; another Heath Minister was later to say that 'it was only when we stopped that we realised how tired we were'. As the incumbent Prime Minister, the initiative properly lay with Heath. Some like Maurice Macmillan urged him to announce that as nobody else had won, and as his Party had got the most votes, he would meet Parliament as Prime Minister; this would challenge the other parties to defeat him on the Queen's Speech – as Baldwin had done in similar circumstances in 1923 and Salisbury in 1885. That would have been constitutionally correct, and would have placed on the Liberals and Nationalists the onus of putting Labour into office or finding an alternative; it would also, as in 1923, have bought time in which options could have been weighed. But such a strategy would have risked a constitutional crisis with the Palace, could have seemed an undignified attempt to hang on to power, and would have thrown away in advance the Conservatives' acknowledged constitutional right' to one attempt to form a government before another election need be called. More significantly, it would almost guarantee the formation of a new Labour Government, committed to more left-wing policies than had been practised before 1970, and to a renegotiation of the terms of entry – which could take Britain out of the EEC. In assessments of Conservative politics in the year from February 1974, and in interpreting Heath's role in those events, too little attention has been paid to Tory fears of the damage that a Bennite Labour Government would do both to Britain and to Britain's position in Europe.[1]

With this reasoning, the tired men who surrounded Heath resolved to make an attempt to keep Labour out of power by assembling a coalition that would rest on the large majority of votes cast against Labour in the Election, a strategy that was constitutionally proper but perhaps politically unwise. Heath later wrote that 'no party was in a position automatically to form a government. Therefore my responsibility as Prime Minister at the time was to see whether I could form an administration with a majority.' His talking was with the Liberals, who represented 6 million votes (a fact that would add more authority to a new Cabinet than their fourteen MPs), and whose policy position overlapped with Heath's on the need for an incomes policy, on British participation in Europe, and on support for power-sharing in Ulster. Heath therefore called a meeting with the Liberal Leader, Jeremy Thorpe, which duly took place on the Sunday following the Election. A number of Ministers now recall this as a fairly desperate throw, a chance worth taking but not one on which they had ever placed much hope. Keith Joseph on the other hand opposed the idea of a deal with the Liberals at the time.[2]

There was common ground between Thorpe and Heath, and their talks hypothesised a relationship which both men could envisage accepting; Thorpe

---

1 Central Office Chairman's department file, CCO 20/8/17, Correspondence with Heath; Norman St John Stevas, *The Two Cities* (1984), 71; William Whitelaw, *The Whitelaw Memoirs* (1989), 134; Robert Behrens, *The Conservative Party from Heath to Thatcher*, Farnborough (1980), 23; Stephen Fay and Hugo Young, *The Fall of Heath* (1976), 30; Central Office *Notes on Current Politics* [hereafter *NCP*] 25 Mar. 1974.
2 D.E. Butler and Dennis Kavanagh, *The British General Election of February 1974* (1974), 253; interviews with Lord Howe, Lord Barber, Lord Carr and Lord Gilmour.

would have joined the Cabinet, with other Liberal MPs in more junior posts, and policy agreement might well have been reached on areas of domestic policy. There were though three large difficulties. First, Thorpe's followers were less keen on a deal with Heath than he was, particularly those Liberal MPs who needed to attract Labour votes to hold their seats; when informal talks took place again in July the message that came back from Thorpe was that he 'could not deliver' because half of his Party's voters preferred Labour to the Conservatives. Liberal MPs might have been persuaded to go along with a coalition though if the second problem, electoral reform, could have been overcome. Heath had not consulted his Party over these discussions, except for those in his outgoing Cabinet (even Ministers outside the Cabinet were being kept in the dark), and any deal with the Liberals might well have been repudiated by right-wingers, as both Norman Tebbit and John Peyton later argued. The more extreme right would certainly have done so; the Luton branch of the Monday Club resolved on 3 March to disown Heath altogether – 'after innumerable political "about turns" in office, it appears that he is now prepared to compromise his party even further by entering into unholy alliances in order to continue to hold power'. The chairman of the National Union Executive suggested in May that the Party would not now stand for 'electoral pacts with the Liberals, as memories of previous ones were so bitter', and in June, du Cann told a Central Office meeting that MPs in the 1922 Committee remained 'anxious that we might do a deal with the Liberals'. When a further Election was called for October, the Executive of the 1922 decided that it would meet as soon as results were declared, so that it would have a chance to intervene in any coalition-making, which suggests that there were indeed worries about what had been discussed in March; on 13 September, du Cann asked Heath on behalf of the 1922 for some *early* guidance on 'the way which discussions with persons of goodwill would take if we are successful in winning', but received a reply that was both non-commital and extremely cool. Whitelaw, back in his Chief Whip days in 1969, had told Cecil King that 'in circumstances of great crisis an emergency coalition might be possible, but it would cause a great uproar in the Tory Party, whose members still regard office as a prize they have no wish to share with others'. What is clear enough is that Heath knew well, even without asking his MPs, that they would not support proportional representation – against which the Party had been committed for as many years as Liberals had supported it. Heath was prepared to promise a Speaker's Conference on electoral reform, but stopped short of any more generous offers of the sort that did succeed in enticing Liberals into a parliamentary pact with Labour in 1977 (but on which the Labour Party did not and could not deliver the goods). Peter Walker has argued that Heath was too honest to make an offer that he could not achieve in practice, and this may well be fair, but it is surely also true that Heath realised that the offer of proportional representation would anyway cause such a Party row on his own side as to wreck a coalition before it ever got started. There was a double irony in all of this, for one of the consequences of proportional representation would have been a much-increased chance of bringing about the national consensus for which Heath was hoping and for which he would increasingly work while he remained Leader. Even after his fall from the leadership, when some Conservatives began to campaign actively for electoral reform, Heath remained opposed until 1992 to this one mechanism that would have been most likely to have promoted the political alignment and policies that he favoured.[3]

All such considerations were in any case subordinate to the third and most crucial problem in coalition-making, the fact that the Conservatives and Liberals had only 311 seats between them, when 318 were needed for a parliamentary majority. This inescapably meant that there was an unreality about the Heath–Thorpe talks: why should Liberals compromise their party's new-found popularity by combining with an unpopular Prime Minister who had just lost an election, when the combination could only be short and unstable anyway? And why should Conservatives surrender the long-term interest of their Party by accepting electoral reform, for the short-term gain of a few weeks in office without a majority? The politics of coalitionism would have seemed dramatically different if the combined Conservative–Liberal forces had been 320 or more MPs, and if there had thus been a reasonable chance of making a combination that would last, from which both partners might expect lasting benefits to offset any short-term concessions.

The arithmetic of the Commons therefore worked against success in coalition-making, unless a third group would also join. Here the position was especially frustrating for Conservatives. Ulster had just elected eleven Unionists, seven of whom were men who had either taken the Conservative whip in the past or who represented a similar persuasion. The problem was that those seven had fought their own election in alliance with other Unionists whose position was more militant, and four of these had also been elected, including Ian Paisley of the Democratic Unionists and William Craig, whose Vanguard Party had been suspected of too close an affinity with Protestant paramilitaries. These eleven MPs met shortly after the Election to elect the relatively moderate Captain Harry West as their chairman, and a ritual dance of mutual misunderstanding then took place. West and his ten colleagues, as

---

3 Butler and Kavanagh, *General Election of February 1974*, 255–7; Central Office Chairman's department file, CCO 20/78/1, Michael Wolff; Phillip Whitehead. *The Writing on the Wall: Britain in the Seventies* (1985), 114; Norman Tebbit, *Upwardly Mobile* (1989), 170; Central Office Chairman's department files, CCO 20/43/6, Monday Club, CCO 20/61/5, Wednesday morning meetings, and CCO 20/8/17, Correspondence with Heath; Advisory Committee on Policy minutes [hereafter ACP], 2 May 1974; Cecil King, *The Cecil King Diary, 1970–1974* (1975), 350; Cecil King, *The Cecil King Diary, 1965–1970* (1972), 242; John Campbell, *Edward Heath* (1993), 617, 805; Peter Walker, *Staying Power: An Autobiography* (1991), 125; Trevor Russel, *The Tory Party: Its Policies, Divisions and Future* (Harmondsworth, 1978), 142.

frightened of a Labour Government as were the Conservatives, made clear that they were willing to take the Conservative whip: they tried to get this message to Heath through intermediaries like Cecil King, and on the Monday the Ulster Unionist Council telephoned through to Central Office a definite offer that all eleven would take the Tory whip, so that no final decision could be taken by Heath before their formal letter arrived. On behalf of the Council, its chairman Sir George Clerk implored Heath to reflect on the long tradition of cooperation, on 'the general United Kingdom political situation', on the fact that all eleven MPs now elected were supported by the Council which was still affiliated to Heath's Party, and on the fact that the Ulster electorate had rejected 'previous policies here'. The 'proper position' was that 'seven Ulster Unionists with four colleagues in coalition have been returned. We request you to examine this situation and support Unionist associations affiliated to the Conservative and Unionist Central Party'. There would have been a price to pay for such support, for the eleven MPs in this Unionist coalition were united in their opposition to power-sharing in the province and had all been elected on that platform. It would have been theoretically possible for Heath to accept the suggestion that their election, with the backing of more than half of Ulster's voters, had anyway repudiated his Ulster policy and made it unworkable (as Maurice Macmillan kept reminding Heath in his own arguments for coalition even after the March talks had collapsed), so that collaboration with them need not now be impossible; and, since power-sharing in Northern Ireland collapsed only a few weeks later, such a decision would not have changed the constitutional future of Ulster either. But such a reversal of front would have been deeply unpopular on the Conservative left, and in this area as in others Heath was far from ready to abandon his Government's policies – even if the electors had repudiated them already. In any case, a change of policy on Ulster and an alliance with men such as Craig would in itself have removed any chance of a deal with the Liberals, so that the arithmetic of 1–3 March 1974 still did not add up (though in the longer term, Ulster Unionism might just have been kept in the Tory camp if Heath had signalled a symbolic preference for West rather than Thorpe as his partner). Heath offered the Conservative whip only to seven Ulster MPs, a number that in combination with the Liberals would still have left him with a majority of only one vote – but which might have enabled him to govern for a time against a fragmented opposition. This insensitive invitation to West to disown four of his colleagues was stiffly rejected by the Unionists, who saw in it another demonstration that the Conservatives did not understand what was now going on in Ulster. The eleven Ulster MPs remained a separate party, and the last chance of healing the Conservative–Unionist split – still less than two years old after a century of cooperation and still far from final – was lost.[4]

---

[4] King, *Diary 1970–74*, 348–50; Whitelaw, *Memoirs*, 135; Butler and Kavanagh, *General Election of February 1974*, 235; Central Office file, CCO 500/55/4, Northern Ireland.

Questioned on the BBC's *Today* radio programme, and asked whether he or any of his colleagues had residual sympathy for the Conservatives, West now replied, 'No, I don't think so' and emphasised that they had all been elected to take an independent line. The Party was then pressed by the YCs finally to sever all organisational connections, but in May the issue was further postponed; the Ulster Unionists simply ceased to attend National Union functions and meetings to avoid being expelled, and the constitutional issues involved were again ducked. Meanwhile, the Party's strategists were worrying about the 'semantics of Ulster' and deciding that they should not concede to the Unionists the self-description 'loyalist'; efforts would be made to get Party spokesmen and the press to use the phrase 'protestant extremists' instead. This last tactical decision, which must have set Lord Randolph Churchill and Andrew Bonar Law spinning in their graves, reflected the parting of the ways between the old allies more clearly than any other development in 1974.[5]

When Thorpe reported on Monday 4 March that Liberal MPs would not agree to a deal, unless all parties were represented, this was a polite way of turning down Heath's offer, for Labour had already said that it would take part in no coalition. Heath consulted his Cabinet again and decided to resign. An exchange of letters between Heath and Thorpe then put on the record the substance of what they had been discussing since the Election. Ministers who had taken part in these discussions have recorded that they felt great relief when they failed. An unstable government with an unreliable or non-existent Commons majority would clearly have been in a very weak position, particularly since it would still have to deal with the miners' strike and the related industrial problems that had prompted Heath to call the Election. Their relief at getting out of office in such unpromising circumstances was understandable, but it also reflected a lack of confidence which could be deeply damaging when it seeped through to the electorate. In September, just after the next Election was called, ORC found that less than half even of Conservative voters thought that the best outcome of the Election would be a Conservative Government. When the Party lost again in October, in still difficult economic circumstances, there was again some relief; it had been, according to a phrase circulating in Central Office, 'a good election to lose'. These were not the attitudes of a party in good heart and convinced of its mission to govern.[6]

There was in the Party, as more widely in the country, a deep pessimism inculcated by the fall of the Heath Government. The combination of poor economic performance and uncontrollable trade union militancy was good reason to be gloomy; during the eight months between the two Elections of

[5] Central Office file, CCO 20/55/4.
[6] *NCP* 25 Mar. 1974; Campbell, *Heath*, 618; Jim Prior, *A Balance of Power* (1986), 95; Butler and Kavanagh, *General Election of February 1974*, 259, 280.

1974, prices rose by 8 per cent and real wages at twice that rate; the market value of shares fell by a third in the same period, and over the two years from their high point in 1972, their value fell by more even than in the Great Crash of 1929. Peter Jenkins wrote in the *Guardian* in June 1974 of the

> utter gloom . . . to be encountered in Whitehall. . . . From senior officials comes a chorus of fateful foreboding remarkable in its unison. Uncontrollable inflation and political disintegration are subjects of no longer purely academic discussion. . . . When Sir Douglas Allen, head of the Treasury, imagines walking to work one morning to find the tanks drawn up on Horseguards Parade nobody is quite sure he is joking. Nobody knows what to do, few any longer pretend to know what to do.

Within a year, Anthony King was defining 'overload' as a congenital problem of British Cabinet government, in which 'our image of government is [now] that of the sorcerer's apprentice. The waters rise. The apprentice rushes about with his bucket. And none of us know when, or whether, the magician will come home.' Samuel Brittan predicted that the inability of governments to meet the rising expectations of an affluent workforce would lead to the end of liberal democracy within a generation. In the Party, such downbeat assessments were equally commonplace; a Bow Group pamphlet of January 1974 mournfully summarised the European perception of Britain as 'the poorest country in Europe in ten years . . . the worst strike record in the world . . . old fashioned and living in the past . . . educationally backward . . . industrially weak because of indifferent management and militant unions . . . lazy . . . nobody works as hard as people on the Continent . . . poor workmanship . . . terrible cooking . . . the most promiscuous girls in Europe'. David Howell, writing in January 1974, was impressed by the decline of optimism over the previous ten years: 'now we see a universal fear about the trend of events, about what will happen next'. An article in *Crossbow* in December 1974 asked 'Can Governments Cope?' and, for his CPC lecture in 1975, Alastair Burnet posed the question 'Is Britain Governable?'[7]

Any understanding of why Conservatives were prepared to flirt either with coalition or with more drastic economic policies than had been traditional must take account of this diagnosis of the country's peril. A similar *kulturpessimismus* had occasioned both a deeply ideological political debate in the Party in the decade before 1914 and a readiness to consider all-party solutions. As Michael Heseltine was to put it in a 1979 Election broadcast, 'Forward or Back? Because we cannot go on as we are.' The *conservative* option of preserving the status quo suddenly seemed to be irrelevant. The

---

[7] D.E. Butler and Dennis Kavanagh, *The British General Election of October 1974* (1975), 13, 18; *Crossbow*, Jan. 1974, 26, and Dec. 1974, 13; Brian Harrison, 'Mrs. Thatcher and the Intellectuals', in *Twentieth Century British History*, vol. 5, no. 2 (1994), 213; Peter Hennessy, *Whitehall* (1990), 318–19; Nick Brittain, 'Britain's Image', in *Europe: The First Year*, published by the Bow Group (1974), 1.

depressing final days of the Heath Government added to this heady brew by seemingly discrediting once and for all the Keynesian and consensual stance that Heath had been trying to pursue, much as the same policies were to be damaged on the Labour side by Callaghan's last limping months in office in 1979; a Tory candidate who declared that 'the Powellite criticisms are wholly misconceived and represent a positively harmful element in the Party' nevertheless also told Robert Carr in March 1974 that 'I am one of many that feel that the [Heath] Government was drifting into an indefensible position over the past few months.' On the eve of the October 1974 campaign, the Party's Vice Chairman for candidates, Anthony Grant, wrote to Whitelaw that 'industrial relations and cooperation in fighting inflation will dominate the election. How on earth can we pour scorn on [Labour's] social contract if that is precisely what *we* are seeking. . . . If the trade unions won't work with Labour why should they work with us? This feeble approach encourages the monetarists (of whom there are fair number among the brighter young candidates) to present what on the face of it appears to be a real alternative to the present morass'. Recent history had enfeebled the Party's moderate wing at precisely the moment when the right had gained a confidence they had not known since 1945.[8]

Memories of the February Election and the March attempt to form a coalition dominated the political landscape for the rest of 1974. The Conservatives' defeat shaped perceptions through and beyond the second 1974 Election in October, with the idea that the Party could not get on with the trade unions being impossible to shift from the popular mind; a leading Conservative told Butler and Kavanagh that for the electorate 'there was a Passchendaele mentality there. You don't understand the 1930s if you don't know what Passchendaele did to people twenty years earlier. Similarly, you won't understand October if you don't know what February did to us.' Lord Hailsham was far from alone in the Autumn in concluding that the Tories had already as good as lost the October Election in February. The idea of coalition lingered on too. In part, it was just not possible for Conservatives to rubbish in the Spring and Summer an idea that they had tried to bring off in March; in part it reflected the voters' wishes, for polls showed a clear majority favouring a coalition – only to fall to about 40 per cent in favour when the Conservatives actually developed such a definite policy in the Summer; in part it was because the idea took root in the minds of Heath and his closest advisers as a genuinely better way of conducting the nation's business than the adversarial politics they had endured since 1971. Heath kept up the 'national' rhetoric; responding to the Labour Government's programme in the Commons on 12 March, he announced that 'We shall judge this

---

8 John Ramsden, *The Age of Balfour and Baldwin, 1902–1940* (1978), 6; Central Office Chairman's department files, CCO 20/16/11, Correspondence with Fraser, and CCO 20/48/5, Candidates.

Government by the test of the national interest. We shall subject each item of policy to that test'; in an economic debate in July, he called on the Government (as Churchill had done before 1951) to abandon nationalisation plans as a threat to national unity, to give up ideas about leaving the EEC as contrary to the national interest, and to lead 'a national effort of a kind never before asked of the British people in time of peace'. The case for coalition received a powerful reinforcement when ORC produced a detailed analysis of the February figures which showed how damaging had been the Party's confrontational reputation with the public – as had Heath's own. Ian Gilmour began to trail the idea of a renewed commitment to a government of more than one party in May, when it seemed likely to evoke a positive response. When Peter Walker called in June for a 'government of national unity' he envisaged that it would be supported not only by Conservatives and Liberals but also by a third of Labour MPs. Such predictions underestimated the tactical skills of Harold Wilson, both in reinserting the Bennite genie into its bottle and in reconverting the Labour majority to Europe by the time it mattered in 1975, and so postponing the departure of people like Roy Jenkins and Shirley Williams until 1981. In 1974 such a departure seemed to be imminent, and would while Heath led the Conservatives have allowed room for a very different political realignment from the one that took place in the 1980s. The fact that such calls for 'a ministry of all the talents' were also made in Summer 1974 by Julian Amery from the Tory right and Maurice Macmillan from the left indicated both the range of appeal that the idea could have and – to suspicious minds – the fact that through his son and his son-in-law Harold Macmillan's influence for consensus politics was still at work; imaginative minds even speculated on Macmillan returning like de Gaulle to head a government of national regeneration. Informal discussions with the Liberals did not though identify any more viable basis of cooperation than that which had failed in March, partly because Liberals wanted a say in who would lead such a government; Conservative attempts spearheaded by Nigel Lawson to work out a basis for a Conservative–Liberal election pact also ran into the ground, as they were perhaps bound to do when the parties were mainly fighting for the same seats. There were clear limits to Heath's own perception of the new approach; he was not prepared to step down to facilitate the cooperation of MPs from other parties, and he was in any case not offering a coalition as such, but but a Conservative government pursuing the national interest, possibly with a few members added from outside. This was scarcely different from what he himself thought he had done between 1970 and 1974.[9]

---

[9] Butler and Kavanagh, *General Election of October 1974*, 25, 44, 61, 259, 280; Campbell, *Heath*, 633–4, 637–8; *NCP* 1 Apr. and 5 Aug. 1974; Morrison Halcrow, *Keith Joseph: A Single Mind* (1989), 69–70.

Heath and his Party critics

Heath emerged from his February defeat a bruised man, with much of the confidence that his unexpected 1970 victory had given now knocked out of him. The very fact of defeat, depriving him of the authority and patronage of a Prime Minister, gave added opportunities to his critics and disheartened his supporters; when he made a fine off the cuff speech in response to Denis Healey's first Budget, in March, he was received almost in silence on his own side of the House. Meanwhile, the undeniable fact that he had now lost two of the three campaigns he had fought as Leader provided support for the most insidious argument against him, that he was a born loser, a poor communicator and a bad television performer; this view was really dangerous because if it became widespread then it would trump all the arguments that pointed the other way – there was after all no especial point in having a far-sighted international statesman as Leader if he just could not win elections. The Eastern Area Council debated the question on 27 April; while it pledged its continued support to Heath as Leader, it also called on the Party to take a hard look at its communications in the context of the General Election defeat, and an amendment urging that 'the leadership should change its negative approach' was defeated only by fifty-seven votes to fifty three. Press critics became more open in their attacks, and in some dangerous places for a Conservative Leader; *The Economist* continued its loyal backing of Heath and derided his opponents, but the *Daily Telegraph* reported his critics with increasing regularity and gave them editorial support too. *The Times* devoted space to attacks on his Government's policy, and the *Spectator* was especially polemical in its hostility. When his March coalition attempt fell through, it attacked 'the squatter in No. 10 Downing Street' and proclaimed that 'Mr. Heath must now depart the Tory leadership as quickly as possible'.[10]

This Heath was not going to do, and as the inquest on his Government began to adopt a more critical tone, he became ever more determined to remain in the one place from which his record could be best defended; only by remaining Leader could he get back into office and prove that he had been right – by carrying the same policies through to success. He was also firmly convinced that he had to stay at the top to safeguard his great achievement of taking Britain into Europe, which would otherwise be imperilled by the shady political manoeuvring of Wilson. Increasingly, he was able to convince himself that the February result had been a sort of 'we was robbed' mistake, a tactical error perhaps but not a real repudiation of what he had tried to do, and that he alone could save the Party and country from the isolationist socialism

[10] Eastern Area Council, 27 Apr. 1974; Rupert Morris, *Tories: From Village Hall to Westminster* (1991), 158; Campbell, *Heath*, 618; John Barnes and Richard Cockett, 'The Making of Party Policy', in A. Seldon and S. Ball (eds), *Conservative Century: The Conservative Party since 1900* (Oxford, 1994), 381; interview with Lord Gilmour.

for which it had not voted. Gradually the shock of rejection wore off and confidence returned, reinforced by a personal triumph on the international scene, when in May he became one of the first Western statesmen to visit China and be received by its government.[11]

Heath's wish to continue with minimal concessions to the fact of defeat, and the weakness of that stance, were both indicated by the team he assembled in opposition. A front bench that had not been thought impressive in office was now weakened by the announcement that Sir Alec Douglas-Home would not seek re-election (though he remained in the shadow cabinet until October), by Barber's anticipated departure from active politics for the City (remaining in the shadow cabinet until June), by the loss at once of Christopher Chataway (for industry), and shortly afterwards of Maurice Macmillan and Lord Windlesham from the front bench. This was something like the atrophying of the leadership that took place on the Labour side after defeat in 1959, another occasion when a major party lacked confidence in its future. Heath's response was to reshuffle the remaining old faces, to promote juniors and to bring in a few from outside, but even this was done in a safe way. Joseph was disappointed of his wish to become shadow chancellor and decided instead to take on no specific duty, so as to remain free to rove widely over policy formulation; instead Robert Carr became shadow chancellor and was outgunned by Denis Healey in the Commons. The Research Department, as so often when the Party has returned to Opposition, was at first understaffed from the viewpoint of giving detailed policy advice to frontbenchers suddenly deprived of civil service briefing; 1974 is the only occasion in its history when the CRD has had no real time to repair this position before a second Election took place. Whitelaw shadowed industrial relations, again reinforcing the 'business as usual' look of the front bench. Geoffrey Rippon as foreign affairs spokesman was more robust, but the appointment also reflected Heath's Euro-centric view of foreign policy for Rippon had himself negotiated Britain's entry and was not likely to be favourable to Labour's attempt to reopen the question. Some of the younger men now promoted were to prove major figures in the future, but this was but dimly perceived at the time; Michael Heseltine was for example given the task of looking after trade and industry, but it was not until October 1975 that he established himself as the darling of Party Conferences and thereby acquired a power-base much like Hailsham had once enjoyed. Where Heath did seek heavyweight reinforcement, it was usually just as safe; later in the year Maudling agreed in principle to rejoin the front bench but felt that a longer interval was needed before the reasons for his earlier departure could be forgotten, so reinforcement was delayed; Edward Boyle, whose return would doubtless have been equally welcome to Heath, had ruled himself out

---

[11] Campbell, *Heath*, 626, 635.

by distancing himself from the Party in 1972, had resigned from the ACP, and was no longer even taking the Tory whip in the Lords.[12]

Such a team inevitably revived old criticisms: John Biffen, commenting on the same old faces in November 1974, remarked tartly that Heath must have been devoting his attention to the scriptures since he had decided to make the team in his own image. John Campbell is one of many who have defended Heath from the charge that he promoted only those who did not challenge his authority, by asking who were the men of talent who *should* have been promoted – and came up with few names. But surely, it was unwise even now to provide no portfolios for Edward du Cann, Angus Maude, Christopher Soames, John Biffen or Peter Thorneycroft, all men of independent mind and considerable weight in the Party, four of whom were given responsibilities by Margaret Thatcher within a year? Inclusion of any of these men, or the more rapid promotion of younger men like Heseltine or Nott, would have done something to head off the Party's discontent, and would thus have been in Heath's own interest too. But they would also no doubt have been likely to argue.[13]

Parliamentary tactics were difficult. If the opposition parties took up too strong a position, they could tempt Wilson into dissolving parliament at once and blaming them for a second election, while if they did not oppose Labour's measures, their own supporters would become restive. As a shadow minister told Robert Behrens, 'It was all rather frustrating. We wanted to defeat the Government but knew that if we did it might be electorally disastrous.' The debate on Wilson's Queen's Speech set the tone for what was to come; when a Tory amendment critical of Labour's proposal to abandon Heath's incomes policy was tabled, the decision of the Liberals to support it threatened a Labour defeat, only for the Conservatives to be saved from bringing down the Government by an even deeper embarrassment; forty Tory MPs organised by the Selsdon Group refused to back Heath and the idea of incomes policy anyway – a significant increase on the number who had ever opposed incomes policies when the Party had been in office. After this the Party leaders were careful to avoid taking up positions that could produce such difficulties, and Tory MPs were not whipped strongly into opposing Labour's plans; Norman Tebbit later joked that a one-line whip was taken to mean 'turn up if you wish', but a three-line whip meant 'for God's sake stay away or we might defeat the Government'. Labour MPs were merciless in deriding about such tactics and Conservatives were increasingly unhappy. In March, Peter Tapsell told his Horncastle association that the next election would probably be on

12 Campbell, *Heath*, 627–8; Reginald Maudling, *Memoirs* (1978), 206; Butler and Kavanagh, *General Election of October 1974*, 41; Julian Critchley, *Heseltine: The Unauthorised Biography* (1987), 46; Christopher Knight, *The Making of Tory Education Policy in Post-War Britain* (1990), 72.
13 Campbell, *Heath*, 518–19; Behrens, *Heath to Thatcher*, 32.

16 June, and Central Office made plans on the same assumption. Only in June itself, with the possibility of a Summer election now gone, did tactics change; on 19 June, Tories, Unionists and Liberals united to defeat a Labour proposal to repay to trade unions fines levied under the Industrial Relations Act, and there were eighteen further Government defeats before the end of July, which in effect guaranteed an election in Autumn. This had some effect in improving Tory morale, and the Party's position in the polls improved too.[14]

One figure remained an influence from out of doors, Enoch Powell, now out of parliament altogether. His own account of his reaction to the result of the February Election was characteristic; finding the morning newspaper headlined 'Heath's gamble fails', Powell 'took it up with me to the bathroom and sang the Te Deum'. There were many Conservatives who could never forgive Powell for his contribution to the February defeat, or for the undisguised pleasure with which he received it, but there remained an awareness that the votes he had mobilised demonstrated that his influence was far from over. On the week-end after the February Election, Powell was on the BBC's *Any Questions* panel alongside Norman St. John Stevas; when it was suggested that he had reduced his right to speak on the issues because he had not contested the Election, Powell replied, 'Fought it? I *won* it!' When he added that it was still his ambition to lead the Party, St. John Stevas remarked, 'I see that there are worse things than losing an election'. A *Crossbow* editorial in June argued that 'it will take a long time for the Rt. Hon. J. Enoch Powell to live down his betrayal at the last election', but went on to urge that, 'the Tory Party would be equally wrong to bolt and bar the door for ever. The tragedy has been that the gap between Party and Powell has grown so wide. Powell speaks for many in the country and it would be foolish for the Party to ignore the reasons behind his support.' Powell was still a Conservative, and had indeed proclaimed his continuing loyalty to the Party when advising electors to vote against it in February. There remained the worrying possibility that he would be selected by a constituency association to fight a marginal seat – and so prove his greater personal capacity than Heath's to pull in the vote. In May Powell made a conciliatory speech, in which he accepted that both sides in recent disputes had acted honourably and called for the 'unity of purpose which the party seemed to lose in the years after 1970', but even this was a hit at Heath, and the EEC remained a barrier between them, perhaps more so when the Labour Government reopened the question of how final Britain's accession had been. Nevertheless, some continued to hope for Powell's return to the Tory fold, and there were invitations to him to return as a candidate; when asked in June by Westhoughton Conservatives whether he would be available for selection as their candidate, he replied that he was 'always prepared to

---

[14] Behrens, *Heath to Thatcher*, 24; Campbell, *Heath*, 625, 632, 636; Tebbit, *Upwardly Mobile*, 171; Butler and Kavanagh, *General Election of October 1974*, 42; Horncastle CA minutes, 22 Mar. 1974; *NCP*, 9 Sept. 1974.

give earnest consideration' to any proposal from a Conservative association or its selection committee, but that he was not willing to be considered unless he was the only candidate. He was not selected there or anywhere else on those conditions, which were against National Union guidelines for selection procedures. Since he had been in touch with the Ulster Unionists since March, it is likely that Powell's response to Westhoughton had more to do with courtesy than ambition, but the prospect that it presented of him storming back into parliament by taking a Labour seat on his personal and policy appeal rang deafeningly loud warning bells in Central Office. On the eve of the October Election, he was adopted as Unionist candidate for South Down, which act took him practically outside the Conservative Party (even if the Unionist associations' disaffiliation was not yet technically achieved). He was from February 1974 personally no longer a member of the Conservative Party (except as President of the Hackney Tories), but regular invitations to him to address Conservative meetings caused embarrassment for Heath and then Thatcher for years to come.[15]

There were plenty of critics of Heath still within the ranks, though in the expectation of an early election such complaints were usually guarded. An MP who tried to call for a new leader at the 1922 Committee in March was shouted down, but as many as a hundred MPs apparently told the whips that Heath should step down at a suitable time since he could not win elections. The problem was that those same MPs feared that, as soon as the Party began a leadership crisis, Wilson would smartly dissolve parliament and catch them unprepared. Throughout the Spring, the issue was fairly easily postponed, and by Summer Heath was again confident and impossible to dislodge; with an Autumn election inevitable, the issue of the leadership was therefore left to the voters. The question did though keep bobbing to the surface, as when Joan Quennell MP, no natural rebel, pointed out in the *Daily Telegraph* in April that if Heath was admired at the grass-roots of the Party he was not regarded with warmth. When asked to become an additional PPS to the Leader, a proposal that in itself reflected a wish to improve Heath's communications with backbenchers, Kenneth Baker was advised by friends among Conservative MPs not to become 'a rare example of a rising politician joining a sinking ship'.[16]

What had brought about such disaffection? Sara Morrison, a friend of Heath's who had been appointed by him as a Party Vice Chairman, believed that from the start there had been 'a sort of crackable quality in the relationship between Ted, the Party organisation, the people out there in the sticks . . . and

---

15 Whitehead, *Writing on the Wall*, 113; St John Stevas, *The Two Cities*, 72; *Crossbow*, June 1974, 7; Central Office Chairman's department file, CCO 20/48/5, Candidates; Butler and Kavanagh, *General Election of October 1974*, 46.
16 Butler and Kavanagh, *General Election of October 1974*, 37; Campbell, *Heath*, 624–5; Behrens, *Heath to Thatcher*, 23–4, 36; Kenneth Baker, *The Turbulent Years: My Life in Politics* (1993), 41.

those who wished the new order of things in the Tory Party well'. The backbench wits declared that Sara Morrison had been appointed with the brief 'to turn Ted into a human being', but without much success. At a Party Conference, as Julian Critchley recalls,

> they both attended the agents' annual dinner [and] Sara noticed that conversation between the Prime Minister and the wife of the chief agent had dried up, so she wrote on her napkin, 'For God's sake say something', folded it carefully and passed it up through the diners to the top table. Ted received it, opened it, glanced at the message and wrote 'I have' before passing it back.

Heath's supporters were driven to distraction in 1974 by Heath's lack of the graces that lubricate political loyalties. Returning from the hard-fought February campaign, Jim Prior was dining Norman Fowler, Julian Critchley and David Walder when Heath interrupted them to consult Prior; he then left without a word to the others, all men who had spent the past few weeks defending Heath and his policies on the hustings, and for whom a word of thanks would have been appropriate; 'What on earth can I do with him?' was Prior's despairing question. When visiting Party workers during the October 1974 campaign, Heath would often reply in monosyllables and leave the making of conversation entirely to those that he had supposedly come to encourage, while, at a reception for Tory agents, his minders discovered him alone in a corner, unwilling even to approach men that he did not know and whose names he could not remember. Peter Rawlinson recorded the 'probably apocryphal' but much-repeated tale that Heath's advisers were always urging him to chat approvingly to backbenchers who had spoken in the House that day. 'But, so the story goes, he demurred. He had not heard the speech himself; he could not readily accept the judgement of others; and he was too honest to pretend.' The wide circulation of the story was significant, whether or not it was true. Reginald Maudling felt that,

> Ted's great weakness was that he gave the impression to the Members of the House that he did not care for them; that he regarded them merely as troops who were there to support him and that he was the officer in command. He was seldom seen in the smoking room, he never fraternized with the rank and file. And he did not make enough knights. If he had been a more loved leader he would have survived.

Morrison, Maudling, Rawlinson and Prior all supported Heath's continuation as Leader even in February 1975. It is easy to see how the same tales could be made to sound even more damaging in the mouths of those who wanted a change. Edward du Cann remarked of Heath in July 1974, and without apparent regret, that 'Edward has few friends, very few friends. If he falls there will be nobody to pick him up'.[17]

---

[17] Whitehead, *Writing on the Wall*, 31, 325; Julian Critchley, *A Bag of Boiled Sweets: An Autobiography* (1994), 139, 141; Peter Rawlinson, *A Price Too High: An Autobiography* (1989), 245; Maudling, *Memoirs*, 207; Behrens, *Heath to Thatcher*, 32.

A Leader so aloof from a parliamentary party whose support he needed was probably also unaware of the extent to which it had changed in the relatively short period since he had known it so well as Chief Whip. Alec Douglas-Home was now the only Conservative MP who had sat in the Commons before the War, and there were only eleven who had been first elected before Heath's own arrival in 1950; of the meritocratic 'class of 1950', only twenty-five were in the 1970 Parliament (during which two more died), and when Heath needed the votes of his contemporaries to stay on as Leader in February 1975 this had fallen again to fourteen. More surprisingly, barely half of the parliamentary party had experience of the Commons going back before the 1964 Election; after October 1974, this had fallen to only 107 out of 277 Tory MPs with more than ten years in parliament, and very few indeed who remembered Heath as a popular Chief Whip. A different character and attitudes had emerged along with the new generation, as Julian Critchley sharply observed when he returned to parliament in 1970 after losing his seat in 1964. Writing in 1972, he thought 'the Conservative Parliamentary Party has changed. It is less socially cohesive, and more ideological in content. It is clearly less "sound" than it once was.' Among the different manifestations of this change were the facts that MPs generally worked harder and now spent week-ends in their constituencies rather than 'in great houses', and that the 1922 Committee had become more efficient but less fun. More MPs were professional politicians and there were fewer of the knights of the shire who had been the 'ballast' of the Party in previous generations.

> The Member for the City of London wears shirts and ties of the same material, and the suits of the party are paler and off-the-peg. Some even wear suede shoes. It was reported recently that a former Member, who was asked at an extraordinary meeting of the Carlton Club, called to consider its finances, to admit to the club all the party's MPs, said, 'I cannot; they are not all gentlemen.' He might not have said that ten years ago.

Only one Tory MP, he noted, now wore the black jacket and striped trousers which had been the traditionalist backbenchers' uniform in the 1950s. Writing in 1972, the former Conservative MP Humphry Berkeley remarked sharply on the same change:

> There is . . . a type of MP who has been unique to the Conservative Party, of which perhaps Sir Harry Legge-Bourke is a good contemporary example. He is a gentle, honourable man, incapable, I would judge, of telling an untruth, totally without personal ambition, who sees his membership of Parliament as an act of public service. He belongs unhappily to a dying breed. He and those like him are being replaced by human efficiency machines, constructed for utility rather than grace. They reel off figures to anyone who is prepared to listen. . . . They have not learned the art of conversation. They appear to communicate by conducting a series of interviews with each other. . . . For them the House of Commons is a stepping stone to the glittering prizes of office and power.

In this context it is easy to see how and why the retirement of Legge-Bourke as Chairman of the 1922 Committee and his replacement by Edward du Cann seemed a milestone in the parliamentary party's development.[18]

To a considerable extent, the facts bear out these sartorial impressions. In the 1970s for the first time in its history, the Conservatives had more MPs from grammar schools than from Eton; for the first time half of its MPs could reasonably be classified as 'businessmen'. Meanwhile the post-war expansion of Oxford and Cambridge ensured that many of this new type of Tory came out like Mrs Thatcher with a traditional Conservative accent – though few managed the transformation in so extreme a form. The military/landowning/farming group that had made up nearly half the parliamentary party in 1914, and was still almost two-fifths in 1939, was down to a fifth in 1964 and only a twelfth of MPs by 1974; the twenty-two MPs of this type who survived were mainly working farmers without great personal wealth. The departure in 1974 of Sir Robin Turton, whose family had a lengthy tradition of representing the North Riding of Yorkshire, and in 1979 of Jasper More, whose family had represented Shropshire on and off ever since the Long Parliament of 1640, were seen as symbolic of the passing of a tradition of rural politics. As Michael Thompson has shown, the withdrawal of the old elite from county politics and social leadership underlay this retreat from the representation of the shires at Westminster. By 1973, following Walker's local government reforms, less than a third of England's lords lieutenant were from old landed or titled families, while in Scotland it was down to half and in Wales the old guard had gone altogether; in their place had emerged a new generation of county leaders 'dominated by retired generals, naval commanders, and successful businessmen', nearly all of them too old to start new careers as MPs. In 1979, James Margach wrote that in parliament, 'the historic family names among the aristocrats, born to rule and lead by centuries of breeding and experience, have gone.' He compared the situation in the 1930s, when he had first reported politics, with the time of his retirement in the 1970s: in the 1930s, the parliamentary Conservative Party had contained 25 heirs to peerages, 125 knights and baronets, and 128 who liked to be known by their former military rank (almost all of the rank of Major or above); in the late 1970s, there were only eight heirs to titles, twenty-three knights and baronets, and only two who used their military rank to describe themselves. It was commonplace to see this change as the replacement of MPs motivated by public service, who had an independent attitude to life combined with an intense loyalty to the Party, with more professional and better trained politicians for whom both the fruits of office and the ideology of political

[18] Butler and Kavanagh, *General Election of February 1974*, 210; Butler and Kavanagh, *General Election of October 1974*, 213; Julian Critchley, 'Strains and Stresses in the Conservative Party', in *Political Quarterly*, vol. 44, (1973), 240, 242; Humphry Berkeley, *Crossing the Floor* (1972), 26–7.

action were more important than had been usual in the past. Peter Riddell has shown how on the Conservative as well as on the Labour side of the House, the period from 1951 to 1992 was marked by a steady rise, from one in ten in 1951 to almost a third by 1992 of new MPs who had never had any occupation but politics; the new generation of Conservative MPs elected after the clear-out of 1964–66 was a milestone along that road. Whereas, even after the Maxwell Fyfe Report, one in four *new* Tory MPs elected in 1950 and 1951 had been Etonians, that figure had fallen to one in seven by 1959, and to one in ten by 1970; by the time of Heath's fall, only about a third of new Tory MPs at each election had been to both public schools and Oxbridge. Expectations and activity levels of these new Conservative MPs were a long way from those of the generation of Florence Horsbrugh, of whom the Area Agent had reported in 1956 that 'she nurses the [Moss Side] constituency conscientiously, visiting it for interviews once a month'. By contrast, an active MP like Sir Gerald Nabarro was receiving by 1969 some fifteen thousand letters a year, and had little opportunity for such semi-detachment from his constituency. In this context, Peter Rawlinson was lamenting in 1989 the passing of both the miners and the knights of the shires and their replacement by 'polytechnic lecturers and corporate financiers', but the real replacements were often those who had gone straight from university to Westminster. What was now rare was the Member who came into Parliament in middle age and with no ambition but to be a backbencher and represent his own area; even in the 1960s, one such MP had told Philip Buck that for such men 'the atmosphere became more uncongenial with the arrival of increasing numbers of keen young professionals'. The Bow Group, which by the 1970s represented the orthodox path to parliament for the not very privileged but extremely ambitious, had 109 members among the Tory candidates in October – but the Bow Group, as Julian Critchley put it, 'has since its inception been first-generation public school and Oxbridge, and can thus pass for white'. In other words, the Group was like Oxbridge a means of absorbing new blood into an old system, and thereby disguising the change that was taking place. In analysing the simmering discontent that produced what Critchley himself was to call the 'peasants' revolt' against Heath in 1975, it is important to be aware that the character of the peasants themselves had changed so much and so quickly. The whips had long seen coming both the change and its consequence: in November 1957, when Heath himself had been the Chief Whip coping with the Suez crisis, his predecessor Patrick Buchan-Hepburn had written to *his* precedessor James Stuart: 'It is not so easy to deal with a Party of Backroom Boys as with a Party of Backwoods Boys (not so "naice").'[19]

[19] John Ramsden, 'The Changing Base of British Conservatism', in Chris Cook and John Ramsden, *Trends in British Politics since 1945* (1978), 43–4; James Margach, *The Anatomy of Power* (1978), 65–71; Peter Riddell, *Honest Opportunism* (1993), 22, 25; Central
continued

The ultimate irony in all of this lies in the fact that Heath was by background – if never by temperament – more of a 'peasant' than most of those who opposed him. But Heath had through his accent, his army career, his political ascent through the Whips' office and as the Prime Minister's protégé under Macmillan, and in his easy relationship with senior civil servants, become more establishment-minded than the old establishment. It was erroneously said by the press in 1967 that his poor relations with du Cann originated in a disrespectful comment made about Heath's background by the more patrician Party Chairman. Since Heath's only comment on these allegations was to snarl at the press that they were 'damned lies', we have only du Cann's account to go on, given later to James Margach. There had not been, said du Cann, any personal 'friction or anything like that' between them, but a major difference of attitude; 'I have always taken the view that the leader exists to serve his Party. Ted alas takes the other view that the Party exists to serve the leader.' He went on to say that

> it is not quite true that I was sacked as chairman of the Party simply because Ted was angry with me for reminding him of his humble origins and how this could be put across to the Party's advantage. Not quite right. I suggested that we could build him up for the press and TV as the new Conservative leader in one of two ways: as the epitome of the new generation, the abrasive, organisational man, success symbol, new horizons, the pacemaker; or the Party machine could build him up, project him, as an entirely new type of leader, making British history; the prospective Prime Minister who had risen from the most humble surroundings, the son of a small one-man jobbing builder with a wife of similar background. It isn't right that I said to him that we in the Party organisation would do a wonderful job on him for the election, in selling him as the son of a lady's maid. That's journalistic licence touching up history, I'm afraid. But I did tell him that we could project his personality as the son of a lower middle class family. I don't think he approved of my second alternative. Ted prefers, I think, and finds it easier to do so, to identify with the more worldly side of power, public life and success.

The result of this approach to authority that the clash with du Cann exemplified was that Heath lost out in 1975 to a Conservative successor who had come up through the Party the hard way rather than on Heath's inside track, was temperamentally inclined to remember rather than forget her origins, and was therefore always able to half-project herself as still being one of the peasants, an outsider even in 1990. In this way, in the Party's self-projection, the Heath era may be seen – as in so many other ways – as

continued

Office constituency file, CCO 1/11/121; Gerald Nabarro, *Nab 1: Portrait of a Politician* (1969), 90; Byron Criddle, 'Members of Parliament', in Seldon and Ball, *Conservative Century*, 163; Rawlinson, *Price Too High*, 132; P. W. Buck, *Amateurs and Professionals in British Politics* (1963), 82; *Crossbow*, Dec. 1974, 5; F.M.L. Thompson, 'English Landed Society in the Twentieth Century: I, Property, Collapse and Survival', in *Transactions of the Royal Historical Society*, 5th series, vol. 40 (1990), 5; John Ramsden, *The Age of Churchill and Eden, 1940 to 1957* (1995), 328.

a transitional phase, between the patrician, 'ruling-class mystique' (to quote Angus Maude) political style of the Churchill/Eden/Macmillan/Home period, and the aggressively classless 'road from [Grantham or] Brixton' message put across by Heath's successors.[20]

Modernising the machine

Outside parliament too, the Party had changed significantly, and the period since 1970 had been characterised by attempts to modernise it. The Party managers' view was that the organisation was in serious decline, and was in danger of becoming stranded with out-of-date attitudes and practices, but that it was stubborn in its resistance to change. There was a shortage of money for the central funds, but when the constituency associations were in 1972 invited to lend their cash reserves to Central Office, few of them agreed to do so, not having confidence that they would in practice get their money back if they needed it. Financial constraints, both central and local, had enforced a reduction in the number of paid Party employees; the 157 people employed in Central and Area offices in 1963 (already down from more like 200 at the height of Woolton's restoration of the machine) had fallen again to 136 by 1974; there were still over 500 constituency agents in 1963, but under 400 early in 1974; on the eve of the October Election, only 325 constituencies had their own full-time fully-qualified agent, 99 being looked after in pairs or groups by another 40 qualified agents. Ten constituencies were run by trainees, and 189 constituencies had no agent at all, making a total of 365 professional agents even if those who had only intermediate qualifications were included. In the West Midlands, where many marginals lay, the 63 constituencies now had only 26 qualified agents, where there had been 40 as recently as 1966. In the West Country in July 1973, there was only one agent in Bristol, and an advertisement even at scale rates with additional marginal weighting had produced no applicants at all for a vacancy at Exeter; in Wales in 1973, a dozen agents covered thirty-six constituencies. The 1966 Parliament was the first since the War in which there had been no concerted national drive to raise the membership, and as a result overall numbers continued to fall. By 1970, Butler and Pinto-Duschinsky were surprised to report that the total of Party members was still as high as 1.25 million to 1.5 million, but while this was probably about the number that the Party had had in the 1930s, it was only half the figure of 1953; research for the Houghton Committee in 1974 confirmed the membership as being around 1.5 million. In 1968–69, Michael Pinto-Duschinsky had found wide variations between different kinds of constituencies, as Tables 7.1 and 7.2 show; he found the lowest figures were all in the cities.

[20] Margach, *Anatomy of Power*, 166.

Table 7.1   Average Conservative memberships, 1968–69

Safe Conservative constituencies	4,700
Marginal Conservative constituencies	3,400
Marginal Labour constituencies	2,550
Safe Labour constituencies	1,350

Table 7.2   Membership compared to the Conservative vote, 1968–69

Conservative-held rural constituencies	24%
Conservative-held other constituencies	16%
Labour-held rural	18%
Labour-held other	11%

The survey of membership in nine critical marginals done for Central Office in 1974 was consistent with this overall finding but reflected wide individual variations from the norm; only two of these Tory-held seats now had a membership of over 5,000, both of them rural constituencies, while four had less than 1,500 members and the lowest of the nine had only 494. As had been clear ever since the 1950s, membership decline had been concentrated in urban areas and especially in safe Labour seats, where average membership was now well under a thousand per constituency.[21]

YC numbers fell even faster than the seniors; a former chairman, Nicholas Scott, estimated in 1973 that the YC total was down to 40,000 nationally, compared to a peak of 200,000, and still 80,000 in the early 1960s; by 1978 the total had fallen yet further; these figures match those collected by Michael Pinto-Duschinsky. In 1971, the Yorkshire Area amended its rules to reflect that decline in numbers, with YC representation on the Area Executive reduced from five to three. The fact that most YCs were now under 20, where at their height the bulk, and certainly the leaders, had been in their late 20s,

---

[21] Eastern Area Council, 4 Nov. 1972; S.E. Finer, *The Changing British Party System* (Washington, DC, 1980), 102; Central Office files, CCO 500/2/24, Central Employment of Agents, and CCO 500/26/35, Marginal reports; D.E. Butler and Michael Pinto-Duschinsky, *The British General Election of 1970* (1970), 279; D.E. Butler and Michael Pinto-Duschinsky, 'The Conservative Elite, 1918–1978: Does Unrepresentativeness Matter?', in Z. Layton-Henry (ed.), *Conservative Party Politics* (1980), 189; Stuart Ball, 'Local Conservatism and the Evolution of Party Organisation', in Seldon and Ball, *Conservative Century*, 275, 291; West Midlands Area Council, 12 Nov. 1966 and 14 Dec. 1974; Western Area Council, 18 July 1973; Wales Area EC, 14 July 1973; Michael Pinto-Duschinsky, 'The Role of Constituency Associations in the Conservative Party', D.Phil. thesis, Oxford University, 1972, 26.

further weakened the movement's political value. Partly as a consequence of this, partly as a result of increasing university access, the Federation of Conservative Students now spoke for more young Conservatives than the YCs. Scott claimed that the YCs still remained 'the largest voluntary youth movement in the free world', and pointed out that Labour's youth wing had collapsed altogether, but accepted the dangers posed by numerical decline. His explanation was that since 'three out of four YCs were interested in the social rather than the political side', there were now just too many other social activities competing for their attention, as was witnessed by the decline in all types of voluntary organisations. He found some comfort in the fact that the branches that had survived were now more radical and more trenchant in their attitudes, citing as example the Greater London YCs' calls for more democracy in the Party; the modern outlook of the YCs was clear from their chairman's habit of addressing Party Conferences wearing a T-shirt, unthinkable only a few years earlier; and YCs had also been in the forefront of forward-looking campaigns for entry into Europe and for moderate policies in Ulster. Not all were so positive; a 1974 article complained of 'ageing trendies and borrowed ideas', and noted that YCs were now as likely to flirt with ideas from the far right as from the left, which meant that they had no collective identity; 'the old style image of short hair and sports cars has virtually gone for ever, but it is doubtful whether long hair, shouting and banner-waving is proving an original or attractive alternative'.[22]

The overall decline in activity was matched by a deterioration in the Party's finances; income fell, both from constituency quotas and from industrial subscriptions, while inflation pushed up costs; a plan to launch a full-scale appeal at the end of 1973 fell through because of the unfavourable circumstances at that time. Late in 1972, the revised forecast for the period 1971 to 1975 predicted an overall annual deficit of £1.3 million, and reserves that at that rate of attrition would disappear altogether in about 1978.[23]

A particular focus of concern was the state of the Party in Scotland, where the downward spiral had been much steeper than in England. Reporting on the survey commissioned after the SNP won Hamilton in 1968, ORC's chairman reported findings that were 'rather rough on the Scottish Conservative Party', which

> has got an exceedingly bad image. It is thought to be out of touch, a bastion of 'foreign' (English) privilege, Westminster-orientated, associated with recalcitrant landowners. Most people are unfamiliar with the leading figures in the Scottish Conservative Party [which] was the only party which, on mention, often elicited mirthful or mirthless laughter. It was variously described as 'run by Lairds', 'landowners', and 'the business community'. Among the insults heaped upon it were that 'Conservatives are the dregs from England'. . . . Unless changes are

---

[22] *Crossbow*, Jan. 1973, 24, and June 1974, 34; Pinto-Duschinsky, 'Constituency Associations', 24; Yorkshire Area Council, 24 Apr. 1971.
[23] Central Office Chairman's department file, CCO 20/22/18, Treasurers.

made in the image and attractiveness of the Scottish Conservative Party, the SNP is very likely to make substantial inroads into the Scottish vote.

A Scottish Conservative candidate asked in August 1973 'why the Scottish Tories are in such a mess?' He put the problem down to the lack of drive in producing economic benefits such as home ownership in Scotland when the Party had been in power, to the neglect of Clydeside since 1965 by an Edinburgh-based Party organisation (which meant that there was now not even one agent in Glasgow and only eight in the whole Western Area of thirty-five constituencies), and above all to the tactical error of offering devolution, which Scottish Tories did not really want, and then not delivering it anyway. There is no doubt though that the decline was general rather than regional, that the Glasgow-based Western Council had long been a focus of resistance to modernising influences, and that decline did not begin at the time of the 1965 reorganisation anyway; what is quite clear is that Clydeside Unionists believed that their interests had been sacrificed in the transfer of the main Party office to Edinburgh, and were deeply insulted by this. In 1970, an election year, the Scottish Conservatives as a whole raised only £118,350 for their central funds, an average of about £1,700 per constituency, exactly half the equivalent figure for England and Wales; the amount contributed to this total by the constituency parties themselves was £8,744 (£123 per constituency association, less than a quarter of the figure for England and Wales); this pattern is a striking measure of the relative as well as the absolute loss of vitality in Scottish local organisation. In 1970 the Greenock Conservatives refused to fight the parliamentary seat, seeing it as a waste of time, and could be neither coerced nor cajoled into changing their mind. After the local government reorganisation of 1973–74, Scottish Conservatives were still not even putting up candidates in a third of the new council areas, though by then there was a party contest for the regions, cities and industrial areas. When in February 1974, two more Scottish seats were lost and many more made to look vulnerable to the attack of the SNP, a *Crossbow* editorial (by a Scotsman) said bluntly that 'the Scottish Tories are a disaster. Feudal and narrow, they have turned their backs on the middle class which might have given them a new lease of life.' Teddy Taylor's (then) success in digging himself into a strong position in Glasgow Cathcart was contrasted with many others who had 'given up the Scottish Tories as a lost cause and come south'; (Taylor's subsequent departure for Southend after losing his own Glasgow seat in 1979 rather confirmed the point). English Conservatives were warned that unless they took devolution seriously they could suffer a disaster north of the Border. In October five more seats were lost.[24]

[24]   Central Office file, CCO 500/50/1, Nationalists; *Crossbow*, Aug. 1973, 17, and June 1974, 5; Glasgow UA, 30 Nov. 1970; J.T. Ward, *The First Century: A History of Scottish Tory Organisation* (Edinburgh, 1982), 41–3; Michael Pinto-Duschinsky, *British Political Finance, 1830–1980* (1981), 138.

Heath did not give a high priority to organisation when he became Prime Minister. His Party Chairman was Peter Thomas, Secretary of State for Wales, which paid lip service to the idea that a Cabinet Minister should hold the post and was ingenious in giving it to one of the least heavily burdened, but it put at Central Office a genial presence rather than a tough reformer. Thomas was complemented by a forceful Vice Chairman fiercely loyal to Heath, Sara Morrison, who devoted considerable attention to the drive for modernisation. Michael Fraser continued as Deputy Chairman of the Party with special responsibility for the CRD, and again no senior Minister was given Butler's old job as the impresario of policy.[25]

Much time and energy was absorbed in the work of the Chelmer Committee to modernise the Party structure, which had more than sixty meetings before producing its report: it was asked to consider 'the extent, if any, to which the Conservative Party in all its aspects outside Parliament might be made more democratic'. The most urgent task was to provide new selection rules that would deal with the sensitive issues arising from redistribution, and this was successfully done, though the recommendation that the Approved Candidates' List should be more regularly reviewed ran into predictable opposition from those who were on it. The adoption of this interim reform package in 1971 ensured that for the first time all constituencies used precisely the same selection rules, the first time indeed that *any* part of local procedures had been imposed on the constituency associations by the National Union as a condition of affiliation. On the wider issues, constituency evidence submitted to the Committee did not in the main support the case for democratising the Party, and the report made few real recommendations in this field (which had been the reason for its existence in the first place). Chelmer's main finding was that constituency associations were 'the vital unit in the organisation of the Party' and that the whole objective of the Party should be the return of Conservative governments, everything else being secondary. His primary recommendation was therefore the reconstruction of constituency associations, to make them more outward-looking, mainly by requiring them to have 'political committees' whose agendas would not be dominated by administrative and financial matters; this was in effect the promotion of 'Project 67' by other means. Many National Union figures were deeply sceptical, fearing that too much energy would go into political debates divorced from the basic tasks of raising money and keeping up electoral organisation in the branches; the West Midlands' National Union Executive representatives reported that they had been 'driven to ask' how many votes such reforms would win and whether the time spent on them would be worthwhile. When both of the 1974 Elections produced tight results, such traditionalists were able to point to the seats won on postal votes as a

[25] Campbell, *Heath*, 510; John Ramsden, *The Making of Conservative Party Policy: The Conservative Research Department since 1929* (1980), 287–9.

vindication of their own order of priorities. Others simply rejected the ideas behind the proposed reforms and did not want the Party to be made more democratic, and particularly did not want changes that would enhance the authority of the Party Conference. The proposal to change the overall name of the organisation to the 'National Conservative Association', at exactly the moment at which the Unionist connection was fragmenting, outraged another type of traditionalist, and was eventually thrown out by an overwhelming vote of the Central Council in an emotional debate. Discussions ran on for months, and in October 1973 Central Council decided, against the advice of the Executive and the National Union officers, to defer the whole thing again until after the coming Election. It could not then be tackled in 1974 with yet another Election due, and the entire package of proposals gradually ran into the sands. Not until the 1981 'Charter to Set the Party Free' was launched, drawing directly on the experience of 1969–73, did a further head of steam for democratic reform build up.[26]

Having failed to reform structures, Central Office, and Sara Morrison in particular, tried to change practices in the constituencies, with a 1972–73 programme called 'Performance Politics'. The idea was that detailed databases would be collected, to enable constituency newsletters to show the practical benefits for their own voters that had accrued from the existence of a Conservative Government and Tory councillors; survey canvassing outside election times would provide information for constituencies about their target voters. In June 1972, Lord Carrington explained the scheme to constituency chairmen, using Heath's own words, that 'too often in the past . . . we have talked in terms of percentages or in huge sums of many millions of pounds. We have not concentrated on making these figures mean something in terms of ordinary people's practical experience'. Coming from Heath such advice was hardly likely to persuade, since the constituencies thought that their alleged fault was what Heath himself did all the time. Extensive programmes of briefings for Area Agents and chairmen, MPs and constituency agents were laid on, and much paperwork was produced, but most constituencies proved reluctant even to discuss the idea and the overall result was negligible, probably because it was attempted at a time of acute Tory unpopularity, when activists were happier to keep their heads down than to go canvassing when there was not even an election on. The West Midlands reported in April 1973, a year into the scheme, that there was 'only a very limited success', and in May the Yorkshire Area had not even called constituencies to a conference to begin it.[27]

26 National Union papers, NUA 6/2/10, GP Committee papers; Phillips and Wilson, 'The Conservative Party from Macmillan to Thatcher', in N. Nugent and R. King (eds), *The British Right* (1977), 40, 42; Patrick Seyd, 'Democracy within the Conservative Party', in *Government and Opposition*, vol. 10 (1975), 219; Butler and Kavanagh, *General Election of February 1974*, 204, 243; National Union Executive Committee minutes [hereafter NUEC], 10 June 1971; *Crossbow*, Oct. 1973, 10, 19, Summer 1982, 15.

27 West Midlands Area Council, 23 Feb. 1973; Central Office file, CCO 500/21/12, Performance Politics.

Thomas had in 1972 been succeeded as Party Chairman by Lord Carrington, with Prior as a Vice Chairman and Christopher Patten as a highly-political Chairman's assistant. Carrington approached the task with some trepidation, for, having never fought an election for a Commons seat himself, he had only indirect experience of the constituencies, and as Secretary of State for Defence he had only limited time for the job and was frequently out of the country. He was unprepared for, and distressed by, the 'wholly unacceptable degree of resistance and back-biting – the latter, of course, often touching the Leader of the Party, the Prime Minister, personally'. Reflecting later on his time at Central Office he concluded that 'I found it very tough indeed'. Having chosen a Chairman without sufficient time, for which the appointment was roundly criticised, Heath compounded his mistake by making Prior Leader of the House and Vice Chairman, a combination that had never worked in the past and did not work this time either; as Prior wrote, at Central Office he had 'a job which brought me into the front-line of the political battle. Yet as Leader of the House I needed to be non-partisan'.[28]

Carrington resolved to press on with some reforms despite resistance from within Central Office and the National Union, and thereby earned the reputation of a dictatorial Chairman. The key issue here was again the central employment of agents. This old chestnut had been revived in 1970 by Sir Arnold Silverstone, a former Area officer on the National Union Executive who was to become a Party Treasurer in 1974. The shrinking number of agents, combined with the free market, made it likely that there would soon be full-time agents only in safe seats, but the Central Office brief for Thomas was, to say the least, hostile: five lines were devoted to the advantages of central employment and a full page to the arguments against, reinforced by an appendix that described every inquiry since 1947 that had come down against the idea. Silverstone urged that a voluntary scheme be adopted to tempt the best agents from 'lush pasture constituencies' to the marginals where the real battle was to be fought, but as usual the National Society of Agents opposed the scheme and by the end of 1971 it had been talked out. Silverstone then reopened the idea when Carrington took over in July 1972, and the Chairman replied that 'I can say on behalf of Jim and myself that this is really one of the most valuable ideas that has been put before us'. Undeterred by warnings, they steamed ahead and produced a scheme; in July 1973, this was simply announced to the National Union as a decision that the Party Chairman had now made. The scheme could not be imposed on constituencies who would not agree, nor on agents who refused to join, but this time it was at least introduced – effectively without the support of Central Office, the National Union or the National Society of Agents. Central employment came into effect on 1 January 1974, covering just 60 agents at first, but intended to

---

[28] Campbell, *Heath*, 511; Lord Carrington, *Reflect on Things Past: The Memoirs of Lord Carrington* (1988), 259–61; Prior, *Balance of Power*, 78; *Crossbow*, Jan. 1972, 6.

extend to 131 by August. In the end, the August figure was 103, but this did contribute to the effective fight for the marginals in October, for those in the scheme were all men and women of experience. However, serious future problems were built into the scheme; when York Conservatives debated it in January 1974, they noted that it would cost them £800 a year more than they were used to paying for an agent, and they agreed to join only if Central Office made up the difference; this was agreed to, because marginal York clearly needed a good agent, but it was very doubtful whether the Party Treasurers would ever get their money back. After the departure from Central Office of those who had fathered and fought it through, the scheme withered, and there were – as predicted – constituency complaints when the board running the scheme raised salaries and then tried to collect the cash from the associations who received the agents' services, as for example in Burton upon Trent in January 1975; in the event, the considerable cost of transferring large salary bills to central funds was not matched by increased income from the marginal constituencies to pay for it. Financial pressures therefore ensured that the scheme was wound down in 1977, though ten years later there were still a few centrally-employed constituency agents lingering on the national payroll. One of the predicted non-financial drawbacks of central employment was highlighted during the leadership battle of January 1975, when at least one centrally-employed agent who backed Heath had to issue a public denial of claims by his own MP (who backed Thatcher) that he was working up constituency opinion for the incumbent on Central Office's instructions.[29]

Persuasion was also stepped up on the city parties, and financial hardship now caused more of them to surrender their independence; in 1972, Central Council resolved to end the rule that allowed city parties additional members on Area and national bodies, keeping up the pressure on them to hand authority back to the constituencies; the Manchester Conservative Association, after a heated meeting with Chelmer and a public statement dissociating themselves from Carrington's announcement of the new rule, unanimously passed a motion regretting the change, but it went ahead none the less. In other ways too, more modern methods could be enforced at the centre even if they produced only a slow response elsewhere. Under the influence of John Gummer, the Vice Chairman responsible for youth movements, a team of youth development officers was created to encourage more political activity among the YCs. The lack of coloured people among the Conservative ranks was also acknowledged to be an increasing embarrassment. In Central Office, the creation of a Community Affairs Section, to coordinate campaigning towards all such interest groups, was resented by

---

[29] Stuart Ball, 'The National and Regional Party Structure', in Seldon and Ball, *Conservative Century*, 176; Central Office file, CCO 500/2/24; Butler and Kavanagh, *General Election of February 1974*, 202–3; Ball, 'Local Conservatism', 284; Central Office file, CCO 500/32/23, Leader's correspondence; NUEC, 19 July 1973; York CA minutes, 3 Jan. 1974; Burton upon Trent CA minutes, 29 Jan. 1975.

the traditionalists and had an uphill task; Michael Wolff was told in June 1974 that the staff of this section needed his backing, and that 'the Central Office [Area] Agents really must be told tactfully to treat them rather less like visiting cuckoos'.[30]

After the February 1974 defeat – for which Carrington accepted much of the responsibility because of the advice he had given on the dissolution – there could not be an early change of Chairman, once again because of the fear of an early second contest; Prior, who might well have succeeded Carrington, put himself out of the running when he made disparaging remarks about the voluntary side of the Party at an Area chairmen's dinner in March. The Central Office Director of Organisation reported to Heath in May that a meeting of the National Union Executive 'revealed a very real apprehension as to the lack of communication and consultation between sections of the Party' and called for an early meeting with both Heath and du Cann. In improving such communications, the Party Chairman would be vital, and Walker, Carr, Howe and Thatcher were all names mentioned as possible successors to Carrington, but Heath appointed Whitelaw as he had probably always intended. Whitelaw was a popular choice, and as Chief Whip less than four years earlier had worked with the people who still ran Central Office and the National Union. Like Neville Chamberlain as Baldwin's Party Chairman in 1930, Whitelaw at Central Office was a potential successor who had to be Heath's own campaign manager; but Whitelaw would not have opposed Heath anyway and had made no secret of his admiration, saying at one point – to the irritation of the government of Iceland – that he would serve in any post Heath offered him, 'even as ambassador to Reykjavik'. It was not because it balked his own claim on the succession that Whitelaw saw the Chairmanship as 'a poisoned chalice', rather that he thought it would be an uphill task to sustain Party morale while in such a generally defeatist mood, a mood he himself largely shared. Prior remained Vice Chairman and headed a team that included Barber and Walker which devoted considerable attention to the 'super-marginals' on which the next campaign would turn. It was decided to set sights lower than usual and concentrate on forty-five seats rather than the eighty designated as 'critical' in the previous Parliament, a decision greeted with 'howls of anger' in the constituencies, according to Patten. Because time was so short, the actual list was drawn up without consultation with Area officers, and this again occasioned criticism of high-handed methods. The chosen marginals received personal visits, grants in aid for posters, literature and secretarial assistance, canvassers for postal votes, and priority for big speakers. In October, these seats registered a lower adverse swing than other comparable constituencies and limited the Labour advance to a bare majority;

---

[30] Butler and Kavanagh, *General Election of February 1974*, 203, 205; Manchester CA minutes, 29 Feb. and 17 May 1972; Ball, 'National and Regional Party Structure', 210, 214; *Crossbow*, May 1973, 20; Central Office Chairman's department file, CCO 20/78/1.

there is a good case for saying that, for once, organisational efforts from the centre produced a measurable effect on the outcome.[31]

By the time Whitelaw took over, there had already been other important changes of personnel. With the Party once more in Opposition, Michael Fraser had to devote much of his attention to the policy side, and again became secretary to the shadow cabinet; for the first time since 1965 Heath reinforced this activity by appointing a front-bench colleague as Chairman of the Research Department. His selection of Sir Ian Gilmour for this role not only placed a serious Conservative thinker as the link between CRD and front bench, but also put in a key role one who would not be likely to disagree with the Leader on the essentials of policy. The same could be said of Chris Patten who in August took over as Director of the CRD. When Heath wanted a small group to analyse poll findings and to advise him about their message, he gave the task to Douglas Hurd and three MPs who were all former staffers at the CRD. The most controversial appointment though was that of Michael Wolff, who after some time on Heath's personal staff and then as a political adviser in the Cabinet Office now became Director-General of Central Office. Since Wolff's earlier career had been as a journalist, and he had no particular experience of management, this seemed a signal rebuff to the career agents and Area managers who had provided the head of the Central Office administration ever since Maclachlan was made Principal Agent in 1927; briefing Carrington for a meeting with MPs, Chris Patten noted equivocally that 'you are not unaware of the political arguments against this [appointment], but the fact that you have nevertheless gone ahead shows how able you think he is'. Fraser had been effectively demoted by this appointment, since his remit now related only to policy, and Sir Richard Webster, Director of Organisation since 1966, would probably have been retired altogether but for the outcry that had already greeted Wolff's arrival; Webster's unconcealed opposition to ideas of a coalition (on the ground that the Party activists would not stand for it) may well have contributed to the attempts to remove him. Career agents felt that after a Heath statement in early March had made it clear that organisation had not been responsible for the February defeat, the promotion of a non-organiser to run the organisation now suggested just the opposite. Wolff scarcely had time to demonstrate his appropriateness for the task he had been given, but by the Summer there was already some recognition that a single chief executive had produced greater order at Central Office. He also showed an open mind, for example agreeing to commission research into the effectiveness of the Party's advertising, something ORC had wanted to do for some time. A

---

[31] Butler and Kavanagh, *General Election of October 1975*, 37–8, 226–7; Central Office file, 500/32/23, Leader's correspondence; Ernle Money, *Margaret Thatcher: First Lady of the House* (1975) 17; Prior, *Balance of Power*, 96; Whitelaw, *Memoirs*, 136–8; Central Office Chairman's department file, CCO 20/59/2, Meetings with the 1922 Committee.

less successful initiative was a Central Office phrase-making group; well aware that Heath's speeches in particular were said to have gone over the voters' heads, Central Office commissioned in July research on ordinary voters' vocabulary; issues of the *Sun* and *Daily Mirror* for a representative week were analysed and found to contain only about two thousand different words, whereas the average educated person was said to use forty thousand; it was hard though to apply this thesaurus of words understood by tabloid readers to the subtle ideas of coalitionism that the Party was campaigning on in October. But whereas the February Election had caught the organisation off balance, everything was certainly ready in October; only £295,000 was spent by Central Office on the February campaign, about twice as much in October, a difference that reflected the availability of spending plans as much as of money.[32]

There was – inescapably – a sense in which Heath was thought to be putting all the key organisational posts into friendly hands: Whitelaw, Prior, Walker, Barber, Wolff, Gilmour, Patten and Hurd were all utterly loyal to the Leader, and their appointments looked to critics to be the personalisation of the Party machine before a contentious period. Heath did not recognise the scale of the threat to his position, however, and was hardly therefore making dispositions in advance of a battle he did not expect to have to fight. His opponents in the Party did not see it that way, and of all these 1974 appointments, Patten was the only one to survive in office under Thatcher in 1975.

New directions in policy

The need to define Party policy for another election produced early evidence of troubles to come. Heath's Government had had less than one full term in office and had not been turned out on the cry of 'time for a change' as in 1945 and 1964; the Leader was thus strongly opposed to the root and branch policy review that had followed those two defeats, for he saw no need to change the basis on which he had just governed the country. There would be a limited number of policy groups to review areas where there was an acknowledged deficiency, as for example housing policy was agreed to have been; the new shadow Environment minister Thatcher was given the task of bringing forward urgent proposals from the group. Three other groups reviewed the future of the Industrial Relations Act, incomes policy, and devolution, all policy areas on which the Labour Government's actions would make at least some adjustments necessary; only a small increase from

---

32 Butler and Kavanagh, *General Election of October 1974*, 39–40, 43, 198, 242; Central Office Chairman's department file, CCO 20/59/2; Ball, 'Central and Regional Party Structures', 187; Ramsden, *Making of Conservative Party Politics*, 304; Campbell, *Heath*, 629; Central Office Chairman's department file, CCO 20/17/51, October 1974 General Election; interview with Lord Gilmour.

these original four groups ever took place. There was no separate Economic Policy group; such a group would have to have drawn members from the backbench Industry and Finance committees, whose leaders included Ridley and Biffen, so economic policy would continue to be a matter for the shadow cabinet, where Heath could control the debate and where backbenchers would not be involved. Again Heath sought to escape divisions by avoiding discussion of such contentious matters as a policy to contain inflation; as 'an insider' told Butler and Kavanagh, 'we spent an awful lot of time just sitting around and looking at the hole in the table'. There was in any case a delay before serious activity started, some of the groups not meeting before the Summer recess, and detailed survey material on the February campaign was not available for several months; Heath's office asked in July for Fraser to do a presentation to the shadow cabinet, 'as, he says, at the moment discussion of new policy proposals goes on against a background of myth and misunderstanding'. That briefing took place, but the full survey report (which included some disquieting reading on Heath's public image) was not circulated until November when the second 1974 campaign was over. The traditional process of manifesto work through Fraser's Official Group at the CRD does not seem to have enjoyed Heath's confidence as it had done before 1970; it did not meet between July and the Election.[33]

In most areas, policy-making was relatively straightforward. On industrial relations, Heath had left office declaring that the question on which he had fought the Election 'will certainly recur throughout the life of this Parliament and the Party should be neither ashamed of having put it to the electorate in the past nor unready to do so in the future'. In practice though it was clear that he had no intention of fighting again on what had been seen – however inaccurately – as a confrontationist platform. Nor was there much point in defending the Industrial Relations Act as such, which the Conservatives had in February promised to amend and which Labour was now dismantling. The policy group under Prior rapidly recommended a cautious policy, and in June Heath pledged not to reintroduce the Act. By October this had gone further, with a promise to cooperate with the unions, who were said to be 'an important Estate of the Realm', and Heath was even promising to accept Labour's new Trade Union and Labour Relations Act, which markedly increased trade union rights.[34]

Similarly, policy on Scotland and Wales was uncontentious in the Party. In April, the Party reiterated the pledge first given in 1968 to introduce a Scottish Assembly; it would be a delegated body drawn from elected local councillors,

[33] Campbell, *Heath*, 630–1; Butler and Kavanagh, *General Election of October 1974*, 63; LCC papers, July and November 1974; Ramsden, *Making of Conservative Party Policy*, 305.
[34] Butler and Kavanagh, *General Election of February 1974*, 273; Butler and Kavanagh, *General Election of October 1974*, 62; Robert Taylor, *The Trade Union Question in British Politics: Government and the Unions since 1945* (Oxford, 1993), 217.

and would have the right to discuss all Scottish legislation, but Heath did not rule out the idea of a directly-elected body in the future; the Assembly would also be free to determine its own priorities for public spending within Scotland. A lesser form of devolution to a Welsh Council was then promised in June. In October, these ideas were set out as *A Conservative Charter for Scotland* – something that went further than the Scottish edition of the manifesto, which had the distinctively unionist title *Putting Britain First*.[35]

Radical ideas on housing did produce disagreements, but not in public. Peter Walker offered the suggestion that all council houses and flats should be handed over to their tenants without payment, which would have dramatically reduced local authority maintenance costs, produced a spectacular increase in homeownership with favourable political consequences, and balanced measures to benefit middle-class homeowners. But Walker's idea was thought just too risky – and seeming too obviously like an election sweetener; instead there would be a big increase in discounts offered to tenants to persuade them to buy. There is some considerable irony in the fact that this deliberate decision to go all out to extend the ownership of property, one of the few major ideas added to the Selsdon programme between 1974 and 1979 (as John Biffen later described it), was pressed for by Walker – who was generally thought to be on the opposite wing of the Party. An irony in the opposite direction arose from Thatcher gaining exposure and credit for housing policies with which she was not herself in agreement. Here there were determined efforts to counter the middle-class disaffection over mortgage interest and rocketing local government rates, which had caused defections to the Liberals in February. It was decided to go for the abolition of the rates altogether, without waiting for the committee currently considering alternative forms of local taxation, and to commit a Tory Government to keep mortgage interest rates below 10 per cent. Thatcher strongly opposed these incautious and interventionist proposals, and used her formidable debating skills to defend her viewpoint, but ultimately agreed to accept the majority view. Heath told Whitelaw in July that in considering future campaigning strategies, 'I number amongst these the need to say something dramatic on mortgages, on council houses and . . . on rates'. The shadow cabinet's best news for voters would thus fall to Thatcher to announce.[36]

If Heath had hoped to keep economic policy debates under control he was soon disappointed. The harmony that had characterised the collective leadership in office was anyway replaced by considerable friction in Opposition, and in this process disagreements over economic policy were the catalyst. Kenneth Baker's memoirs record a meeting early in the Opposition

[35] *NCP*, 1 July 1974; Central Office *Daily Notes* [hereafter *DN*] 18 Sept. 1974.
[36] Baker, *Turbulent Years*, 41; John Ranelagh, *Thatcher's People* (1991), 92; Halcrow, *Joseph*, 75; Hugo Young, *One of Us: A Biography of Margaret Thatcher* (1989), 83; Central Office Chairman's department file, CCO 20/8/17.

period, at which Joseph called for a full-scale review with economists present to advise on current thinking, receiving some support from Thatcher and Howe (though the memories of others differ in their accounts of the extent to which Thatcher backed Joseph at this stage); Heath, supported by Walker and Gilmour, 'was very cool about this. Most of the others remained silent.' According to John Ranelagh, Joseph's call for a full-dress debate with economists was eventually granted, in a meeting at Heath's Commons office. Sir Donald MacDougall, who had been chief economic adviser at the Treasury until 1973, advised along Keynesian lines, and Alan Walters equally predictably argued that control of the money supply was the key and that market forces were the only long-term salvation for the economy. Heath, who had heard out Walters only with visible impatience, then called on the third economist present, James Ball of the London Business School, who had been close to Heath when in office. Ball surprised most of those present by urging them to follow Walters' advice, but Heath refused to accept this and, after a long meeting, summed up to the effect that 'our policies were right, but . . . we did not persist in them long enough.' This makes a good story, but seems likely to have conflated more than one meeting and to have over-dramatised the clash of personalities. Nevertheless, it is not surprising that Joseph felt after these discussions that there was little point in trying to win the economic argument on the inside.[37]

As Hugo Young has pointed out, the debate over economic policy often incorporated wider issues; Joseph was advocating a break with all recent practice in managing the economy at precisely the moment when Heath's own strategy was moving ever closer to a consensus of all parties; it is no accident that it was the economic heretics like Joseph who were also the most lukewarm on the coalition question; Joseph had therefore been the only Cabinet Minister to oppose talks with the Liberals after the February Election. He now pointed out that if there was a broad consensus on the policies to be pursued then coalition was unnecessary, while if there was not a broad consensus on policy, as he now believed, then coalition would be impossible anyway.[38]

At heart though the disagreement on economic policy was just that, and one in which Heath and his keenest supporters like Walker, who ridiculed Joseph's views as much as they argued against them, had not grasped how fast the intellectual tide was now running against them. Douglas Hurd suggested in 1978 that one reason for the Heath Government's inability to keep to its original course was that it came into office with radical intentions but without a current of informed opinion convinced of the rightness of what it was trying to do. It is easy to forget how suddenly, after the events of 1972–74, and in

[37] Walker, *Staying Power*, 111, 126; Baker, *Turbulent Years*, 41; Campbell, *Heath*, 630–2; Ranelagh, *Thatcher's People*, 125–6; interviews with Lord Howe and Sir Edward Heath.
[38] Young, *One of Us*, 89; Russel, *Conservative Party*, 144; interview with Lord Barber.

part *because* of them, opinions that had seemed wild now became respectable; the then Permanent Secretary of the Treasury recently recalled that it was in 1973 when for him in particular and for Treasury civil servants in general, 'policy thinking began to change' towards a greater attention being given to the money supply and credit control. It was after all only in 1974 and 1977 respectively that Hayek and Friedmann were awarded Nobel Prizes for economics, awards that transformed the authority accorded to their views. It was in the same period that three of the most influential commentators on political economy in Britain, Samuel Brittan (*Financial Times*), Peter Jay (*The Times*) and William Rees-Mogg (editor of *The Times*), of which only the third was even a Conservative, came down on the monetarist side of the argument. Heath was therefore defending an orthodoxy that was itself ceasing to be orthodox, but seemed almost unaware of the fact. As Robert Eccleshall has put it, 'unlike the free marketeers at the turn of the century, who never seized the intellectual initiative, the libertarian right of the 1970s, did help to change the climate of public debate'.[39]

Before examining the way in which Joseph introduced these ideas into mainstream Conservative politics, it is useful to see from whence they came; according to Maurice Cowling in 1989, this success of 'the new right' was the work of only 'about fifty people'. The origins lie in the high noon of Butskellite consensus, the 1950s; it was then that Macleod and Joseph were introduced to Alan Walters by Enoch Powell; it was then that the Mont Pelérin Society was gathering together those who supported the ideas of Hayek; and it was then that the first propagandising body for the new approach, the Institute of Economic Affairs (IEA), was founded. When the Radcliffe report of 1959 came out with its endorsement of Keynesian economic principles, a report whose commissioning owed something to the Treasury resignations of Thorneycroft and Powell, the IEA published *Not Unanimous* to prove that dissenting voices still existed. The IEA was officially non-partisan, but its director Ralph Harris was a former Tory candidate and among party people only Conservatives seemed interested in its free-market philosophy, notably Powell from the 1960s and later Joseph and Howe. It was always an elite body, aiming through lunches and specialist pamphlets to tilt the opinions of the informed in Westminster and Fleet Street rather than attacking public opinion as a whole. Powell's Opposition speeches from 1963 (edited for publication by the IEA's deputy director) helped to give a wider currency to IEA ideas on public spending, interventionism and the causes of inflation, as did a number of favourable journalists after about 1972. The academic climate mainly turned in universities outside Oxbridge (which may explain why front-bench Conservatives underestimated its impact), notably

---

[39] Robert Blake, *The Conservative Party from Peel to Thatcher* (1985), 310, 323; Douglas Hurd, *An End to Promises: Sketch of a Government* (1978), 149; Lord Croham at ICBH witness seminar, 1994; Robert Eccleshall, *English Conservatism since the Restoration* (1990), 207.

at Liverpool, St Andrews and the LSE; the St Andrews' Tory students' alternative manifesto of 1971 was a milestone in the permeation of the Party by such ideas. In part the tide began to turn precisely because the economy was still doing badly when managed by traditional methods; as Arthur Seldon of the IEA put it in 1984: 'Sceptics [used to] say to us, in defence of collectivist policies, "Give them time. They'll work in the end." By the mid 1970s they had been saying it for thirty years and could no longer ask for more time.' This gradual permeation of informed opinion, along with Labour's lurch to the left in the early 1970s, helped to produce converts to the Tory side of politics; Lord Chalfont, who had held office under Wilson, switched sides even during the October 1974 campaign, as did other more minor figures; by 1978, Patrick Cormack was able to assemble eight such politicians and intellectuals who had made that damascene conversion for *Right Turn: Eight Men who Changed their Minds*, and the inclusion of such men as Paul Johnson, former editor of the *New Statesman*, among their number, was some indication of the breadth as well as the strength of the new intellectual right.[40]

A dangerous sign for Heath was the permeation with the new economic orthodoxy of the Bow Group, which had since its formation in 1951, and especially since its re-launch under Macmillan's patronage in 1958, been a bastion of support for the type of politics that Heath practised; the Oxford magazine *Isis* had in 1957 dubbed the Group 'the rising hope of the mild and moderate Conservatives'; when in for a selection contest in a London constituency in 1962, Geoffrey Howe found that, as the Area Agent reported, 'his membership of the Bow Group was looked upon with some slight suspicion because they thought it was Left Wing'. Even when allowance is made for the fact that the Bow Group had no official doctrine on *any* subject and allowed its writers free rein to ask interesting questions, it is clear that, from the time at which Biffen and Howe were chairmen, it was at least open to tough ideas in the economic field; its stance in the 1960s might well be described as 'Home Office left – Treasury right', since (like Keith Joseph) its members were generally persuaded of the need both for a 'sound money' approach to public finance and for a generous approach to protecting the disadvantaged. The former Bow Grouper Russell Lewis, who was director of the CPC between 1965 and 1974, was opening official Party publications more widely to similar ideas in those years. When the monetarist tide began to flow after 1970, the Bow Group was therefore ripe for capture, and the chairmanship of Peter Lilley was important in setting a new course, though ironically he too found that his association with the Group (still remembered for its 'pinko' past by many in the constituencies) was a barrier to his getting

---

[40] Simon Burgess and Geoffrey Alderman, 'The Centre for Policy Studies', in *Contemporary Record*, vol. 4 (1990), 14; Ranelagh, *Thatcher's People*, 74–5; Harrison, 'Mrs. Thatcher and the Intellectuals', 214; Ward, *The First Century*, 41; Dennis Kavanagh, *Thatcherism and British Politics* (Oxford, 1987), 80–1, 84, 118.

elected for a winnable seat. *The Alternative Manifesto* that the Group's officers produced in Autumn 1973 called for the amendment of the 1972 Industry Act to prevent indiscriminate hand-outs to industry and for the introduction of competition within the public sector; it accepted the case for a prices and incomes policy only as an emergency measure, and demanded that 'more fundamental measures' be taken in the longer term, asking for a pledge 'to keep monetary expansion from outstripping the growth in the economy'. Once the Party was out of office, these statements became even less guarded; in June 1974 a paper called *Lessons for Power* proclaimed starkly (in a section over Lilley's name) that

> Conservatives must recognise that Trades Unions do not cause inflation. They may, by pricing workers out of jobs, create unemployment. But it is governments who create inflation, especially if they attempt to reduce unemployment by expanding demand. Such well meaning attempts are in the end always unsuccessful.

This was three months before Joseph's speech at Preston argued the same case. Also in June, a discussion paper entitled *No More Tick* was published by the Group in the names of Alan Walters and two Conservative MPs, one of them a junior spokesman, Marcus Fox: 'what is needed . . . is a three or four year policy for gradual but steadfast return to a balanced budget and concomitant reductions in the rate of growth in the money supply' – which they represented as a moderate alternative to the 'Powellite' demand to eradicate inflation even more quickly. Even if all Group publications were unofficial, the official disclaimer was in itself significant: these papers were said to contain 'facts and opinions which merit consideration by the Conservative Party and by a wider audience'. Among that wider audience receiving this stream of monetarist advice were the fifty Conservative MPs (and in October a sixth of all Tory candidates) who were Bow Groupers. The storm-troopers of Tory progressivism had become the keenest advocates of the new economics, and as a predominantly youthful group they could also be seen as having time on their side. So far had this gone that in early 1975 *The Economist* wrote of the Bow Group as 'a monetarist, free market only shrine', and some members began to question whether it had lost its traditional catholicity. When Thatcher replaced Heath in 1975, the Group rallied to her at once and showed no great regret at the departure of its earlier favourite.[41]

The drift of opinion in the Bow Group was matched by a decline in the voice of PEST, which slumped from fifteen university groups (the strongest of them, in Cambridge, Oxford, Manchester and Lancaster, having large

[41] Central Office file, CCO 3/5/38, Bow Group; Central Office constituency file, CCO 1/14/75; Phillips and Wilson, 'Macmillan to Thatcher', 43; Riddell, *Honest Opportunism*, 107; Richard Cockett, *Thinking the Unthinkable: Think Tanks and the Economic Counter-Revolution, 1931–1983* (1994), 163; Peter Lilley, Patricia Hodgson and Nigel Waterson, *Alternative Manifesto* (1973), 5–6, 9; Patricia Hodgson (ed.), *Lessons for Power* (1974), 3; Tony Durant, Marcus Fox, Cyril Taylor and Alan Walters, *No More Tick: A Conservative Solution to Inflation* (1974), 4; *Crossbow*, Aug. 1975, 4, 31.

numbers of members) to a mere five groups, two of them relatively new, in 1973; by this time it had about fifty MPs and peers in association with it, but was generating little activity at the grass-roots, and was in danger of becoming an all chiefs and no indians organisation. A re-launch was planned for 1975, but by November 1974 the chairman reported that the organisation was in 'acute financial crisis'. As chairman, Nicholas Scott was convinced that PEST had 'a vital role to play in the Party during what could be an extremely difficult time ahead. We have to make sure that the flow of ideas is kept up and that the voice of the progressive wing of the Party is powerfully heard'. Another re-launch, amalgamating PEST with the Macleod Group, did not come until September 1975, by which time the Party had already taken a turn in a direction of which its members did not approve. PEST was not therefore able to ensure that its voice was 'powerfully heard' during the critical period.[42]

Free-market ideas had received apparent official encouragement in the wider Party from the 'Selsdon Man' stance of 1970, and the few Conservatives that came into the open against Heath while still Prime Minister constantly harped on that fact; in 1973 some of them formed the Selsdon Group specifically to fight for free market policies which, it alleged, Heath had espoused but then betrayed. It was the first of a plethora of organisations campaigning specifically within the Party and aiming to set its agenda, paralleled by the Conservative Philosophy Group almost at once and followed by the Centre for Policy Studies in 1974, the Freedom Association and the Middle Class Alliance in 1975, and the Adam Smith Institute and the *Salisbury Review* later in the 1970s, opposed only by the re-formed Tory Reform Group, incorporating the earlier PEST and Macleod Group on the other side of the argument. Since the 'legion of leagues' in the 1906–11 period, the Conservative Party had seen nothing like it.[43]

Beyond this intellectual debate lurked a more basic political instinct for those who were lifelong Conservatives. Now that a respectable body of doctrine in political economy was being propagated that provided an alternative to collectivism, many no doubt grasped it simply as a convenient cover for their instinctive dislike of recent practice. In October 1974, Ronald Butt reminded his *Sunday Times* readers that for a decade 'the whole vocabulary of political and social debate has been captured by the Left. . . . Where the Conservative party has answered back, it has done so by conceding half the case that it should have been rebutting and has usually sought to appease the trend.' This was far from being a new view; T.E. Utley wrote in the *Spectator* in 1963 of the many who believed that the Conservative Party 'has

[42] File in the Boyle papers on 'PEST, 1964–1975', and especially Boyle MSS 24410, 24445, 24485, 24489, 24493.
[43] Kavanagh, *Thatcherism*, 94; Ramsden, *Age of Balfour and Baldwin*, 40–2; Cockett, *Thinking the Unthinkable*, 218.

occasionally checked, but has never fundamentally reversed the trends towards national bankruptcy and imperial and social dislocation which were going on when it came to power'. Four years later, considering the same question, Utley concluded that Powellism was therefore 'the most valuable single ingredient in Conservatism today', for Powell 'regards it as his appointed function to criticise the heresies absorbed by the Conservative Party'. But after the Heath Government's U-turn in 1972, and especially in Opposition after February 1974, such viewpoints were far more confidently argued. They now challenged the nature of post-war Conservatism itself; Butt called for the Conservatives, 'even at the risk of being called reactionary', to reverse some of Labour's policies. Rhodes Boyson, whose own conversion from Labour to the Conservatives owed something to economic liberalism as well as to patriotism, argued that the Party's commitment to 'conserve' was merely appeasement of an ever more left-wing Labour Party. For Angus Maude, 'consensus' meant that Conservatives merely consolidated Labour policies in the intervals between Labour governments. Most persuasively of all, Keith Joseph argued that the 'middle ground' which Rab Butler and Harold Macmillan had wanted the Conservatives to occupy, and which remained Heath's chosen place of residence, was a myth anyway. It was only the mid-point in a spectrum that Labour was always shifting to the left, not a constant political position at all:

> As things worked out, with the socialists of nearly all shades committed to moving towards the promised land at whatever rate seemed practicable, while we Conservatives were basically reconciled to the *status quo* as of that moment, it was inevitable that the pendulum should be replaced by the ratchet. When the socialists were in power they moved it forward as fast as they considered politic; when we were in office, we either kept things as they were, or let them move on under their own momentum.[44]

'The ratchet effect' was a brilliantly effective shorthand analysis to capitalise on years of frustration in the Tory rank and file, and was picked up immediately as a popular catch-phrase. Rhodes Boyson's appeal for an end to the 'slow-quick-quick-slow foxtrot to socialism' was essentially making the same point. A new economic approach that both fitted more into Conservative instincts and also offered to smash the ratchet would have a powerful appeal; it was, said Joseph, simply a matter of 'reversing the trend' so that Labour would be the party that would have to apply a ratchet while the Conservatives set the direction in which the wheel turned – as indeed it turned out after 1979. This approach implied a repudiation not only of the Heath Government, which Joseph at least was ready to concede, but also of much of the record of 1951 to 1964. By 1978, Maurice Cowling was prepared

---

[44] Kavanagh, *Thatcherism*, 72; Charles Moore and Simon Heffer, *A Tory Seer: The Selected Journalism of T.E. Utley* (1989), 5, 21; Behrens, *Heath to Thatcher*, 9; Eccleshall, *English Conservatism*, 230, 232, 235–6.

to accept this price too, though with a Burkeian acknowledgement that a debt was still owed to the previous generation:

> In the 1940s and 1950s Lord Butler may well have been right; it may well be that the Conservative party owes a great deal more of its present existence to his calculating intentions than it is now willing to believe. In the last ten years, however, the climate has changed, and with that change have come intuitions quite different from those he operated with then. It has been calculation as well as instinct that has made it necessary to replace his sort of liberal Conservatism by the new Conservatism of the 1970s. The change is here to stay. There can be no going back on the intuition that what Conservatism should mean in the seventies and eighties is an attempt . . . to give political form to the idea of 'rolling back the frontiers of the state'.

Cowling was writing though when the new ideas had captured the Conservative mainstream under a sympathetic Leader, and when the Party was riding high in public approval. In June 1974 that was all still to be done: the chairman of the Selsdon Group wrote then that the Opposition's task was 'to acknowledge the seriousness of the situation, identify the dirigiste thinking that is responsible for it, make the electorate realise that there is no easy way out, and finally present the idea of a society in which all share the benefits of capitalism. What is called for is in fact a great exercise in political education.' With Powell in political exile, that was the uphill task that fell to Sir Keith Joseph.[45]

Alongside Joseph were two other Privy Councillors now in the open as critics of Heath and his policies, Edward du Cann and Angus Maude. Du Cann picked up on Maude's traditional stance, asking in May 1974 for a restatement of the Party's philosophy and principles in order to raise the morale of MPs and Party activists; in June, at the Party Chairman's Wednesday morning consultations, 'Mr. Du Cann said that many of our supporters felt that there was a need for a more positive statement of our beliefs and attitudes'. But du Cann was mainly asking questions rather than offering solutions. In 1974, Maude used his position as a representative of the 1922 Committee on the Advisory Committee on Policy to criticise the continuation of the policies of 1972–74, giving a clear indication of the sort of policies he would have preferred, and he clearly won support there, but he also turned his pen to a campaign in the press and in Party publications, attacking the very fundamentals of Heath's approach to life, and from a philosophical position rather different from that of Joseph. Maude complained regularly that the Party lacked any real policies except those relating to the economy. The Party's leaders must

> stop boring the pants off people with speeches about 'growth'; and they must open their eyes to the growing mass of evidence that makes a nonsense of their cherished

---

[45] Eccleshall, *English Conservatism*, 206; Maurice Cowling, 'The Present Position', in M. Cowling (ed.), *Conservative Essays* (1978), 14; *Crossbow*, June 1974, 39.

conviction that large institutions and enterprises are always more efficient than smaller ones.

Growth, said Maude, was for most ordinary people a story of inflation and high interest rates. The pursuit of this false god had made the Party 'appear purely materialist to many who believe the Tory Party should stand for rather more than that, while managing to disappoint the material expectations we aroused in the rest.' Maude was certainly a crucial figure in funnelling diversified discontent through the Party machine to the top in the evolution of a distinctive education policy, and he was quite willing to envisage a reactionary break with all recent practice; he wrote that he hoped that the *Black Paper* of 1968 'may really launch a counter-revolution'. With the assistance of many sympathisers in key positions in the Party – Sewill at the CRD, Russell Lewis at the CPC, the National Advisory Committee on Education, the *Swinton Journal*, and the backbench Education committee (with Maude as chairman) – the campaigners for a halt to comprehensivisation had virtually captured the Party by 1974; it was their ideas that shaped the February and October manifestos in their education sections. Maude's ideas also converged with Joseph's on the principle of the ratchet. He wrote in June 1975, that

> what has done most to widen the gap between the Conservative leadership and our supporters (and potential supporters) in the country is the realisation that no action is ever taken to reverse the steady drift to the left. If Labour Governments are always prepared to reverse the actions of Tory Governments, while Conservatives will never reverse what Labour has done in office, it follows that the left always wins. The secular trend is clear. Whether it is nationalisation, the taxation of capital, the abolition of grammar schools, 'progressive' changes in the penal system, or relaxation of legal controls over trade unions, it is only what Labour does in office that remains permanent. What is the point, then, of voting Conservative? It will all be the same in the end.

The conclusion to this line of argument was that if Tories did not promise to reverse and restore, and not merely to conserve, there would be no point in having a Conservative Party anyway, 'better to emigrate – or spend all one's capital and cut one's throat.' Such colourful language, and a long history of oppositionism – even *Enoch Powell* thought Maude 'an irreconcilable' – no doubt reduced the impact of Maude's attacks, just as du Cann could be discounted as a long-term opponent of Heath, hence the greater importance of the more conventional figure of Joseph.[46]

Joseph was an easy man to underestimate, a politician regarded by both colleagues and opponents with more affection than respect, and regarded above all as naive; his fellow MP for Leeds, Denis Healey, thought him to be 'politically a mixture of Hamlet, Rasputin and Tommy Cooper'.

---

[46] Central Office Chairman's file, CCO 20/61/5, Wednesday morning meetings; *Crossbow*, June 1974, 10; Knight, *Tory Education Policy*, 23, 34, 42–3, 49–50, 66–8, 79.

Heathites who dubbed him 'the mad monk' had reached a similar conclusion. *The Economist* derided his economic prospectus as a recommendation 'that Britain should parachute to safety with something closely resembling a pocket handkerchief', and it later thought that he had 'the fatal innocence of the truly innocent'. Others were horrified by the *political* innocence of his breast-beating confessions that 'we were all wrong': Michael Wolff wrote that 'You can't have people who voted for a certain policy suddenly turning back and rending their garments like Old Testament prophets and pouring ash on their heads and saying, "I have sinned, I have sinned!" This is incredible, not only in a political sense, but in a purely human sense.' On the eve of the October Election a front-bench colleague asked in despair, 'Does Keith really think we can fight on controlling the money supply? Try explaining that to the voters.' Later in the year when Joseph was preparing to challenge Heath for the leadership, Heath supporters saw only the funny side of the idea, and Whitelaw thought that the contest would be a good way of seeing off the critics on the right and confirming Heath in office. But Joseph's obvious integrity gave him an appeal that went right across the Party, and some of those like Norman Fowler who backed Joseph for Leader because he seemed an honest man who was prepared to think radically were certainly not right-wingers. Joseph reacted to the loss of office in February 1974 like a man released from a treadmill, free again to pursue things that really mattered, and he was upset by the reaction of his earlier monetarist friends to his sudden reappearance in their ranks, unaware of the depth of their hostility to what he and his colleagues had recently done in office. Alan Walters in particular brought Joseph up short in this way. Joseph was also impressed by the financial difficulties of the family firm, seemingly symptomatic of the plight in which the Heath Government had left British industry. If Walters was at first cool, Alfred Sherman and the IEA were delighted to find in Joseph a willing listener to their belief that, as Sherman told him, 'Keynes is dead'. Under these influences, Joseph moved swiftly back to the position he had taken up in 1969–70, but now with a determination to raise the public profile both of the ideas and of himself as their advocate. If he sometimes later discounted the description of this intellectual progress as a 'conversion', because it was indeed more the return to an old faith than the discovery of the new, at the time he was ready to see it as very new indeed; introducing in mid-1975 the published version of his speeches of the previous year, he wrote that 'it was only in April 1974 that I was converted to Conservatism'. That book, *Reversing the Trend* (another reference to the ratchet), had as its sub-title, 'a critical re-appraisal of Conservative economic and social policies', and this showed more accurately even than the title the breadth of Joseph's new iconoclasm. Whether 'converted' or not, he was certainly ready to throw overboard all previous doctrine and practice in the search for truth: in 1974, speaking of 'thirty years of socialistic fashion', he effectively disowned all public policy since the War. If Powell was the intellectual ancestor of Thatcherism in its economic context, Joseph has a good claim to be seen as the midwife who brought it to birth in the mainstream, and from inside the shadow cabinet.[47]

In this quest to open up new areas of debate, and on the initiative of Sherman, Joseph and Thatcher launched in March 1974 their own research unit, the Centre for Policy Studies, though it opened its doors only in the Summer, with Sherman as its first director. The IEA was happy to have an allied body specifically within the Tory ranks, and Heath reluctantly nominated a member of the Centre's advisory board to keep an eye on things on behalf of the Party. One reason for his reluctance, shared at Central Office, was that the new CPS would syphon off funds that would otherwise go to the Party organisation, so that great care had to be taken to avoid poaching from Party subscribers; another was that the attraction to Joseph of having a research unit to work for monetarism was exactly what did not endear it to the official Party, for it promised to widen the emerging breach. The CPS was formally set up to review the reasons for Britain's economic sluggishness compared to her European partners, which has the sound of a description chosen to persuade Heath to give it the go-ahead, but even this line of inquiry was always likely to lead to contentious zones of debate. In 1975, Joseph wrote that in addition to such international comparisons, he and Thatcher had founded the CPS 'to survey the scope for replacing increasingly interventionist government by social market policies, and to seek to change the climate of opinion in order to gain acceptance of them'. David Howell was one Heathite who was influenced by the CPS from its early days; he told the ACP in December 1974 that 'the seminars organised by the Centre for Policy Studies . . . he had found extremely stimulating and opened up areas that were not often raised'. Nicholas Ridley later thought that the CPS had been 'the furnace in which the new economics were forged', which was scarcely true since it arrived so late in that process, but it might well be correct to see the CPS as forging political weapons from economic ideas already smelted elsewhere. Joseph's own 1974 speeeches were the main case in point.[48]

Joseph would have found it less easy to start this new enterprise if he had not been so generally credited with integrity; nobody saw his initiative as a bid for the leadership, or feared the CPS as a dangerous private army. However, these first reactions gave way to more hostility when Joseph attracted such public attention to his own evolving ideas. To Heath's supporters, Joseph was rocking the boat at a difficult time by questioning in public matters that should have been kept for the shadow cabinet, and he was letting the side

[47] Denis Healey, *The Time of My Life* (1989), 488; Ranelagh, *Thatcher's People*, 122–3, 127, 129, 143, 154; Butler and Kavanagh, *General Election of October 1974*, 95; Whitelaw, *Memoirs*, 142; Norman Fowler, *Ministers Decide* (1991), 10–11; Halcrow, *Joseph*, 57, 59, 62, 64, 67; Keith Joseph, *Reversing the Trend* (1975), 1 ,4.

[48] Cockett, *Thinking the Unthinkable*, 237; Ranelagh, *Thatcher's People*, 129–31; Halcrow, *Joseph*, 65, 70–1; Behrens, *Heath to Thatcher*, 25; Joseph, *Reversing the Trend*, 3; ACP, 4 Dec. 1974; Nicholas Ridley, *My Style of Government* (1991), 7.

down, by disowning retrospectively policies that he had supported between 1970 and 1974; for Joseph and his backers, he had been left with no alternative but to go public after Heath's refusal to have a wide-ranging review within the shadow cabinet; and when shadow ministers *did* discuss the issues, both sides thought they had won the argument anyway, so different were their premises. At Upminster in June, Joseph began what was intended to be a series of seven speeches, only three of which were delivered before the October Election; the theme was that 'this is no time to be mealy-mouthed: intervention is destroying us'. He devoted much of his time to attacking Tony Benn's interventionist policies, but also argued that 'if we stave off Benn and carry on as before, I fear that we shall have more disappointments'. At Leith in August, he argued that inflation had done serious damage to industry, linking his argument to an attack on Labour's tax policies but again casting the net wider in references to 'three decades of almost continuous inflation and erratic government intervention'. Heath cannot have enjoyed reading that 'successive governments – Tory and Labour – with the aid of the unions and with the encouragement of the media, have helped undermine British industry'.[49]

However, it was the third speech of the series, delivered at Preston on 5 September when the Election was imminent, that really caused a stir, and its title, 'Inflation is caused by Governments', goes far to explain why. Joseph accepted 'my full share of the collective responsibility' for what he now portrayed as disastrous past policies, but in doing so he heaped equal blame on to all his Conservative colleagues. Incomes policies were wrong, post-war governments had been obsessed by unemployment, and there had been 'excessive injections of money'. This Preston speech, trailed in advance to the media as a major event and given the rare honour of a verbatim reprint in the quality press (taking up the entire centre page in *The Times*), was deeply embarrassing to the Heath camp, and anyway gave a damaging impression of disunity just before a dissolution; Powell called the Preston speech 'an admirable anthology from my speeches on this subject in recent years', which also cannot have endeared Joseph to Heath. Prior recalls getting advance notice of the speech and trying to get Joseph to moderate its tone, using Howe and Thatcher as intermediaries. But to little effect – their meeting served only to consolidate their emerging sense of being three partners in a struggle to convert the Party. Heath's own response to the speech was to say to Joseph that 'your analysis of [my] Government's record has left me heartbroken', which sounds somewhat ironical. Powell also said of this belated acceptance of his ideas, 'I have heard of death-bed repentance. Perhaps it would be more appropriate to refer to post-mortem repentance.' Was there a little jealousy here? Joseph had after all succeeded in three months in inserting Powell's economic ideas into the mainstream political agenda,

---

[49] Behrens, *Heath to Thatcher*, 26; Whitehead, *Writing on the Wall*, 323; Keith Joseph, *Why Britain Needs a Social Market Economy* (1975), 3, 5, 11, 17.

as Powell had never quite managed to do, largely because Joseph had – unlike Powell – always previously been seen as a good Party man. This was what gave his 'conversion' such newsworthiness. Apart from the loyally Heathite *Economist*, the press gave Joseph's Preston speech at least guarded approval; *The Times* thought that 'the main lines were unquestionably right', and the *Daily Telegraph* was even more positive – under Maurice Green it had since 1964 moved steadily towards economic liberalism. This was an important moment in British political history; in a few weeks, as Alfred Sherman later put it, Joseph had taught the Tory Party that it dare be radical. The role of John the Baptist for Margaret Thatcher's messianic vision was a vital one.[50]

The October 1974 General Election

All the same, within a few days of Joseph's Preston speech the calling of a second General Election occupied all attention; policy and leadership wrangles were both put in abeyance. Though Harold Wilson cited Joseph's speech as proof that 'Tories equal unemployment', Joseph himself attracted little media attention and only thin audiences for his own campaign meetings. The preparation of the manifesto had proceeded alongside the evolution of official policy, though the exact nature of Heath's government-of-national-unity strategy remained unclear until the very end. The ACP and shadow cabinet each looked at final drafts on 2 September and, offered alternative paragraphs on the central theme, opted for the vaguer of the two; the word 'coalition' would not be used, but Heath promised that if returned with a Conservative majority (which was still the stated objective) he would invite 'people from outside the ranks of our party to join with us in overcoming Britain's difficulties'. As a gesture to Joseph, the manifesto promised to use 'every tolerable means available to fight inflation. We will rigorously control public spending and the money supply'. It was easy to see that the word 'tolerable' was a way of reconciling opposed views, for who would want to use intolerable measures – but 'tolerable' was susceptible to a wide range of meanings. The manifesto also incorporated the pledges on mortgage interest and on the abolition of domestic rates. Despite Wilson's continuing negotiations about Britain's place in the EEC, the Tory manifesto made little mention of Europe, which is hardly surprising in the context of current public opinion; by October only 6 per cent of the electorate thought that Britain should stay in the EEC on the terms on which Heath had joined; pro-Europeans like Anthony Grant MP complained that this was in itself a

---

[50] Halcrow, *Joseph*, 71–2, 74; Joseph, *Social Market Economy*, 19–32; Whitehead, *Writing on the Wall*, 323; Harrison, 'Mrs. Thatcher and the Intellectuals', 216; Prior, *Balance of Power*, 97; *Crossbow*, June 1974, 9; Geoffrey Howe, *Conflict of Loyalty* (1994), 87–8; Baker, *Turbulent Years*, 42; Cockett, *Thinking the Unthinkable*, 183, 188; Ranelagh, *Thatcher's People*, 139.

result of the Party's timidity, for 'we seem to be terrified to mention the EEC in anything but apologetic, defensive terms. As a result the "Antis" blame everything upon it with impunity.' The manifesto was leaked to the press, but this only succeeded in attracting an unusual amount of attention, and within a few days the campaign started anyway.[51]

October 1974 was never going to be other than a difficult Election. Polls indicated that two-thirds of the electorate had made up their minds before campaigning started, which still seemed to leave room to influence the result, but deeper surveys of attitudes and policy preferences did not look promising. Labour under Wilson had used its time in office since February to maximise its appeal, and by Autumn had greatly enhanced support for its policies. Only 10 per cent of voters in August thought that Britain's economic difficulties were due to Labour, compared to 25 per cent who blamed the Conservatives and 38 per cent who blamed both parties equally. In Autumn then, the Conservatives were still on the defensive about their legacy from February, and the Party's Tactical Committee had regular debates during the campaign on ways of defusing the 'confrontation' question. On voting intention, every published poll but one put Labour ahead, most of them by a comfortable margin; the private polls were no more encouraging, showing the Conservatives' chosen themes as not getting across well. Nine-tenths of Conservative candidates cited prices and trade unions as issues brought up on the doorstep, while three-quarters mentioned housing, and only half of them the national unity appeal that was the centrepiece of the Tory campaign. Likewise, national unity and coalition was never more than the fifth most prominent issue reported in the media, and had sunk to ninth in the final week. Even so, if they did not report the idea, the newspapers' own unusual lack of partisanship, in a campaign when five national papers failed to endorse any party at all, may have contributed to support for Heath's appeal.[52]

The Conservative campaign was a deliberate reaction to what had been viewed as a confrontationist approach in February and was intended to be low key throughout; Heath announced at the outset that 'we should stop calling each other liars, and put an end to this party political bickering'. The problem in this strategy was that journalists who were having to report the fourth successive contest between the same two potential premiers found it difficult to describe this low-profile Tory campaign in a way that attracted attention. Because, as an adviser put it, 'We had relied too much on the cult of a single personality', this time Heath took only half of the Party's press

---

[51] Ramsden, *Making of Conservative Party Policy*, 306–7; Butler and Kavanagh, *General Election of October 1974*, 66–7, 134, 284; Campbell, *Heath*, 639–40, 643; Central Office Chairman's department file, CCO 20/48/5, Candidates; Roger Jowell and Gerald Hoinville, *Britain into Europe, Public Opinion and the EEC, 1961–1975* (1976), 33.

[52] Robert Worcester, *British Public Opinion* (1991), 58; Butler and Kavanagh, *General Election of October 1974*, 52, 86, 145, 170, 192, 199, 233; Central Office Chairman's department file, CCO 20/17/49, October 1974 Election.

conferences and was generally subdued in tone; in his first major speech, he was so unprovocative that he spoke for three-quarters of an hour without even raising applause until the end. In the final week his attacks on Labour's plans did raise the temperature, and Hailsham was brought into a press conference specifically to raise Tory voters' morale by highlighting law and order in an aggressive way. At the end it seemed increasingly as if Heath – as in 1966 – was laying down markers for the future in his insistence that there was a major economic storm on the horizon. Attempts to present a collective leadership were again frustrated by the media's concentration only on the parties' leaders; Heath was quoted on national TV and radio more than all the other Conservative leaders added together, while Thatcher attracted under 4 per cent of the Party's news coverage in the last campaign before she became Leader. She did play a major role in the Party's own television campaigning, however, featuring in two broadcasts and beginning her media partnership with Gordon Reece. On the other hand, the two pledges that she had been persuaded to make did not add much to the Party's credibility; polls showed that a high proportion of voters saw them as irresponsible, even as bribes to the electorate.[53]

Low-profile campaigning was unlikely to satisfy party activists, and when the Election was lost some were inclined to blame the lacklustre campaign for the Party's defeat. But this approach was necessary if the proposal for a government of national unity was to be highlighted. Though he had been a late convert, and though he continued to hedge it round with qualifications, Heath had become an enthusiast for the principle. There was also some evidence that this had an effect on voters: near the end of the campaign, a poll found that 69 per cent knew of Heath's pledge to invite non-Conservatives into his government, and about a fifth of voters said that this made them more likely to vote Conservative; it may well have tempted some Liberals in marginals to vote against Labour candidates in the reasonable hope of producing Liberal–Tory cooperation. Much of the Party's campaigning made the assumption that the stance was a vote-winner; there was, for example, a newspaper advertisement in which the block letter message 'VOTE FOR NATIONAL UNITY' entirely dwarfed the tiny slogan 'Vote Conservative'. During the campaign, a far more radical coalitionist initiative was being discussed: the new pressure group Conservative Action for Electoral Reform (CAER) proposed on 10 September that, now that the Liberals had refused a deal, the Conservatives should force one on them. The plan was that, at the last moment before the close of nominations, if it were clear that the Conservatives were unlikely to win on their own, forty-nine Conservative candidates in Labour seats should be withdrawn, to allow the

53 Butler and Kavanagh, *General Election of October 1974*, 102, 115, 122, 131, 134, 143, 156–7, 260–1; Campbell, *Heath*, 645; Michael Cockerell, *Live from Number Ten: The Inside Story of Prime Ministers and Television* (1988), 212–13.

Liberals a free run against Labour. This would, it was claimed, 'seize the initiative in the last few days of the campaign', it would greatly increase the chance of Labour failing to win the Election and of there being a combined Liberal/Conservative majority (the lack of which had wrecked the talks in March); it would also allow targeted efforts to defeat Labour left-wingers like Tony Benn, it would impress Liberal voters in Conservative–Labour marginals with the honesty of the Conservatives' coalitionist intentions, and it would ensure that most Liberal MPs would know that they now depended on Tory votes (and would therefore be more favourable to a coalition with the right than the left). As an electoral tactic this had quite a lot in common with the strategy that Joseph Ball and Neville Chamberlain had pursued successfully in 1931, except that in 1931, crucially, the deal had been done before the campaign, and covered sitting Liberal MPs, rather than candidates – who in 1974 had in some places come third only six months earlier. This superficially-attractive idea seems to have generated quite a serious debate among the Party managers; Wolff commissioned a professional statistician to check the assumptions behind the proposal (he said that it would not work), and the Research Department was also asked for its evaluation (James Douglas thought it 'statistically and politically naive'); Wolff reported to Whitelaw, with some apparent regret, that the CAER proposal was 'politically unrealistic'; there is no evidence of Heath's views about this proposed electoral buccaneering, but it is unlikely that so much time would have been devoted to evaluating it at such a busy time without at least his knowledge of its existence. It would though have been impossible to implement with the Party already in such a mutinous state, for a number of those candidates required to withdraw would surely have refused to do so at such short notice and the public split on strategy that this would have created would have vitiated any positive results anyway.[54]

In the absence of such a headline-grabbing démarche, the main difficulties of the coalition strategy were the lack of definition of the policy itself and the refusal to accept that it might require a Prime Minister other than Heath to bring it off. Some advisers suggested that Heath should offer to make 'the supreme sacrifice' of standing aside in the interests of national unity, arguing that this involved little risk: if there was a Conservative majority, then he would not need to stand aside, and if there were not he would probably have to withdraw anyway. But Heath's reluctance to make such an offer, and Whitelaw's determination as Party Chairman not to allow the idea to be publicly debated, ensured that the question was never directly faced. In the final week Heath issued a message to Conservative candidates in which he called for a 'National Coalition Government', the first time that the word

[54] Butler and Kavanagh, *General Election of October 1974*, 124–6, 128–9; Behrens, *Heath to Thatcher*, 28; DN, 25 and 29 Sept., 2 Oct. 1974; Central Office Chairman's department file, CCO 20/78/1.

had been used. Three days before polling, Heath hinted that the 'supreme sacrifice' might be made, telling a caller on a radio phone-in that 'I am not the obstacle to any coalition', but it was still far from clear what he meant. While the Central Office *Daily Notes* for candidates offered guidance on how to answer such questions, it never convincingly solved the dilemma. Whitelaw's final ambiguous statement was that this was an appeal to the country 'to give us a majority to form a government of national unity'. After the campaign, Gillian Peele was highly critical of the muddled thinking behind this 'rather woolly and nebulous programme'; even if Heath had had 'the charisma of a Churchill or a de Gaulle he would have had difficulty in rousing enthusiasm for a cause which was predicated on the assumption that the party could not cope with the economic and other problems facing the nation'. John Campbell's view in 1993 was that 'for the second time in seven months the party committed itself to a risky but potentially popular strategy, then threw away the dividend by pressing its case weakly.' But it was easier for others to say that Heath should have been more explicit about his proposal, than it was for him to do it at the time; Party activists did not like the idea of fighting for something less than a Tory victory, and some shadow cabinet colleagues were already hostile to Heath's apparent willingness to sacrifice some of their posts and their policies even if the Party won a majority; asked during the campaign whether 'her' pledges on mortgages and domestic rates were items that might be negotiated away in the process of coalition-making, Thatcher made it clear that these at least were not negotiable. In the circumstances, Heath went as far as he could if he was to avoid a Party row in mid-campaign.[55]

The post-election meeting of the ACP, not held until 4 December when other matters were on members' minds, tends to confirm this view. Heath, in the chair, began by saying that the Party's manifesto had been 'acclaimed by the press', and suggested that this success was due in no small part to the hard work put in by the ACP earlier in the year. The subsequent debate indicated the extent of disagreement on Heath's viewpoint, and the extent to which trades union policy and coalitionism were inextricably entangled in the minds of politicians no longer confident of their ability to deal with the one without the other. Professor Esmond Wright, principal of Swinton College, argued that 'the national unity theme had worried some of our own supporters in that it seemed to conflict with Party loyalty, and supporters did not know how to react to it'. Others agreed with this and Lord Chelmer added that 'the lack of presentation of the implications of this policy came under a good deal of fire', suggesting that lack of definition had cost the Party support. Angus Maude then launched the main attack; at its pre-election meeting, on 2 September,

55 Campbell, *Heath*, 647; *DN*, 8 Oct. 1974; *Crossbow*, Dec. 1974, 6; Russel, *Conservative Party*, 145; Young, *One of Us*, 90–1.

the ACP (like the shadow cabinet later on the same day) had been offered a clear choice between two alternatives:

> the first being a clear, specific commitment to coalition government and the second being little more than a statement of willingness to consult with all sides. The second alternative had been preferred by the ACP and had in fact been adopted [for the manifesto]. As the campaign had progressed, however, spokesmen had been forced to adopt something more like the first alternative of coalition because of probing questions. Then, at the end of the campaign it was felt that the Party stood for something rather different than that stated in the Manifesto.

From the chair, Heath rejected the claim that different things had been said as the campaign went on, but reminded the ACP that the public and press 'had undoubtedly been for coalition. This was due to a widespread feeling that no single party was going to be able to cope with the country's problems, and deal with the trade unions'. Maude then reminded the committee that he had often asked at earlier meetings

> what answer could be given to queries about what the Party would do in the event of another major confrontation with the unions. He had warned that this would be the major question during the campaign, as indeed it was, but no fully convincing answer had been forthcoming. The chairman said the truth was there was no simple answer to the question. It was the major constitutional problem of our time.

This last was not a very satisfactory answer when given in mid-campaign, and did not satisfy Heath's critics afterwards either. At the National Union Executive, there was similar 'criticism of the way in which policy was developed during the campaign'.[56]

In the event, the election results on 10 and 11 October were better than had been feared, and Whitelaw was surely justified in his later claim that the Party's performance at the polls was a success against the odds; *Labour Weekly* took the same view, arguing a week after polling day that 'Labour failed in many of the key marginals it hoped to win. . . . It was evident that the Tories had mounted very determined efforts to hold their marginals [and] the election had proved the wisdom of concentrating on the marginals.' Despite Labour's continuous poll leads during the campaign, and a BBC exit poll that foreshadowed a Labour landslide, the first prediction based on actual results was of a Labour majority of twenty, and this then fell steadily as results were declared, leaving Wilson in the end with an overall majority of three. There was a uniform regional swing to Labour of about 2 per cent (except, crucially, in the most marginal Conservative-held constituencies), and twenty fewer Conservative MPs were elected than in February, the only prominent casualty being Tom Boardman, Coal Minister under Heath. The large Liberal vote of February fell slightly, and this helped Conservatives to hold some seats that

---

[56] ACP, 4 Dec. 1974; NUEC, 9 Nov. 1974.

would have fallen on the average national swing; the Party again did worse than average in inner cities, though there was a tiny swing to Conservative in the London suburbs.[57]

It was easy to argue after 1979 that Tory voters' tenacity in the marginals had so blunted Labour's attack as to deny it the full fruits of victory. A majority of three would not last a full Parliament, and the unstable government in 1977–79 that followed the loss of Labour's majority through by-election defeats did indeed set up Callaghan's Commons defeat in 1979, which in turn produced an Election at a time he would not have chosen, and the Conservatives' return to office. That silver lining was nowhere apparent in 1974. Labour's majority of three was for a time perfectly adequate, for the fragmentation of the anti-Labour forces into five parties and assorted individuals made it fairly straightforward for Labour to govern. And the Conservative 'success' was apparent only when compared to their gloomy expectations; the 277 Conservative MPs elected was a smaller number than at any post-war election except the landslides of 1945 and 1966. The regional pattern also gave cause for concern; where the Party had held half the Scottish seats in 1955, it now held under a quarter. A lesser but still serious devastation had occurred in urban England; even in 1945 there had been seven Conservatives elected by the cities of Birmingham, Manchester, Liverpool and Leicester, and there had been nine in 1966, but now there were only four. Despite much contemporary discussion of the opening up of a North–South divide, this was at best half true; if Ulster Unionists are left out of the calculation, the proportion of Tory MPs elected north and west of the Severn-to-the-Wash line had scarcely changed since 1950; the real division was between inner cities everywhere and the suburbs, rural areas and mixed constituencies; the North West Area Agent pointed out that between 1970 and October 1974, the swing to Labour in Manchester and in Liverpool was more than three times as great as in the rest of his Area – and in those cities the Party's position had already been seriously weakened before 1970. To underline this point, a comparison between 1950 and October 1974 is instructive, for in both elections the Tories took 252 English seats: the number of seats won in Inner London and the fourteen largest provincial cities had been 36 in 1950 but was now 14; the share in London's suburbia was 33 in both years; but the share in the rest of England had risen from 183 seats to 205. There had thus been areas of long-term growth as well as areas of decline; in some places where traditional nonconformity had once been a barrier to Conservative success, as in Norfolk or in the Pennine region of Lancashire and Yorkshire, the Party was now doing as well as at any time in the twentieth century. But there was no denying the failure of Conservatives in the cities, and what was particularly ominous was the fall in the size of

57 Whitelaw, *Memoirs*, 141; Worcester, *Public Opinion*, 194; *NCP* 11 Dec. 1974; Butler and Kavanagh, *General Election of October 1974*, 136, 138, 276.

Conservative majorities even where city seats were held; after October, there were only two or three such constituencies in cities outside Greater London that could be counted as safe. The need to renew the appeal to the provincial cities was a running theme in Conservative politics over the next few years. A further sign of Conservative pessimism about the results of the 1974 Elections is to be found in growing support in 1975–76 for Conservative Action for Electoral Reform, a group that based its pragmatic argument for proportional representation on the fear of Labour governments being regularly elected on minority votes. For the first time since the immediate post-war years, Conservatives began seriously to ask whether the rules would have to be changed before their Party would prosper again.[58]

Heath and his critics after October

Such calculations were now largely beside the point, for the Party had to settle to a full Parliament in Opposition, with a Leader who had now lost three of the four contests he had fought; two defeats in one year was exactly what had forced Arthur Balfour out in 1910. Moreover, even supporters of Heath's leadership like Reginald Maudling and Nigel Fisher had found on the doorstep in London that voters did not like him and that his presence made them less likely to vote Tory; Fisher (but not Maudling) decided on the strength of this that there must be a change. Julian Critchley's doorstep experiences in Basingstoke had had a similar effect and were to turn this left-wing Tory into a voter for Thatcher in the following February: Critchley had been piqued by Heath's snubs and disappointed by his lack of preferment, but 'more creditably, I had come to the conclusion that Ted Heath had not the quality that Napoleon demanded of his marshals: he was not lucky.' Two hundred miles away, Michael Alison (a moderate Tory, made a Minister by Heath) had been forced to the same conclusion; he told his constituency association in Yorkshire that Heath 'had had a good innings' and reminded his supporters of 'the canvassing at the last election which showed him beyond doubt that as a leader Heath had become a liability'. Opinion polls confirmed this message, for Heath was the only party leader to be consistently less popular than his Party, and his approval rating was now down to a disastrous 27 per cent. The press almost unanimously predicted that Heath would have to step down, a view encouraged by Carrington's reported visit to Heath's constituency on polling day to tell him that he should go quickly and with dignity. Most saw Whitelaw as the most likely successor. Heath was now besieged by conflicting advisers. On the one hand, Walker, Hailsham and Whitelaw all urged him to defy his critics and soldier on; on the other, Pym,

---

[58] Campbell, *Heath*, 653; Butler and Kavanagh, *General Election of October 1974*, 281; *NCP* 11 Nov. 1974; North West Area Council, 16 Nov. 1974; Ramsden, 'Changing Base of British Conservatism', 30–1, 33–4; *Crossbow*, Oct. 1975, 2.

Prior, Gilmour, his PPSs and Sara Morrison, as well as Carrington, offered the less welcome advice that if his leadership was to be saved (which many doubted anyway), he must arrange for a quick contest that he might win before a serious challenger emerged. That latter group were all devoted supporters of Heath and his policies, worried that a refusal to recognise the vulnerability of his position would both increase the threat to him and remove the chance of an orderly handover to a successor of whom both he and they could approve. Patrick Jenkin, another loyalist who owed his promotion to Heath and who would still support Heath in the February 1975 ballot, agreed on 29 October with a branch chairman's demand for a new Leader. 'I just do not think we can go into another General Election with him as our leader. What seems to me to be necessary is a period of reflection so that the changes may be effected decently and in a way that allows Ted to go on playing a major role in the Party and the shadow cabinet'. [59]

Battered and angry, Heath was not ready to take a cool judgement of the situation; he therefore resolved to sit it out, convincing himself that it was his duty to do so in defence of sensible politics in the Party – and especially over Europe where a national referendum was likely in 1975; he told Prior, with the convoluted logic of a trapped man, that he did not intend to fight a leadership contest because he wanted to stay on to resist the right wing, which made sense only if he thought he would *lose* a contest; he told Kenneth Baker that he would stay on 'to save the Party from extremism'. He therefore battled on as if his election defeat conveyed no message; replying to the new Queen's Speech, he continued to stress the need for national unity and offered to cooperate with Wilson if he governed in a non-partisan way; he was saying much the same in an economic debate in the House in December. This reluctance to give ground on policy was as damaging as the refusal to stand for re-election; in the *Spectator*, Patrick Cosgrave argued in January 1975 that, 'Mr. Heath clearly intends to do nothing whatever – whatever others do – about examining the record of the party during his government'. Since 1975 it has often been argued that Heath's refusal to get an early confirmation of his leadership after October 1974 was what led to his fall, much as it had done for Sir Alec in 1964–65, but surely this underestimates the groundswell of resistance now building up to his policies as well as to him in person, and which would have evicted him sometime in the next four years, come what may? What is quite clear though is that Heath's refusal either to resign *or* to seek re-election in October 1974, by binding all loyal Heathites to his doomed cause, ensured that when a contest came it would be in circumstances in which neither he nor any of his supporters could win.

59 Money, *Margaret Thatcher*, 20; Butler and Kavanagh, *General Election of October 1974*, 136, 266; Maudling, *Memoirs*, 206; Critchley, *Bag of Boiled Sweets*, 142, 146; Barkston Ash CA minutes, 7 Feb. 1975; Whitehead, *Writing on the Wall*, 325; Francis Pym, *The Politics of Consent* (1984), 4; Patrick Jenkin to the author, 29 Oct. 1974.

This tactic can be variously interpreted as ill-judged or simply egotistical; a story circulating on the backbenches was that Whitelaw had told friends, 'in total confidence . . . that Ted was not behaving like a gentleman'. In either case, the effect was to be fifteen years of Conservative Party politics of which Heath himself thoroughly disapproved; his own apparent irritability for much of that time no doubt owed at least something to a belated recognition of his personal responsibility for what had happened.[60]

Outsiders could see clearly enough what lay ahead. On the morrow of the October defeat, *The Times* printed a cartoon showing Labour supporters looking at a pile of 'Down with Heath!' banners, with one of them saying, 'Perhaps we could sell them to the Tories?' At the Eastern Area Council on 3 November, 'some members expressed the view that the question of the party leadership was of paramount importance, but the chairman stressed that it was vital that no hasty decision should be taken'. Years of latent hostility now erupted and pleas for calm and delay were swept aside in the process; a senior backbencher, although known as a critic, shocked Norman Fowler by saying that there should *not* be an early leadership challenge, because so far 'Heath has not suffered enough'. Where previous muted criticism of Heath's policies and style had been coded attacks on his leadership, critics now appeared without fear. Among Tory MPs, right-wingers like John Cordle, Neil Marten and Nicholas Winterton all called openly for a new leader; these were anti-Europeanists rather than economic Powellites. but the latter were gathering too, and while their grouping included traditional rebels like Ridley, it also now included Geoffrey Howe and Ian Gow, both men who had previously cast no vote against Heath's economic policy. Howe had even had ministerial responsibility for the prices and incomes policy, but, as Gow later put it, 'Howe and Gow both wanted Keith'. On 15 October, Andrew Bowden was reported as the first Tory MP outside the Monday Club to call openly for Heath to resign; ten days later, a group of disaffected Tories took advertisements in the *Daily Mail* and *The Times*, cunningly disguised to look like an official Central Office statement, with the heading 'In the name of God, Go!'[61]

A *Crossbow* editorial published in December, written by the new editor Peter Lloyd, just back from two 1974 contests in a Nottingham marginal, put the accumulating case against Heath at its squarest. He began by stating as fact that 'the bulk of the parliamentary party' wanted Heath to go and that even loyal Party workers in the country 'do not look forward to fighting the next election with him at their head'; he then attacked Heath's policy record as inconsistent and confusing:

---

[60] Prior, *Balance. of Power*, 98; Baker, *Turbulent Years*, 43; Campbell, *Heath*, 655–7; *NCP* 11 Nov. and 30 Dec. 1974; *Spectator*, 18 Jan. 1975; Critchley, *Bag of Boiled Sweets*, 140.

[61] Money, *Margaret Thatcher*, 12; Eastern Area Council, 3 Nov. 1974; Fowler, *Ministers Decide*, 7; Behrens, *Heath to Thatcher*, 28; Central Office file, CCO 500/32/23, Leader's correspondence.

The major argument against Mr. Heath's leadership is not that the Party with him at its head will find it much harder to win elections, but that under him it has ceased to know where it is going and what it stands for. This confusion is not so much the product of the celebrated U-turns, which it has followed with varying degrees of heart-searching, but rather the deepening conviction that these reversals revealed the absence of a clear view of how the economy and society work and what the relationship of the Government should be to both.

Finally, Lloyd thought that 'Mr. Heath's trouble-shooting managerial style has placed such great strains on the loyalty of the Party that it can never be enthusiastically reunited while he remains at its head'; he should stand down without a fight and thereby allow himself to serve under his successor without loss of face. This encapsulated the three repeated strands of criticism: (1) Heath's lack of electoral appeal, (2) his inability to articulate the firm conviction that lay behind apparently contradictory policies, and (3) the fact that his leadership was now in itself a barrier to Party unity. A great many in the Party did not share the third of these beliefs, and many – probably still a majority – did not share the second either, but the acceptance of the first was near universal and was the real foundation of the 'anyone but Ted' mood now emerging, while the fact that even a large minority articulated the second point would sooner or later make the third one self-fulfilling.[62]

Against such a weight of feeling, it was not sensible of Heath to cause offence to the 1922 Committee. The Executive had planned to meet three days after polling day for reasons that had more to do with a possible coalition than with the Party leadership, but even by then its members had been on the receiving end of a steady stream of demands for action from Tory MPs. It therefore empowered its chairman, du Cann, to call on Heath and report the Executive's view that there should be a contest for the leadership, in the near future if not at once. The 1922 Executive was not regarded as sympathetic or representative by Heath and his supporters – Chris Patten had warned Carrington in 1973 that 'the Executive has more than its quota of embittered souls' – and du Cann himself was regarded by Heath as a personal foe, with some justification, though Heath had himself contributed to the antagonism. It was though extraordinarily unwise of Heath to reject the Executive's advice, for they were the elected representatives of the MPs whose backing he needed. It was even more rash to refuse to discuss the issue at all until the Executive had been confirmed in office for the new Parliament, for Heath was thereby imposing on them exactly the test of re-election to which he himself was refusing to submit. This problem was exaggerated when the subsequent Executive meeting, called so that du Cann could report Heath's reply and arranged to take place at du Cann's City office so as *not* to attract attention, burst on to the front pages after news of it was leaked to the press, apparently

---

[62] *Crossbow*, Dec. 1974, 3; Ranelagh, *Thatcher's People*, 119, 132–5.

by Heath supporters at Central Office anxious to expose people they saw as disloyal plotters; this was not the last of the attempts by Heathites to place damaging stories about du Cann, Joseph and Thatcher in the press, invariably with results that were counter-productive. The 'Milk Street mafia' photographed leaving du Cann's office were embarrassed by their sudden fame, but the news of the 1922's breach with Heath which was thereby publicised was worse news for the Leader than for his critics; questioned at the next full 1922 Committee, du Cann reported that the Executive and officers had continued to meet since the dissolution, 'in accordance with precedent', and his reply satisfied the committee. The re-election en bloc of the Executive on 3 November (its twelve members including Maude, Neave, Marten and Biffen), with the rejection in the process of several candidates put up by Heath supporters, and the ovation that greeted the news that du Cann had been returned unopposed as chairman, was therefore public evidence of the wrongness of Heath's claim that the 1922's leaders no longer represented Tory MPs. At a packed meeting of the 1922, nearly every Member who spoke was critical of Heath, and Kenneth Lewis, not a regular critic, attracted much applause for the contention that the Party leadership was 'a leasehold not a freehold'. This was a revolutionary view of the constitutional position of the Tory Leader, but it was what MPs wanted to hear.[63]

It is also clear that many of the constituency associations wanted a change. In Peckham, the October canvass was said to have shown strong backing for Heath among Tory voters, but a resolution of confidence in the Leader attracted only eight votes from the sixteen committee members. In Ashford, the association appointed on 29 October two representatives from each branch to convey to the MP the weight of feeling on the subject. In West Derbyshire, the meeting called to review the October campaign heard strong criticisms of Heath's leadership, which was 'discussed at length'. In the neighbouring High Peak constituency, after a similar debate, the chairman agreed to pass on to the MP 'the general dissatisfaction with the present leadership', and made elaborate plans to consult over a thousand local activists in the event of a ballot. In Sheffield Hallam, some members wanted an immediate local ballot, but this was staved off by the agent until it had been overtaken by national events. Harrow West still had many active Heath supporters, who in December 'spoke of his sincerity and single-mindedness and believed he should stay because no obvious successor had emerged', but the association Executive nevertheless passed by fourteen to five a motion stating that 'it would be beneficial to the Party if a change of leadership were seriously considered at the appropriate time'. It was reported in Ruislip that the YCs were 100 per cent against Heath, as were the 'under-35s' generally, while Heath's supporters could not deny his lack of electoral appeal, arguing just

63 Campbell, *Heath*, 656–8, 661–2; Central Office Chairman's department file, CCO 20/59/2, Meetings with the 1922 Committee; 1922 Committee minutes [hereafter 1922], 31 Oct. and 7 Nov. 1974; Halcrow, *Joseph*, 78; Blake, *Conservative Party*, 317.

that he was the best man in the Commons. Nor did these demands for a change take place only in constituencies with a tradition of passing right-wing resolutions or with MPs hostile to Heath; Francis Pym's Cambridgeshire association, which had as recently as April 1974 rejected (or amended beyond recognition) branch resolutions critical of Heath and had actually passed one calling for stronger policies to 'curb those abuses of capitalism that are no longer tolerable in this day and age', now came to some very different conclusions: asked on 28 November whether 'on the whole do you consider that the Party would be better off or worse off during the next six months under the leadership of Edward Heath?' (the key question that the Party had to confront), eleven of the Executive voted for 'better', twelve for 'worse', and nine abstained. At Horncastle on 10 December, a branch resolution withdrawing support from Heath was not endorsed, and the association resolved that this was entirely a matter for the parliamentary party, but the debate indicated a great deal of dissatisfaction. [64]

How can this accumulated evidence of disaffection be reconciled with the fact that most constituency parties advised that Heath be re-elected when the actual contest came in January 1975? Perhaps because, like Harrow West, they desperately wanted Heath to solve their dilemma by stepping down, so that a contest could take place 'at the appropriate time', and without a split; perhaps because they still did not see even in January 1975 where the next leader was going to come from. Even in late January, many still did not see Thatcher as anything other than a disloyal breaker of ranks. Then suddenly, but only in early February, they recognised something that they liked. Saffron Walden demanded on 2 December a leader who would pursue true Conservatism and not the 'watered down socialism' that members felt to be personified by Whitelaw – quite a reversal since the heyday of their own MP Rab Butler – but they also lamented the lack of 'a leading personality' who could offer them what they wanted; on 7 January there were some very anti-Heath views expressed in the association, but there was virtually no mention of Thatcher who was by then already running as a candidate; by 10 February it was reported that the final soundings had produced overwhelming backing for Thatcher from the association. In December 1974, the local associations wanted a change but not an enforced change, and not a change to a leader about whom most of them knew very little. [65]

Heath now had no option but to give ground. His efforts to widen the base of the shadow cabinet were one attempt to strengthen the position, but Maudling would not yet agree to return, du Cann 'could not be bought

---

[64] Ashford CA minutes, 29 Oct. 1974; Peckham CA minutes, 16 Oct. 1974; West Derbyshire CA minutes, 4 Nov. 1974; High Peak CA minutes, 29 Oct. 1974 and 4 Mar. 1975; Sheffield Hallam CA minutes, 15 Nov. 1974; Harrow West CA minutes, 12 Dec. 1974; Ruislip CA minutes, 1 Nov. 1974; Cambridgeshire CA minutes, 28 Nov. 1974; Horncastle CA minutes, 10 Dec. 1974.

[65] Saffron Walden CA minutes, 2 Dec. 1974, 7 Jan. and 10 Feb. 1975.

off now' (as John Campbell put it), and only the independent right-winger John Peyton could be added to vary the old faces. In the hope of sharpening up the attack on Labour in the House, Margaret Thatcher was transferred from the Environment portfolio to second Robert Carr on Treasury affairs; since this was just the launching pad that had started Heath's own final spurt for the leadership in 1965, it is evidence of how far in November Heath still discounted any threat to him from Thatcher. More significant even than this, Heath attended a 1922 Committee meeting on 14 November, and announced that the opportunity of a leadership contest would be provided.[66]

Heath versus Thatcher

It would first be necessary though to revise the election rules, since they did not provide for contests except where a vacancy already existed, and Heath did not intend to create one. Heath therefore also explained on 14 November that Lord Home of the Hirsel (as Sir Alec now was) would chair a committee to undertake this task; after a quick programme of five meetings, the committee reported on 11 December and the new rules were circulated to MPs just before Christmas. The committee recommended one of the elements of Humphry Berkeley's 1964 proposals that had not been adopted at that time; henceforth there would be an opportunity to challenge the incumbent leader at the start of each parliamentary session; a few months later, Wiiliam Deedes pointed out that the Party Leader 'has ceased to be an owner occupier. She or he is now on an annual tenancy agreement, without the Rent Acts.' This was to be a significant provision in 1989 and 1990, but other changes mattered more in 1975. It has often been claimed that the revised 1974 rules allowed for new candidates on the second ballot because Heath supporters wanted a second bite at the cherry if their candidate failed to win, but this provision had in fact already been there since 1965. What was new was a formal mechanism for informing MPs of the views of Tory peers and of activists in the country before each ballot for the leadership, and a provision that slightly raised the hurdle that was required for outright victory on the first ballot. Instead of the need to get a majority of votes cast and a 15 per cent lead over the runner up, as prescribed in 1965, a winner now needed a majority of all Tory MPs plus the same 15 per cent lead. This last change was jocularly christened 'Alec's revenge' (against Heath – for the events of 1965) because, by counting abstentions as if they were votes against the winner, the new rule made it more difficult for an incumbent to be re-elected without general enthusiasm. In 1990 this was to be the rule that brought Thatcher down, but it scarcely mattered at all in 1975, for there were very few abstentions and the new rule was not invoked.[67]

---

[66] Campbell, *Heath*, 661–2.
[67] George Hutchinson, *Edward Heath: A Personal and Political Biography* (1970), 221, 223; Campbell, *Heath*, 664; William Deedes, 'No Reversing the Sundial', *Crossbow*, Apr. 1975, 6.

As in 1965 the new rules were technically a matter only for the Leader's approval, but the inclusion of du Cann, the Chief Whip and National Union leaders in Home's committee ensured that the rest of the Party had already signified agreement; the 1922 formally approved the new scheme on 16 January, along with their Executive's view that there should now be an election 'as soon as possible within the time limits set out in the draft procedure', though some MPs felt that even this did not go far enough and called for an election to be at 'the earliest possible opportunity'. With the new rules in place, and opinion on the backbenches reported to him by du Cann, Heath had no option but voluntarily to submit himself for early re-election rather than wait for the next new session in the Autumn. He formally announced his own candidature on 23 January, with the first ballot fixed for 4 February: 'I offer myself to the party. I offer myself on the first ballot, and if there are further ballots after that I offer myself in those as well.'[68]

During the long round of informal campaigning between 11 October and the last week of January, it was unclear until very late who Heath's challenger(s) would be. Attention initially focused on du Cann, for his position in the 1922 Committee indicated breadth of support, and the fact that he had not served in Heath's Government relieved him of all responsibility for recent events, and on Joseph, whose speeches had done so much to mobilise the policy alternative to Heath. Although du Cann had substantial support in the National Union, dating back to his time as Party Chairman, he had never held Cabinet office, and his City connections had run into some difficulties during the recent runaway credit boom; he hesitated for weeks before finally ruling himself out on 13 January.[69]

Joseph though was quickly into the race and quickly out again. He was certainly not running a campaign for the leadership, but when asked to stand by sympathetic backbenchers, he immediately accepted the responsibility. Within a week, another 'great speech' by Joseph himself had torpedoed his own campaigners before they could set sail. Speaking at Birmingham on 19 October, for once on a non-economic theme, he called for a return to traditional spiritual and moral values, and for a campaign of political education across the whole nation. A good speech that would have attracted support to him from people not interested in monetarist economics was wrecked by a final section, by way of example and from the evidence of single-parent families, arguing the need for birth control in deprived groups. The basic point, and his attendant references to 'our human stock' and to 'these classes of people', caused an outcry, typified by the *Evening Standard*'s headline – 'Sir Keith in "Stop Babies" Sensation'. Few thought that Joseph was really

[68] Campbell, *Heath*, 670; 1922, 16 Jan. 1975.
[69] Campbell, *Heath*, 660–1, 666; Young, *One of Us*, 95; Tebbit, *Upwardly Mobile*, 177–8; Behrens, *Heath to Thatcher*, 39.

advocating any form of eugenics, but many questioned his judgement in raising the matter in this way. (It is notable that when, earlier in 1974, a senior backbencher tried with Central Office backing to put exactly the same issues on to the agenda of the Party's Environment committee, Thatcher refused to have anything whatsoever to do with them, and ensured that they never came near to surfacing as Party policy.) Joseph compounded the error of the Birmingham speech, the memory of which would have faded quickly enough if left alone, by insisting that he had been misunderstood and that the record must be put straight, in television interviews and letters to the press; the result was that the issue rumbled on for a full fortnight. Joseph, hurt both by original reactions to his speech and by the subsequent debate, now began to doubt his own fitness for the highest office and to wonder whether persisting with his candidature might not actually reduce support for the views he now held so fervently; by late November he had decided not to stand. Interviewed in 1985, he concluded of Birmingham, with characteristic humility, that 'I did it wrong. Just as well I did, because it killed off any idea that I might be a suitable leader of the Conservative Party.'[70]

In 1990, Joseph was to say that, 'I only came into anyone's mind because of the apparent poverty of choice, not because of my virtues.' The casting around by Heath's critics for such unlikely alternative candidates as Christopher Soames, out of Parliament since 1966, and Julian Amery, for whom support at this late stage of his career would surely have been minimal, indicates indeed how desperate they had become. On 20 January 1975, the York Conservatives had 'a very full discussion . . . regarding the lack of leadership in the Party and the unfortunate absence of any alternative'. There was though one potential candidate who did offer a real alternative, who supported Joseph's economic prospectus, and who was quite prepared to fight it out; when informed by Joseph on 21 November that he would not be standing, Thatcher responded, 'If you are not, I shall'. Talking later to an interviewer about critics of Joseph's Birmingham speech, she remarked that 'they broke Keith, but they won't break me'. When she called on Heath to tell him formally that she would stand for the leadership, a two-minute interview in which, characteristically, he neither stood up nor invited her to sit, he responded by saying 'If you must. You'll lose'. He was by no means the only one who formed that opinion; *The Economist* thought Thatcher to be 'precisely the sort of candidate . . . who ought to be able to stand, and lose, harmlessly'. Ladbrokes thought the odds against her winning the leadership were fifty to one, and Willie Whitelaw, who as Party Chairman really ought to have been better informed, 'simply thought such a challenge was good, in that it would clear the air and that Ted Heath would win'. Heath's supporters did not underestimate the gravity of the situation for them or (as they saw it) for the Party if Thatcher were

[70] Halcrow, *Joseph*, 80–4, 86–7; Whitehead, *Writing on the Wall*, 327; Ranelagh, *Thatcher's People*, 133.

to win, but they did enormously underestimate the chances of her getting elected, and so until very late on did her supporters. Airey Neave, whose management of her campaign was in the end to be crucial, was looking for *any* candidate who could unseat Heath, but he offered his services to Thatcher only in early January when all his other runners had withdrawn, six weeks after she had decided to stand. It was in two factors that her opportunity lay: she had a free run against Heath because all his other opponents withdrew, and her own courage was demonstrated precisely because she stood against what seemed enormous odds. Powell later thought that she 'didn't rise to power. She was opposite the spot in the roulette wheel at the right time, and didn't funk it'. Luck and courage were to be her principal assets for years to come.[71]

What in Thatcher's career to date had put her into this position? From early on she had impressed other MPs with her determination and professionalism, but it was only when Macleod picked her out to support him as shadow Chancellor in 1965 that her career really began to take off; she had in any case to be an unusually accomplished politician to fight her way through the spoken and unspoken prejudices against career women in the Party in the 1950s and 1960s, and to rise to the top; in 1970 she was only the second woman ever to hold Cabinet office in a Tory Government, and was to be the first to stay there for a full Parliament. There is though a paradox between her trenchant expressions of opinion throughout this prelude and her actual career in office before 1974. In an important lecture to the CPC in 1968, she had dwelt at length on the evils of consensual politics, which 'could be an attempt to satisfy people holding no particular views about anything', and in the *Daily Telegraph* in 1969 she was quoted arguing of industrial policies that, 'the test of their correctness is the market place'. She was certainly often perceived to be instinctively on the right of the Party on economics; Arthur Seldon at the IEA thought her in October 1969 to be 'one of a small group of Tory politicians like Enoch, Keith and [Geoffrey Howe] who saw the value of the market in economic affairs'. It was equally clear that not everyone saw it that way; a short appreciation of her for a book on the incoming Ministers of 1970 concluded that she was 'a middle of the roader in all things'. Perhaps it was clearer though by 1974, from her words if not from her actions; the Economic Dining Club, a group of twelve MPs supportive of Powell's economic thinking, had to find a replacement for Powell himself after his breach with the Party in February 1974, and selected Thatcher to fill his place. She was already thought to be 'one of them'; only four club members had been promoted by Heath, and only to junior posts, but eight went on to serve in Thatcher's Cabinet. Yet from within Heath's

---

[71] Ranelagh, *Thatcher's People*, 137, 140; Money, *Margaret Thatcher*, 28; York CA minutes, 20 Jan. 1975; Campbell, *Heath*, 663; Morris, *Tories*,198; Whitelaw, *Memoirs*, 142; D.E. Butler and Dennis Kavanagh, *The British General Election of 1979* (1980), 62; Whitehead, *Writing on the Wall*, 330.

Government, despite occasional outbursts against the Industry Bill or the failure to reduce the public sector, she was in public a loyal Minister who toed the Party line; as late as October 1974 she was promoting a Party pledge that she had little regard for, even if by then she was also dropping hints, for example in statements on coalition, which suggested that her patience was wearing thin. Perhaps the resolution of the paradox lies in Enoch Powell's 1989 description of a little observed trait of Thatcher's political character.

> The consonance between thoughts and words is something in which she is basically not interested. This – as well as being a woman – enables her year after year to live with something, with a cross on a paper at the back of her mind saying, 'I don't agree with that; I don't like it; it's rotten awful; but I can't do anything about it at the moment.' It's not exactly the mood of a person who says, 'I'm trapped'; it's more the mood of a person who says, 'I don't like that. When I can settle accounts with that, I will settle accounts with it.'

On this reading, Thatcher would never have been a trailblazer for the new economic ideas, but the emergence into political respectability for those ideas through Joseph and the Centre for Policy Studies in 1974 enabled her to think she might now 'settle some accounts'. Alfred Sherman later drew a distinction between Joseph who was excited intellectually by ideas, and Thatcher who 'does not think. She thinks to do.' Such ideas as Sherman was now pressing for seemed ideas on which action could at last be taken.[72]

The opportunity of a one to one contest against Heath gave Thatcher a quite different opportunity to settle scores. Until February 1974 she had been kept in a single Cabinet post from which she could not easily rove into other Ministers' territories, and in a department that was a traditional woman's job in government anyway. Heath had refused all requests to widen her experience by giving her a different post. Peter Rawlinson thought that there was,

> such obvious antagonism between Ted and Margaret that anyone could have foretold that if ever opportunity presented itself, the political dagger would be cheerfully slipped out of the stocking-top and into the substantial frame of her Leader. They were enemies, naked and unashamed, and they had been from the start.

If 'enemy' is a word that some of their colleagues dispute, it is clear that there was no empathy between Heath and Thatcher; even when promoting her to the Environment portfolio in March 1974, Heath was careful to change the draft seating plan for shadow cabinet meetings so that Thatcher would be

---

[72] Joni Lovenduski, Pippa Norris and Catriona Burns, 'The Party and Women', in Seldon and Ball, *Conservative Century*, 630; Young, *One of Us*, 63, 67; Robert Shepherd, *Iain Macleod* (1994), 429; Cockett, *Thinking the Unthinkable*, 171–2; James Margach and Rowland St Oswald, 'Cabinet Ministers in Waiting', in T. Stacey and R. St Oswald (eds), *Here Come the Tories* (1970), 94; Cecil Parkinson, *Right at the Centre* (1992), 124–5; Ranelagh, *Thatcher's People*, 28, 35; Andrew Alexander and Alan Watkins, *The Making of the Prime Minister, 1970* (1970), 100.

placed not across the table from him but in a far corner from whence she would not easily catch the chairman's eye; when the shadow cabinet was again reconstituted after the October Election, Heath still placed Thatcher only tenth in the formal order of precedence, a month before she was challenging for the leadership. Many have in their memoirs recalled Heath slapping Thatcher down rudely in Cabinet and shadow cabinet, and Rawlinson felt that Heath 'did not treat her well. Or rather, he did not treat her right.' But he also conceded that 'she was, probably, always quite impossible to handle'.[73]

In his final year as Leader Heath inadvertently gave Thatcher every opportunity to advance herself as a possible rival. Giving her the Environment portfolio between the two 1974 Elections guaranteed her maximum exposure in the presentation of the Party's most imaginative new policy proposals; putting her into the Treasury team at the crucial time in which the leadership contest was brewing gave her an opportunity to use her specialised knowledge as a tax barrister to good effect, and to shine where it was most needed, in the Commons Chamber where MPs were the only real audience; Carr had asked for a second shadow minister for his Treasury team, but was amazed when the choice fell on Thatcher, recognising exactly the threat that the Leader had created to his own position. Just as Heath had done in 1965, Carr assembled a formidable team to fight Denis Healey's budget, nine of them going on to join the Thatcher Cabinet, but the limelight was stolen from Carr by Thatcher herself, who was more often to be found in colloquy with Joseph than with Carr himself. She was scornfully dubbed by Denis Healey 'the La Pasionara of Privilege', an epithet that was as useful to her on her own side as being called 'the iron lady' by the Soviet leader a few years later. She was particularly noticed for a blistering and highly offensive speech attacking the Chancellor of the Exchequer, an attack which set the Tory benches cheering; the *Daily Telegraph*'s parliamentary reporter noted with satisfaction that they had cheered 'from genuine enthusiasm rather than the hopes of distant knighthoods or peerages'. As she told Cecil Parkinson about this very speech, 'in parliament, it's not what you say but the way you say it', a doctrine that was about as far from Heath's concept of a parliamentary performance as it was possible to go. In 1975 Conservative MPs were looking as much as anything for a fighting Opposition leader; as in 1965 they looked with an increased respect on a front-bencher who could be so rude to Labour Ministers. A few weeks earlier, Norman Tebbit had been thinking of supporting Geoffrey Howe for Leader, 'but I could not see in him the bite and sharp cutting edge needed to scythe down Harold Wilson'. With such priorities in his mind, it is hardly surprising that he now joined the Thatcher campaign. Nicholas Ridley remembered that 'in 1974 the Conservative Party had lost its way; it was beaten and humiliated.

[73] Rawlinson, *Price Too High*, 246, 248; shadow cabinet seating, 2 Apr. 1974 and order of precedence, Nov. 1974, LCC papers.

Here was a senior figure who didn't seem beaten at all; she exuded confidence and certainty. She made a lot of converts.' From among her later critics, Francis Pym put it in much the same way: 'amidst the shambles and doubts of that time, here was one person who could articulate a point of view with conviction.' Patrick Cosgrave argued a fortnight before the ballot that

> it is the conviction that she stands for something recognisable as Conservatism which has gained so much much support for her in recent weeks, not merely on the right of the party but in the solid centre, and among the ranks of the more senior and experienced backbenchers.

Even when allowance is made for tactical voting in her favour on the first ballot, the sheer number of votes she received (with practically no *front*-bench support) confirms the accuracy of this diagnosis. As in so many Party crises – 1922 and 1940 being obvious examples – it was the plumping of much of the solid centre for Thatcher that made her challenge so formidable.[74]

The tide was not running all one way. Peter Walker had recently warned against 'retreating into the bunkers and bolt-holes of narrow middle-class politics'. Ian Gilmour joked that if Thatcher were elected, 'we would all have to take refuge in our clubs', but argued seriously that a Thatcher-led Party would be a 'permanent opposition, a class-based rump'; in a vein that satirised Thatcher's surburban political identity as the Member for Finchley, he also warned that Conservatives must not 'retire behind a privet hedge into a world of narrow class interests and selfish concerns'. Heath himself argued that there was a danger of the Party deteriorating into a middle-class protection society, a claim given some substance by the formation by her supporter John Gorst of a Middle Class Alliance. Thatcher was adept at the deflection of such attacks; when asked on television how someone with her accent and manner would be able to win back the Tory votes lost in the North, she replied that 'it wasn't I who lost them, except by being a member of Mr. Heath's administration and bearing the same responsibility as he does'. When Walker publicised the fact that Thatcher had hoarded food during the miners' strike, the whole idea backfired; it seemed that Heath's followers were getting desperate, and in any case, if the story were true, then as Jim Prior put it, 'most of us thought this seemed an eminently sensible thing for her to have done'. The incident did though allow the Thatcher camp to claim that dirty tricks were being used against her, and to add the claim that Central Office had also been stirred up against her by Michael Wolff. The *News of the World* reported on 26 January that Wolff was conducting a purge of 'the old faithfuls' at Central Office to ensure even greater loyalty to Heath there. [75]

[74] Parkinson, *Right at the Centre*, 127; Cockerell, *Live from Number Ten*, 213; Baker, *Turbulent Years*, 42; Tebbit, *Upwardly Mobile*, 177; Ridley, *My Style of Government*, 8–9; Pym, *Politics of Consent*, 5; *Spectator*, 18 Jan. 1975; interview with Lord Carr.
[75] Critchley, *Bag of Boiled Sweets*, 143; Halcrow, *Joseph*, 91; Ranelagh, *Thatcher's People*, 143; Cockerell, *Live from Number Ten*, 216; Prior, *Balance of Power*, 100; Behrens, *Heath to Thatcher*, 40; Central Office file, CCO 500/32/23.

The official Heath campaign was more confident but equally ineffective. Peter Walker, who had run such a skilled campaign for Heath in 1965, was asked to stand back, on the principle that having ex-Ministers running the Leader's campaign would seem like a panic measure. In the hands of Heath's PPSs, Baker and Kitson, his campaign managed to be complacent and over-aggressive at the same time, mainly because they just could not believe that their master might be unseated by such an inexperienced woman candidate. Campaigners for incumbents always have difficulty in this type of contest, as Thatcher was to find in 1990, and Maudling (who as Deputy Leader was virtually the incumbent) had done in 1965. MPs seeking future preferment would pledge their support to be on the safe side, whatever their actual intentions, and bullying could only antagonise them. As Norman Tebbit put it, 'Ted Heath's friends . . . too easily fell into the trap of putting junior colleagues into a position where answers were given to please rather than to inform'. By comparison, the quiet observations of the Thatcher team were not even always visible; Kenneth Clarke did not even know that he had been sounded and written off as an unconvertible Heathite. The campaign also failed to turn to good effect the outside support that Heath still enjoyed; a survey in October had found that most constituency chairmen wanted him to stay on; a poll in November found that he was still backed by more than half of Tory voters and another late in January found that 70 per cent of Conservatives preferred him to Thatcher; the National Union's soundings of constituency opinion came down strongly in his favour, as did the Conservative peers. But none of these people had votes, and the Heath campaign signally failed to canvass effectively those who did. Taking out a newspaper advertisement in the name of 'The Friends of Ted Heath', which urged supporters to write in to their MP, was a traditional US practice, but much resented by backbenchers as an attempted act of coercion. Heath's quoted determination to stay on, however many ballots it took to get him re-elected, seemed like another coercive act. Nor were the attempts to involve Heath himself very effective; it just did not work to have him suddenly appearing in the lobbies, full of joviality after years of neglect, and he was not happy with the genial role that such campaigning needed; after a dinner for potential supporters, a Heath supporter concluded his letter of thanks with the suggestion that 'perhaps it would be better if you just let us get on with it, without actually producing the leader'. Kenneth Baker recalled that when MPs were invited to meet Heath, so that he could talk them round, 'it was rather like being summoned to the Head-master's study . . . it was rather uncomfortable, and the sooner it was over the better'. In a *Daily Telegraph* article written to explain his idea of the Party's future, he continued to stress in very general terms the old themes of moderation, balance and national unity, on which the Party had *lost* in 1974, whereas Thatcher used her equivalent opportunity to convey the fact that she at least wanted to do something *different*.[76]

Thatcher's campaign deployed the skills that the Heath campaign had shown in 1965 – and Michael Heseltine's was to have in 1990. Her agent in Finchley loyally told *The Times* that local supporters all wanted her to be Leader, and added for good measure a sharp attack on Heath's judgement for calling the February Election at the wrong time and then for wrecking Party morale in October with talk of coalitions: 'that sort of offer smacks of defeatism, it is not being positive. The grass roots Tory wants something more positive than that.' The candidate used her own opportunities expertly to rally those who just felt that something different should be done. She had often been seen around the lobbies and cafeterias of the Commons, at least since February 1974, so her discreet campaigning now drew less attention than Heath's was bound to do. To her Finchley constituents, but with a different audience in mind, she wrote in a published letter that, because previous Tory Governments had not been tough enough in limiting state power, 'Britain is now set on a course towards inevitable socialist mediocrity. That course must not only be halted. It must be reversed.' This was, she explained, because the Heath Government had not listened sufficiently to its supporters (a popular belief among even those Conservatives who did not share Thatcher's economic beliefs), and she pledged to do things differently in future. In the *Daily Telegraph*, she mounted an even more direct attack on Heath's 'failure' by pointing out his inability to explain away election defeats. 'To deny that we failed the people is futile, as well as arrogant. Successful Governments win elections. So do parties with broadly acceptable policies. We lost.' This all focused attention on the need-for-a-change-in-order-to-win theme. She admitted the failure and felt that 'one of the reasons for our electoral failure is that people believe that too many Conservatives have become socialists already'. On television on the day before the first ballot, a profile by Granada's *World in Action* showed a sharp-edged campaigner who knew her own mind and was a born fighter, a performance much lauded in the press and cheered by MPs crowded around television sets in the Commons. For those looking to replace Heath with a better communicator, she suddenly seemed to be rather a good bet.[77]

Alongside this public campaigning went a more subtle and even devious canvass for votes. When Airey Neave came into her camp, a month before the ballot, he brought with him fifteen or twenty votes that had previously

[76] Walker, *Staying Power*, 128; Behrens, *Heath to Thatcher*, 40; Tebbit, *Upwardly Mobile*, 179; Malcolm Balen, *Kenneth Clarke* (1994), 95; Baker, *Turbulent Years*, 44; Campbell, *Heath*, 659, 667, 669–72.

[77] Fowler, *Ministers Decide*, 3; Central Office Chairman's department file, CCO, 500/32/23; Russel, *Conservative Party*, 15; Behrens, *Heath to Thatcher*, 39; Whitehead, *Writing on the Wall*, 328; Cockerell, *Live from Number Ten*, 217; Campbell, *Heath*, 670–1.

been committed to du Cann, extensive contacts built up in preparation for any anti-Heath campaign, and a burning hatred of Heath himself occasioned by a slight during Heath's days as Chief Whip. Some who came over to Thatcher at this time, like Nigel Fisher, committed themselves only to vote for her on the first ballot, in order to get rid of Heath, but reserved their right to put their support elsewhere if other candidates were then to emerge. Neave capitalised brilliantly on the factor that this highlighted: the only way to make other candidates available was for Heath not to win first time round, and the only way to achieve this was for people who did not like Heath to vote for Thatcher. (A third candidate, Hugh Fraser, representing the more traditional, misogynist right, was never thought likely to get more than a handful of votes.) Michael Alison found on 7 February that some Barkston Ash Conservatives feared that Thatcher was too much associated with the suburban south east, and others thought her too right wing; their MP assured the latter that she was 'by no means a right-winger and would seek to unify the Party'; but his chief response was to explain that there would anyway be a clear majority of MPs against Heath and to review the alternatives: Joseph had 'neither the right temperament nor the stamina to stand the strain' but Thatcher was 'a tough debater in the House, able to hold her own against anyone, and a woman with a man's mind'; however, the clinching argument was clearly that 'she was the only one who had the courage to come forward and challenge Mr. Heath'. Since the Barkston Ash Tories also wanted Heath to go, they accepted Alison's conclusion. This was a widespread process of reasoning, but what seems to have been particularly effective in promoting it was Neave's black propaganda as campaigning drew to a close. Thatcher was attracting enough votes to do well, but not necessarily enough to win. Thus, while the Heath campaigners exaggerated their optimism in order to make their candidate's victory look inevitable, Neave took the opposite tack, telling enquirers that she was doing fairly well but not enough to win. While he himself put her vote at about 120, he was telling others that it would be about 70. Cecil Parkinson was deputed by Neave to tell the Chief Whip that Heath would win and that he should prepare to give Thatcher a major job to match her new status. Intelligence of this sort reverberated around the lobbies – and was meant to – and forced those who had reluctantly decided to vote for Heath, but did not want him to be able to claim an encouraging victory, to re-examine their position. It seems that the tactic persuaded a number to switch to Thatcher at the last moment to stop Heath winning outright. Norman Tebbit, for example, remembered that he and John Nott had persuaded Michael Heseltine, a Whitelaw supporter, to back Thatcher on the first ballot because that was the only way to have a second ballot in which Whitelaw could stand. The fact that Julian Critchley's insider biography of Heseltine states unequivocally that he actually voted for Heath is a useful reminder that, after all the lobbying was over, the vote was secret. There must therefore remain much supposition about what actually happened and who voted for whom.[78]

Since most newspapers had come down for Heath and none for Thatcher, and since both campaign teams had sought for their own reasons to tell the world that Heath was winning, the actual result was a sensation. Heath was advised by Kitson that he would get at least 129 votes, and that 17 more were good hopes; the final prediction was 125–30, but Peter Walker was said to have put it as high as 138–44. Neither of these scores would have put him over both of the thresholds needed for victory under the new rules, and even the more optimistic prediction would imply that nearly half of all Conservative MPs had refused to vote for him, which would surely have necessitated his early retirement after a decent interval. In the event, Thatcher led the poll with 130 votes out of 277 Conservative MPs; Heath had 119 and Fraser 16; five MPs spoiled their ballot papers and six abstained or were absent – not necessarily a deliberate act, since a delayed train meant that Jim Prior was one of them. Reactions to the result were, to say the least, mixed. A Party Vice Chairman was reported as having said, 'My God! The bitch has won!' and Reginald Maudling was seen by Kenneth Baker, 'uncharacteristically rushing down the corridor and muttering, "The Party's taken leave of its senses. This is a black day".' On the other side of the House, Barbara Castle told her diary that she 'felt a sneaking feminist pleasure. Damn it, that lass *deserves* to win. Her cool and competent handling of the cheaper mortgages issue in the last election campaign gave us our only moment of real anxiety. All right, it was dishonest as a policy, but she dealt with it like a professional.' Privately Heath raged that, 'They are absolutely mad to get rid of me, absolutely mad', but in public he was dignified and equally professional. Discounting the arithmetical possibility that he could rally all those MPs who had not voted for Thatcher – he would have needed twenty more votes from the twenty-seven who had voted for neither Thatcher nor himself in order to win the second ballot – he announced his immediate withdrawal from the contest. He also made it clear that he would take neither a peerage nor a European job but stay in the Commons, adding in ominously Gaullist tones, 'I'm in reserve'. Robert Carr became acting Leader until a successor had been elected. Just how unexpected the result had been emerges from the fact that Central Office had made no plans at all to deal with enquiries on the evening of the ballot, since they did not expect much press interest in Heath's re-election. In the event, as the Head of Administration minuted on the next day, 'until about 0300 hours on the night of 4/5 February the telephone was ringing continuously. Many of the calls were for the press office. Our (Polish) night-watchman obviously could not cope adequately.'[79]

There was now a panic among those who had backed Heath and wanted to continue with his policies. There would be only a week to the second ballot, and Thatcher was now clearly the front-runner who needed only nine more votes to win; those that had gone to the other right-wing candidate Fraser would easily be enough. She had also acquired great credit simply by having forced the Party into the decision it had now taken, to get rid of Heath; the votes on the first ballot proved to MPs that without her determination they would have taken a decision that most of them did not actually want. Thatcher therefore now had a broader base of support, and other candidates looked like the threat to Party unity; a *Daily Telegraph* editorial almost suggested that there was something improper in having a second ballot at all: 'A whole crowd of faint hearts left it to a courageous and able woman. If they ganged up to deny her her just reward it would smell.' Whitelaw was the obvious alternative candidate now that his loyalty to Heath no longer held him back, but in the confusion of 5 February three others emerged as well, Prior, Howe and Peyton. All of these were to an extent standing in each other's way, but all were laying down markers for the future. Hugo Young argued that the standing of Prior as well as Whitelaw proves that they did not see yet Thatcher as an ideological enemy, since otherwise they would not have risked splitting Whitelaw's vote, but this surely underestimates their lack of clear thinking in decisions made in a hurry after the shock of the first ballot result. In any case, though they recognised her ideological position well enough, the Heathites still believed that they would be able to talk her round once she had the responsibility, and that office would in itself tame her – as many well-informed political commentators continued to believe right up to 1981. The 'Cambridge mafia' of Clarke, Fowler and Brittan were instrumental in persuading Howe to stand, seeing in it little chance of stopping Thatcher but feeling that Howe could be (in Clarke's words) 'the intelligent man's abstention', since 'he combined right-wing economics with left-wing social policy, the old Bow Group combination'. There was a scramble for public attention by the four new candidates, a scramble that had to be undignified if they were to attract notice in just a few days from a standing start. John Ranelagh has suggested that for the first ballot Heath had been caught with his planes on the ground; if this was so, then the new candidates never even got their own planes off the drawing board. Thatcher on the other hand had all the velocity needed, even though many of those who had voted for her on the first ballot had not actually wanted her to win at that time. Barbara Castle, by 5 February

---

[79] Campbell, *Heath*, 672–5; Ranelagh, *Thatcher's People*, ix; Baker, *Turbulent Years*, 44; Barbara Castle, *The Barbara Castle Diaries, 1964–1976* (1990), 557; Money, *Margaret Thatcher*, 30; Central Office Chairman's department file, CCO 500/32/23.

a real Thatcher admirer, noted 'how many brave warriors have crept out of hiding to rush to climb on the second ballot bandwagon! Margaret looks the epitome of cool courage compared with them.' Whispering the question, she asked a Tory backbencher, Stephen MacAdden, whether he had voted for Thatcher, and he replied *loudly* that he had. When Castle said, 'I think she might win', he replied 'I am sure she will.' The Thatcher campaign now had all the confidence.[80]

Over the week-end before the second ballot the new candidates strove to impress for the television cameras, Whitelaw in the unconvincing pose of a man who did his own washing up. Thatcher, on the other hand, having established her lead, now almost withdrew from the hurly-burly. She was booked to address the YC Conference at Eastbourne, and used the occasion for another cheer-leading speech, calling for 'workers not shirkers', and for liberty without licence. But she declined to appear on a BBC television *Panorama* programme to be broadcast on the evening before the second ballot; the four male candidates were left to appear as fractious outsiders while the 'incumbent' stood aloof. Her growing status as effective incumbent after the first ballot was also indicated in the support for her in the soundings taken by the National Union this time. When the press identified him as a Howe supporter, Norman Fowler found his Sutton Coldfield constituents keen to tell him that they supported Thatcher, where a week earlier they had backed Heath. This dramatic rise in Thatcher's support among Party activists was a common pattern; in Bury St Edmunds, the first ballot consultation was even between Thatcher and Heath, the second overwhelmingly for Thatcher; in Totnes a vote of twelve to six for Heath over Thatcher now became eight to six for Thatcher over Whitelaw; on the first round in Brentford and Isleworth, Thatcher had only one supporter out of twenty-five, but on the second round eleven votes to Whitelaw's fifteen; in Denbigh, a wider consultation had found more than two-thirds for Heath on the first round, but Thatcher and Whitelaw tied on the second; other constituency associations backing Thatcher by the second ballot were Burton upon Trent, Fife Central and Upminster; and in the whole South East Area, the natural heartland of Selsdon Man, voting first time was three-quarters for Heath, but at the second time of asking Thatcher was backed by twenty-eight constituencies, with only six for Whitelaw, and no constituency opting clearly for anyone else; the Area chairman in the East reported that opinion in his constituencies had 'had a pronounced effect on the first ballot, and on the second it was overwhelming', in support of Thatcher. Where Thatcher was already preferred, her support rose further; in Truro the vote on 31 January was eleven for Thatcher against three for Heath, but on 7 February she had sixteen votes against one for Whitelaw and one for Howe. By early February, quite staggeringly, Thatcher, who was only tenth in precedence in the shadow cabinet, had made herself the establishment candidate. Reviewing her campaign afterwards, William Deedes (shortly to be *Private Eye*'s [Dear] 'Bill' as a result of Thatcher's election) noted that her advisers alone had spotted that 'the Mark II ballot put everyone into a different ball game'.

> Mrs. Thatcher not only advertised herself, but did so professionally. Both will take it as a compliment if one says that Mrs. Thatcher has forgotten more about RADA than Mr. Whitelaw ever wished to learn – and as if to reassure us on that point he allowed himself to be caught, absurdly, scrubbing pots at the sink. 'As soon catch me on a golf course', observed Mrs. Thatcher later that week to the Young Conservatives. When on stage, she knows what every woman knows and male top Tories do not wish to find out . . . Tories cannot have it both ways. If they insist, as they have done for years, that star quality on television is essential for the Leader, then they must avoid muttering behind their hands that, when it proves successful it is vulgar. Perhaps it is vulgar. So at times was Disraeli. He is the only Tory leader from the past century who might have beaten Margaret Thatcher at her own game.[81]

The results of the second ballot on 11 February did not quite match up to such hype. Her vote among MPs rose only from 130 to 146, exactly the number who had voted either for her or for Fraser a week earlier. But that correspondence in the figures was misleading, for some who voted for her first time now went to Whitelaw (as they had always intended) and others switched directly from Heath on the first round to Thatcher on the second; this last group, including for example Norman St. John Stevas, were those whose transfer of support actually made Margaret Thatcher Leader. She had got seven more votes than were needed for a majority, and was well ahead of any other candidate, so she was declared elected under the new rules. Whitelaw scored seventy-nine, Prior and Howe nineteen each, and Peyton eleven; this time only two Tory MPs failed to cast valid votes. But if the second ballot was not overwhelming in its endorsement of Thatcher personally, Conservative MPs, now freed from the restraints of loyalty, rejected Heathite politics even more comprehensively than they had done a week earlier; Peyton and Howe represented like Thatcher reactions against Heath's incomes policies, so that all but a hundred MPs were voting for – or at least acquiescing in – a change from the way the Party had recently been led, more than two-thirds of the parliamentary party. Julian Critchley called this 'the peasant's revolt' because few of their betters had joined the rebellion. Of the front bench, only Thatcher, Joseph, St. John Stevas and Godber had apparently voted for her

81 Money, *Margaret Thatcher*, 31; Fowler, *Ministers Decide*, 15, 18; Bury St Edmunds CA minutes 31 Jan. and 18 Mar. 1975; Totnes CA, papers filed in minute book; Brentford and Isleworth CA, 3 and 10 Feb. 1975; Denbigh CA minutes, 6 Feb. 1975; West Fife UA minutes, 11 Feb. 1975; Burton upon Trent CA minutes, 1 and 8 Feb. 1975; Upminster branch minutes, 11 Feb. 1975; South East Area Council, papers for February 1975; Eastern Area Council, 26 Feb. 1975; Truro CA minutes, 7 Feb. 1975; *Crossbow*, Apr. 1975, 6.

to become Leader, though Howe was certainly a sympathiser with her politics. *Mutatis mutandis*, she was to be, as Harold Wilson more implausibly claimed of himself in 1963–64, 'a Bolshevik in a [Shadow] Cabinet of Tsarists'.[82]

How had this happened? Above all because on the first ballot the Party wanted to be rid of Heath, to have 'anyone but Ted', and she alone had forced it into the corner where that decision had to be taken. On the second ballot the alternative candidates were tainted with their cowardice (which had in fact been loyalty) a week earlier, and did not begin to approach the professionalism and determination with which she stretched out her hand for the crown. In that second week too, the idea of a woman Leader actually took hold of opinion as an exhilaratingly bold step forward that would show how modern the Party had become, much as the bold choices of Disraeli, Bonar Law and Heath himself had enlivened the Party on earlier occasions, and in similarly unlikely circumstances. As John Ranelagh has put it, 'The Parliamentary Party, surprised by what it had done on the first ballot, was carried away by the thrill of the new.' Was this then a vote for 'Thatcherism'? Clearly not, if by 'Thatcherism' is meant all that that concept had come to mean by and after 1981, but it seems clear enough that a political manner and style that were sharply different from Heath's, in content of policy as well as in rhetoric, was one of the factors that pulled in the vote on the first ballot, and then held it on the second, so making Thatcher the Leader. She told MPs what to expect, and it was scarcely her fault if so many did not believe that she meant it.[83]

The formal election of Margaret Thatcher as Leader of the Party took place a week later, the motion proposed in the traditional form by politicians who had opposed the decision just made, in this case Hailsham and Whitelaw. Party unity in practice was less easy to achieve. Several MPs noticed the picture of the frail (looking) woman Leader dwarfed by the Party's male grandees on the platform, and left the meeting with an emotional loyalty to the new regime. Whitelaw rapidly came to the conclusion that he owed it to the Party to agree to serve under her and accepted her invitation to become her deputy, and all the other candidates on the second ballot followed him in accepting places in the shadow cabinet. This loyalty to the Party by Whitelaw, Carrington, Pym, Maudling and Prior, all men who had severe reservations about the turn of events and none of whom but Whitelaw were ever close to the new Leader, did much to restore unity at the top. Peter Walker was less easily accommodated, and his removal from the front bench by Thatcher probably only prevented his resignation; over the next few years Walker wrote and worked to expose what he saw as the fallacies of the monetarist position, and became the chief advocate of the Heathite 'government over the water' (as *Crossbow* lampooned it in deference to Heath's interest in sailing). Robert Carr had wanted to return

---

[82] Ranelagh, *Thatcher's People*, 148; St John Stevas, *The Two Cities*, 17.
[83] Ranelagh, *Thatcher's People*, 149.

to industry but had been persuaded by Whitelaw that they must all offer Thatcher their services so as to minimise any appearance of a Party split, only for him to be then sacked by Thatcher herself; he therefore left the shadow cabinet too and became an occasional critic from the outside. On the other hand, Thatcher reinstated Maude, brought back into the collective leadership from the pre-Heath period Soames and Thorneycroft, and paid attention to du Cann. These and similar changes meant, with some irony, that the Grantham housewife's accession to the leadership coincided with the largest proportion of old Etonians and top public school men on a Tory front bench since Home had been Prime Minister in 1963; the social revolution would have to wait until Thatcher had a Prime Minister's patronage at her disposal.[84]

But if she had to live mainly with the spokesmen she inherited, in other ways Thatcher used the powers of patronage she had immediately at her disposal to strengthen her position, an example that ought to have indicated to her opponents the attitude that she was likely to take when in due course she controlled government appointments too. The new seating plan for shadow cabinet meetings had Thatcher seated with Whitelaw, Joseph, Thorneycroft and Howe around her, and with men like Prior exiled to the far corners from which she herself had just come. In the organisation, there was an abrupt clear-out of Heath supporters inserted in the previous year. Whitelaw wanted to leave Central Office where he had not been happy, but the choice of Thorneycroft to succeed him was extremely imaginative, for he was a man who owed nothing to Heath and whose 1958 resignation from the Treasury even allowed him to be claimed as having paternity rights to Conservative monetarism; he was also to be the most avuncular and long-serving presence at Central Office since Woolton, a Party Chairman who would prove extremely popular with the constituencies, at least partly because he slowed down or abandoned the drastic reforms that Carrington had tried to push through. One of his first acts was the summary dismissal of Michael Wolff, whose support for Heath had made him deeply unpopular in the rival camp; Michael Fraser's retirement later in the year snapped another cord of continuity with the recent as well as the more distant past at Central Office; Sara Morrison, who had, said the *Evening Standard*, 'downright chilly relations' with Thatcher, also departed. Chris Patten survived as Director of the Research Department, but the CRD's activities were treated with some suspicion as a result, and in 1979 its independent role came to an end with a merger into Central Office. In any case, its political direction changed straightaway in 1975 when Gilmour was sacked as chairman of the ACP and CRD, and replaced by Joseph in one job and Maude in the other. The levers of Party power were by the middle of

[84] Critchley, *Bag of Boiled Sweets*, 146; Whitelaw, *Memoirs*, 143; Prior, *Balance of Power*, 103; Walker, *Staying Power*, 132; Ranelagh, *Thatcher's People*, 154–7; *Crossbow*, Apr. 1975, 15 and Spring 1977, 12; Phillips and Wilson, 'The Conservative Party from Macmillan to Thatcher', in Nugent and King, *The British Right*, 36; Howe, *Conflict of Loyalty*, 94; interview with Lord Carr.

1975 firmly in the hands of those who had been critics until February. In place of economic policy formulation at shadow cabinet, under Heath's personal guidance, Joseph reported to Thatcher on 4 March that he and Howe would jointly chair 'the Economic and Social Strategy Committee which you and I thought should be the centre of the policy-making organisation'. To Howe, the new Leader explained that the three of them would need to work closely together, 'for we're the ones who have the same idea of where we need to go'.[85]

Where did Thatcher herself see her election leading the Party? Mainly, she responded to her elevation with the same mixture of conviction and presentational pragmatism that had projected her upwards so spectacularly over the previous eleven months and would help to sustain her at the top for the next fifteen years. She explained to a BBC television audience, tears in her eyes, that 'with my predecessors, Edward Heath, Sir Alec Douglas-Home, Harold Macmillan, Anthony Eden, then of course the great Winston, it is like a dream. Wouldn't you think so? I almost wept when they told me. I did weep.' With press photographers, she revolved obediently so that each could take a good picture from their various angles, but finished the session with the words, 'And now I am going to take a turn to the right, which is very appropriate'. In private she could be less guarded, less coy. Listening to a briefing, on traditional 'middle way' lines, from a CRD staffer a few weeks later, she could barely contain her impatience; eventually she drew out of her handbag Hayek's *The Constitution of Liberty* and slammed it down on the table with the declaration, 'This is what we believe'.[86]

Back on 4 February, Tony Benn had received the news of the first ballot result with mixed feelings:

> So Heath resigned and that's the end of him. Very sad in a way. Politics is a brutal business and I think we would be foolish to suppose that Mrs. Thatcher won't be a formidable leader; and Harold [Wilson] couldn't pour scorn on a woman because the people wouldn't have it. I think the quality of debate will be raised because the Tory Party will be driven to the right and there will be a real choice being offered to the electorate.

Her own statement of the immediate situation was presented at the formal meeting that elected her as Leader of the Party: there must be determined policies to deal with such threats as inflation, and there must be a clear vision of the Britain that the Conservatives wanted to build; 'but if we need purpose and vision, we also need a third thing and that is presentation. It is no good having a first class product unless people know about it. And they won't know about it unless we tell them.' Ernle Money noted what

---

[85] Ball, 'Central and Regional Structures', 178; Blake, *Conservative Party*, 327; Central Office Chairman's department file, CCO 500/32/23; Ramsden, *Making of Conservative Party Policy*, 308; LCC papers; Howe, *Conflict of Loyalty*, 94.

[86] Cockerell, *Live from Number Ten*, 219; Ranelagh, *Thatcher's People*, ix.

happened when a week later Harold Wilson first faced Margaret Thatcher across the despatch box. 'After offering his congratulations he went on to say: "From a study of her speeches I have formed the opinion that there may be a deep gulf between the Right Honourable Lady and myself." This remark was greeted with Conservative cheers.' It is important to remember that in choosing Thatcher over Heath as a strong-minded person who seemed to know what she wanted, the Conservatives were still, as ever since 1963, trying to find an electorally successful way of reacting to Harold Wilson's methods and manner as leader of the Labour Party. They certainly did not foresee that Wilson would retire a year later but that Thatcher would be there for a generation.[87]

What was very widely felt was that the decision that the Party had made was a rather important one. Although he subsequently came to feel that 'she gave us the courage of our convictions', Kenneth Clarke's immediate reaction to Margaret Thatcher's election in 1975 was that, 'the reaction starts here'. On the other wing of the Party, joy was more or less unconfined for much the same reason. The *Daily Telegraph* and most other Conservative papers reacted to Thatcher's election with great enthusiasm, and the *Spectator* which had campaigned hard against Heath and latterly for Thatcher to succeed him, was especially euphoric. Its editorial of 15 February urged Mrs Thatcher to campaign in the North and in Scotland to win back lost votes, and to set in train early work on economic policy, but,

> though the devising of an economic policy must be the first charge, everything will come far better, and be more readily accepted, from a leader who is obviously and sincerely a thinking and believing Conservative, who knows what has gone wrong, and who knows how to put it right. The party could hardly have chosen better. The quarrels of the recent past can now be put behind it, and a new future can begin.[88]

The *Telegraph*, noting that Mrs Thatcher was 'a bonny fighter', who 'believes in the ethic of hard work and big rewards of success', also admired the fact that 'she owes nothing to inherited wealth or privilege'. Since this exempted her from middle-class guilt, Mrs Thatcher ought therefore to be able to exert a strong moral lead on the Conservative Party in its battle with socialism. 'If she does so, her accession to the leadership could mark a sea-change in the whole character of the party political debate in this country.'[88]

[87] Tony Benn, *Against the Tide: Diaries 1973–1976* (1990), 311; Money, *Margaret Thatcher*, 33–4.
[88] Balen, *Clarke*, 97, 99; *Spectator*, 15 Feb. 1975; *Daily Telegraph*, 12 Feb. 1975.

Bibliography

Primary sources (private papers)

Avon MSS: diaries and papers of Sir Anthony Eden, Earl of Avon, Library of Birmingham University

Boyle MSS: papers of Sir Edward Boyle Bt, University of Leeds

Butler MSS: papers of R.A. Butler, Lord Butler of Saffron Walden, Trinity College, Cambridge

Cilcennin MSS: papers of J.P.L. Thomas, Viscount Cilcennin, Carmarthenshire County Record Office

Hailes MSS: papers of Patrick Buchan-Hepburn, Lord Hailes, Churchill College, Cambridge

Kilmuir MSS: papers of David Maxwell Fyfe, Earl of Kilmuir, Churchill College, Cambridge

Margesson MSS: papers of David Margesson, Viscount Margesson, Churchill College, Cambridge

Swinton MSS: papers of Philip Cunliffe-Lister, Earl of Swinton, Churchill College, Cambridge

Woolton MSS: diary and papers of Frederick Marquis, Earl of Woolton, Bodleian Library, Oxford

Conservative Party papers (parliamentary)

Minute Books of the 1922 Committee, 1950–75, Bodleian Library, Oxford

Minute Books and associated papers of the Leader's Consultative Committee, 1964–70 and 1974–75, Bodleian Library, Oxford

Conservative Party papers (National Union)

Party Conference agendas, minutes, and reports of meetings with Leaders to discuss resolutions, Bodleian Library, Oxford

Central Council agendas and minutes, Bodleian Library, Oxford

Executive Committee minutes and secretary's notes, Bodleian Library, Oxford, and at Conservative Central Office

General Purposes Committee, secretary's notes, Bodleian Library, Oxford

Minutes of ad hoc National Union Committees, Bodleian Library, Oxford

Conservative Party papers (minute books of Area Organisations, seen at Area Offices)

London Conservative Union to 1963, and Greater London Area from 1963; Home Counties South East Area to 1963, and South Eastern Area from 1963; Eastern Area; West Midlands Area; East Midlands Area; North West Area; Yorkshire Area; Northern Area; Wessex Area; Western Area; Wales and Monmouthshire Area

Conservative Party papers (Local Organisations, seen at Constituency Office unless otherwise noted, listed in Conservative Party Areas as at 1965)

Battersea South Conservative Association (CA), Brentford and Chiswick CA, Dulwich CA, Hampstead CA, Harrow West CA, Holborn and St Pancras South CA, Ilford CA, Islington South West CA, Ruislip Northwood CA, St Marylebone CA, Shoreditch and Finsbury CA, Twickenham CA, Upminster Branch, Uxbridge CA, Wanstead and Woodford CA (at the Essex County Record Office)

Ashford CA, Brighton Kemptown CA, Gravesend CA (at the Kent County Record Office), Lewes CA, Guildford CA, Maidstone CA (at the Kent County Record Office), Reigate and Banstead CA (at the Surrey County Record Office)

South Bedfordshire CA, Bury St Edmunds CA, Cambridgeshire CA, Hemel Hempstead CA, King's Lynn CA, Saffron Walden CA

Birmingham CA, Burton upon Trent CA, Coventry North East CA, Coventry North West CA, Coventry South CA, Lichfield and Tamworth CA, Rugby CA, Shrewsbury CA, Solihull CA, Walsall South CA, Warwick and Leamington CA

Derby North CA, Derbyshire West CA (at the Derbyshire County Record Office), High Peak CA, Horncastle CA, Kettering CA, Newark CA, City of Nottingham CA

Accrington CA, Bolton West CA, Liverpool Constitutional Association, City of Manchester CA, Manchester Cheetham CA, Manchester Exchange CA, Manchester Wythenshawe CA, Nelson and Colne CA, Newton le Willows CA, North Fylde CA, Southport CA, Wirral CA

Barkston Ash CA, City of Bradford CA, Bradford West CA, City of Leeds CA, Leeds North West CA, Pontefract CA, Ripon CA, Sheffield Hallam CA, York CA

Darlington CA, Easington CA, Hexham CA, Middlesbrough West CA, City of Newcastle upon Tyne CA, Tynemouth CA, Workington CA

Aylesbury CA, Basingstoke CA, Newbury CA (at the Berkshire County Record Office), Oxford CA, Swindon CA

Bath CA, City of Bristol CA, Bristol West CA, Cirencester and Tewkesbury CA, Cornwall North CA, Dorset West CA, Totnes CA, Truro CA

Barry CA, Cardiff South East CA, Denbigh CA (at the Clwyd County Record Office), Flint East CA, Monmouth CA

Aberdeen South Unionist Association (UA), Angus South UA, Dunbartonshire West UA, Edinburgh East UA, Edinburgh North UA, Fife West UA, Galloway UA, City of Glasgow UA, Glasgow Bridgeton UA, Glasgow Craigton UA, Glasgow Pollok UA, Glasgow Scotstoun UA, Kirkcaldy UA

Conservative Party papers (Central Office, at the Bodleian Library, Oxford)

CCO 1 series (constituency correspondence)
CCO 2 series (Area correspondence)
CCO 3 series (correspondence with outside organisations)
CCO 4 series (subject files)
CCO 20 series (Party Chairman's office files)
CCO 120 series (General Director's office files)
CCO 500 series (Chief Organisation Officer's files)

Party publications (various)

Conservative Agents' Journal
Crossbow
Notes on Current Politics and *Daily Notes*
National Society of Agents, *Annual Reports*

Secondary sources: books, theses and articles

All books cited were published in London unless stated otherwise.

Keith Alderman, 'Harold Macmillan's Night of the Long Knives', in *Contemporary Record*, vol. 6, no. 2 (1992), 243–65

Andrew Alexander, 'Reginald Maudling', in *Here Come the Tories*, eds T. Stacey and R. St Oswald, Tom Stacey (1970)

Andrew Alexander and Alan Watkins, *The Making of the Prime Minister, 1970*, Macdonald (1970)

David Alexander, 'Sentimental Journey or Selsdon Revisited', in *Crossbow*, June (1974), 37

Arthur Aughey, 'The Role of the Conservative Political Centre', *Hull Papers in Politics* (1981)

Kenneth Baker (ed.), *The Faber Book of Conservatism*, Faber (1993)

Kenneth Baker, *The Turbulent Years: My Life in Politics*, Faber (1993)

Malcolm Balen, *Kenneth Clarke*, Fourth Estate (1994)

Stuart Ball, 'The National and Regional Party Structure', in *Conservative Century: The Conservative Party since 1900*, eds A. Seldon and S. Ball, Oxford, OUP (1994)

Stuart Ball, 'Local Conservatism and the Evolution of Party Organisation', in *Conservative Century: The Conservative Party since 1900*, eds A. Seldon and S. Ball, Oxford, OUP (1994)

John Barnes and Richard Cockett, 'The Making of Party Policy', in *Conservative Century: The Conservative Party since 1900*, eds A. Seldon and S. Ball, Oxford, OUP (1994)

M.J. Barnett, *The Politics of Legislation: The Rent Act of 1957*, Weidenfeld and Nicolson (1969)

Alan Beattie, *English Party Politics, vol. II, 1906–1970*, Weidenfeld and Nicolson (1970)

Robert Behrens, *The Conservative Party from Heath to Thatcher*, Farnborough, Saxon House (1980)

Max Beloff, 'Reflections on the General Election of 1966', in *Government and Opposition*, vol. 1, no. 4 (1966), 529

Max Beloff, 'The Crisis and its Consequences for the British Conservative Party', in *Suez, 1956*, eds Roger Louis and Roger Owen, Oxford, OUP (1989)

Tony Benn, *Out of the Wilderness: Diaries 1963–1967*, Arrow (1988)

Tony Benn, *Office Without Power: Diaries 1968–1972*, Arrow (1989)

Tony Benn, *Against the Tide: Diaries 1973–1976*, Arrow (1990)

Alan Bennett, Peter Cook, Jonathan Miller and Dudley Moore, *The Complete Beyond The Fringe*, Methuen (1987)

M. Benney, A.P. Gray and R.H. Pear, *How People Vote: A Study of Electoral Behaviour in Greenwich*, Routledge and Kegan Paul (1956)

Humphry Berkeley, *Crossing the Floor*, Allen and Unwin (1972)

Hugh Berrington, 'The Conservative Party: Revolts and Pressures, 1955–1961', in *Political Quarterly*, vol. 32 (1961), 363

Reginald Bevins, *The Greasy Pole*, Hodder and Stoughton (1965)

John Biffen, 'Party Conference and Party Policy', in *Political Quarterly*, vol. 32 (1961), 257

John Biffen, 'The Conservative Party Today', in *The Conservative Opportunity*, ed. M. Wolff, Batsford (1965)

Tessa Blackstone and William Plowden, *Inside the Think Tank*, Heinemann (1988)

Robert Blake, 'Principles in Practice: The Absence of Emotion', in *Crossbow*, Jan. (1972) 8

Robert Blake, *The Conservative Party from Peel to Thatcher*, Faber (1985)

Jean Blondel, 'The Conservative Association and the Labour Party in Reading', in *Political Studies*, vol. 6 (1958), 101

Jean Blondel, *Voters, Parties and Leaders: The Social Fabric of British Politics*, Harmondsworth, Penguin (1963)

Vernon Bogdanor, 'Devolution', in *Conservative Party Politics*, ed. Zig Layton-Henry, Macmillan (1980)

Vernon Bogdanor, 'The Selection of the Party Leader', in *Conservative Century: The Conservative Party since 1900*, eds A. Seldon and S. Ball, Oxford, OUP (1994)

John Boyd-Carpenter, *Way of Life*, Sidgwick and Jackson (1980)

Nick Brittain, 'Britain's Image', in *Europe: The First Year*, Bow Group (1974)

Samuel Brittan, 'Some Thoughts on the Conservative Opposition', in *Political Quarterly*, vol. 39 (1968), 145

Samuel Brittan, *Steering the Economy*, Secker and Warburg (1969)

Jock Bruce-Gardyne, *Whatever Happened to the Quiet Revolution?*, Charles Knight (1974)

Jock Bruce-Gardyne, 'A Court in Exile', in *Crossbow*, Spring (1977), 12

P.W. Buck, *Amateurs and Professionals in British Politics, 1918–59*, University of Chicago Press (1963)

Martin Burch, 'Approaches to Leadership in Opposition: Edward Heath and Margaret Thatcher', in *Conservative Party Politics*, ed. Zig Layton-Henry, Macmillan (1980)

Martin Burch and Michael Moran, 'The Changing British Political Elite: MPs and Cabinet Ministers', in *Parliamentary Affairs*, vol. 38 (1985), 1

Simon Burgess and Geoffrey Alderman, 'The Centre for Policy Studies', in *Contemporary Record*, vol. 4 (1990), 14

D.E. Butler, *The Electoral System in Britain since 1918*, 2nd edn., Oxford, OUP (1963)

D.E. Butler, *British General Elections since 1945*, Oxford, Blackwell, 1989.

D.E. Butler and G. Butler, *British Political Facts, 1900–1986*, Macmillan (1986)

D.E. Butler and Dennis Kavanagh, *The British General Election of February 1974*, Macmillan (1974)

D.E. Butler and Dennis Kavanagh, *The British General Election of October 1974*, Macmillan (1975)

D.E. Butler and Dennis Kavanagh, *The British General Election of 1979*, Macmillan (1980)

D.E. Butler and Anthony King, *The British General Election of 1964*, Macmillan (1965)

D.E. Butler and Anthony King, *The British General Election of 1966*, Macmillan (1966)

D.E. Butler and Michael Pinto-Duschinsky, *The British General Election of 1970*, Macmillan (1971)

D.E. Butler and M. Pinto-Duschinsky, 'The Conservative Elite 1918–78: Does Unrepresentativeness Matter?' in *Conservative Party Politics*, ed. Zig Layton-Henry, Macmillan (1980)

D.E. Butler and Richard Rose, *The British General Election of 1959*, Macmillan (1960)

Lord Butler of Saffron Walden, *The Art of the Possible: The Memoirs of Lord Butler*, Hamish Hamilton (1971)

Lord Butler of Saffron Walden, *The Art of Memory: Friends in Perspective*, Hodder and Stoughton (1982)

John Campbell, *Edward Heath*, Cape (1993)

Lord Carrington, *Reflect on Things Past: The Memoirs of Lord Carrington*, Collins (1988)

Barbara Castle, *The Barbara Castle Diaries, 1964–1976*, Macmillan (1990)

Randolph Churchill, *The Fight for the Tory Leadership*, Mayflower (1964)

Alan Clarke, 'What's Wrong with the Tory Party?', in *Crossbow*, June (1974), 31

Ian Clarke, 'The Tory Party after Chelmer: Half a Reform is Better than None', in *Crossbow*, October (1973) 19

Michael Cockerell, *Live from Number Ten, the Inside Story of Prime Ministers and Television*, Faber (1988)

Richard Cockett, *Thinking the Unthinkable: Think Tanks and the Economic Counter-Revolution, 1931–1983*, HarperCollins (1994)

Richard Cockett, 'The Party, Publicity and the Media', in *Conservative Century: The Conservative Party since 1900*, eds A. Seldon and S. Ball, Oxford, OUP (1994)

Lord Coleraine, *For Conservatives Only*, Tom Stacey (1970)

Chris Cook and John Ramsden (eds), *By-Elections in British Politics*, Macmillan (1973)

Patrick Cosgrave, 'Heath as Prime Minister', in *Political Quarterly*, vol. 44 (1973), 435

Patrick Cosgrave, *R.A. Butler: An English Life*, Quartet (1981)

Mary Cotton, 'Sovereignty', in *Europe: The First Year*, Bow Group (1974)

Anthony Courtney, *Sailor in a Russian Frame*, Johnson (1968)

Maurice Cowling, 'The Present Position', in *Conservative Essays*, ed. M. Cowling, Cassell (1978)

F.W.S. Craig (ed.), *British General Election Manifestos, 1918–66*, Chichester, Political Reference Publications (1970)

F.W.S. Craig (ed.), *British Parliamentary Election Statistics, 1918–70*, Chichester, Political Reference Publications (1971)

F.W.S. Craig (ed.), *British Parliamentary Election Results, 1950–70*, Chichester, Political Reference Publications (1971)

F.W.S. Craig (ed.), *The Boundaries of Parliamentary Constituencies, 1885–1972*, Chichester, Political Reference Publications (1972)

Aidan Crawley, *Leap Before You Look*, Collins (1988)

Byron Criddle, 'Members of Parliament', in *Conservative Century: The Conservative Party since 1900*, eds A. Seldon and S. Ball, Oxford, OUP (1994)

Julian Critchley, 'The Intellectuals', in *Political Quarterly*, vol. 32 (1961), 267

Julian Critchley, 'Strains and Stresses in the Conservative Party', in *Political Quarterly*, vol. 44 (1973), 403

Julian Critchley, *Westminster Blues*, Futura (1986)

Julian Critchley, *Heseltine: The Unauthorised Biography*, Deutsch (1987)

Julian Critchley, *A Bag of Boiled Sweets: An Autobiography*, Faber (1994)

J.A. Cross, *Lord Swinton*, Oxford, OUP (1982)

Richard Crossman, *The Crossman Diaries, 1964–1970*, ed. Anthony Howard, Magnum, 1979

Christie Davies and Russell Lewis (eds), *The Reactionary Joke Book*, Wolfe (1973)

Nicholas Deakin (ed.), *Colour and the British Electorate, 1964*, Pall Mall Press (1965)

David Dean, 'Preservation or Renovation? The Dilemmas of Conservative Education Policy, 1955–1960', in *Twentieth Century British History*, vol. 3, no. 1 (1992), 3–31

William Deedes, 'Conflicts within the Conservative Party', in *Political Quarterly*, vol. 44 (1973), 391

William Deedes, 'No Reversing the Sundial', in *Crossbow*, April (1975), 6

John Dickie, *The Uncommon Commoner: A Study of Sir Alec Douglas-Home*, Pall Mall Press (1964)

Piers Dixon, 'Eden after Suez', in *Contemporary Record*, vol. 6 (1992), 178

Michael Dockrill, *British Defence Policy since 1945*, Oxford, Blackwell (1988)

Gerald Dorfman, *Wage Politics in Britain, 1945–1967*, Charles Knight (1974)

Gerald Dorfman, *Government Versus Trades Unionism in British Politics since 1968*, Macmillan (1979)

R.E. Dundas, 'Why the Scottish Tories are in a Mess', in *Crossbow*, June (1973), 17

Tony Durant, Marcus Fox, Cyril Taylor and Alan Walters, *No More Tick: A Conservative Solution to Inflation*, Bow Group (1974)

David Dutton, 'Living with Collusion: Anthony Eden and the Later History of the Suez Affair', in *Contemporary Record*, vol. 5 (1991), 201

David Dutton, 'Anticipating Maastricht: The Conservative Party and Britain's First Application to Join the European Community', in *Contemporary Record*, vol. 7 (1993), 522

Robert Eccleshall, *English Conservatism since the Restoration*, Unwin Hyman (1990)

Ruth Dudley Edwards, *The Pursuit of Reason: The Economist, 1843–1993*, Hamish Hamilton (1993)

Lord Egremont, *Wyndham and Children First*, Macmillan (1968)

Peter Emery, 'Bow Group Dawn', in *Crossbow*, Summer (1981), 5

Harold Evans, *Downing Street Diary: The Macmillan Years, 1957–63*, Hodder and Stoughton (1981)

B.J. Evans and A.J. Taylor, 'The Rise and Fall of Two-Party Electoral Co-operation', in *Political Studies*, vol. 23 (1984), 257

Arthur Fawcett, *Conservative Agent: A Study of the National Society of Conservative Agents*, Driffield, Yorkshire, NSA (1967)

Stephen Fay and Hugo Young, *The Fall of Heath*, Sunday Times (1976)

S.E. Finer, *The Changing British Party System*, Washington, DC, American Enterprise Institute (1980)

Nigel Fisher, *Iain Macleod*, Purnell (1973)

Nigel Fisher, *The Tory Leaders, their Struggle for Power*, Weidenfeld and Nicolson (1977)

Paul Foot, *The Politics of Harold Wilson*, Harmondsworth, Penguin (1968)

Norman Fowler, *Ministers Decide*, Chapman (1991)

R. Frasure and A. Kornberg, 'Constituency Agents and British Politics', in *British Journal of Political Science*, vol. 5 (1975), 459

David Frost and Ned Sherrin (eds), *That Was The Week That Was*, W.H. Allen (1968)

Andrew Gamble, *The Conservative Nation*, Routledge and Kegan Paul (1974)

Ian Gilmour, *The Body Politic*, Hutchinson (1969)

Ian Gilmour, *Inside Right*, Hutchinson (1977)

Ian Gilmour, Review of Alistair Horne's *Macmillan, 1957–1986*, in *London Review of Books*, 27 July (1989)

R.S. Goldstone, 'Patronage in British Government', in *Parliamentary Affairs*, vol. 30 (1977), 80

Philip Goodhart, *The 1922: The Story of the 1922 Committee*, Macmillan (1973)

W. Gore Allen, *The Reluctant Politician: Derick Heathcoat Amory*, Christopher Johnson (1958)

J.R. Greenwood, 'Promoting Working Class Candidates', in *Parliamentary Affairs*, vol. 41 (1988), 456

John Selwyn Gummer, 'The Social Services', in *Political Quarterly*, vol. 44 (1973), 425

Lord Hailsham, *The Door Wherein I Went*, Collins (1975)

Lord Hailsham, *A Sparrow's Flight: Memoirs*, Collins (1990)

Morrison Halcrow, *Keith Joseph: A Single Mind*, Macmillan (1989)

Max Hanna, 'Where are the Coloured Tories?', in *Crossbow*, May (1973), 20

Michael Harrington, 'Sir Keith Joseph', in *Here Come the Tories*, eds T. Stacey and R. St. Oswald, Tom Stacey (1970).

Nigel Harris, *Competition and the Corporate Society: British Conservatives, the State and Industry, 1945–64*, Methuen (1972)

Brian Harrison, 'Mrs. Thatcher and the Intellectuals', in *Twentieth Century British History*, vol. 5, no. 2 (1994), 206

Ian Harvey, *To Fall Like Lucifer*, Sidgwick and Jackson (1971)

Denis Healey, *The Time of My Life*, Michael Joseph (1989)

Edward Heath, *The Great Divide in British Politics, Speeches*, CPC (1966)

Peter Hennessy, *Cabinet*, Oxford, Blackwell (1986)

Peter Hennessy, *Whitehall*, Fontana (1990)

Charles Hill, *Both Sides of the Hill*, Heinemann (1964)

Judy Hillman and Peter Clarke, *Geoffrey Howe: Quiet Revolutionary*, Weidenfeld and Nicolson (1988)

Patricia Hodgson (ed.), *Lessons for Power*, Bow Group (1974)

Patricia Hodgson and David Rigg, *Can the Tory Party Survive?*, Bow Group (1975)

Christopher Hollis, 'The Conservative Party in History', in *Political Quarterly*, vol. 32 (1961), 214

Martin Holmes, *Political Pressure and Economic Policy*, Butterworths (1982)

Martin Holmes, 'Heath's Government Reassessed', in *Contemporary Record*, vol. 3, no. 2 (1989), 26

R.T. Holt and J.E. Turner, *Political Parties in Action: The Battle of Barons' Court*, Macmillan (1968)

Lord Home, *The Way the Wind Blows*, Collins (1976)

Richard Hornby, 'The Influence of the Backbencher: A Tory View', in *Political Quarterly*, vol. 36 (1965), 286

Alistair Horne, *Macmillan, 1894–1956*, Macmillan (1988)

Alistair Horne, *Macmillan, 1957–1986*, Macmillan (1989)

Anthony Howard, *RAB: The Life of R.A. Butler*, Cape (1987)

Anthony Howard and Richard West, *The Making of the Prime Minister*, Cape (1965)

Geoffrey Howe, *Conflict of Loyalty*, Macmillan (1994)

David Howell, 'What Conservatism Means Now', in *Crossbow*, Jan. (1974) 25

Douglas Hurd, *An End to Promises: Sketch of a Government, 1970–74*, Collins (1978)

George Hutchinson, *Edward Heath: A Personal and Political Biography*, Longman (1970)

George Hutchinson, *The Last Edwardian at No. 10: An Impression of Harold Macmillan*, Quartet (1980)

M.J. Hyslop, 'The Role of the Annual Conference in the Conservative Party', MA thesis, University of Durham, (1973–74)

ICBH witness seminar, 'The Trade Unions and the Fall of the Heath Government', in *Contemporary Record*, vol. 2, no. 1 (1988), 36

ICBH witness seminar, '1961–1964: Did the Conservatives Lose Direction?', in *Contemporary Record*, vol. 2, no. 5 (1989), 26

ICBH witness seminar, 'Conservative Party Policy Making, 1964–70', in *Contemporary Record*, vol. 3, no. 3 (1990), 36; vol. 3, no. 4 (1990), 34

ICBH witness seminar, 'The Heath Government', in *Contemporary Record*, vol. 9, no. 1 (1995), 188.

Richard Ingrams (ed.), *The Life and Times of Private Eye*, Harmondsworth, Penguin (1971)

Clive Irving, Ron Hall and Jeremy Wallington, *Scandal '63: A Study of the Profumo Affair*, Heinemann (1963)

R.J. Jackson, *Rebels and Whips: Dissension, Discipline and Cohesion in British Parliamentary Parties since 1945*, Macmillan (1968)

Peter Jenkins, *The Battle of Downing Street*, Charles Knight (1970)

Donald Johnson, *A Cassandra at Westminster*, Johnson (1967)

Keith Joseph, *Why Britain Needs a Social Market Economy*, Centre for Policy Studies,(1975)

Keith Joseph, *Reversing the Trend*, Chichester, Barry Rose (1975)

Roger Jowell and Gerald Hoinville, *Britain into Europe: Public Opinion and the EEC, 1961–75*, Croom Helm (1976)

Wolfram Kaiser, 'Using Europe and Abusing the Europeans: The Conservatives and the European Community', in *Contemporary Record*, Vol. 8, no. 2 (1994), 381

Dennis Kavanagh, *Thatcherism and British Politics*, Oxford, OUP (1987)

Dennis Kavanagh and Peter Morris, *Consensus Politics from Attlee to Thatcher*, Oxford, Blackwell (1989)

James Kellas, 'The Party in Scotland', in *Conservative Century: The Conservative Party since 1900*, eds A. Seldon and S. Ball, Oxford, OUP (1994)

Richard Kelly, *Conservative Party Conferences: The Hidden System*, Manchester, Manchester University Press (1989)

Richard Kelly, 'The Party Conferences', in *Conservative Century: The Conservative Party since 1900*, eds A. Seldon and S. Ball, Oxford, OUP (1994)

V.O. Key Jr, 'A Theory of Critical Elections', in *Journal of Politics*, vol. 17 (1955), 3–18

Earl of Kilmuir, *Political Adventure*, Weidenfeld and Nicolson (1964)

Cecil King, *The Cecil King Diary, 1965–1970*, Cape (1972)

Cecil King, *The Cecil King Diary, 1970–1974*, Cape (1975)

Uwe Kitzinger, *Diplomacy and Persuasion: How Britain Joined the Common Market*, Thames and Hudson (1973)

Christopher Knight, *The Making of Tory Education Policy in Post-War Britain, 1950–1986*, Falmer (1990)

Richard Lamb, *The Failure of the Eden Government*, Sidgwick and Jackson (1987)

Zig Layton-Henry, 'Political Youth Organisations in Britain', PhD thesis, Birmingham University (1972)

Zig Layton-Henry, 'The Young Conservatives', in *Journal of Contemporary History*, vol. 8 (1973), 143

Zig Layton-Henry, 'Immigration', in *Conservative Party Politics*, ed. Zig Layton-Henry, Macmillan (1980)

Anthony Lejeune (ed.), *Enoch Powell, Income Tax at 4/3 in the £*, Tom Stacey (1970)

Bernard Levin, *The Pendulum Years: Britain and the Sixties*, Pan (1977)

Roy Lewis and Angus Maude, *The English Middle Classes*, Harmondsworth, Penguin (1953)

Peter Lilley, 'Controlling Inflation', in *Lessons for Power*, ed. P. Hodgson, Bow Group (1974)

Peter Lilley, Patricia Hodgson and Nigel Waterson, *Alternative Manifesto*, Bow Group (1973)

T.F. Lindsay and M. Harrington, *The Conservative Party, 1918–70*, Macmillan (1974)

Joni Lovenduski, Pippa Norris and Catriona Burns, 'The Party and Women', in *Conservative Century: The Conservative Party since 1900*, eds A. Seldon and S. Ball, Oxford, OUP (1994)

Vincent McKee, 'Conservative Factions', in *Contemporary Record*, vol. 3, no. 1 (1989), 30

David McKie, 'By-Elections of the Wilson Government', in *By-Elections in British Politics*, eds Chris Cook and John Ramsden, Macmillan (1973)

Harold Macmillan, *Riding the Storm, 1956–59*, Macmillan (1971)

Harold Macmillan, *Pointing the Way, 1959–61*, Macmillan (1972)

Harold Macmillan, *At the End of the Day, 1961–63*, Macmillan (1973)

David Mahony, 'Can Governments Cope?', in *Crossbow*, Dec. (1974) 13

James Margach, 'Iain Macleod', in *Here Come the Tories*, eds T. Stacey and R. St Oswald, Tom Stacey (1970)

James Margach, 'Anthony Barber', in *Here Come the Tories*, eds T. Stacey and R. St Oswald, Tom Stacey (1970)

James Margach, *The Anatomy of Power*, W.H. Allen (1978)

James Margach and R. St Oswald, 'Cabinet Ministers in Waiting', in *Here Come the Tories*, eds T. Stacey and R. St. Oswald, Tom Stacey (1970)

Angus Maude, 'The Conservative Party and the Changing Class Structure', in *Political Quarterly*, vol. 24 (1953), 139

Angus Maude, 'What the Tory Party Must Do Now', in *Crossbow*, June (1974), 9

Reginald Maudling, *Memoirs*, Sidgwick and Jackson (1978)

Keith Middlemas, 'The Party, Industry and the City', in *Conservative Century: The Conservative Party since 1900*, eds A. Seldon and S. Ball, Oxford, OUP (1994)

R.S. Milne and H.C. Mackenzie, *Straight Fight: A Study of Voting Behaviour in the Constituency of Bristol North East at the General Election of 1951*, Hansard Society (1954)

Ernle Money, *Margaret Thatcher: First Lady of the House*, Leslie Frewin (1975)

Charles Moore and Simon Heffer (eds), *A Tory Seer: The Selected Journalism of T.E. Utley*, Hamish Hamilton (1989)

Janet Morgan (ed.), *The Backbench Diaries of Richard Crossman*, Hamish Hamilton/Jonathan Cape (1981)

Rupert Morris, *Tories: From Village Hall to Westminster, A Political Sketch*, Mainstream (1991)

Sara Morrison, 'Remaking the Party Machine', in *Crossbow*, Oct. (1973), 10

Ferdinand Mount, 'Edward Heath', in *Here Come the Tories*, eds T. Stacey and R. St. Oswald, Tom Stacey (1970)

Gerald Nabarro, *Nab 1: Portrait of a Politician*, Maxwell (1969)

Gerald Nabarro, *Exploits of a Politician*, Barker (1973)

Joanna Nash, 'The YCs Today: Ageing Trendies and Borrowed Ideas', in *Crossbow*, June (1974), 34

Nigel Nicolson (ed.), *Harold Nicolson: Diary and Letters, 1945–1962*, Collins (1968)

K.D. Northrop, 'Factionalism within the Conservative Party: An Examination of the Selsdon Group', *Hull Papers in Politics*, Hull (1982)

Philip Norton, *Dissension in the House of Commons, 1945–74*, Macmillan (1975)

Philip Norton, *Conservative Dissidents: Dissent within the Parliamentary Conservative Party, 1970–74*, Temple Smith (1978)

Philip Norton, 'Kingston upon Hull Conservative Party: A Case Study of an Urban Tory Party in Decline', *Hull Papers in Politics*, Hull (1980)

Philip Norton and Arthur Aughey, *Conservatives and Conservatism*, Temple Smith (1981)

Robin Oakley and Peter Rose, *The Political Year, 1970*, Pitman (1970)

Robin Oakley and Peter Rose, *The Political Year, 1971*, Pitman (1971)

Peter Oppenheimer, 'Muddling Through: The Economy, 1951–1964', in *The Age of Affluence, 1951–1964*, eds V. Bogdanor and R. Skidelsky, Macmillan (1970)

Keith Ovenden, *The Politics of Steel*, Macmillan (1978)

Cecil Parkinson, *Right at the Centre*, Weidenfeld and Nicolson (1992)

M. Parkinson, 'Central–Local Relations in British Parties', in *Political Studies*, vol. 19 (1971), 440

Peter Paterson, *The Selectorate*, McGibbon and Kee (1967)

Chris Patten, 'R.A. Butler: What We Missed', unpublished R.A. Butler Memorial Lecture (1994)

Gillian Peele, 'Election Campaign: Well Judged or Damp Squib?', in *Crossbow*, Dec. (1974), 6

H.R. Penniman (ed.), *Britain at the Polls: The Parliamentary Elections of 1974*, Washington, DC, American Enterprise Institute (1975)

Maurice Peston, 'Conservative Economic Policy', in *Political Quarterly*, vol. 44 (1973), 411

D.J. Phillips and M. Wilson, 'The Conservative Party from Macmillan to Thatcher', in *The British Right*, eds N. Nugent and R. King, Farnborough, Saxon House (1977)

Ben Pimlott (ed.), *The Political Diary of Hugh Dalton, 1918–40, 1945–60*, Cape (1986)

Ben Pimlott, *Harold Wilson*, HarperCollins (1992)

Michael Pinto-Duschinsky, 'Bread and Circuses? The Conservatives in Office, 1951–1964', in *The Age of Affluence, 1951–1964*, eds V. Bogdanor and R. Skidelsky, Macmillan (1970)

Michael Pinto-Duschinsky, 'The Role of Constituency Associations in the Conservative Party', D.Phil. thesis, Oxford University (1972)

Michael Pinto-Duschinsky, *British Political Finance, 1830–1980*, American Enterprise Institute (1981)

Enoch Powell, *Reflections: Selected Writings and Speeches of Enoch Powell*, Bellew (1992)

Jim Prior, *A Balance of Power*, Hamish Hamilton (1986)

Francis Pym, *The Politics of Consent*, Hamish Hamilton (1984)

Timothy Raison, *Why Conservative?*, Harmondsworth, Penguin (1964)

John Ramsden, 'From Churchill to Heath', in *The Conservatives*, ed. Lord Butler, Allen and Unwin (1977)

John Ramsden, *The Age of Balfour and Baldwin, 1902–40*, Longman (1978)

John Ramsden, 'The Changing Base of British Conservatism', in *Trends in British Politics since 1945*, eds C. Cook and J. Ramsden, Macmillan (1978)

John Ramsden, *The Making of Conservative Party Policy: The Conservative Research Department since 1929*, Longman (1980)

John Ramsden, 'A Party for Owners or a Party for Earners? How Far did the British Conservative Party really Change after 1945?' in *Transactions of the Royal Historical Society*, 5th series, vol. 37 (1987), 49–63

John Ramsden, 'The Conservative Party since 1945', in *UK Political Parties since 1945*, ed. A. Seldon, Hemel Hempstead, Philip Allan (1990)

John Ramsden, *The Age of Churchill and Eden, 1940–57*, Longman (1995)

John Ranelagh, *Thatcher's People* (1991)

Peter Rawlinson, *A Price Too High: An Autobiography*, Weidenfeld and Nicolson (1989)

William Rees-Mogg, 'The Selection of Parliamentary Candidates: The Conservative Party', in *Political Quarterly*, vol. 31 (1959), 215

Robert Rhodes James, *Ambitions and Realities: British Politics 1964–1970*, Weidenfeld and Nicolson (1972)

Robert Rhodes James, *Anthony Eden*, Weidenfeld and Nicolson (1986)

Robert Rhodes James, *Bob Boothby: A Portrait*, Headline (1989)

Peter G. Richards, *Patronage in British Government*, Allen and Unwin (1963)

Peter Riddell, *Honest Opportunism*, Hamish Hamilton (1994)

Nicholas Ridley, *My Style of Government: The Thatcher Years*, Hutchinson (1991)

Richard Rose, 'Tensions in Conservative Philosophy', in *Political Quarterly*, vol. 32 (1961), 275

Andrew Roth, *The Business Background of Members of Parliament*, Parliamentary Profiles (1963)

Andrew Roth, *Enoch Powell: Tory Tribune*, Macdonald (1970)

Andrew Roth, *Heath and the Heathmen*, Routledge and Kegan Paul (1972)

Andrew Rowe, 'Conservatives and Trades Unionists', in *Conservative Party Politics*, ed. Zig Layton-Henry (1980)

Trevor Russel, *The Tory Party: Its Policies, Divisions and Future*, Harmondsworth, Penguin (1978)

K. Sainsbury, 'Patronage and Honours and Parliament', in *Parliamentary Affairs*, vol. 19 (1965/66), 346

Norman St. John Stevas, *The Two Cities*, Faber (1984)

Anthony Sampson, *The Anatomy of Britain*, Hodder and Stoughton (1962)

Anthony Sampson, *Macmillan: A Study in Ambiguity*, Harmondsworth, Penguin (1968)

Nicholas Scott, 'Have the YCs Really Changed?', in *Crossbow*, Jan. (1973), 24

Roger Scruton (ed.), *Conservative Texts: An Anthology*, Macmillan (1991)

Arthur Seldon, *The Emerging Consensus*, Institute of Economic Affairs (1981)

Arthur Seldon, *The State is Rolling Back*, E and L Books (1994)

Brendon Sewill, *British Economic Policy, 1970–74: A View from the Inside*, Institute of Economic Affairs (1975)

Patrick Seyd, 'Factionalism within the Conservative Party: The Monday Club', in *Government and Opposition*, vol. 7 (1972), 464

Patrick Seyd, 'Democracy within the Conservative Party', in *Government and Opposition*, vol. 10 (1975), 219

Patrick Seyd, 'Factionalism in the 1980s', in *Conservative Party Politics*, ed. Zig Layton-Henry, Macmillan (1980)

Robert Shepherd, *Iain Macleod: A Biography*, Hutchinson (1994)

Norman Shrapnel, *The Seventies*, Constable (1980)

Larry Siedentop, 'Mr. Macmillan and the Edwardian Style', in *The Age of Affluence 1951–1964*, eds V. Bogdanor and R. Skidelsky, Macmillan (1970)

Fred Silvester, 'Where the Tory Left has Failed', in *Crossbow*, Aug. (1973), 15

William P. Snyder, *The Politics of British Defense Policy, 1945–1961*, Columbus, Ohio State University Press (1964)

Gerald Sparrow, *Rab, Study of a Statesman*, Odhams (1965)

Frank Stacey, *British Government 1966–1975: Years of Reform*, Oxford, OUP (1975)

Tom Stacey and R. St Oswald (eds), *Here Come the Tories*, Tom Stacey (1970)

M. Stenton and S. Lees, *Who's Who of British Members of Parliament, 1945–79*, Brighton, Harvester (1981)

James Stuart, *Within the Fringe*, Bodley Head (1967)

Andrew Taylor, 'Conservatives and Trade Unions since 1945', in *Contemporary Record*, vol. 4 (1990), 15

Andrew Taylor, 'The Party and the Trade Unions', in *Conservative Century: The Conservative Party since 1900*, eds A. Seldon and S. Ball, Oxford, OUP (1994)

Robert Taylor, *The Trade Union Question in British Politics: Government and Unions since 1945*, Oxford, Blackwell (1993)

A.L. Teasdale, 'The Conservative Leadership under Challenge', B.Litt. thesis, Oxford University (1983)

Norman Tebbit, *Upwardly Mobile*, Futura (1989)

William Teeling, *Corridors of Frustration*, Johnson (1970)

Philip Tether, 'Clubs: A Neglected Aspect of Conservative Organisation', *Hull Papers in Politics*, no. 42, Hull (1988)

Alan Thompson, *The Day before Yesterday*, Panther (1971)

F.M.L. Thompson, 'English Landed Society in the Twentieth Century: I,

Property; Collapse and Survival', in *Transactions of the Royal Historical Society*, 5th series, vol. 40 (1990), 1–24.

G. Thomson, 'Parties in Parliament 1959–63, II, A Tory View', in *Political Quarterly*, vol. 34 (1963), 249

D.R. Thorpe, *Selwyn Lloyd*, Cape (1989)

David Thurlow, *Profumo: The Hate Factor*, Robert Hale (1992)

Ian Trethowan, *Split Screen*, Hamish Hamilton (1984)

John Turner, *Macmillan*, Longman (1994)

D.W. Urwin, 'Scottish Conservatism: A Party Organisation in Transition', in *Political Studies*, vol. 14 (1966), 145

T.E. Utley, 'The Significance of Mrs. Thatcher', in *Conservative Essays*, ed. M. Cowling, Cassell (1978)

John Vaizey, *In Breach of Promise* [includes essays on Iain Macleod and Sir Edward Boyle] Weidenfeld and Nicolson (1984)

David Walder, *The Short List*, Heinemann (1964)

Peter Walker, 'What They Never Tell You', in *Crossbow*, April (1975), 15

Peter Walker, *Staying Power: An Autobiography*, Bloomsbury (1991)

William Wallace, 'The British General Election of 1970', in *Government and Opposition*, vol. 6, no. 1, (1971), 36

Dennis Walters, *Not Always with the Pack*, Constable (1989)

J.T. Ward, *The First Century: A History of Scottish Tory Organisation*, Edinburgh, Scottish Conservative and Unionist Association (1982)

Harold Watkinson, *Turning Points: A Record of our Times*, Salisbury, Russell (1986)

Phillip Whitehead, *The Writing on the Wall: Britain in the Seventies*, Michael Joseph (1985)

William Whitelaw, *The Whitelaw Memoirs*, Aurum (1989)

Philip Williams (ed.), *The Diary of Hugh Gaitskell, 1945–56*, Cape (1983)

D.J. Wilson, *Power and Bureaucracy: Regional Organisation in the Conservative and Labour Parties*, Saxon House (1975)

M. Wilson, 'Grass Roots Conservatism: Motions to the Party Conference', in *The British Right*, eds N. Nugent and R. King, Farnborough, Saxon House (1977)

Lord Windlesham, *Communication and Political Power*, Cape (1966)

Lord Windlesham, *Politics in Practice*, Cape (1975)

Michael Wolff (ed.), *The Conservative Opportunity*, Batsford (1965)

Bruce Wood, *The Process of Local Government Reform, 1966–74*, Allen and Unwin (1976)

John Wood (ed.), *A Nation Not Afraid: The Thinking of Enoch Powell*, Batsford (1965)

John Wood (ed.), *Powell and the 1970 Election*, Kingswood, Surrey, Elliott Right Way Books (1970)

Earl of Woolton, *Memoirs*, Cassell (1959)

Robert Worcester, *British Public Opinion*, Oxford, Blackwell (1991)

Esmond Wright, 'The Future of the Conservative Party', in *Political Quarterly*, vol. 41 (1970), 387

Hugo Young, *One of Us: A Biography of Margaret Thatcher*, Macmillan (1989)

John Young, *Britain and European Unity, 1945–1992*, Macmillan (1993)

Kenneth Young, *Sir Alec Douglas-Home*, Dent (1970)

Ken Young, 'Orpington and the "Liberal Revival"', in *By-Elections in British Politics*, eds C. Cook and J. Ramsden, Macmillan (1973)

Ken Young, 'The Party and English Local Government', in *Conservative Century: The Conservative Party since 1900*, eds A. Seldon and S. Ball, Oxford, OUP (1994)

Wayland Young, *The Profumo Affair: Aspects of Conservatism*, Harmondsworth, Penguin (1963)

Index